ECONOMICS TODAY
The Micro View

ECONOMICS TODAY
The Micro View

FOURTH EDITION

Roger LeRoy Miller
Professor of Economics
Department of Economics
and
Associate Director
Law and Economics Center
University of Miami

1817

HARPER & ROW, PUBLISHERS, New York
Cambridge, Philadelphia, San Francisco,
London, Mexico City, São Paulo, Sydney

We gratefully acknowledge the following sources for providing photographs used in this book: page *15,* Grace, Stock, Boston; *32,* The Mansell Collection; *39,* Rastelli, Woodfin Camp; *61,* UPI; *76,* The American Red Cross; *119,* Laffont, Sygma; *133,* Silverstone, Magnum; *182,* Powers, Jeroboam; *200,* Grace, Stock, Boston; *207,* Lubin, Jeroboam; *215,* Ramsey & Muspratt, London; *229,* Green, Sygma; *247,* Smolan, Stock, Boston; *270,* Mahon, Monkmeyer; *297,* UPI; *314,* Beckwith Studios; *331,* Davidson, Magnum; *347,* Uzzle, Magnum; *368,* Brody, Stock, Boston; *387,* Laffont, Sygma; *404,* The Mansell Collection; *406,* Ira Kirschenbaum; *423,* Grant Heilman; *455,* The Mansell Collection; *460,* Arnold, Magnum.

Sponsoring Editor: John Greenman
Development Editor: Johnna G. Barto
Project Editor: David Nickol
Designer: Robert Sugar
Manager of Production: Kewal K. Sharma
Photo Researcher: Mira Schachne
Compositor: Lehigh/Rocappi
Printer and Binder: The Murray Printing Company
Art Studio: Vantage Art, Inc.
Cover: Direction by Robert Sugar, Concept and Design by Infield D'Astolfo Associates

Economics Today: The Micro View,
Fourth Edition

Library of Congress Cataloging in Publication Data

Miller, Roger LeRoy.
Economics today—the micro view.

Includes bibliographies and indexes.
1. Microeconomics. I. Title.
HB172.M63 1982 338.5 81-13403
ISBN 0-06-044491-6 AACR2

Contents

Preface

To the Instructor

Today there are few people who would not agree that economic issues rank at or near the top of the list of problems confronting Americans. There is no news telecast, newspaper edition, or weekly news magazine that does not report on some new economic datum which shows that either things are getting worse or things are getting better. Those "things" obviously have something to do with the rates of inflation and unemployment, the length of food stamp lines, the number of individuals still on welfare rolls, the amount of racial discrimination still being practiced, the cost of cleaning up the air, or the handling of corporate profits.

Many, if not most, of the current social issues are involved with economics in some way or another. However, for students to understand and apply economic reasoning to social issues, they must have a solid foundation in economics. *Economics Today: The Micro View* was written both to provide that necessary foundation and to demonstrate the application of economic reasoning to the problems around us.

THE FOURTH EDITION

This edition incorporates numerous theoretical and pedagogical changes while keeping the flavor of the previous three editions. In a sentence, the fourth edition again deepens the theoretical content while expanding the pedagogical aids to make the theory more understandable to the student reader.

Significant Changes in Theory Chapters

While the number of new chapters has been kept to a minimum, virtually all of the theory chapters have been reworked to expand coverage of theoretical concepts and make them more understandable.

1. Chapter 6, "Demand and Supply Elasticity," has been further simplified while still maintaining its rigorous nature.
2. The following chapters have been expanded: Chapter 7, "Consumer Choice"; Chapter 9, "The Firm in Competition"; Chapter 11, "In Between Monopoly and Competition."
3. Chapter 19, "Conservation and Energy," has been completely updated and revised to take account of new information on our energy problems worldwide.
4. Chapter 21, "Agriculture," has been completely updated and revised.

Chapter 5 is completely new; it concerns private business organizations and financing. The chapter gives students an introduction to the organization of business.

A Word About the Appendixes

This edition has more appendixes than any previous edition, and those that remain from the third edition have been completely reworked.

1. The appendix to Chapter 1, "Reading and Working with Graphs," has been expanded.
2. The appendix to Chapter 5, "Simplified Accounting with and Without Inflation," introduces students to one of the most important changes in the business world—taking account of inflation when doing the books.
3. The appendix to Chapter 7, "Analyzing Consumer Choice with Graphs," has been expanded.
4. There is a new appendix to Chapter 19 presenting a brief view on discounting and present value.

Issues and Applications

In keeping with the flavor of the first three editions, this edition contains extensive application of economic theory to real-world problems. All chapters have a section titled ***Issues and Applications.*** One or more current topics are covered in a manner that reveals how economic theory can be used to analyze what is happening around us. There are over 30 *Issues and Applications* from which the professor can choose. Each is self-contained with two useful pedagogical aids that show the student how it links up with the preceding theoretical materials. Each *Issue and Application* is introduced by a boxed item titled ***Concepts Applied,*** which tells the student which theoretical concepts will be used in the following *Issue and Application.* At the end of each *Issue and Application,* there are two or three ***Questions,*** again attempting to guide the student in applying theory to what he or she has just read. To avoid confusion in assignments and in reading graphs and tables, and also to show the closer link between the *Issues and Applications* and the chapter materials, all *Issues and Applications* are contained within each chapter, and a sequential numbering system for all graphs and tables is used.

Professors can use as many *Issues and Applications* as deemed appropriate. In other words, the theoretical parts of the text can stand alone. Students, however, often seem to understand the theory better after seeing it applied to real-world problems.

Some New and Altered Issues and Applications. Many of the *Issues and Applications* have significant changes in them, and others are completely new, including the following:

- "The Market for Home Computers," in Chapter 3
- "Antitrust Actions: The Case of 'Shared' Monopoly" in Chapter 12
- "Bringing the Draft Back" in Chapter 14
- "Should We Market the Right to Pollute?" in Chapter 18

THE FOURTH EDITION IS NOW A TOTAL LEARNING SYSTEM

There have been significant pedagogical improvements in the fourth edition, which now allow all pedagogical devices to be interacting. There are no empty questions without answers and no pedagogical aid stands alone without being linked to the rest of the system. The elements of the total system are as follows:

1. ***For Preview and Study:*** Each chapter has five *For Preview and Study* questions. What is truly unique about these questions is that they are repeated at the end of the chapter *with the answers.* The student is given total reinforcement.

2. ***Topics for Review:*** Beginning with Chapter 2 accompanying the *For Preview and Study* section, there is a *Topics for Review* section listing the key concepts that must be mastered before going on to the new chapter. What is unique here is that the student is referred to specific *Concepts in Brief* (described below) by number. In other words, the number refers to the specific boxed set of *Concepts in Brief* that the student previously studied. Since all of the *Concepts in Brief* boxes have been numbered, the student can quickly go back to them.

3. ***Concepts in Brief:*** Included after each major section within the chapter is a boxed set of brief summary statements that are numbered sequentially.

4. ***Issues and Applications*** that are linked to the chapter concepts: As pointed out above, each *Issue and Application* is introduced by a boxed item entitled *Concepts Applied,* which tells the student which theoretical concepts will be used in the following *Issue and Application.* At the end of each *Issue and Application,* questions are asked which relate to the *Concepts Applied* that started the *Issue and Application.* Finally, answers to the two or three questions are presented in the *Instructor's Manual* so that the instructor can use them as quiz items or class discussion items.

5. ***Glossary of Terms:*** All important terms when they first appear in a chapter are in boldface. All such boldface terms are clearly defined in the *Glossary of Terms* that appears at the end of the chapter.

6. ***Chapter Summary:*** For ease of review and for testing of knowledge, a chapter summary is given in point-by-point format.

7. ***Answers to Preview and Study Questions:*** As mentioned above, the preview and study questions are repeated and the answers are given at the back of each chapter.

8. ***Problems:*** Almost every chapter has from two to six problems, most of which require graphic or arithmetic manipulation. These problems are self-teaching devices because all of them have answers at the back of the text. This provides total reinforcement.

9. ***Selected References:*** Numerous newly selected references are given for each chapter to help the more adventurous student continue his or her studies.

TEACHING AIDS AND SUPPLEMENTS

Economics Today: The Micro View is part of an entire teaching package, which includes the following items:

1. **Instructor's Manual:** A completely new *Instructor's Manual* has been developed by Professor Robert Pulsinelli of Western Kentucky University. In the manual, the instructor is provided with:
   a. Complete chapter overview and lecture notes
   b. A new section entitled "For Those Who Wish to Stress Theory"
   c. Answers to the questions that appear at the end of each *Issue and Application* in the text
   d. Further questions for class discussion or essay tests
   e. Selected references and films

The *Instructor's Manual* is three-hole punched and fits into a three-ring binder so that transparency masters, test questions, newsletters, and other items can be added as appropriate.

2. **Learning Guide:** A completely new *Student Learning Guide* has been written by Professor Otis Gilley of the University of Texas at Austin. Included in this manual are:

a. Four to six learning objectives specifying goals the student should be able to accomplish after completing the exercises
b. An overview of the content of the chapter, identifying the most important topics and how they relate to material previously studied
c. A programmed-learning section, which requires the student to fill in key terms in statements reviewing the coverage of the chapter. Some of these programmed-learning sections are presented in the form of crossword puzzles, which add some fun to the learning experience
d. A review test including ten or more multiple choice items per chapter
e. Two to four problems per chapter, which require computation and graphical analysis by the student to apply the theories discussed in the chapter
f. Several essay questions as a final test of the student's understanding of the theories and applications covered in the chapter

In addition to including a list of key terms and concepts within each chapter, a complete alphabetical glossary appears at the end of the *Student Learning Guide.* This is a self-contained learning aid; answers to all exercises (with explanations) appear at the back of the guide.

3. **Independent Study Modules (ISMs).** A complete and heavily pretested audio/graphic learning system is available to instructors who have available classrooms or student learning centers that are equipped with tape playback facilities. These unique materials were independently developed in conjunction with the use of the first edition by their authors, James Mason, Mike Melvin, and Craig Justice. The ISM package includes thirty separate cassettes, virtually one for each chapter in this book. Besides the graphic packets and cassette tape materials, there are self-tests that can be used in a programmed-learning manner.

The weekly ISM materials can be used in a variety of ways. One way is as a substitute for one lecture period. ISM materials can also be used to reinforce a full lecture schedule on an assigned or even a voluntary basis. The emphasis of the system tends toward integrating it with chapter theory while giving specific examples of problems that are different from those in the text.

We have found from extensive field testing that the ISM supplements develop positive student responses to learning economic theory. Students have a greater appreciation of the opportunity to learn the complex material objectively at their own individual pace. The instructors who have used the system contend that students come to lectures better prepared and with positive expectations.

4. **Test Bank:** A *Test Bank,* developed by Professor Edward John Ray of Ohio State University, is available in printed form and in a computerized service system permitting effective and simple examination. Approximately 90 percent of these questions were written specifically for the Fourth Edition. *Each item is graded according to difficulty.*

5. **Transparency Masters.** All important graphs are available in a set of transparency masters that is free to adopters. These graphs have been completely redone so that they are visually most appealing and useful.

6. **An Occasional Newsletter:** Several times a year, an *Economics Today Newsletter* will be sent out to all adopters for inclusion in their *Instructor's Manual.* It will be three-hole punched and will bring the text up to date on any new areas as necessary.

To the Student

How to Learn Economics Using *Economics Today: The Micro View*

For many beginning economics students, fear can best describe their feelings prior to taking the course. Economics has often been labeled a "hard" subject to master. But it need not be. In the next few paragraphs, a plan of study is presented that will allow you to learn the course material, be able to apply economics to the world around you, and dispel the myth that economics is a more difficult topic to understand than others.

1. Read the *For Preview and Study* questions. Can you think of any answers to them? Do you have any preconceived notions about the topics to be discussed in each chapter?

2. Read the *Topics for Review* section. (All chapters except Chapter 1 have this section.) Have you mastered all of the concepts listed there? If not, go back to the *Concepts in Brief* boxes whose numbers are given after the appropriate review concepts.

3. Read the assigned chapter relatively rapidly without attempting to understand portions of it that you find difficult. Put it away for a few hours or even a day.

4. Reread the chapter, stopping at each point where you have difficulty and noting such difficulties on a separate sheet of paper. Look at the *Concepts in Brief* when you first encounter them. Do they make sense? If they don't, it means that you missed an important theoretical concept or its application. Go back and reread the appropriate sections.

5. Draw the graphs yourself, reading their legends in the book as you do so. Do they make sense? How do they apply to the chapter materials?

6. Read each assigned *Issue and Application,* first looking at the *Concepts Applied.* Do the concepts mean anything to you? If they do, try to see where they are fit into the analysis in the materials that follow. Try to answer the two or three *Questions* that appear at the end of each issue or application. How do the *Questions* relate to the *Concepts Applied* that started the issue or application? You should be able, in most cases, to see a link.

7. Read through the glossary items in the *Definition of Terms* section. By now they should all be familiar.

8. Read the point-by-point *Chapter Summary.* Do all the points make sense? If they don't, go back to the appropriate sections.

9. Go back to the *For Preview and Study* questions. Try to write down some ideas on your answers. Now refer to the answers given at the end of the chapter after the *Chapter Summary.*

10. Work through each available *Problem.* Do not look at the answers in the back of the book until you have worked the problem through to the best of your ability. It is essentially a self-test system that shows you whether you have mastered one or more of the theoretical points in the chapter.

11. Use the *Learning Guide.* This may be particularly appropriate just prior to examinations. If you have mastered the chapter materials, the *Learning Guide* will reinforce your mastery of them and also improve your ability to do well on exams. You may wish to write your answers to the *Learning Guide* questions on a separate piece of paper the first time you do them, then use the *Guide* as a refresher for the final examination, marking your answers one final time in the book and checking them with the correct answers.

12. Additionally, in your preparation for midterm and final exams, you should reread the chapter once again, then go back and look at the *Preview* questions, answering them with ease this time. Look at the *Concepts in Brief* highlighted throughout each chapter. Then go to the point-by-point *Chapter Summary.* All the concepts covered should be well understood by now.

13. After midterm examinations, find out which questions you did not answer correctly. Go back to the appropriate sections in the text and the *Learning Guide.* Remember, use the midterm exams as a learning device rather than as a pure testing device.

The above study program is not necessarily rigid and can be done in a different order. Depending on your ability to understand the material, you can skip various steps. The program outlined is basically for a student who wishes to *fully* master all the materials assigned by the instructor.

Acknowledgments

THE FIRST EDITION

John R. Aidem, Miami-Dade Junior College
Glen W. Atkinson, University of Nevada
Charles A. Berry, University of Cincinnati
Conrad P. Caligaris, Northeastern University
Warren L. Coats, Jr., University of Virginia
Ed Coen, University of Minnesota
Alan E. Ellis, De Anza College
Grant Ferguson, North Texas State University
Peter Frost, University of Miami
Martin D. Haney, Portland Community College
Timothy R. Keely, Tacoma Community College
Norman F. Keiser, California State University at San Jose
E. R. Kittrell, Northern Illinois University
John L. Madden, University of Kentucky
John M. Martin, California State University at Hayward
E. S. McKuskey, St. Petersburg Junior College
Herbert C. Milikien, American River College
Jerry L. Petr, University of Nebraska at Lincoln
I. James Pikl, University of Wyoming
Richard Romano, Broome Community College
Augustus Shackelford, El Camino College
Howard F. Smith, California Polytechnic State University at San Luis Obispo
William T. Trulove, Eastern Washington State College
Robert F. Wallace, Washington State University
Henry C. Wallich, Yale University
James Willis, California State University at San Jose
Shik Young, Eastern Washington State College

THE SECOND EDITION

G. Jeffrey Barbour, Central Michigan University
Thomas Borcherding, Simon Frazer University
Maryanna Boynton, California State College, Fullerton
Ralph T. Byrns, Clemson University
Thomas Curtis, University of South Florida
Barry Duman, West Texas State University
G. B. Duwaji, University of Texas at Arlington
Mike Ellis, North Texas State University
Frank Emerson, Western Michigan University
James Foley, University of Miami
Nicholas Grunt, Tarrant County Junior College
Demos Hadjiyanis, College of St. Thomas
E. L. Hazlett, Kansas State University
David Jones, College of St. Thomas
Daniel Joseph, Niagara Community College
Craig Justice, Chaffey College
E. D. Key, Stephen F. Austin State University
Bruce Kimzey, New Mexico State University
Terrence W. Kinal, College of St. Thomas
Glen Marston, Utah State University
James Mason, San Diego Mesa College
G. Hartley Mellish, University of South Florida
Mike Melvin, San Diego Mesa College
Herbert Milikien, American River College
Claron Nelson, University of Utah
John Rapp, University of Dayton
Larry Ross, Anchorage Community College
Richard Sherman, Ohio State University
Lee Spector, State University of New York, Buffalo
George Spiva, University of Tennessee
J. M. Sullivan, Stephen F. Austin State University
Robert P. Thomas, University of Washington
Wylie Whalthall, College of the Alameda
Raburn M. Williams, University of Hawaii
Travis Wilson, De Kalb Community College

THE THIRD EDITION

G. Jeffrey Barbour, Central Michigan University
Charles Berry, University of Cincinnati
Thomas W. Bonsor, Eastern Washington University
Diane Dumont, University of New Mexico
Morton Hirsch, Kingsborough Community College
Tomotaka Ishimine, California State University, Long Beach
J. Paul Jewell, Kansas City, Kansas, Community College
Robert S. Rippey, Central Connecticut State College
Thomas N. Schaap, Clemson University
David Schauer, University of Texas, El Paso
Richard Sherman, Ohio State University

THE FOURTH EDITION

As usual, I received a large number of comments from adopters which aided me greatly in revising for the fourth edition. I could not hope to list everyone who has written or called me about proposed changes. Nonetheless, I will attempt to list here in alphabetical order some of the major reviewers for the fourth edition.

Glen Beeson, Duquesne University
Tom Boston, Atlanta University
Ronald Brandolini, Valencia Community College
Elba Brown, University of Texas, El Paso
Dancy R. Carr, Coastal Carolina College
Gary Clayton, Northern Kentucky University
Frank Fato, Westchester Community College
John Foreman, Westmoreland County Community College

Otis Gilley, University of Texas, Austin
Jack Goddard, Northeastern Oklahoma State University
John Hensel, University of Cincinnati, University College
Philip Jacob, University of South Carolina
Paul A. Joray, Indiana University, South Bend
Daniel A. Joseph, State University College at Buffalo and Niagara County Community College
Michael Kupilik, University of Montana
Keith Langford, Macon Junior College
Howard J. McBride, University of Cincinnati
Stephen Morrell, Auburn University
Timothy Perri, Appalachian State University
Robert Pulsinelli, Western Kentucky University
Ron Reddall, Allan Hancock College
Patricia Sanderson, Mississippi State University
William Schaniel, West Georgia College
Dan Segebarth, Triton College
Richard Sherman, Jr., Ohio State University
David Shorow, Richland College
Allan D. Stone, Southwest Missouri State University
John Vahaly, University of Louisville
Terence West, County College of Morris
George Wilson, Central Missouri State University
Donald J. Yankovic, University of Toledo
Alex Yguado, Mission College

Finally, I wish to thank Professor Robert Pulsinelli for helping me in the arduous task of checking copyedited manuscript and proofreading galley proofs and page proofs, as well as helping me proofread all of the artwork. Of course, neither he nor anyone else is responsible for any remaining errors. I continue to welcome all comments and criticisms from adopters and students alike.

RLM

PART

I

INTRODUCTION TO ECONOMICS AND THE PRICING SYSTEM

1

What Economics Is All About

scarcity

FOR PREVIEW AND STUDY

1. Nations with high per capita incomes and individuals who are wealthy are referred to as affluent. Do affluent people face the problem of scarcity?
2. Fresh air and clean water can often be consumed in the United States free of charge. Does this mean that these "goods" are free or costless to *society*?
3. Why does the scarcity problem force people to consider opportunity costs?
4. What are some costs and benefits of specialization?
5. What is the difference between positive and normative economics?

The reason that we face economic problems individually and as a nation is that none of us can have all that we want—we live in a world of *scarcity*. Economic problems face you, me, your friends, the nation, and the world. It is impossible to avoid these problems personally or as a nation. They involve choosing a career and where to live, what price to pay for a house, how to solve the simultaneous problems of unemployment and rising prices, plus thousands of other decisions.

This book is about economics and economic problem-solving. Consequently, it relates to you as an individual who must decide how to earn income and how to spend it. It relates to you as an individual who must vote for political candidates who decide how much of your income to tax and how to spend tax revenues. Finally, it relates to your country and how much it buys from and sells to the rest of the world. We study economics because the primary economic decision—what type of system do we choose—helps determine our political, social, religious, and personal environment.

Scarcity—the Bane of Civilization

Would you like to be able to study more and also to have more time to go to the student union and drink coffee with your friends? Would you like to have a bigger house or apartment or a bigger room in your dorm or fraternity or sorority house? Would you like to have more clothes but not give up any evenings out on the town? For most people, the answer to all of these questions is a resounding *yes.* Why can't we have more of everything? Because individually and collectively we face a constraint called scarcity. **Scarcity** is the most basic concept in all of economics. Scarcity means that we do not and cannot have enough income or wealth to satisfy our every desire. Note that we are not referring to any *measurable* standard of wants; rather, we are referring to the way people believe—what people want, need, or desire *relative* to what is available at any moment. If the world were such that everyone could have as much of everything as is desired, without sacrifice, then economics would no longer exist as a meaningful intellectual or practical pursuit. But there is scarcity. And we have not just recently moved into the "age of scarcity," as many people seem to believe. Scarcity has always been with us and will be with us as long as we cannot get everything we want at a zero price.

RESOURCES ARE SCARCE

The concept of scarcity arises from scarce resources, or simply resources, for short. We define **resources** as the inputs, or factors, used in the production of those things that we desire. Resources can therefore be classified in a variety of ways. Every classification scheme is, to some extent, arbitrary. We can, nonetheless, consider natural, human, and manufactured resources as broad categories.

Natural Resources = Land and Mineral Deposits

Basically, **land** with its inherent mineral deposits is the natural resource we think of most often. The original fertility of land is also a natural resource. Some land can grow phenomenal amounts of crops without any addition of fertilizer; other land is incapable of growing anything in its natural state.

Human Resources = Labor

In order to produce the things we desire, a human resource must be used. That human resource consists of the productive contributions of **labor** made by individuals who work—for example, steelworkers, ballet dancers, and professional baseball players.

Manufactured Resources = Capital

When labor is applied to land to grow corn, for example, something else is used. Usually it is a plow or a tractor. That is to say, land and labor are combined with manufactured resources in order to produce the things that we desire. These manufactured resources are called **capital,** which consists of machines, buildings, and tools. Additionally, capital consists of improvements to natural resources, such as irrigation ditches.

Another Human Resource = Entrepreneurship

There is, in effect, a fourth type of input used in production. It is a special type of human resource; it consists of entrepreneurial ability, or **entrepreneurship.** The best way to define entrepreneurship is by listing what an entrepreneur does:

1. Takes the initiative in combining land, labor, and capital in order to produce a good or service.
2. Undertakes basic decision-making for the business.
3. Takes risks of losing money or going bankrupt.
4. Forms a business and introduces new products and new techniques.

Without entrepreneurship, virtually no large-scale business organizations could operate. Clearly, entrepreneurship as a human resource is scarce: not everyone is willing to take risks or has the ability to do successful business decision-making.

We see the classification of resources in Exhibit 1–1.

EXHIBIT 1–1

Resource Classification. We can arbitrarily classify resources into those that are natural, human, and manufactured. We have denoted specific names within those three classifications.

Natural Resources	*Human Resources*	*Manufactured Resources*
Land	Labor and entrepreneurship	Capital

Scarce resources produce what are called **economic goods**—the subject of our study throughout this book.

Economic Goods

Any good (or service) produced from scarce resources is also scarce and is called an economic good. Because economic goods are scarce, we constantly face decisions about how best to use them. After all, the desired quantity of an economic good, by definition, exceeds the amount that is directly available from nature at a zero price.

However, not all goods are economic; some are free.

Free Goods

There are, of course, some things around that are free. We call them **free goods,** as opposed to economic goods. Not many are left. Old economics textbooks used to call air a free good, but that is really no longer true, because in many cities pollution makes air unfit to breathe. In many mountain areas, clean air is still a free good (once you are there); you can have all of it you want at a zero price, and so can anybody else who bothers to hike up to where you are. You and anybody else who hikes there do not have to worry about how free goods, including air and running water in many wilderness areas, should be or have to be allocated among competing demanders. There is no scarcity involved. Who is interested in free goods, then? Certainly not most economists. Perhaps physicists, hydrologists, biologists, and chemists are interested in free air and water, but the economist steps in only when the problem of scarcity arises, and people become concerned about allocating the scarce resource. We have seen throughout our history that as population and production increase over time, many "free" goods become "economic" goods, such as land for mining, water and air for industrial uses, and water for hydroelectric power. To the population of native American Indians, tobacco leaves were a free good before the time of Sir Walter Raleigh. The Indians could have all that they wanted. Later, however, tobacco leaves became (and remain) an economic good.

Choice

Scarcity forces us to choose. You had to choose whether to go to college or to go to work. You have to choose between going out on a date or studying. Your government policymakers have to choose between using more resources in the production of military goods or using more resources in the production of, say, educational services. In fact, the concept of choice forms the basis of our formal definition of **economics:**

Economics is the study of how individuals and societies choose among the alternative uses of scarce resources to produce goods.

As we will see throughout our study of economics, the choices we make affect not only how we live today, but how we will live in the future. Moreover, the choices that we can make are constrained not only by scarcity, but also by political, legal, traditional, and moral forces.

In other words, there are numerous noneconomic forces that determine and mold our decision-making processes. In this text, however, we will concentrate on how economic forces affect our choices. We are not, though, denying that the others are important, too.

Concepts in Brief 1-1

- Scarcity exists because we cannot have all that we want from nature without sacrifice.
- We use scarce resources, such as land, labor, capital, and entrepreneurship, to produce economic goods—that is, goods that are desired but are not directly obtainable from nature to the extent demanded or desired.
- Scarcity requires us to choose, and economics is the study of how we make those choices.

Choice and Opportunity Costs

Choosing one thing requires giving up something else. When you sit down to read this book, you are making a choice. You have chosen not to do at least a thousand other things with your time. You could have read your English text, you could have watched television, you could have slept, or you could have gone to the movies. Thus, the time scarcity that you face requires you to choose between reading this book and doing something that is presumably less valuable. In other words, there is a cost associated with spending time reading these words. Economists call it **opportunity cost.**

Let's assume that of all the other things you could have done instead of reading this book, the thing you *most* wanted to do, but didn't do, was to watch television. If that's the case, then watching television is the opportunity cost of reading this book. *Opportunity cost is defined as the highest valued alternative that had to be sacrificed for the option that was chosen.* Opportunity cost is a powerful concept that allows us to place a value on the resources that are used to produce something.

Now let's look at an example of opportunity cost in the business world. Suppose that you own a firm that uses a large expensive machine to make bolts. What is the opportunity cost of that machine? One place to look is elsewhere in the factory. What else could you do with the machine? Could you make nuts, or screws, or hairpins, or something else? The value, or income, that the machine would generate in making the most profitable alternative in your factory gives you some (but not a total) indication of its opportunity cost. You must also look to the outside. Is there another firm that might be willing to rent that machine or even to buy it so that you could invest the proceeds from the sale in something else? Let's say that you could rent the machine to a factory around the corner for $10,000 a month and that this is more than its value in producing any alternative in your own factory. Then $10,000 is its opportunity cost. This gives us a rule:

Opportunity cost does not depend on who might use the resource. It is the resource's highest value in *any* of the alternative uses not chosen.

THE TRADE-OFFS FACING YOU

Whatever you do, you are trading off one use of a resource for one or more alternative uses. The value of these **trade-offs** is represented by the opportunity cost just discussed. Let's go back to the opportunity cost of reading this book. Let us assume that you have a maximum of ten hours per week to spend studying just two topics—economics and accounting. The more you study economics, the higher will be your expected grade; the more you study accounting, the higher will be your expected grade in that subject. There is a trade-off, then, between spending one more hour reading this book and spending that hour studying and doing accounting problems. This can be more clearly brought out in a graph[1] that clearly shows the trade-off involved.

[1] Readers needing a refresher on graphical techniques should now read the appendix to this chapter.

GRAPHICAL ANALYSIS

In Exhibit 1–2, we have put the expected grade in accounting on the vertical axis of the diagram and the expected grade in economics on the horizontal axis. In this simplified world, if you spend all of your time on economics, you will get an A in the course, but you will fail accounting. On the other hand, if you spend all of your time on accounting, you will get an A in that subject and you will flunk economics. The trade-off is a special case: one to one. A one-to-one trade-off means that in this case the opportunity cost of receiving one grade higher in economics (for example, improving from a C to a B) is one grade lower in accounting (falling from a C to a D in our example).

PRODUCTION POSSIBILITIES CURVE

The diagram in Exhibit 1–2 illustrates the relationship between the possible results that can be produced in each of two activities, depending on how much time you choose to put into each activity. Economists call this kind of diagram a **production possibilities curve.**

If you consider that what you are producing is a grade when you study economics and accounting, then the diagram in Exhibit 1–2 can be related to the production possibilities that you face. The line that goes from *A* on one axis to the *A* on the other therefore becomes a production possibilities curve. It is defined as all possible combinations of the maximum amount of any two goods or services that can be produced from a fixed amount of resources. In the example, your time for studying was limited to ten hours per week. The two possible outputs were grades in accounting and grades in economics. The particular production possibilities curve presented in Exhibit 1–2 is a graphic representation of the opportunity cost of studying one more hour in one subject. If the student decides to be at point x in Exhibit 1–2, then five hours of study time will be spent on accounting and five hours will be spent on economics. The expected grade in each course will be a C. If the student is more interested in getting a B in economics, then he or she will go to point y on the production possibilities curve, spending only 2.5 hours on accounting but 7.5 hours on economics. The expected grade in accounting will then drop from a C to a D. Note that these trade-offs between expected grades in accounting and economics are given holding constant total study time as well as all other factors that may influence the student's

EXHIBIT 1–2
Production Possibilities Curve for Grades in Accounting and Economics. On the vertical axis, we measure the expected grade in accounting; on the horizontal axis, the expected grade in economics. We assume that there are only ten hours total time that can be spent per week on studying. If all ten hours are spent on economics, an A is received in economics and an F in accounting. If all ten hours are spent on accounting, an A is received in that subject and an F in economics. There is a one-to-one trade-off. If the student is at point *x*, equal time (5 hours a week) is spent on both courses and equal grades of C will be received. If a higher grade in economics is desired, the student may go to point *y*, thereby receiving a B in economics, but a D in accounting. At point *y*, 2.5 hours are spent on accounting, 7.5 hours on economics.

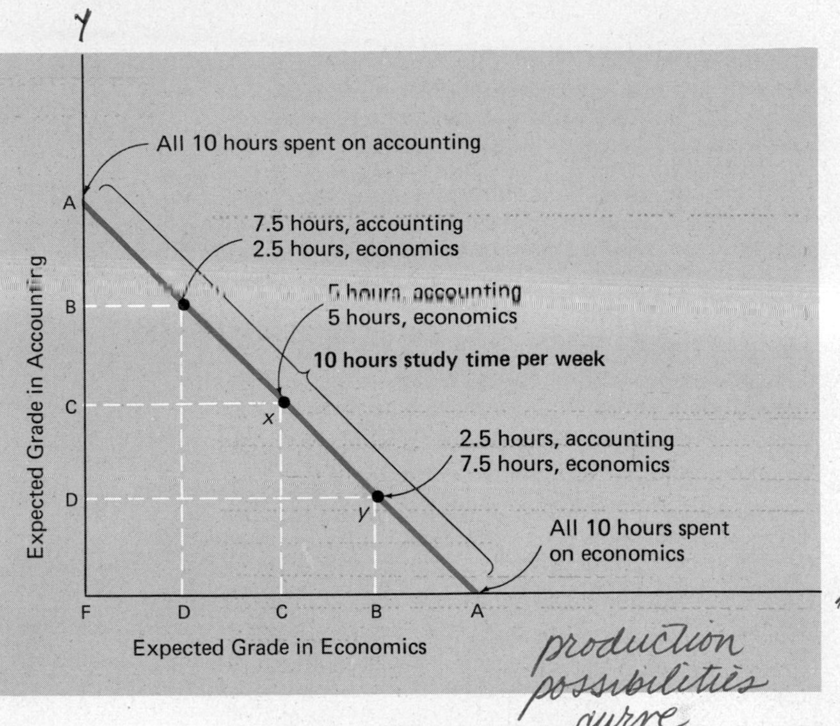

ability to learn. Quite clearly, if the student wished to spend more total time studying, then it would be possible to have higher grades in both economics and accounting. However, then we would no longer be on the specific production possibilities curve that is illustrated in Exhibit 1–2. We would have to draw a new curve in order to show the greater total study time and a different set of possible trade-offs.

> ***Concepts in Brief 1-2***
> - Any use of a resource involves an opportunity cost because an alternative use, by necessity, was sacrificed.
> - We look only at the highest valued alternative to determine opportunity cost.
> - Evaluating opportunity cost does not depend on who uses a resource, or on whose resource is used, but rather on its maximum value in some other use.
> - The graphic conceptualization of trade-offs that must be made is displayed in a production possibilities curve.

Society's Choices

The straight-line curve in Exhibit 1–2 can be generalized to the choices facing an entire nation. When a nation chooses more military goods, it is, by reason of the scarcity constraint, choosing to produce fewer civilian goods. In Exhibit 1–3(a) look at the hypothetical numerical trade-offs expressed in billions of dollars per year for military versus civilian goods for the American economy. If no civilian goods are produced, all of our resources will be used in the production of military goods that will have a value of $1.8 trillion per year. On the other hand, if no military goods are produced, all of our resources will create $2 trillion of civilian goods per year.[2] In between, there are various combinations that are possible. These combinations are plotted as points *A, B, C, D, E,* and *F* in Exhibit 1–3(b). When these points are connected with a smooth curve, we come up with society's production possibilities curve showing the trade-off between military and civilian goods. These trade-offs occur *on* the production possibilities curve. Remember, we use military and civilian goods in our example, but the analysis holds for any two goods. This concept could be applied to *all* types of goods, but that is not graphically possible. We use two types of goods in our model to illustrate trade-offs that exist in choosing *any* combinations of any number of goods.

[2] Note that if all resources are used for civilian goods, $2 trillion per year can be produced, but only $1.8 trillion can be produced when all resources are used for military goods. The assumption in our example is that our total resources are less well suited to the production of military goods than to the production of civilian goods.

EXHIBIT 1–3

Society's Trade-off Between Military and Civilian Goods. Both military and civilian goods are measured in billions of dollars per year. We look at six combinations from *A* through *F*. The first one is 0 civilian goods, which allows us to produce $1.8 trillion per year of military goods. At the other extreme, combination *F*, society produces 0 military goods, which allows it to produce $2 trillion of civilian goods. These combinations are plotted in panel (b). We connect points *A* through *F* with a smooth line. It is society's production possibilities curve for military and civilian goods. Point *R* lies outside the production possibilities curve and is therefore unattainable; point *S* lies inside and therefore represents an inefficient use of resources.

Panel (a)

Combination	*Military Goods (billions of dollars)*	*Civilian Goods (billions of dollars)*
A	$1800	$ 0
B	$1710	$ 400
C	$1540	$ 800
D	$1100	$1200
E	$ 620	$1600
F	$ 0	$2000

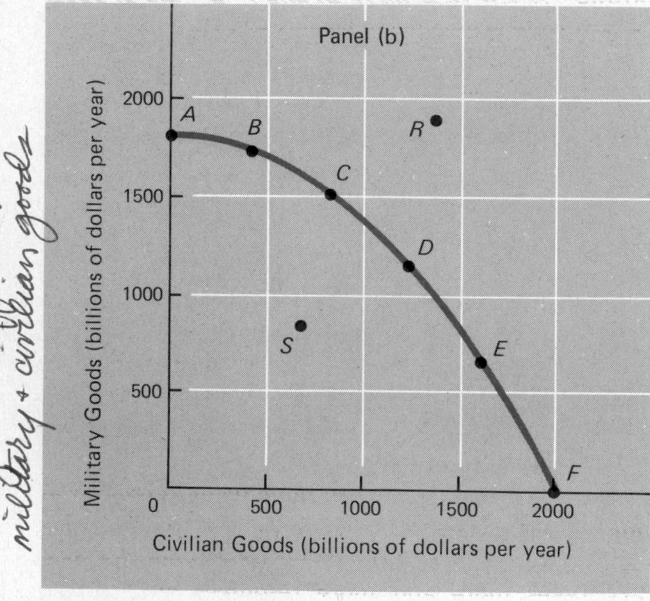

ASSUMPTIONS UNDERLYING THE PRODUCTION POSSIBILITIES CURVE

There are a number of assumptions underlying the production possibilities curve. The first one relates to the fact that we are referring to the output possible on a *yearly* basis. In other words, we have specified a time period over which the production takes place.

Second, we are assuming that resources are *fixed* over this time period. To understand fully what is meant by a fixed amount of resources, consider that there are (1) factors that influence labor hours available for work and (2) factors that influence productivity, or the output per unit of input.

Factors Influencing Labor Hours Available for Work

Hours available for work are determined by:

1. Labor force size.
2. The percentage of available individuals who choose to work.
3. Population, both its growth and trends.
4. Custom and tradition.

Factors Influencing Productivity

There are a number of factors influencing productivity, of which we can name at least four:

1. Quantity and quality of capital.
2. Quantity and quality of natural resources.
3. Health, education, motivation, and skill levels of the labor force.
4. Research and development.

Basically, then, we assume when drawing a production possibilities curve that no earthshaking invention that would reduce significantly the cost of producing either military or civilian goods in our example has occurred. We are further assuming that the labor force size remains the same over the time period, that the health, motivation, and skill levels remains the same, and so on. If any one of the factors influencing labor hours or productivity changes, then the production possibilities curve will shift. Any improvement in technology (productivity) will move the entire curve outward to the right, as in Exhibit 1–4(a). Any significant reduction in the labor force, all other things held constant, will shift the entire production possibilities curve inward to the left, as in Exhibit 1–4(b).

Being Off the Production Possibilities Curve

Point *R* lies outside the production possibilities curve in Exhibit 1–3(b). Any point outside the curve is impossible to achieve during the time period used. By definition, the possibilities curve relates to a specific unit of time. Additionally, the production possibilities curve is drawn for a given resource base. Under these two constraints, the production possibilities curve therefore indicates, by definition, the maximum quantity of one good available, given some quantity of the other. Point *R*, lying outside the production possibilities curve, occurs because we live in a world of scarcity. Look at point *S* in Exhibit 1–3(b). It is inside the curve,

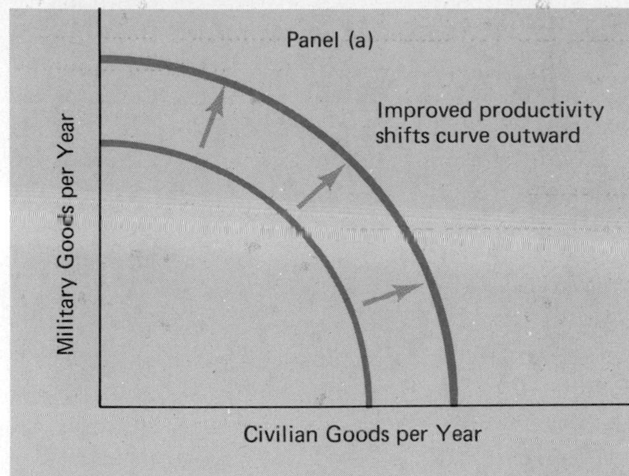

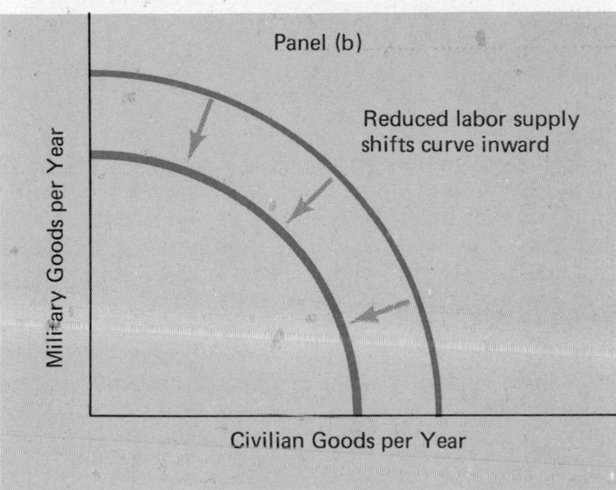

EXHIBIT 1–4
Shifting Production Possibilities Curves. In panel (a), we see that improved productivity will shift the entire production possibilities curve outward over time. In panel (b), a reduced amount of labor available to the economy will shift the entire production possibilities curve inward over time.

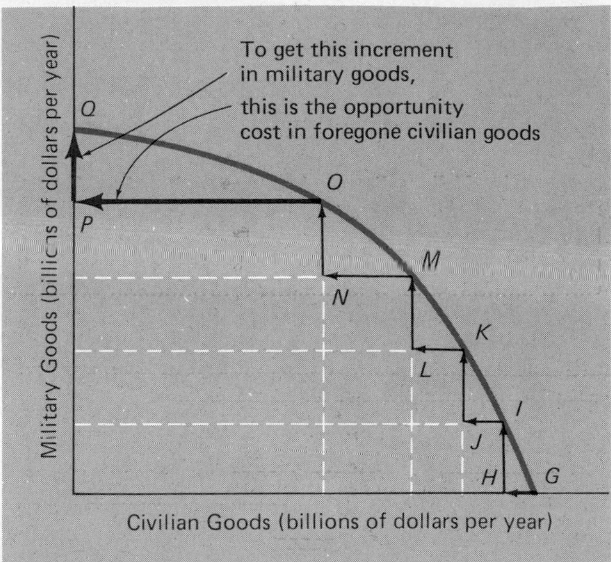

EXHIBIT 1–5
The Law of Increasing Costs. Consider equal increments in military goods production, as measured on the vertical axis in this diagram. Thus, all of the vertical arrows—*H–I, J–K, L–M, N–O,* and *P–Q*—are of equal length. What is the cost to society of obtaining the first such increment in military goods? It is a reduction in civilian goods, *G–H.* This cost for additional equal increments in military goods rises, however. Finally, to get the last increment in military goods—*P–Q*—society must give up the entire distance *O–P.* The opportunity cost of each additional increase in military goods rises.

which means that society's resources are not being fully utilized. This could be due to unemployment.

WHY THE PRODUCTION POSSIBILITIES CURVE IS BOWED OUTWARD

In the example in Exhibit 1–2, the trade-off between a grade in accounting and a grade in economics was one to one. The trade-off ratio was fixed. That is not the case in Exhibit 1–3. The opportunity cost of obtaining more and more units of military goods rises. That is to say, each additional unit costs society more in foregone alternatives than the previously produced unit. We can see this more clearly in Exhibit 1–5. Each increment in military output is the same, but look at what we have to *give up* in civilian goods when we go from the next to the last unit of military output to the last unit where the entire economy is producing just military goods. The opportunity cost is very large relative to what a one-unit increase in military goods costs the society when we start with none being produced at all. Exhibit 1–5 can also be labeled a representation of the **law of increasing relative costs.** As society takes more and more resources and applies them to the production of any specific item, the opportunity cost for each additional unit produced increases at an increasing rate.

Why are we faced with the law of increasing relative costs? Why is the production possibilities curve bowed outward? The answers to these questions are basic, and are related to the fact that some resources are just better suited for the production of some things than they are for other things. We start in a world with *no* military goods. We can at first relatively easily transfer engineers, mechanics, and technicians who are producing television sets, cars, and refrigerators in the private sector to produce guns, tanks, and bombs in the military sector. Many, if not most, of these engineers, mechanics, and technicians will be doing a job in the military sector that is quite similar to the one that they were doing in the private sector. Thus, their productivity will be approximately the same as it was prior to the move.

Eventually, however, we will have to transfer college economics professors, Sunday school teachers, day-care center operators, and rock singers into the factories making war goods. (This was indeed the case during World War II.) Their talents will be relatively poorly suited to such tasks. We might have to use 25 economics professors to get the same increment in output that we got when we hired an engineer to build us the first tank. Thus, the opportunity cost of an additional unit of war-related goods will be much higher when we use resources that are ill-suited to the task. That cost—of using poorly suited resources—will increase as we attempt to produce more and more military output. Basically, we can say that the more specialized the resources are, the more bowed the production possibilities curve will be. If all resources were equally suitable to produce both military and civilian goods, then the curves in Exhibits 1–3, 1–4, and 1–5 would approach a straight line, as in Exhibit 1–2.

Specialization is a fact of life and a topic we must cover.

> ***Concepts in Brief 1-3***
>
> ■ Trade-offs are represented graphically by a production possibilities curve showing the maximum output combinations obtainable over a one-year period from a given set of resources.
>
> ■ Since many resources are better suited for certain productive tasks than for others, society's production possibilities curve is bowed outward following the law of increasing relative cost.
>
> ■ Points outside the production possibilities curve are unattainable; points inside represent an inefficient use of or underutilization of available resources.

Specialization

All resources are better suited for some uses than for others. They are specialized. Most of us will engage in **specialization.** As a labor resource, each of us will become specialized in a particular field. Generally, the reason we allow ourselves to become specialized is so that we can attain a higher living standard. We prefer to specialize in one endeavor, such as accounting, teaching, selling, writing, or whatever, and trade with other specialists. Perhaps the easiest way to see the benefits from specialization is to look at a simple numerical example.

Look at Exhibit 1–6. Here we show total output available for two productive workers in a small world where they are the only individuals. At first, they do not specialize; rather, each works an equal amount of time, 8 hours each day, harvesting soybeans and cabbage. Ms. Jones chooses to harvest 2 pounds of soybeans in 4 hours of work and an additional 2 pounds of cabbage with the additional 4 hours. Mr. Smith chooses to harvest 3 pounds of soybeans in his first 4 hours of work but only 1 pound of cabbage in his second 4 hours. The total

EXHIBIT 1–6

Before Specialization: Here we show the relationship between Ms. Jones and Mr. Smith's daily work effort and the harvesting of soybeans and cabbage. When Ms. Jones works on her own without specializing in either activity, she devotes 4 hours a day to soybean harvesting and 4 hours a day to cabbage harvesting. For her efforts, she obtains 2 pounds of each. On the other hand, Mr. Smith, again not specializing, will harvest in the same two 4-hour periods 3 pounds of soybeans and 1 pound of cabbage. Their total output will be 5 pounds of soybeans and 3 pounds of cabbage.

Daily Work Effort	*Ms. Jones*
4 hours	2 lbs. soybeans
4 hours	2 lbs. cabbage
	Mr. Smith
4 hours	3 lbs. soybeans
4 hours	1 lb. cabbage
Total = 5 lbs. soybeans, 3 lbs. cabbage	

After Specialization: If Ms. Jones specializes in the harvesting of cabbage, she can harvest 4 pounds for every 8 hours of daily work effort. Mr. Smith, on the other hand, specializing in the harvesting of soybeans, will harvest 6 pounds. Their grand total of production will be 6 pounds of soybeans and 4 pounds of cabbage, a pound more of each good than before they specialized.

Daily Work Effort	*Ms. Jones*
8 hours	4 lbs. cabbage
	Mr. Smith
8 hours	6 lbs. soybeans
Total = 6 lbs. soybeans, 4 lbs. cabbage	

amount that the two can and choose to harvest without specialization is 5 pounds of soybeans and 3 pounds of cabbage.

Now look at what happens when they specialize. We see, in Exhibit 1–6, that after specialization, when Ms. Jones spends all her day harvesting cabbage, she can harvest 4 pounds (since she can harvest 2 pounds in 4 hours). Mr. Smith, on the other hand, spending all his work day harvesting soybeans, produces 6 pounds (since he can produce 3 pounds in just 4 hours). The total output of this two-individual world has now increased to 6 pounds of soybeans and 4 pounds of cabbage. With the same two people using the same amount of resources, the total output of this little economy has increased from 5 pounds of soybeans per day to 6, and from 3 pounds of cabbage per day to 4. Obviously, Ms. Jones and Mr. Smith would be better off (in a material sense) if they each specialized and exchanged. Ms. Jones would exchange cabbage for soybeans, Mr. Smith would do the reverse. (Our discussion, of course, has not dealt with the *disadvantages* of specialization—monotony and drudgery in one's job.)

After specialization, each individual would be doing what he or she could do *comparatively* better than the other. This leads us to the concept of comparative advantage.

Comparative Advantage

Specialization, as outlined in our example of soybeans and cabbage harvesting, rests on a very important fact: different individuals, communities, and nations are indeed different, at least when it comes to the skills of each in producing goods and services. In our simple two-person example, if these persons could do both jobs equally well, there would have been no reason for specialization, since total output could not have been increased. (Go back to Exhibit 1–6 and make Mr. Smith equally physically productive in harvesting both soybeans and cabbage, producing say, 1 pound of each in 4 hours, and then see what happens to our example after specialization.)

In fact, people are not uniformly talented. Even if individuals or nations had the talent to do everything better (for example, by using fewer resources, especially labor hours), they would still want to *specialize in the area of their greatest advantage,* that is, in their **comparative advantage.** A good example involves former President William Howard Taft. Before he became president, he was probably the country's fastest stenographer. He might have been at the same time the country's best typist, best violin player, and best everything else, but he decided to become president, because that was where his comparative advantage lay. Had he declined the presidency to remain a stenographer, the cost to him of that action would have been tremendous.

To continue the example, consider the hypothetical dilemma of the president of a large company. Suppose that he or she can type better than any of the typists, file better than any of the file clerks, drive a truck better than any of the truck drivers, and wash windows better than any of the window washers. That just means that the president has an **absolute advantage** in all of these endeavors—he or she uses fewer labor hours for each task than anyone else in the company. However, his or her *comparative* advantage lies in managing the company, not in doing the aforementioned tasks. How is it known that that is where the comparative advantage lies? The answer is quite easy: The president is *paid* the most for being president, not for being a typist or a file clerk or a truck driver or a window washer for the company. The same is true of the simple two-person economy we previously discussed. If someone were paying Ms. Jones and Mr. Smith, Mr. Smith would obviously be paid more to specialize in harvesting soybeans rather than cabbage. In fact, he could figure that out all by himself. To get 1 more pound of cabbage, he would have to give up 3 pounds of soybeans. However, for Ms. Jones to get 1 more pound of soybeans, she only has to give up 1 pound of cabbage. She therefore has a comparative advantage in harvesting cabbage, and he therefore has a comparative advantage in harvesting soybeans, because in both cases the cost of *not* harvesting the other commodity is lower.

Basically, *one's comparative advantage is found by choosing that activity that has the lowest opportunity cost.* Mr. Smith had the lowest opportunity cost in harvesting soybeans. He therefore specialized in soybeans while Ms. Jones specialized in cabbage harvesting.

The Division of Labor

Within any given firm that includes specialized human and nonhuman resources, there is a **division of labor** among those resources. The most famous example of all time comes from one of the earliest and perhaps one of the most famous economists of all time, Adam Smith, who illustrated the benefits of a division of labor with this example:

> One man draws out the wire, another straightens it, a third cuts it, a fourth points, a fifth grinds it at the top for receiving the head; to make the head requires two or three distinct operations; to put it on is a peculiar business, to whiten the pins is another; it is even a trade by itself to put them into the paper.[3]

Making pins this way allowed ten workers without very much skill to make almost 48,000 pins "of a middling size" in a day. One worker, toiling alone, could have made perhaps 20 pins a day; therefore, ten workers could have produced 200. Division of labor allowed for an increase in the daily output of the pin factory from 200 to 48,000! (Smith did not attribute *all* of the gain to the division of labor according to talent, but also to the use of machinery, to the fact that less time was spent shifting from task to task, and so on.)

What we are referring to here involves a division of the resource called labor into different kinds of labor. The different kinds of labor are organized in such a way as to increase the amount of output possible from the fixed resources available. We can therefore talk about an organized division of labor within a firm leading to increased output.

Concepts in Brief 1-4

- With a given set of resources, specialization results in higher output; in other words, there are gains to specialization in terms of higher material well-being.
- Individuals and nations specialize in their comparative advantages in order to reap the gains of specialization.
- Comparative advantages are found by determining which activities have the lowest opportunity cost or, otherwise stated, which activities yield the highest return for the time and resources used.
- A division of labor occurs when different workers are assigned different tasks. Together, the workers produce a desired product.

Economics as a Science

Economics is a social science that makes use of the same kinds of methods used in other sciences, such as biology, physics, and chemistry. Like these other sciences, economics uses models, or theories. Economic models and theories are simplified representations of the real world that we use to help us understand, explain, and predict economic phenomena in the real world.

For many centuries, most people thought that the world was flat. Using this model, they predicted that if one sailed to the edge of the world, one would fall off into space. Columbus, however, applied a new model. His **model,** or **theory,** postulated that the world was round. He predicted that one could sail around the world without falling off an edge, because there were no edges. He tested his model, or theory, by sailing and sailing and sailing. He did not fall off any edges, and thereby refuted the flat-earth model empirically.

MODELS AND REALISM

At the outset, it must be emphasized that no model in *any* science, and therefore no economic model, is complete in the sense that it captures every detail and interrelationship that exists. Indeed, a model, by definition, is an abstraction from reality. It may be conceptually impossible to construct a perfectly realistic model. For example, in physics we cannot account for every atom and its position and certainly not for every molecule and subparticle. Not only is such a model impossibly expensive to build, but it would also be impossible to work with it. No model of the solar system, for example, could possibly take into account all aspects of the entire solar system.

The nature of scientific model building is such that the model should capture only the *essential* relationships that are sufficient to analyze the particular problem or answer the particular question with which we are concerned.

What is essential is open to debate; hence, we observe competing models developed by those who may disagree on what relationships are essential. For example, when we attempt to construct a model of how consumers behave in the face of changing prices for a particular commodity, there are at the very least a million determinants of how each consumer will respond to such changes in prices. However, most of these determinants are left out of our model. It is not because they are meaningless; rather, the model that we usually use, which includes: (1) the price of the particular commodity, (2) the income of the consumer, and (3) the price of substitutes for the commodity in question, seems to be adequate. That is, just taking into account the magnitudes of these three determinants of consumer demand works "well," even though the model is "unrealistic" because it does not capture *all* the potential determinants of how consumers

[3]Adam Smith, *The Wealth of Nations* [1776] (New York: Random House, 1937).

will respond to a change in price. And since most of economics is concerned with the behavior of groups, we can ignore factors that are peculiar to specific individuals. For example, when we wish to predict how much ice cream people will buy when its price falls, we can safely ignore the fact that some people won't buy *any* more ice cream because their doctor told them not to eat it.

In sum, then, an economic model cannot be faulted as unrealistic merely because it doesn't represent every detail of the real world. That same model may be very realistic in terms of elucidating the *central* issue at hand or forces at work. Every theory is an abstraction of reality.

ASSUMPTIONS

Every model, or theory, must be based on a set of assumptions. Assumptions define the set of circumstances in which our model is most likely to be applicable. When scientists predicted that sailing ships would fall off the edge of the earth, they used the assumption that the earth was flat. Columbus did not accept the implications of such a model. He tested the predictions of his own model, which was based on the assumption that the world was round. He sailed and did not fall off any "edge." The empirical test of his own model refuted the flat-earth model. Indirectly, then, it was a test of the assumption of that model that the earth was flat.

Models in physics and chemistry, for example, contain numerous assumptions. In physics, for instance, there is a model that uses a "perfect gas." A perfect gas is one whose molecules are so far apart that you can ignore any interaction between them, except when they collide. Of course, no gas in the real world behaves like a perfect gas. Nonetheless, the model that is based on this assumption of a perfect gas is well known and accepted. It is called Boyle's Law. The assumption of the model is unrealistic as are the physicists' models that assume a frictionless world. We still accept these assumptions and the resulting models, provided that they *work* well. Now, you ask, what does "work well" mean?

DECIDING ON THE USEFULNESS OF A MODEL

We generally do not attempt to determine the usefulness of a model or how "good" it is merely by evaluating how realistic its assumptions are. Rather, we consider that a model is "good" if it yields usable predictions and implications for the real world. In other words, can we predict what will happen in the world around us with the model? Are there implications in the model of how things will happen in our world?

Once we have determined that the model does predict real-world phenomena, then the scientific approach to analysis of the world around us requires that we consider evidence. Evidence is used to test the usefulness of a model. This is why we call economics an empirical science—empirical meaning that real evidence (data) is looked at to see whether we are right.

Consider two competing models that concern themselves with the following strange occurrence: every time that I leave paper currency (money) on a table in the student union, it disappears. The first model is based on several assumptions, including that of self-interest—making oneself as well off as possible. This model predicts that if it doesn't take too much effort to take possession of the paper currency (which can then be spent), individuals will engage in this clearly worthwhile activity. The competing model sounds a little kooky, but we'll go along with it anyway. It uses a theory of magnetic attraction: paper currency emits a magnetic force that causes people's hands to pick it up. A testable (that is, refutable) implication of the first model is that money will disappear faster the larger the denomination of the bills left. The implication of the magnetic attraction model, on the other hand, is that no matter what the size of the denomination of the bills, they will disappear equally fast. We can run an experiment now to test the predictive capacity of these two models. On some days we randomly leave a dollar bill on a table at different time intervals. Then we keep increasing the possible take, leaving next \$5 at a time, then \$10, then \$50, then \$100. If we observe that more individuals hang around the student union as the denomination of the bills gets larger, we have an observed fact that does not refute the implication or prediction of the first model. It does, however, refute the second model, which would predict that the number of students who hang around will be the same no matter what the denomination of the bill is, because denomination does not determine magnetic force. In this case, we would then choose the first model and reject the second.

MODELS OF BEHAVIOR, NOT THOUGHT PROCESSES

Take special note of the fact that economists' models do not relate to the way people *think*. Rather, they relate to the way people *act,* to what they do in life with their limited resources. Models tend to generalize human behavior. In no way does the economist attempt to predict how people will think about a particular topic, such as the high price of oil products, accelerated inflation, higher taxes, or the like. Rather, the task at hand is to predict how people will act, which may be quite different from what they say they will do.

Positive Versus Normative Economics—What *Is* Versus What *Ought to be*

Economics is a social science; it uses *positive* analysis. This is a scientific term that relates to the value-free nature of the inquiry; no subjective or "gut" feelings enter into the analysis. Positive analysis relates to basic statements, such as *If A, then B.* For example, if the price of gasoline goes up relative to all other prices, then the amount of it that people will buy will fall. That is a positive economic statement. It is a statement of *what is.* It is not a statement of anyone's value judgment or subjective feelings. "Hard" sciences, such as physics and chemistry, are considered to be virtually value-free. After all, how can someone's values enter into a theory of molecular behavior? But economists face a different problem. They deal with the behavior of individuals, not molecules. Thus, it is more difficult to stick to what we consider to be value-free or **positive economics** without reference to our feelings.

When our values are interjected into the analysis, we enter the realm of **normative economics,** or normative analysis, which is defined as analysis containing, whether explicitly or implicitly, the values of someone. A positive economic statement is: "If the price of gas goes up, people will buy less." If we add to that analysis the following statement—"and therefore we *should* not allow the price to go up"—we have entered the realm of normative economics; we have expressed a personal opinion or value judgment. In fact, any time you see the word *should,* you will know that values are entering into the discussion.

USING POSITIVE ECONOMICS IN NORMATIVE ANALYSIS

Even though this economics textbook, along with virtually all others, contains mostly positive economic analyses, such analyses can be used when one passes into the realm of policymaking in which values enter. Suppose, for example, that you desire to raise the income of unemployed teenagers. That is a normative judgment (that is, a value judgment) that you have made and in which you believe. Assume that you are a policymaker with many options available to you. One is to get Congress to raise the minimum wage. Here is where positive analysis can come to your aid.

Suppose that you construct a model of the teenage labor market. Your examination of real-world evidence tells you that in the past raising the minimum wage has not led to higher incomes for unemployed teenagers. In fact, you find out that it can even cause increased unemployment among teenagers. Even though your normative goal is to help unemployed teenagers, you may use positive economic analysis to decide that you must seek an alternative policy to raising the minimum wage. Hence, positive economics can be used as the basis for deciding on the appropriate policies to carry out one's goals or the goals of the nation.

A WARNING

It is easy to define positive economics. It is quite another matter to catch all unlabeled normative statements in a textbook like this one, even though an author goes over the manuscript many times before it is printed. Therefore, do not get the impression that a textbook author will be able to keep his or her values out of the book. They will slip through. In fact, the choice itself of which topics to include in an introductory textbook involves normative economics. There is no value-free or objective way to decide which ones to use in a textbook. The author's "gut feelings" ultimately make a difference when choices have to be made. From your own personal standpoint, what you might hope to do is to be able to recognize *when* you are engaging in normative as opposed to positive economic analysis. Reading this text should equip you for that task.

Concepts in Brief 1-5

- A model, or theory, uses assumptions and is by nature a simplification of the real world.
- Models in economics relate to behavior rather than individuals' thought processes.
- Positive economics indicates what *is,* whereas normative economics tells us what *ought to be.*

ISSUES AND APPLICATIONS

Does It Cost Only $3.34 a Day to Go to College?

Concepts Applied
- Opportunity cost and trade-offs

An ad in one local newspaper read as follows: "It will cost you $3.34 a day to go to Sunshine College. That's based on today's prices where you will spend $1,068 to attend this community college for two years, including tuition fees and textbooks. It comes out to $3.34 a day."

That sounds like a pretty good deal, doesn't it?

A typical college student might look at the cost of going to school as including a little bit more, because the student would pay for food, clothing, and recreation. His or her yearly cost accounting might be as follows for one year:

1. Tuition fees: $450
2. Books: $184
3. Room: $1,200
4. Food: $1,200
5. Recreation: $200

   TOTAL: $3,234 per year

If you were then to multiply this total by four, you would come up with a sizable number, and in this particular example a four-year program would cost 4 × $3,234, or $12,936. That sounds like a lot, but is in fact relatively little. If you put in the one-year tuition fee at Harvard or Stanford or some other private four-year school, the total would be even greater.

What is the Opportunity Cost of Going to School?

Does $12,936 represent the true cost of going to school for four years? Remember that the cost of doing anything is its opportunity cost. Right away, you can see that a major cost was left out of the first calculations and, by implication, left out of the very misleading ad for a local community college. The alternative to going to school is working and earning income. If, with the same effort, you could make after taxes, say, $8,000 a year, then the opportunity cost of your time of going to school is $8,000 times the number of years you stay in school. Further, room, board, and recreation do not represent a cost of going to school, because you don't have any alternative. You eat, sleep, and have fun no matter what you are doing; thus, the calculation given above is grossly inaccurate. What it should include is (1) the opportunity cost of not working, (2) tuition fees, and (3) textbooks and incidentals related strictly to schooling. The revised figures for one year might look like this:

1. Foregone after-tax earnings: $8,000 (opportunity cost of your time)
2. Tuition fees: $450
3. Books: $184

   TOTAL: $8,634 per year

The full cost of education at this school for four years would then be 4 × $8,634, or $34,536. That's quite a bit more than the original calculation, isn't it? But it's more accurate in terms of the true cost to you as an individual with alternatives in a world of scarcity. Now answer the question at the head of this Issue.

Questions

1. Why is the opportunity cost of going to school measured by *after-tax* income?
2. If you are given a scholarship that pays all tuition fees, does that affect your opportunity cost? Does it affect your calculation of the full cost of education?

Is It Possible to Have More Guns and More Butter Simultaneously?

Concepts Applied
- Trade-offs and production possibilities curve

A number of years back, when the United States was involved in a war in Vietnam, the late President Johnson made a speech in which he assured the American public that the United States would not sacrifice butter for guns. In other words, we could have more guns for the war and also more domestic social programs. Is that possible? At a given time, it is not, at least not starting from full employment. Look at Exhibit 1-7. It is a production possibilities curve: on one axis is measured guns per year, on the other, butter per year. If the nation moves from point *A* to point *B*, we clearly sacrifice butter in order to have more guns. There are, in fact, only two ways in which President Johnson could have been correct, and then only in a very loose way.

Unemployment and Inefficiency

If we were "inside" the production possibilities curve, we might be at a point such as *U* in Exhibit 1-8. Then it would be possible to have more guns and more butter simultaneously. But consider how far inside the production possibilities curve we would have to be to observe a significant increase in more of each of these commodities with no additional cost to society. When President Johnson spoke, this nation was not suffering a great depression, nor can we assume

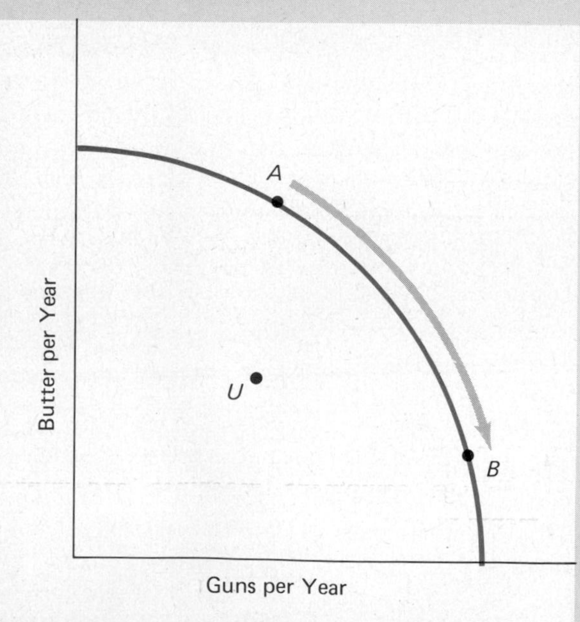

EXHIBIT 1–7
The Trade-off Between Guns and Butter. It is impossible to have more guns and more butter at the same time during any given period starting from a full-employment situation such as at points *A* and *B*. When we move from point *A* to point *B*, we indeed have more guns but, unfortunately, less butter. A choice must be made.

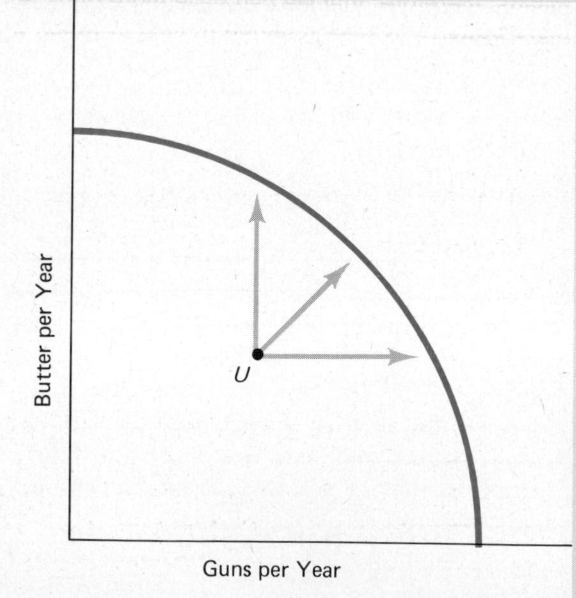

EXHIBIT 1–8
Being Inside the Production Possibilities Curve. If we are at point *U* within the production possibilities curve, then it is possible to have more guns and more butter simultaneously. We can be inside the curve because resources are underutilized.

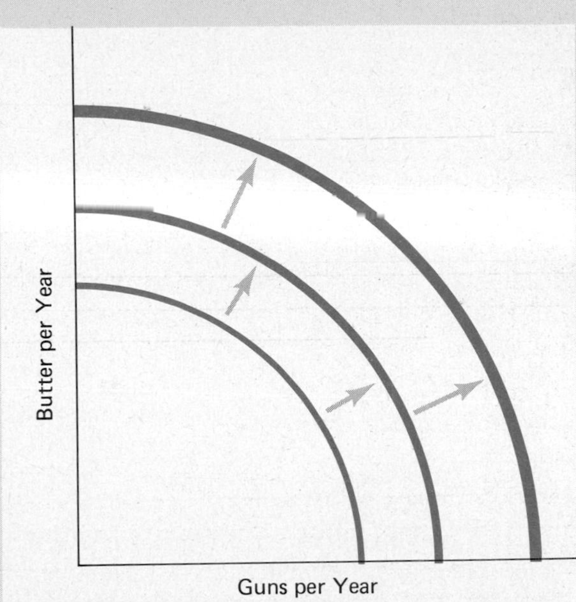

EXHIBIT 1–9
Economic Growth Allows for More of Everything. If the nation experiences economic growth, the production possibilities curve between guns and butter will move out, as is shown. This takes time, however, and it does not occur automatically. It means, therefore, that we can have more guns and more butter only after a period of time in which we have experienced economic growth.

that at that time resources were so poorly organized that we were inside the production possibilities curve.

Economic Growth

Over time, it is possible to have more guns and more butter. This is through economic growth. In Exhibit 1–9, we see the production possibilities curve for guns and butter shifting outward. There are two additional curves shown. These represent new choices open to an economy that has experienced economic growth. Such growth comes about because of productive investments in both humans and equipment. If all of us decided to spend more time in school to make ourselves more productive in the future, we could, taken together, move the production possibilities frontier outward. If more income is spent on research and development and improved techniques of production, then there is a good chance that the production possibilities curve will continue to move outward. That is what economic growth is all about.

Scarcity still exists. Note, however, that no matter how much economic growth there has been, we will still be at a point on some production possibilities curve. Thus, we will always face trade-offs. The more we want of one thing, the less we will have of others. Scarcity cannot be escaped.

Questions
1. What possible reasons would cause the country to be at point *U* in Exhibit 1–7?
2. Why are the production possibilities curves shown in Exhibits 1–7, 1–8, and 1–9 bowed outward?

Definition of Terms

Scarcity A reference to the fact that at any point in time there exists only a finite amount of resources—human and nonhuman. Scarcity of resources therefore means that nature does not freely provide as much of everything as people want.

Resources Inputs used in the production of the goods and services that we desire.

Land The natural resources that are available without alteration or effort on the part of humans. Land as a resource includes only original fertility and mineral deposits, topography, climate, water, and vegetation.

Labor Productive contributions of humans who work, which involve both thinking and doing.

Capital All manufactured resources, including buildings, equipment, machines, and improvements to land.

Entrepreneurship The fourth factor of production involving human resources that perform the functions of raising capital, organizing, managing, assembling other factors of production, and making basic business policy decisions. The entrepreneur is a risk-taker.

Economic good Any good or service that is scarce.

Free good Any good or service that is available in quantities larger than are desired at a zero price.

Economics The study of the way in which individuals and societies choose among alternative uses of scarce resources.

Opportunity cost The highest valued alternative that must be sacrificed to attain something or satisfy a want.

Trade-off A term relating to opportunity cost. In order to get a desired economic good, it is necessary to trade off some other desired economic good whenever we are in a world of scarcity. A trade-off involves a sacrifice, then, that must be made in order to obtain something.

Production possibilities curve A curve representing all possible combinations of total output that could be produced assuming (a) a fixed amount of productive resources and (b) efficient use of those resources.

Law of increasing relative costs This law is an economic principle that states that the opportunity cost of additional units of a good generally increases as society attempts to produce more of that good.

Specialization The division of productive activities among persons and regions so that no one individual or one area is totally self-sufficient. An individual may specialize, for example, in law, medicine, or automobile production. A nation may specialize in the production of coffee, computers, or cameras.

Comparative advantage The ability to be able to produce a good or service at a lower opportunity cost than someone else.

Absolute advantage The ability to produce a good or service at an "absolutely" lower cost, usually (but not necessarily) measured in hours of work required to produce the good.

Division of labor The segregation of a resource into different specific tasks; for example, one automobile worker puts on bumpers, another doors, and so on.

Models, or theories Simplified representations of the real world used to make predictions or to better understand the real world.

Positive economics Analysis that is strictly limited to making either purely descriptive statements or scientific predictions; for example, *If A, then B*. A statement of *what is*.

Normative economics Analysis involving value judgments about economic policies; relates to whether things are good or bad. A statement of *what ought to be*.

Chapter Summary

1. All societies at all times face the universal problem of scarcity because we cannot all obtain everything that we want from nature without sacrifice.
2. The resources that we use to produce desired goods and services can be classified into land, labor, capital, and entrepreneurship.
3. Desired goods and services that are not freely available in nature are called scarce goods.
4. Goods and services freely available in excess of the quantity desired at a zero price are called free goods, such as clear air once you are in the mountains.
5. Because we are faced with virtually unlimited wants but scarce resources, we must choose among alternatives. Economics is the study of how people, individually and jointly, make these choices.
6. Scarcity and poverty are not synonymous. Scarcity faces even the richest nation and person because even they have to make choices among alternatives.
7. We measure the cost of anything by what has to be given up in order to have it. This cost is called opportunity cost; it does not depend on where the sacrificed alternative resource would be used or who would be using it.
8. The trade-offs facing you as an individual and all of us as a society can be represented graphically by a production possibilities curve. It shows the maximum combinations of two goods that can be produced with society's given resources over a specified period, usually a year.
9. Since resources are generally specialized, production possibilities curves bow outward. That means that each additional increment of one good can only be obtained by giving up more and more of the other good. This is called the law of increasing relative costs.
10. It is impossible to be outside the production possibilities curve, but we can be on the inside. When we are, we are in a situation of underemployment, unemployment, inefficiently organized resources, or some combination of the three.
11. Individuals end up specializing in fields in which they have a comparative advantage because their material standard of living can then be higher.
12. Within a production organization is division of labor in which resources are assigned specific tasks.
13. One finds one's comparative advantage by looking at that activity which has the lowest oppor-

tunity cost. That is, one's comparative advantage lies in that activity which generates the highest income.

14. We use models or theories in order to explain and predict behavior.
15. Models or theories are never completely realistic because, by definition, they are simplifications using assumptions that are not *directly* testable.
16. We decide upon the usefulness of a model and, by implication, its assumptions, if it seems to predict real-world phenomena relatively accurately.
17. None of the models in economics relate to individuals' thought processes; rather, they relate to what people do, not what they think or say they will do.
18. Much of economic analysis involves positive economics; that is, it is value-free. Whenever statements embodying values are made, we enter the realm of normative economics.
19. The true cost of going to college does not include just books and matriculation fees. Nor does it include room and board.
20. The true cost of going to college includes the opportunity cost (foregone income) of not working at some alternative.
21. It is impossible to have more guns and more butter simultaneously at any point in time unless we are inside the production possibilities curve.
22. The only way we can have more of everything is through economic growth, which can be represented by an outward shift in a production possibilities curve.

Selected References

Blaug, Mark. *Methodology of Economics.* New York: Cambridge University Press, 1980.
Crouch, Robert. *Human Behavior: An Economic Approach.* North Scituate, Mass.: Duxbury Press, 1979.
Friedman, Milton. *Essays in Positive Economics.* Chicago: University of Chicago Press, 1953.
Keynes, J. N. *The Scope and Method of Political Economy.* 4th ed. New York: Macmillan, 1930.
Koopmans, Tjalling C. "Economics among the Sciences." *American Economic Review* 69 (March 1979): 1–13.
Kuhn, Thomas S. *The Structure of Scientific Revolutions.* 2nd ed. Chicago: University of Chicago Press, 1970.
Lekachman, Robert. *Economists at Bay.* New York: McGraw-Hill, 1976.

Answers to Preview and Study Questions

1. Nations with high per capita incomes and individuals who are wealthy are referred to as affluent. Do affluent people face the problem of scarcity?

It is important to distinguish between the concepts "relative" and "absolute." Scarcity is a relative concept; scarcity exists because wants are great relative to the means of achieving those wants (wealth or income). Thus, even though affluent people have absolutely high levels of income or wealth, they nevertheless typically want more than they can have (in luxury goods, power, prestige, and so on). Even the richest person in the world faces scarcity—if only with respect to time. That person does not have time to do everything that he or she wants to do.

2. Fresh air and clean water can often be consumed in the United States free of charge. Does this mean that these "goods" are free or costless to society?

Economists distinguish between private costs (costs to specific individuals) and social costs (costs to society). Air is free to *individuals* in the United States; specific individuals are not charged a price for the use of this good. Yet, this good is not free to society. If a good were free to society, every person would be able to use all that he or she wanted to use; no one would have to sacrifice anything in order to use that good, and people would not have to compete for it. In the United States different groups compete for air and water. Environmentalists and concerned citizens compete with automobile drivers for clean air and with businesses for clean water. Note that as automobiles, consumers, and businesses pollute the environment, they impose costs (sacrifices) upon others who sacrifice health, cleanliness, the beauty of nature, and so on. In short, while air and water may (in many cases) be free to individuals, they are not free goods with respect to society.

3. Why does the scarcity problem force people to consider opportunity costs?

Since neither an individual nor society can have everything desired, each must make choices. Individuals have limited incomes; as a consequence, an expenditure on, say, an automobile necessarily precludes expenditures on *other* goods and services. If Mr. Smith spends $7,000 on a new car, he cannot spend that same $7,000 on other goods; Smith therefore is forced to choose between the automobile or $7,000 worth of other goods and services. The same is true for society, which also faces the scarcity problem; if society allocates specific resources to the production of a steel mill, *those same resources* cannot be allocated elsewhere. Since resources are limited, society is forced to decide how to allocate its available resources; scarcity means that the costs of allocating resources to produce specific goods is ultimately assessed in terms of other goods which are necessarily sacrificed. Since there are millions of ways in which the resources allocated to a steel mill might otherwise be allocated, one is forced to consider the *highest* valued alternative. We define the opportunity cost of a good as its highest valued alternative; the opportunity cost of the steel mill to society is the highest valued output which those *same* resources could otherwise have produced; the opportunity cost of the $7,000 auto to Mr. Smith is the highest valued alternative purchase he could have made for $7,000. Is there an opportunity cost involved in your reading this book? How would you assess it?

4. What are some costs and benefits of specialization?

People are different. They have different abilities, skills, levels of intelligence, coordination, and so on. Nonhuman resources also exhibit differences; differences in land fertility, regional rainfall, machine quality, richness in ores, and so on exist. As a consequence, different resources are better suited for specific jobs. Specialization allows specific resources to be allocated toward those jobs to which they are best suited. As a consequence, the benefits of specialization accrue in the form of increased efficiency—output increases in quantity and quality. On the other hand, specialization is not an unmixed blessing; specialization has costs (disadvantages) as well as benefits. For example, a much discussed cost is monotony and drudgery resulting from repetitive behavior. Another important cost is increased dependence; specialization requires that the specializing parties exchange outputs. Clearly the "jack of all trades" is less dependent on others than is the specialist. Regions or nations may specialize and be forced to depend upon other regions for "strategic" goods such as oil, steel, and aluminum. Another cost of specialization is increased risk; an individual or region may specialize in something that may later turn out to be unwanted by buyers. It is important to note that economists approach many issues via cost-benefit analysis; since few economic events (or policies) are all "good" or all "bad," economists often attempt to assess whether the benefits of some policy outweigh the costs.

5. What is the difference between positive and normative economics?

Ideally, positive economics deals with what *is,* whereas normative economics deals with what *ought* to be. Positive economic statements are of the "if—then" variety; they are descriptive and predictive and are not related to what *should* happen. Normative economics, on the other hand, is concerned with what ought to be and is intimately tied to value judgments. Of course, the two can work together; if full employment is desirable (a normative statement), then if *x, y,* and *z* are done, full employment will probably result (a positive statement). Since economics is a social science, economists sometimes engage in normative economics unwittingly—they sometimes confuse what *is* with what *ought* to be. It is very difficult to be value-free when the subject matter is people.

Problems

(Answers at the back of the book)

1. Construct four separate models to predict the probability that a person will die within the next five years. Include only one determining factor in each of your models.

2. The following sets of numbers represent a set of hypothetical production possibilities for a nation in 1984.

Butter	*Guns*
4	0
3	1.6
2	2.4
1	2.8
0	3.0

Plot these points on a piece of graph paper. Does the law of increasing relative costs seem to hold? Why? On the same graph, now plot and draw the production possibilities curve that will represent 10 percent economic growth.

3.

Daily Work Effort	*Ms. Jones*
4 hours	8 jackets
4 hours	12 ties
	Mr. Jones
4 hours	8 jackets
4 hours	12 ties

Total Daily Output = 16 jackets, 24 ties

Given the above information, answer the following questions.

a. Who has an absolute advantage in jacket production?
b. Who has a comparative advantage in tie production?
c. Will Ms. and Mr. Jones specialize?
d. If they specialize, what will total output equal?

4.

Daily Work Effort	*Ms. Jones*
4 hours	8 jackets
4 hours	12 ties
	Mr. Jones
4 hours	4 jackets
4 hours	12 ties

Total Daily Output = 12 jackets, 24 ties

Given the above information, answer the following questions.

a. In what does Ms. Jones have an absolute advantage?
b. In what does Mr. Jones have an absolute advantage?
c. In what does Ms. Jones have a comparative advantage?
d. In what does Mr. Jones have a comparative advantage?
e. If they specialize according to their comparative advantages, what will total output equal?

APPENDIX

A

Reading and Working with Graphs

"A picture is worth a thousand words . . ." And so is a graph! It is often easier to communicate an idea by using a picture than to read or listen to a lengthy description. A graph performs much the same function as a picture. A graph is a visual representation of the relationship between two or more variables. In this appendix, we'll stick to just two variables—an *independent* variable, which can change in value freely, and a *dependent* variable, which changes in value according to changes in the value of the independent variable.

Before we present the "picture," that is, a graph, let's return to the "thousand words," that is, a table. A table is a "list" of values showing the relationship between two variables. Any table can be converted into a graph, which is a visual representation of that list. Once you understand how a table can be converted to a graph, you will understand what graphs are and how to construct and use them.

Consider a practical example. A conservationist may try to convince you that driving at lower highway speeds will help you conserve gas. The following table, labeled Exhibit A–1, showing the relationship between speed—the independent variable—and how far you can go on a gallon of gas—the dependent variable—at that speed might be presented.

EXHIBIT A–1

Miles per Hour	*Miles per Gallon*
45	25
50	24
55	23
60	21
65	19
70	16
75	13

This table does show a pattern of sorts. As the data in the first column get larger in value, the data in the second column get smaller in value.

Now let's take a look at the different ways variables can be related.

Direct and Inverse Relationships

Two variables can be related in different ways, some simple, others more complex. For example, a person's weight and height are often related. If we measured the height and weight of thousands of people, we would surely find that taller people tend to weigh more than shorter people. That is, we would discover that there is a *direct relationship* between height and weight. By direct relationship, we simply mean that an *increase* in one variable is usually associated with an *increase* in the related variable. This can easily be seen in panel (a) of Exhibit A–2.

Let's look at another simple way two variables can be related: Much evidence indicates that as price rises for a specific commodity, the amount purchased decreases—there is an *inverse relationship* between the variable's "price per unit" and "quantity purchased." A table listing the data for this relationship would indicate that for higher and higher prices, smaller and smaller quantities would be purchased. We see this relationship in panel (b) of Exhibit A–2.

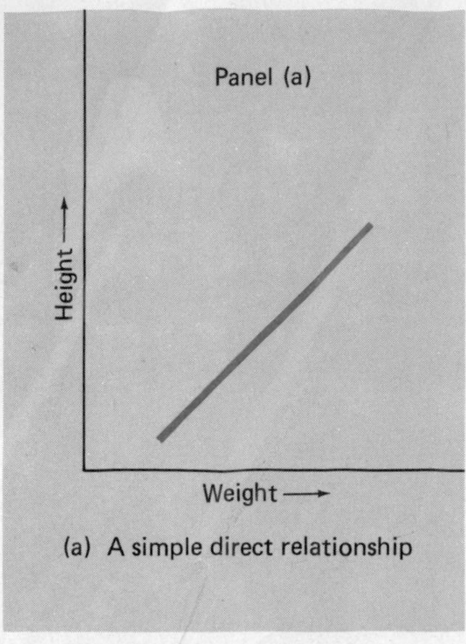

(a) A simple direct relationship

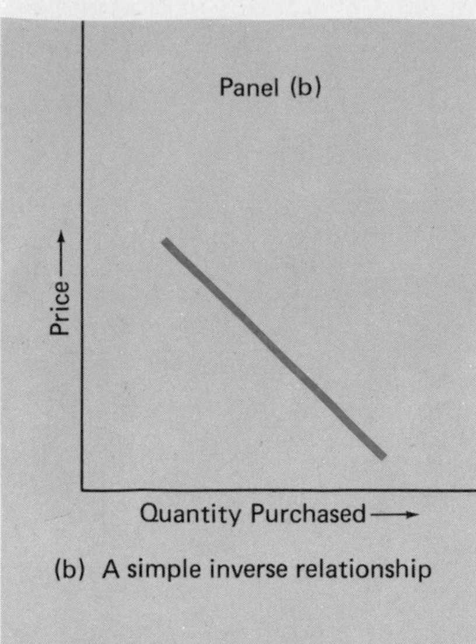

(b) A simple inverse relationship

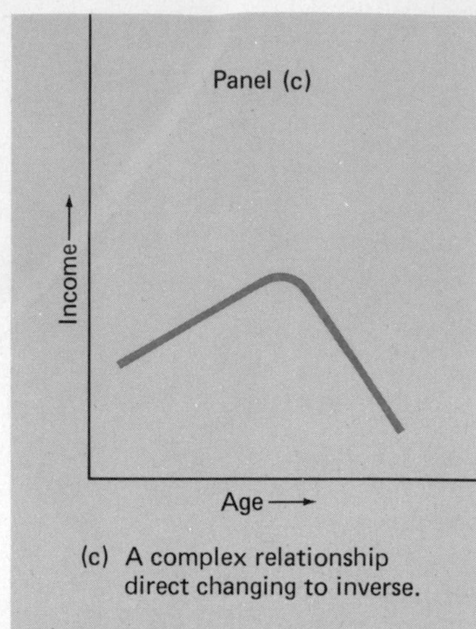

(c) A complex relationship direct changing to inverse.

EXHIBIT A–2

Now for a slightly complicated relationship between two variables: Beginning with the average person's first job, earnings increase each year up to a certain age, then beyond that age, earnings decline each year. This is not a surprising economic research finding. Most people are more energetic and productive in the early and middle years of life. In this example, the two variables—earnings and age—would yield a more complex pattern. At earlier ages, these variables are directly related—earnings increase as age increases—and at later ages these variables are inversely related—earnings decline as age increases. We have also implied the concept of *maximum*—that is, there is an age at which annual earnings are at a maximum over the lifetime of annual earnings. We see all this in panel (c) of Exhibit A–2.

Constructing a Graph

Up to this point, we have been describing with words some patterns or relationships that may exist between two variables. However, if you were paying attention, you should have noticed that we cheated—we didn't confine our description only to words. We also presented three graphs to describe the three preceding examples. Did you get the feeling that the graphs were indeed a way to "see" the idea presented by each example? If so, then you're on your way to learning how to read and work with graphs. We will now show you how to construct a graph to illustrate a relationship between two variables.

A NUMBER LINE

The first step is to become familiar with what is called *a number line.* Consider the number line shown in Exhibit A–3. There are several things that you should notice about it.

1. The points on the line divide the line into segments.
2. All the line segments are equal.
3. The numbers associated with the points on the line increase in value from left to right, or saying it the other way around, the numbers decrease in value from right to left. However you say it, what we're describing is formally called an ordered set of points.

On the number line we have shown the line segments, that is, the distance from 0 to 10 or the distance between 30 and 40. They all appear to be equal and, indeed, are equal to one-half inch. When we use a distance to represent graphically a quantity, such as barrels of oil, we are "scaling" the number line. In the example shown, the distance between 0 to 10 might represent 10 barrels of oil, or

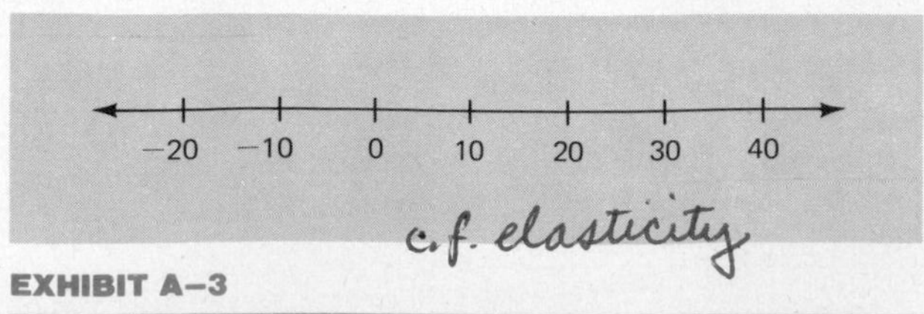

EXHIBIT A–3

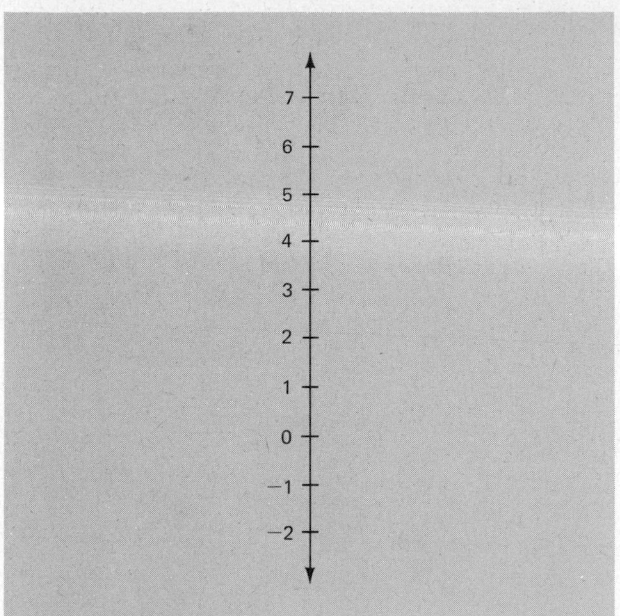

EXHIBIT A–4

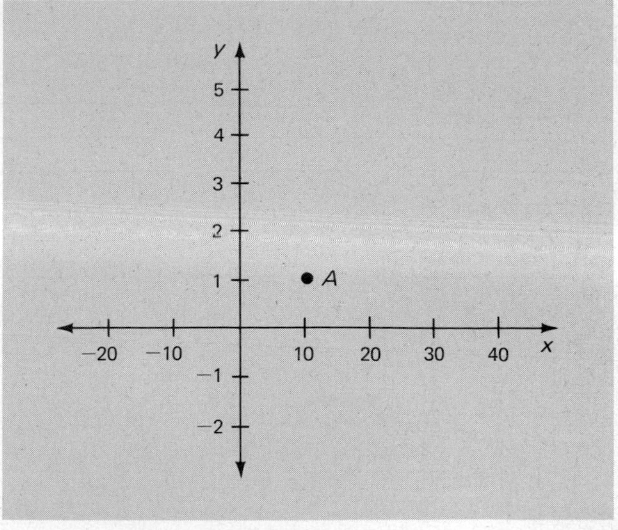

EXHIBIT A–5

the distance from 0 to 40 might represent 40 barrels. Of course, the scale may differ on different number lines. For example, a distance of one inch could represent 10 units on one number line or 5,000 units on another.

Notice that on our number line points to the left of 0 correspond to negative numbers, and points to the right of 0 correspond to positive numbers.

Of course, we can construct a vertical number line. Consider the vertical number line in Exhibit A-4. As we move up this vertical number line, the numbers increase in value; or, conversely, as we descend, the numbers decrease in value. Below 0 the numbers are negative; and above 0 the numbers are positive. And like the horizontal number line, all the line segments are equal. This line is divided into line segments such that the distance between -2 and -1 is the same as the distance between 0 and 1.

COMBINING THE VERTICAL AND HORIZONTAL NUMBER LINES

By now, you may have thought that it is by combining the horizontal and vertical number lines that we are able to represent graphically the relationships between variables in our earlier examples.

We combine the horizontal and vertical number lines as shown in Exhibit A–5.

When we combine a vertical number line with a horizontal number line so that they intersect (1) at each other's 0 point and (2) perpendicular to each other, we get what is called a set of coordinate axes, or a coordinate number system—the basis for a graph.

With a number line, you need only one number to specify a point on the line; or conversely, when you see a point on the line, you know that it represents one number, or one value. With a coordinate value system, you need two numbers to specify a single point in the system; or, when you see a single point on a graph, you know that it represents two numbers, or two values.

The basic things that you should know about a coordinate number system are: The vertical number line is referred to as the *y-axis;* the horizontal number line is referred to as the *x-axis;* and the point of intersection of the two lines is referred to as the *origin.*

Any point such as A in Exhibit A–5 represents two numbers—a value of x and a value of y. But we also know more than that; we also know that point A represents a positive value of y because it is above the x axis, and we know that it represents a positive value of x because it is to the right of the y axis.

Point A represents a "paired observation" of the variables x and y; in particular, in Exhibit A–5, A represents an observation of the pair of values $x = 10$ and $y = 1$. Every point in the coordinate system corresponds to a paired observation of x and y, which can be simply written (x,y)—as in the alpha-

EXHIBIT A–6

COLUMN 1 Price of T-Shirts	COLUMN 2 Number of T-Shirts Purchased per Week
$10	20
9	30
8	40
7	50
6	60
5	70

bet, the x value is always specified first, then the y value.

Later in this text, instead of the general variables x and y, we will be talking about specific pairs of related variables, such as prices and quantities, interest rates and the amount of credit, and other things that economists measure. Most of the variables that we deal with in economics will have positive values.

Graphing Numbers in a Table

Consider the table above, labeled Exhibit A–6. Column 1 shows different prices for T-shirts, while Column 2 depicts the number of T-shirts purchased per week at these prices.

Notice the "pattern" of these numbers. As the price of T-shirts falls, the number of T-shirts purchased per week increases. Therefore, an *inverse* relationship exists between these two variables and as soon as we represent it on a graph, you will be able to "see" the relationship. We can graph this relationship using a coordinate number system, using a vertical and horizontal number line for each of these two variables. Such a graph is shown in Exhibit A–7.

In economics, it is conventional to put dollar values on the y axis. We therefore construct a vertical number line for a price and a horizontal number line, the x axis, for quantity of T-shirts purchased per week. The resulting coordinate system shows each of the "paired observation" points; we have also repeated the table which shows an additional column representing the paired data (x,y) form. For example, point J is the paired observation (30, $9). It indicates that when the price of a T-shirt is $9, 30 will be purchased per week.

If it were possible to sell parts of a T-shirt (1/2 or 1/20 of a shirt), we would have observations at every possible price. That is, we would be able to connect our paired observations, represented as lettered points. Let's assume that we can make "T-shirts"

EXHIBIT A–7

Panel (a)

Price	T-Shirts per Week	Point on Graph
$10	20	R (20, 10)
9	30	J (30, 9)
8	40	K (40, 8)
7	50	L (50, 7)
6	60	M (60, 6)
5	70	N (70, 5)

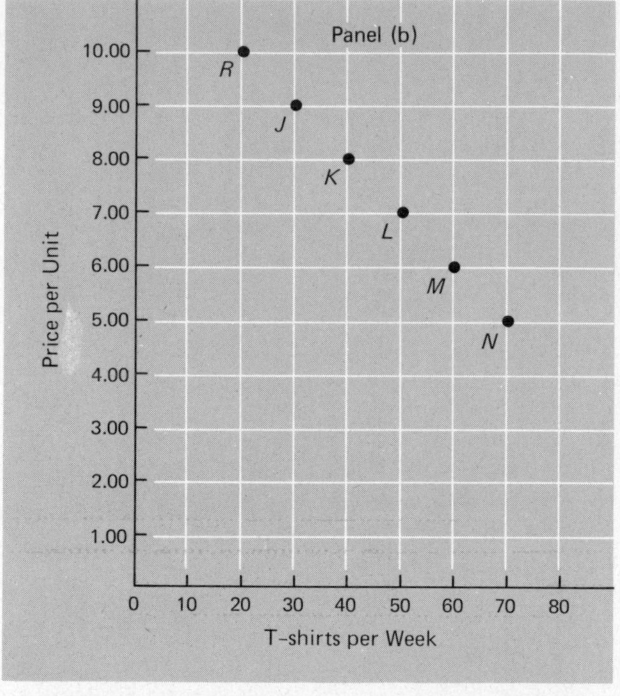

perfectly divisible. We would then have a line that connects these points, as shown in the graph in Exhibit A–8.

In short, we have now represented the data from the table in the form of a graph. Note that an inverse relationship between two variables shows up on a graph as a line or curve that slopes downward, that is, from left to right. (You may as well get used to the idea that economists call a straight line on a graph, a "curve," even though it may not "curve" at all. Much of economists' data turns out to be curves, so they refer to everything represented graphically as curves, even straight lines.)

The Slope of a Linear Line (A Linear Curve)

An important property of a curve represented on a graph is its *slope*. Consider the table and its corresponding graph shown below in Exhibit A–9. The

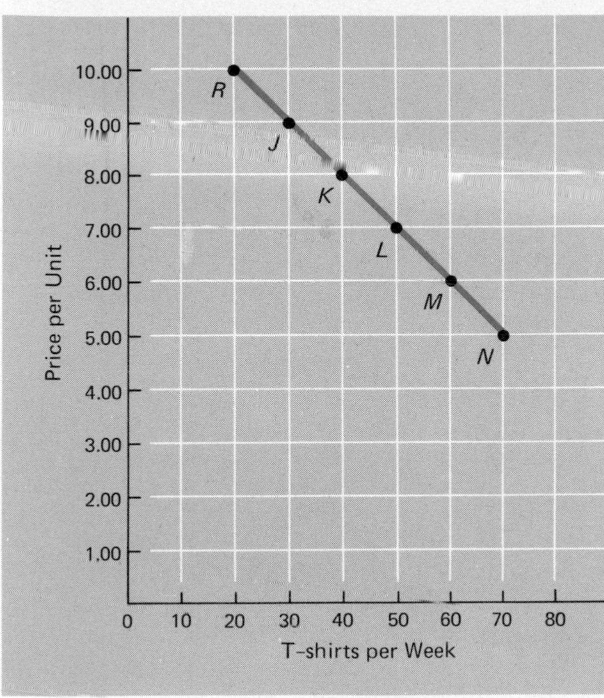

EXHIBIT A-8

EXHIBIT A-9

Panel (a)

Price	*Quantity of Shoes Offered per Week*	*Point on Graph*	
$100	400	A	(400, 100)
80	320	B	(320, 80)
60	240	C	(240, 60)
40	160	D	(160, 40)
20	80	E	(80, 20)

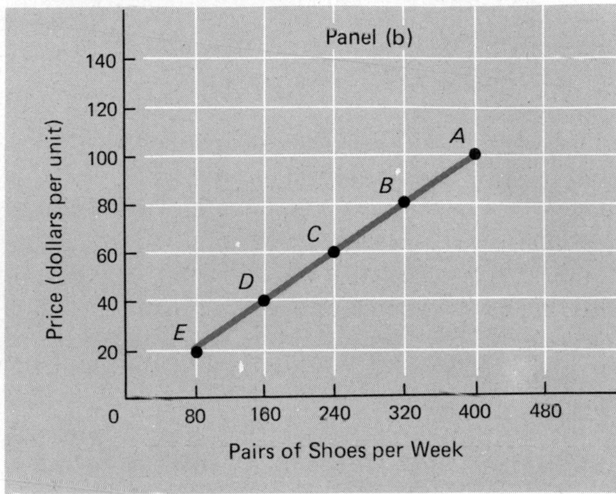

table and graph represent the quantities of shoes per week that a seller is willing to offer at different prices.

The slope of a line is defined as the change in the *y* values, divided by the corresponding change in the *x* values, as we move along the line. In Exhibit A–9, let's move from point *E* to point *D*. As we do so, we note that the change in the *y* values, which is the change in price, is +$20, since we have moved from a price of $20 to $40 per shoe pair. As we move from *E* to *D*, the change in the *x* values is +80; the number of pairs of shoes willingly offered per week rises from 80 to 160 pairs. The slope calculated as a change in the *y* values divided by the change in the *x* values is therefore:

$$\frac{20}{80} = +\tfrac{1}{4}$$

It may be helpful for you to think of slope as "rise" (movement in the vertical direction) over a "run" (movement in the horizontal direction). We show this abstractly in Exhibit A–10. The slope is measured by the amount of rise divided by the amount of run. In the example in Exhibit A–10, and of course A–9, the amount of rise is positive and so is the amount of run. That's because it's a direct relationship. We show an inverse relationship in Exhibit A–11. The slope is still equal to the rise divided by the run, but in this case, the rise is negative because the curve is sloping downward. That means that the slope will have to be negative, and that means that we are dealing with an inverse relationship.

Now let's calculate the slope for a different part of the curve back in Exhibit A–9. We will find the slope as we move from point *B* to point *A*. Again, we note that slope, or rise/run, from *B* to *A* equals:

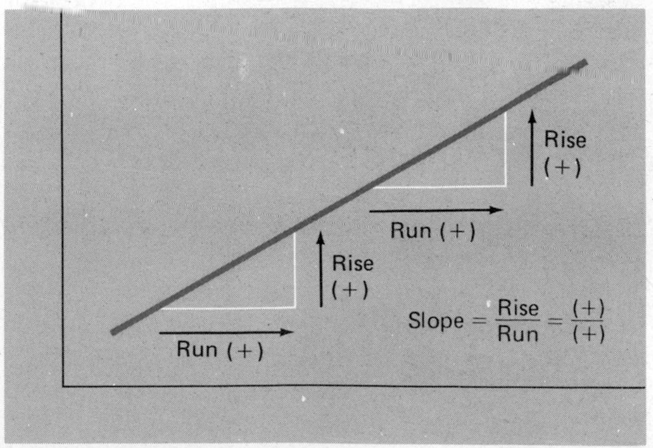

EXHIBIT A–10

$$\frac{20}{80} = +\frac{1}{4}$$

A specific property of a straight line is that its slope is the same between any two points; or, a slope is constant at any point on a straight line on a graph.

We conclude that for our example in Exhibit A–9, the relationship between the price of a pair of shoes and the quantity of pairs of shoes willingly offered per week is "linear," which simply means straight line, and our calculations indicate a constant slope. Moreover, we calculate a direct relationship between these two variables, which turns out to be an upward-sloping (from left to right) curve, that is, straight line. Upward-sloping curves have positive slopes—in this case, it is $+\frac{1}{4}$.

We know that an inverse relationship between two variables shows up as a downward-sloping curve—"rise" over "run" will be a negative slope because the "rise" is really a fall, as shown in the graph. When we see a negative slope, we know that increases in one variable are associated with decreases in the other. Therefore, we refer to downward-sloping curves as negative slopes. Can you verify that the slope of the graph representing the relationship between T-shirt prices and the quantity of T-shirts *purchased* per week in Exhibit A–8 is $-\frac{1}{10}$?

SLOPES OF NONLINEAR CURVES

The graph presented in Exhibit A–12 indicates a nonlinear (which simply means not a straight line) relationship between two variables, total yearly profits and output per year. Inspection of this graph indicates that, at first, increases in output lead to increases in total profits; that is, total profits rise and output increases. But beyond some output level, further increases in output cause decreases in total profits.

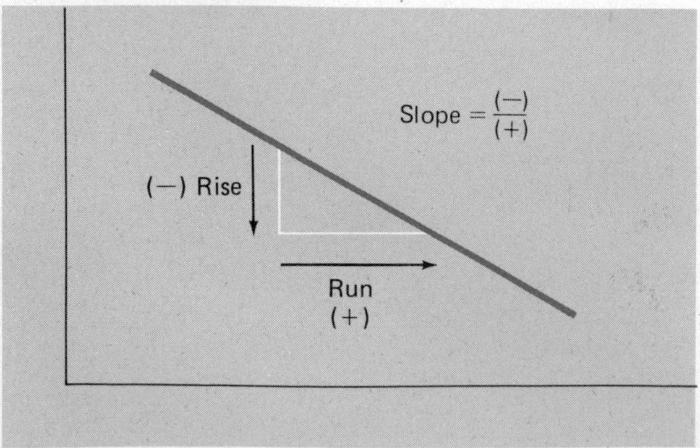

EXHIBIT A–11

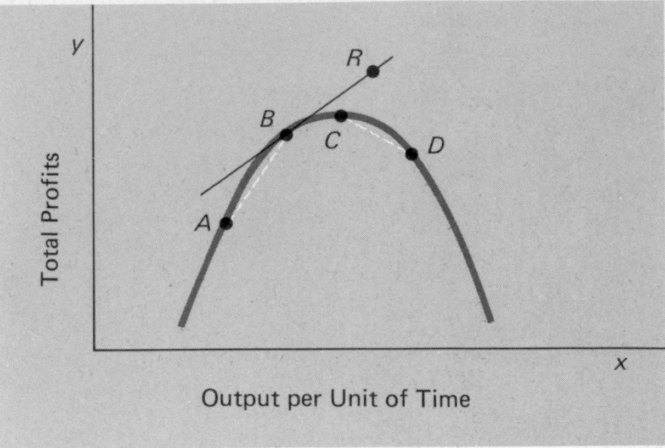

EXHIBIT A–12

Can you see how this curve rises at first, reaches a peak, and then falls? This curve relating total annual profits to annual output levels appears "mountain shaped," doesn't it?

Since this curve is nonlinear (it obviously is not a straight line), should we expect a constant slope when we compute changes in y divided by corresponding changes in x in moving from one point to another? A quick inspection, even without specific numbers, should lead us to conclude that the slopes of lines joining different points in this curve, such as between A and B, or B and C, or C and D, will *not* be the same. In fact, the slope of the line between any two points on this curve will be different from the slope of the line between any two other points. Every slope will be different as we move along the curve.

Instead of using a line between two points to discuss slope, mathematicians and economists prefer to discuss the slope at a particular point, rather than the slope between points. The slope at a point on the curve, such as point B in the graph in Exhibit A–12, is the slope of the line *tangent* to that point. A tangent line is a straight line that touches a curve at only one point. For example, it might be helpful to think of the tangent at B as the straight line which just "kisses" the curve at point B.

To calculate the slope of a tangent line, you need to have some additional information besides the two values of the point of tangency. For example, in Exhibit A–12, if we knew that the point R also lay

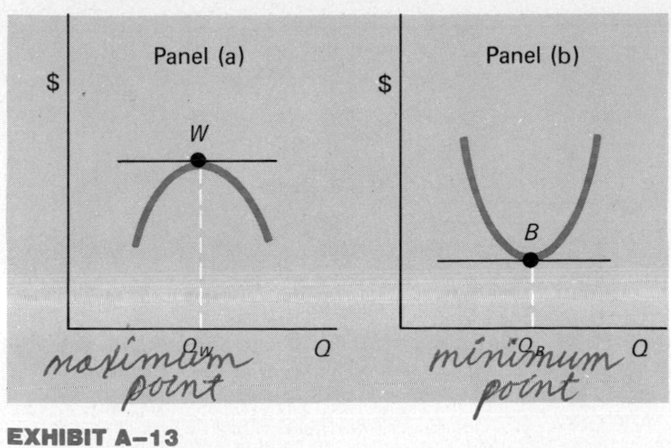

EXHIBIT A–13

on the tangent line, and we knew the two values of that point, we could calculate the slope of the tangent line. We could calculate rise over run between points *B* and *R*, and the result would be the slope of the line tangent to the one point *B* on the curve.

From now on, we will refer to the slope of the line tangent to a curve at a point as a slope at that point. Furthermore, you should realize that every point on a nonlinear curve will have a different tangent line.

Maximum and Minimum Points

Observe the two graphs above labeled panel (a) and panel (b) of Exhibit A–13. In panel (a) of Exhibit A–13, point *W* is a point at the peak of the curve. The slope of the tangent line to point *W* is 0, since there is zero rise for any run, that is, there is no change in the *y* value for any given change in the *x* value. Notice that at any value of *Q* less than Q_W, the curve is rising, and at any value of *Q* greater than Q_W, the curve is falling. Therefore, we refer to the peak point, *W*, as the maximum point.

On the graph in panel (b), the tangent line at point *B* also has a zero slope. That is, the slope at *B* = 0. Inspection of this graph reveals that at values of *Q* greater than Q_B, the curve is rising; at any value of *Q* less than Q_B, the curve is falling. Point *B*, therefore, is referred to as a minimum point. It is important for you to realize that there are many kinds of nonlinear curves. Some may have neither a minimum point nor a maximum point; some may have both; others may have several of either or both. Don't fear, we don't stress these complicated nonlinear curves in this text.

However, you should be aware that direct relationships can be linear or nonlinear; and, of course, inverse relationships can be linear or nonlinear. You should be aware of them because we do use them. Here are examples in Exhibit A–14. In panel (a) of Exhibit A–14, we show a nonlinear inverse relationship between *y* and *x*. In panel (b) of Exhibit A–14, we show a nonlinear direct relationship between *y* and *x*.

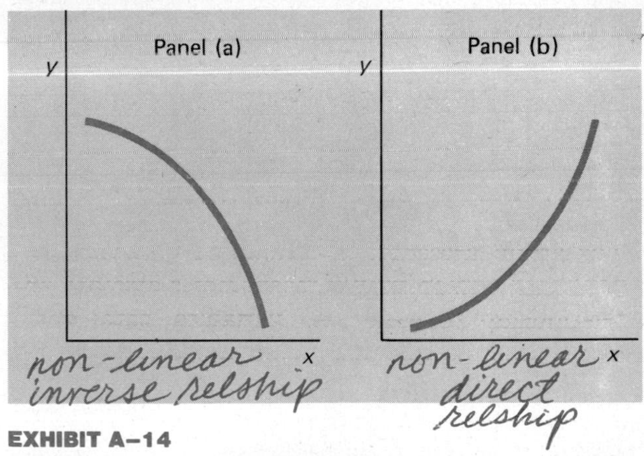

EXHIBIT A–14

2

Capitalism and the American Economy

TOPICS FOR REVIEW

The topics listed below, which we have already analyzed, are applied in this chapter. You may find it worthwhile to review them. For your convenience each topic is followed by the number identifying the specific "Concepts in Brief." For example, "Specialization (1–4)" indicates that a review of specialization can be found in Chapter 1 in the fourth "Concepts in Brief" box.

a. Scarcity (1–1)

b. Opportunity costs, trade-offs (1–2)

c. Production possibilities curve (1–3)

d. Specialization (1–4)

FOR PREVIEW AND STUDY

1. Capitalist economies are associated with great economic freedoms, with regard to ownership and use of private property. Why doesn't all this freedom lead to chaos and anarchy? That is, what gives *direction* and *regulation* to a capitalist economy?
2. It is said that *all* real-world economies are mixed economies. What does this mean?
3. A trade-off exists between present consumption and future consumption. Why?
4. Money economies are more advanced than barter economies. Why?
5. The circular flow models yield the same fundamental insight, whether they are circular flows of a barter or of a money economy. What is this insight?

The American economy is huge. In a typical year, it produces 2 billion bushels of wheat, 6 billion bushels of corn, 140 million tons of steel, 9 million new automobiles, several million new housing units, and 4 million gallons of beer, plus a variety of services from doctors, lawyers, mechanics, and educators. Consider the transportation industry alone.

Over 9 million new automobiles are produced and marketed each year. Employment in the automobile industry alone is over a quarter million workers. In addition, over 19,000 trucks and buses, 21,000 aircraft, and 54,000 railroad cars are produced each year. The production of tires and inner tubes employs 113,000 workers and yields an output valued at over $10 billion each year.

The Pieces in Our Economic Puzzle

Transportation is just one sector in our economy. There are many more. We can look at the nation in terms of industries, which we have done in Exhibit 2-1.

Another way we can look at our system is in terms of the private sector and the government sector. The latter consists of local, state, and federal governments combined. In the United States, the government sector accounts for at least one-fourth of all economic activity in terms of the *purchases* of goods and services. If we wish to look at what you and I and every other American citizen pay in total taxes, the figure is about 40 percent of all income because government also collects funds that it *redistributes* as, for example, welfare payments. Government clearly is an important aspect in the American economy.

The private sector consists of more than 12 million business firms, plus all of the individuals who work in those firms. The total private labor force numbers 79 million. When we add workers in the government sector (plus the unemployed), we get a total labor force of almost 110 million out of a population close to 230 million.

The United States Compared to the Rest of the World

During the earliest years of this country, the colonists' economic situation in North America was at the bare minimum to sustain life. Certainly their standard of living was below that of the Native Americans. From these meager beginnings, the standard of living soon began an upward climb. By the eve of the American Revolution, the population was over 2.7 million. Income had risen even more rapidly.

By 1777, Americans had an average income that rivaled that of the wealthiest, most advanced countries in the world. At that time, average income per person in England was the highest in the world, with France, Holland, and the thirteen colonies close behind. It was only because of the relative preponderance of a small percentage of very wealthy individuals in England that *average* incomes there were higher than in the colonies. Actually, the average worker in England fared less well

EXHIBIT 2–1
The Industries in the United States.

Transportation
Communication
Chemicals
Alcohol
Plastics and resin materials
Electric power
Gas
Alcoholic beverages
Dairy products
Grain and grain products
Livestock
Meats
Poultry and eggs
Miscellaneous food products
Fats, oils, and related products
Tobacco
Hides and skins
Leather
Leather manufacturers
Lumber—all types
Iron and steel
Nonferrous metals and products
Machinery and equipment
Electrical equipment
Gas equipment
Coal
Petroleum and products
Paper and paper products
Rubber
Tires and tubes
Clay construction products
Glass and glass products
Gypsum and products
Fabric
Cotton and manufacturers
Synthetic fibers and manufacturers
Wool and manufacturers
Floor coverings
Apparel
Aerospace vehicles
Motor vehicles
Railroad equipment

than the average worker in the colonies. That is why North America has been labeled by historians as the best "poor person's" country in the late 1700s. It was in the British North American colonies that wages were highest and land most abundant.

It is important to emphasize the fact that the level of income per free person[1] at the time of the birth of the United States was relatively high. The annual average income per person in the colonies was in excess of $1,000, measured in terms of today's purchasing power. Compared to countries today, the thirteen colonies were quite advanced; few countries at the beginning of the 1980s enjoy average annual incomes that match or exceed those achieved in the thirteen colonies on the eve of the Revolution. Indeed, countries holding more than two-thirds of the world's population today live with average annual incomes below that earned by free people in the thirteen colonies over 200 years ago.

Whether or not we can continue to grow as we have in the past is an issue facing citizens and politicians alike. In any event, some of the forces that have caused our growth in the past have a common basis—they are rooted in our capitalist system and the ideology of capitalism, to which we now turn.

An Analysis of Capitalist Ideology

Capitalism is a type of economic system that is typically characterized by limited involvement of government in the economy, coupled with individual ownership of the means of production. We might further add that in a capitalist system, individuals can pursue their own self-interest without many constraints. Actually, it is quite difficult to define capitalism exactly. What we will do in this chapter is first look at economic systems in general and then look explicitly at the ideology, or bodies of ideas and philosophies, underlying capitalism as an economic system.

ECONOMIC SYSTEMS

We might formally wish to characterize an **economic system** as all the institutional means through which national resources are used to satisfy human wants. By **institutions,** we mean principally the laws of the nation, but also the habits, ethics, and customs of its citizenry. From the outset, you should be aware that all economic systems are artificial; none of them is God-given or sent from the stars. All institutions in an economy are exactly what human beings have made them. And when modifications of laws and other institutions occur, they are made by human beings—the judges, workers, government officials, consumers, and legislators are the ones who change, destroy, create, renovate, and resuscitate economic institutions.

Analyzing the Institutions and Assumptions of Capitalist Ideology

Capitalist ideology is based on a set of fundamental assumptions. These assumptions are not, of course, accepted by all, but they must be understood in order to understand what capitalist ideology is all about. The institutions of capitalist ideology are, in many senses, abstract but play an important role in determining the way in which individuals can act in a pure capitalist system.

Our analysis will be limited to a discussion of:

1. The system of private property.
2. Free enterprise and free choice.
3. Self-interest.
4. Competition and unrestricted markets.
5. The pricing system in those markets.
6. The limited role of government.

The System of Private Property

The ownership of most property under a capitalist system is usually vested in individuals or in groups of individuals. The state is not the owner of, for example, productive resources that are important forms of property. In the United States, the government does own certain property, but in general we live within a system of private property. Private property is controlled and enforced through the legal framework of laws, courts, and police. Under capitalism, individuals have their property rights protected; individuals are usually free to use their private property as they choose, so long as they do not infringe on the legal property rights of others. Individuals are usually allowed to enter into private contractual agreements that are mutually satisfying.

Free Enterprise and Free Choice

Another attribute of a capitalistic system is free enterprise, which is merely an extension of the concept of property rights. **Free enterprise** exists when private individuals are allowed to obtain re-

[1] The data exclude nonfree persons, such as those in slavery and indentured servants.

sources, to organize those resources, and to sell the resulting product in any way the person chooses. In other words, there are no artificial obstacles or restrictions that a government or other producers can put up to block a business's choice in the matter of purchasing its inputs and selling its outputs.

Additionally, all members of the economy are free to choose to do whatever they wish. Workers will be free to enter any line of work for which they are qualified and consumers can buy the desired basket of goods and services that they feel is most appropriate for them. The ultimate voter in the capitalist system is the consumer, who votes with dollars and decides which product "candidates" will survive; that is, there is **consumer sovereignty** in that the ultimate purchaser of products and services determines what, in fact, is produced.

Self-Interest and "The Invisible Hand"

In 1776, Adam Smith, the author of *The Wealth of Nations,* described a system in which government had a limited role and individuals pursued their own self-interest. Smith reasoned that, in so doing, individuals will be guided as if by an invisible hand to achieve maximum social welfare for the nation. In his own words:

> [An individual] generally, indeed, neither intends to promote the public interest, nor knows how much he is promoting it. . . . He intends only his own gain, and he is in this, as in many other cases, led by an invisible hand to promote an end which was no part of his intention. Nor is it always the worst for the society that it was no part of it. By pursuing his own interest he frequently promotes that of the society more effectually than when he really intends to promote it.[2]

What does self-interest entail? For the businessperson, it normally means maximizing profits or minimizing losses. For the consumer, it means maximizing the amount of satisfaction possible from spending a given amount of money income. From the worker's point of view, it means obtaining the highest level of income possible for a given amount of work. For the owner of a resource, it means obtaining the highest price possible when that resource is sold, or the greatest rent if it is rented.

Capitalism, therefore, presumes self-interest as the fundamental way that people operate in the system. Self-interest is the guiding light in capitalism.

[2] Adam Smith, *The Wealth of Nations* [1776] (New York: Random House, 1937), Book IV, chap. 2, p. 423.

Competition and Unrestricted Markets

Competition is rivalry among sellers who wish to attract customers and rivalry among buyers to obtain desired goods. In general, competition exists among buyers and sellers of all resources who wish to obtain the best terms possible when they transact their business.

Competition requires, at a minimum, two things:

1. A relatively large number of independently acting sellers and buyers.
2. The freedom of sellers and buyers to enter or exit a particular industry.

1. Diffusion of power. The presence of a large number of buyers and sellers means that power is diffuse, that no one buyer or one seller can noticeably influence the price that a particular product fetches in the marketplace. Consider the selling side of the story. If there are many, many sellers, no one of them can arbitrarily affect the price of the product, for with attempts to raise the price, potential buyers will go to one of the many other sellers. On the buyer's side, the same analysis holds. No single buyer can manipulate price or purchase to individual advantage.

Basically, economic competition—rivalry among buyers and sellers—imposes limits on the self-interest of buyers and sellers. Competition, then, is the regulating force in capitalism.

2. Easy entry and exit. Another thing that makes competition a regulatory force is the ability of individuals to enter an industry that is profitable. Furthermore, those who feel that they could earn more profits in another industry must have the legal ability to leave the industry they are in now. We say, then, that there are weak barriers to entry and exit from industries so that competition can prevail throughout.

The Market System

Capitalism is a **market economy** defined as one in which buyers and sellers express their opinions through how much they are willing to pay for or how much they demand of goods and services. In a market economy, prices are used to *signal* the *value* of individual resources. Prices are the guideposts to which resource owners, businesspersons, and consumers refer when they make their choices as they attempt to improve their lives. In other words, the market system, also called the price system, is the organizing force in our economy. When we refer to

Adam Smith

SCOTTISH ECONOMIST (1723–1790)

OF MARKETS AND MEN

"I have never known much good done by those who affected to trade for the public good," Adam Smith once remarked. If he put little stock in good intentions, Smith did invest heavily in demonstrating that selfish intentions could lead to public good. In *The Theory of Moral Sentiments* (1759), his first book, Smith tried to show how altruism could come out of self-interest. In his second and more famous book, Smith attempted to reveal how the self-interest of private individuals could be transformed by the sleight of an invisible hand (the unfettered market) into social harmony and public benefit, producing the wealth of the nation in the best of all possible ways. The result of this effort was *An Inquiry into the Nature and Causes of the Wealth of Nations* (1776), perhaps the most influential economics treatise ever written, one that has set the tone for capitalist ideology for the past two centuries.

Adam Smith himself was a notoriously absent-minded Scotsman, eccentric, and not very handsome. He was born in the small town of Kirkaldy in 1723, attended Oxford, then returned to Scotland to teach moral philosophy at the University of Glasgow. An invitation to tutor a young duke on his grand tour of Europe gave Smith an opportunity to meet some of the leading economic thinkers of his

day. It was while on this trip that Smith started *The Wealth of Nations,* which would take him 12 years to complete. Two years after its publication, Smith was appointed commissioner of customs for Edinburgh, where he spent his remaining days: a quiet, uneventful life when compared to the revolution he effected in economic thinking.

In one book, Smith was able to change the face of economics, synthesizing the thoughts of previous writers and adding considerable insights of his own about the workings of the market, the division of labor, and the labor theory of value. Published the same year that the American colonies declared independence from Britain, *The Wealth of Nations* celebrated the economic freedom of being able to sell one's labor and to enjoy the fruits thereof. This principle was enough to guarantee prosperity, Smith asserted: "The natural effort of every individual to better his own condition, when suffered to exert itself with freedom and security, is so powerful a principle, that it is alone, and without any assistance . . . capable of carrying on the society to wealth and prosperity." He went on to show how a market made up of competing individuals, when free from government intervention, could normally regulate the allocation of resources and distribution of commodities efficiently and in accordance with the best interests of society.

Smith's conception of the market reflected England of the eighteenth century—a "nation of shopkeepers," he called it. But according to his critics, his model fit less well the England of a century later, when the nation was in the midst of the industrial revolution, and fits even less today's economy, in which the state plays a large role and large corporations have replaced the shopkeeper. This has led some economists, like Milton Friedman, to push for a return to the "efficiency" of Smith's model of little government involvement, and led other economists, like Joan Robinson, to argue that the Smithian conception is quite outmoded. But all agree on Smith's central role in the development of economic thought.

organization, we mean the coordination of individuals, often doing different things, in the furtherance of a common end.

Resources tend to flow where they yield the highest rate of return, or highest profit. Prices generate the signals for resource movements, they provide information cheaply and quickly, and they affect incentives.

A market system is only one type of social organization for production and distribution. A *political* or *hierarchical* organization is another. Within this very broad category of political systems, there are a large number of variants—majority rule and dictatorship, for example. Actually, within most countries a combination of market and political systems is used: a hybrid social organization that determines production and distribution thus exists. Some decisions are made by politicians and their organizations; some are made in the market by businesses and consumers.

The Limited Role of Government

Even in an "idealized" capitalistic system there is still a role for government, for someone has to define and enforce private property rights. The government protects the rights of individuals and businesspersons to keep private property private and to keep the control of that property vested with the owners. Even Adam Smith, the so-called father of free enterprise, described in detail the role of government in a purely capitalistic system. He suggested the need for government in providing national defense and in eliminating monopolies that would restrain trade. Smith further suggested that the functions of a government within a capitalist system might include such things as issuing money, prescribing standards of weights and measures, raising funds by taxation and assorted other means for public works, and settling disputes judicially. Government thus is essential to the existence of even a purely capitalist system.

> ***Concepts in Brief 2-1***
>
> - An idealized capitalist system works within the institution of private property that is controlled and enforced through the legal framework of laws, courts, and police.
> - Further, such a system is one of free enterprise, where producers freely choose the resources they use in the products they produce. Consumers have freedom of choice also, as do workers and owners of resources in general.
> - Individuals and producers express their desires through the market system, where prices are signals about the relative scarcities of different goods, services, and resources.
> - The role of government is a limited one.

Finally—A Definition of Capitalism

We are now in a position to formally define in more detail what we mean by **capitalism:**

Capitalism is an economic system in which individuals privately own productive resources and possess the right to use these resources in whatever manner they choose, subject to certain (minimal) legal restrictions.

Notice here that we use the words *productive resources,* rather than capital. This takes into account not only machines and land, but also labor services.

Our Mixed Economic System

We have been talking about the capitalist ideology, or pure capitalism in theory. How well does this ideal system fit the American economic scene? Does Adam Smith's "invisible hand" perform all of its tasks well and rapidly, resulting in maximum welfare for society? The answers to these questions have to be partly yes and partly no. We no longer (if we ever did) have a purely capitalist economy. Rather, we have tended more and more through the years toward one in which the government plays a more influential role. We have a **mixed system**—a market system coupled with government control and intervention.

INCREASED GOVERNMENT

The role of government in our economic system has expanded greatly, especially since World War II. When we speak of government—federal, state, and local—we are referring to the collective total of all individuals who, in one way or another, are paid by our tax dollars, who decide what should be done with other tax dollars, and who regulate private transactions. Not only does government control an important share of total income, but it has entered into many aspects of hitherto private economic dealings. For example, governments step in to help out (subsidize) certain industries (e.g., loan guarantees to Lockheed and Chrysler) or to tax others (e.g., a windfall profits tax on oil companies). As another example, the government has put many restrictions on the working of our agricultural sector. Additionally, through its many departments and agencies, the government controls numerous aspects of energy, transportation, communication, and commerce in general. In the last several decades, the government has increased its welfare programs—tax dollars are redistributed to those who are deemed "needy." Finally, education has become primarily a government activity.

> ***Concepts in Brief 2-2***
>
> ■ The American economy is not an "idealized" capitalist system. Nor is it a political system of pure government control over all resources. Rather, we can say that it is a *mixed system* in which private individuals and government influence what happens in the marketplace.

Other Characteristics of the American Economic System

Many of the institutions and assumptions we just outlined for an idealized capitalist system do characterize the American economic system. There are other characteristics of the U.S. economy (and other advanced economies) that can now be examined. These involve (1) a large capital base, (2) a high degree of specialization, and (3) the extensive use of money.

OUR IMMENSE CAPITAL STOCK

One of the reasons that the American workers are among the highest paid in the world is that they have so much capital with which to work. The capital per worker in this country is probably greater than anywhere else in the world. When you think about capital, just think about all of the open-hearth furnaces in Gary, Indiana; Pittsburgh, Pennsylvania; and Cleveland, Ohio. Think about the huge railroad yard in Chicago. Think about all of the buildings in the middle of your city where office workers go every day. When you have stopped thinking about those examples of capital, you will have just touched the tip of the capital iceberg. Capital also includes the unused raw materials and as yet unsold products that producers have on hand, equipment throughout the country, and much, much more.

Scarcity Revisited

At this point, it is useful to remember the scarcity constraint. Productive resources are limited. Thus, we must make choices about how we use them. We have to decide how much of which goods we will produce with our resources. For our purposes here, there will be only two choices: those goods that we consume directly, called **consumer goods**—food, clothes, cars—and those that we consume indirectly, called **capital goods**—machines, plants, equipment. Everyone acts as a consumer in using consumer goods. On the other hand, capital goods, such as machines, factories, trucks, and ships, are used to make the consumer goods to which we just referred.

Why We Make Capital Goods

Why would we be willing to use productive resources to make things—capital goods—that we cannot consume directly? One of the reasons we use productive resources to make capital goods is that the latter enable us to produce larger quantities of consumer goods or to produce them more inexpensively than we otherwise could. Before fish are produced for the market, fishing boats, nets, and poles are first produced. Now imagine, for example, how expensive it would be to obtain fish for market without using these capital goods. Getting fish with one's hands is not an easy task. The price per fish would be very high if capital weren't used.

Foregoing Current Consumption

Whenever we use productive resources to make capital goods, we are implicitly foregoing current consumption. We are waiting for some time in the future to consume the fruits that will be reaped from the use of capital goods. Indeed, if we were to produce only consumer goods now and no capital goods, then our capacity to produce consumer goods in the future would suffer. Here we see a trade-off situation, one which lends itself to the sort of graphical analysis that we developed in the first chapter.

The Trade-off Between Consumption Goods and Capital Goods

In order to have more consumer goods in the future, we must accept fewer consumer goods today. With the resources that we don't use to produce consumer goods for today, we invest in capital goods that will produce more consumer goods for us later. The trade-off is depicted in Exhibit 2-2. On the left-hand side of panel (a), you can see this trade-off depicted as a production possibilities curve between capital goods and consumption goods. If we decide to use all of our resources to produce goods and services for consumption today, we can produce \$2 trillion worth per year, which is represented as point *B*. In this extreme case, using all our productive resources for only consumption goods leads to no future growth.

Now assume, however, that we are willing to give up, say, \$200 billion worth of consumption today.

EXHIBIT 2–2
Capital Goods and Growth.

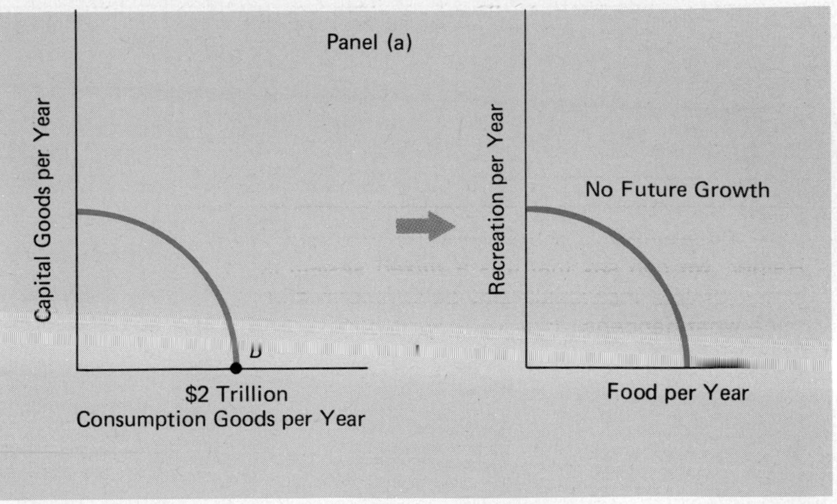

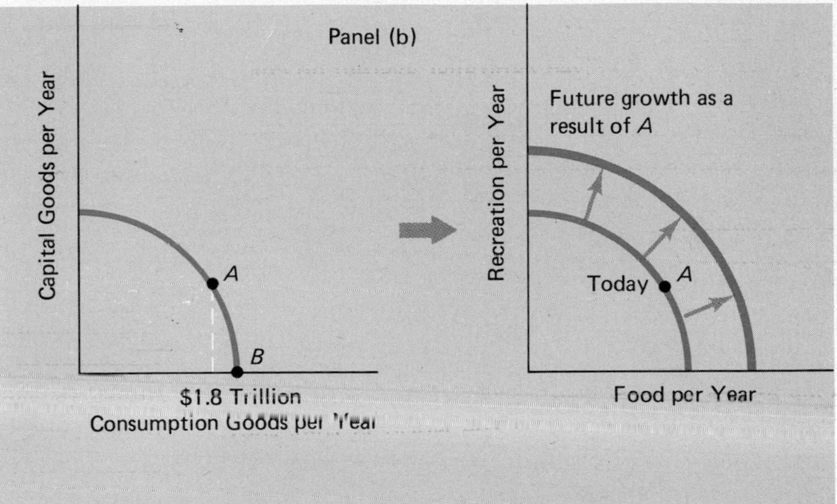

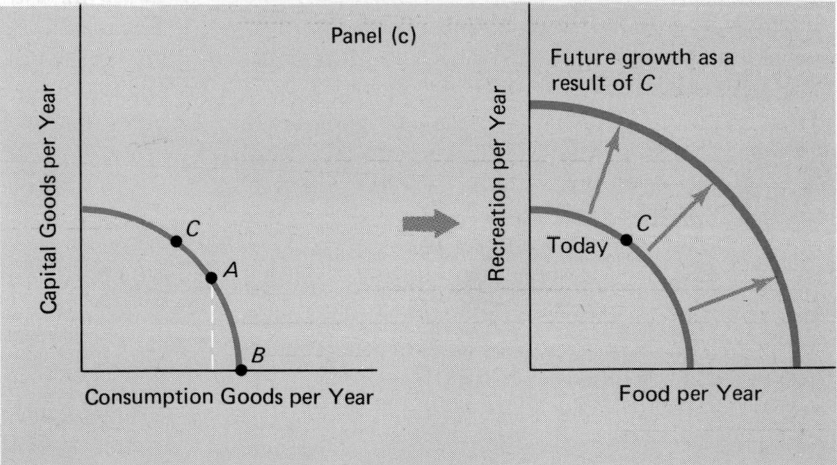

We will be at point *A* in the left-hand diagram of panel (b). This will allow the economy to grow. We will have more future consumption because we invested in more capital goods today. In the right-hand diagram of panel (b), we see two goods represented—food and recreation. The production possibilities curve will move outward if we collectively decide to restrict consumption each year and invest in capital goods—that is, if we agree to be at point *A*.

In panel (c), we show the results of our willingness to forego quite a bit more current consumption. We move to point *C*, where we have many fewer consumer goods today, but produce a lot more capital goods. This leads to more future growth in this simplified model, and thus the production possibilities curve in the right-hand side of panel (c) shifts outward more than it did in the right-hand side of panel (b).

In other words, the more we give up today, the more we can have tomorrow.

> ***Concepts in Brief 2-3***
> ■ The use of capital requires using productive resources to produce capital goods that in turn will later produce consumer goods.
> ■ A trade-off is involved between current consumption and capital goods, or alternatively, between current consumption and future consumption, because the more we invest in capital goods today, the greater the amount of consumer goods we can produce in the future.

SPECIALIZATION

Chapter 1 introduced the concept of specialization. The extent to which this nation relies on specialization is truly extraordinary. In our American economy, you do not have to be self-sufficient. We each can specialize in one thing, and we then depend on the specialized outputs of many other people. Ours is clearly not a society of self-sufficient individuals doing "their own thing" (although there is a relatively small number of people who are largely self-sufficient).

Regional Specialization

Ours is a nation of varied regions with varied resources, and hence we find regional specialization. The Midwest is the breadbasket where large amounts of grain are produced. The Northeast is the main financial center of the country. Specialization allows each area in the country to turn out those goods and services that its resources can most efficiently produce. We started specializing as a country from the very beginning. The South specialized in tobacco, indigo, and rice. The middle colonies were made up of the fertile agricultural areas of Pennsylvania, New York, and New Jersey, where livestock and grain could be more cheaply produced than in New England or the South. That is, the middle colonies' comparative advantage lay in the production of livestock and grain goods. In the New England area, the comparative advantage of the colonists lay in their proximity to ocean waters that were filled with fish and their proximity to the vast acreage of forest lands. Hence, we find the New Englanders exporting ship timbers, whale oil, and codfish. Later on, they became extremely efficient shipbuilders, and many New Englanders became world traders and sailors.

The Cost of Specialization

Specialization does not come free of charge. The more specialized we become as individuals, as regions, or as a nation, the more interdependent (and therefore more vulnerable) we become. Additionally, specialization can lead to monotony in one's work. Increased specialization requires increased risk-taking. Why? Because, to specialize, one must choose something in which to specialize. That means making an investment, in advance, in particular types of resources and/or training. When tastes change, for example, the area in which you specialize may no longer be as profitable. Your training and investment in that area may prove to have been a mistake. You will end up poorer than you would have been had you not made the investment; but you didn't know, because you did not have perfect information about the future. Consider the possibility of your going to law school and specializing in federal income taxation. You would invest a number of years learning all of the ins and outs of the tax code. What would happen to the value of that investment in time and money if a tax reform act came along and simplified every aspect of the federal tax system such that few people demanded your services anymore? You would have to switch to another field where your services would be in higher demand.

> ***Concepts in Brief 2-4***
> ■ Our mixed economic system involves specialization; individuals and regions engage in the activities in which they have the greatest, or comparative, advantage.
> ■ Specialization involves disadvantages such as monotony in one's work, increased risk-taking, and increased interdependence.

THE USE OF MONEY

In our economic system, money is used as a *medium of exchange*. In other words, we have one standard good that everyone knows everyone else is willing to accept in exchange for all other goods and services. Money also serves many other functions that are described in later chapters.

EXHIBIT 2–3
The Circular Flow—A Barter Economy. In this economy, money is not used as a medium of exchange. There are just two sectors, households and businesses. Households provide to businesses the services of the land, labor, capital, and entrepreneurship that they own. Businesses, in turn, pay the households with goods and services. What cannot be shown in this simplified circular flow diagram is the bartering that must go on among households as they attempt to obtain the desired mix of goods and services that probably will not coincide with the mix of goods and services paid to them by businesses.

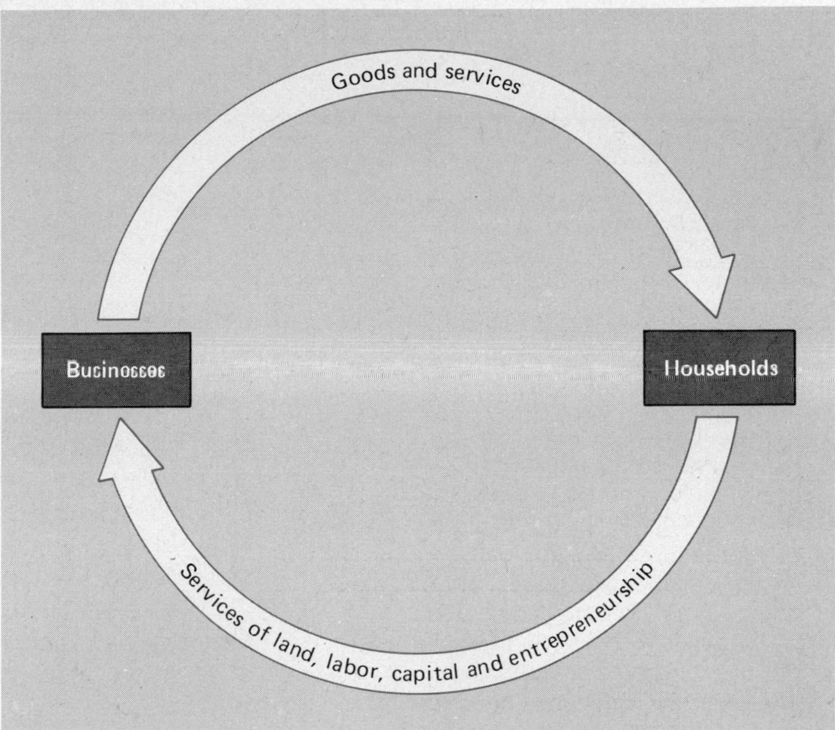

Using money as a medium of exchange facilitates specialization and exchange among people. In fact, it is necessary that there be a convenient means of exchanging goods and services in order for us to be able to specialize. Consider the alternative to using money—barter—where we exchange goods for goods, or services for goods, or services for services.

Bartering has been around a long time. However, it requires a double coincidence of wants between two individuals or businesses.

Suppose that you make frying pans and I make shoes. I decide I want a frying pan. If you, at the same time, want shoes, then we can probably make a barter exchange. Suppose, though, that you want a couple of new hats. I must go seek someone who wants some shoes in exchange for some hats. When I finally get the hats, then perhaps I can exchange them for your frying pans.

Sounds pretty complicated, doesn't it? Well, it is, and it is costly. The time involved is tremendous compared to the facility with which exchange takes place when money is used. Money is one of the most important inventions created by humans. It has existed in many forms, such as stones, shells, pieces of metal, cigarettes, and more recently, paper bills, and checks. The only characteristic that it must have in order to facilitate exchange is that it must be generally acceptable by sellers in exchanges. Whatever fits this definition can be called money.

Our willingness to accept paper money, metal money, or any other type of money allows each person and each region to specialize in production despite a noncoincidence of wants.

Concepts in Brief 2-5

■ Money is any generally accepted medium of exchange. It facilitates exchange and thereby allows for increased specialization.

The Circular Flow of Income

Now that we have talked about what makes up our American economy, we can put it into a simple model. We will first look at an utterly simplified economy where no money exists, and in which there is only barter.

A PURE BARTER ECONOMY

In a barter economy, households own all economic resources and supply these resources to businesses. That means that households provide all the land, labor, and capital. This is seen in Exhibit 2–3 on the bottom flow. Businesses wish to obtain these resources because they want them to produce goods and services. Now, in exchange for the resources made available to businesses, households receive payments in kind. That is to say, households will receive goods and services that they have helped to produce. This is shown in the top flow in Exhibit 2–3. What the diagram does not show is what the

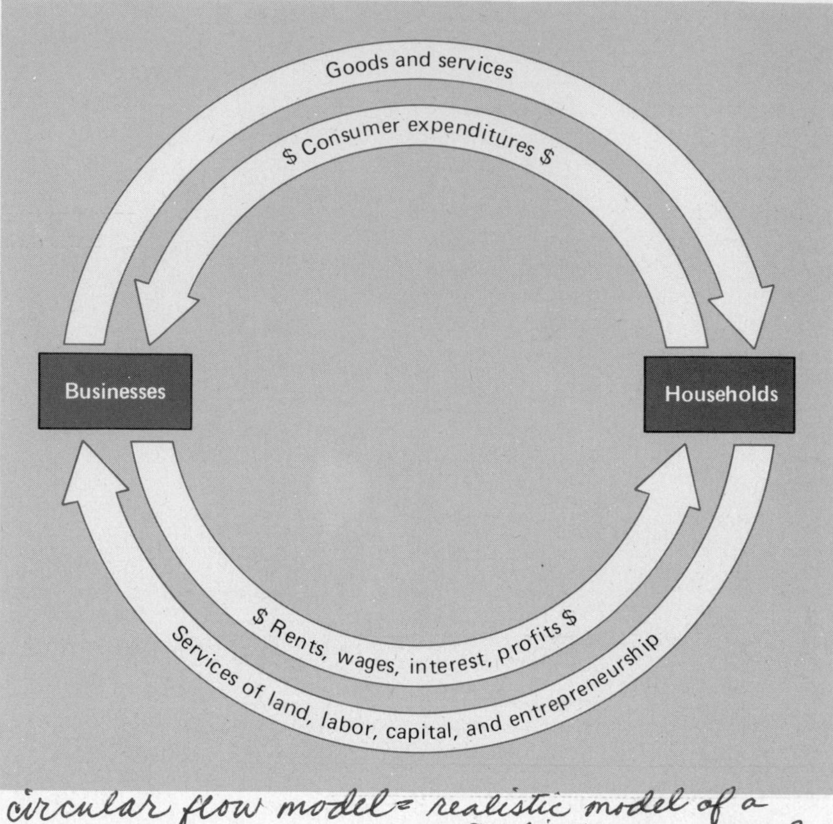

EXHIBIT 2–4
The Circular Flow—A Monetary Economy. In this simplified model, again, there are only households and businesses. Money is used as the medium of exchange. Households sell the services of land, labor, capital, and entrepreneurship that they own to businesses. Businesses, in turn, pay households rent, wages, interest, and profits. Businesses also sell goods and services to households for which the businesses receive payment in the form of consumer expenditures of money income.

households have to do to receive payments of goods and services. They will have to go around the countryside swapping goods for goods with one another in order to satisfy their wants.

Exhibit 2–3 can be called a model of *real* flows within the economy. That is, it demonstrates the flow of resources and the flow of goods and services within a capitalist system. It is called the **circular flow model.**

A MONETARY ECONOMY

Now we come to a more realistic model of the capitalist economy. Money is used as a medium of exchange. Households sell economic resources to businesses, and in return they are paid money income in the form of wages, interest, rents, and profits. They receive wages for their labor services, interest for the capital services that they provide, rents for the land that they own, and profits for their entrepreneurial abilities. This is shown in the bottom loops in Exhibit 2–4. Businesses, on the other hand, sell finished goods and services to households, for which, in exchange, they are paid money. This is shown in the top loop in Exhibit 2–4.

LIMITATIONS IN SIMPLE CIRCULAR FLOW MODELS

Of course, the model of our monetary economy given in Exhibit 2–4 is an extreme simplification of the workings of capitalism. For example, it has the following shortcomings:

1. Nothing is said about transactions or exchanges that occur within the business sector and within the household sector. The whole distribution chain between manufacturers of intermediate parts is ignored, as is the chain of events that goes from manufacturer to wholesaler to retailer. For example, the model ignores the many steps it takes for a loaf of bread to get to market. It ignores the selling of refined flour to the baker, the baker selling the bread to a wholesaler, and then the wholesaler selling the bread to the various retailers.
2. The model makes no mention of the economic role of government which does, of course, tax and spend, as well as regulate. In a purely capitalist world, we would have a self-regulated economy in which the government's role would

be minor anyway. In a more complete model of our actual economy the role of government cannot be ignored.

3. The model does not include saving and investment nor the foreign sector of the economy.
4. Nothing is said about how resources and products come into existence and at what prices they are sold. That is the job of our supply and demand analysis and also requires an explanation of our pricing system, which is what we turn to in the next two chapters.

Concepts in Brief 2-6

- In a pure barter economy, the circular flow of goods and services is strictly between households and businesses. Households provide all productive resources in exchange for payments in kind made by businesses. This is a model of real flows within the economy.
- With money added, households sell their productive resources for money income; they purchase finished goods and services that constitute their consumer expenditures.

ISSUES AND APPLICATIONS

Capitalism Creeps into China

Concepts Applied

- Profit, economic system, capitalism

For most of this chapter we have described what capitalism is all about. For many years, the supposed antithesis of capitalism has been the Chinese economic system in which there has been public ownership of all industries, agricultural cooperatives, communes, and massive central planning. Until 1979, we had no trouble stating categorically that all the decisions regarding investment versus consumption, how labor should be supplied to different sectors of the economy, and what the prices of various goods and services should be were made by the state government.

A Little History

After taking power in 1949, the communists under Mao Tse-tung devised plans to help put their devastated country back onto the road to economic prosperity. The first Five Year Plan was instituted in 1952. It stressed investment in heavy industry, retention of small-scale and handicraft industries, and a land reform policy that took land from wealthy Chinese and gave it to poor peasants. Farms were also collectively organized. In 1958, the second plan was put into effect. It started out with the so-called Great Leap Forward, a plan by Chinese economic policymakers to increase individual output by over 25 percent per year and develop heavy industry even more rapidly than they had in the previous five years. The plan called for labor to be used more intensively in order to reduce *under*employment (as opposed to *un*employment) of the labor force. Instead of directing all heavy indus-

Capitalism was reintroduced to China in 1980 with the opening of the first privately owned restaurant since 1949. If the experiment succeeds, perhaps others will invest in additional private establishments to serve consumers.

trial plants from the central government, there was to be some decentralization—in the sense that local managers would have more control over what their plants bought and sold and what production methods would be used.

From the very beginning, there were unexpected and tragic consequences of the Great Leap Forward. The program was, in a word, too ambitious. Many goods were being produced that were not really wanted in the economy, and many large-scale irrigation projects that were undertaken were poorly planned and managed. The result was often a complete fiasco. Steel was being made by many unskilled workers in unsafe, often quite primitive production environments. Often the steel produced was of such poor quality that it could not be used.

A food shortage began to develop. Many workers had been transferred from agriculture to the city to help in the great industrial expansion program. The consequence was too little production of food. Finally, the much needed New Economic Policy was begun.

The new policy. The leaders of China finally realized that agriculture had to be built up before rapid industrialization could be attempted. The only way that urbanization—growth in the cities—can occur is for productivity in the agricultural sector to rise fast enough to allow those who stay in agriculture to feed those who go to the city. The Chinese leaders finally realized this. Agriculture then became the foundation of the entire economy.

One of the most interesting aspects of the agricultural program in China is a system of communal farming in which work teams are essentially self-governing and the workers are paid work points. In a communal system, the workers live together on the same site where they work. Not all the communes work out well, however. Fewer communes have been started in recent years.

China Today: Profits and Capitalism—Well, at Least a Little

The economic system in China is changing, although not rapidly, perhaps quite radically. The concept of profit has been reintroduced. That concept was last heard of prior to 1949. An experiment was started in 1980 in Sichuan. Five companies were then allowed to make their own production plans, to do their own marketing and purchasing, and to set their own prices, as well as to make decisions on hiring and firing. In reality, the managers there didn't really get to do all of that, but they did get to do some planning. The five firms in Sichuan have been allowed to keep their profits after paying a profit tax to the government. In the past, the government simply kept all profits or subsidized any losses. These companies still must satisfy a state plan for production, but once it is satisfied, they can tailor their production directly to the domestic market.

As an example, consider the Chongquing Watch and Clock Company. In 1979, it produced 700,000 clocks and 300,000 watches. Its profits were almost $3 million; the state received them all. In 1980, they were again supposed to produce for the state the same number of clocks and watches. By September of 1980, they fulfilled that government requirement and turned out an additional 200,000 clocks and 300,000 watches that they were able to sell directly. The profits? Five-and-a-half-million dollars, of which 60 percent went to the state as a profits tax.

Unrestricted capitalism is not quite what you'd call it, though. While the experiment with complete freedom, except for satisfying a state production quota, looks good on paper, the five factories that participated in the experiment did not have as much freedom as promised. They were able to dismiss or lay off workers who violated discipline rules. If, on the other hand, they laid off a worker because of automation, they had to pay him or her 75 percent of salary anyway. And prices weren't really as flexible as promised. Any of the five firms could lower prices below the state price but a price increase over that government limit had to be approved.

Investors won't get rich. One of the first privately financed companies was the Patriotic Construction Company of Shang-hai that raised $36 million from former capitalists. These investors, however, are not strictly equivalent to those in the United States. All they get is the usual bank interest of 5 percent, regardless of how profitable the company becomes. Nonetheless, the company vice-president, Mr. Yang

Yanxiu, claims that "If we need money, a lot more people will be willing to invest."[3]

At the other end of the scale of business size is the first privately owned restaurant and tea shop in all of China since 1949. It started in 1980. It is run by a family of five. No bigger than a large walk-in closet, the first postrevolution capitalist eatery is doing a thriving business in Peking.

Does this signal the end of the Chinese "experiment"? Probably not, according to China watchers. Since Mao's death, there has been a gradual drift toward a freer economy, but the strong anticapitalist, antifree enterprise Maoist legacy will undoubtedly live on for many years. In the meantime, we'll probably hear about more extensive forays into that economic system that we know as capitalism.

[3] *Wall Street Journal,* January 14, 1981, "China's Pre-1949 Capitalist Pitch-in," p. 5.

Questions

1. Do you think that the high profits tax imposed on the participants in the "experiment" in Sichuan had any effect on productivity? Why or why not?
2. If firms cannot easily charge higher than state prices for their manufactured products, which products will they want to produce and which will they avoid?

Definition of Terms

Economic system The institutional means through which resources are used to satisfy human wants.

Institutions The laws of the nation as well as the habits, ethics, mores, folkways, and customs of the citizens of that nation.

Free enterprise A system in which private business firms are able to obtain resources, to organize those resources, and to sell the finished product in any way they choose.

Consumer sovereignty The concept of the consumer as the one who, by his or her dollar votes, ultimately determines which goods and services will be produced in the economy. In principle, competition among producers causes them to adjust their production to the changing desires of consumers.

The consumer decides wh goods will be produced.

Competition Rivalry among buyers and sellers of outputs, or among buyers and sellers of inputs.

Market economy An economy in which prices are used to signal firms and households about the value of individual resources. It is also called the price system.

Organization The coordination of individuals, each doing different things in the furtherance of a common end.

Capitalism An economic system in which individuals privately own productive resources; these individuals can use the resources in whatever manner they choose, subject to common protective legal restrictions.

Mixed system An economic system in which the decision about how resources should be used is made partly by the private sector and partly by the government or public sector.

Consumer, or consumption, goods Goods that are used directly by consumers to generate satisfaction. To be contrasted with capital goods.

Capital goods Goods that are used in the production of other goods. Examples include trucks, factories, foundries, and so on. We do not directly consume capital goods.

Barter A system of exchange in which goods or services are exchanged for goods or services without the use of money.

Circular flow model A model of the flows of resources, goods, and services, as well as money, receipts, and payments for them in the economy.

Chapter Summary

1. Very early the American economy established a relatively high level of income per person. Today two-thirds of the world have average incomes per person less than those we had on the eve of our Revolution.
2. Capitalist ideology rests on: (a) a system of pri-

vate property, (b) free enterprise and free choice, (c) self-interest as a guiding force, (d) competition within unrestricted markets, (e) a market system in which prices and profits are signals, and (f) a very restricted role for government.

3. All economic systems have some capital, because it is impossible to produce with labor alone.
4. We have a "mixed" economic system in which government plays an important role in both spending resources and regulating private transactions.
5. The United States has an immense capital stock. To get it, we have had to sacrifice consumption.
6. There is a trade-off between consumption goods and capital goods. The more resources we devote to capital goods, however, the more consumption goods we can have in the future (and less currently).
7. In this nation we have seen areas of specialization from colonial times on.
8. Specialization, however, does involve costs, including monotony and tedium in one's work.
9. Specialization also requires risk-taking because the area in which one has chosen to specialize may turn out to be unprofitable in the future.
10. In our mixed economy, we use money as an exchange medium; before that barter was used, but it was a costly way to make exchanges.
11. A simplified flow-of-income model shows the flows of resources from households to businesses and goods and services from businesses to households. Also, payments for those resources in the form of wages, rents, interest, and profits are shown, along with consumer expenditures in money terms.

Selected References

Ebenstein, William, and E. Fogelman. *Today's Isms.* 8th ed. Englewood Cliffs, N.J.: Prentice-Hall, 1980, chap. 3.
Feldstein, Martin, ed. *The American Economy in Transition.* Chicago: University of Chicago Press, 1980.
Friedman, Milton. *Capitalism and Freedom.* Chicago: University of Chicago Press, 1963.
Gilder, George. *Wealth and Poverty.* New York: Basic Books, 1980.
Haag, E. van den, ed. *Capitalism: Sources of Hostility.* New York: Epoch Books, 1979.
Heilbroner, Robert L. *The Worldly Philosophers.* Rev. ed. New York: Simon & Schuster, 1972.
Smith, Adam. *The Wealth of Nations.* New York: Dutton, 1978.

Answers to Preview and Study Questions

1. Capitalist economies are associated with great economic freedoms, with regard to ownership and use of private property. Why doesn't all this freedom lead to chaos and anarchy? That is, what gives *direction* and regulation to a capitalist economy?

Self-interest and competition give much direction and therefore act as regulating forces in capitalist economies. While businesses are free to produce anything legal, it is in their own self-interest to produce the most profitable goods; competition forces them to do so. Laborers are free to work at any job for which they can be hired—but self-interest directs them to the higher-paying jobs. Most nonhuman resources are owned, and owners find it in their own self-interest to sell to the highest bidder. All of this self-interest is kept in check by competition; individual sellers cannot charge higher and higher prices because buyers can buy from their competitors; individual buyers cannot use their power to squeeze lower and lower prices out of sellers, since sellers have the option to sell to other buyers. Thus, competition acts as a regulating force.

2. It is said that *all* real-world economies are mixed economies. What does this mean?

No advanced economies in the real world are purely capitalistic or purely socialistic. As a practical matter, all advanced economies are mixed; resource allocation decisions are made by both private individuals and governments. Even under an idealized capitalistic economy, important roles are played by the government; it is generally agreed that government is required for (some) income redistribution, national defense, maintenance of competition, protection of property rights, and so on. On the other hand, socialistic economies have found it convenient to allow for private property rights regarding labor and personal property items (clothing, housing, consumer durables, etc.).

3. A trade-off exists between present consumption and future consumption. Why?

The main manner in which increased future consumption can come about is through increased output of machinery, plants, and equipment today (investment). Since we live in a world of scarcity, increased investment in the present necessarily means less output of consumer goods in the present; the opportunity cost of increased investment is loss of present consumption. Conversely, increased present consumption comes at the expense of fewer investment goods—and therefore reduced future consumption. Since we assess the opportunity cost of present consumption in terms of foregone future consumption, and we assess the opportunity cost of future goods in terms of foregone present consumption, we say that a trade-off exists between present and future consumption.

4. Money economies are more advanced than barter economies. Why?

Barter economies require a coincidence of wants. For example, a fisher who wants shoes must find a shoemaker who wants fish. Obviously, the costs of exchanging goods and services in a barter economy are high, since it takes time and effort to find such coincidence of wants. Barter economies, therefore, encourage individuals to be "jacks of all trades." In a money economy workers can work for money because money has the power to purchase any goods—in the present or in the future. Since people are freed from the necessity for a coincidence of wants, exchange costs are lowered and people are more inclined to specialize and trade. Specialization is a necessary condition for economic advancement.

5. The circular flow models yield the same fundamental insight, whether they are circular flows of a barter or of a money economy. What is this insight?

In a circular flow model of a barter economy, the insight is that, ultimately, households trade productive services for final goods and services. In a money economy, households pay money for final goods, and businesses pay money for productive services. In the final analysis, however, households exchange their productive services for final goods and services.

Problems

(Answers at the back of the book)

1. Some critics believe and have attacked consumer sovereignty as nonexistent in our economy. List the possible reasons that consumer sovereignty might not exist. Also, can you distinguish between consumer sovereignty and consumer choice? (Hint: the consumer could be "sovereign" but have few choices.)
2. List the various institutional means through which resources in our economy are used to satisfy human wants. Pick one institution that has changed over the last several hundred years. How has that change altered our economic system?
3. List the main characteristics of a capitalistic economy.
4. List some major characteristics of advanced economies, such as the U.S. economy.

3

Demand and Supply

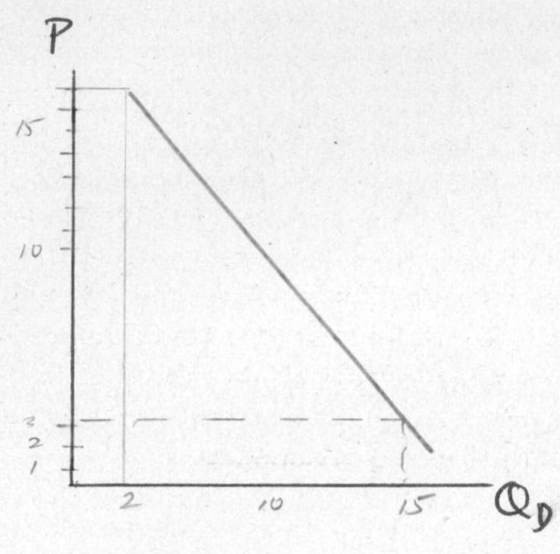

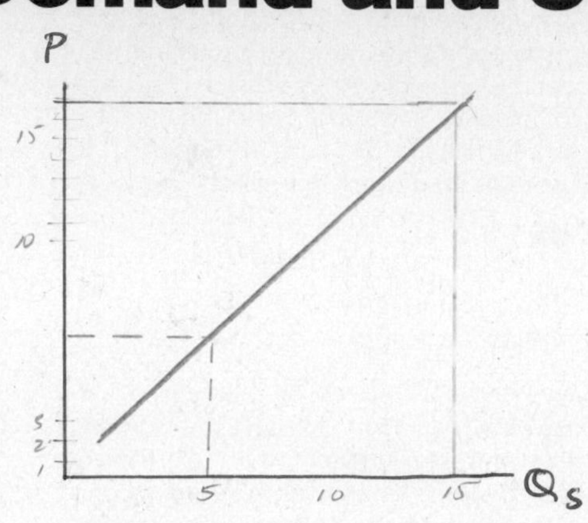

TOPICS FOR REVIEW

The topics listed below, which we have already analyzed, are applied in this chapter. You may find it worthwhile to review them. For your convenience the topic is followed by the number identifying the specific "Concepts in Brief."

a. Scarcity (1–1)

b. Increasing extra cost (1–3)

c. Model (1–5)

FOR PREVIEW AND STUDY

1. The law of demand indicates that an inverse relationship exists between price and quantity demanded, other things constant. Why?
2. Distinguish between (a) a change in demand and (b) a change in quantity demanded, with a given demand curve. Use graphs to aid you.
3. The law of supply indicates that a direct relationship exists between price and quantity supplied, other things constant. Why?
4. Why will the market clearing (equilibrium) price be set at the point of intersection of supply and demand—and not at a higher or lower price?
5. Since 1973 the United States has periodically experienced shortages of gasoline and heating oil, two distillates of crude oil. Some people think this is so because the world is running out of crude oil. Does our analysis of supply and demand suggest an alternative explanation to these shortages?

One cornerstone of economic analysis is the simple demand and supply model. Understanding what demand is, what supply is, and the relationship between the two is essential for understanding virtually all of economics. Demand and supply are two ways of categorizing the influences on the price of goods that you buy. This chapter is an introduction to the study of demand and supply. First, we will look at demand, then supply, and then put them together. In the Issues and Applications section of this chapter, we will use demand and supply analysis to examine illegal markets and activities. We will see that our analysis will allow us to predict what will happen to the price of goods that are made illegal. We look also at the market for home computers.

Law of Demand

The **law of demand** can be stated succinctly as follows:

> **At higher prices, a lower quantity will be demanded than at lower prices, other things being equal.**
>
> Or, looked at another way:
>
> **At lower prices, a higher quantity will be demanded than at higher prices, other things being equal.**

The law of demand, then, tells us that the quantity demanded of any commodity is inversely related to that commodity's price, other things being equal. When we talk about a relationship being inverse, we mean that when one variable moves up in value, the other will move down. Thus, the law of demand states that the price and the quantity demanded move in opposite directions. Price goes up, quantity demanded goes down; price goes down, quantity demanded goes up. You can perhaps think of other inverse relationships. The longer the time that an air conditioner is left on, the lower the temperature in the room will become—within broad limits. The more miles you run every day, holding your intake of food constant, the lower will be your body weight.

OTHER THINGS BEING EQUAL

Notice that at the end of the law of demand, there is the phrase *other things being equal.* Otherwise stated, we are assuming that "other things are held constant." Price is not the only thing that affects purchases. There are many others, which we will look at in detail later on. One, for example, is income. If, while the price of a good is changing, income is also changing, then we would not know whether the change in the quantity in the marketplace was due to a change in the price change or to a change in income. Therefore, we hold income constant, as well as any other factor that might affect the quantity of the product demanded.

Since we are holding all other things equal, or constant, that obviously means that we are holding the prices of all other goods constant when we state the law of demand. Thus, when the price of the good in question goes up, we are assuming that the prices of all other goods have not gone up. Implicitly, therefore, we are looking at a price change of the good under study *relative* to all other prices. An understanding of the concept of *relative prices* is important in the study of economics.

RELATIVE PRICES

The **relative price** of any item is its price compared to the price of other goods, or relative to a (weighted) average of all other prices in the economy. The prices that you and I pay in dollars and cents for any good or service at any point in time are called **absolute,** or **nominal,** prices. Consumer buying decisions, however, depend on relative, not absolute, prices. To drive this point home, let's consider the absolute and relative prices of hamburgers and hot dogs, which we do in Exhibit 3-1. We show the absolute prices of hamburgers and hot dogs three years ago and today. They have both gone up in price. That means that we have to pay out in today's dollars and cents more for hamburgers and for hot dogs. If we look, however, at the relative price of hamburgers to hot dogs, we find that three years ago, hamburgers were twice as expensive as hot dogs, but today they are only one and a half times as expensive. Conversely, if we compare hot dogs to hamburgers three years ago, they cost only half as much as a hamburger, but today they cost two-thirds as much. In the three-year period, while both prices have gone up absolutely, the relative price of hamburgers has fallen (and, conversely, the relative price of hot dogs has risen). If our law of demand holds, then in the economy over this three-year period, a larger quantity of hamburgers will be demanded, while a smaller quantity of hot dogs will be demanded, other things being equal.

Once this distinction is made between absolute and relative prices, there should be no confusion

EXHIBIT 3–1

Absolute Versus Relative Price. The absolute price of both hamburgers and hot dogs has risen. But the relative price of hamburgers has fallen (or, conversely, the relative price of hot dogs has risen).

	ABSOLUTE PRICE		RELATIVE PRICE	
	Price Three Years Ago	*Price Today*	*Price Three Years Ago*	*Price Today*
Hamburgers	$1.00	$3.00	$\frac{\$1.00}{\$0.50} = 2$	$\frac{\$3.00}{\$2.00} = 1.5$
Hot Dogs	$0.50	$2.00	$\frac{\$0.50}{\$1.00} = 0.5$	$\frac{\$2.00}{\$3.00} = 0.67$

about the meaning of price during a period of generally rising prices. Someone not familiar with this distinction may contend that the law of demand clearly does not hold because, say, the price of washing machines went up last year by 5 percent, but the quantity demanded did not go down at all. Assuming that other things in the economy didn't change, this indeed may have been a possible refutation of the law of demand, except for the fact that last year's prices in general may have gone up by as much as or more than 5 percent. It is the price of washing machines *relative* to all other prices that is important for determining the relationship between price and the quantity demanded.

TWO REASONS WHY WE OBSERVE THE LAW OF DEMAND

There are two fundamental reasons that explain why the quantity demanded of a good is inversely related to its price, other things being equal.

Substitution Effect

Let's assume now that there are several goods, not exactly the same, or perhaps even very different from one another, but all serving basically the same purpose. If the price of one particular good falls, we most likely will substitute in favor of the lower-priced good and against the other similar goods we might have been purchasing. Conversely, if the price of that good rises relative to the price of the other similar goods, we will substitute in favor of them and not buy as much of the higher-priced good. Consider an example: The prices of tacos, hamburgers, and hot dogs are all about the same. Each of us buys a certain amount (or none) of each of these three substitutable fast foods. What if the price of tacos increases considerably, while the prices of hamburgers and hot dogs do not? What will we do? We will buy more hamburgers and hot dogs and fewer tacos, since tacos are relatively more expensive, while hot dogs and hamburgers are now relatively cheaper. In effect, we will be substituting hamburgers and hot dogs for tacos *because* of the relatively higher price of tacos. Thus, you can see how the substitution effect affects the quantity demanded of a particular good.

Real Income Effect

If the price of something that you buy goes up while your money income and other prices stay the same, then your ability to purchase goods in general goes down. That is to say, your effective purchasing power is reduced even though your money income has stayed the same. If you purchase ten tacos a week at $1 apiece, your total outlay for tacos is $10. If the price goes up by 50¢, you would have to spend $15 in order to purchase ten tacos. If your money income and the prices of other goods remained the same, it would be impossible for you to purchase ten tacos a week at $1.50 apiece (as you used to do at the lower price) and still purchase the same quantity of all other goods and services that you were purchasing. You are poorer, and hence it is likely that you will buy less of a number of things, including the good whose price rose. The converse will also be true. When the price of one good that you are purchasing goes down without any other prices changing and without your money income changing, you will feel richer and undoubtedly will purchase a bit more of a number of goods, including the lower-priced good.

> ***Concepts in Brief 3-1***
>
> - There is an inverse relationship between the quantity demanded of a good and its price, other things being equal.
> - We hold constant other determinants of quantity demanded, such as income.
> - The law of demand holds because when the price of a good goes down: (1) we substitute in favor of it and (2) we are now richer and buy more of everything, including it.

The Demand Schedule

Let's take a hypothetical demand situation to see how the inverse relationship between the price and the quantity demanded looks. What we will do is consider the quantity of French fries demanded by American college students *per year.* Without stating the *time dimension,* we could not make any sense out of this demand relationship, because the numbers would be different if we were talking about the quantity demanded per month or the quantity demanded per decade.

CONSTANT QUALITY UNITS

Look at Exhibit 3–2(a). Here we show the price per constant-quality bag of French fries. Notice the words *constant quality.* We tack on this qualification in order to take care of the problem of varying qualities of French fries when we wish to add up all of the bags of French fries sold or that could be sold every year. Consider the fact that a bag of French fries at a local fast food place might cost 40¢, whereas in a lavish restaurant an order of beautifully done, perfectly cut up Idaho French fries might cost $2; one of those beautiful French fries might cost the same as a whole bag at the local fast food outlet. Clearly, we do not wish to consider both orders of French fries as exactly the same thing. Therefore we pick some standard such as the bag you usually get at, say, McDonald's. Then we compare all others to that standard. The Idaho French fries in the lavish restaurant might be given the same weight—that is, constant quality—as, say, four bags of McDonald's. We don't have to worry about actually figuring out how we might statistically complete such a task. It is sufficient that you realize that we are correcting conceptually for differences in the qualities of French fries purchased.

What we see in Exhibit 3–2(a) is that if the price were 10¢ per bag, 10 million bags would be bought by American college students each year; but if the price were 50¢ per bag, only 2 million would be bought. This reflects the law of demand. Exhibit 3–2(a) is also called a **demand schedule** because it gives a schedule of alternative quantities demanded per year at different possible prices.

EXHIBIT 3–2(a)
The Demand Schedule and Demand Curve for French Fries by American College Students. Column 1 represents the price per constant-quality bag of French fries. Column 2 represents the quantity demanded by American undergraduates, again measured in constant-quality bags per year of French fries. The last column merely labels these various price/quantity demanded combinations. Notice that as the price rises, the quantity demanded per year falls.

Price per Constant-Quality Bag (cents)	*Quantity Demanded of Constant-Quality Bags per Year*	*Combination*
50	2 million	A
40	4 million	B
30	6 million	C
20	8 million	D
10	10 million	E

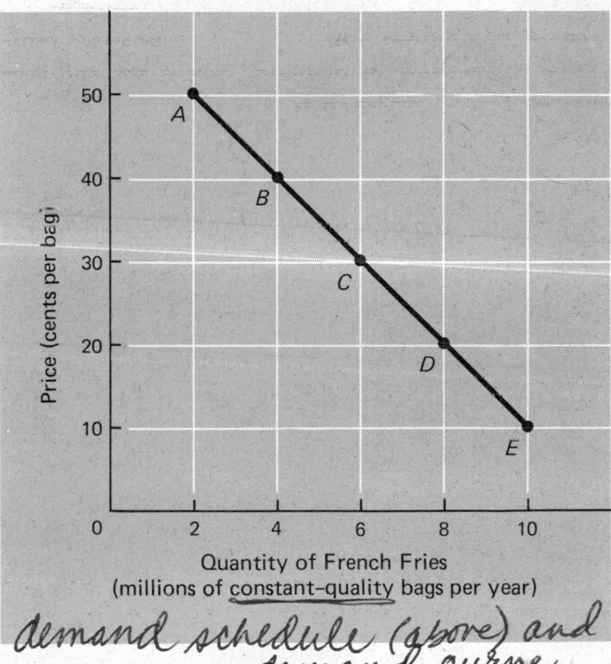

EXHIBIT 3–2(b)
We measure the quantity of French fries in millions of constant-quality bags per year on the horizontal axis and the price per constant-quality bag on the vertical axis. We then take the price/quantity combinations from Exhibit 3–2(a) and put them in this diagram. These points are *A, B, C, D,* and *E.* When we connect the points, we obtain a graphic representation of a demand schedule. It is downward sloping to show the inverse relationship between quantity demanded and price.

THE DEMAND CURVE

Tables expressing relationships between two variables can be represented in graphic terms. To do this, we need only construct a graph that has the price per constant-quality bag on the vertical axis and the quantity measured in constant-quality bags per year on the horizontal axis. All we have to do is take combinations *A, B, C, D,* and *E* from in

Exhibit 3-2(a) and plot those points in Exhibit 3-2(b). Now we connect the points with a smooth line, and *voilà,* we have **a demand curve.**[1] It is downward-sloping (from left to right) to indicate the *inverse* relationship between the relative price of French fries and the quantity demanded per year by American undergraduates. Our presentation of demand schedules and curves applies equally well to all commodities, including toothpicks, hamburgers, textbooks, credit, and labor services.

Determinants of Demand

The demand curve in Exhibit 3-2(b) is drawn with other things held constant, that is, with all of the other nonprice factors that determine demand held constant. There are many such determinants. The major nonprice determinants are: (1) income, (2) tastes and preferences, (3) the price of related goods, (4) changes in expectations of future relative prices, and (5) population (that is, market size).

CHANGES IN DEMAND

If one of the above five determinants of demand changes, then the entire demand curve *shifts,* either to the right or the left. Consider, for example, how we might represent a dramatic increase in the quantity of French fries demanded at *all* prices because of a medical discovery that French fry consumption increased life expectancy! The demand curve presented in Exhibit 3-2(b) would not be an accurate representation of demand now. What we have to do is shift the curve outward, or to the right, to represent an increase in demand. That is to say, there will now be an increase in the quantity demanded at *each and every possible price.* We do this in Exhibit 3-3. The demand curve has shifted from *DD* to *D'D'*. Take any price, say, 30¢. Originally, before the great medical discovery, the quantity demanded at 30¢ was 6 million bags per year. After the discovery, however, the new amount demanded at 30¢ is 10 million bags per year. Thus, we have witnessed a shift in the demand for French fries. We could use a similar analysis when discussing a shift inward, or to the left, of the demand curve for French fries. This might happen, for example, in the case of a medical discovery that French fry consumption actually decreased life expectancy. The demand curve would shift to *D''D''*; quantity demanded would now be less at each and every possible price.

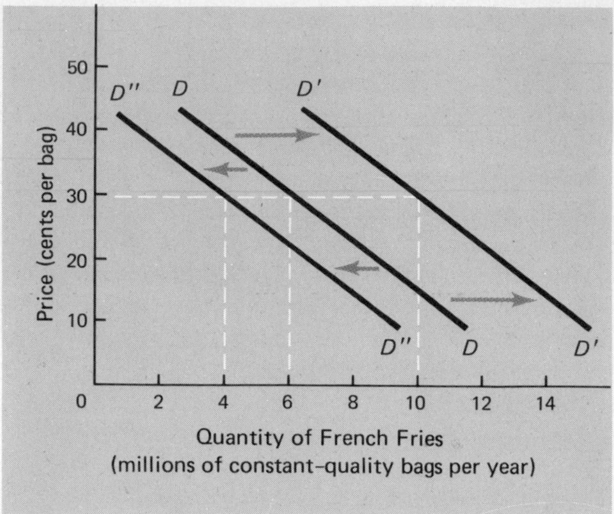

EXHIBIT 3–3
A Shift in the Demand Curve. If only the price of French fries changes, we move to a different point (coordinate) along a given demand curve. However, if some factor other than price changes, the only way we can show its effect is by moving the entire demand curve from *DD* to *D'D'*. We have assumed in our example that the move was precipitated by a medical discovery showing that French-fry consumption led to a greater life expectancy. That meant that at *all* prices a larger quantity would be demanded than before. For example, at a price of 30¢, instead of 6 million bags per year being demanded, 10 million would be demanded. If there were a medical discovery indicating shorter life because of French-fry consumption, the demand curve would shift inward to *D''D''*. At a price of 30¢, for example, now only 4 million bags per year would be consumed. Curve *D''D''* represents reduced demand.

THE DETERMINANTS OF DEMAND

We mentioned that there are five major nonprice determinants of demand.

Income

For most goods, an increased income will lead to an increase in demand. The phrase *increase in demand* always refers to a comparison between two *different* demand curves. Thus, an increase in income for most goods will lead to a rightward shift in the position of the demand curve from, say, *DD* to *D'D'* in Exhibit 3-3. You can avoid confusion about shifts in curves by always relating an increase in demand to a rightward shift in the demand curve and a de-

[1] Even though we call them curves, for the purposes of exposition, we only draw straight lines. In many real-world situations, demand and supply "curves" will in fact be lines that do curve. In order to connect the points in panel (b) with a smooth line, we assume that for all prices in between the ones shown, the quantities demanded will be found along that line.

crease in demand to a leftward shift in the demand curve. Goods for which the demand increases when income increases are called **normal goods.** Most goods are "normal" in this sense. There are some goods for which demand *decreases* as income increases. These are called **inferior goods.** Potatoes might be an example. Assume that we are in a very poor nation and that potatoes are eaten in large quantities by most families. The nation gets richer and richer. With most families on average having higher incomes, more people will be able to afford meat. Thus, instead of buying more potatoes as their income rises, the nation will substitute more meat. An increase in income will have caused a shift inward in the nation's demand curve for potatoes. (The terms *normal* and *inferior* are merely part of the economist's terminology; no value judgments are associated with them.)

Tastes and Preferences

A change in consumer tastes in favor of a good can shift its demand curve outward to the right. When Frisbees became the rage, the demand curve for them shifted to the right; when the rage died out, the demand curve shifted inward to the left. Fashions depend to a large extent on people's tastes and preferences. Economists have little to say about the determination of tastes; that is, we don't have any "good" theories of taste determination or why people buy one brand of product rather than others.

Price of Related Goods: Substitutes and Complements

Demand schedules are always drawn with the prices of all other commodities held constant. That is to say, we assume that only the price of the good under study changes. For example, when we draw the demand curve for butter, we assume that the price of margarine is held constant. When we draw the demand curve for tennis rackets, we assume that the price of tennis balls is held constant. When we refer to *related goods* we are talking about those goods whose demand is interdependent. In other words, if a change in the price of one good shifts the demand for another good, we say that those two goods are related.

There are two types of related goods: **substitutes** and **complements.** We can define and distinguish between substitutes and complements in terms of how the change in price of one commodity affects the demand for its related commodity.

Consider butter and margarine. Generally, we think of butter and margarine as substitutes. Let's assume that each originally costs $1 per pound. If the price of butter remains the same and the price of margarine falls from, say, $1 per pound to 50¢ per pound, people will buy more margarine and less butter. The demand curve for butter will shift inward to the left. If, on the other hand, the price of margarine rises from $1 per pound to $2 per pound, people will buy more butter and less margarine. The demand curve for butter will shift outward to the right. In other words, an increase in the price of margarine leads to an increase in the demand for butter, and an increase in the price of butter will lead to an increase in the demand for margarine. Thus, for substitutes, a price change in the substitute will cause a change in the same direction in the demand for the good under study.

With complementary goods, the situation is reversed. Consider tennis rackets and tennis balls. We draw the demand curve for tennis rackets with the price of tennis balls held constant. If the price of tennis balls decreases from, say, $5 a can to $2 a can, that will encourage more people to take up tennis, and they will now buy more rackets, at any given price, than before. The demand curve for tennis rackets will shift outward to the right. If the price of tennis balls increases from $5 a can to $8 a can, fewer people will play tennis. The demand curve for tennis rackets will shift inward to the left. A decrease in the price of balls leads to an increase in the demand for rackets. An increase in the price of balls leads to a decrease in the demand for rackets. Tennis rackets and tennis balls are thus said to be complementary goods.

The relationship between prices of related goods is shown in Exhibit 3–4.

Changes in Expectations About Future Relative Prices

Expectations about future relative prices play an important role in determining the position of a demand curve because many goods are storable. If all of a sudden there is an expectation of a rise in the future relative price of *x*, then we might predict, all other things held constant, that people will buy more now and the present demand curve will shift from *DD* to *D′D′* in Exhibit 3–3. If, on the other hand, there is a new expectation of a future decrease in the price of *x*, then people will buy less now and the present demand curve will shift instead to *D″D″* in Exhibit 3–3.

Note that we are talking about changes in expectations of future *relative* prices rather than *absolute* prices. If all prices have been rising at 10 percent a year, year in and year out for 100 years, this now fully anticipated price rise has no effect on the

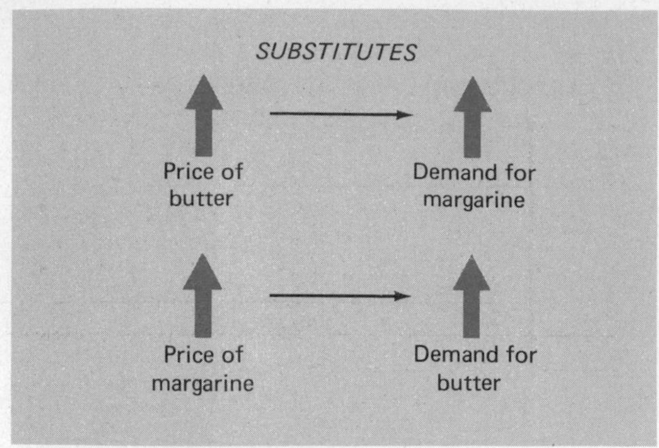

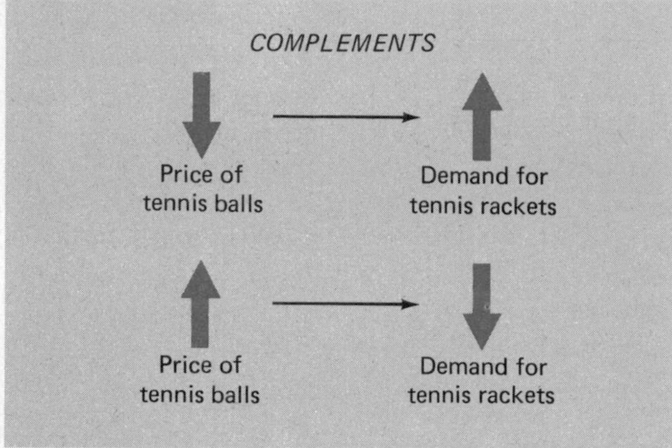

EXHIBIT 3–4
Related Goods.

position of the demand curve for a particular commodity (if the price is measured in *relative* terms on the vertical axis).[2] Consider, for example, what would happen to the demand curve for new automobiles if it were known that their price would rise by 10 percent next year. If it were anticipated that the prices of all other goods would also rise by 10 percent, then the price of new cars relative to an average of all other prices would not be any different next year than it is this year. Thus, the demand curve for new cars this year would not increase just because of the *anticipated* 10 percent price rise in absolute price.

(5) Population

Often an increase in the population in an economy (holding per capita income constant) shifts the market demand outward for most products. This is because an increase in population leads to an increase in the number of buyers in the market. Conversely, a reduction in the population will shift most demand curves inward because of the reduction in the number of buyers in the market. An example of the impact of a change in the number of consumers in a market is the effect of birthrates on the baby food industry. As birthrates dropped in the United States, firms dealing in baby food started to diversify. They moved into other fields because of an anticipated shift inward in the market demand curve for their product.

> ***Concepts in Brief 3-2***
>
> ■ Demand curves are drawn with nonprice determinants held constant. The major nonprice determinants are: (1) income, (2) tastes, (3) prices of related goods, (4) expectations of future relative prices, and (5) population (number of buyers in the market). If any one of these determinants changes, the demand schedule will shift to the right or to the left.

DISTINGUISHING BETWEEN CHANGES IN DEMAND AND CHANGES IN QUANTITY DEMANDED

We have been referring to *changes in demand*—shifts in the entire demand curve so that the quantity demanded at each and every price changes. The term *demand* always relates to the entire demand schedule or curve. *Demand, therefore, refers to a schedule of planned rates of purchase.* Demand—the demand schedule or curve—depends on many nonprice determinants, such as those just discussed.

On the other hand, a change in the quantity demanded can only come about because of a change in price. Look at panel (a) in Exhibit 3–5. We draw a given demand schedule for any good, say, good X. At a very high price, P_1, a small quantity will be demanded, Q_1. This is shown as point A on the demand curve DD. On the other hand, at a very low price, say, P_2, a very large quantity will be demanded, Q_2. We show this on the demand curve as point B. *A change in the quantity demanded occurs when there is a movement to a different point (coordinate) along a given demand curve.* This movement occurs because the price of the product changes. In panel (b) of Exhibit 3–5, let us assume that we start off at a price of 30¢. If the price falls to 10¢, the quantity demanded will increase from 6

[2] We assume that *all* prices have been rising, including the value of all the things that you own and the price you are paid for your labor, that is, your income.

Change in demand
Change in quantity demanded

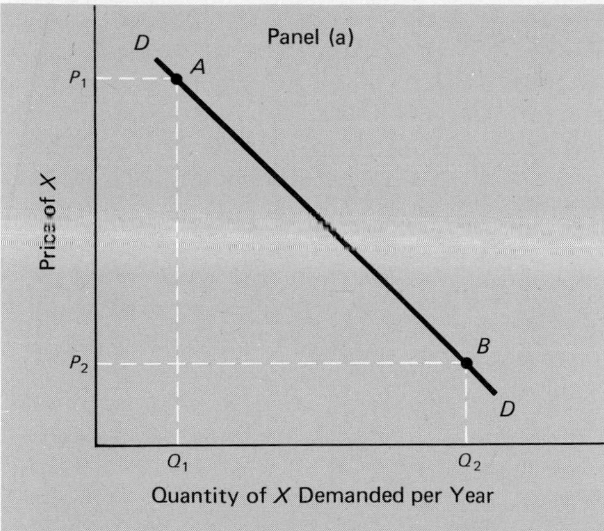

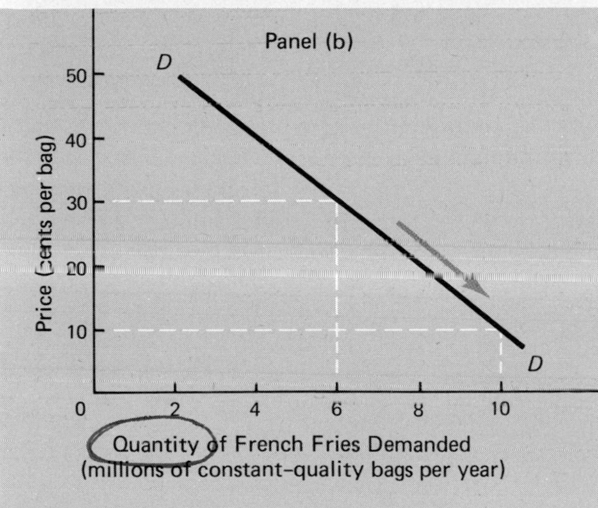

EXHIBIT 3–5

Movement Along a Given Demand Curve. In panel (a), we show the demand curve *DD* for a hypothetical good, *X*. If price is P_1, then the quantity demanded will be Q_1; we will be at point *A*. If, on the other hand, the price is relatively low, P_2, then the quantity demanded will be relatively high, Q_2. We'll be at point *B* on *DD*. Now look at panel (b). Here we show distinctly that a change in price changes the quantity of a good demanded. It is a movement along a given demand schedule. If, in our example, the price of French fries falls from 30¢ a bag to 10¢, the quantity demanded will increase from 6 million bags per year to 10 million.

million bags per year to 10 million bags per year. You can see the arrow moving *down* the given demand schedule *DD* in panel (b).

In economic analysis, it is extremely important to distinguish between changes in demand and changes in the quantity demanded.

> ***Concepts in Brief 3-3***
>
> ■ A change in demand comes about only because of a change in the nonprice determinants of demand.
>
> ■ A change in the quantity demanded comes about only when there is a change in the price.
>
> ■ A change in demand shifts the demand curve and is caused by changes in the determinants of demand; a change in quantity demanded involves a movement along a *given* demand curve and is caused by a change in price.

The Law of Supply

Just as there is a law of demand, so, too, is there a **law of supply,** which is defined as follows:

> **At higher prices, a larger quantity will generally be supplied than at lower prices, all other things held constant.**
>
> Or, stated otherwise:
>
> **At lower prices, a smaller quantity will generally be supplied than at higher prices, all other things held constant.**

In other words, there is a direct relationship between quantity supplied and price. This is the opposite of the relationship we saw for demand. There, price and quantity demanded were inversely related. Here they are directly related. Other direct relationships include, for example, those that exist between caloric intake and body weight, between temperature and the length of time a heater is left on, between fingernail length and time between manicures, and many others. For supply, as the price rises, the quantity supplied rises; as the price falls, quantity supplied also falls. Producers are willing to produce and sell more of their product at a higher price than at a lower price, other things being constant.

WHY A DIRECT, OR POSITIVE, RELATIONSHIP?

There are several reasons why there is a direct, or positive, relationship between price and quantity supplied.

Greater Incentive

The higher the price of a good, all other things remaining constant, the greater the incentive for a

EXHIBIT 3–6

The Supply Schedule and Supply Curve for French Fries by American Producers. In panel (a) at higher prices, suppliers will be willing to provide a greater *quantity supplied* of French fries. We see, for example, in column 1 that at a price per constant-quality bag of 10¢, only 2 million bags will be supplied; but at a price of 50¢ per bag, 10 million will be forthcoming from suppliers. We label these price/quantity combinations in the third column. In panel (b) the horizontal axis measures the quantity of French fries supplied, expressed in millions of constant-quality bags per year. The vertical axis, as usual, measures price. We merely take the price/quantity combinations from panel (a) and plot them as points *F, G, H, I,* and *J.* Then we connect those points to find the supply curve for French fries. It is positively sloped, demonstrating the law of supply. At higher prices, a larger quantity will be forthcoming.

Panel (a)

Price per Constant-Quality Bag (cents)	*Quantity Supplied of French Fries (Measured in Constant-Quality Bags) per Year*	*Combination*
10	2 million	F
20	4 million	G
30	6 million	H
40	8 million	I
50	10 million	J

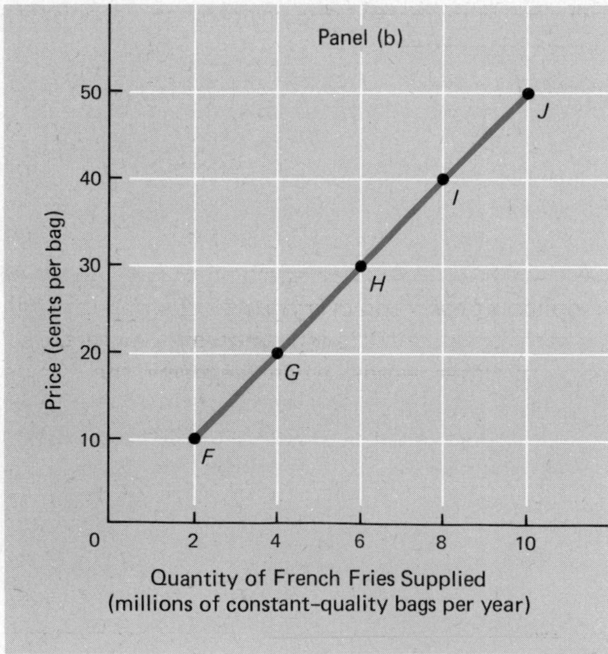

producer to produce more. If the producer's per unit costs have remained the same but, for whatever reason, that producer can sell as much, or more, of the product at a higher price, then, clearly, this would generate higher profits for the producer. Additionally, at a higher price of a good, a producer could incur even higher per unit costs as that producer expands output if, indeed, the output can be sold at a higher price to cover these rising costs. Indeed, it is only when the price has risen that the producer has any incentive to increase production when that producer is faced with rising costs of production. For this reason, we anticipate that producers will be willing to offer for sale greater output at higher prices.

Substitution

When the price of a good goes up, consumers substitute away from it and in favor of other items. The opposite occurs in terms of the resources that producers can use in the production of the higher-priced product. Consider a farmer who uses land, labor, and capital to produce corn, wheat, and barley. If the price of corn goes up, that farmer can shift resources into the production of this higher-priced good and out of the production of the relatively lower-priced products, wheat and barley (assuming similar costs).

> ***Concepts in Brief 3-4***
>
> ■ There is a direct relationship between price and quantity of a good supplied, other things held constant. This direct relationship results from the fact that at higher prices, producers have a greater incentive to produce; at higher prices, they will substitute away from producing less profitable products.

SUPPLY SCHEDULE

Just as we were able to construct a demand schedule, so we can construct a **supply schedule,** which is a table relating prices to the quantity supplied at each price.

It is a set of planned production rates that depends on the price of the product. In Exhibit 3–6 panel (a), we show the supply schedule of French fries.

SUPPLY CURVE

We can convert the supply schedule in panel (a) of Exhibit 3–6 into a **supply curve,** just as we earlier created a demand curve in Exhibit 3-2. All we do is take the price-quantity combinations from panel (a) of Exhibit 3-6 and plot them in panel (b). We have labeled these combinations *F* through *J*. Now we connect these points with a smooth line and we have a "curve." It is upward-sloping to show the direct relationship between price and the quantity supplied. Again, we have to remember that we are talking about quantity supplied *per year,* measured in constant-quality units.

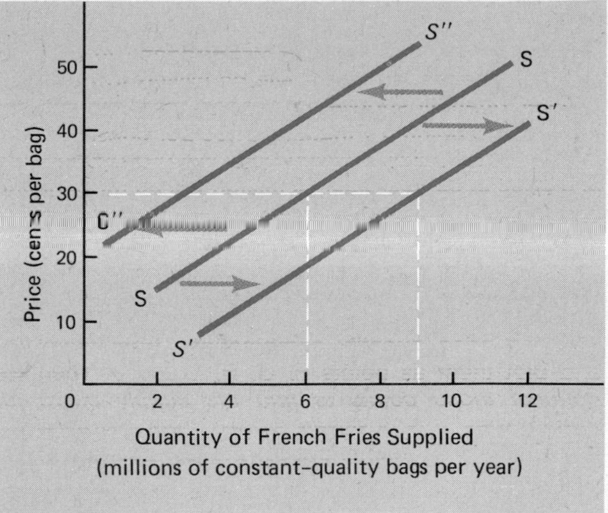

EXHIBIT 3–7

A Shift in the Supply Schedule. If only the price changes, we move along a given supply schedule. However, if, for example, the cost of production of French fries were to fall dramatically, the supply schedule would shift rightward from *SS* to *S'S'* so that at all prices a larger quantity would be forthcoming from suppliers. Conversely, if the cost of production rose, the supply curve would shift leftward to *S''S''*.

THE DETERMINANTS OF SUPPLY

When supply curves are drawn, only the price changes, and it is assumed that other things remain constant. The other things assumed constant are: (1) the prices of resources used to produce the product, that is, the cost of production, (2) technology, (3) taxes and subsidies, (4) price expectations of producers, and (5) the number of firms in the industry. These are the major nonprice determinants of supply. If any of them changes, there will be a shift in the supply curve.

Shifting Supply

A change in the price of the good itself will cause a movement along the supply curve. A change in the nonprice determinants, however, will shift the entire curve.

Consider an example: If a new method of cooking French fries reduces the cost of cooking them by 98 percent, suppliers will supply more at all prices because their cost of supplying French fries has fallen so dramatically. Competition among sellers to produce more at all prices will shift the supply schedule of French fries outward to the right, as we see in Exhibit 3–7. At a price of 30¢, the quantity supplied was originally 6 million per year, but now the quantity supplied at 30¢ a bag will be 9 million per year. This is like what has happened to the supply of electronic calculators in recent years.

The opposite case will make the point even clearer. Suppose that a pair of potato bugs sneak into the U.S. from Ireland in someone's backpack, and that within a matter of months, they and their offspring have destroyed 80 percent of the American potato crop. When French-fry makers try to buy potatoes, they will find an incredibly reduced supply. They—in competition, of course, with other businesspersons who buy and use raw potatoes in other markets—will bid up the price of potatoes. Ultimately, then, French-fry makers will have to pay greatly increased prices for raw potatoes. The supply curve will shift inward to *S''S''*. At all prices, the quantity supplied will fall dramatically due to the greatly increased costs of resources used to produce French fries.

THE DETERMINANTS IN DETAIL

The Prices of Resources Used to Produce the Input

If one or more input prices fall, the supply curve will shift outward to the right; that is, more will be supplied at each and every price. The opposite will be true if one or more inputs become more expensive. In other words, when we draw the supply curve of cars, we are holding the price of steel (and other inputs) constant. When we draw the supply curve of blue jeans, we are holding the price of cotton fixed.

Technology

Supply curves are drawn by assuming a given technology or "state of the art." When the types of production techniques available change, the supply curve will shift. For example, if a better production technique becomes available, the supply curve will shift to the right. A larger quantity will be forthcoming at each and every price.

(3) Taxes and Subsidies

Certain taxes, such as sales taxes, are effectively an addition to production costs and therefore reduce the supply. Thus, if the supply curve were *SS* in Exhibit 3-7, a sales tax increase would shift it to *S″S″*. A subsidy would do the opposite; it would shift the curve to *S′S′*. Every producer would get a "gift" from the government of, say, a few cents for each unit produced.

(4) Price Expectations

A change in the expectation of a future relative price of a product can affect a producer's current willingness to supply, just as price expectations affect a consumer's current willingness to purchase. As an example, consider that some owners of natural gas wells may have kept them capped in anticipation of the federal government raising the legal maximum price for natural gas. Farmers may withhold from market part of their current wheat crop if they anticipate a higher wheat price in the future. In either example, the current quantity supplied at each and every price will decrease.

(5) The Number of Firms in the Industry

In the short run when firms can only change the number of employees they use, we hold the number of firms in the industry constant. In the long run, the number of firms may change. If the number of firms increases, the supply curve will shift outward to the right. If the number of firms decreases, it will shift inward to the left.

> ***Concepts in Brief 3-5***
>
> ■ The supply curve is drawn with other things held constant. If nonprice determinants of supply change, then the supply curve will shift. The major nonprice determinants are: (1) input costs, (2) technology, (3) taxes and subsidies, (4) expectations of future relative prices, and (5) the number of firms in the industry.

Change in Quantity Supplied and Change in Supply

We cannot overstress the importance of distinguishing between a movement along the supply curve—which occurs only when the price changes—and a shift in the supply curve, which occurs only with changes in other nonprice factors. A change in price always brings about a change in quantity supplied. We move to a different coordinate on the existing supply curve. This is specifically called a change in quantity supplied.

But a change in technology, for example, will shift the curve such that there is a change in the quantity supplied at each and every price. This is called a change in supply. A rightward shift represents an increase in supply; a leftward (inward) shift represents a decrease in supply.

> ***Concepts in Brief 3-6***
>
> ■ If the price changes, we *move along* a curve—there is a change in quantity demanded and/or supplied. If something else changes, we *shift* a curve—there is a change in demand and/or supply.

Putting Demand and Supply Together

In the preceding sections on supply and demand, we tried to confine each discussion only to supply or to demand. But you have probably already gotten the idea that we can't view the world just from the supply side or just from the demand side. There is an interaction between the two. In this section, we will discuss how they interact and how that interaction determines the prices that prevail in our economy.

Let's first combine the demand and supply schedules, and then we will combine the curves.

THE DEMAND AND SUPPLY SCHEDULES COMBINED

Let's place Exhibit 3-2(a) (the demand schedule) and panel (a) from Exhibit 3-6 (the supply schedule) into Exhibit 3-8(a). Column 1 shows the price; column 2, the quantity supplied per year at any given price; and column 3, the quantity demanded. Column 4 is merely the difference between columns 2 and 3, or the difference between the quantity supplied and the quantity demanded. In column 5, we label those differences as either an excess quantity demanded or an excess quantity supplied. For example, at a price of 10¢, there would be only 2 million bags of French fries supplied, but the quantity demanded would be 10 million. The difference would be a negative 8 million, which we label an excess quantity demanded. At the other end of the scale, a price of 50¢ per bag would elicit a 10 million

EXHIBIT 3–8

Putting Demand and Supply Together. In panel (a) we combine Exhibits 3–2(a) and 3–6(a). Column 1 is the price per constant-quality bag, column 2 is the quantity supplied, and column 3 is the quantity demanded, both on a per year basis. The difference is expressed in column 4. For the first two prices, we have a negative difference; that is, there is an excess quantity demanded, as expressed in column 5. At the price of 40¢ or 50¢ we have a positive difference; that is, we have an excess quantity supplied. However, at a price of 30¢, the quantity supplied and the quantity demanded are equal, so there is neither an excess quantity demanded nor an excess quantity supplied. We call this price the equilibrium, or market clearing, price. In panel (b) the intersection of the supply and demand curves is at *E*, at a price of 30¢ per constant-quality bag of fries and a quantity of 6 million bags per year. At point *E* there is neither an excess quantity demanded nor an excess quantity supplied. At a price of 10¢ the quantity supplied will be only 2 million bags per year, but the quantity demanded will be 10 million. The difference is excess quantity demanded at a price of 10¢. There are forces that will cause the price to rise, so we will move from point *A* up the supply curve to point *E*. At the other extreme, 50¢ elicits a quantity supplied of 10 million, with a quantity demanded of 2 million. The difference is excess quantity supplied at a price of 50¢. Again, forces will cause the price to fall, so we will move down the demand and the supply curves to the equilibrium price, 30¢ per bag.

Panel (a)

(1) Price (cents)	(2) Quantity Supplied (Bags per Year)	(3) Quantity Demanded (Bags per Year)	(4) Differences (2)–(3) (Bags per Year)	(5) Excesses
10	2 million	10 million	−8 million	Excess quantity demanded
20	4 million	8 million	−4 million	Excess quantity demanded
30	6 million	6 million	0	Market clearing price—equilibrium
40	8 million	4 million	4 million	Excess quantity supplied
50	10 million	2 million	8 million	Excess quantity supplied

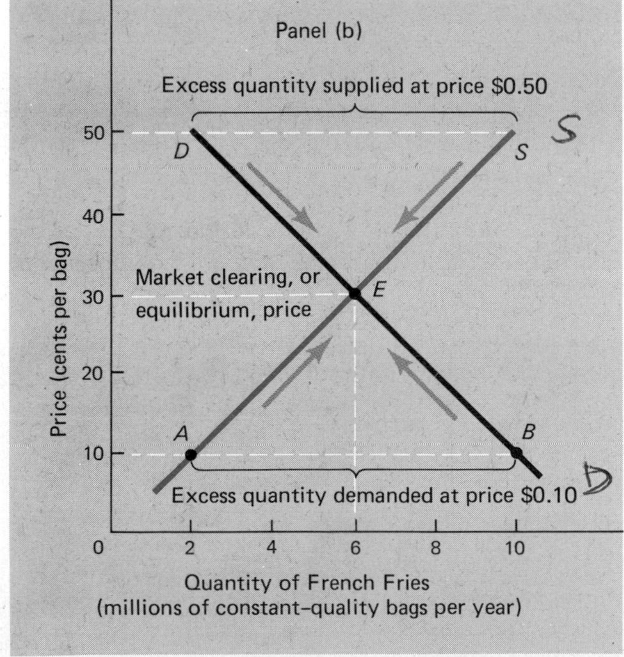

quantity supplied, but quantity demanded would drop to 2 million, leaving a difference of (plus) 8 million, which we call an excess quantity supplied.

Now, do you notice something special about a price of 30¢? At that price, both the quantity supplied and the quantity demanded per year are 6 million bags of French fries. The difference then is zero. There is neither an excess quantity demanded nor an excess quantity supplied. Hence, this price of 30¢ is very special. It is called the **market clearing price**—it clears the market of all excess supply or excess demand. There are no willing demanders who want to pay 30¢ but are turned away from hamburger stands, and there are no willing suppliers who want to provide French fries at 30¢ but cannot sell all they want to sell at that price. The market clearing price is also called the **equilibrium price,** or the price at which there is no tendency for change. Demanders are able to get all they want at

note my error re measurement of surplus + shortage

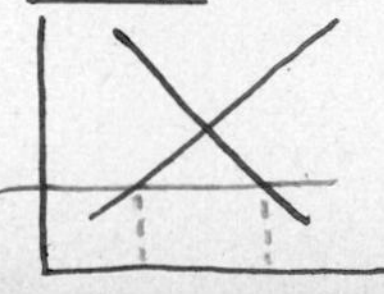

that price; and suppliers are able to sell the amount that they want to at that price.

THE DEMAND AND SUPPLY CURVES COMBINED

Perhaps we can better understand the concept of an equilibrium or market clearing price by looking at the situation graphically. What we want firmly established is the understanding that in the market, a commodity's price will tend toward its equilibrium or market clearing price. Once that price is reached, the price will remain in effect unless either supply or demand changes.

Let's combine panel (b) in Exhibit 3–2 and panel (b) in Exhibit 3–6 into panel (b) in Exhibit 3–8. The only difference now is that the horizontal axis measures both the quantity supplied and the quantity demanded per year. Everything else is the same. The demand curve is labeled *DD,* the supply curve *SS.* We have labeled the intersection of the supply curve with the demand curve as point *E,* for equilibrium. That corresponds to a price of 30¢, at which both the quantity supplied and the quantity demanded per year are 6 million. There is neither an excess quantity supplied nor an excess quantity demanded. Point *E,* the equilibrium point, always occurs at the intersection of the supply and demand curves. Now let's see why we said that this particular price is one toward which the market will automatically tend to gravitate.

Shortages

Suppose we were at a price of 10¢, where the quantity supplied was 2 million and the quantity demanded was 10 million. We would have a situation of an excess quantity demanded at a price of 10¢. This is usually called a **shortage.** Demanders of French fries would find that they could not buy all the French fries they wanted at that price. We can surmise what would happen. Some demanders would sneak around the back of the hamburger stands and offer the owners a tip or a gift to get the French fries they wanted to buy. This would effectively raise the price received by the owner, who could then be induced to supply a larger quantity (remember that the supply curve slopes upward). We would move from points *A* and *B* toward point *E.*

The process would indeed come to a halt when the price reached 30¢ per bag. The hamburger stand owners as a group would not be getting any more orders for fries than they could handle, and French-fry eaters would be able to buy all the French fries they wanted to buy at the going price of 30¢. We would move from a situation of excess quantity demanded at a price of 10¢ to a situation of no excess quantity demanded at a price of 30¢.

Surpluses

Now let's repeat the experiment with the price at 50¢ per bag. We draw a horizontal line at 50¢ to find out what the quantities demanded and the quantities supplied are. As can be expected, the quantity demanded has fallen and is now only 2 million bags per year, but the quantity supplied has risen greatly, to 10 million. There is an excess quantity supplied at a price of 50¢; this is usually called a **surplus.** There is one simple way for that excess quantity supplied to be eliminated. All that has to happen is for the price to fall from 50¢ to 30¢. As the price falls—that is, as the hamburger stand owners compete by offering French fries as a "special" to customers to get rid of the excess quantities they want to supply consumers—the consumers will indeed demand a larger quantity.

THE QUESTION OF PRICE FLEXIBILITY

We have used as an illustration for our analysis a market in which prices are quite flexible. In reality, there are markets in which this is the correct analysis. There are others, however, where price flexibility may take the form of indirect adjustments such as by way of hidden payments or quality changes. For example, the published price—the one that you pay in dollars and cents—for an airline seat may remain the same throughout the year. Nonetheless, the price per constant-quality unit of airline services differs, depending on how crowded the airplane is. In a sense, then, you pay a higher price for airline services during the peak holiday periods than during off-peak periods.

Concepts in Brief 3-7

- When we combine the demand and supply curves, we can find the market clearing, or equilibrium, relative price at the intersection of those two curves. The equilibrium price is one from which there is no tendency to change and toward which price will gravitate if it is higher or lower.
- At prices above the market clearing price, there will be an excess quantity supplied, or a surplus.
- At prices below the market clearing price, there will be an excess quantity demanded, or a shortage.

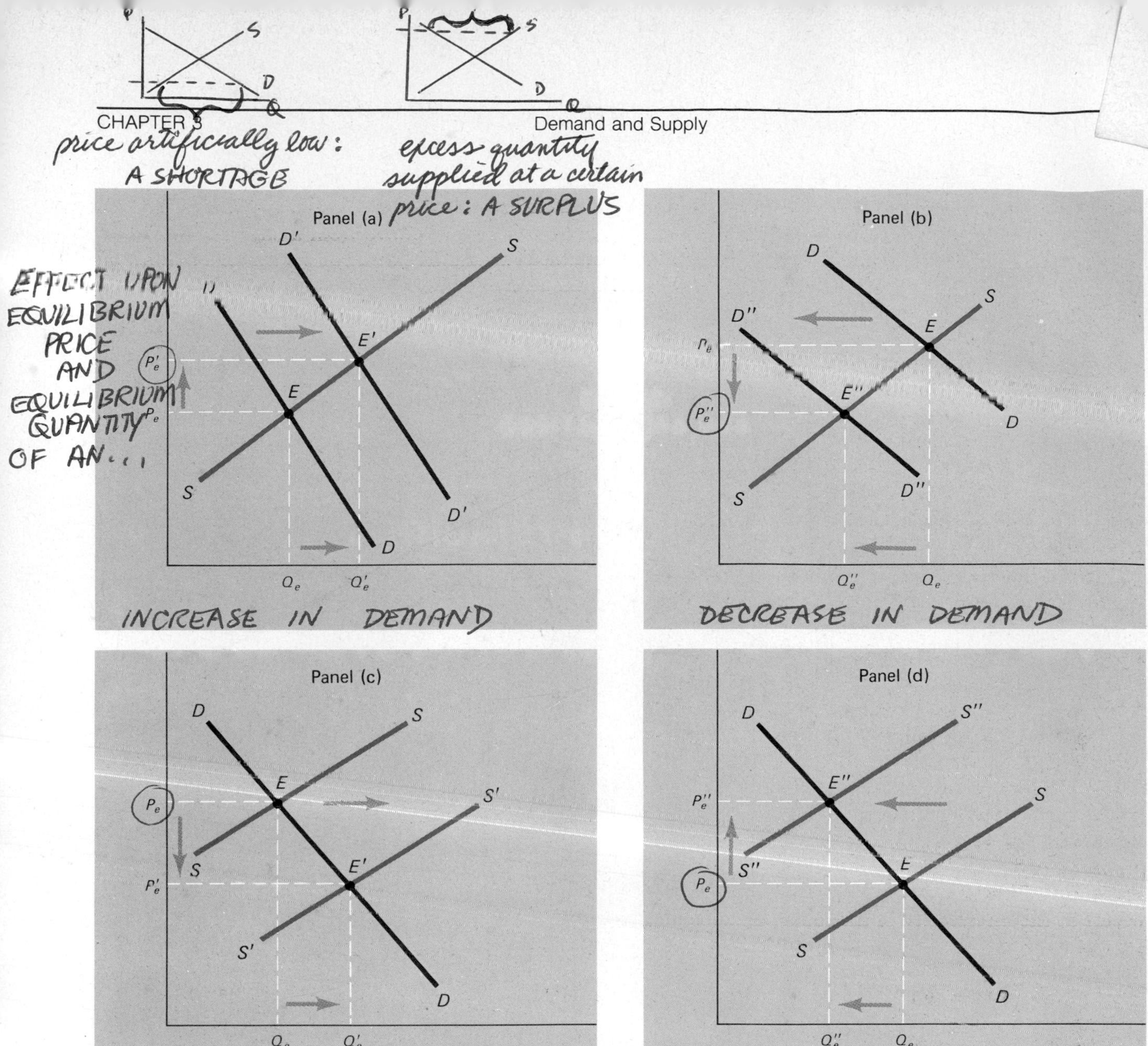

EXHIBIT 3–9

Shifts in Demand and in Supply. In panel (a), the supply curve is stable at *SS*. The demand curve shifts out from *DD* to *D′D′*. The equilibrium price and quantities rise from P_e, Q_e to P_e', Q_e', respectively. In panel (b), again, the supply curve remains stable at *SS*. The demand curve, however, shifts inward to the left showing a decrease in demand from *DD* to *D″D″*. Both equilibrium price and equilibrium quantity fall. In panel (c), the demand curve now remains stable at *DD*. A supply increase is shown by a movement outward to the right of the supply curve from *SS* to *S′S′*. The equilibrium price falls from P_e to P_e'. The equilibrium quantity increases, however, from Q_e to Q_e'. In panel (d), the demand curve is stable at *DD*. Supply decreases, as shown by a leftward shift of the supply curve from *SS* to *S″S″*. The market clearing price increases from P_e to P_e''. The equilibrium quantity falls from Q_e to Q_e''.

Changes in Demand and Supply

Now that we have combined both demand and supply on one graph, we can analyze the effects of changes in supply and changes in demand. In Exhibit 3–9, there are four panels. In panel (a), the supply curve remains stable, but demand increases from *DD* to *D′D′*. Note that the result is both an increase in the market clearing price from P_e to P_e' and an increase in the equilibrium quantity from Q_e to Q_e'.

In panel (b) there is a decrease in demand from *DD* to *D′D′*. This results in a decrease in both the relative price of the good and the equilibrium quantity.

Panels (c) and (d) show the effects of a shift in

the supply curve while the demand curve is stable. In panel (c), the supply curve has shifted rightward—supply has increased. The relative price of the product falls; the equilibrium quantity increases. In panel (d) supply has shifted leftward—there has been a supply decrease. The product's relative price increases; the equilibrium quantity decreases.

ISSUES AND APPLICATIONS

The Effects of Prohibition

Concepts Applied

- Shifts in supply and demand curves

On January 17, 1920, the Eighteenth Amendment to the United States Constitution was put into effect. It prohibited "manufacture, sale or transportation of intoxicating liquors within, or the importation thereof into, or exportation thereof from the United States . . . for beverage purposes." The Eighteenth Amendment therefore was a legislative attempt to eliminate the *supply* of alcoholic beverages.

We know, though, that there are two sides to every coin: no law is effective without enforcement, and Congress was aware of this. In 1919, while the Eighteenth Amendment was being ratified by the various states, the National Prohibition Act, or Volstead Act, was passed to enforce the amendment. This 73-section act tried to prevent trade in liquor by making it illegal to "manufacture, sell, barter, transport, import, export, deliver, furnish or possess any intoxicating liquor." Legislation therefore had also attacked the *demand* side of the alcohol question by making possession illegal.

From the supply side

Before the passage of the Eighteenth Amendment, business people entered into the liquor business if they thought as large a profit could be made in distilling, importing, exporting, wholesaling, or retailing alcoholic beverages as could be made in some other line of commercial endeavor. Take, for example, the cost involved in distilling and wholesaling bourbon. A bourbon distillery usually consisted of distilling, blending, and bottling plants; each plant contained highly specialized equipment such as stainless steel tanks (where the mash was heated to convert starch to sugars), cypress wood fermenting vats, large patent or column stills, and new charred white oak barrels for aging.[3] The owner had to pay for all this equipment and also had to pay employees at least the amount they could earn by working for someone else in a similar job.

When the bourbon manufacturer went to sell the product to wholesalers or even to retailers, if the manufacturer wanted to eliminate the middleman, the bottles of whiskey had to be provided with familiar labels that customers could use to identify this particular brand of spirits. The manufacturer had to package the trademarked bottles of bourbon in cartons so that they could be transported to the buyer. In order to make wholesalers, retailers, and the public aware of this particular product, the manufacturer also had to spend money on some sort of advertising. When wholesalers and retailers demanded the product, the manufacturer either had to rent delivery trucks or to purchase trucks. The manufacturer then had to pay the wages of the drivers. To guard against losses due to theft or accident, the manufacturer needed to purchase some form of insurance.

During Prohibition, one way to minimize the risk of being caught was to extend payoffs to the

[3] Old Carolina moonshiners assert that one can get by with considerably less equipment: a copper pot and worm, a section of garden hose, and some fruit jars, at a minimum. Suggested also was a rifle.

police and officials who were responsible for preventing the illegal manufacture and sale of alcohol. In December 1921—only one year after the start of Prohibition—about 100 federal agents in New York City were dismissed for the "abuse of permits for use of intoxicants." One New York speakeasy proprietor estimated that about 30 percent of his operating costs went for protection money to law enforcement agencies. Of course, it was no longer possible to buy the usual insurance against economic losses from theft and accidents. Apparently, the only insurance against theft was to pay off organized crime. Indeed, the "take" in any individual's business dealings with alcoholic beverages was rumored to be substantial.

Briefly, as manufacturing and distributing spirits became illegal, the cost of doing business increased. The amount of alcohol that businesspersons were willing to supply at any given price thus had to decrease.

From the demand side

Even though the purchase and consumption of spirits became illegal after the passage of the Volstead Act, the demand for intoxicating beverages did not disappear. Before Prohibition, the demand for alcohol was dictated, at least in part, by people's *preferences,* their *incomes,* and the *prices* they had to pay for what they wanted to drink. Let's look at the aspect of price first.

We all know that the price of any product or service represents what we have to give up in order to purchase it. Give up what? you might ask. Someone buying a fifth of bourbon in 1918 would have to give up $2 of purchasing power over other goods and services that were then being sold. For the price of a single fifth of bourbon, our whiskey drinker could have bought perhaps 12 bottles of beer, or 2 steak dinners, or 5 passes to the movies, or 6 new ties. The higher the price, the more you have to give up of all other things. Before the Prohibition period, the higher the price of alcohol, the less of it was sold. During Prohibition, the same relationship continued to hold.

When Prohibition made the purchase of alcohol illegal, certain of the determinants of the demand for spirits changed drastically. Costs that were unknown before Prohibition suddenly faced the potential drinker. When bourbon was legal, manufacturers advertised openly the various qualities that could be found in each individual product. The prices of different brands were well known and widely publicized. The courts upheld trademark laws, so consumers were fairly certain that a particular brand they bought was made by the particular manufacturer. If the product was of a certain quality the last time it was purchased, it would probably be of the same quality the next time. Manufacturers attempting to sell low-quality alcohol would not be successful in such a situation unless they lowered their price accordingly to induce buyers to buy their "inferior" product.

When Prohibition came, there was no more advertising. Brand names were not as numerous as before, and the possibility of fraudulent use of a brand name was now very high. A distiller couldn't very well go to the authorities to complain about some other bootlegger using its brand name. In a phrase, the cost of information about prices and quality went up drastically after alcohol production and consumption became illegal. So even if the price of a fifth of bourbon had remained the same, the actual cost to drinkers would still have gone up because they could not be sure about what they were buying. In fact, they risked the possibility of blindness or even death from drinking bootlegged liquor. Since information was so difficult and costly to come by, bootleggers could get away with producing an occasional batch of lethal bourbon and still stay in business—something that would likely have been impossible before Prohibition. Competitors would have made sure that consumers found out about such behavior, even if bourbon drinkers didn't take the time to inform themselves.

Another cost to imbibers was the risk of being involved in a speakeasy raid. After all, purchase of spirits was illegal. Even though the authorities did not arrest all whiskey drinkers during the Prohibition period, in its first 10 years, the enforcement of the National Prohibition Act did result in about half a million arrests. One might ask which people were most likely to be caught in a speakeasy raid. Who were the people least able to find out about the best whiskey? Or, who were the people most likely to pay intermediaries to go to Canada to purchase high-quality Canadian whiskey? Obviously, we would not be surprised to learn that richer whiskey drinkers ended up with consistently high-quality bourbon and did not run a very high risk of being blinded, killed, or jailed by consuming it. As we shall point out on numerous occasions in this book, when the cost of information goes up, the people who suffer the most are usually those who are less well-off. The poor are usually the ones who suffer the most from our attempts to legislate morality.

The final outcome

What would economists predict as the final outcome? Would the price of liquor go up? Would the quantity demanded go down? Would society be better off? Very few things can be said with certainty in economics. However, predictive and analytical statements can be made with a high degree of reliability if qualifications are tacked on. We know that the cost of providing alcohol went up during Prohibition because of the risk of jail sentences or fines, the price of paying off the police or organized crime, and the difficulty of product differentiation in a market where open advertising was forbidden. Hence, if everything else had remained the same, we could state that the higher costs of production and distribution would have resulted in higher prices for alcoholic beverages, and smaller quantities of alcoholic beverages would have been demanded than before.

Everything else didn't remain the same, though. On the demand side, the implicit cost of purchasing spirits went up due to higher information costs and the possibility of being jailed, fined, blinded, or killed. In this case, if everything else had remained the same, less alcohol would have been demanded. We assume, for the moment, that income and preferences did remain the same. We see, then, that we could have predicted a *lower equilibrium quantity* of alcohol after the passage of the Eighteenth Amendment.

A Graphic Analysis

It's fairly straightforward to translate our verbal analysis into a graph. We do that in Exhibit 3–10, where we show the demand and supply of alcoholic beverages before and after Prohibition. The "before" situation is represented by curves *DD* and *SS*; the "after" situation, by curves *D′D′* and *S′S′*. If our analysis is correct, what happened after Prohibition was a shift of the supply curve leftward because of the increased risk to the supplier, among other things. The shift in the demand curve leftward is less certain. Presumably, because of the stigma attached to the illegality of drinking, a lower quantity would be demanded at all prices, and hence the shift inward to *D′D′*. But demanders were rarely if ever punished like suppliers, so that the shift leftward of the supply curve probably predominated. The market clearing or equilibrium price would rise from P_L to P_I because that is the price at which the relevant supply and demand curves intersect. That is to say, it is the forces underlying demand and supply that yield these two market clearing prices. During Prohibition, the equilibrium price was higher and the equilibrium quantity was lower. Remember that we are talking in terms of constant-quality units per time period. In our case, we can deal with a constant-quality liter of alcoholic beverage per year.

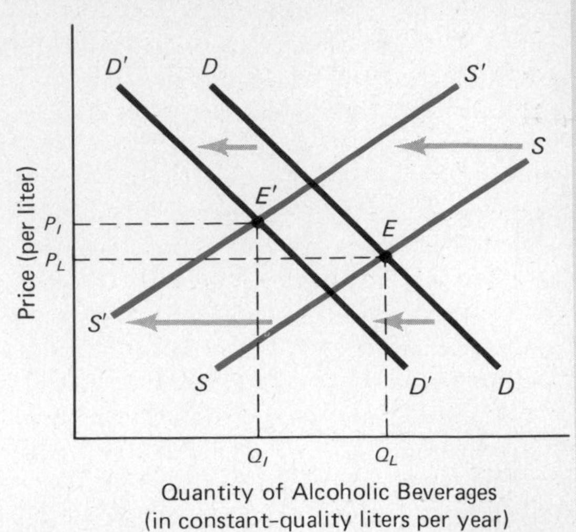

EXHIBIT 3–10
The Effects of Prohibition. We show the original supply and demand curves for alcoholic beverages as *SS* and *DD*. The equilibrium is established at their intersection, *E*. The market clearing price when alcoholic consumption is legal is P_L. Now Prohibition comes into effect. The supply schedule shifts leftward to *S′S′*, and the demand schedule, presumably, shifts leftward to *D′D′*. A new intersection occurs at *E′*. The market clearing price after Prohibition has come into effect is P_I, which is greater than P_L. The equilibrium quantity falls from Q_L to Q_I.

Questions

1. Under what circumstances could Prohibition lead to a larger equilibrium quantity in the marketplace? (Hint: look at the curves in Exhibit 3–10.)
2. Can you apply the analysis of Prohibition to other illegal goods and services? What differences exist among other such goods that would cause your analysis to be different from the one just presented here?

The Market for Home Computers

Concepts Applied

- The law of demand, the law of supply, shifts in demand and supply

Buy an Apple II Plus. Or maybe buy a TRS-80. Or should you get an Atari? In other words, should you buy a home computer, otherwise known as a microcomputer? This question wouldn't have made much sense to most individuals ten years ago, for the market for home computers actually didn't exist then. If it did, it was only a few electronics "freaks" who were playing with computers in their own homes. But let's look at the situation today. "The times, they are a changin'," that's for sure. During the 1980s, industry experts predict that 6,500,000 home computers will be sold. The situation today can be depicted graphically.

Improvements in technology have made microcomputers available at prices affordable by small businesses and individuals for home use.

Graphic Analysis of Today's Home Computer Market

In Exhibit 3–11, the current demand curve for home computers is labeled *DD*. The current supply curve is labeled *SS*. The equilibrium price, P_e, is probably around $750 per constant-quality unit of home computer. (After all, we do have to correct for quality changes. An Apple, according

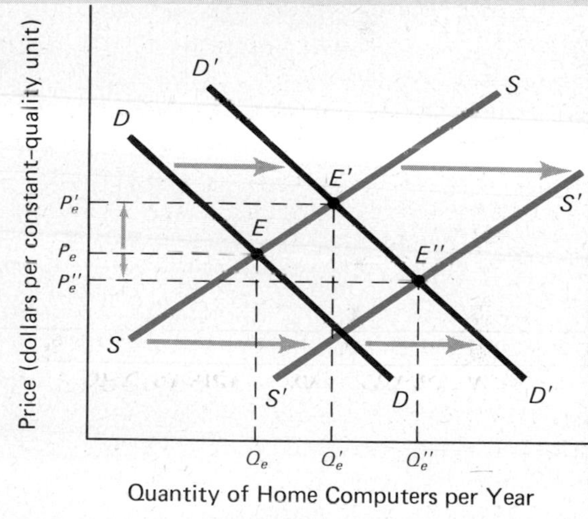

EXHIBIT 3–11
Changes in the Market for Home Computers. We assume that the current demand curve for home computers is *DD* and the current supply curve is *SS*, with an equilibrium at point *E*. The equilibrium price is P_e, with an equilibrium quantity of Q_e. Greater familiarity and rising real income will cause the demand curve to shift to *D'D'*. The new equilibrium shifts from *E* to *E'*. The equilibrium price rises to P_e' and the equilibrium quantity to Q_e'. Improvements in technology, and entry by new firms, however, cause an outward shift in the supply curve to *S'S'*. The new equilibrium is at point *E''*. The new equilibrium price drops to P_e''; the new equilibrium quantity increases to Q_e''.

to some, is "better" than the less expensive TRS-80, made by Radio Shack.) The equilibrium quantity is given by Q_e.

A shift in demand. We can expect, though, that the demand curve for home computers will be shifting out for at least two reasons:

1. As real (inflation-corrected) incomes rise, more people will be willing to buy microcomputers.
2. As individuals become more familiar with the capacity and the ease of using a home computer, the demand curve will also shift outward to the right. After all, many younger people are becoming familiar and unafraid of computers very early in their schooling. Older individuals are experimenting in neighbors' homes with microcomputers and finding out that they aren't that hard to use.

We would expect the demand curve to shift outward to the right from DD to a new curve like $D'D'$. If nothing were to happen to the supply curve, the new equilibrium would move from E to E'. The new equilibrium price would go from P_e to P_e', with a greater equilibrium quantity of Q_e'.

Improvements in Technology

Remember that one of the nonprice determinants of supply is a change in technology. The computer industry has been experiencing what can be termed "phenomenal" increases in technology. The use of better memories, improvements in semiconductor technology, and so on, are allowing computer manufacturers to make computers with greater and greater capacity at the same, or even lower, cost. We can predict, therefore, that as a result of these technological advances and because high profits in existing firms will cause more and more firms to enter the industry that there will be a significant increase in the supply curve from SS to $S'S'$. The new equilibrium will shift from E' to E''. The equilibrium price will fall from P_e' to P_e''. The equilibrium quantity will further increase to Q_e''.

What we have depicted here is how to analyze questions about future events—improvements in the technology for making computers—and their impact on the price and quantity demanded of a particular product.

Questions

1. "I'm going to wait until more people get interested in buying that new product. Then the price will fall." This common statement seems consistent with what is happening (or predicted to happen) in the home computer industry. Nonetheless, the reasoning may be incorrect. What is the correct reasoning?
2. Under what circumstances, even given dramatic improvements in the technology of making home computers, could our prediction about a lower price in the future be wrong?

Definition of Terms

Law of demand Quantity demanded and price are inversely related—more is bought at a lower price, less at a higher price (other things being equal).

Relative price The price of a commodity expressed in terms of the price of another commodity or the average price of all other commodities.

Absolute or nominal prices The prices that we observe today in terms of today's dollars. Also called nominal or current prices.

Demand schedule A set of pairs of numbers showing various possible prices and the quantities demanded at each price; this is a schedule showing the rate of planned purchase per time period at different prices of the good.

Demand curve A graphic representation of the demand schedule. A negatively sloped line showing the inverse relationship between the price and the quantity demanded.

Normal goods Goods for which demand increases as income increases. Most goods that we deal with are normal.

Inferior goods Those goods for which demand decreases as income increases.

Substitute Two goods are considered substitutes when a change in the price of one causes a shift in demand for the other in the same direction as the price changes. For example, if the price of butter goes up, the demand for margarine will rise; if the price of butter goes down, the demand for margarine will decrease.

Complement Two goods are considered complements if a change in the price of one causes an opposite shift in the demand for the other. For example, if the price of tennis rackets goes up, the demand for tennis balls will fall; if the price of tennis rackets goes down, the demand for tennis balls will increase.

Law of supply There is a direct relationship between the price and the quantity supplied (other things being equal).

Supply schedule A set of numbers showing prices and the quantity supplied at those various prices; a schedule showing the rate of planned production at each relative price for a specified time period, usually one year.

Supply curve The graphic representation of the supply schedule; a line showing the supply schedule, which slopes upward (has a positive slope).

Market clearing, or equilibrium, price The price that clears the market where there is no excess quantity demanded or supplied. The price at which the demand curve intersects the supply curve.

Shortage Another term for an excess quantity demanded or insufficient quantity supplied. The difference between the quantity demanded and the quantity supplied at a specific price below the market clearing price.

Surplus Another name for an excess quantity supplied or insufficient quantity demanded. The difference between the quantity supplied and the quantity demanded at a price above the market clearing price.

Chapter Summary

1. It is important to distinguish between the relative price of a good or service and its absolute price. During a period of rising prices, such as we are now experiencing in the United States, almost all prices go up, although some go up faster than others.
2. The law of demand is one of the most fundamental propositions in economics. It merely states that at a higher price, individuals will purchase less of a commodity, and at a lower price they will purchase more.
3. When stating the law of demand, we must be careful to add the phrase *other things being equal.*
4. When discussing the law of demand (and supply), we must be careful to talk in terms of constant-quality units of the commodity in question. In other words, we have to correct for quality differences.
5. The law of demand holds because when a price changes: (a) there is a substitution effect and (b) we are poorer or richer. (income effect)
6. The law of demand can be seen in the demand schedule, which shows the relationship between various possible prices and the respective quantities of an item purchased per unit time period. In graphic terms, the demand schedule is shown as a demand curve that is downward sloping.
7. The nonprice determinants of demand are: (a) income, (b) tastes and preferences, (c) the price of related goods, (d) expectations of future relative prices, and (e) the population, or market size.
8. Whenever any of the nonprice determinants of demand changes, the demand curve shifts so that the quantities demanded at each and every price change.
9. Where the demand and supply curves intersect, we find the equilibrium, or market clearing, price at which the quantity demanded equals the quantity supplied.
10. It is important to distinguish between a movement along a demand or supply curve and a shift in one of those curves. Whenever the price changes, we move along the curve. However, if something else changes, such as income, preferences, or population, then there is a shift in one or both of the curves.
11. The supply curve is generally an upward-sloping line, showing that at higher prices more will be forthcoming from suppliers. Again, we must

talk in terms of constant-quality units of measurement, and we must specify a time period for our analysis.

12. The two reasons that we empirically observe the law of supply are: (a) greater incentive to produce at higher prices and (b) substitution of resources into the more profitable good when price rises.
13. The nonprice determinants of the position of the supply schedule are: (a) technology, (b) taxes and subsidies, (c) price expectations, (d) input prices, and (e) entry and exit of firms.
14. When the price of a good is greater than its market clearing price, there is an excess quantity supplied at that price. This is usually called a surplus.
15. When the price is below the market clearing price, there is an excess quantity demanded at that price. This is usually called a shortage.
16. Illegal markets can be analyzed from a supply and demand point of view. Making the sale of a good illegal usually shifts the supply curve leftward; making the purchase and consumption of a good illegal often shifts the demand curve leftward. The after-illegality market clearing price usually rises, and the equilibrium quantity falls. This was the case after Prohibition became effective.
17. The market for home computers can be analyzed in terms of, first, the shift in the demand curve outward to the right caused by more familiarity and rising real income. This leads to an increase in the equilibrium price, given a stable supply curve. Technological improvements and entry by new firms cause the supply curve to shift outward to the right, ultimately resulting in a lower-than-original equilibrium price.

Selected References

Henderson, Hubert. *Supply and Demand.* Chicago: University of Chicago Press, 1958, chap. 2.

Schultz, Henry. *The Theory and Measurement of Demand* (Reissue). Chicago: University of Chicago Press, 1957.

Watson, Donald S., and Malcolm Getz. *Price Theory and Its Uses.* 5th ed. Boston: Houghton Mifflin, 1981, chap. 2.

Answers to Preview and Study Questions

1. The law of demand indicates that an inverse relationship exists between price and quantity demanded, other things constant. Why?

Economists maintain that the real-income effect and the substitution effect help explain the law of demand. Let's see how as we trace through the effects of a reduction in the price of hamburgers, other things being constant. Suppose that when the price of hamburgers was $1 per unit, Mr. Smith purchased 10 hamburgers per week; Mr. Smith spent $10 per week on hamburgers. Let's further assume, for simplicity, that Smith spent *all* his weekly income of $100 per week. Now, if the price of hamburgers falls to 50¢ per unit, and all other things remain constant, what will happen? If Smith makes exactly the same number of purchases he made the week before, he would now be spending the same amount on nonhamburgers and only $5 on hamburgers. In short, Mr. Smith has experienced an increase in his real income of $5; his $100 weekly income can buy everything he purchased last week and he still has $5 left over. We predict that he will spend some of this $5 on hamburgers.

Now, what if this $5 extra real income were taxed away from Smith (as a windfall profit tax)? In effect we have eliminated the real-income effect. Yet we *still* predict that Smith will buy more hamburgers. Why? The prices of all other goods, such as hot dogs and roast beef sandwiches, remain constant by assumption. As a consequence the *relative* price of hamburgers has fallen, and the *relative* prices of hamburger substitutes have increased (note that the *absolute* prices of hamburger substitutes have remained constant). We predict that Mr. Smith will buy more hamburgers and, since more money spent on hamburgers means less to spend on other goods, fewer hamburger substitutes.

In short, a reduction in the price of hamburgers, other things being constant, leads to an increase in the quantity demanded for hamburgers. This is due to the real-income effect and the substitution effect—two distinct effects.

2. Distinguish between (a) a change in demand and (b) a change in quantity demanded, given demand. Use graphs to aid you.

A change in demand, since demand is a curve, is equivalent to a *shift* in the demand curve. Changes in demand result from changes in the nonprice determinants of demand, such as money income, tastes and preferences, expectations, prices of related goods, and population. A change in quantity demanded, given demand, is a movement along a demand curve and results from a change in the price of the commodity in question.

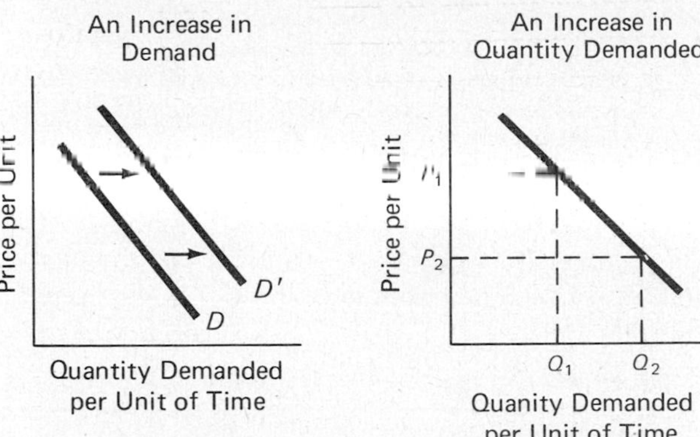

3. The law of supply indicates that a direct relationship exists between price and quantity supplied, other things constant. Why?

Economists maintain that the incentive effect and the substitution effect account for the law of supply. In general, businesses experience increasing *extra* (or marginal) costs as they expand output in the short run. This means that later units of output, which may be quite similar in physical attributes to earlier units of output, actually cost the firm more to produce. Consequently, firms often require a higher and higher price (as an incentive) in order to produce more in the short run; the incentive effect maintains that higher prices, other things being constant, lead to increases in quantity supplied.

Moreover, if a given business (manufacturer or farmer) has the option of producing *more* than one commodity, it will respond to relative price differences in selling price. That is, if the price of ties rises, while the price of shirts remains constant, the relative price of ties has increased. We would expect the shirt-tie manufacturer to reallocate resources in order to produce more ties and fewer shirts. Our producer will substitute some more tie production for less shirt production; an increase in the price of ties, other things being constant, leads to an increase in the quantity of ties supplied. Both the incentive effect and the substitution effect imply that an increase in price, other things being constant, leads to an increase in quantity supplied.

4. Why will the market clearing (equilibrium) price be set at the point of intersection of supply and demand—and not at a higher or lower price?

Consider the graph in the next column.

In order to demonstrate that the equilibrium price will be at P_e, we can eliminate all other prices as possibilities. Consider a price above P_e, $8 per unit. By inspection of the graph we can see that at that price the quantity supplied exceeds the quantity demanded for this product ($B > A$). Businesses are not able to sell all they want to sell at a price of $8 per unit and so inventories will be rising unintentionally, at the rate of B − A per unit of time. For that number of units produced, costs are incurred but no revenues are forthcoming. Also, storage costs for increased inventories will be rising through time as inventories accumulate. Clearly sellers are not maximizing total profits and they therefore find it profitable to lower price and decrease output. In fact this surplus situation exists at *all* prices above P_e.

Consider a price of $4 per unit, where the quantity demanded exceeds the quantity supplied ($F > C$); a shortage of this commodity exists at a price of $4 per unit. Buyers will not be able to get all they want at that relatively low price. Since buyers are competing for this good, those buyers who are willing to give up more of other goods in order to get this one will offer higher and higher prices. By doing so they eliminate buyers who are not willing to give up more of other goods. An increase in price encourages sellers to produce and sell more. A shortage exists at *any* price below P_e, and therefore price will rise if it is below P_e.

At P_e the quantity supplied equals the quantity demanded, Q_e, and both buyers *and* sellers are able to realize their intentions. Since neither group has an incentive to change its behavior, equilibrium exists at P_e.

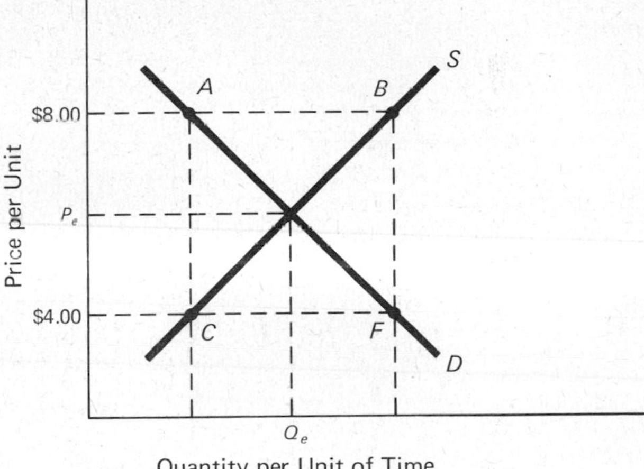

5. Since 1973 the United States has periodically experienced shortages of gasoline and heating oil, two distillates of crude oil. Some people think this is so because the world is running out of crude oil. Does our analysis of supply and demand suggest an alternative explanation to these shortages?

Our analysis of supply and demand indicates to us that a shortage is a situation in which the quantity demanded exceeds quantity supplied at a price *below* equilibrium. A shortage situation can exist if price is not allowed to rise to the equilibrium position. Thus, an alternative explanation to the periodic gasoline and heating oil shortages is that price has not been allowed to rise to equilibrium or market clearing levels. If the prices of these oil distillates were allowed to rise, then quantity supplied would rise and quantity demanded would fall; a rise in the price of gasoline and heating oil would eliminate their shortages. Indeed, independent evidence indicates that, in fact, price controls *have* existed on these items. Governments have disallowed these prices from rising; shortages have resulted.

Problems

(Answers at the back of the book)

1. Construct a demand curve and a supply curve for skateboards, based on the data provided in the following tables.

Price per Skateboard	*Quantity Demanded per Year*
$75	3 million
$50	6 million
$35	9 million
$25	12 million
$15	15 million
$10	18 million

Price per Skateboard	*Quantity Supplied per Year*
$75	18 million
$50	15 million
$35	12 million
$25	9 million
$15	6 million
$10	3 million

What is the equilibrium price? What is the equilibrium quantity at that price?

2. "Drugs are obviously complementary to physicians' services." Is this statement always correct?

3. Five factors, other than price, that affect the demand for a good were discussed in this chapter. Place each of the following events in its proper category, and state how it would shift the demand curve in question.

a. New information is disclosed that large doses of vitamin C prevent common colds. (The demand for vitamin C.)

b. A drop in the price of tape recorders occurs. (The demand for stenographic services.)

c. A fall in the price of pretzels occurs. (The demand for beer.)

4. Examine the table below, then answer the questions below it.

	Price (per Unit) Last Year	*Price (per Unit) Today*
Heating Oil	$1.00	$2.00
Natural Gas	$ .80	$3.20

What has happened to the absolute price of heating oil? Of natural gas? What has happened to the price of heating oil relative to the price of natural gas? What has happened to the relative price of heating oil? Will consumers, through time, change their relative expenditures? If so, how?

5. Suppose that the demand for oranges remains constant, but that a frost occurs in Florida, which could potentially destroy one-third of the Florida orange crop. What will happen to the equilibrium price and quantity for oranges?

4
The Price System

TOPICS FOR REVIEW

The topics listed below, which we have already analyzed, are applied in this chapter. You may find it worthwhile to review them. For your convenience the topic is followed by the number identifying the specific "Concepts in Brief."

a. Scarcity (1–1)

b. Positive versus normative economics (1–5)

c. Demand (3–1)

d. Supply (3–4)

e. Changes in demand lead to changes in price (3–7)

FOR PREVIEW AND STUDY

1. Why does the scarcity problem force all societies to answer *what, how,* and *for whom*?
2. Under ideal capitalism, exchange is voluntary. What are some implications of this?
3. How do markets lower the transactions costs of exchange?
4. What is consumer sovereignty? Is consumer sovereignty worthwhile?
5. What is the difference between technical efficiency and economic efficiency?

The price system, or market system, is one of the basic elements of capitalism. We learned that back in Chapter 2. In Chapter 3, we showed how demand and supply interact to determine the relative prices of resources, goods, and services. In this chapter we will look at the price system in more detail. For example, we will see that demand and supply interact to determine relative prices and that relative prices determine how resources are allocated. In other words, how do we end up using our resources to produce cars instead of buggies? By what mechanism was the pulp, ink, and glue funneled into the textbook industry for *Economics Today,* Fourth Edition? We will also look at other aspects of the price system along with the arguments for and against it.

Resource Allocation

Because we live in a world of scarcity, decisions must be made, whether implicitly or explicitly, about how resources shall be allocated. The problem of **resource allocation** is solved by the economic system at work in a nation. We will study how the price system in our mixed economy (capitalism mixed with socialism) allocates our resources. We will see how our price system answers the three questions—*what? how?* and *for whom?* goods and services will be produced.

1. *What and how much will be produced?* There are literally billions of different things that could be produced with society's scarce resources. Some mechanism must exist that causes some things to be produced and others to remain as either inventors' pipe dreams or individuals' unfulfilled desires.
2. *How will it be produced?* There are many ways to produce a desired item, once the decision has been made to produce it. It is possible to use more labor and less capital and vice versa. It is possible to use lots of unskilled labor or fewer units of skilled labor. Somehow, some way, a decision must be made as to the particular mix of inputs and the way they should be organized.
3. *For whom will it be produced?* Once a commodity is produced, who shall get it? In other words, what mechanism is there to distribute commodities (and income) once they are produced?

We shall see that in a price system, literally millions of individuals are involved in solving these three fundamental questions. The interaction among the individuals within the price system is done without the use of centralized decision-making. Rather, the price system involves decentralized decision-making. Each decision in a price system is made by the interaction of the millions of people involved in the decision. In the American economy, much of the decision-making that goes on about *what, how,* and *for whom* is carried out in markets by voluntary exchange.

EXCHANGE TAKES PLACE IN MARKETS

As a society we have unlimited wants, but we must make choices among the limited alternatives available to us. When you start trading with other individuals, choices arise because you have to pick among alternative **exchanges** that you could make. Individuals in societies have been exchanging goods and services for hundreds of thousands of years. For example, archaeologists tell us that during the Ice Age, hunters of mammoths in the Great Russian Steppe were trading for Mediterranean shells.

Voluntary Exchange

For the most part, our discussion of exchange will center on voluntary exchanges among individuals and among nations. By necessity, prior to the undertaking of every voluntary exchange, the act of exchange itself appears to make both parties to the exchange better off. In other words, exchange is mutually beneficial or it would not be entered into. By assumption, if it were not mutually beneficial, individuals and nations would not bother exchanging.

To be sure, involuntary exchanges do occur and some are quite unpleasant for the losing parties. Involuntary exchanges occur where coercion is used to alter the behavior of another person or nation. When individuals are robbed, they suffer exchange of goods that must be deemed involuntary. We make the assumption that only a very small part of all exchanges are involuntary and, hence, such involuntary exchanges will not affect our analysis of the price system.

The **terms of exchange**—the opportunity cost or price we pay for the desired item—are determined by the interaction of the forces underlying demand and supply. This statement, of course, relates only to an unrestricted price system. Many of the terms of exchange—the prices we pay—are determined by laws and regulations that are a result of the political process. Additionally, some items of exchange are determined by custom and by tradition. While custom does not play a significant role in determining prices in our society, in traditional societies it has been an important determinant. Customs, regulations, and laws are established by individuals acting in some type of collective manner. Thus, in a sense, all terms of exchange are determined ultimately by individuals.

In our economy, the allocation of resources takes place through voluntary exchanges in *markets.*

MARKETS AND INFORMATION

Economists talk about markets a lot. The concept of a **market** is abstract, for it encompasses the exchange arrangements of both buyers and sellers that underlie the forces of supply and demand. In other words, demand and supply work themselves out in markets. As a general term, the word *market* refers to any arrangement or arrangements that individuals have for exchanging with one another. Economists, therefore, typically talk about the labor market, the automobile market, and even the education market.

One of the major factors involved in the market is the exchange of information about prices, quantities, qualities, and so forth. Different markets have different degrees of information and speed with which that information is transmitted. The stock market, for example, has information about the prices and quantities of stocks being bought and sold. This information is transmitted almost instantaneously throughout the United States at least, if not the world. Profit-seeking entrepreneurs are constantly looking for ways to make more profits by improving on the information network within markets. That's why every stockbroker can now tell you instantly the last price and quantity traded of any stock listed on a major stock exchange.

WHY WE TURN TO MARKETS

The reason individuals turn to markets to conduct economic activities or exchanges is that markets reduce the costs of exchanging. These costs are generally called **transactions costs** because they are associated with transacting economic exchange. We can define transactions costs as all of the costs enabling exchanges to take place. Thus, they include the cost of being informed about the qualities of a particular product, its price, its availability, its durability record, its servicing facilities, its degree of safety, and so on. Consider, for example, the transactions costs in shopping for a ten-speed bicycle. Such costs would include phone calls or actual visits to sellers in order to learn about product features and prices. In addition to these costs, we must include the cost of negotiating the sale. The specification and execution of any sales contract is thus included, and ultimately transactions costs must include the cost of enforcing such contracts.

The transactions costs in the most highly organized markets are relatively small. Take, for example, the New York Stock Exchange. It is quite easy to obtain immediate information on the price of listed stocks, how many have been bought and sold in the last several hours, what the prices were the day before, and so on.

Generally, the less organized the market, the higher the transactions costs. No market can completely eliminate transactions costs, but some markets do a better job of reducing them than do others. Historically, as it has become less costly to disseminate information through technological improvements, transactions costs have fallen. Think how costly, in terms of time and money, it was years ago for someone in California to find out in a hurry the price of stocks being sold in New York.

Concepts in Brief 4-1

- Any economic system must answer the questions: (1) *what* will be produced, (2) *how* it will be produced, and (3) *for whom* it will be produced.
- Within a price system, supply and demand determine the prices at which exchanges shall take place.
- The price system is also called a market system because exchanges take place in markets where market mechanisms have reduced transactions costs, defined as all costs associated with exchange.

Relative Prices Revisited

We have often referred to prices as relative prices. This is even more important in understanding how the price system solves the basic allocation of resources problem. In the broad sense of the term, the relative price of a good is defined as the price of that good expressed in terms of how much of other goods must be given up to purchase a unit of the good in question. To establish relative prices, comparison with other prices must be made. Virtually all economic models, like supply and demand, relate individual behavior to changes in relative, not absolute, prices.

PRICES AND INFORMATION

Relative prices are the conveyors of information in the marketplace. For the buyers, the relative price of a good indicates what the individual purchaser must give up in order to obtain that good. Consider an example. You are told that a loaf of bread will cost you $100. That sounds outrageous, doesn't it? But what if you are then told that you will be making $500 per hour? Does that $100 loaf of bread still sound so expensive? Is it any more expensive than, say, a current price of $1 for the loaf and a wage rate of $5 per hour? In both cases, you only have to work one-fifth of an hour to pay for the loaf of bread. It is the relative price of the loaf of bread—in this case, relative to the price of your labor—that tells you how expensive it *really* is (or what your real purchasing power is).

Now consider the relative value of the resources used to produce the bread. Its relative price will, in most cases, indicate the amount of resources given up to produce that good. Hence, when the relative price of a commodity goes up, that bit of information tells the buyer and the seller that the good is now relatively scarcer. Note that neither the producer nor the consumer has to know *why* that particular commodity has become relatively scarcer. It may not matter to you as a consumer, when allocating your budget, whether the price of gasoline has gone up *because* of a restriction on imports or *because* of a new law that requires gasoline refineries to install more expensive pollution abatement equipment. The only thing that definitely matters to you is the higher relative price, for that is the basis on which you will make your decision about the quantity to purchase. The message is transmitted by the higher relative price. Of course, how you respond to the message is impossible to predict on an individual basis, for there are probably an infinite number of ways that a consumer can "conserve" on a relatively scarcer good.

Changes in relative prices convey information on changing relative scarcity to both buyers and sellers. Of course, buyers respond differently than sellers. Sellers may see a rise in the relative price of a particular good as an opportunity to increase profits, and eventually such information may be translated into a larger amount of resources going to the production of that now relatively higher-priced good. It is in this manner that resources are allocated in a system that allows prices to convey the information about relative scarcities. We call it a market system: prices convey the information to the individuals—both sellers and buyers—in the marketplace. There is no need for a central agency to produce information or to allocate resources. This does not mean that problems will not arise and that certain economic activities could not be better handled by other than unrestricted market processes. What it does mean is that spontaneous coordination occurs in a decentralized price system; resource allocation ideally requires no outside management.

> ***Concepts in Brief 4-2***
>
> ■ Individuals respond to changes in *relative* prices, not absolute prices. Therefore, changes in the general price level—the average of all prices—must be purged from our analysis of the price system.

Markets, Prices, and the Determination of What Is to Be Produced

The decision about *what* is to be produced depends on the incentives generated within an economic system. Within the price system, the incentive that is foremost is *profit:* the search for higher profits causes decision-makers to produce a mix of goods whose total effective demand is the greatest relative to the scarce resources available for the production of all goods and services.

PROFITS

A businessperson seeks **profits.** We define profits as the difference between the cost of producing something and the price that it fetches in the marketplace. (Remember: The only way we are strictly able to define cost is *opportunity cost*—the value of the resources in their next highest, or best, alternative use.) Another way of looking at profits is as the income generated by buying cheap and selling dear. A businessperson buys factors of production—land, labor, and capital—at a cost that is less than the price obtainable when the finished product is sold. This definition of profit also includes the income received by the buying of anything at a lower price than the price for which it is sold. If you buy a used Honda motorcycle for $800 from a friend and then sell it two hours later to someone else for $1,200, you have made a profit of $400.

Let's take two examples to see how changes in profitability cause resources to be reallocated, and hence determine what is to be produced.

THE PROFITABILITY OF MAKING SAILBOATS

Not too many years back, there was a fear that gasoline would no longer be available for use in pleasure boats powered by internal combustion engines. This fear (among other things) translated itself into a reduction in the demand for powerboats. We see this as a shift inward to the left in the demand curve for powerboats in panel (a) of Exhibit 4-1. What happened? The relative price of powerboats fell from its original price of P_e to P_e'.

Many individuals contemplating the purchase of a powerboat decided against it. Many individuals already owning powerboats wanted to sell them. One substitute to which they looked was sailboats, which required little, if any, gasoline. Thus, the demand curve for sailboats increased. It moved outward to the right, as shown in panel (b) of Exhibit 4-1. The relative price rose from P_e to P_e''.

Assuming now that the cost of inputs into powerboat manufacturing hasn't changed, the lower market clearing price will mean less profit (or maybe even losses) for the manufacturers of such boats. On the other hand, assuming again that there's been no change in input prices, when the market clearing price of sailboats goes up, the profit per unit will also rise.

The profitability of powerboat manufacturing clearly fell. The profitability of sailboat manufacturing clearly increased. In time, the increased profitability of sailboat manufacturing caused an increase in the number of new firms coming into the industry. Very likely, people started making sailboats in their backyards and setting up small sailboat manufacturing companies. Moreover, powerboat manufacturers switched some production facilities for making powerboats to making sailboats. Soon, the output of sailboats increased dramatically and the output of powerboats fell.

What caused the decision to be made to produce more sailboats and fewer powerboats? It was not a decree by a central political figure. Rather, the incentive of earning higher profits in sailboat making caused resources to flow into that activity. The incentive to minimize losses in powerboat manufacturing caused resources to flow out of that activity.

> ***Concepts in Brief 4-3***
>
> ■ Within a market economy, businesses seek profits. In their quest for profits, they move resources out of declining industries into expanding industries.

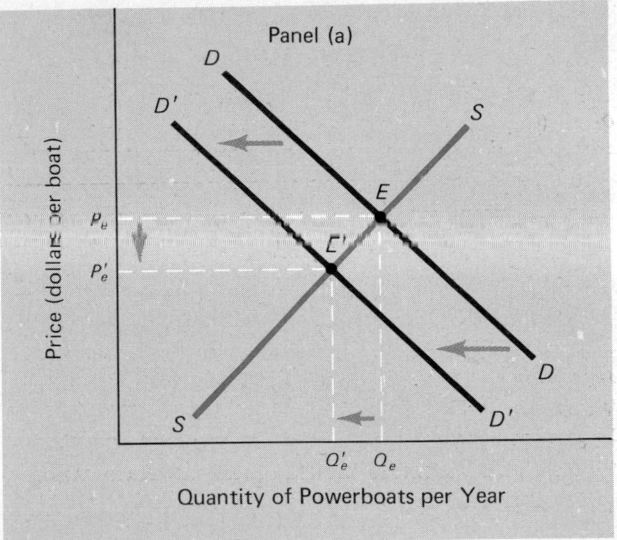

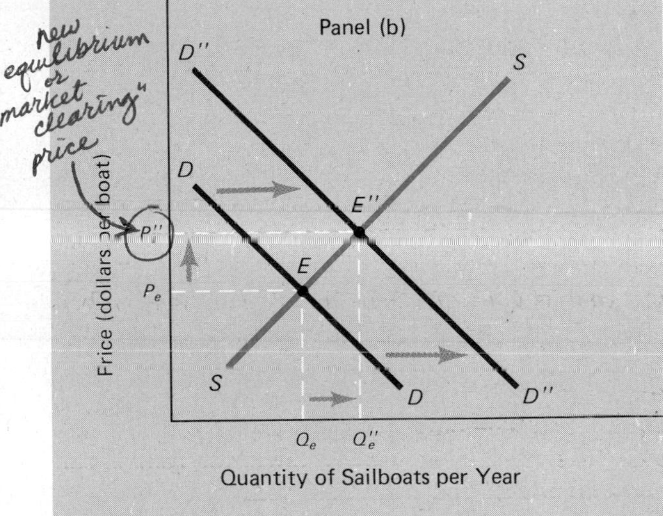

EXHIBIT 4–1
Shifts in Demand Cause Prices to Change. In panel (a) we show the supply and demand for powerboats. At the original equilibrium, the market clearing relative price is P_e. When, because of an anticipated gasoline shortage, the demand curve shifts leftward from DD to $D'D'$, the relative price, and hence profitability, of manufacturing powerboats will fall. The new market clearing price after adjustment would become P_e' with the smaller quantity Q_e' produced. In panel (b), just the opposite has happened for sailboats. The demand curve has shifted from DD to $D''D''$. The market clearing price has gone up from P_e to P_e'' with the larger quantity Q_e'' produced. The profitability of making sailboats has risen. More resources will flow into the sailboat industry; fewer will be used in the powerboat industry.

Moving Resources from Lower- to Higher-Valued Uses

The above examples may not mean much until we realize that the movement of resources in search of higher profits for businesses is simultaneously a movement of resources from lower- to higher-valued uses. When consumers no longer wanted to buy as many powerboats, the demand curve shifted inward to the left [panel (a) of Exhibit 4–1]. Thus, powerboats were no longer as valuable from a subjective point of view as they were prior to the shift in demand. Had all of the resources remained in the powerboat industry, they would be generating a lower subjective value to consumers than they could elsewhere in the economy.

Another incentive to shift production would involve the piling up of unsold inventories of powerboats. When no boats are back-ordered but, rather, many remain unsold, that is information which encourages the manufacturer to switch resources to the production of something else.

When some of these resources were moved from powerboat manufacturing to sailboat manufacturing, they were, by necessity, being moved to a use that generated a higher value to consumers. How do we know this? Because the demand curve for sailboats shifted outward to the right. With a given supply curve, this dictated a higher relative price, which gave an indication that consumers now valued marginal resources in the sailboat industry more than in the past.

CONSUMER SOVEREIGNTY REVISITED

The movement of resources from lower- to higher-valued uses depends crucially on consumer sovereignty. Consumer sovereignty means that the ultimate determiners of how much of what is produced are consumers, not politicians or businesses. In other words, in a world of consumer sovereignty, consumers are the decision-makers. Final production is destined to fulfill their wants and no one else's. In a pure market economy, or price system, each consumer expresses his or her desires (constrained by income) by "voting" in the marketplace with dollars. When fewer consumers were voting for powerboats, this was translated into a shift leftward of the demand curve. When more consumers were expressing their votes for sailboats, this was shown by a shift rightward of the demand curve for sailboats.

Note that the consumer voting system is not the same as a majority voting system. No firm has to receive 51 percent of the available dollar votes in order to produce a particular product. There are, for example, specialty customized car companies that probably receive on the order of four 1,000ths of one percent of the total dollar votes for new cars each year. They continue to exist because that is a sufficient demand to make them profitable. On the other hand, there are many products that are not produced even though they could receive 100 percent of all of the dollar votes by all of a small group of people who desire those goods. Why? Because even with 100 percent of the dollar votes, there would not be enough buyers for a businessperson to make a profit on the product. Consider someone desiring a French meal regularly in a nice restaurant in town. If that gourmet lives along with, say, thirty others in a small town, chances are that even if they all would go regularly to a high-quality French restaurant, there still wouldn't be enough business to make it profitable. Often when you think of goods or services that you want to buy but can't find, you are in a similar position.[1]

In sum, in a pure market economy, consumers vote with their dollars, but it is proportional (as opposed to majority rule) voting. If you have a spendable income of $100 per week, then you can vote with it in any way you want: $1 for each of 100 different things; or $50 for one thing, $30 for another, and $20 for a third thing. The point is that manufacturers will respond and resources will be allocated proportionally to the way the total population spends its money, or votes with its income.

THE MARKET SYSTEM AND EFFICIENCY

Consumer sovereignty in a pure price system means that resources will be used as efficiently as possible. The efficient use of resources will occur because businesspersons in each industry are competing for the dollar "votes" of consumers. Consequently, each firm (and hence the economy taken as a whole) will fully utilize its available resources and will generate maximum consumer satisfaction by

[1] Note another difference between political voting and dollar voting. In a market system, you do not have to "vote" for an entire package at one single time. Rather, you "vote" for different parts—goods and services—of your total consumption package a little at a time. In a political arena, you make your decision, at most, once a year, and sometimes only once every four years.

fulfilling the largest number of consumer desires reflected by money income spent.

There are really two parts of efficiency—**technical efficiency** and **economic efficiency,** both of which are satisfied in a pure market economy.

Technical Efficiency

Technical efficiency relates to utilizing production techniques that do not waste inputs. In other words, we can assume that within the market economy businesses will never waste inputs: they will never use ten units of capital, ten units of labor, and ten units of land when they could produce the same amount of output with only eight units of capital, seven units of labor, and nine units of land.

Economic Efficiency

This concept relates to maximizing the total subjective valuation of our available resources. That means that resources are moved to their highest-valued uses, as evidenced by consumers' willingness to pay for the final products. As we saw above, profits signal resources to move around so that economic efficiency occurs. The forces of demand and supply guide resources to their most efficient uses. In a sense, it is the invisible-hand concept again. Individuals as businesspersons seeking their own self-interest end up, consciously or unconsciously, generating maximum economic value from their activities.

Let's repeat these two efficiency concepts and then apply them to one example.

1. Technical efficiency means that resources will never be wasted in producing a given output.
2. Economic efficiency means that resources will be used in their highest-valued uses.

Now let's distinguish between the two with an example that involves lumber (ash, pine, oak, and redwood), shipping crates, and furniture.

Technical efficiency. Oranges will be shipped in crates made with the minimum amount of lumber necessary. No lumber will be wasted. Crates will not, for example, be made with three-inch thick wood when three-eighths will do just as well (and possibly also save on shipping costs because it is lighter).

Economic efficiency. Ash or pine will be used rather than oak or redwood, which have a higher-valued use today for, say, furniture. Perhaps in the past, when the demand for furniture was relatively less compared to the more abundant supply of oak and redwood, it might have been economically efficient to use those types of wood in orange crates instead of ash or pine. How do we know that oak and redwood will now be used for furniture? Because furniture-makers will be willing to pay a lot more for that type of wood than will crate-makers.

> ***Concepts in Brief 4-4***
>
> ■ If consumer sovereignty exists, proportional dollar voting by consumers determines the output mix. Thus, within a pure market economy, resources flow from lower- to higher-valued uses. In the process, the price system attains both technical and economic efficiency.
>
> ■ With technological efficiency, inputs are not wasted.
>
> ■ With economic efficiency, total subjective valuation of all resources is greatest. Resources are used in their highest-valued uses.

Organizing Production—How Will Goods Be Produced?

The second function of an economic system, which was mentioned at the beginning of this chapter, relates to *how* goods will be produced.

HOW OUTPUT WILL BE PRODUCED

The question of how output will be produced relates to the efficient use of scarce resources. Consider the possibility of only using two types of resources—capital and labor. A firm may have the following options given in Exhibit 4–2. It can use various combinations of labor and capital in order to produce the same amount of output. Two hypothetical combinations are given in that exhibit. How, then, is it decided which combination should be used? In the price system, the *least-cost combination* (which is technique *B*) will in fact be chosen, because in this manner, profits will be the highest possible. To be sure, different production techniques will have to be utilized depending on which combination is selected. We are virtually guaranteed that the least-cost production technique will be chosen because if any other technique were chosen, firms would then be sacrificing *potential* profit.

Moreover, in a price system, competition will in effect *force* firms to use least-cost production techniques. Any firm that fails to employ the least costly technique will find that other firms can undercut its price. In other words, other firms that choose the least-cost production technique will be

EXHIBIT 4–2

Production Costs for 100 Units of Product *X*. Technique *A* or *B* can be used to produce the same output. Obviously, *B* will be used because its total cost is less than *A*'s.

		A		B	
Inputs	*Input Unit Price*	*Production Technique A (input units)*	*Cost*	*Production Technique B (input units)*	*Cost*
Labor	$10	5	$50	4	$40
Capital	$ 8	4	$32	5	$40
Total cost of 100 units of product *X*			$82		$80

able to offer the product at a lower price and still make a profit. The lower price that they offer the product for will induce consumers to shift sales from the higher-priced firm to them. Inefficient firms will be forced out of business.

All of this discussion assumes that technology and resource prices are held constant. If the cost of capital remained the same and the cost of labor were to decrease considerably in our example in Exhibit 4–2, another production technique such as *A* might then be less costly. Firms would shift to that production technique in order to obtain the highest profits possible.

The Distribution of Total Output

The last question that any economic system must solve is distribution—*how* is total output distributed among competing claimants? The problem of distribution of total output can be separated into two parts, one relating to the distribution of products to consumers and the other relating to the distribution of money income to individuals.

WHICH CONSUMERS GET WHAT?

The distribution of finished products to consumers is based on the consumers' ability and willingness to pay the market price for the products. If the market clearing price of TV dinners is $2.50, those consumers who are able and willing to pay that price will get those TV dinners. Those consumers who are not will not.

Here we are talking about the *rationing* function of market clearing prices in a price system. Rather than have a central political figure decide which consumers will get which goods, those consumers who are willing to pay the market clearing price obtain the good. That is to say, relative prices ration the available resources, goods, and services at any point in time among those who would like to have the scarce items. If scarcity didn't exist, then we would not need any system to ration available resources, goods, and services. All of us could have all of everything that we wanted without taking away from what anyone else obtained.

THE DETERMINATION OF MONEY INCOME

In a price system, a consumer's ability to pay for consumer products is based on the size of his or her money income. That, in turn, depends on the quantities, qualities, and types of the various human and nonhuman resources that the individual owns and supplies to the marketplace. Additionally, the prices, or payments, for those resources influence total money income. When you are selling your human resources as labor services, your money income is based on the wage rate, or salary, that you can fetch in the labor market. If you own nonhuman resources—capital and land, for example—the level of interest and rents that you would be paid for your capital and land will clearly influence the size of your money income and thus your ability to buy consumer products.

Evaluating the Price System

It is now possible to take a normative look at the price system. (Remember that normative economics involves using value judgments, or "gut" feelings.) Is it the "best" means of deciding what, how, and for whom? Clearly, there is no scientific answer to this question. We can, however, present a few of the arguments for and against the price system.

THE CASE IN FAVOR OF THE PRICE SYSTEM

The supporters of the price system base their support on two key aspects: freedom and efficiency.

Freedom

The price system normally places emphasis on individual, or personal, freedom. The coordination of social organization through a price system does not require central direction or the use of force by any governmental authority. The price system allows for a type of spontaneous coordination via the mechanism described by Adam Smith as the invisible hand. The price system permits, as it were, the freedoms of choice and enterprise. Individuals are free to further their self-interest. One of the contemporary champions of the price system has laid out this normative argument very clearly:

> So long as effective freedom of exchange is maintained, the central feature of the market organization of economic activity is that it prevents one person from interfering with another in respect of most of his activities. The consumer is protected from coercion by the seller because of the presence of other sellers with whom he can deal. The seller is protected from coercion by the consumer because of other consumers to whom he can sell. The employee is protected from coercion by the employer because of other employers for whom he can work, and so on. And the market does this impersonally and without centralized authority.[2]

Efficiency

The price system leads to both technical and economic efficiency. Competition among firms forces them to choose the least-cost production techniques, thus avoiding waste. In the absence of restraints and imperfections in the system, we find that maximum economic value is obtained from a given set of resources at any given point in time. Thus, the proponents of the price system see it as harnessing self-interest in order to provide society with the greatest possible output of desired goods. Additionally, the price system leads to an automatic transfer of resources from lower- to relatively higher-value use. Thus, resources will not stay in an industry the demand for whose product has withered away because of a change in consumer tastes.

THE CASE AGAINST THE PRICE SYSTEM

There are certainly as many, if not more, critics of the price system as there are supporters. Opponents of the price system point out that the market does not always work. In other words, there is market failure that prevents the price system from attaining both allocative efficiency and individual freedom. These market failures have to do with what are called externalities and social goods.

Externalities

If the price system does not register all of the costs and benefits associated with the production and/or consumption of commodities, then an externality arises. We define an externality as a cost or benefit external to an exchange. In other words, the external benefits or costs accrue to parties other than the immediate seller and buyer in a transaction. An obvious example of an external cost is the pollution of air and water. These are externalities because they result from production and consumption activities in which the parties involved do not take account of such ill effects on others. The point to be made is that whenever supply and demand do not fully reflect all costs and all benefits of production and consumption, the price system cannot be expected to bring about an efficient allocation of resources. (Externalities are an extremely important topic in economics; we treat them in detail in a later chapter.)

Social Goods

The price system relates to the tabulation of individual wants only. Many goods and services are not, however, financed by individuals through the marketplace. Flood control programs and national defense cannot be purchased in small amounts by households and individuals. They can be consumed only on a social, or collective, basis. The opponents of the price system argue that it is incapable of providing such social goods in optimal quantities.

Efficiency and Unequal Income Distribution

There are many opponents of the price system who point out that even though it may be economically

[2] Milton Friedman, *Capitalism and Freedom* (Chicago: University of Chicago Press, 1962), pp. 14–15.

efficient, it can lead to a very unequal distribution of income. Perfect economic efficiency may still allow certain individuals to starve to death if they do not have sufficient resources that are valued in the marketplace. Now questions of fairness and equity arise. Should those who have the most resources be allowed to reap large benefits from the price system while others who are less fortunate barely survive? Should the more cunning and entrepreneurial among us be allowed to accumulate, particularly over generations, large holdings of property resources with which tremendous incomes can be earned? For many critics of the price system the answer is no, and that is why they believe it should not be allowed to work without restrictions and regulations.

Lack of Competition

Finally, critics of the price system point out that competition, particularly the type outlined by such a laissez-faire economist as Adam Smith, no longer exists, if it ever did. Even Adam Smith realized that competition, although desirable from a social point of view, was undesirable from individual business firms' points of view. Hence, he stated that "People of the same trade seldom meet together for fun and merriment, but the conversation ends in a conspiracy against the public, or in some contrivance to raise prices."[3] Smith's fear of conspiracies and monopolies that would hurt consumers is a fear that still is with us today. For many, this fear has taken on the form of reality, for they believe that there is little competition left in many parts of the American economy. The price system cannot work to its fullest advantage if there are restraints on trade through monopoly. Whenever the degree of competition declines, the price system becomes less of a perfect mechanism for efficiently allocating resources. The invisible hand works correspondingly less well.

[3] Adam Smith, *The Wealth of Nations* [1776] (New York: Random House, 1937), p. 128.

ISSUES AND APPLICATIONS

A Prisoner-of-War Camp Develops a Market

Concepts Applied

- Demand and supply, markets, marketplaces, market mechanisms, and transactions costs

Supply and demand operate at any time that transactions are made, even when money is not present. When supply and demand interact, prices may change. How can prices be determined if no coin or currency is used in the trading? During World War II in prisoner-of-war camps in Germany, barter replaced the kind of exchange described in this chapter, and as time passed, more complex exchange systems developed in the camps. In the article that is excerpted in the following paragraphs, you can read about what actually took place. It is a fascinating and instructive first-hand account of how markets, money, and supply and demand developed *spontaneously* in World War II prisoner-of-war camps:

Prisoners of war used cigarettes for money. It was the medium of exchange, even in poker.

We reached a transit [prisoner-of-war] camp in Italy about a fortnight after capture and received ¼ of a Red Cross food parcel each a week later. At once exchanges, already established, multiplied in volume. Starting with simple direct barter, such as a non-smoker giving a smoker friend his cigarette issue in exchange for a chocolate ration, more complex exchanges soon became an accepted custom. Stories circulated of a padre who started off round the camp with a tin of cheese and five cigarettes and returned to his bed with a complete parcel in addition to his original cheese and cigarettes; the market was not yet perfect. Within a week or two, as the volume of trade grew, rough scales of exchange values came into existence. Sikhs [followers of an Indian monotheistic religion that rejects idolatry and the caste system of India] who had at first exchanged tinned beef for practically any other foodstuff began to insist on jam and margarine. It was realised that a tin of jam was worth ½ lb. of margarine plus something else; that a cigarette issue was worth several chocolates issues, and a tin of diced carrots was worth practically nothing.

In this camp we did not visit other bungalows very much and prices varied from place to place; hence the germ of truth in the story of the itinerant priest. By the end of a month, when we reached our permanent camp,[4] there was a lively trade in all commodities and their relative values were well known, and expressed not in terms of one another—one didn't quote bully [canned beef] in terms of sugar—but in terms of cigarettes. The cigarette became the standard of value. In the permanent camp people started by wandering through the bungalows calling their offers—"cheese for seven" (cigarettes)—and the hours after parcel issue were Bedlam. The inconveniences of this system soon led to its replacement by an Exchange and Mart notice board in every bungalow, where under the headings "name," "room number," "wanted" [bid] and "offered" [offer] sales and wants were advertised. When a deal went through, it was crossed off the board. The public and semi-permanent records of transactions led to cigarette prices being well known and thus tending to equality throughout the camp. . . . With this development everyone, including non-smokers, was willing to sell for cigarettes, using them to buy at another time and place. Cigarettes became the normal currency, though, of course, barter was never extinguished.

The unity of the market and the prevalence of a single price varied directly with the general level of organisation and comfort in the camp. A transit camp was always chaotic and uncomfortable: people were overcrowded, no one knew where anyone else was living, and few took the trouble to find out. Organisation was too slender to include an Exchange and Mart board, and private advertisements were the most that appeared. Consequently a transit camp was not one market but many. The price of a tin of salmon is known to have varied by two cigarettes in 20 between one end of a hut and the other. Despite a high level of organisation in Italy, the market was [broken up] . . . in this manner at the first transit camp we reached after our removal to Germany in the autumn of 1943. In this camp—Stalag VIIA at Moosburg in Bavaria—there were up to 50,000 prisoners of all nationalities. French, Russians, Italians, and Jugo-Slavs were free to move about within the camp; British and Americans were confined to their compounds, although a few cigarettes given to a sentry would always procure permission for one or two men to visit other compounds. The people who first visited the highly organised French trading centre with its stalls and known prices found coffee extract—relatively cheap among the tea-drinking English—commanding a fancy price in biscuits or cigarettes, and some enterprising people made small fortunes that way. (Incidentally we found out later that much of the coffee went "over the wire" and sold for phenomenal prices at black market cafes in Munich: some of the French prisoners were said to have made substantial sums in RMk.s. [Reich Marks, the German currency]. This was one of the few occasions on which our normally closed economy came into contact with other economic worlds.)

Eventually public opinion grew hostile to these monopoly profits—not everyone could make contact with the French—and trading with them was put on a regulated basis. Each group of beds was given a quota of articles to offer and the transaction was carried out by accredited representatives from the British compound, with monopoly rights. The same method was used for trading with sentries elsewhere, as in this trade secrecy and reasonable prices had a peculiar importance, but as is ever the case with regulated companies, the interloper proved too strong.

[4] Notice the difference between a transit camp and a permanent camp. A transit camp is where prisoners of war were first taken but not where they were permanently going to stay. After they were at the transit camp for some time, it was decided where their permanent "home" would be in a permanent prisoner-of-war camp.

The permanent camps in Germany saw the highest level of commercial organisation. In addition to the Exchange and Mart notice boards, a shop was organised as a public utility, controlled by representatives of the Senior British Officer, on a no profit basis. People left their surplus clothing, toilet requisites and food there until they were sold at a fixed price in cigarettes. Only sales in cigarettes were accepted—there was no barter—and there was no higgling. For food at least there were standard prices: clothing is less homogeneous and the price was decided around a norm by the seller and the shop manager in agreement; shirts would average say 80, ranging from 60 to 120 according to quality and age. Of food, the shop carried small stocks for convenience; the capital was provided by a loan from the bulk store of Red Cross cigarettes and repaid by a small commission taken on the first transactions. Thus the cigarette attained its fullest currency status, and the market was almost completely unified.

Public opinion on the subject of trading was vocal if confused and changeable, and generalisations as to its direction are difficult and dangerous. A tiny minority held that all trading was undesirable as it engendered an unsavoury atmosphere; occasional frauds and sharp practices were cited as proof. Certain forms of trading were more generally condemned; trade with the Germans was criticised by many. Red Cross toilet articles, which were in short supply and only issued in cases of actual need, were excluded from trade by law and opinion working in unshakable harmony. At one time, when there had been several cases of malnutrition reported among the more devoted smokers, no trade in German rations was permitted, as the victims became an additional burden on the depleted food reserves of the Hospital. But while certain activities were condemned as anti-social, trade itself was practised, and its utility appreciated, by almost everyone in the camp.

More interesting was opinion on middlemen and prices. Taken as a whole, opinion was hostile to the middleman. His function, and his hard work in bringing buyer and seller together, were ignored; profits were not regarded as a reward for labour, but as the result of sharp practices. Despite the fact that his very existence was proof to the contrary, the middleman was held to be redundant in view of the existence of an official Shop and the Exchange and Mart. Appreciation only came his way when he was willing to advance the price of a sugar ration, or to buy goods spot and carry them against a future sale. In these cases the element of risk was obvious to all, and the convenience of the service was felt to merit some reward. . . . Opinion notwithstanding, most people dealt with a middleman, whether consciously or unconsciously, at some time or another.

There was a strong feeling that everything had its "just price" in cigarettes. While the assessment of the just price, which incidentally varied between camps, was impossible of explanation, this price was nevertheless pretty closely known. It can best be defined as the price usually fetched by an article in good times when cigarettes were plentiful. The "just price" changed slowly; it was unaffected by short-term variations in supply, and while opinion might be resigned to departures from the "just price," a strong feeling of resentment persisted. A more satisfactory definition of the "just price" is impossible. Everyone knew what it was, though no one could explain why it should be so. . . .[5]

Questions

1. What substitutes for currency and coin were used by the prisoners? Did the fact that substitutes were used mean that a price system was not operating?
2. How did supply and demand operate within the prisoner-of-war camp?

[5] R. A. Radford, "The Economic Organisation of a P.O.W. Camp," *Economica,* new series, vol. 12, November 1945, p. 189–201. Reprinted by permission.

Definition of Terms

Resource allocation The assignment of resources to specific uses. More specifically, it means determining what will be produced, how it will be produced, who will produce it, and for whom it will be produced.

Exchange The act of trading, usually done on a voluntary basis in which both parties to the trade are subjectively better off.

Terms of exchange The terms under which the trading takes place. Usually the terms of exchange are given by the price at which a good is traded.

Market An abstract concept concerning all of the arrangements that individuals have for exchanging with one another. Thus, we can speak of the labor market, the automobile market, and the credit market.

Transactions costs All of the costs associated with exchanging, including the informational costs of finding out price and quality, service record, durability, etc., of a product, plus the cost of contracting and enforcing that contract.

Profit The income generated by selling something for a higher price than was paid for it. In production, the income generated as the difference between total revenues received from consumers who purchase the goods and the total cost of producing those goods.

Technical efficiency The utilization of the cheapest production technique for any given output rate; no inputs are willfully wasted.

Economic efficiency The use of resources that generate the highest possible value of output as determined in the market economy by consumers.

Chapter Summary

1. The price system answers questions relating to: (a) what will be produced, (b) how it will be produced, and (c) for whom it will be produced.
2. Exchanges take place in marketplaces. The terms of exchange—prices—are registered in marketplaces.
3. There are numerous market mechanisms that facilitate exchange within markets. These include all techniques for reducing the transactions costs associated with exchanging, such as improved communication systems, better enforcement of contracts, and so on.
4. The less "organized" the market, the higher the transactions costs of exchanging.
5. Relative prices indicate what a consumer has to give up in order to purchase a specified quantity of a specified good. Under some circumstances, relative prices also indicate the amount of resources in the economy that were used to produce the product.
6. Changing profitability induces movements of resources from less to more profitable industries. In the process, resources are moved from relatively lower-valued uses to relatively higher-valued uses.
7. In a world of consumer sovereignty, this movement of resources leads to economic efficiency, or maximum subjective valuation from a given set of resources.
8. Technical efficiency means not wasting productive resources when producing a desired output. Economic efficiency relates to resources flowing to where they generate the highest-valued use.
9. Within a price system, competition forces producers to seek least-cost production techniques. Thus, the problem of how resources are produced is solved.
10. Final output is distributed according to willingness and ability to pay, which, in turn, is a function of money income, which is, in the price system, a function of the ownership of human and nonhuman resources.
11. Those in favor of the price system cite personal freedom and economic efficiency as arguments.
12. Critics of the price system believe that market failures cannot be ignored. Externalities such as air and water pollution will exist, according to them. On the other hand, social goods will not be produced in sufficient quantities. Opponents of the price system also believe there is a lack of competition in our economy and an unjust distribution of income.
13. A price system can operate even in the absence of coins and currency; this is clear when one examines how the economy of a prisoner-of-war camp developed in World War II.

Selected References

Friedman, Milton. *Free to Choose.* New York: Harcourt Brace Jovanovich, 1980.

Heilbroner, Robert L. *The Worldly Philosophers.* 4th ed. New York: Simon & Schuster, 1972, chap. 3.

Klaasen, Adrian, ed. *The Invisible Hand.* Chicago: Henry Regnery, 1965.

Answers to Preview and Study Questions

1. Why does the scarcity problem force all societies to answer *what, how,* and *for whom*?

Scarcity is a relative concept; scarcity exists for a society because people want more than their resources will allow them to have. As a result, people are forced to choose; if people want literally unlimited goods and services from their limited resources, they must choose which wants to satisfy and which to forego. In short, society must answer *what* to produce because of scarcity. If wants are severely restricted and resources are relatively superabundant, *what* to produce is trivial—society simply produces *everything* that everyone wants. Superabundant resources relative to restricted wants also make the *how* to produce question trivial. If scarcity doesn't exist, then superabundant resources can be combined in *any* manner; waste or efficiency have no meaning without scarcity. Similarly, *for whom* is meaningless without scarcity; people can consume *all* they want.

2. Under ideal capitalism, exchange is voluntary. What are some implications of this?

The fact that exchange is voluntary implies that both parties to a transaction perceive benefit; voluntary exchange makes it possible for people to benefit without imposing costs on others. Thus one person need not gain at the expense of others; before economic transactions will occur and be renewed, both sides must feel that they are gaining. Moreover, "exploitation" is difficult if exchange is voluntary. As long as buyers are not forced to purchase (or sellers not forced to sell), it is difficult to imagine how exploitation can take place—at least in its more extreme forms—when competition exists.

3. How do markets lower the transactions costs of exchange?

Markets transmit information; the more efficient the market, the better the information and the sooner this information is transmitted. Buyers and sellers are freed from time-consuming and costly "shopping" and information searches. The net result is that the cost of making transactions is lowered for both buyers and sellers; trade, specialization, and division of labor are facilitated.

4. What is consumer sovereignty? Is consumer sovereignty worthwhile?

Consumer sovereignty refers to the fact that the ultimate determiners of output are consumers; consumers rule, or are "sovereign," in ideal capitalism. In effect, millions of consumers cast their "dollar votes" for goods and services daily. If not enough dollar votes are cast to make producing a given product profitable, that product will disappear from the marketplace. Conversely, if dollar votes are sufficient to make some commodity profitable to produce, the commodity will appear in the marketplace. If consumer tastes change in favor of small autos and away from "gas guzzlers," consumer sovereignty requires that output of small cars expand, and output of large, heavy cars contract. Whether consumer sovereignty is "worthwhile" or not is a value judgment; we leave the realm of positive economics and enter normative economics when we say whether or not consumer sovereignty is "good." In the communist countries consumer sovereignty is replaced by "party sovereignty"; the leaders of the communist party answer the *what* question. In effect, communist countries have rejected consumer sovereignty as being desirable.

5. What is the difference between technical efficiency and economic efficiency?

Technical efficiency exists when inputs are not wasted. Thus, a given output level will be produced with a minimum number of inputs; conversely, a given quantity of inputs will produce the maximum output level. Economic efficiency is more subjective and requires normative statements; economic efficiency exists when resources are allocated so as to maximize the (subjective) value of goods and services. Resources will be allocated to their highest-valued use.

Problems

(Answers at the back of the book)

1. Assume that in 1980 a quart of beer cost 50¢ while a quart of tequila cost $5. By 1984, the respective absolute prices had risen to 70¢ and $6.30. What happened to the relative price of tequila in relation to beer? Suppose that the average of all other prices rose by 70 percent over the same period. That is to say, in 1984 it cost $170 to buy the same goods and services that would have cost $100 in 1980. What has happened to the relative prices of beer and tequila in comparison to all other consumer goods and services?

2. List the types of transactions costs that are involved in locating and buying a home. After you have listed them, can you think of ways to economize on such transactions costs?

3. Assume that a business has found that its most profitable output occurs when it produces $172 worth of output of a particular product. It can choose from three possible techniques, *A*, *B*, and *C*, that will produce the desired level of output. Below we see the amount of inputs these techniques use along with each input price.

Price of Input (per unit)		PRODUCTION TECHNIQUES *A (units)*	*B (units)*	*C (units)*
$10	Land	7	4	1
$ 2	Labor	6	7	18
$15	Capital	2	6	3
$ 8	Entrepreneurship	1	3	2

a. Which technique will the firm choose and why?
b. What would the firm's maximum profit be?
c. If the price of labor increases to $4 per unit, which technique will be chosen and why? What will happen to profits?

4. List the alleged advantages and disadvantages of a price system. Can we decide whether the advantages outweigh the disadvantages by adding up the two lists and comparing the total sums?

5

Private Business Organizations and Financing

TOPICS FOR REVIEW

The topic listed below, which we have already analyzed, is applied in this chapter. You may find it worthwhile to review it. For your convenience the topic is followed by the number identifying the specific "Concepts in Brief."

a. Specialization, division of labor (1–4)

FOR PREVIEW AND STUDY

1. What is the distinction between a plant, a firm, and an industry?
2. How has the composition of industry changed in the United States?
3. What is the distinction between a sole proprietorship, a partnership, and a corporation?
4. How does corporate common stock differ from preferred stock?

The American economy can be categorized by groups that perform economic functions. In our mixed economy, the first distinction we make is between the public, or government, sector and the private sector. Within the private sector, there are two major categories: households and businesses. In this chapter, we wish to examine the business sector in more detail. Specifically, we will look at the various legal forms of business organization in the United States today. Then we will examine the ways in which private businesses can be financed. In the Issues and Applications section, some practical information is offered about whether you should ever consider becoming a corporation. (That's right, you can personally become a corporation.) In Appendix B, you will find some hints on how to read business firms' standard accounting statements, as well as how accountants must grapple with the fact that we live in an inflationary environment.

Before we start our more detailed discussion of business organizations, let's make a distinction between plants, firms, and industries, and then let's see what has happened to the industrial structure of America over time.

Making the Distinction Between a Plant, a Firm, and an Industry

When you are walking or riding down the street and pass a large building with smokestacks coming out of it, trucks coming and going, and with the sign of some business name on the side of the building, you are probably looking at a **plant.** We define a plant as the actual physical establishment that performs some manufacturing or distribution function. Thus, a plant is found in the forms of mines, farms, factories, warehouses, and stores. The business **firm,** though, is the organization that owns and operates one or more plants. Many business firms own and operate just one plant, but many others operate numerous plants. General Motors has plants around the country. So, too, do the larger steel companies.

The definition of an **industry** is not as clear-cut as the definition of a plant or a firm. In general, we define an industry as a group of firms producing similar products. The problem is, how do we define "similar" products? Depending on how specific you wish to make your definition of "similar products," the industry you define will be larger or smaller. The more particular you are about how similar the products should be, the smaller will be the number of firms that you include in your definition of an industry. Another problem resides in the fact that most business firms in the United States, particularly the large ones, produce numerous products, some of which are totally unrelated.

The Changing Character of American Industry

When this nation started, the industry of America was almost 100 percent agriculture. After all, it was simply a question of eking out a subsistence existence. By 1870, agriculture had fallen in importance, accounting for only 53 percent of total output. The manufacturing sector, on the other hand, was up to 33 percent. The remaining 14 percent was accounted for by mining and construction.

By the turn of the century, the importance of agriculture and manufacturing switched places. Agriculture accounted for 33 percent of the nation's output; manufacturing, 53 percent, with the remainder in mining and construction. Today, agriculture accounts for a mere 3.4 percent of the nation's yearly output. Manufacturing accounts for 28 percent and mining and construction for 6 percent. But 3.4 plus 28 plus 6 does not equal 100 percent. What about the rest? The rest is taken up by what we now call the *service sector* of the economy—medical care, legal work, repairs, and so on. The service sector is the fastest growing sector of the economy. Indeed, we can predict that if our nation continues to grow economically, the manufacturing sector will become smaller and smaller relative to the service sector.

Now let's look at the various forms of business organization in America.

Forms of Business Organizations

There are basically three types of business organizations—sole proprietorships, partnerships, and corporations. Additionally, there are two types of partnerships—limited and general—and various classifications of corporations.

SOLE PROPRIETORSHIP

A **sole proprietorship,** also called an individual proprietorship, is a business owned by one person. It is the oldest form of business organization; it is also the most common. Today there are more than 10 million sole proprietorships in the United States. You may know of hundreds in your area—beauty parlors, fruit stands, repair shops, drugstores, hobby shops, liquor stores, and so on. Many doctors, dentists, lawyers, and accountants also practice as sole proprietors.

Advantages of a sole proprietorship. There are many advantages to operating a sole proprietorship. Here are a few.

1. *The proprietor receives all profits.* As the only owner, the proprietor gets all the profits because he or she takes all the risks.
2. *Pride of ownership.* Because a proprietorship is owned by one individual, that person has full pride in owning it. The person is his or her own boss and makes the business whatever it is.
3. *Ease of starting a business.* Since the proprietor makes all decisions, starting a proprietorship is less difficult than forming those types of businesses that require agreement with the people involved.
4. *Freedom from corporate income taxes.* A proprietor does not pay corporate income taxes, which we will discuss later. The proprietor does have to pay personal income taxes on any profits made. But personal income tax rates may be lower than the rates that would have to be paid on the profits derived from the corporate type of business organization.

Disadvantages of a sole proprietorship. Obviously, a proprietorship has disadvantages. Many people must perceive that the benefits outweigh the disadvantages, however, since proprietorships are so widespread in the United States.

1. *Responsibility for all losses.* As the only owner, the proprietor bears the risk of all losses.
2. *Limited money capital.* The proprietor is limited by his or her own funds and those that others will lend. This is perhaps the greatest disadvantage. It is very difficult for a business to grow with limited money capital.
3. *Unlimited liability.* The proprietor has liability, or legal responsibility, for all debts and damages incurred in doing business. For example, if the proprietor of a repair service wired a television set incorrectly and it blew up, he or she could be held responsible and sued for damages. If someone were injured, the legal responsibility might extend to all of the proprietor's personal wealth.

A PARTNERSHIP

A **partnership** is any form of business enterprise that two or more individuals own and operate for profit. A written agreement is usually (but not necessarily) drawn up when a partnership is formed. You probably know of numerous partnerships in your area. Many lawyers, doctors, and dentists, as well as small retail stores, form partnerships.

Advantages of a partnership. Partnerships are formed because they offer advantages not found in a sole proprietorship.

1. *More money capital.* A partnership combines the money capital of two or more people. It makes more money available to operate a larger and perhaps more profitable business. If each partner has a good credit rating, the partnership can generally borrow more money than a sole proprietorship.
2. *Greater efficiency.* Partnerships are usually more efficient than proprietorships. They allow each partner to specialize in certain aspects of the business. We pointed out in Chapter 1 that specialization led to greater productivity. As an example, consider partnerships in law offices. Different partners specialize in different aspects of the law. They are able to generate more revenues per total number of hours worked by not individually having to keep up with all areas of the law.

Disadvantages of a partnership. A partnership also has disadvantages, which we list below. We leave it up to you to decide whether these may offset the advantages to a particular firm.

1. *Unlimited liability.* Complete legal responsibility is a major disadvantage in a sole proprietorship. As a partner, however, one is responsible for the debts of the business that were created by the partners. Therefore, as a partner, one may have an even greater legal responsibility for debts than as a sole proprietor.
2. *Profits must be shared.* Obviously, since partners share the risks of the business, they also share the profits. In many situations, one partner may receive an equal share of the profits but feel that he or she has contributed more than that to the success of the business. Partnership arrangements constantly run into this problem. In such cases, one partner will think that he or she would have done better as a sole proprietor.
3. *Possible disagreement.* In partnerships, disagreements regarding necessary decisions can lead to severe problems in running the business. Often such disagreements can lead the partnership to an impasse, where no decision is made. In that case, a very profitable business opportunity may be missed.

ARTICLES OF INCORPORATION
OF

____

(name of corporation)

We, the undersigned, of full age, for the purpose of forming a corporation under and pursuant to the provisions of Chapter 301 Minn. Statutes, known as the Minnesota Business Corporation Act, and laws amendatory thereof and supplementary thereto, do hereby associate ourselves as a body corporate and adopt the following Articles of Incorporation:

ARTICLE I

The name of this corporation is: ____

Note: The corporate name must end with "Incorporated," "Inc." or "Corporation" or contain "Company" or "Co." not immediately preceded by "and" or "&."

ARTICLE II

The purpose of this corporation are: ____

ARTICLE III

The period of duration of corporate existence of this corporation shall be:

Note: The duration may be perpetual or for a specified period of time.

ARTICLE IV

The location of the registered office of this corporation in this state is:

Note: Give street or post office address, city or town, county and zipcode number.

ARTICLE V

The amount of stated capital with which this corporation will begin business is:

Note: The stated capital must be at least $1000.

ARTICLE VI

The total authorized number of shares of par value is: ____________________

and the par value of each share is: ____________________

The total authorized number of shares without par value is: ____________________

ARTICLE VII

The description of the classes of shares, the number of shares in each class, and the relative rights, voting power, preferences and restrictions are as follows: ____________________

EXHIBIT 5–1
Sample Articles of Incorporation

4. *Death of a partner.* If a partner dies or leaves the business, the business must be reorganized.

> ***Concepts in Brief 5-1***
>
> ■ A plant is the physical establishment that performs manufacturing and distribution; a firm is an organization that owns and operates one or more plants; an industry is a group of firms producing similar products.
>
> ■ There are basically three types of business organizations: sole proprietorships, partnerships, and corporations.
>
> ■ The advantages of a sole proprietorship are: (1) ease of starting, (2) pride of ownership, (3) the proprietor receives all profits, and (4) freedom from corporate income taxes.
>
> ■ The disadvantages of a sole proprietorship are: (1) responsibility for all losses, (2) limited money capital, and (3) unlimited liability.
>
> ■ The advantages of a partnership are: (1) more money capital, and (2) greater efficiency.
>
> ■ The disadvantages of a partnership are: (1) unlimited liability, (2) profits must be shared, (3) possible disagreement among partners, and (4) death of a partner terminates a partnership.

THE CORPORATE WORLD

In terms of the volume of business transacted in the United States today, by far the most important type of business operation is the **corporation.** Corporations provide most of the goods that people buy. Although they constitute only *10 to 12 percent* of all business firms, they collect almost *75 percent* of all business receipts.

The corporate form has made possible large-scale business. It was a key to the development of American industry and to America's growth as the most industrial nation in the world.

A corporation is legally separate from the human beings who own and who control it. However, it enjoys many of the same legal powers, such as the rights to buy and sell property, enter into contracts, and sue or be sued.

Forming a corporation. In order to form a corporation, you must sell shares of stock in a business. The shares represent ownership rights to a certain proportion of the profits of a corporation. There are two things you must do to start a corporation and sell stock.

1. *Register the corporation.* State and federal laws govern the formation of all corporations. Most state laws are similar, although they vary according to the type of corporation to be formed. People who are forming corporations generally need to consult a lawyer to have him or her draw up articles of incorporation. These articles include four items: (a) the name, address, and purpose of the corporation, (b) the names and addresses of the initial board of directors, (c) the number of directors, and (d) the amount of capital to be put into the corporation. Exhibit 5–1 shows a sample articles of incorporation. The articles of incorporation and an application for a charter (or certificate) of incorporation are sent to the appropriate state or federal agency. If the articles comply with the laws, a charter will be granted.
2. *Choose a board of directors.* Every corporation must be controlled by a board of directors. The board is elected by the stockholders, the people who own the corporation. The bylaws of the corporation govern the election. The bylaws describe the time and place of the stockholders' meeting at which the board of directors is elected. The directors are responsible for supervising and controlling the corporation. However, they do not generally perform daily business operations. Rather, the board selects company officers—a president, vice-president(s), secretary, and treasurer—to run the business. Exhibit 5–2 shows the organizational chart for IBM.

Advantages of a corporation. There are several major advantages to the corporate form of business. The chief advantage concerns the greater facility for raising capital.

1. *Greater money capital.* The corporate form of organization allows the business to use either debt (bonds) or equity (common stocks) financing that can be offered to a large number of people. Basically, such corporate financing can bring small amounts of capital from many people who are willing to invest because of the limited liability, long life, and easy transfer of ownership of the corporation. A corporation can raise more capital than either a sole proprietorship or a partnership.
2. *Limited liability.* A stockholder in a corporation generally limits his or her liability to the money invested. Many people consider limited liability to be the major advantage of the corporate form of business. If a corporation goes bankrupt or is sued, the most that the stockholders can lose is the volume of their stock.

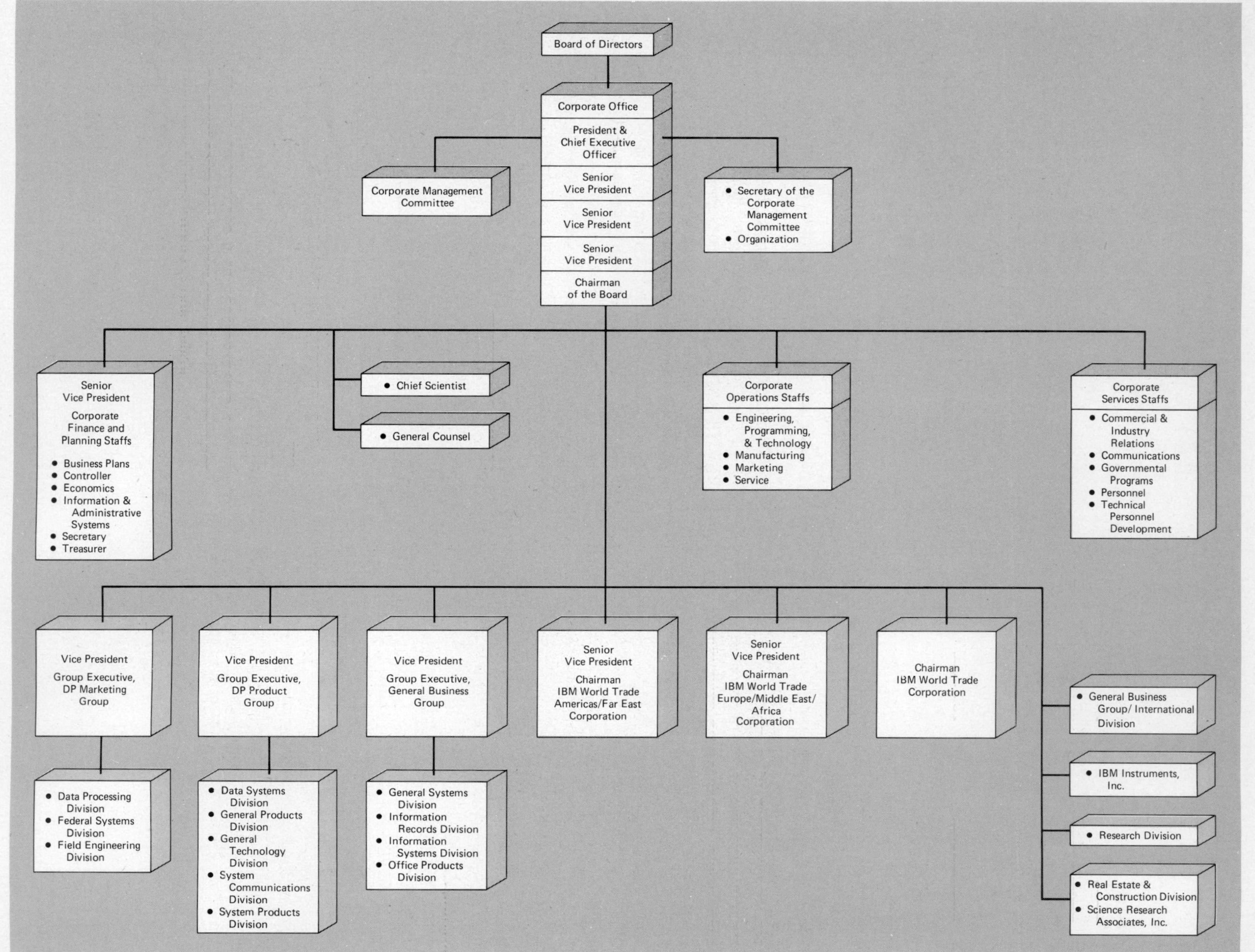

EXHIBIT 5–2
Organizational Chart for IBM

EXHIBIT 5–3
The Top Ten U.S. Industrial Corporations (ranked by sales)

Rank		Company	Sales	Assets		Net Income		Employees	
'80	'79		(thousands of dollars)	(thousands of dollars)	Rank	(thousands of dollars)	Rank	Number	Rank
1	1	**Exxon**	103,142,834	56,576,558	1	5,650,090	1	176,615	9
2	3	**Mobil**	59,510,000	32,705,000	3	3,272,000	3	212,800	6
3	2	**General Motors**	57,728,500	34,581,000	2	(762,500)	490	746,000	1
4	5	**Texaco**	[illegible]	[illegible]	5	[illegible]	4	66,745	50
5	6	**Standard Oil of California**	40,479,000	22,162,000	7	2,401,000	5	40,218	112
6	4	**Ford Motor**	37,085,500	24,347,600	6	(1,543,300)	491	426,700	2
7	7	**Gulf Oil**	26,483,000	18,638,000	9	1,407,000	11	58,900	61
8	8	**International Business Machines**	26,213,000	26,703,000	4	3,562,000	2	341,279	5
9	10	**Standard Oil (Ind.)**	26,133,080	20,167,474	8	1,915,314	6	56,401	68
10	9	**General Electric**	24,959,000	18,511,000	10	1,514,000	10	402,000	3

Source: Adapted from *Fortune,* May 4, 1981 pp. 324–325

3. *Unlimited life.* When the owner of a sole proprietorship dies, his or her business ceases to exist. When one partner in a partnership dies, the partnership ceases to exist. It must be re-formed. A corporation, however, can exist indefinitely if it continues to be profitable. The life of the corporation is not affected by the death of its owners, because the shares are transferable.
4. *Specialized and professional management.* Corporations, usually because of their size, are able to hire highly specialized and professional management to carry out the important management duties of the firm. Most smaller sole proprietorships and partnerships have to use more generalized management personnel or "jacks-of-all-trades."

Disadvantages of a corporation. The corporate form of business has two chief disadvantages.

1. *Federal and state taxes.* The federal income tax on corporations is a problem that proprietorships and partnerships do not face. The corporate profits tax is levied on the profits of all corporations. In addition, some states and localities tax corporation profits or property. A state may also tax a corporation for the right to carry on business within its boundaries. Additionally, dividends received by individual stockholders are taxed along with other personal income by the federal government and by some state governments. This has been called "double taxation" in that the same income is taxed once as corporate profits and again as personal income.
2. *Increased government control.* Since corporations are chartered by government agencies, these agencies are generally more concerned with corporate activities than with those of other forms of business. Therefore, there are numerous laws and enforcement procedures that affect corporations but not partnerships or proprietorships. For firms that require large amounts of capital, the corporate organization is the logical choice. Thus, corporations dominate the business scene in the United States today. Some of them are larger than the economies of many nations. Exhibit 5–3 lists the ten largest industrial corporations in the United States. You may already be familiar with most of them. Some of them employ a virtual army of workers and control a kingdom of assets. The financial pages of most daily newspapers will give the latest stock quotations for these corporations.

Concepts in Brief 5-2

- The advantages of a corporation are: (1) greater money capital, (2) limited liability, (3) unlimited life, and (4) specialized professional management.
- The disadvantages of a corporation are: (1) the necessity of paying federal and state taxes on corporate profits, and (2) increased government control.

COMPARING A PARTNERSHIP WITH A CORPORATION

In Exhibit 5–4 we show a comparison of partnerships and corporations.

EXHIBIT 5–4
Comparing a Partnership with a Corporation

Characteristic	Partnership	Corporation
1. Method of Creation	Created by agreement of the parties.	Charter issued by state—created by statutory authorization.
2. Legal Position	Not a separate legal entity in many states.	Always a legal entity separate and distinct from its owners—a legal fiction for the purposes of owning property and being party to litigation.
3. Liability	Unlimited liability (except for limited partners in a limited partnership).	Limited liability of shareholders—shareholders are not liable for the debts of the corporation.
4. Duration	Terminated by agreement of the partners, by the death of one or more of the partners, by withdrawal of a partner, or by bankruptcy.	Can have perpetual existence.
5. Transferability of Interest	Although partnership interest can be assigned, assignee does not have full rights of a partner.	Shares of stock can be transferred.
6. Management	Each general partner has a direct and equal voice in management unless expressly agreed otherwise in the partnership agreement. (Limited partner has no rights in management in a limited partnership.)	Shareholders elect directors who set policy and appoint officers.
7. Taxation	Each partner pays pro rata share of income taxes on net profits, whether or not they are distributed.	Double taxation—corporation pays income tax on net profits, with no deduction for dividends, and shareholders pay income tax on disbursed dividends they receive.
8. Organizational Fees, Annual License Fees, and Annual Reports	None.	All required.
9. Transaction of Business in Other States	Generally no limitation.	Normally must qualify to do business and obtain certificate of authority.

Financing Corporations

Corporations obtain necessary long-term financing by selling **securities** to individuals and institutions. We define a security as the tangible evidence—a certificate—of an investment by individuals and institutions in the affairs of business firms and governments. Stocks and bonds are the two major types of securities. Stocks represent the purchase of ownership in business firms, whereas bonds represent the lending of money to firms and governments. In what follows, we examine first stocks and then bonds in more detail.

Stocks

A *stock* is a legal document giving its owner the claim on a certain portion of the profits of the company that issued it. Why would a company want to give away part of the rights to profits made in the future? Let us look at an example to see why.

Suppose a woman owns Keepfit, a health food company worth $1 million. She wants to raise $200,000 in cash for expansion. To obtain the money, she is willing to sell stock. She has 100,000 shares of Keepfit stock. Thus, to raise $200,000, she would have to put 20,000 new shares of her stock on the market. That is, she would have to sell an additional 20,000 shares at $10 a share. If all of the stock were sold, Keepfit would get the money for expansion, and the people who bought stock (called stockholders or shareholders) would receive stock certificates for the number of shares they purchased. As part owners, they would collectively have a claim to one-sixth of whatever profits the

Keepfit Company earned (for they own 20,000 of 120,000 shares of stock).

Stocks represent equity capital in a company. The concept of equity might best be understood in terms of the equity that homeowners have in their homes. If you own a house that has a market value (the price at which you could sell your house after all selling costs) of $100,000 and you owed $60,000 on your home mortgage, then you would have an equity of $40,000 in your home. Stockholders have an equity share of a company.

COMMON STOCKS

Most stock is **common stock,** usually called equity. The above example of Keepfit referred to common stock. The business that issues common stock does not guarantee any rate of return to the purchasers of those stocks. Indeed, because corporations are organized as ongoing entities, there is no intent to return the original investment per share to each shareholder.

Retained earnings. The earnings of a corporation are either paid out in the form of cash dividends to common stock shareholders or are retained in the business to finance expansion and thereby enhance future earnings.

Shareholders get the residuals. Common stock shareholders, then, are a group of investors who assume the *residual* position in the overall financial structure of a business. In terms of receiving payment for their investment, they are last in line. The earnings to which they are entitled also depend on all of the other groups—suppliers, employees, managers, bankers, governments, bondholders, and preferred stock shareholders—first being paid what is due them. Once those groups are paid, however, common stock shareholders are entitled to *all* of the remaining earnings that are to be distributed. This is the central feature of ownership in any business, be it a corner newsstand, a retail store, an architectural firm, or a giant international oil corporation. In each instance, the common stock owners occupy the riskiest position relative to all constituent groups. But, as a result, they can potentially earn a return on their investment that is greater than that accruing to the other groups.

Voting rights. Usually each investor who owns common stock in a particular firm has one vote per common share. Voting rights in a corporation apply to the election of the firm's board of directors and to any proposed changes in the ownership structure of the firm. For example, if you are a common stock shareholder in Keepfit, you might be asked to vote on a decision about merging Keepfit with Cosmos, a natural health cosmetics company.

PREFERRED STOCK

The owners of **preferred stock** have no voting rights as do common stock shareholders. From an investment standpoint, preferred stock is more similar to bonds than it is to common stock. It is not included among the liabilities of a business because there is no fixed maturity time when the preferred shares must be retired by the firm. As a preferred stock shareholder, you get your investment back by selling your shares to another investor rather than to the issuing firm. Occasionally, firms do retire preferred stock, but they are not legally obligated to do so. As a preferred stock shareholder, you also receive periodic dividend payments, usually established as a fixed percentage of the face amount of each preferred share. A 7 percent preferred stock with a face amount of $100 per share would pay its owner a $7 dividend each year. But, again, this is not a legal obligation on the part of the firm, as are the interest payments legally due bondholders.

Stock is "preferred" in the sense that its owners must be paid their dividends before common stock owners may be paid a dividend and also because preferred stock owners have a prior claim on the assets of the corporation should the firm be liquidated.

Bonds

A **bond** is basically an IOU or a promissory note of a corporation or government, usually issued in multiples of $1,000 with a specific maturity date. A bond is evidence of a debt in which the issuing company usually promises to pay the bondholders a specified amount of interest for a specified length of time, and then to repay them the loan (principal) on the maturity date. In every case, a bond represents debt: its holder is a creditor of the corporation and not a part owner as is the stockholder.

Because debt financing represents a legal obligation on the part of the corporation, various features and terms of a particular bond issue are specified in a lending agreement called a bond indenture. A corporate trustee, often a commercial bank trust department, represents the collective well-being of all bondholders in ensuring that the terms of the bond issue are met by the corporation. The bond indenture specifies the maturity date of the bond and the pattern of interest payments until maturity. Most corporate bonds pay semiannually a coupon rate of interest on the $1,000 face amount of the bond. If you owned a 6 percent corporate bond, you would receive $30 interest every six months. The indenture, i.e., written agreement, also indicates if any portion of the bond is to be retired each year. Any collateral for the bond issue, such as buildings or equipment, also is indicated. Additionally, the indenture indicates how you as a bondholder would fare—along with other creditors of the business firm—should the firm get into serious financial difficulty and not be able to meet all of its legal obligations.

STOCKS VERSUS BONDS FOR LONG-TERM FINANCING OF PRIVATE BUSINESSES

A corporation has two major roads it can take for long-term financing—the sale of bonds or the sale of common stocks (to make the comparison easy, we'll ignore preferred stock). We cannot do the careful analysis necessary for a major corporation here. All we can do is give the pros and cons of the two types of long-term financing avenues.

COMMON STOCK: PROS AND CONS

This type of financing has the lowest risk for the corporation. There is no legal obligation to make dividend payments to common stock shareholders. Common stock shareholders do not have to be repaid at some future date. On the other hand, it is a relatively expensive way to finance a company since there are a great deal of selling costs involved in placing the stock. Dividends are paid out of corporate earnings from which federal, state, and corporate taxes have *already* been paid. Additionally, whenever new common stock is sold, the original stockholders find that they hold a smaller percentage of total stock than before the sale of new stock. Thus, the original stockholders' ownership is diluted. The initial stockholders will find that their claim on future residual earnings will be less.

BONDS: PROS AND CONS

Many financial managers of large corporations prefer to raise additional capital through the sale of long-term bonds. An advantage of bonds is that they may be a cheap way of financing, because bond interest is tax deductible to the corporation. Additionally, bondholders have no voice in management and, therefore, no loss in control to management occurs. The original stockholders' rights to residual earnings are also left untouched.

A disadvantage of bonds is that they are highly risky. Holders of bonds have senior rights to the stream of earnings of any company. If a company is unable to make interest payments, it may be forced into bankruptcy by its bondholders. Common stock owners cannot do this, however.

We compare stocks and bonds in Exhibit 5-5.

EXHIBIT 5-5
Comparing Stocks and Bonds

Common Stocks	*Bonds*
1. Stocks represent ownership.	1. Bonds represent owed debt.
2. Stocks do not have a fixed dividend rate.	2. Interest on bonds must legally be paid, whether or not any profit is earned.
3. Stockholders can elect a board of directors, which controls the corporation.	3. Bondholders usually have no voice in, or control over, the management of the corporation.
4. Stocks do not have a maturity date; the corporation does not usually repay the stockholder.	4. Bonds have a maturity date, at which time the bondholder is to be repaid the face value of the bond.
5. All corporations issue or offer to sell stocks. This is the usual definition of a corporation.	5. Corporations are not required to issue bonds.
6. Stockholders have a claim against the property and income of a corporation after all creditors' claims have been met.	6. Bondholders have a claim against the property and income of a corporation that must be met before the claims of stockholders.

ISSUES AND APPLICATIONS

Should You Be a Corporation?

Concepts Applied
- Legal status of a corporation

Should you be a corporation? That's not such a silly question. There are many benefits of incorporating, provided, however, that you have a high enough income to justify the cost. Incorporation for individuals with regular jobs, however, is limited to those who also have substantial outside, or "moonlighting," income that can be funneled through the corporation. This income cannot be salaried income; it must be in the form of payments that can go directly into a corporation. (Any checks that the individual receives from which Social Security and federal withholding taxes are deducted generally cannot be deposited into the corporation as corporate income.) A family cannot incorporate simply because it is a family; it must be engaged in a bona fide business from which it receives nonsalaried income.

The Costs of Incorporating

Just about anyone in any state can start a corporation. There are, however, numerous expenses associated with starting and running such a venture. Below is a list of the possible expenses:

1. *Lawyers' fees.* These can range from a minimum of $250 to as much as $3,000.
2. *Accountants' fees.* It can cost several hundred dollars to establish a bookkeeping system for a corporation.
3. *Fees to the state.* The state can require an annual corporate fee ranging from a few dollars to several hundred dollars.
4. *Unemployment insurance taxes.* Even if the corporation has only one employee, and it is clearly set up for tax reasons only, it must still pay unemployment insurance taxes, either to the state in which it is registered or to the federal government.
5. *Employer's contribution to Social Security.* Even if a person is a salaried employee of some other company, as an employee of his or her own corporation, he or she must pay an employer's "contribution" to Social Security. This "contribution" is nonrefundable and seems to be on the rise.
6. *Annual legal and accounting fees.* Many forms must be filed for corporations in the different states. In addition, corporate records and detailed books must be maintained. Typically, an accountant or a lawyer does this. Annual fees for such services can run into many hundreds of dollars. Numerous forms must be filled out every year for retirement funds alone.

The Benefits of Incorporating

One of the major advantages of incorporating is the tax savings derived from pension or profit-sharing plans; another is the tax-related benefit associated with fringe benefits.

Pension and profit-sharing plans. The IRS routinely allows pension plans consisting of two parts—a 10 percent retirement plan and a 15 percent profit-sharing plan. The 10 percent and 15 percent numbers refer to the percentage of the gross salary paid to the corporation's individual employees in any one year. Assume that you decide to incorporate under the laws of your state. You make the firm a closely held corporation in which you are the sole shareholder. Let's say that in the year after you have incorporated, you are able to take out $50,000 as income. In other words, you pay yourself a salary as the president and sole employee. If you had started a legally acceptable pension and profit-sharing plan, then your closely held corporation could contribute $5,000 to your corporate pension plan and $7,500 to your corporate profit-sharing plan. These two contributions would be tax deductible to the corporation but not taxable to you in that year. Rather, you would pay taxes on those contributions when you retired and took out the benefits from your corporate pension plan and corporate profit-sharing plan.

The Benefits of Pension and Profit-sharing Plans

The tax-sheltered pension or profit-sharing plan allows the individual to save before-tax dollars as opposed to saving after-tax dollars. If the individual is in the 50 percent tax bracket, for example, a pension tax shelter will allow that person to save twice as many before-tax dollars as after-tax dollars.

A tax-exempt savings plan does not, however, allow the individual to avoid paying taxes indefinitely on the savings put into the plan. Eventually, the individual will have to pay taxes, but they will be paid as they are taken out of the plan. Thus, the individual saves on taxes because he or she is usually in a lower tax bracket after retirement. Moreover, the individual puts off having to pay those taxes, which allows savings to grow at compounded rates. This is a key aspect of tax-exempt pension and profit-sharing plans. By deferring taxes until a future date, interest can be earned on those deferred taxes since they are not being paid (and the taxes on those earnings are deferred). In other words, the government lends the individual the taxes owed for a number of years and does not charge interest on the loan. This "loan" must be repaid *eventually* (usually starting at retirement), but until then extra income can be earned on it. A simple numerical example follows to illustrate the point.

Fringe Benefits

An individual who starts a corporation can take advantage of a number of fringe benefits that provide items that might otherwise have to be bought with after-tax dollars.

Term life insurance. An individual, through his or her own corporation, can purchase up to $50,000 of term life insurance every year with dollars out of the corporation. Because these dollars are a cost to the corporation, they are not taxable. If the person is in the 50 percent tax bracket, for example, that means that he or she is buying $50,000 of term insurance for "50¢ dollars." In this example, the cost of that insurance is essentially one-half what it would have been if it had been purchased outside the corporate structure.

A medical plan. An individual can set up a completely comprehensive medical plan to cover virtually all kinds of medical expenses. Thus, the corporation can reimburse the individual with before-tax dollars for any payments made for medical insurance. The corporation can pay for all medicines, dental work, and anything that relates to physical well-being. For someone with a large family, this comprehensive medical plan can mean substantial savings every year. If, in general, an individual spends $2,000 more each year in medical expenses than his or her medical plan covers and if the individual is in the 50 percent tax bracket, he or she gets a "kickback" of $1,000.

The benefit of a medical plan is reduced by the availability of medical deductions that the individual could have taken off his or her income before figuring federal income taxes. Part of the person's medical insurance plus any medical expenses exceeding 3 percent of the adjusted gross income can be itemized as specific deductions on his or her personal federal income tax return. Essentially, then, a medical plan within the corporation for the individual and dependents eliminates the medical expenses that generally are not deductible.

The Revenue Act of 1978 requires that a medical plan not discriminate among employees. In other words, if it is made available for the president of the corporation, it must also be made available for all employees in the corporation.

Disability insurance. An individual can purchase, with before-tax dollars, long-term disability insurance through the corporation. In other words, a person can buy a salary continuation policy with before-tax dollars that might otherwise have to be bought with after-tax dollars. Such policies pay a certain amount of money every month if the person becomes disabled and is unable to work.

Questions

1. If you were to incorporate, would your corporation show up in the government records along with General Motors and IBM? In other words, would you be on equal footing, at least statistically?

Definition of Terms

Plant The physical establishment that manufactures or distributes a commodity.

Firm An organization that owns and operates one or more plants.

Industry A group of firms producing similar commodities.

Sole proprietorship A business owned by only one person. Also called an individual proprietorship.

Partnership A business entity involving two or more individuals who join together for business purposes, but who have not incorporated. In most instances, each partner is liable for the debts of the business to such an extent that he or she can lose his or her personal wealth if the business incurs debt.

Corporation A legal entity owned by stockholders. The stockholders are liable only for the amount of money they have invested in the company.

Security The tangible evidence of an investment by individuals and institutions in the affairs of business firms and governments.

Common stock A security that indicates the real ownership in a corporation. It is not a legal obligation for the firm and does not have a maturity. It has the last claim on dividends each year and on assets in the event of firm liquidation.

Preferred stock A security that indicates financing obtained from investors by a corporation. It is not a legal obligation for the firm and does not have a maturity, but pays a fixed dividend each year. It has preferred position over common stock, both for dividends and for assets in the event of firm liquidation.

Bond An interest bearing certificate issued by a government or a corporation. This type of security represents debt.

Chapter Summary

1. We make the distinction between a plant, a firm, and an industry in which a firm consists of one or more plants, and an industry consists of firms producing similar products.
2. American industry has a changing character. Agriculture has fallen in importance. Manufacturing gained in importance until relatively recently but now is falling in importance compared to the service sector of the economy where medical care, legal work, repairs, and so on, are carried out.
3. The three most important forms of business organization are sole proprietorships, partnerships, and corporations.
4. The advantages of a sole proprietorship are: (a) the proprietor receives all profits, (b) there is pride in ownership, (c) such businesses are easy to start, and (d) there is freedom from corporate income taxes on any profits.
5. The disadvantages of a sole proprietorship are: (a) responsibility for all losses, (b) limited money capital, and (c) unlimited liability.
6. The advantages of a partnership are: (a) more capital, and (b) greater efficiency; they allow for specialization.
7. The disadvantages of a partnership are: (a) unlimited liability, (b) profits must be shared, (c) the partners may disagree about management decisions, and (d) the death of a partner requires reorganization of the partnership.
8. To form a corporation it must be registered with the appropriate state agency and a board of directors must be chosen.
9. The advantages of a corporation are: (a) greater capital, (b) limited liability, (c) unlimited life, and (d) specialized and professional management.
10. The two disadvantages of a corporation are: (a)

the necessity of paying federal and state taxes on profits, and (b) increased government control and regulation.

11. A corporation can obtain long-term financing by selling stocks or bonds to individuals and institutions.

12. The two types of stock are common and preferred. A common stock represents ownership in a firm. A preferred stock is more like a bond. The owner gets dividends before owners of common stock get dividends, and the owner of a preferred stock has a prior claim to any assets if the firm is liquidated.

13. A bond is basically a promissory note of a government or corporation and is evidence of a debt to the bondholder.

14. Long-term financing by common stocks has the lowest risk for the corporation because there is no legal obligation to make dividend payments.

15. The sale of long-term bonds, however, has an advantage in that they may be the cheapest way of financing because bond interest paid out is tax deductible to the corporation.

16. There are numerous reasons to consider incorporation; however, there are numerous costs that must be incurred.

Selected References

Baratz, Morton S. *The American Business System in Transition.* New York: Crowell, 1970.

Green, Mark, and Robert K. Massie, Jr., eds. *The Big Business Reader.* New York: The Pilgrim Press, 1980.

Trebing, Harry M., ed. *The Corporation in the American Economy.* Chicago: Quadrangle Books, 1970.

Answers to Preview and Study Questions

1. What is the distinction between a plant, a firm, and an industry?

A plant is a physical establishment that performs some manufacturing or distribution function. A firm is the organization that operates one or more plants. An industry is a group of firms producing similar products. Thus, General Motors is a firm that has many plants located throughout the world and is in the automobile industry.

2. How has the composition of industry changed in the United States?

When the United States was founded in 1776, somewhere between 80 and 90 percent of the people lived and worked on farms. Through time, agriculture was replaced by manufacturing in importance; by 1900 agriculture accounted for 33 percent of the nation's output while manufacturing accounted for over 50 percent of total output. Today, fewer than 5 percent of the U.S. population is on the farm, and the service sector is growing the most rapidly. Projections are that the service sector will eventually surpass the manufacturing sector in contribution to the value of total output.

3. What is the distinction between a sole proprietorship, a partnership, and a corporation?

A sole proprietorship is a business owned by one person and is the most common form of business organization. A partnership is any form of business enterprise that two or more individuals own and operate for profit. A corporation is a business, comprised of an association of stockholders, that is legally separate from the people who own and control it. Whereas sole proprietorships account for the largest number of business firms in the United States, corporations provide the great majority of the goods purchased—corporations constitute some 12 percent of all business firms but collect almost 75 percent of all business receipts.

4. How does corporate common stock differ from preferred stock?

Common stock is that form of corporate stock that vests a firm's ownership rights in the stockholders; owners of common stock have voting power and are the ultimate owners and residual profit receivers. Preferred stock owners have a claim against a firm's assets; this claim is placed ahead of claims by common stock owners. Preferred stock normally earns a specified amount of annual interest.

Problems

(Answers at the back of the book)

1. List each of the following under one of the following headings: plant, firm, industry.
   a. The McDonald's at the corner of 12th Street and Somerset
   b. General Motors
   c. A factory
   d. All the plants owned by Ford
   e. All the producers of steel, aluminum, and other metals
   f. Producers of automobiles, trucks, buses, jeeps, and motorcycles
   g. Prudential Insurance Company
   h. A drugstore

2. List the advantages and disadvantages of the corporate form of business organization.

3. List the advantages and disadvantages of long-term corporate financing by selling stock instead of selling bonds.

APPENDIX

B

Simplified Accounting, with and without Inflation

In this chapter you have looked at the organization of the private business firm in the United States. Firms are assumed to exist to make a profit. Therefore, determining the profitability of a firm is important to businesspeople—those who run the firm—and also to investors—those who buy shares of ownership of the firm or lend money to it.

To determine the profitability of a firm, we need information provided by accountants. The profitability for any firm can be learned from two basic financial statements—the *balance sheet* and the *income statement,* sometimes called the *statement of earnings*—which accountants use to describe the financial condition of the firm. Learning how to analyze these financial statements, which form the basis of a firm's *annual report* to its stockholders and investors, will help you when you are either involved in running a firm or are thinking about investing in a particular firm.

What we will do first in this appendix is look at firm accounting under the unrealistic assumption that there is no inflation. Then we will examine the accounting system used that explicitly deals with our inflationary times. Prior to 1979, accounting standards did not require that inflation-adjusted data be presented in company annual reports. But in October of 1979, the Financial Accounting Standards Board (commonly referred to as the FASB), an organization that sets standards for the accounting profession, ruled that corporations must indeed take account of inflation.

The FASB's ruling on inflation accounting affected some 1,300 firms. To explain and demonstrate the accounting for financial information without and with inflation-adjusted data, we will use and closely analyze the balance sheet and income statement for International Business Machines Corporation (IBM). IBM operations are mostly in the field of information-handling systems; its products include data-processing machines and systems, information processors, office systems, electric and electronic typewriters, copiers, dictation equipment, and related supplies and services.

The Balance Sheet

Take a look at the IBM balance sheet shown in Exhibit B–1 and observe that the date, December 31, 1980, is printed so that it appears to be a rather important part of the title. That's because the date is important. The balance sheet is a statement of the financial well-being of a firm at a *specific* point in time. In this case, the balance sheet is a statement of a financial condition, or well-being, of IBM exactly on that day, December 31, 1980.

Typically, balance sheets are published annually, although there are situations in which a company will publish balance sheets more frequently, particularly if an important event has occurred or if the firm is making a large purchase of another firm, and so on.

THE PARTS OF A TYPICAL BALANCE SHEET

A typical balance sheet is made up of three main sections.

EXHIBIT B–1
Balance Sheet: IBM, December 31, 1980 (all figures in millions of dollars)

Assets		
Current Assets:		
Cash	$ 281	
Marketable securities, at lower of cost or market	1,831	
Notes and accounts receivable—trade, less allowance: 1980, $195; 1979, $188	4,562	
Other accounts receivable	315	
Inventories, at lower of average cost or market	2,293	
Prepaid expenses	643	
		$ 9,925
Rental Machines and Parts	15,352	
Less: Accumulated depreciation	6,969	
		8,383
Plant and Other Property	11,018	
Less: Accumulated depreciation	4,384	
		6,634
Deferred Charges and Other Assets		1,761
		$26,703

Liabilities and Stockholders' Equity		
Current Liabilities:		
Taxes	$ 2,369	
Loans payable	591	
Accounts Payable	721	
Compensation and benefits	1,404	
Deferred income	305	
Other accrued expenses and liabilities	1,136	
		$ 6,526
Deferred Investment Tax Credits	182	
Reserves for Employees' Indemnities and Retirement Plans		1,443
Long-Term Debt		2,099
Stockholders' Equity:		
Capital stock, par value $1.25 per share		3,992
Shares authorized, 650,000,000		
Issued: 1980–584,262,074; 1979–583,973,258		
Retained earnings	12,491	
	16,483	
Less: Treasury stock, at cost	30	
Shares: 1980–455,242; 1979–378,715		16,453
		$26,703

a. Assets
b. Liabilities
c. Owners' equity, more commonly referred to as shareholders' or stockholders' equity.

By definition, assets must equal liabilities plus owners' equity. That is,

Assets = liabilities + owners' equity

Assets. Assets are those things owned by the company, or to which it has property rights. For example, the assets of the company might include cash in the bank, land and buildings, and such intangible things as the rights to patents and the value of copyrights and trademarks.

Liabilities. Liabilities include all debts owed by the company. Examples of common liabilities are debts such as taxes and salaries that the company owes, loans payable to banks, reserves for employee retirement plans, and so on.

Owners' equity. Owners' equity is the difference between assets and liabilities. That is, whatever is left over after all debts are paid, or at least taken account of, is owned by the stockholders in the company. In the IBM balance sheet, the stockholders' equity was $16,453,000,000 on December 31, 1980. That means that if all debts were paid on that date, the book value of the IBM Corporation was worth almost $16½ billion to its owners!

Current and fixed assets. Under assets, note the subheading "Current Assets." Current assets are assets that are either in the form of cash right now or will be turned into cash within one year. On the other hand, fixed assets include things that have a life longer than one year. IBM lists them as "Plant, Rental Machines, and Other Property."

Current and fixed, or long-term liabilities. Current liabilities have the same time framework as current assets. Current liabilities are those that must be paid within the following year. Fixed, or long-term, liabilities are those that must be paid sometime after one year or during a period of years.

THE BALANCING ACT

A balance sheet is exactly what it says it is. It must balance. The two totals on the bottom of each part of the ledger must always be equal. Remember:

Assets = liabilities + shareholders' equity

That means that, should IBM borrow to build another plant, the balance sheet for next year would show the value of another plant as an asset, and it would also show a liability equal to the cost of the plant because it was bought on credit.

The Income Statement

The income statement for IBM is its "statement of earnings." The income statement focuses on the financial activities of a firm during an entire one-year period. For example, if the balance sheet reports a firm's financial condition specifically on December 31, the income statement will normally report its financial activities between January 1 and December 31.

The statement of earnings reports a firm's revenues, its costs, and its profits during the year. Profit, of course, is the difference between total revenues and total costs. Unfortunately, there may be cases where costs are greater than revenues and when this happens, a negative profit—that is, a loss—results. Losses are represented within parentheses in income statements.

Look at Exhibit B–2. The first three lines in this IBM income statement, "Sales" and "Rentals" and "Services," represent all the money income received for the products or services sold. In 1980, IBM had a gross income from sales plus rentals and services of $26,213,000,000, or about $26 billion.

COSTS

Next on the income statement is a listing of costs. These costs are related to the earning of the revenues from sales and rentals and services.

The Effect of Inflation on Accounting

Economists and accountants have long known that inflation makes a firm's profits, or earnings, appear greater from one year to another than they actually are. Consider an example. Assume that Corporation X in, say, 1980, had total sales revenues of $10 and total costs of $8. Profits, or earnings, would be $2. Now suppose that during the following year the price level doubles, and, in 1981, Corporation X realizes total sales of $20 and total costs of $16. Total profits for 1981 would be $4. It might seem that in one year profits have doubled. Of course, only

EXHIBIT B–2
Income Statement: IBM, 1980 (In millions of dollars except per share amount)

Gross Income:		
Sales	$ 10,919	
Rentals	10,869	
Services	4,425	
		$ 26,213
Cost of sales	4,197	
Cost of rentals	3,771	
Cost of services	2,181	
Selling, development and engineering, and general and administrative expenses	10,324	
Interest expense	273	
		20,746
		5,467
Other income, principally interest		430
Earnings before income taxes		5,897
Provision for U.S. Federal and non-U.S. income taxes		2,335
Net Earnings		$ 3,562
Per share (Average number of shares outstanding: 1980–583,516,764)		$ 6.10

nominal profits—those reported on the books—have doubled; *real* profits—profits adjusted for inflation—have remained unchanged.

No matter how you look at profits, if you don't take inflation into consideration, *nominal* profits look bigger than profits really are. The maximum distortion would occur if assets were valued at their historic, that is, their original, purchase price. For instance, continuing with our example, suppose Corporation X's productive assets were purchased for $20 in 1980. The ratio of earnings to assets for 1980, in our example, would be

$$\$2 \div \$20 = 10 \text{ percent.}$$

In 1981, if we use the original purchase price as the value of the asset, this ratio would be

$$\$4 \div \$20 = 20 \text{ percent.}$$

But the real value of the assets is their *current* price. Thus, if we did the calculation using the current, inflation-adjusted, value of assets, the ratio of earnings to assets would be

$$\$4 \div \$40 = 10 \text{ percent.}$$

This rate is the same as for 1980.

In short, inflation "overstates" (makes figures appear larger than in reality) the absolute value of profits as well as the ratio of earnings to assets, when assets are valued at their historic (or purchase) value.

OTHER PROFIT ILLUSIONS

Inflation overstates profits in other ways, too. We will look at some of them here.

Inventory profits. If we look at profits through "inventory profits," they will tend to be overstated unless adjusted for inflation.

The problem with inventory profits arises when a unit of some product produced in the past is sold in the present—with inflation occurring in the meantime. For example, suppose Corporation X had been selling its output for 10¢ per unit, while costs were 8¢ per unit. Each unit, therefore, contributed 2¢ to total profits. Suppose, however, that inflation occurs so that a unit that previously cost 8¢ is still in inventory and can now be sold for 20¢. Assume that the cost for new units going into inventory has risen to 16¢ per unit. In effect, the firm has realized what is called an "inventory profit" on the unit produced earlier, for 20¢ minus 8¢ equals 12¢. However, inventory profits are in a sense "fictitious," because in order to *replace* this unit in inventory, Corporation X would have to pay the higher cost (16¢ in our example).

Homeowners who understand this phenomenon

wisely observe that inflation may have increased the value of their house, but if they sold the house and realized this "profit," the profit would vanish upon the purchase of a house that is similar to the one they just sold. The key here is that replacement costs make the "profit" only an illusion caused by inflation.

Last-In, First Out, or LIFO. Accountants, recognizing how inflation causes the illusion of inventory profit, have devised an accounting practice to maintain reality in treating the costs and income from inventories. This accounting practice is called LIFO, which stands for Last-In, First-Out. This means that the accountants will use the costs of the most recently (Last-In) produced goods as the costs of goods sold in any profit calculations. In effect, where there is inflation, the most costly goods are those which were produced most recently.

Using LIFO in our example, when Corporation X sold that unit which "really" only cost 8¢ one year before, it would have a "cost of goods sold" of 16¢. Most firms use LIFO, thereby reducing fictitious inventory profits to some extent.

Depreciation. Inflation also affects depreciation entries in accounting. It makes profits appear larger than they really are. For example, when a firm purchases a factory, it is realized that this asset—the factory—will wear out, that is, it will *depreciate* over time. Thus, a machine, for example, that costs, say, $1,000 and still works but wears out over ten years, can be assumed to depreciate at roughly $100 per year. This $100 per year is a legitimate expense, and it is common accounting practice to subtract this annual expense from sales receipts in order to calculate earnings or profits. In times of inflation, however, the replacement cost of the machine rises. As an example, let's assume that it doubles. Now, by subtracting only $100 as a depreciation expense, we are *understating* replacement cost—and therefore *overstating* profits.

To see how this happens, let's assume that the firm before inflation has $100 of depreciation expense plus $100 of other costs of doing business, and $250 income. Its profit would be

$$\$250 - (\$100 + \$100) = \$50.$$

Now let's assume that during the next year, when the firm still deducts $100 depreciation expense, income doubles and so do all other costs of doing business. Thus, profit would seem to be

$$\$500 - (\$100 + \$200) = \$200.$$

But, something is wrong with this calculation because, if inflation has caused all prices to double, it would have cost twice as much to replace the machine that we are depreciating. That means that the $100 depreciation expense is not enough to replace the present annual cost of buying a new machine. Can you see now how inflation, through depreciation expenses, causes a fictitious increase in profits?

Unfortunately, no accounting technique comparable to LIFO has been devised to account for depreciation to make profits more realistic in times of inflation.

Interestingly enough, not all firms have complained about the fictitious profits earned during periods of inflation. This may be because the annual stockholder meetings are more pleasant when "profits" are rising, especially for firms earning low *real* profits! That is, fictitious profits that are adjusted for inflation turn out to be relatively small.

Unfortunately, not only do illusory profits *not* put money in the pockets of stockholders—that is, provide them with real income—rather, the illusion of higher profits results in a higher real cost—takes money out of their pockets. This happens because taxes must be paid on nominal profits—the illusory higher profits—not on real profits—which would be lower if depreciation and inventories were fully adjusted for inflation. Many studies indicate that after adjusting for inflation, many firms paid higher tax rates than they should have.

Accounting for Inflation

Now that you have some idea of the havoc inflation can cause to financial data, you can appreciate why the Financial Accounting Standards Board made its historic ruling in 1979. To restore precision, meaning, and consistency in financial data reported by corporations, the FASB ruled that their data must report data that are adjusted for inflation. To understand what "adjusted for inflation" means and how corporations must now report their data, see Exhibit B–3. We use in that exhibit the income statement for IBM for 1980, both with and without adjustments for inflation. The comparison is a fascinating confirmation of what we have discussed above. The figures are in thousands of dollars except for the per-share amounts. We are considering a price rise over the 1980 period. Compare the un-

EXHIBIT B–3
1980 IBM Statement of Earnings (in millions of dollars except per share amounts)

	Unadjusted		*Adjusted For Inflation*	
Gross Income from sales, rentals and services		$26,213		$26,213
Cost of sales, rentals and services	$10,149		$11,064	
Other Expenses	10,167		10,335	
Provision for U.S. Federal and non-U.S. Income Taxes	2,335		2,335	
TOTAL COSTS		22,651		23,734
NET EARNINGS		$ 3,562		$ 2,479
EARNINGS PER SHARE		$ 6.10		$ 4.25
DEPRECIATION EXPENSE		$ 2,362		$ 3,041
NET ASSETS		$16,453		$19,176
AFTER TAX RETURN TO NET ASSETS		21.6%		12.9%
EFFECTIVE TAX RATE		39.6%		48.5%

adjusted side, in the top half of the table, to the adjusted side. The only change for adjustment involves the "Cost of Sales, Rentals, and Services" and "Other Expenses." This is because IBM raised its prices during the year (in response to inflation, that is, to keep pace with everyone else's price increases). Because its taxes are a percentage of its income, both income and taxes paid increase at exactly the same rate as inflation. Thus, income and taxes require no adjustment.

On the other hand, inventory, plant, rental machines and other property, cost of sales, rentals and services, and depreciation expenses had to be converted, or adjusted, for inflation. These original costs were adjusted upward to take account of inflation that occurred from the purchase date to 1980. In other words, if a factory, built five years ago for $1 million, costs $2 million to replace in 1980, the annual depreciation expense for that factory is doubled to be correctly adjusted for inflation. All fictitious inventory profits were eliminated in the column labeled "Adjusted for Inflation." Note that adjusting for inflation raises the cost of sales, rentals, and services from $10,149 million to $11,064 million. Adjustment for inflation also raises other expenses from $10,167 million to $10,335 million. In other words, total costs, adjusting for inflation, rise from $22,651 million to $23,734 million—or a difference of $1.083 billion. Over half of that adjustment was due to increased depreciation expenses, which were adjusted from $2,362 million to $3,041 million, or an increase in depreciation of $649 million.

Gross revenue minus an inflation-adjusted upward cost of sales, of course, lowers net earnings. Moreover, a lowered net earnings, combined with an adjusted upward asset value (higher replacement expenses), lowers the after-tax rate of return to assets—ratio of earnings to assets—from 21.6 percent to 12.9 percent. Also note that the effective tax rate jumps from 39.6 percent to 48.5 percent. In other words, IBM in 1980, was actually paying a higher rate of taxes than the 46 percent statutory limit on corporations!

PART

MARKETS, THE FIRM, AND RESOURCE ALLOCATION

6

Demand and Supply Elasticity

TOPICS FOR REVIEW

The topics listed below, which we have already analyzed, are applied in this chapter. You may find it worthwhile to review them. For your convenience each topic is followed by the number identifying the specific "Concepts in Brief."

a. Demand (3–1, 3–2)

b. Shifts versus movements along demand curves (3–3)

c. Supply (3–4, 3–5)

FOR PREVIEW AND STUDY

1. What is price elasticity of demand?
2. How is total revenue related to price elasticity of demand?
3. What are the determinants of price elasticity of demand?
4. What is price elasticity of supply?
5. What is income elasticity of demand?

In Chapter 3, we learned that the law of demand stated that at higher relative prices smaller quantities are demanded, and at lower relative prices larger quantities are demanded, other things being equal. We also looked at the law of supply, which tells us that, in most cases, suppliers will be *willing* to supply greater quantities at higher than lower prices, other things being equal. Knowing the laws of demand and supply is not enough, however, to answer important questions.

Put yourself for a moment in the place of the leaders of the Organization of Petroleum Exporting Countries (OPEC). You must make a decision about how much to raise the price of crude oil next year, if at all. In order to make an intelligent decision, you have to know how consumers will respond to the higher price. If consumers buy *a lot less* when you raise the price, your total revenues may fall. On the other hand, if consumers don't change their buying decisions very much when you raise the price, your total revenues may increase. For example, if OPEC raises prices by 10 percent, will total revenues fall, remain constant, or rise? That depends on how much quantity demanded changes due to the price rise. Thus, from the seller's point of view, knowing that consumers behave according to the law of demand is certainly insufficient information on which to make pricing decisions. Sellers also have to know how the price change and resultant change in quantity demanded will affect their total revenues.

Now suppose you are in Congress, drafting energy legislation. Consider the possibility that a 10 percent rise in the price of oil and oil products will lead to a reduction in quantity demanded of only 1 percent. What this higher price and small reduction in quantity demanded means is that consumers would then be spending larger portions of their total budgets on oil products. This has important government policy implications, particularly with respect to low-income families who would have a hard time finding where to cut back in their other purchases. In other words, knowing that quantity demanded will not fall very much when there is a large percentage increase in the price of petroleum products might lead Congress to pass additional legislation aimed at helping out low-income families. Congress might want to adopt special subsidies for energy consumption by these people.

In this chapter, we wish to find out how we can measure the *responsiveness* of quantities demanded and supplied to changes in relative prices. Economists have given such price responsiveness a special name—elasticity.

Price Elasticity

To begin to understand what "elasticity" is all about, just keep in mind that it means "responsiveness." Here we are concerned with the price elasticity of demand and the price elasticity of supply. We wish to know the extent to which a change in the relative price of, say, petroleum products will cause the quantity demanded and the quantity supplied to change. Let's restrict our discussion at first to the demand side. For convenience we may occasionally write only "price," but we can agree that we always mean relative price throughout our price elasticity discussion.

PRICE ELASTICITY OF DEMAND

We will formally define the **price elasticity of demand,** which we will label e_d, as follows:

$$e_d = \frac{\text{percentage change in quantity demanded}}{\text{percentage change in price}}$$

What will price elasticity of demand tell us? It will tell us the relative amount by which the quantity demanded will change in response to a change in the relative price of a particular good.

Consider the example we just used above where a 10 percent rise in the price of oil leads to a reduction in quantity demanded of only 1 percent. Putting these numbers into the formula, we find that the price elasticity of demand of oil equals the percentage change in quantity demanded divided by the percentage change in price, or,

$$e_d = \frac{-1 \text{ percent}}{+10 \text{ percent}} = -.1$$

Notice that this number is pure—that is, dimensionless, a percentage divided by a percentage.[1]

An elasticity of $-.1$ means that a 1 percent *decrease* in the price would lead to a mere one-tenth of 1 percent *increase* in the quantity demanded. If you were now told that the price elasticity of demand for oil was, say, -1, then you would know that a 1 percent increase in the price of oil would lead to a 1 percent decrease in the quantity demanded.

Basically, the greater the numerical price elasticity of demand, the greater the demand responsive-

[1] Miles divided by gallons gives the ratio "miles per gallon." But when you see a ratio without such a dimension, that means that the ratio is comparing two identical dimensions.

ness to relative price changes—a small change in price has a great impact on quantity demanded. The smaller the numerical price elasticity of demand, the smaller the demand responsiveness to relative price changes—a large change in price has little effect on quantity demanded.

Price Elasticity of Demand Is Always Negative

Remember that the law of demand states that quantity demanded is *inversely* related to the relative price. Thus, in the preceding example, an increase in the price of oil led to a decrease in the quantity demanded. Alternatively, we could have used an example of a decrease in the relative price of oil, in which case the quantity demanded would increase a certain percentage. The point is that price elasticity of demand will always be negative. By convention, we will ignore the negative sign in our discussion from this point on.

Relative Quantities Only

Notice that in our elasticity formula, we talk about *percentage* changes in quantity demanded divided by percentage changes in price. We are not, therefore, interested in the absolute changes, but only in relative amounts. This means that it doesn't matter if we measure price changes in terms of cents, dollars, or hundreds of dollars. It also doesn't matter whether we measure quantity changes in, for example, ounces, grams, or pounds. The percentage change will be the same.

> ***Concepts in Brief 6-1***
>
> ■ Elasticity is a measure of the price responsiveness of the quantity demanded and supplied.
>
> ■ The price elasticity of demand is equal to the percentage change in quantity demanded divided by the percentage change in price.
>
> ■ The law of demand states that quantity demanded and relative price are inversely related. Therefore, the price elasticity of demand is always negative, since an increase in price will lead to a decrease in quantity demanded and a decrease in price will lead to an increase in quantity demanded.
>
> ■ Price elasticity of demand is calculated in terms of relative percentage changes in quantity demanded and in price. Thus, we end up with a unitless, scaleless number.

CALCULATION OF ELASTICITY

In order to calculate the price elasticity of demand, we have to compute percentage changes in quantity demanded and in relative price. To obtain the percentage change in quantity demanded, we can look at

$$\frac{\textbf{change in quantity demanded}}{\textbf{original quantity demanded}} \times \textbf{100 percent}$$

To find the percentage change in price, we can look at

$$\frac{\textbf{change in price}}{\textbf{original price}} \times \textbf{100 percent}$$

There is a slight problem with computation of percentage changes in this manner. We get a different answer depending on whether we move up the demand curve or down the demand curve.

Columns 1 and 3 of Exhibit 6–1(a) are simply the quantity demanded and price data for the demand curve represented graphically as Exhibit 6–1(b) and (c). Columns 2 and 4 show changes in quantity demanded corresponding to changes in price.

Let's start with a quantity of one unit demanded at the price of $10 per unit and *move down the demand curve.* If we start at a price of $10 with one unit demanded, price then falls to $9. Quantity demanded increases to two. The percentage change in price is:

[($10 − $9)/$10] × 100 percent, or:
[$1 ÷ $10] × 100 percent = 10 percent

The percentage change in quantity demanded is:

[(2 − 1)/1] × 100 percent, or:
[1 ÷ 1] × 100 percent = 100 percent

Thus, price elasticity of demand is equal to:

100 percent ÷ 10 percent = 10

Now let's calculate the price elasticity of demand when we *move up the demand curve.* We start at a price of $9 with two units demanded. The price goes up to $10 and one unit is demanded. The percentage change in price is now equal to:

[($10 − $9)/$9] × 100 percent =
[$1 ÷ $9] × 100 percent = 11.11 percent

The percentage change in quantity demanded is:

[(2 − 1)/2] × 100 percent, or:
[1 ÷ 2] × 100 percent = 50 percent

EXHIBIT 6–1(a)
Numerical Calculation of Price Elasticity of Demand for Oil. Column 1 is the quantity demanded at different prices. Column 2 is the change in the quantity demanded. In other words, we merely subtract the smaller from the larger quantity. In each case, the change is 1 million barrels per day. Column 3 is the price per barrel, and column 4 is the change in the price, which happens to be $1 in each case. Columns 5 and 6 are the average quantities and prices, e.g., $(Q_1 + Q_2)/2 = (0 + 1)/2 = .5$ and $(P_1 + P_2)/2 = (\$11 + \$10)/2 = \$10.5$ for the first row. Column 7 presents an approximation of the price elasticity of demand, e_d.

(1) Quantity Demanded (Q) (millions of barrels per day)	(2) Change in Q (millions of barrels per day)	(3) Price (P)	(4) Change in P	(5) $\frac{Q_1 + Q_2}{2}$	(6) $\frac{P_1 + P_2}{2}$	(7) $e_d = \frac{\text{change in Q}}{(Q_1 + Q_2)/2} \div \frac{\text{change in P}}{(P_1 + P_2)/2}$
0		$11				
	1		$1	0.5	$10.5	1/.5 ÷ 1/10.5 = 21
1		10				
	1		1	1.5	9.5	1/1.5 ÷ 1/9.5 = 6.333
2		9				
	1		1	2.5	8.5	1/2.5 ÷ 1/8.5 = 3.4
3		8				
	1		1	3.5	7.5	1/3.5 ÷ 1/7.5 = 2.143
4		7				
	1		1	4.5	6.5	1/4.5 ÷ 1/6.5 = 1.444
5		6				
	1		1	5.5	5.5	1/5.5 ÷ 1/5.5 = 1
6		5				
	1		1	6.5	4.5	1/6.5 ÷ 1/4.5 = .692
7		4				
	1		1	7.5	3.5	1/7.5 ÷ 1/3.5 = .467
8		3				
	1		1	8.5	2.5	1/8.5 ÷ 1/2.5 = .294
9		2				
	1		1	9.5	1.5	1/9.5 ÷ 1/1.5 = .158
10		1				

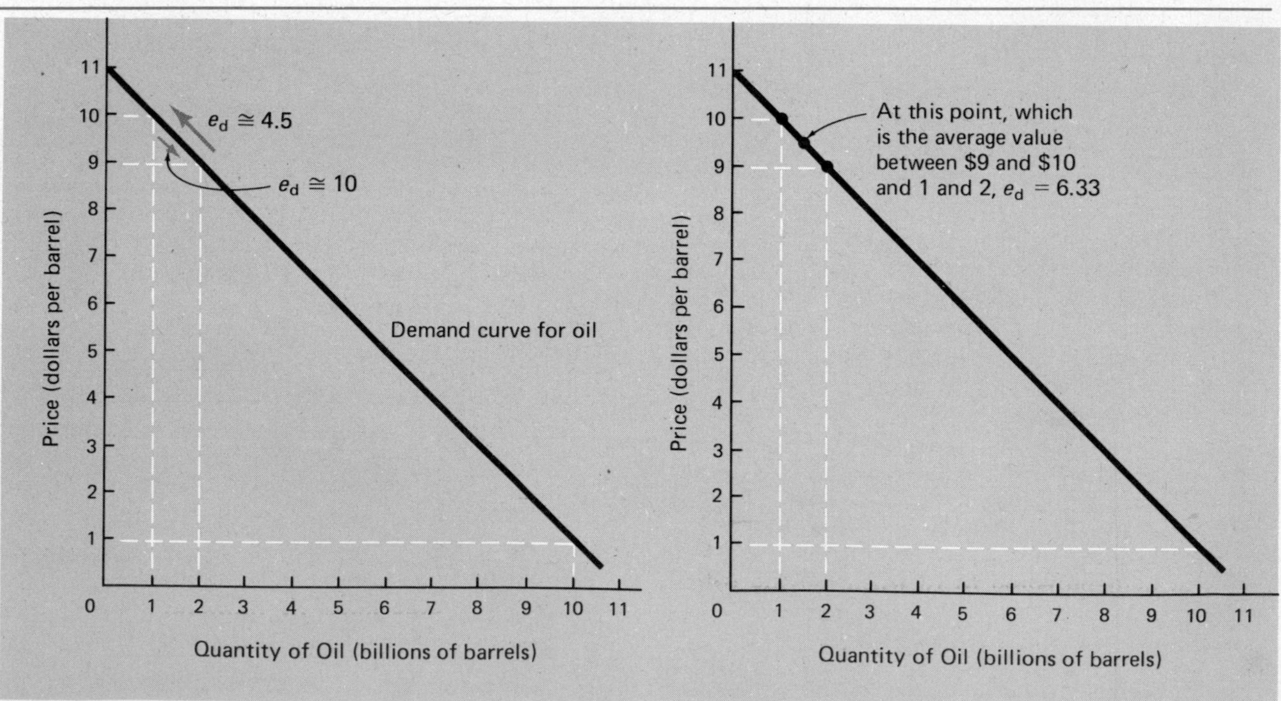

EXHIBIT 6–1(b)
Two Different Elasticities.

EXHIBIT 6–1(c)
Using Average Values.

Thus, the price elasticity of demand is now equal to:

$$50 \text{ percent} \div 11.11 \text{ percent} = 4.5$$

Quite a difference! We show this in panel (b) of Exhibit 6–1.

Using average values. For the same segment of the demand curve, we get different values of price elasticity of demand because the original prices and quantities depend on whether we move up or down the demand curve. The *absolute* changes in price and quantity are the same size regardless of direction. But when moving down the demand curve, the *original* price is higher than when moving up the demand curve. When moving up the demand curve, the original quantity demanded is greater. Since a percentage change depends on the size of the original value, the percentages we calculate for price elasticity of demand will be affected by choosing a higher price and smaller quantity, or a lower price and greater quantity. One way out of this difficulty is to take the average of the two prices and the two quantities over the range we are considering and compare the change to the average, instead of comparing it to the price or quantity at the start of the change.

The formula for computing price elasticity of demand then becomes:

$$e_d = \frac{\text{change in quantity}}{\text{sum of quantities}/2} \times 100 \text{ percent} \div \frac{\text{change in price}}{\text{sum of prices}/2} \times 100 \text{ percent}$$

We can rewrite this more simply if we do two things: (1) We can let Q_1 and Q_2 equal the two different quantities demanded before and after the price change, and P_1 and P_2 equal the two different prices; and (2) because we will be dividing a percent by a percent, we simply use the ratio, or the decimal form, of the percent. Therefore,

$$e_d = \frac{\text{change in } Q}{(Q_1 + Q_2)/2} \div \frac{\text{change in } P}{(P_1 + P_2)/2}$$

Let's redo the example that showed a price elasticity of demand equal to 10 when moving from a \$10 price to a \$9 price, but gave an elasticity of 4.5 when moving from \$9 to \$10. We insert our numbers in the average formula just given, so that price elasticity of demand becomes, in either case:

$$e_d = \frac{1}{\left(\frac{1+2}{2}\right)} \bigg/ \frac{1}{\left(\frac{9+10}{2}\right)} = \frac{1}{\left(\frac{3}{2}\right)} \bigg/ \frac{1}{\left(\frac{19}{2}\right)} = \frac{2}{3} \bigg/ \frac{2}{19}$$

$$= \frac{38}{6} = 6.33$$

We show this in panel (c) of Exhibit 6–1.

Thus, calculating the price elasticity of demand, using the midpoint (or average) formula, yields $e_d = 6.33$. This calculation is not affected by the direction of movement along the demand curve; that is, $e_d = 6.33$ whether we move up or down the demand curve over the range we have been considering.

Consider the hypothetical data presented in the rest of Exhibit 6–1 for the quantities of OPEC oil demanded by American consumers at various prices. Columns (2) and (4) show the changes in quantities and in prices. Columns (5) and (6) give us the average quantities and the average prices. And finally, in the last column, a numerical example of price elasticity of demand is given.

We see that the computation of elasticity ranges from 21 down to .158. What does that mean? Simply that at very high prices for oil, such as between \$10 and \$9 a barrel, the response to a 1 percent decrease in price will be a 21 percent increase in the quantity demanded. At the other extreme, at relatively low prices for oil—say, between \$2 and \$1 per barrel—the elasticity of .158 means that a 1 percent reduction in price will be followed by only .158 of a 1 percent increase in the quantity demanded. Thus, in our example, elasticity falls as price falls.

Different Kinds of Elasticities

We have names for the varying ranges of price elasticities, depending on whether a 1 percent change in price elicits more or less than a 1 percent change in the quantity demanded:

1. **Elastic demand.** We say that a good has an elastic demand whenever the price elasticity of demand is greater than 1. A 1 percent change in price causes a response greater than 1 percent change in quantity demanded. Candidates for elastic-demand sections of our demand schedule in Exhibit 6–1 are obviously an e of 1.444 and above.
2. **Unitary elasticity of demand.** In this situation, a 1 percent change in price causes a response of exactly 1 percent change in the quantity demanded.

EXHIBIT 6–2

The Relationship Between Price Elasticity of Demand and Total Revenues. Here we reproduce in different form, parts of Exhibit 6–1. In panel (a), we show the elastic, unit elastic, and inelastic sections of the demand schedule according to whether a reduction in price increases total revenues, causes them to remain constant, or causes them to decrease, respectively. In panel (b), we show graphically what happens to total revenues, and we have labeled the sections elastic, unit elastic, and inelastic, which we have also done in the accompanying demand curve shown in panel (c).

Panel (a)

(1) Price of Oil ($ per unit)	(2) Units Demanded (per time period)	(3) Total Revenue $TR = P \times Q$ [(1) × (2)]	(4) Elasticity $e_d = \dfrac{\text{change in } Q / \frac{(Q_1 + Q_2)}{2}}{\text{change in } P / \frac{(P_1 + P_2)}{2}}$	
11	0	0		
			21	elastic
10	1	$10		
			6.333	elastic
9	2	18		
			3.4	elastic
8	3	24		
			2.143	elastic
7	4	28		
			1.444	elastic
6	5	30		
			1	unit elastic
5	6	30		
			.692	inelastic
4	7	28		
			.467	inelastic
3	8	24		
			.294	inelastic
2	9	18		
			.158	inelastic
1	10	10		

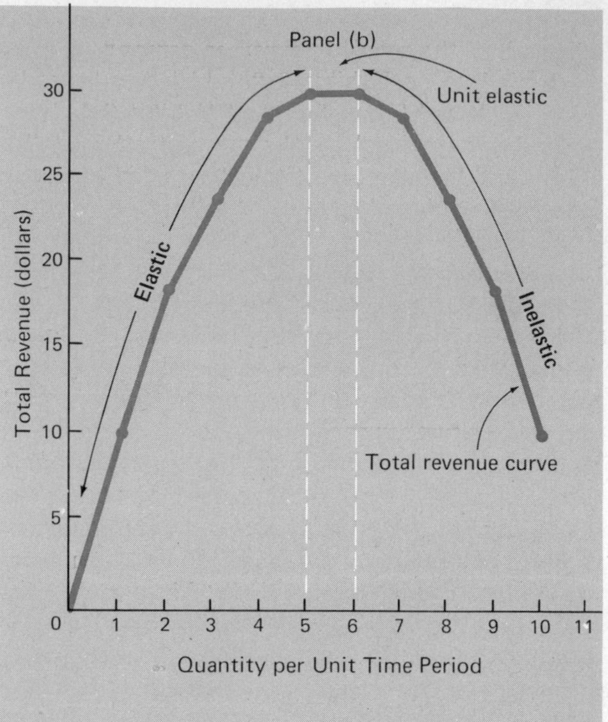

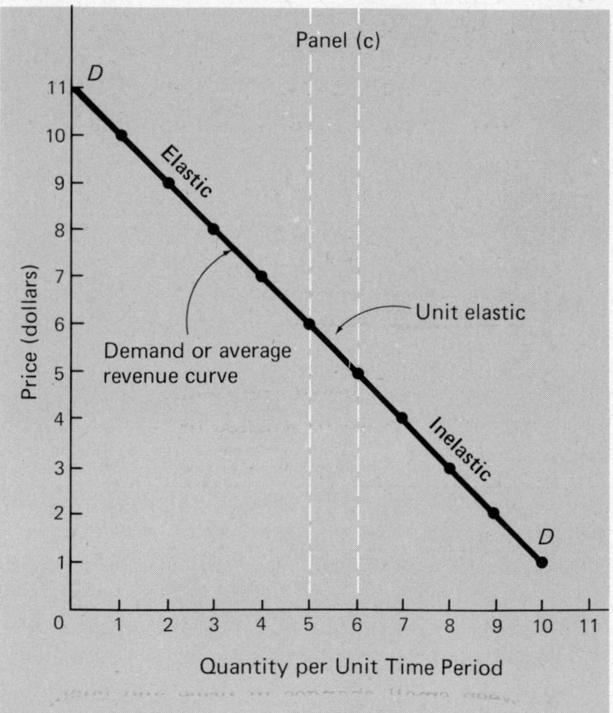

3. **Inelastic demand.** Here, a 1 percent change in price causes a response of less than 1 percent change in quantity demanded. An elasticity of .692 and below in the last four rows of Exhibit 6–1(a), represents a situation of inelastic demand. In brief, a 1 percent change in price causes a less than 1 percent change in quantity demanded.

Elasticity and Total Revenues

We started off this chapter by considering a decision faced by OPEC leaders. Should the price of crude oil be raised and, if so, by how much? Part of the decision rests on what will happen to total revenues for the oil-producing countries as a result of the price change. It is commonly thought that the way to increase total receipts is to increase price per unit. But is this always the case? Is it possible that a rise in price per unit could lead to a decrease in total revenues? The answers to these questions depend on the price elasticity of demand.

Let's look at Exhibit 6–2, which is a reproduction in altered form of part of Exhibit 6–1. In column 1, we again show the price of oil in dollars. Column 2 lists the quantities demanded (we ignore that each value shown is actually in millions, for simplicity's sake). In column 3, we multiply column 1 times column 2 to derive total revenues; and in column 4, we copy the values of elasticity from Exhibit 6–1. Notice what happens to total revenues throughout the schedule. They rise steadily as the price rises from $1 to $5 per unit; then, when the price rises further to $6 per unit, total revenues remain constant at $30. At prices per unit higher than $6, total revenues actually fall as price is increased. So it is not safe to assume that a price hike is always the way to greater revenues. Indeed, if prices are above $6 per unit in this example, total revenues can only be increased by cutting prices—not by raising them.

LABELING ELASTICITY

The relationship between price and quantity on the demand schedule is given in columns 1 and 2 of panel (a) in Exhibit 6–2. In panel (c), the demand curve, *DD*, representing that schedule, is drawn. In panel (b), the total revenue curve representing the data in column 3 is drawn. Notice first the level of these curves at small quantities. The demand curve is at a maximum height, but total revenue is zero, which makes sense according to this demand schedule—at maximum price, no units will be purchased and therefore total revenue will be zero. As price is lowered, we travel down the demand curve, total revenues increase up to a price of $6 per unit, remain constant from $6 to $5 per unit, and then fall for lower unit prices. Corresponding to those three sections, demand is price elastic, unit elastic, and price inelastic. Hence, we have three relationships among the three types of price elasticity and total revenues.

1. **Price elastic demand.** A negative relationship between small changes in price and changes in total revenues. That is to say, if it lowers price, total revenues will rise when the firm faces demand that is price elastic. And if it raises price, total revenues will fall.
2. **Unit price elastic demand.** Small changes in price do not change total revenues. In other words, when the firm is facing demand that is unitary price elastic, if it increases price, total revenues will not change; if it decreases price, total revenues will not change either.
3. **Price inelastic demand.** A positive relationship between small changes in price and total revenue. In other words, when the firm is facing demand that is price inelastic, if it raises price, total revenues will go up; if it lowers price, total revenues will fall.

We can see in Exhibit 6–2 the areas in the demand curve that are elastic, unit elastic, and inelastic. For prices from $11 per unit to $5 per unit, as price decreases, total revenues rise from zero dollars to $30. Clearly, demand is price elastic. When prices change from $6 to $5, however, total revenues remain constant at $30; demand is unit elastic. Finally, when price falls from $5 to $1, total revenue decreases from $30 to $10; demand is price inelastic. In panels (b) and (c) of Exhibit 6–2, we have labeled the sections of the demand curve accordingly, and we have also shown how total revenues first rise, remain constant, and then fall.

The relationship between price elasticity of demand and total revenue brings together some important microeconomic concepts. Total revenue, as we have noted, is the product of price per unit times quantity of units sold. The law of demand states that, along a given demand curve, price and quantity changes will move in opposite directions: one increases as the other decreases. Consequently, what happens to the product of price × quantity depends on which of the opposing changes exerts a greater force on total revenue. But this is just what price elasticity of demand is designed to measure—responsiveness of quantity to a change in price.

The relationship between price elasticity of demand and total revenue, TR, is summarized in Exhibit 6–3.

Concepts in Brief 6-2

- Price elasticity of demand is related to total revenues (and total consumer expenditures).
- When demand is elastic, the change in price elicits a change in total revenues (and total consumer expenditures) in the opposite direction to the price change.
- When demand is inelastic, a change in price elicits a change in total revenues (and in consumer expenditures) in the same direction as the price change.
- When demand is unit elastic, a change in price elicits no change in total revenues (or in total consumer expenditures).

EXHIBIT 6–3
The Relationship Between Elasticity and Total Revenues. Here we show in summary form the relationship between price elasticity of demand and total revenues.

	Price Elastic Demand	Unitary Elastic Demand	Price Inelastic Demand
Price Increase	↑ × ↓ → ↓ P × Q = TR	↑ × ↓ → No change P × Q = TR	↑ × ↓ → ↑ P × Q = TR
Price Decrease	↓ × ↑ → ↑ P × Q = TR	↓ × ↑ → No change P × Q = TR	↓ × ↑ → ↓ P × Q = TR

Changing Price Elasticity

We have seen in the example of the demand for oil that the price elasticity changes as we move along the demand curve. That is to say, price elasticity is high when price is high and low when price is low. (Look again at columns 3 and 7 in Exhibit 6–1(a).) As a general rule, along any demand curve that is a straight line, price elasticity declines as we move down that demand curve. Consider the reason why. In our example in Exhibit 6–1(a), the change in price was always \$1 and the change in the absolute quantity demanded was always 1 million barrels per day. Remember that here we are talking about absolute changes only. What about percentage changes? At the upper end of the demand curve, a \$1 price change is in percentage terms relatively small (\$1/[\$9 + \$10)/2] = 10.5%) whereas the 1 million change in quantity demanded is a large percentage change of the small quantity demanded (1/[(1 + 2)/2] = 66.7%).

Thus, at the top of the demand curve, the elasticity formula will have a large numerator and a small denominator; therefore, price elasticity is relatively elastic (66.7 percent/10.5 percent = 6.33). At the lower end of the curve, the price elasticity formula will have a small numerator and a large denominator; thus, the demand curve is relatively inelastic (10.5 percent/66.7 percent = 0.158).

We can indicate the relationship between price and elasticity very concisely if we use some basic arithmetic manipulations. Recall that the elasticity of demand, e_d, is defined as:

$$e_d = \frac{\text{percentage change in quantity demanded}}{\text{percentage change in price}}$$

$$= \frac{\dfrac{\text{change in quantity demanded}}{\text{original quantity demanded}}}{\dfrac{\text{change in price}}{\text{original price}}}$$

therefore

$$e_d = \frac{\text{change in quantity demanded}}{\text{original quantity demanded}} \times \frac{\text{original price}}{\text{change in price}}$$

$$e_d = \frac{\text{change in quantity demanded}}{\text{change in price}} \times \frac{\text{original price}}{\text{original quantity demanded}}$$

But the slope of a demand curve is given as[2]

$$\text{slope} = \frac{\text{change in price}}{\text{change in quantity demanded}}$$

so

$$e_d = \frac{1}{\text{slope}} \times \frac{\text{original price}}{\text{original quantity demanded}}$$

[2] Refer back to Appendix A on graphical analysis for a refresher explanation on the meaning of slope.

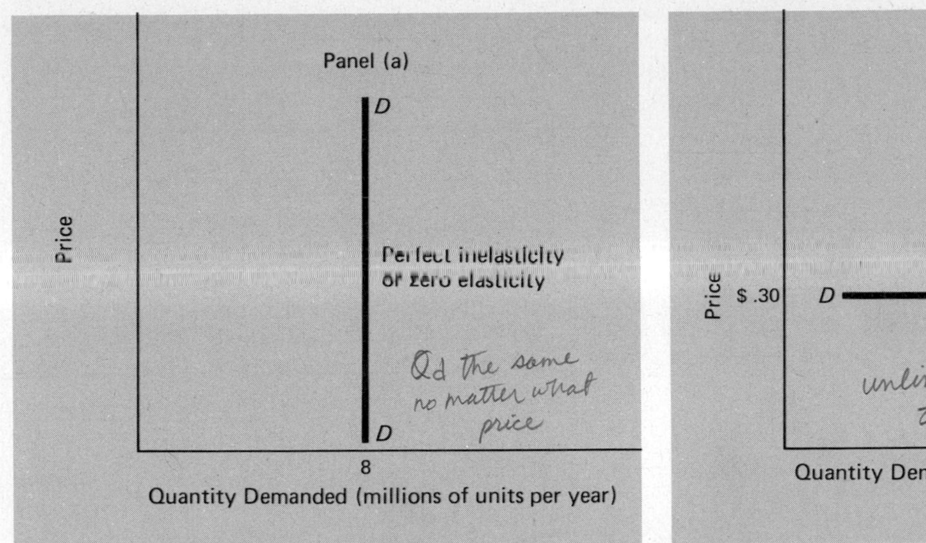

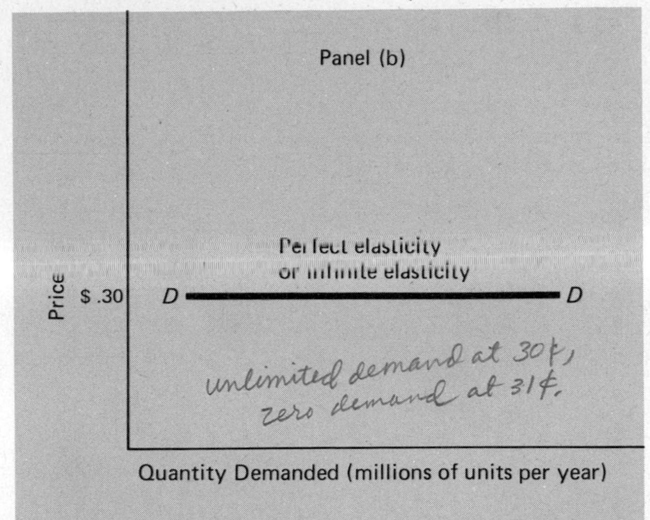

EXHIBIT 6–4
Two Extreme Price Elasticities. In panel (a), we show complete price unresponsiveness. The demand curve is vertical at the quantity of 8 million units per year. That means that price elasticity of demand is zero. Consumers will demand 8 million units of this particular commodity no matter what the price. In panel (b), we show complete price responsiveness. At a price of 30¢ in this example, consumers will demand an unlimited quantity of the particular good in question. This is a case of infinite price elasticity of demand.

Note that because we assumed a linear demand curve, slope (and therefore 1/slope) is a constant. However, as price falls quantity demanded rises; therefore the *ratio* of price to quantity demanded must fall. As price falls we calculate e_d by multiplying a constant (1/slope) times a decreasing ratio (price/quantity demanded); as price falls, e_d falls.

ELASTICITY AND SLOPE

Students often confuse elasticity and slope. As the preceding analysis clearly indicates, however, they are not the same. We demonstrated that along a linear demand curve (that is, a straight line that has a *constant* slope, by definition) elasticity continuously falls with price. As a matter of fact, the calculated elasticity along a downward-sloping *straight-line* demand curve goes numerically from infinity to zero as we move down the curve. We therefore must always specify the *price range* when discussing price elasticity of demand, since most goods have ranges of both elasticity and inelasticity. The only time we can be sure of the elasticity of a straight-line demand curve by looking at it is if it is either perfectly horizontal or perfectly vertical. The horizontal straight-line demand curve has infinite elasticity at every quantity (it has only one price for every quantity). The vertical demand curve has zero elasticity at every price (it has only one quantity demanded at every price). Then we know that it has infinite elasticity or zero elasticity, respectively.

EXTREME ELASTICITIES

There are two extremes in price elasticities of demand: one is total unresponsiveness, which is called a *perfectly inelastic demand* situation or zero elasticity, and the other is complete responsiveness, which is called an unlimited, infinite, or *perfectly elastic demand* situation.

We show perfect inelasticity in panel (a) of Exhibit 6–4. Notice that the quantity demanded per year is 8 million units, no matter what the price. Hence, for any percentage price change, the quantity demanded will remain the same, and thus the change in the quantity demanded will be zero. Look at our formula for computing elasticity. If the change in the quantity demanded is zero, then the numerator is also zero, and anything divided into zero results in an answer of zero, too. Hence, perfect inelasticity.

At the opposite extreme is the situation depicted in panel (b) of Exhibit 6–4. Here we show that at a price of 30¢, an unlimited quantity will be demanded. At a price that is only slightly above 30¢, none will be demanded. In other words, there is complete, or infinite, responsiveness here, and hence we call the demand schedule in panel (b) of Exhibit 6–4 infinitely elastic.

Most estimated demand-schedule elasticities lie between the two extremes. For example, in Exhibit 6–5 we present demand elasticities for selected goods. None of them is zero, and the largest one is 4.6—a far cry from infinity. Remember, again, that even though we are leaving off the negative sign, there is an inverse relationship between price and quantity demanded and that the minus sign is implicit. Also, remember that these elasticities represent average elasticities over *given* price ranges. Presumably, different price ranges would yield different elasticity estimates for these goods.

EXHIBIT 6–5
Demand Elasticity for Selected Goods. Here we have obtained the estimated demand elasticities for selected goods. All of them are negative, although we have not shown a minus sign. For example, the price elasticity of demand for shoes is .4. That means that a 1 percent increase in the price of shoes will bring about a .4 percent decrease in the quantity of shoes demanded.

	Estimated Elasticity
Food Items:	
White potatoes	.3
Green peas, fresh	2.8
Green peas, canned	1.6
Tomatoes, fresh	4.6
Tomatoes, canned	2.5
Other Nondurable Goods:	
Shoes	.4
Stationery	.5
Newspapers and magazines	.1
Gasoline and oil, short-run	.2
long-run	.7
Durable Goods:	
Kitchen appliances	.6
China and tableware	1.1
Jewelry and watches	.4
Automobiles, long-run	.2
Tires, short-run	.4
long-run	.6
Radio and television receivers	1.2
Sports equipment, boat, pleasure aircraft, short-run	.6
long-run	1.3
Services:	
Physicians' services	.6
Legal services	.5
Taxi	.4
Rail commuting	.7
Airline travel, short-run	.06
long-run	2.4
Foreign travel, short-run	.7
long-run	4.0

Sources: H. S. Houthakker and L. D. Taylor, *Consumer Demand in the United States, 1929–1970* (Cambridge, Mass.: Harvard University Press, 1966); U.S. Department of Agriculture, 1954; and H. Schultz, *Theory and Measurement of Demand* (Chicago: University of Chicago Press, 1938).

Concepts in Brief 6-3

- The price elasticity of demand changes as we move down a straight-line demand curve; it becomes relatively more inelastic.
- Price elasticity of demand cannot be determined by looking at the *slope* of a straight-line demand curve. There are two extreme exceptions:
- When a demand curve is perfectly vertical, it has zero price elasticity of demand; it is completely inelastic.
- When a demand curve is perfectly horizontal, it has completely elastic demand; its price elasticity of demand is infinite.

Constant Price Elasticity of Demand

It is possible to have a demand curve that actually curves such that price elasticity of demand is constant. We give just one example in Exhibit 6–6.

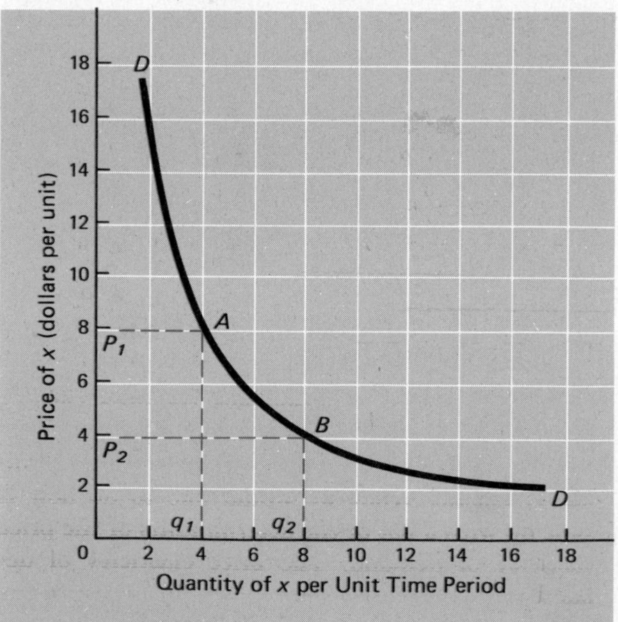

EXHIBIT 6–6
Constant Price Elasticity of Demand. If the demand curve is curved in such a way that total revenues (and consumer expenditures) remain constant no matter what the price, then we have a demand curve that is everywhere unit elastic. This is what we show here.

That demand curve, *DD*, exhibits unitary elasticity at any point. We can tell this by using the total revenues approach. At a price of $8 for this product, 4 will be purchased for total revenues of $32. At a price of $4, the quantity demanded will be 8, for total revenues of $32 again. At $2, 16 will be bought for total revenues of $32. A reduction in price leads to no change in total revenues; hence, price elasticity of demand is equal to one. And this is true all along the curve because of its special curved shape. (If we extended *DD* in Exhibit 6–6 outward, it would become a very flat line at the extreme ends, but, nonetheless, the elasticity at the extreme ends would be just the same as anywhere else on the curve.)

The way in which we found out the total revenues is an important tool that you should understand for the rest of this section. Remember the formula for total revenues:

total revenues = price × quantity

Thus, in Exhibit 6–6, we measured total revenues by looking at the *rectangle* formed from the price to the demand curve to the quantity axis. The vertical side of the rectangle was always equal to the price, and the horizontal side of the rectangle was always equal to the quantity. Thus, if asked how to determine total revenue for any price/quantity combination off of a demand curve, you simply form the appropriate rectangle. The *area* of that rectangle is equal to total revenues for the particular quantity under consideration.

The Determinants of the Price Elasticity of Demand

We have learned how to calculate the price elasticity of demand. We know that it ranges numerically from zero—completely inelastic—to infinity—completely elastic. What we would like to do now is come up with a list of the *determinants* of the price elasticity of demand. The price elasticity of demand for a particular commodity at any price depends on, at a minimum, the following:

1. The existence and closeness of substitutes.
2. The "importance" of the commodity in the consumer's total budget.
3. The length of time allowed for adjustment to changes in the price of the commodity.

EXISTENCE OF SUBSTITUTES

The closer the substitutes for a particular commodity, the greater will be its price elasticity of demand. At the limit, if there is a perfect substitute, the price elasticity of the commodity will be infinity. Thus, even the slightest increase in the commodity's price will cause an enormous reduction in the quantity demanded; quantity demanded will fall to zero. We are really talking about two goods that the consumer believes are exactly alike and equally desirable, like dollar bills, whose only difference is serial numbers. When we talk about less extreme examples, we can only speak in terms of the number and the closeness of substitutes that are available. Thus, we will find that the more narrowly we define a good, the closer and greater will be the number of substitutes available. Take an example. If we talk about food and drinks in general, there aren't many substitutes. If we talk about tea, there are certainly lots of substitutes, including coffee, milk, soft drinks, and so on. Thus, the more narrowly we define the good, the more substitutes there are available and the greater will be the price elasticity of demand. In this example, the price elasticity of demand for all beverages will be numerically much less than it is for, say, Constant Comment tea. If the price of Constant Comment tea increased by 20 percent, a lot of people might switch over to another brand of tea. On the other hand, if the price of all beverages went up on average by 20 percent, certainly a smaller percentage of beverage consumers would switch over to beverage substitutes, such as food or recreation or whatever else might conceivably be considered a substitute for beverages.

THE IMPORTANCE OF THE COMMODITY IN THE CONSUMER'S BUDGET

If we mean by *importance* the percentage of total expenditures that the individual allocates to a particular commodity, we can speculate that the greater the *percentage* of a total budget spent on the commodity, the greater the person's price elasticity of demand for that commodity. The demand for salt is thought to be very inelastic merely because individuals spend so little on it relative to their total budgets. In contrast, the demand for things like transportation and housing is thought to be certainly more elastic because they occupy a large part of people's budgets—changes in their prices cannot be so easily ignored without sacrificing a lot of other alternative goods that could be purchased.

Consider a numerical example. A household earns $20,000 a year. It purchases $20 of pepper per year and $2,000 of transportation services. Now consider the spending power of this family when the price of pepper and the price of transportation both go up by 100 percent. If the household buys the same amount of pepper, it will now spend $40. It thus will have to reduce other expenditures by $20. This $20 represents only one-tenth of 1 percent of the entire household budget. On the other hand, a doubling of transportation costs requires that the family spend $4,000, or $2,000 *more* in transportation if it is to purchase the same quantity. That increased expenditure on transportation of $2,000 represents 10 percent of total expenditures that must be switched from other purchases. We predict that the household will react differently to the doubling of prices for pepper than it will for transportation. It will buy about the same amount of pepper, but will spend less on transportation.

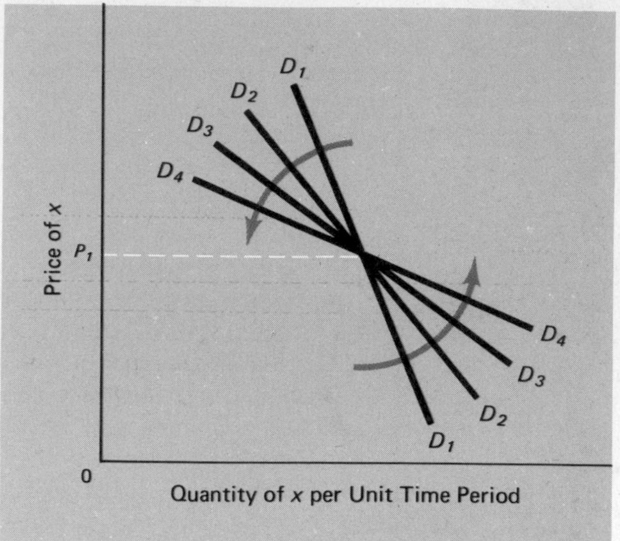

EXHIBIT 6–7
Long- and Short-Run Price Elasticities of Demand. The longer the time allowed for adjustment, the greater the price elasticity of demand. We therefore have a whole family of demand curves, depending on the time allowed for adjustment. D_1D_1 is a demand curve for a shorter adjustment period than D_4D_4. At prices slightly above or below P_1, the steeper the slope, the less the elasticity, and vice versa.

THE TIME FOR ADJUSTMENT IN RATE OF PURCHASE

When the price of a commodity changes and that price change persists, more people will learn about it. Further, consumers will be better able to revise their consumption patterns, the longer the time they have to do so. And, in fact, the longer the time they do take, the less costly it will be for them to engage in this revision of consumption patterns. Consider a price decrease. The longer the time that the price decrease persists, the greater will be the number of new *uses* that consumers will "discover" for the particular commodity, and the greater will be the number of new *users* of that particular commodity.

It is possible to make a very strong statement about the relationship between the price elasticity of demand and the time allowed for adjustment: *The longer any price change persists, the greater the price elasticity of demand.* Otherwise stated, price elasticity of demand is greater in the long run than in the short run.

Let's take an example. Suppose the price of electricity goes up 50 percent. How do you adjust in the short run? You can turn the lights off more often, you can stop running the stereo as much as you used to, and so on. Otherwise, it's very difficult to cut back on your consumption of electricity. In the long run, though, you can devise methods to reduce your consumption. Instead of using electric heaters, the next time you have a house built you will install gas heaters. Instead of using an electric stove, the next time you move you will have a gas stove installed. You will purchase fluorescent bulbs because they use less electricity. The longer you have to figure it out, the more ways you will find to cut electricity consumption. We would expect, therefore, that the short-run demand curve for electricity would be highly inelastic (in the price range around P_1), as demonstrated by D_1D_1 in Exhibit 6–7. However, the long-run demand curve may exhibit much more elasticity (in the neighborhood of P_1), as demonstrated by D_4D_4. Indeed, we can think of an entire family of demand curves such as those depicted in that diagram. The short-run demand curve is for that period when there is no time for adjustment. As more time is allowed, the demand curve becomes flatter, going first to D_2D_2 and then all the way to D_4D_4. Thus, *in the neighborhood of* P_1, elasticity differs for each of these curves. It is greater for the less-steep curves (but remember, slope alone does not measure elasticity for the *entire* curve).

> ***Concepts in Brief 6-4***
>
> ■ Demand curves can be linear or nonlinear. Linear demand curves have constantly changing elasticities as we move along them. Nonlinear demand curves *may* be drawn with constant elasticities of any desired value. We have constructed one that exhibits unit elasticity everywhere on the curve.
>
> ■ The determinants of price elasticity of demand are: (1) the number and closeness of substitutes, (2) the percentage of the total budget spent on the good in question, and (3) the length of time allowed for adjustment to a change in prices.

Elasticity of Supply

The **price elasticity of supply** is defined in a similar way as the price elasticity of demand. Supply elasticities are generally positive; this is because the law of supply indicates that at higher prices, larger quantities will be forthcoming from suppliers. Our definition of the price elasticity of supply, e_s, is the following:

$$e_s = \frac{\textbf{percentage change in quantity supplied}}{\textbf{percentage change in price}}$$

We use some hypothetical data to illustrate the price elasticity of supply for oil. This is done in Exhibit 6-8. Note that the price elasticity of supply remains constant and equal to one in this particular example. This is a special feature of any *straight-line* supply curve that passes through the origin, that is, whose intercept is zero.[3]

CLASSIFYING SUPPLY ELASTICITIES

Just as with demand, there are different types of supply elasticities. They are similar in definition.

If a 1 percent increase in price elicits a greater than 1 percent increase in the quantity supplied, we say that at the particular price in question on the supply schedule *supply is elastic.*

If, on the other hand, a 1 percent increase in price elicits a less than 1 percent increase in the quantity supplied, we refer to that as an *inelastic supply* situation.

If the percentage change in the quantity supplied is just equal to the percentage change in the price, then we talk about *unitary elasticity of supply.*

We show in Exhibit 6-9 two supply schedules, *SS* and *S′S′*. Can you tell at a glance, without reading the caption, which one is infinitely elastic and which one is perfectly inelastic?

As you might expect, most supply schedules exhibit elasticities that are somewhere between the range of zero to infinity.

PRICE ELASTICITY OF SUPPLY AND LENGTH OF TIME FOR ADJUSTMENT

We pointed out earlier that the longer the time allowed for adjustment, the greater the price elastic-

[3] If the straight-line supply curve has a vertical intercept, then price elasticity of supply is greater than 1 (elastic throughout); if a straight-line supply curve intersects the horizontal axis, then its price elasticity of supply is less than 1 (inelastic throughout).

EXHIBIT 6–8

Calculating the Price Elasticity of Supply for Oil. We use some hypothetical data to demonstrate how to calculate price elasticity of supply. We use the midpoint, or average, formula. Column 2 gives the change in quantity of oil supplied derived from column 1. Column 4 gives the change in price derived from column 3. Columns 5 and 6 give the average quantity and price values. Column 7 presents the price elasticity of supply, which is constant and equal to one because the curve intercepts the origin.

(1) Quantity Supplied (millions)	(2) Change in Q (millions)	(3) Price	(4) Change in P	(5) $\frac{Q_1 + Q_2}{2}$	(6) $\frac{P_1 + P_2}{2}$	(7) $e_s = \frac{\text{change in } Q}{(Q_1 + Q_2)/2} \Big/ \frac{\text{change in } P}{(P_1 + P_2)/2}$
0		$.00				
	2		$.10	1	$.05	(2/1) ÷ (.10/.05) = 1.00
2		.10				
	2		.10	3	.15	(2/3) ÷ (.10/.15) = 1.00
4		.20				
	2		.10	5	.25	(2/5) ÷ (.10/.25) = 1.00
6		.30				
	2		.10	7	.35	(2/7) ÷ (.10/.35) = 1.00
8		.40				
	2		.10	9	.45	(2/9) ÷ (.10/.45) = 1.00
10		.50				

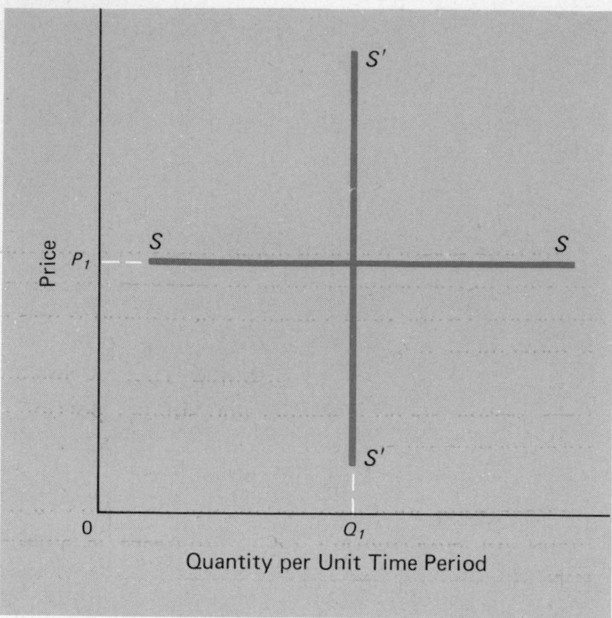

EXHIBIT 6–9
The Extremes in Supply Curves. Here we have drawn two extremes of supply schedules: *SS is a perfectly elastic supply curve, S′S′ is a perfectly inelastic one.* In the former, an unlimited quantity will be forthcoming at the price P_1. In the latter, no matter what the price, the quantity supplied will be Q_1. An example of $S'S'$ might be the supply curve for fresh fish on the morning the boats come in.

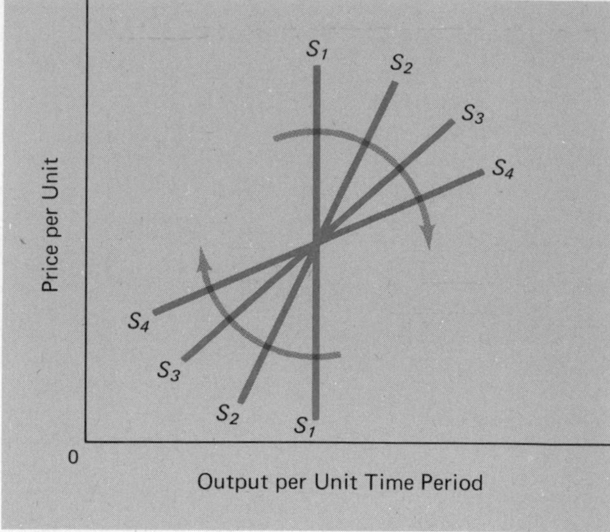

EXHIBIT 6–10
Short- and Long-Run Supply Curves. In the very short run, the quantity supplied cannot respond to a change in price, so the supply curve is S_1S_1. As more time is allowed for adjustment, the supply curve becomes more elastic, moving to S_2S_2, S_3S_3, and, finally, to S_4S_4.

ity of demand. It turns out that the same proposition applies to supply. The longer the time for adjustment, the more price elastic is the supply curve. Consider why this is true:

1. The longer the time allowed for adjustment, the more firms are able to figure out ways to increase production in an industry.

2. The longer the time allowed, the more resources can flow into an industry through expansion of existing firms.

We therefore talk about short- and long-run price elasticities of supply. The short run is defined as the time period during which full adjustment has not yet taken place. Thus, the long run is the time period during which firms have been able to adjust fully to the change in price.

Consider an example—an increase in the price of housing. In the very short run, when there is no time allowed for adjustment, the amount of housing services offered for rent or for sale is relatively inelastic. However, as more time is allowed for adjustment, current owners of the housing stock can find ways to increase the amount of housing services they will offer for rent from given buildings. The owner of a large house can decide, for example, to have two of his or her children move into one room so that a "new" extra bedroom can be rented out. This can also be done by the owner of a large house who decides to move into an apartment and rent each floor of the house to a family. Thus, the quantity of housing services supplied will increase. We can show a whole set of supply curves similar to the ones we generated for demand. In Exhibit 6–10 when nothing can be done in the short run, the supply curve is vertical, S_1S_1. As more time is allowed for adjustment, the supply curve rotates to S_2S_2, S_3S_3, and then S_4S_4, becoming more elastic as it rotates.

Real-World Estimates of Price Elasticity of Supply

We were able to give some real-world estimates of the price elasticity of demand. In Exhibit 6–11, we give some real-world estimates of the price elasticity of supply for both the short and the long run.

EXHIBIT 6–11
Estimated Price Elasticities of Supply.

Commodity	ELASTICITY e_s Short Run	Long Run
Cabbage	0.36	1.20
Carrots	0.14	1.00
Cucumbers	0.29	2.20
Onions	0.34	1.00
Green peas	0.31	4.40
Tomatoes	0.16	0.90
Watermelons	0.23	0.48
Beets	0.13	1.00
Cauliflower	0.14	1.10
Celery	0.14	0.95
Eggplant	0.16	0.34
Spinach	0.20	4.70

Source: M. Nerlove and W. Addison, "Statistical Estimation of Long-Run Elasticities of Supply and Demand," *American Journal of Agricultural Economics* (formerly *Journal of Farm Economics*), Vol. 40 (November 1958), pp. 861–880.

Notice that most short-run elasticities are considerably less than their long-run counterparts. Clearly, then, it is important to distinguish between short- and long-run price elasticities. A policymaker who looks only at the short-run price elasticity of supply, for example, will incorrectly predict changes in supplies in the future, and therefore an improper policy decision might be made.

> ***Concepts in Brief 6-5***
>
> - Price elasticity of supply is given by the percentage change in quantity supplied divided by the percentage change in price.
> - Usually, price elasticities of supply are positive—higher prices yield larger quantities supplied.
> - Long-run supply curves are more elastic than short-run supply curves because the longer the time allowed, the more resources can flow into or out of an industry when price changes.

Income Elasticity of Demand

In Chapter 3, we talked about the determinants of demand. One of those determinants was income. Briefly, we can apply our understanding of elasticity to the relationship between changes in income and changes in demand. We measure the responsiveness of quantity demanded to income changes by the **income elasticity of demand:**

$$e_r = \textbf{income elasticity of demand} = \frac{\textbf{percentage change in the amount of good purchased}}{\textbf{percentage change in income}}$$

We will denote the income elasticity of demand by e_r.

Income elasticity of demand refers to a *horizontal shift* in the demand curve in response to changes in income (while price elasticity of demand refers to a movement *along* the curve in response to price changes). We know, for example, that as income rises, people spend a smaller and smaller portion of total income on supermarket food purchases and a rising portion of their income on recreation. Thus, we have some idea that the income elasticity of demand for supermarket food purchases is smaller than the income elasticity of demand for purchases of recreation. What we would like to do now is to be able to calculate income elasticity of demand.

A simple example will demonstrate how income elasticity of demand can be computed. In Exhibit 6–12, we give the relevant data. The product in question is stereo records. We assume that the price of stereo records remains constant relative to other prices. In period 1, six records per month are purchased. Income per month is \$200. In period 2, monthly income is increased to \$300 and the quantity of records demanded per month is increased to eight. We can apply the following calculation:

$$\textbf{income elasticity of demand} = e_r$$

$$= \frac{(8-6)/6}{(300-200)/200} = \frac{\frac{1}{3}}{\frac{1}{2}} = \frac{2}{3} = .667$$

Hence, measured income elasticity of demand for record albums for the individual represented in this example is .667. Note that this holds only for the move from six records to eight records purchased per month. In the move for decreased income from

EXHIBIT 6–12
How Income Affects Quantity of Records Demanded.

Time Period	Quantity of Stereo Albums Demanded per Month	Income per Month
Period 1	6	\$200
Period 2	8	\$300

\$300 to \$200 per month and from eight to six records per month, the calculation becomes:

$$\frac{(6-8)/8}{(200-300)/300} = \frac{-2/8}{-100/300} = \frac{-\frac{1}{4}}{-\frac{1}{3}} = \frac{3}{4} = .75$$

Thus, the measured income elasticity of demand is equal to .75.

To get the same income elasticity of demand over the same range of values, regardless of which direction the change (increase or decrease), we can use the same midpoint formula that we used in computing the price elasticity of demand. When doing so, we have the following:

$$e_r = \frac{\dfrac{\text{change in quantity}}{\text{sum of quantities}/2}}{\dfrac{\text{change in income}}{\text{sum of incomes}/2}}$$

ISSUES AND APPLICATIONS

The Short and the Long of Rent Control

> *Concepts Applied*
>
> ■ The law of demand and supply, and short- versus long-run price elasticity of supply

There has been rent control in New York City for a long time. Many argue that it is necessary in order to provide low-cost housing to city residents. Others contend that rent control creates more problems than it solves. The issue at hand really turns out to concern the *long-run* price elasticity of supply of housing.

Before we tell this story, it will help to describe briefly the way in which a market adjusts to changes in supply and demand both in the short run and in the long run. By the short run, we mean a period of time that is too short for the building of new housing units. Now that does not mean that the supply is perfectly inelastic. Why not? The answer is that a higher price for housing will encourage people who own homes or housing units to be willing to rent part of the units out rather than keep them all for themselves. Therefore, there is some short-run elasticity of supply. A shift in demand, reflecting (as it did in New York City in wartime) a sudden increase in the number of people seeking apartments, would lead to a sharp rise in price and some increase in the quantity of units available.

Long-Run Effects

The consequence, in the long run, is to set in motion the forces that make for a new equilibrium, which is the heart of the way in which a market system works. The sharp rise in the price of apartments makes it very attractive for people to invest their money in building new housing. Additionally, the use of land will change. As rents go higher, the profitability of putting up high-rise apartment buildings with numerous rental units increases relative to the profitability of putting up smaller buildings with fewer rental units. Therefore, more capital will flow into high-rise apartment buildings. To put it another way, the rate of return for investing in the housing stock has increased as compared to other ways investors could use their capital. This results in new construction, which in turn leads to a downward movement in the price of housing as the supply increases, until ultimately an equilibrium is reached. Note, therefore, that the implication is that the long-run supply of housing is relatively elastic under these conditions in contrast to the short run. The long-run equilibrium is one in which the rate of return on investing in one more unit of housing is just equal to that of investing in any other similar economic activity with the same degree of risk. Now back to our story of housing in New York City.

Skirting controls. The federal government imposed rent control as a temporary wartime measure in 1943. While the federal program ended after the war, it was continued in New York City (and in a few other locations). The law in the city kept rent for certain categories of existing apartments at fixed levels, allowing a 15 percent increase in rent only when a tenant moved out. Needless to say, an immediate consequence was that landlords tended to encourage such departures in any way, from pounding on the pipes to cutting off the heat. Since there were many more people wanting apartments than there were apartments available, a longer-run consequence was the development of a vast array of devices to attempt to get around the restrictions. The most obvious was what was called key money, which was a way to charge a prospective renter a larger amount of money simply to get a key to the apartment. Or one could hire the landlord's son to repaint the apartment at a substantial fee. In still other cases, the landlord would discriminate among prospective tenants on the basis of race, religion, dogs, children, or whatever. Still another consequence was that landlords simply failed to maintain apartments. Another device was that tenants would inform someone about the then-current tenant's intentions to move. In exchange for that information, the person receiving it would "buy" the furniture in the apartment at prices exceeding the furniture's market value.

All of these policies, of course, suggest that landlords and tenants were simply finding a way to get around the artificially low price and in fact move toward a de facto equilibrium. That is, the real value of apartments deteriorated and fell and/or the tenant in fact paid an extra price. One obvious consequence was that there was widespread noncompliance with the law. Thus, laws were passed in an attempt to force landlords to maintain apartments, but these were widely evaded. Similarly, there were laws passed that were designed to prevent subletting for higher prices. And these, too, were widely evaded; so much so that a 1960 survey showed that 25 percent of renters were paying more than was legal for the rent-controlled apartments. Note that this did not include bribes or cuts in quality. These were simply people paying above the amount stipulated. What we observe in such cases is that the market does seek its own equilibrium.

In the long-run rent control can result in deterioration of housing. The landlord cannot afford the increasing costs to make necessary repairs because his rent income remains fixed.

Apartments abandoned. That the market seeks its own equilibrium does not mean that there are not significant consequences for renter and landlord. Clearly, the landlord suffers in terms of a drop in income, and a renter suffers in terms of a quality reduction in apartments. But that is not nearly the end of the story. As of 1975, some 642,000 apartments in New York City were rent controlled. Another 650,000 were covered by another complex form of regulation called rent stabilization. During the whole period since World War II, there has been almost no construction of apartments that would be subject to rent control. Moreover, apartments deteriorated because it was not worthwhile for landlords to maintain them. Eventually the annual taxes on the apartment houses exceeded the income that the landlord could receive and the apartments were simply abandoned. In 1970, 33,000 housing units were abandoned in that year alone. And as late as 1974, 10,000 were abandoned in one year. In some parts of the Bronx and on Manhattan's lower East Side, whole rows of abandoned apartment houses stood gutted and stripped by vandals. During his tenure in office as president, Carter made a highly publicized walking tour of the South Bronx area, commenting to the press and the public about the horrors that he saw. He promised to get the federal government to help rebuild that area but was unsuccessful in following through.

Thus, the long-run consequences in New York City have been a decay in the housing stock and a decline in the amount of available space for middle- and lower-income tenants (luxury apartments that were exempted from rent control have continued to be built).

Questions

1. What is the difference between the short- and the long-run price elasticity of supply of housing services?
2. Who benefits most from effective rent controls?

Is Water Different?

Concepts Applied

■ Law of demand, short- versus long-run price elasticity of demand

The water industry is one of the oldest and largest in the United States. The philosophy surrounding the water industry bears some analysis. Many commentators believe that water is unique, that it should not be treated as an economic good, that is, a scarce good. Engineering studies that concern themselves with demand for residential water typically use a "requirements" approach. The forecaster simply predicts population changes and then multiplies those estimates by the currently available data showing the average amount of water used per person. The underlying assumption for such a forecast is that no matter what the price charged for water in the future, the same quantity will be demanded. Implicitly, then, both the short- and long-run price elasticities of demand are assumed to be zero.

Flat Rate Versus Metered Rate: A Case Study

Many residential water systems charge a flat monthly rate. Each household pays a specified amount of dollars per month no matter how much water is used. This was the case in Boulder, Colorado, prior to 1961.

An alternative approach to determine the amount of payment for water involves using meters at each residence. In 1961, in Boulder, Colorado, the water utility had water meters installed in every home (and business) that it supplied. Each residence was charged 35¢ per thousand gallons of water used. In essence, the flat fee charged prior to 1961 meant that a zero price was charged at the margin (for any incremental use of water). Since a rate per thousand gallons was charged, a positive price for the marginal unit of water was now imposed.

Economist Steve Hanke looked at the quantity of water demanded both before and after the meters were installed in Boulder.[4] Hanke first developed what he calls "ideal" use of water for each month throughout the year. He completed his "ideal" use estimates by taking account of average irrigable area per residence, the average temperature during the month, the average number of daylight hours, and the effect of rainfall. The term *ideal* implies nothing from an economic point of view, but rather indicates the minimum quantity of sprinkling water required to maintain the aesthetic quality of each residence's lawn.

What the Data Show

Looking at the different physical routes (each one was numbered), we find in Exhibit 6–13 that

[4] "Demand for Water under Dynamic Conditions," *Water Resources Research*, Vol. 6, No. 5 (October 1970): 1253–1261.

EXHIBIT 6–13
Comparing Water Usage with and without Metering of Actual Usage. In this table we show the results of imposing a metering system that charged consumers in Boulder, Colorado, according to the actual quantity of water utilized. Column 1 presents the arbitrarily assigned meter route numbers; column 2 shows how much water was used before metering; and column 3 shows how much water was used after metering. Water usage is expressed as a percentage of "ideal" sprinkling, which was calculated on the basis of number of days of sun, area to be sprinkled, and so forth.

(1) Meter Routes	(2) Actual Sprinkling to Ideal Sprinkling, Flat Rate Period	(3) Actual Sprinkling to Ideal Sprinkling, Metered Rate Period
16, 18	128	78
37	175	72
53, 54	156	72
70, 71, 72	177	63
73, 75	175	97
74	175	102
76, 78	176	105
79	157	86

Source: Steve Hanke, "Demand for Water under Dynamic Conditions," *Water Resources Research*, Vol. 6, No. 5 (October 1970).

individuals sprinkled their lawns much more under a flat-rate system than they did under a metered-rate system. These data presented in column 3 in Exhibit 6–13 are for a one-year period after the metering system was put into effect.

In column 1, we see the particular meter route numbers that have been arbitrarily assigned by the municipality. Column 2 shows how much water was used in the different routes during the period when a flat rate was charged for water usage, irrespective of the quantity of usage. It is expressed in terms of actual sprinkling compared to "ideal" sprinkling. In column 3, actual sprinkling is compared to "ideal" sprinkling but under a system of metered-rate pricing in which each user is charged a price commensurate with the actual amount of water used.

These data allow us to test our demand hypothesis, which in effect predicts that if people are faced with the higher price of a commodity, they will demand a smaller quantity. So now the important question is, "Did residential consumers of water for sprinkling go back to their old habits?" Otherwise stated, what was the long-run price elasticity of demand?

The Long-Run Price Elasticity of Demand

One important postulate we gave concerning price elasticities was that the longer the time for adjustment, the greater the price elasticity. It turns out that for Boulder, Colorado, the long-run responsiveness of quantity demanded to a change in the price of water was indeed greater than in the short run. Look at Exhibit 6–14. Here we show the amount of water consumed relative to the "ideal" amount required for keeping lawns green. Right after metering was instituted, the amount used dropped below the "ideal" amount. For several years after that, from 1963 to 1968, it continued to drop. What did that mean? Simply that given the increased cost per thousand gallons of water, the residents of Boulder, Colorado, decided to use less water and have browner lawns.

EXHIBIT 6–14
Actual Sprinkling to Aggregate Ideal Sprinkling. In this figure we show graphically the results of the imposition of a metering system for water usage in Boulder, Colorado. After metering was introduced just prior to 1962, the amount of cumulative sprinkling usage dropped dramatically and remained at the lower rate of usage throughout the period studied. Indeed, usage rate even dropped consistently from 1962 to 1968.

Source: Steve Hanke, *Ibid.*

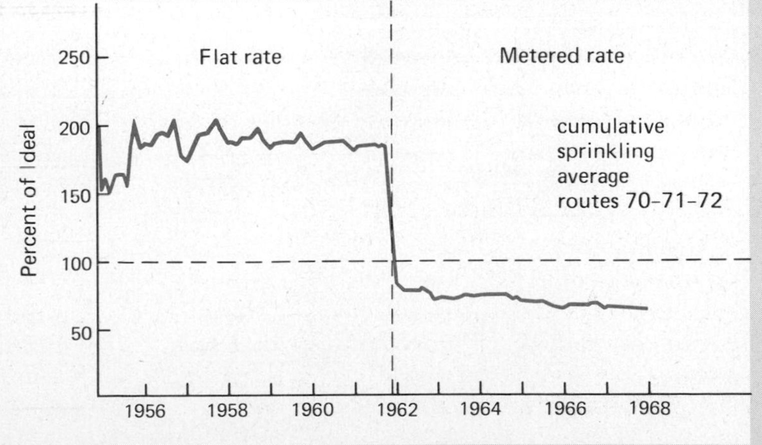

Questions

1. Do the data presented in Exhibits 6–13 and 6–14 refute the "water-is-different" philosophy?
2. If the price elasticity of demand for water in the short run and in the long run were equal, how would Exhibit 6–14 look?
3. Do the data from Boulder, Colorado, give any indication about how water shortages can be solved?

Definition of Terms

Price elasticity of demand The responsiveness of the quantity demanded for a commodity to changes in its price per unit. The price elasticity of demand is defined as the percentage change in quantity demanded divided by the percentage change in price.

Elastic demand A characteristic of a demand curve in which a given percentage change in price will result in a larger percentage change in quantity demanded, in the opposite direction. Total revenues and price are inversely related in the elastic portion of the demand curve.

Unitary elasticity of demand A property of the demand curve, where the quantity demanded changes exactly in proportion to the change in price. Total revenue is invariant to price changes in the unit elastic portion of the demand curve.

Inelastic demand A characteristic of a demand curve in which a given change in price will result in a less-than-proportionate change in the quantity demanded, in the opposite direction. Total revenue and price are directly related in the inelastic region of the demand curve.

Price elasticity of supply The responsiveness of quantity supplied of a commodity to a change in its price. Price elasticity of supply is defined as the percentage change in quantity supplied divided by the percentage change in price.

Income elasticity of demand The percentage change in the quantity demanded divided by the percentage change in money income; the responsiveness of the quantity demanded to changes in income.

Chapter Summary

1. We measure price responsiveness by calculating the price elasticity of demand or the price elasticity of supply.
2. Price elasticity is a measure of percentage change in quantity demanded or supplied relative to the percentage change in price. Therefore, it is a pure number; it has no dimension. Because of the law of demand, price elasticity of demand is always negative.
3. We classify demand as: elastic if a 1 percent change in price leads to a more than 1 percent change in quantity demanded; unit elastic, if exactly 1 percent change in quantity demanded; inelastic, if less than 1 percent change in quantity demanded.
4. We can also classify price elasticity of demand as elastic, unit elastic, and inelastic, depending on whether a decrease in price leads to an increase, no change, or a decrease in total revenues.
5. Price elasticity of demand falls as we move down a straight-line demand curve. It goes from infinity to zero.
6. It is possible to have constant price elasticity of demand along a particular curved demand curve.
7. Elasticity and slope are not equivalent, because the slope of a straight-line curve is always constant, whereas elasticity changes as we move down the straight-line curve.
8. A vertical demand curve is perfectly inelastic; a horizontal demand curve is perfectly elastic.
9. The price elasticity of demand depends on: (a) the existence and closeness of substitutes, (b) the "importance" of the commodity in the total budget, and (c) the length of time allowed for adjustment.
10. The longer the time allowed for adjustment, the greater the price elasticity of demand.
11. Price elasticity of supply is given by the percentage change in quantity supplied divided by the percentage change in price.

12. The greater the time allowed for adjustment, the greater the price elasticity of supply.
13. The income elasticity of demand is given by the percentage change in quantity demanded divided by the percentage change in income.
14. Rent control may have little effect in the short run because the price elasticity of supply of housing is relatively small. However, in the long run, rent control can lead to a decrease in the rate of growth of available housing, thereby ultimately raising the average price of housing in a rent-controlled city.

Selected References

Henderson, Hubert. *Supply and Demand.* Chicago: University of Chicago Press, 1958.
Kaish, Stanley. *Microeconomics: Logic, Tools, and Analysis.* New York: Harper & Row, 1976, chap. 3.
Watson, Donald S., and Malcolm Getz. *Price Theory and Its Uses.* 5th ed. Boston: Houghton Mifflin, 1981, chaps. 3 and 4.

Answers to Preview and Study Questions

1. What is price elasticity of demand?

Price elasticity of demand measures the responsiveness of buyers to changes in price. Granted that buyers will buy less as relative price rises, and more as relative price falls—*how much* less or more? Technically, price elasticity of demand is defined as the percentage change in quantity demanded divided by the percentage change in price; if the absolute value of the resulting coefficient is greater than, equal to, or less than the number one, we refer to demand as elastic, unitary elastic, or inelastic, respectively. Along most demand curves price elasticity of demand changes with price. As a consequence, it is very misleading to refer to a commodity as being price inelastic or price elastic; one should be careful to specify the *price range* when discussing elasticity coefficients. In general, price elasticity of demand falls with price.

2. How is total revenue related to price elasticity of demand?

Total revenue is defined as price times quantity demanded; since price changes lead to changes in quantity demanded, total revenue and elasticity are intimately related. If, over the price range in question, demand is inelastic, this means that buyers are not responsive to price changes. Intuitively then, if price rises and quantity demanded doesn't fall by much, total revenue will rise. On the other hand, if price falls and quantity demanded rises only slightly, total revenue will fall. If, over the price range in question, demand is elastic, then buyers will be quite responsive to price changes. Intuitively, if price rises and quantity demanded falls greatly, then total revenue will fall. Similarly, if price falls and quantity demanded rises greatly, then total revenue will rise. Finally, if we are in the range of unitary elasticity, then given percentage changes in price will lead to equal percentage changes in quantity. Thus, for small price changes, total revenue remains unaffected in the unitary elasticity range.

3. What are the determinants of price elasticity of demand?

Three major determinants of price elasticity of demand are: (a) the existence and closeness of substitutes, (b) the importance of the commodity in the consumer's budget, and (c) the length of time buyers have to react to price changes. Clearly, the more substitutes and the better they are, the higher will be the price elasticity of demand. Thus, price elasticity of demand rises as we consider the commodities "fruit," then "oranges," then "Sunkist oranges"; more and better substitutes exist for a specific brand of oranges than for the fruit group. Also, when a commodity takes up a small percentage of the consumer budget (other things being constant) we expect price elasticity of demand to be relatively lower—as compared to items important to a budget. Presumably buyers will have more incentive to shop around and seek substitutes for high-cost items than for low cost items. Finally, for a given percentage change in price, quantity responsiveness (and therefore elasticity) will increase with the time period allowed for adjustment. With the passage of time buyers are better able to find, and implement the use of, substitutes.

4. What is price elasticity of supply?

Price elasticity of supply refers to the responsiveness of sellers to changes in price. Technically, price elasticity of supply is defined as the percentage change in quantity supplied divided by the percentage change in price. The resulting coefficient can be greater than, equal to, or less than the number one—referred to as elastic, unitary elastic, and inelastic price elasticity of supply, respectively. The longer the period of adjustment time, the greater will be the quantity responsiveness (and therefore the price elasticity of supply) of sellers to given price changes.

5. What is income elasticity of demand?

Income elasticity of demand refers to the responsiveness of buyers to income changes. Technically, income elasticity of demand is defined as the percentage change in quantity demanded divided by the percentage change in income. The resulting coefficient is referred to as being income elastic, unitary elastic, or income inelastic, depending on whether it is greater than, equal to, or less than one. Income elasticity of demand provides one means to classify goods as "necessities" or "luxuries"; presumably, very low-income elastic goods are necessities and high income elastic goods may be thought of as luxuries.

Problems

(Answers at the back of the book)

1. Use the following hypothetical demand schedule for tea to answer the following questions:

Quantity demanded/week	*Price/oz.*	*(Elasticity)*
1,000 oz.	$ 5	
800	10	______
600	15	______
400	20	______
200	25	______

   a. Using the above demand schedule, determine the elasticity of demand for each price change. (Example: when price changes from $5 to $10, quantity demanded changes from 1,000 to 800 oz., so the elasticity of demand, using average values, is 1/3 or .33.)
   b. The data given in the demand schedule would plot as a straight-line demand curve. Why is demand more elastic the higher the price?

2. Calculate the price elasticity of demand for the product below using average values for the prices and quantities in your formula. Over the price range in question, is this demand schedule price inelastic, unitary elastic, or elastic? Is total revenue greater at the lower price or at the higher price?

Price (per unit)	Quantity demanded
$4	22
6	18

3. Calculate the income elasticity of demand for the product below, using average values for incomes and quantities.

Quantity of video tape recorders per year	*Per capita annual group income*
1,000	$15,000
2,000	20,000

   a. Is the demand for this product income elastic or inelastic?
   b. Would you consider this commodity a luxury or a necessity?

7

Consumer Choice

TOPICS FOR REVIEW

The topics listed below, which we have already analyzed, are applied in this chapter. You may find it worthwhile to review them. For your convenience each topic is followed by the number identifying the specific "Concepts in Brief."

a. Marginal analysis (1–3)

b. Demand, income, and substitution effects (3–1)

c. Change in demand versus change in quantity demanded (3–2, 3–3)

FOR PREVIEW AND STUDY

1. What is utility?
2. What is the law of diminishing marginal utility?
3. How does a consumer maximize his or her total utility?
4. What happens to consumer equilibrium when price changes?
5. How can the law of diminishing marginal utility account for the law of demand?

When we first discussed the law of demand in Chapter 3, we gave several reasons why the quantity demanded went up when the price of something went down. We pointed out that as the price of a good falls, individuals will *substitute* some of that good for other things. Additionally, when the price of one good in a consumer's budget goes down with all other prices remaining the same, that person's buying power will actually be greater. A person not only *feels* richer, he or she *is* richer. With a constant money income, when the price of one good falls, the person clearly has more real spending power.

The law of demand is important and so, too, is its derivation, because it allows us to arrange the relevant variables, such as prices, incomes, and tastes, in such a way so as to generate predictions about the real world.

Another way of deriving the law of demand involves an analysis of the logic of consumer choice in a world of limited resources. In this chapter, therefore, we will discuss *utility analysis.* As throughout this book, we will be dealing with a world of scarce resources in which individuals must choose among alternatives.

Utility Theory

When you buy something, you buy it because of the satisfaction you expect to receive from having and using it. For just about everything that you like to have, the more you have of it, the higher the level of satisfaction you receive. Another term can be used for satisfaction—namely, **utility,** or want-satisfying power. This is a property that is common to all goods that are desired. The concept of utility is purely subjective, however. There is no way that you or I can measure the amount of utility that we or another consumer might be able to obtain from a particular good, for utility does not mean "useful" or "utilitarian" or "practical." For this reason, there cannot be true scientific assessment of the utility that someone may receive by consuming, say, a TV dinner or a movie relative to the utility that another person might receive. Furthermore, even though illegal activities may be considered morally wrong by many people, they can still be analyzed in terms of the utility that those activities generate for their consumers.

We can analyze in terms of utility the way consumers decide what to buy, just as physicists have analyzed some of their problems in terms of what they call force. No physicist has ever seen a unit of force, and no economist has ever seen a unit of utility. In both cases, however, these concepts have proven useful for analysis.

Utility and Utils

Economists used to believe that utility could be measured. They therefore first developed utility theory in terms of units of measurable utility, to which they applied the term **util.** Thus, the first chocolate bar that you eat might yield you four utils of satisfaction; the first peanut cluster, six utils; and so on. Today, no one really believes that we can actually measure utils, but the ideas forthcoming from such analysis will prove useful in our understanding of the way in which consumers choose among alternatives.

Total and Marginal Utility

When you consume one bottle of Coca-Cola, you obtain a certain amount of satisfaction, or utility. Let's say that shortly after the first Coke you consume another and then another. With each successive Coke you obtain some additional units of utility. Clearly, the total amount of satisfaction, or utility, that you derive from drinking more Cokes is going up, but what about the additional utility for each Coke?

That additional, or incremental, utility is called **marginal utility,** where *marginal* is another term for incremental, or additional. Understanding the concept of marginal is important in economics, because we make decisions at the margin. This means that at a particular point, we compare additional benefits with additional costs.

The way to understand more clearly the distinction between total utility and marginal utility is to take the specific example presented in Exhibit 7-1. Here we show the total and marginal utility of drinking Cokes. The marginal utility is seen to be the difference between the total utility derived from a specific quantity of Cokes, say, Q, and the total utility derived from one more, $Q + 1$. In our example, when a person already has consumed two Cokes and drinks another, total utility increases from 16 utils to 19. Therefore, the marginal utility (of drinking one more Coke after having already consumed two) is equal to three utils.

EXHIBIT 7–1

Total and Marginal Utility of Cokes. If we were able to assign specific numbers to the utility derived from the consumption of Cokes, we could then obtain a marginal utility schedule that would probably be similar in pattern to the one below. In column 1 is the quantity of Cokes consumed; in column 2, the total utility from each quantity; in column 3, the marginal utility, which is defined as the increment in total utility due to the consumption of one more unit consumed.

(1) Quantity of Good (Cokes per day)	(2) Total Utility (utils per day)	(3) Marginal Utility (utils per day)
0	0	
		10
1	10	
		6
2	16	
		3
3	19	
		1
4	20	
		0
5	20	
		−2
6	18	

GRAPHIC ANALYSIS

We can transfer the information in Exhibit 7–1 into graphic form, which we do in panels (a) and (b) of Exhibit 7–2. Total utility, which is represented in column 2 of Exhibit 7–1, is transferred in blocks (represented by dashed outlines) to Exhibit 7–2(a).

Total utility continues to rise until four Cokes are consumed per day. This measure of utility remains at 20 utils through the fifth Coke, and at the sixth Coke falls to 18 utils because we assume that at *some* quantity consumed, per unit of time, dislike sets in. If we connect the tops of the total utility blocks with a smooth line, we come up with a representation of the total utility curve associated with the consumption of Cokes during a one-day period. This is shown in panel (a) of Exhibit 7–3.

Marginal Utility

If you look carefully at both panels (a) and (b) of Exhibit 7–2, the notion of marginal utility and what it is can be seen very clearly. In economics, marginal always refers to a change in the total. The marginal utility, for example, of consuming three Cokes a day as opposed to two Cokes is the increment in total utility and is equal to three utils per day. Marginal utility is represented by the shaded portion of the blocks in panel (a) of Exhibit 7–2. We

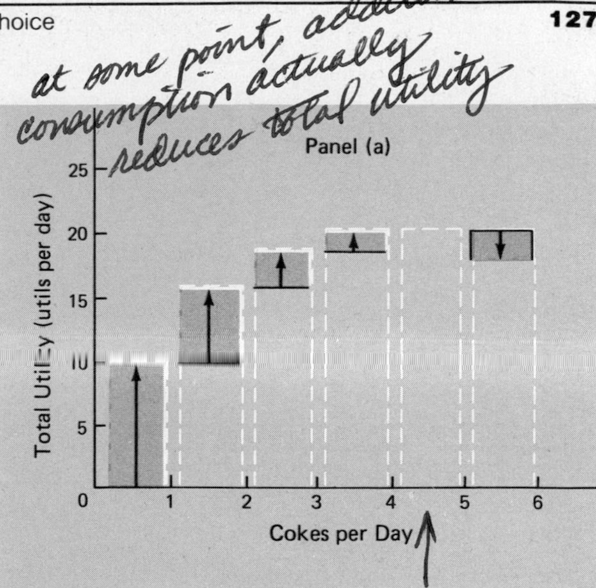

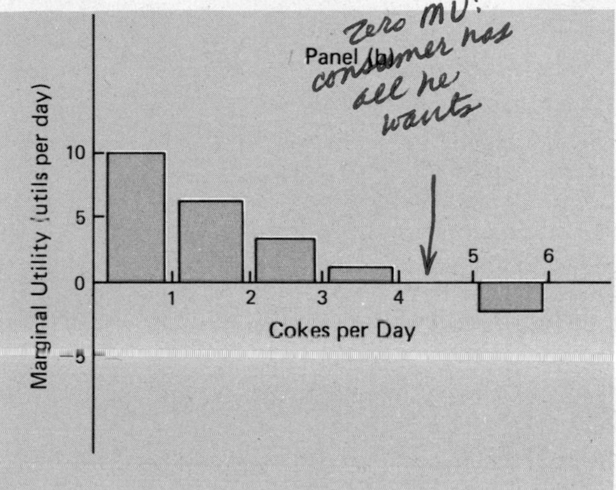

EXHIBIT 7–2

Total and Marginal Utility in Discrete Units. In panel (a), the dashed outline indicates the total utility for each rate of consumption of Cokes per day. The shaded portion of each dashed box indicates the marginal utility for each additional Coke. When we transfer the shaded boxes to panel (b), we have a diagram of discrete marginal utility.

can transfer these shaded portions down to panel (b) of Exhibit 7–2 and come up with a graphic representation of marginal utility. When we connect the tops of these marginal utility rectangles in panel (b) of Exhibit 7–3, we come up with a smoothly sloping marginal utility curve. Notice that that curve hits zero at a consumption rate beyond four Cokes per day. At zero marginal utility, the consumer has all that he or she wants and doesn't want any more. The last unit consumed at zero marginal utility gives the consumer no additional satisfaction, or utility.

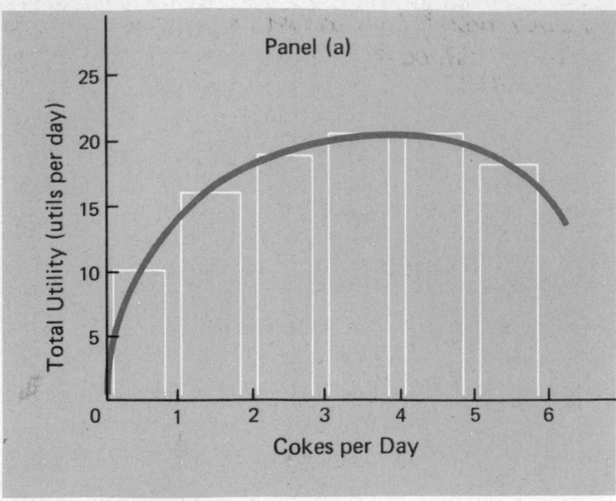

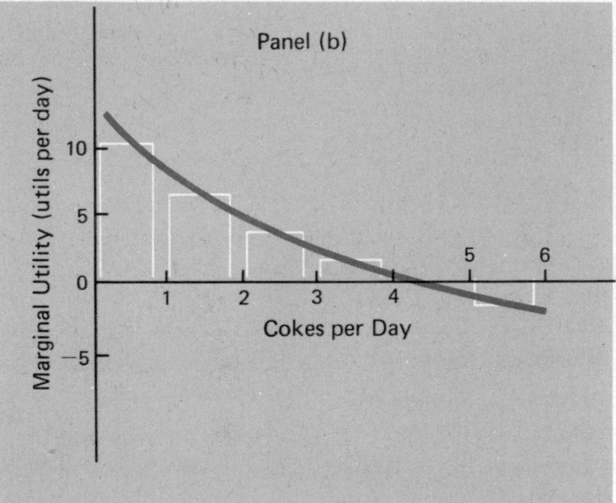

EXHIBIT 7–3

Total and Marginal Utility. If we take the total utility units from column 2 in Exhibit 7–1, we obtain rectangles like those presented in Exhibit 7–2(a). If we connect the tops of those rectangles with a smooth line, we come up with a total utility curve that peaks somewhere between four and five Cokes per day and then slowly declines [panel (a)]. Marginal utility is represented by the increment in total utility, shown as the shaded blocks in Exhibit 7–2(b). When these blocks are connected by a smooth line in panel (b), we obtain the marginal utility curve.

When marginal utility becomes negative, such as it does in this example after the consumption of four Cokes per day, it means that the consumer is fed up with Cokes and will require some form of compensation to drink any more. When marginal utility is negative, the additional unit consumed actually lowers total utility by becoming a "nuisance."

> ***Concepts in Brief 7-1***
>
> - Utility is defined as want-satisfying power; it is a property common to all desired goods and services.
> - We arbitrarily measure units of utility in utils.
> - It is important to distinguish between total utility and marginal utility. Total utility is the total satisfaction derived from the consumption of a given quantity of a good. Marginal utility is the change in total utility due to a one-unit change in the consumption of the good.

Diminishing Marginal Utility

Notice that in panel (b) of Exhibit 7–3, marginal utility is continuously declining. This property of marginal utility has been named **diminishing marginal utility.** There is no way we can prove diminishing marginal utility; nonetheless, economists and laypersons for years have believed strongly in the assertion of diminishing marginal utility. Diminishing marginal utility has even been called a "law." This supposed law concerns a psychological, or subjective, utility that you receive as you consume more and more of a particular good. Stated formally, the law is:

As an individual consumes more of the same good per unit of time, utility increases (up to a point, at least). However, the extra utility added by an extra (marginal) unit of that good does not increase at a constant rate. Rather, as successive new units of the good in question are consumed, after some point the total utility will grow at a slower and slower rate. Otherwise stated, as the amount of a good consumed per unit of time increases, the marginal utility of the good tends to decrease.

HOW DOES THE CONSUMER MAXIMIZE SATISFACTION?

Consider a simple example in which an individual has a specific income and two desired goods on which to spend that income. Should the individual allocate the whole of that income on the first good and none on the second? Should the individual allocate all of the income on the second good and none on the first? Or should the individual choose to be somewhere between those two extremes? In many cases, the answer is that the individual chooses to consume some of each good. We observe this in the real world. Now, how can we explain it?

If we start with the assumption that the consumer wishes to maximize total satisfaction, or utility, then we can derive a way to view his or her behavior. Only when the consumer is maximizing total utility will he or she be in equilibrium. Remember that equilibrium is a situation from which there is no tendency to change. Do you think equilibrium will occur when the marginal utility you received from the last bottle of Coke you bought equals the marginal utility you received from the last pair of blue jeans you purchased? Probably not, for the price of a pair of blue jeans is usually much higher than the price of a bottle of Coke.

Wouldn't it make more sense if the marginal utility received from the last dollar spent on each item in a person's budget were equal all around? That way, the individual would be assured that there is no way to increase further total utility for a given level of income by reallocating expenditures in any other way. After all, if the marginal utility received from the last dollar spent on Cokes is greater than the marginal utility received for the last dollar spent on blue jeans, the consumer could increase total utility by spending less on blue jeans and more on Cokes, that is, by adjusting his or her spending pattern accordingly.

Let's take a purely hypothetical numerical example. You have a certain amount of income to spend and you are consuming both Cokes and blue jeans. The price of Cokes and the price of blue jeans are unaffected by your purchases. We let *MU* equal marginal utility and *P* equal price. It turns out that you know you are receiving in satisfaction, or utility, 15 utils per last dollar spent on Cokes and 10 utils per last dollar spent on blue jeans, or:

$$\frac{MU_{\text{cokes}}}{P_{\text{cokes}}} = \textbf{15 utils per last dollar spent}$$

$$\frac{MU_{\text{blue jeans}}}{P_{\text{blue jeans}}} = \textbf{10 utils per last dollar spent}$$

Could you possibly be in equilibrium here? You are getting a greater marginal utility per last dollar spent for Coke consumption than you are for blue jean consumption. With a fixed income and with given prices for goods to be purchased, the way to obtain maximum utility is to equate marginal utilities per last dollar spent on each good. This is sometimes known as the **principle of equal marginal utilities per dollar.** According to this principle, each good will be demanded up to the point where the marginal utility per dollar spent is exactly the same as the marginal utility per dollar spent on any other good. Or[1]

$$\frac{\textbf{marginal utility of good } x}{\textbf{price of good } x} = \frac{\textbf{marginal utility of good } y}{\textbf{price of good } y}$$

What does this mean? Simply that the last dollar spent on good x must yield the same satisfaction as the last dollar spent on good y. If such were not the case, then the consumer could increase total utility by shifting his or her consumption pattern. For example, assume the marginal utility per dollar spent was lower on one good than on another. Let's continue our example. The marginal utility of the last dollar spent on Coke was equal to 15 utils, and the marginal utility of the last dollar spent on blue jeans was only 10 utils. If the consumer transferred one dollar of income from blue jeans to Coke, that individual would give up 10 units of utility but gain 15. Hence, total utility would increase by (approximately) five units of utility by changing the pattern of a *given* level of money expenditures. Only when the marginal utility per dollar spent on both Cokes and blue jeans is equal will the consumer be obtaining maximum utility, given a fixed income and constant prices.

We show the process of attaining consumer equilibrium in Exhibit 7-4. In panel (a), we initially start off with Coke consumption of Q_C and marginal utility of 15 utils per last dollar spent. In panel (b), we show initial blue jean consumption of Q_B and marginal utility of 10 utils per last dollar spent. We increase Coke consumption to Q'_C so that marginal utility falls to 12 utils per last dollar spent (remember the law of diminishing marginal utility). We cut back on blue jean consumption to Q'_B so that the marginal utility increases to 12 utils per last dollar spent. Our net gain is two utils (+12 − 10 = +2), even though *total expenditures* have remained constant. Q'_C and Q'_B are the equilibrium quantities demanded of Cokes and blue jeans for this consumer. This principle of equal marginal utilities is also applicable to activities other than the purchase of goods and services.

[1]The principle of equal marginal utilities per dollar can be generalized to include all goods in addition to x and y.

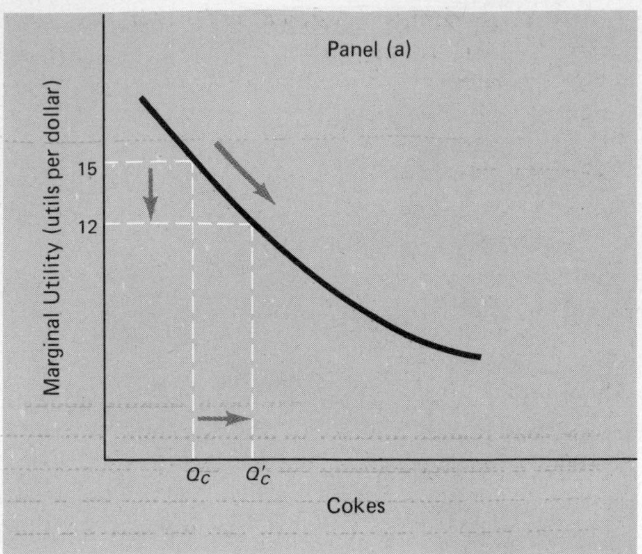

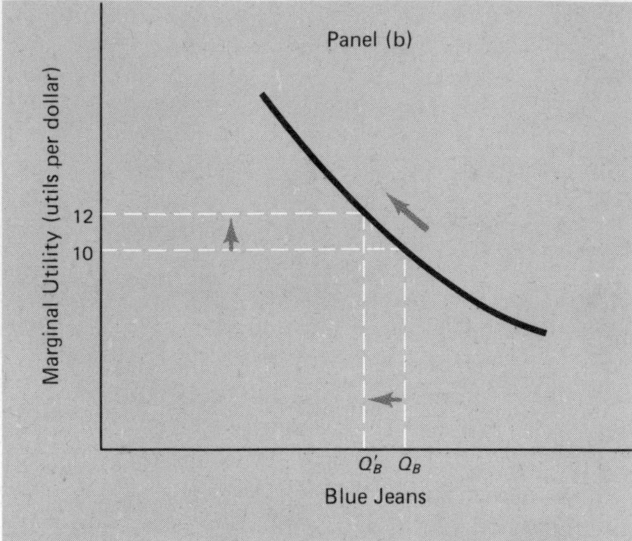

EXHIBIT 7–4

Attaining Maximum Utility. In panel (a), we start out with an initial quantity of Cokes consumed of Q_C. At that quantity, the marginal utility expressed in utils is 15 per dollar. The initial quantity of blue jeans consumed is Q_B. The initial marginal utility expressed in utils is 10 per dollar. The consumer can increase total utility by increasing his or her consumption of Cokes and decreasing his or her consumption of blue jeans. We show this as a movement in panel (a) to quantity of Cokes consumed of Q'_C and in panel (b) to Q'_B. Now the consumer is maximizing satisfaction because the marginal utilities per last dollar spent on each of the two items are equal. By spending more dollars on Cokes, and correspondingly fewer on blue jeans, total expenditures remain constant, but total utility rises by approximately two utils.

We can apply it to the way people use their time. Every individual must make a choice among all possible uses of time. The marginal utility received from the last minute used, for example, to study economics should not be radically different from the marginal utility received from the last minute used to study English literature (assuming, of course, that the student is maximizing grades while faced with a time constraint). If these marginal utilities are greatly out of line, then obviously you should change the time mix. You should spend more or less time with one than the other.

Remember here that we are not clearly assuming that the student receives utility from spending time studying either economics or English literature (although this is a possibility). Rather, it is the outcome of the time spent studying—higher grades and perhaps a better job in the future—that generates the utility.

Consumer Equilibrium and Price Changes

Let us assume for the moment that the consumer is in equilibrium; that is, the marginal utilities per dollar spent on each item in the consumer's budget are the same. Now one item, let's say Cokes, becomes more expensive. The consumer can no longer be in equilibrium. It is no longer true that the marginal utility per dollar spent on Cokes is equal to the marginal utility per dollar spent on anything else. At a higher price, the marginal utility *per dollar spent* on Cokes has got to fall because one dollar now buys a smaller quantity of Coke. The consumer can get back into equilibrium, after the relative price of Cokes has gone up, only by purchasing less of them.

This situation is due to the law of diminishing marginal utility. When the price of Cokes rises, the only way to raise its marginal utility is to purchase fewer Cokes; that is, we move back up that marginal utility curve shown in Exhibit 7–3(b).[2] If the relative price of Cokes falls, of course, the opposite would have to occur to bring the consumer back into equilibrium—more would have to be purchased. We move back down the marginal utility

[2] In equilibrium $MU_{\text{Coke}}/P_{\text{Coke}}$ equals the MU-to-P ratio of all other goods. But if P_{Coke} increases, these ratios are no longer equated. To get back into equilibrium, MU_{Coke} must increase. This is accomplished by buying fewer Cokes.

curve shown in Exhibit 7–3(b), thereby lowering the marginal utility of Cokes.

The Demand Curve Revisited

Linking together the law of diminishing marginal utility and the law of equal marginal utilities per dollar gives us a negative relationship between the quantity demanded of a good or service and its price. As the relative price of Cokes, for example, goes up, the quantity demanded will fall; and as the relative price of Cokes goes down, the quantity demanded will rise. Exhibit 7–5 shows this demand curve for Cokes. As the relative price of Cokes falls, the consumer can maximize total utility only by purchasing more of them, and vice versa. In other words, the relationship between price and quantity desired is simply a downward-sloping demand curve. Note, though, that this downward-sloping demand curve (the law of demand) is derived under the assumption of constant tastes and incomes. You must remember that we are keeping these important determining variables constant when we simply look at the relationship between price and quantity demanded.

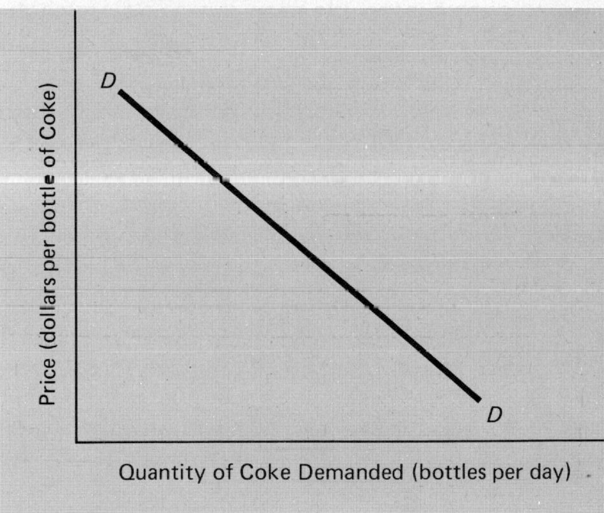

EXHIBIT 7–5
Hypothetical Demand Curve for Cokes. Here we have the quantity of Cokes demanded per day on the horizontal axis, and the price per bottle on the vertical axis. The demand curve slopes downward by virtue of diminishing marginal utility. At a lower price, the last dollar spent on Cokes now will yield more utility than the last dollar spent on other things. In order to maximize total utility we buy more Cokes as its price falls. As we buy and drink more Cokes, the marginal utility falls—that is, we move down the demand curve—until the marginal utility of the last dollar spent on Cokes again equals the marginal utility of the last dollar spent on other things. Thus, the law of diminishing marginal utility predicts that demand curves will be downward sloping, from left to right, for people who wish to maximize their total utility.

DERIVING THE MARKET DEMAND CURVE

The demand curve we have been talking about is one that relates directly to an individual. But what about a *market* demand curve—that is, the demand curve that represents the entire market for a particular good or service? How can we derive a market demand curve from the individual ones we've analyzed?

Actually, deriving a market demand curve from individual demand curves is not difficult. What we have to do is add together all the individual demands horizontally (assuming that each individual's decisions are made independently of others'). We know that not all people are alike. We know, for example, that even at very, very low prices, certain individuals will demand no Cokes whatsoever. So, to derive a demand curve for the entire market, we must add up each individual's demand. This is what we do in Exhibit 7–6. The exhibit shows explicitly that the demand curves are fitted together to obtain the market demand curve for Cokes by what we call "horizontal addition." Notice that the good's demand is expressed in quantity per time period. We include a time period to the demand analysis because we are talking about a flow through time of a demand for a specific good.

EXHIBIT 7–6(a)
Cokes Demanded per Day. Individuals *A*, *B*, and *C* present us with the various quantities of Coke they intend to purchase at various relative prices: 20¢, 30¢, and 40¢. When we add quantities demanded by these individuals, we get the total or market quantity demanded at each of these various prices.

	20¢	*30¢*	*40¢*
Individual *A*'s quantity demanded	4	3	2
Individual *B*'s quantity demanded	2	1	0
Individual *C*'s quantity demanded	1	0	0
Market quantity demanded	7	4	2

EXHIBIT 7–6(b)
Deriving the Market Demand Curve. Individual *A*'s demand curve is shown first, then individual *B*'s and individual *C*'s. By adding these three demand curves horizontally, we obtain the market demand curve represented by the heavily shaded line in the right-hand graph.

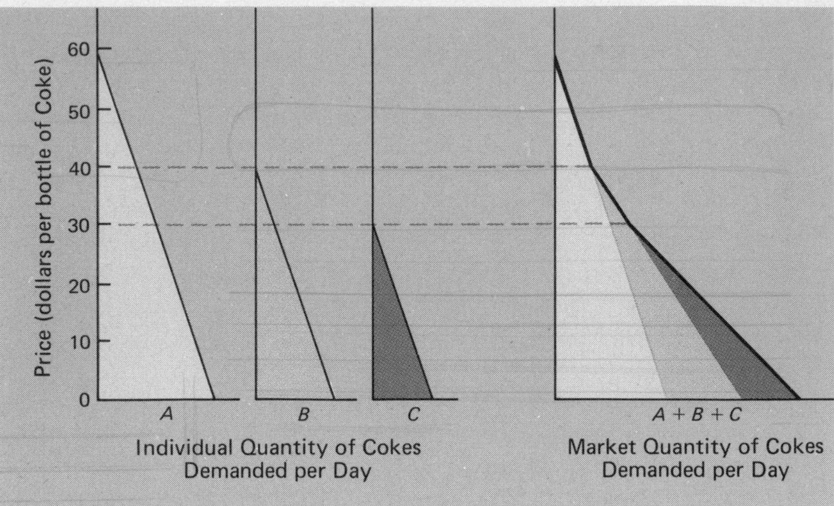

Utility Analysis—A Summary

The analysis of consumer demand using utility theory may appear abstract. That, of course, must be true every time we attempt to hypothesize anything about people's behavior. But utility theory was developed for a very specific reason. It allowed economists to understand the importance of the factors that influence demand and that influence quantity demanded.

The theory of consumer choice is a theory that helps economists predict how consumers will react to changes in price, income, and so on. The goal of this analysis, as well as of any other in this text, is to allow the reader to predict what will happen when an important determining variable changes. Just because we have used an example concerning consumer choice about Cokes, that does not mean that the analysis stops there. It can be extended to any good or service.

Concepts in Brief 7-2

- The law of diminishing marginal utility tells us that the extra utility added by the marginal unit of a good consumed falls.
- The consumer maximizes total utility by equating the marginal utility of the last dollar spent on one good with the marginal utility per last dollar spent on all other goods. He or she is then in consumer equilibrium.
- In order to remain in consumer equilibrium, a price decrease requires an increase in consumption; a price increase requires a decrease in consumption.
- Assuming that we can measure utility, and further assuming that the law of diminishing marginal utility holds, the demand curve must slope down—quantity demanded and price are inversely related.

ISSUES AND APPLICATIONS

Why Are Diamonds More Expensive Than Water?

Concepts Applied

- Total and marginal utility, supply and demand

Water is essential to life. Diamonds are quite unessential to life. Nonetheless, water is cheap relative to diamonds. In economics this is called the diamond-water paradox. For many years, there was no acceptable solution to this paradox, par-

Water is relatively plentiful, inexpensive, and necessary for life; diamonds are relatively scarce, expensive, but unnecessary for life. The key to understanding the price of water and diamonds is in their marginal utilities.

ticularly during the period when economists used to explain the value of things by the amount of labor that was required to produce them. This was called the labor theory of value. If five hours of a given quality of labor were required to produce one hat, but ten hours were required to produce a pair of shoes, the labor theory of value would indicate that the shoes were twice as valuable as the hat. We know now that such a theory is inadequate and inaccurate. Goods that require countless hours of labor to produce will have little or no market value if few people desire to consume them.

We can use marginal utility analysis to solve the diamond-water paradox. In so doing, we must distinguish between total and marginal utility.

Total versus marginal utility. It is not the total utility of water or of diamonds that determines the price of either. To be sure, the total utility of water greatly exceeds the total utility derived from diamonds. However, in economics what determines price is what happens on the margin, and what happens on the margin is quite simple. Since we have so much water, its marginal utility (because it is diminishing) is quite small, given the total quantity that we consume. Because we have relatively few diamonds, the marginal utility of that last diamond consumed is quite high. Moreover, the price of water is the same, more or less, for everyone who buys it in a particular market situation. We find also that the price of the diamond, in another market situation, is the same for everyone who buys it. In other words, every unit must be sold for what the last (marginal), and hence least useful, unit sells for. By *least useful* we mean in terms of individual subjective or psychological marginal utility.

So the diamond-water paradox is only a paradox if one confuses total utility with marginal utility. Total utility does not determine what people are willing to pay for a particular commodity. Marginal utility does.

Graphical Analysis

Let us examine Exhibit 7-7. Here we show the demand curve for diamonds, labeled $D_{diamonds}D_{diamonds}$. The demand curve for water is labeled $D_{water}D_{water}$. We plot quantity in terms of kilograms per unit time period on the horizontal axis. On the vertical axis is plotted price in dollars per kilogram. We use kilograms as our common unit of measurement for water and for diamonds. We could have just as well used gallons, acres, feet, or liters.

Notice that we have drawn the demand curve for water with a break in it to illustrate that the demand for water is many, many times the demand for diamonds. We draw the supply curve of water as SS at a quantity of Q_{water}. The supply curve for diamonds is given as $S'S'$ at quantity $Q_{diamonds}$. Clearly, at the intersection of the supply curve of water with the demand curve of water, the price per kilogram is P_{water}. The intersection of the supply curve of diamonds with the demand curve of diamonds is at $P_{diamonds}$. Notice that $P_{diamonds}$ exceeds P_{water}. Diamonds sell at a higher price than water.

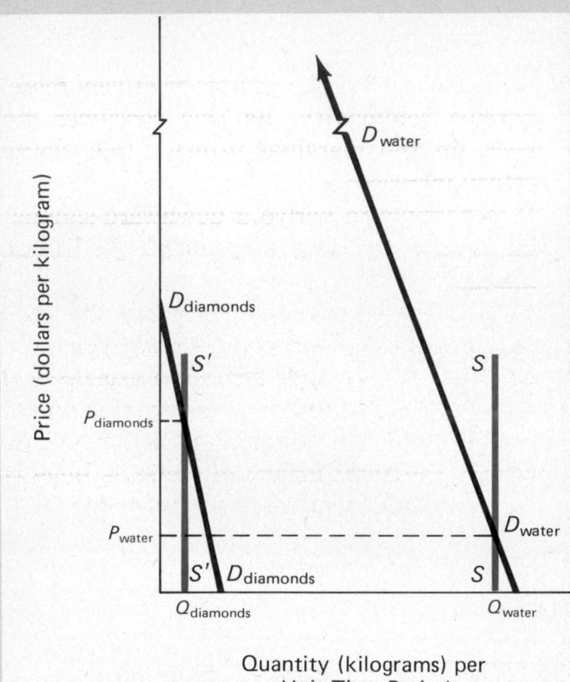

EXHIBIT 7–7
The Diamond-Water Paradox. We pick as a common unit of measurement kilograms for both water and diamonds. The demand curve for water is way to the right of the demand curve for diamonds. To demonstrate that the demand for water is immense, we have put a break in the demand curve, $D_{water}D_{water}$. We have also put a break indication on the vertical axis to show that it goes much higher than indicated on this graph. Although the demand for water is much greater than the demand for diamonds, the marginal valuation of water is given by the marginal value placed on the last unit of water consumed. To find that, we must know the supply of water, which is given as SS. At that supply, the price of water is P_{water}. But the supply for diamonds is given by $S'S'$. At that supply, the price of diamonds is $P_{diamonds}$. The total valuation that consumers place on water is tremendous relative to the total valuation consumers place on diamonds. What is important for price determination, however, is the marginal valuation, or the marginal utility received.

Measuring marginal valuation. If we assume that at any point along the demand curve we can infer marginal valuation of that particular quantity of the good, then we can make a determination of relative "value." In other words, the point gives an indication of the consumer's monetary evaluation of the last unit consumed. The marginal valuation (marginal utility) of diamonds exceeds the marginal valuation of water. Clearly, the total value of water has got to be huge. After all, look how far over to the left the demand curve is. But price is determined by marginal utility, or marginal valuation. Since water is plentiful, as indicated by the supply curve SS, it intersects demand at a relatively low price.

If, for some reason, the supply curve of water shifted inward to the left from SS in Exhibit 7-7, then its price could eventually far exceed the price of diamonds. In other words, what is important is relative scarcity, that is, supply relative to demand. That is how we explain the diamond-water paradox.

Questions

1. Would the analysis just presented apply to other "necessities" such as food?
2. Why is the marginal utility of diamonds so high?

Definition of Terms

Utility The want-satisfying power that a good or service possesses.

Util An artificial unit by which utility is measured.

Marginal utility The change in total utility due to a one-unit change in the quantity of a good consumed.

Diminishing marginal utility The increase in total utility from the consumption of a good or service becomes smaller as more is consumed.

Principle of equal marginal utilities per dollar Each commodity is demanded up to the point where the marginal utility per dollar spent equals the marginal utility per dollar spent on all other goods and services.

Chapter Summary

1. As an individual consumes more of a particular commodity, the total level of utility or satisfaction derived from that consumption increases. However, the rate at which it increases diminishes as more is consumed. This is known as the law of diminishing marginal utility.
2. A consumer reaches equilibrium when the marginal utility per last dollar spent on each commodity consumed is equal to the marginal utility spent on every other good. This is known as the law of equal marginal utilities per dollar.
3. When the relative price of a particular commodity goes up, the law of equal marginal utilities per dollar spent is violated. For the consumer to get back into equilibrium, he or she must reduce the consumption of the now relatively more expensive commodity. As this consumer moves back up the marginal utility curve, marginal utility increases.
4. It is possible to derive a downward-sloping demand curve by using the principle of diminishing marginal utility.
5. The market demand curve is merely the horizontal summation of individual demand curves.
6. The reason diamonds are more expensive than water is that the marginal utility of diamonds is greater than the marginal utility of water. Of course, the total utility of water is huge compared to the total utility of diamonds.

Selected References

Becker, Gary S. *The Economic Approach to Human Behavior.* Chicago: University of Chicago Press, 1978.
Leftwich, Richard H. *The Price System and Resource Allocation.* 7th ed. New York: Dryden Press, 1979, chap. 5.
Watson, Donald S., and Malcolm Getz. *Price Theory and Its Uses.* 5th ed. Boston: Houghton Mifflin, 1981, chap. 5.

Answers to Preview and Study Questions

1. What is utility?

Utility is simply another word for satisfaction; a good or service is said to have utility if it has the power to satisfy wants. A unit of utility is arbitrarily defined—and called a util. Total utility is defined as the sum of all the individual utils resulting from consumption. Marginal utility is defined as the change in total utility resulting from the consumption of one more unit of a commodity or service; total utility for some commodities can also be defined as the sum of all the individual marginal utilities.

2. What is the law of diminishing marginal utility?

The law of diminishing marginal utility states that as an individual consumes more and more units of a commodity per unit of time, eventually the extra benefit derived from consuming successive units will fall. Thus, the fourth hamburger consumed in an 8-hour period yields less satisfaction than does the third, and the third less than the second. The law is quite general and holds for almost any commodity; it is difficult to think of an exception to this "law."

3. How does a consumer maximize his or her total utility?

This question deals with the maximization of utility derived from the consumption of not *one* commodity, but from the consumption of all commodities that the individual wants—subject to his or her income constraint. The rule is that maximization of total utility requires that the last dollar spent on each commodity consumed by the individual should have the same marginal utility. Stated differently, the consumer should purchase goods and services up to the point where the consumer's marginal utilities *per dollar's* worth (marginal utility divided by price) for all commodities are equated—and all income is spent (of course, one can save and "spend" for future consumption). For example, assume that Mr. Romano has spent all of his income but discovers that the marginal utility per dollar's worth for bread was 10 utils and the marginal utility per dollar's worth of milk was 30 utils. This means that the last dollar he spent on bread increased his total utility by 10, while the last dollar he spent on milk increased his total utility by 30. By spending one more dollar on milk and one dollar less on bread his total utility rises by about 20 utils, while his total dollar expenditures remain constant. This reallocation causes the marginal utility per dollar's worth of milk to fall, and the marginal utility per dollar's worth of bread to rise. In order to maximize, Mr. Romano will continue to buy more or less of each commodity until the marginal utilities per dollar's worth of all goods he consumes are equated.

4. What happens to consumer equilibrium when price changes?

Assume that Mr. Romano in the above example is in equilibrium; the marginal utilities per dollar's worth for all the goods he purchases are equated. Assume that the last dollar spent on each of the commodities he purchases increases his total utility by 20 utils. Now, suppose the price of bread falls—all other prices remaining constant. Note that since the price of bread has fallen, the last dollar spent on bread now has a higher marginal utility. This will be true because at a lower price for bread a one dollar bill can purchase a greater quantity of bread. Thus, it is true that marginal utility per dollar's worth for bread now *exceeds* 20 utils, whereas the marginal utility per dollar's worth of each of the other goods he purchases still equals 20 utils. In short, Mr. Romano is no longer in equilibrium; his old pattern of expenditures does not maximize his total utility. Mr. Romano can *now* increase his total utility by purchasing more bread; note that a reduction in the price of bread (other things constant) led to Mr. Romano's purchasing more bread per unit of time.

5. How can the law of diminishing marginal utility account for the law of demand?

When a consumer is in equilibrium, total utility is maximized. An increase in expenditures on any specific commodity will necessarily lead to a reduction in expenditure on another commodity—and a reduction in overall total utility. Why? Because of the law of diminishing marginal utility. For example, suppose that Mr. Romano is maximizing his overall total utility, and that the marginal utility per dollar's worth of each commodity he purchases is 20 utils. Suppose he experiments and spends another dollar on bread—and therefore spends one less dollar on, say, milk. His total utility must fall because he will receive less than 20 utils for the next dollar's worth of bread, and he loses 20 utils from a dollar's less expenditure on milk. Thus, on net balance, he loses utility. Intuitively then, since Mr. Romano gets less and less additional benefit from consuming more and more bread (or any other commodity), the price of bread (or any other commodity) *must fall* before he will voluntarily purchase more and more of it. In short, diminishing marginal utility implies the law of demand.

Problems

(Answers at the back of the book)

1. Suppose that you are standing in the checkout line of a grocery store. You have 5 pounds of oranges and 3 ears of corn. Oranges cost 30¢ a pound; so, too, does an ear of corn. You have $2.40 to spend. You are satisfied that you have reached the highest level of satisfaction, or total utility. Your sister comes along and tries to convince you that you have to put some of the corn back and replace it with additional pounds of oranges. From what you know about utility analysis, how would you explain this disagreement?
2. In order to increase marginal utility, the consumer must decrease consumption (other things constant). This sounds paradoxical. Why is it a correct statement, nonetheless?
3. Assume that Mr. Warfield's marginal utility is 100 utils for the last hamburger he consumed. If the price of hamburgers is $1 apiece, what is Warfield's marginal utility per dollar's worth of hamburger? What is his marginal utility per dollar's worth if the price were 50¢ per hamburger? If the price were $2? How do we calculate marginal utility per dollar's worth of specific commodities?
4. Consider a two-person economy in which the following tables indicate each person's demand for hamburgers.

Price per hamburger	*Mr. Smith: Quantity demanded per week*	*Mr. Johnson: Quantity demanded per week*
$2.00	2	0
1.50	3	1
1.00	4	2
.50	5	3

a. Construct a group demand schedule (table).
b. Graph Mr. Smith's, Mr. Johnson's, and the group's demand curves.
c. Why might Mr. Smith and Mr. Johnson have different demand curves for hamburgers?

APPENDIX

C

Analyzing Consumer Choice with Graphs

It is certainly possible to analyze consumer choice verbally, as we did for the most part in Chapter 7. The theory of diminishing marginal utility can be fairly well accepted on intuitive grounds and by introspection. If we want to be more formal and perhaps more elegant in our theorizing, however, we can translate our discussion into graphic analysis with what are called "indifference curves" and "the budget constraint." Here we discuss these terms and their relationship and demonstrate consumer equilibrium in geometric form.

On Being Indifferent

What does it mean to be indifferent? It usually means that you don't care one way or the other about something—you are equally disposed to either of two alternatives. With this interpretation in mind, we will turn to the two choices, Cokes and 7-Ups. In Exhibit C–1(a), we show several combinations of Cokes and 7-Ups that our representative soft-drink consumer considers to be equally satisfactory. That is to say, for each combination, *A, B, C,* and *D,* this soft-drink consumer will have exactly the same level of total utility.

EXHIBIT C–1(a)

Combinations that Yield Equal Levels of Satisfaction. The combinations *A, B, C,* and *D* represent varying combinations of Cokes and 7-Ups that give an equal level of satisfaction to this consumer. In other words, the consumer is indifferent among these four combinations.

Combination	*Cokes*	*7-Ups*
A	1	7
B	2	4
C	3	2
D	4	1

The simple numerical example which we used happens to concern Cokes and 7-Ups. This example is used to illustrate general features of indifference curves and related analytical tools that are necessary for deriving the demand curve. Obviously, we could have used any other two commodities. Just remember that we are using a *specific* example to illustrate a *general* analysis.

We can plot these combinations graphically in Exhibit C–1(b), with 7-Ups on the horizontal axis and Cokes on the vertical axis. These are our consumer's indifference combinations—the consumer finds each combination as acceptable as the others. Each one carries the same level of total utility. When we connect these combinations with a smooth curve, we obtain what is called the "con-

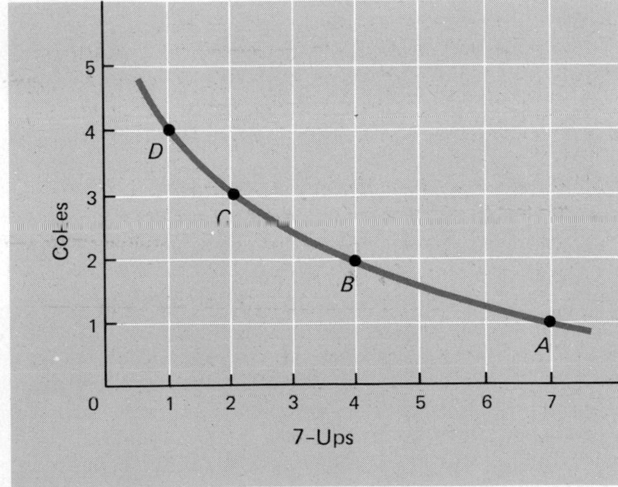

EXHIBIT C–1(b)

An Indifference Curve. If we plot the combinations *A, B, C,* and *D* from panel (a), we obtain the curve *ABCD*, which is called an indifference curve.

sumer's indifference curve." Along the indifference curve, every combination of the two goods in question yields exactly the same level of total utility. Every point along the indifference curve is equally desirable to the consumer; for example, four Cokes and one 7-Up will give our representative consumer exactly the same satisfaction as, say, two Cokes and four 7-Ups.

THE SHAPE OF THE INDIFFERENCE CURVE

The indifference curve that we have drawn in Exhibit C–1(b) is special. Notice that it is curved. Why didn't we just draw a straight line as we have usually done for a demand curve? To find out why we don't posit straight-line indifference curves, consider the implications. We show such a straight-line indifference curve in Exhibit C–2. Start at point *A*. The consumer has no 7-Ups and five Cokes. Now the consumer wishes to go to point *B*. He or she is willing to give up only one Coke in order to get one 7-Up. Now let's assume that the consumer is at point *C*. That consumer is consuming one Coke and four 7-Ups. If the consumer wants to go to point *D*, he or she is again willing to give up one Coke in order to get one more 7-Up. In other words, no matter how many Cokes the consumer has, he or she is willing to give up one Coke in order to get one 7-Up. That does not seem to be plausible. According to the law of diminishing marginal utility, the more of something that a consumer has, the lower will be its marginal utility. Thus, doesn't it make sense to hypothesize that the more Cokes that the consumer drinks, the less he or she will value an additional Coke? Presumably, when the consumer has five Cokes and no 7-Ups, he or she should be willing to give up more than one Coke in order to get one 7-Up. Therefore, once we accept diminishing marginal utility of Coke consumption, a straight-line indifference curve as shown in Exhibit C–2 no longer seems possible. Diminishing marginal utility implies curved indifference curves like the one shown in Exhibit C–1(b).

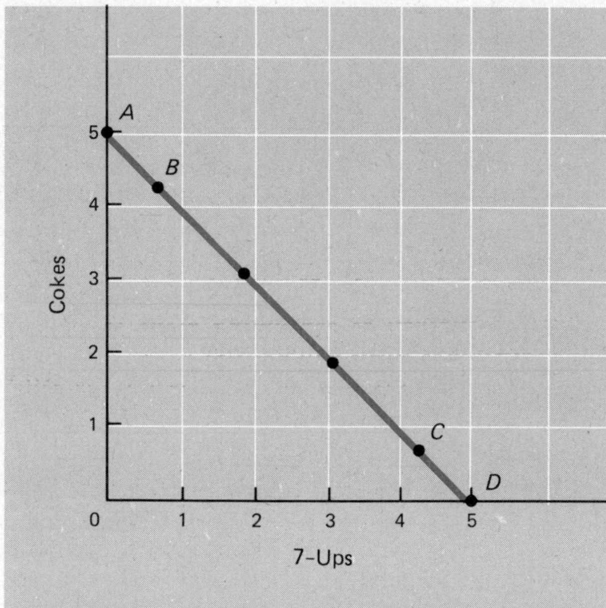

EXHIBIT C–2
The Implications of a Straight-Line Indifference Curve. If the indifference curve is a straight line, the consumer will be willing to give up the same number of Cokes (one for one in this simple example) to get one more 7-Up, whether the consumer has no 7-Up or a lot of 7-Up. For example, the consumer at point *A* has five Cokes and no 7-Up. He or she is willing to give up one more Coke in order to get one more 7-Up. At point *C*, for example, the consumer has only one Coke and four 7-Ups. Because of the straight-line indifference curve, this consumer is willing to give up the last Coke in order to get one more 7-Up even though he or she already has four.

In mathematical jargon, an indifference curve is convex with respect to the origin. The reason for this is the law of diminishing marginal utility, which we discussed in Chapter 7.[1] As the individual consumes more of a particular item, the marginal utility of consuming one additional unit of that item falls, or, conversely, as the person consumes less of it, that good will have a higher marginal utility.

We can measure the marginal utility of something by the quantity of a substitute good that would leave the consumer indifferent. Let's look at this in Exhibit C–1(a). Starting with combination *A*, the consumer has one Coke but seven 7-Ups. To remain indifferent, the consumer would be willing to give up three 7-Ups to obtain one more Coke (as shown in combination *B*). However, to go from combination *C* to combination *D*, notice that the consumer would be willing to give up only one 7-Up for an additional Coke. In other words, the quantity of the substitute considered acceptable changes as the relative scarcity of the original item changes.

Diminishing marginal utility exists throughout this set of choices, and consequently the indifference curve in Exhibit C–1(b) will be convex when

[1] Actually, it can be shown that only diminishing marginal rates of substitution are required.

EXHIBIT C–3
Calculating the Marginal Rate of Substitution.

Combination	7-Ups	Cokes	Marginal Rate of Substitution of 7-Ups for Cokes
A	7	1	
			1/3
B	4	2	
			1/2
C	2	3	
			1/1
D	1	4	

viewed from the origin. If it were a straight line, marginal utility would not be diminishing but constant; if it were curved the other way (concave), marginal utility would be increasing.

THE MARGINAL RATE OF SUBSTITUTION

Above we discussed marginal utility in terms of the marginal rate of substitution between 7-Ups and Cokes. More formally, we can define the consumer's marginal rate of substitution as follows:

MRS = the change in the quantity of one good that just offsets a one-unit change in the consumption of another good, such that total well-being remains constant.

We can see numerically what happens to the marginal rate of substitution in our example if we rearrange Exhibit C–1(a) into Exhibit C–3. Here we show 7-Ups in the second column and Cokes in the third. Now we ask the question: What change in the consumption of 7-Ups will just compensate for a one-unit change in the consumption of Cokes and leave the consumer's total utility constant? The movement from *A* to *B* reduces 7-Up consumption by three and increases Coke consumption by one. Here the marginal rate of substitution of 7-Ups for Cokes is 1 to 3. We do this for the rest of the table and find that as Coke consumption increases, the marginal rate of substitution goes from 1-to-3 to 1-to-1. The marginal rate of substitution of 7-Ups for Cokes rises, in other words, as the consumer obtains more Cokes. This is sometimes called the *law of substitution.*

When a good is consumed in smaller quantities, it has greater value in substitution.

In geometric language, the slope of the consumer's indifference curve (actually, the "negative of the slope") measures the consumer's marginal rate of substitution. Notice that this marginal rate of substitution, or MRS, is purely subjective or psychological. We are not talking about financial capabilities, merely about a consumer's particular set of preferences.

The Indifference Map

Let's now consider the possibility of consuming both more Cokes *and* more 7-Ups. When we do this, we can no longer stay on the same indifference curve that we drew in Exhibit C–1. That indifference curve was drawn for equally satisfying combinations of Cokes and 7-Ups. If the individual now has the possibility of consuming *more of both,* a new indifference curve will have to be drawn *above* and to the right of the one shown in Exhibit C–1(b). Alternatively, if the individual is faced with the possibility of consuming *less of both* Cokes and 7-Ups, an indifference curve would have to be drawn *below* and to the left of the existing one in Exhibit C–1(b). Thus, we can map out an entire set of indifference curves corresponding to these different possibilities. What we come up with is an indifference map.

Exhibit C–4 shows several possible indifference curves. Indifference curves that are higher than others necessarily imply that more of both goods in question can be consumed. Looked at another way, if one goes from, say, indifference curve I_1 to I_2, it is possible to consume the same number of 7-Ups but be able to consume more Cokes. This is shown as a movement from point *A* to point *B* in Exhibit C–4. We could do it the other way. When we move from a lower to a higher indifference curve, it is possible to consume the same number of Cokes and more

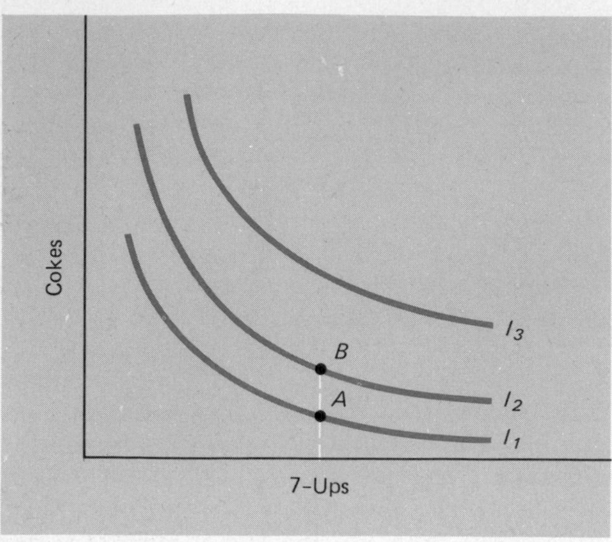

EXHIBIT C–4
A Set of Indifference Curves. There are an infinite number of indifference curves that can be drawn. We show three possible ones. You should realize that a higher indifference curve represents the possibility of higher rates of consumption of both goods. Hence, a higher indifference curve is preferred to a lower one because "more" is preferred to "less." Look at points *A* and *B*. Point *B* represents more Cokes than point *A*; therefore, indifference curve I_2 has to be a preferred one, since the number of 7-Ups is the same at points *A* and *B*.

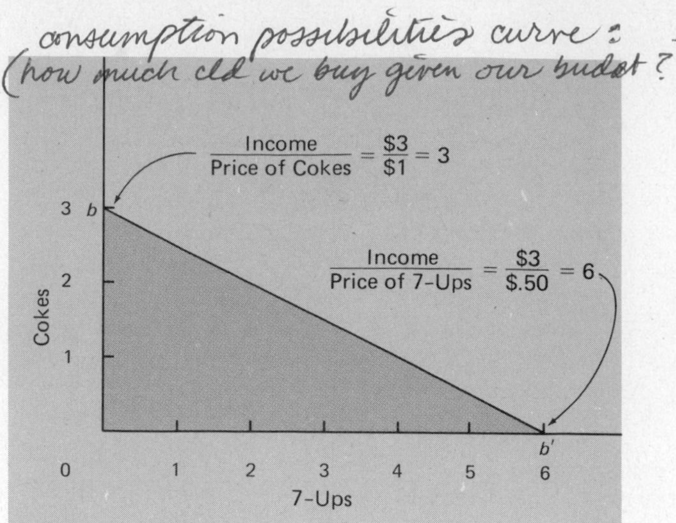

EXHIBIT C–5
The Budget Constraint. The line *bb′* represents this individual's budget constraint. Assuming that Cokes cost $1 each and 7-Ups 50¢ and that the individual has a budget of $3, a maximum of three Cokes or six 7-Ups could be bought. These two extreme points are connected to form the budget constraint. All combinations within the shaded area are feasible.

7-Ups. Thus, the higher a consumer finds himself or herself on the indifference curve map, the greater that consumer's total well-being—assuming, of course, that the consumer does not become satiated.

The Budget Constraint

Our problem here is to find out how to maximize consumer satisfaction. In order to do so, we must consult not only our *preferences*—given by indifference curves—but also our *opportunities*—given by our available income, called our budget constraint. We might want more of everything, but for any given budget constraint we have to make choices or trade-offs among possible goods. Everyone has a budget constraint; that is, everyone is faced with a limited consumption potential. How do we show this graphically? We must find the prices of the goods in question and determine the *maximum* consumption of each allowed by our consumer's budget. For example, let's assume that Cokes cost $1 apiece and 7-Ups cost 50¢. Let's also assume that our representative soft-drink consumer has a total budget of $3. What is the maximum number of Cokes the consumer can buy? Obviously, three. And the maximum number of 7-Ups? Six. So we now have, in Exhibit C–5, two points on our budget line, which is sometimes called the "consumption possibilities curve." The first point is at *b* on the vertical axis; the second at *b′* on the horizontal axis. The line is straight because the prices do not change.

Any combination along line *bb′* is possible; and, in fact, any combination in the grey area is possible. We will assume, however, that the individual consumer completely uses up his or her available budget, and we will consider as possible only those points along *bb′*.

THE SLOPE OF THE BUDGET CONSTRAINT

The budget constraint is a line that slopes downward from left to right. The slope of that line has a special meaning. To see this, look carefully at the budget line in Exhibit C–5. How far up that line do we have to move to get a one-unit movement up the vertical axis? Well, when we move from four to three 7-Ups, there is a movement from one Coke to one-and-a-half Cokes. This is a slope, in absolute terms, of 1:2, which is also the ratio of the prices of Cokes to 7-Ups—Cokes cost $1 and 7-Ups cost 50¢. That is, Cokes cost twice as much as 7-Ups.

The numerical slope of the budget constraint therefore represents the rate of exchange between Cokes and 7-Ups in the marketplace, that is, the realistic rate of exchange given their prices.

Now we are ready to determine how the consumer achieves equilibrium.

CONSUMER EQUILIBRIUM REVISITED

Consumers, of course, will attempt to attain the highest level of total utility possible, given their budget constraint. How can this be shown graphically? We draw a set of indifference curves similar to those given in Exhibit C–4, and we bring in reality—the budget constraint, *bb'*. Both are drawn in Exhibit C–6. Now, since a higher level of total satisfaction is represented by a higher indifference curve, we know that the consumer will strive to be on the highest indifference curve possible. However, the consumer cannot get to indifference curve I_3, because his or her budget will be exhausted before any combination of Cokes and 7-Ups represented on indifference curve I_3 is attained. This consumer can maximize total utility, subject to the budget constraint, only by being at point E on indifference curve I_2, because here the consumer's income is just being exhausted. Mathematically, point E is called the tangency point of the curve I_2 to the straight line *bb'*.

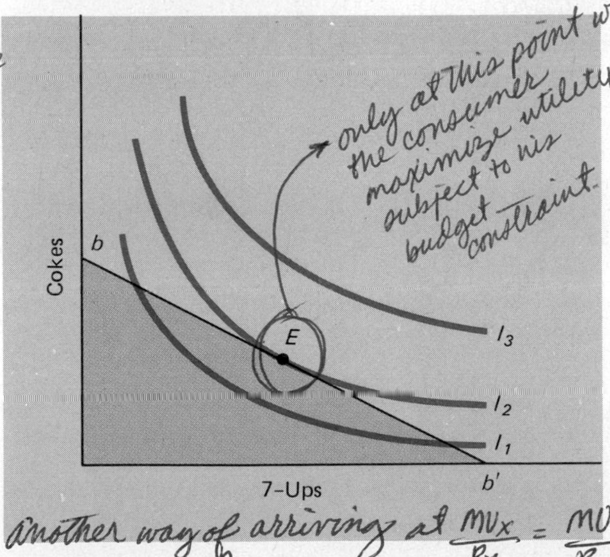

EXHIBIT C–6
Consumer Equilibrium. A consumer reaches equilibrium when he or she ends up on the highest indifference curve possible, given a limited budget. This occurs at the tangency between an indifference curve and the budget constraint. In this diagram, the tangency is at *E*.

Consumer equilibrium is achieved when the marginal rate of substitution (which is subjective) is just equal to the feasible, or realistic, rate of exchange between Cokes and 7-Ups. This realistic rate is the ratio of the two prices of the goods involved. It is represented by the absolute value of the slope of the budget constraint. At point E, the point of tangency between indifference curve I_2 and budget constraint *bb'*, the rate at which the consumer wishes to substitute Cokes for 7-Ups (the numerical value of slope of the indifference curve) is just equal to the rate at which the consumer *can* substitute Cokes for 7-Ups (the slope of the budget line).

What Happens When Income Changes?

A change in income will shift the budget constraint *bb'* in Exhibit C–6. Consider only increases in income and no changes in price. The budget constraint will shift outward. Each new budget line will be parallel to the original one because we are not allowing a change in the relative prices of Cokes and 7-Ups. We would now like to find out how an individual consumer responds to successive increases in income when nominal and relative prices remain constant. We do this in Exhibit C–7. We start out with an income that is represented by a budget line *bb'*. Consumer equilibrium is at point E, where the consumer attains his or her highest indifference curve I, given the budget constraint *bb'*. Now we let money income increase. This is shown by a shift outward in the budget line to *cc'*. The consumer attains a new equilibrium at point E'. That is where a higher indifference curve, II, is reached. Again, the consumer's income is increased so that the new budget line facing him or her is *dd'*. The new equilibrium now moves to E''. This is where the indifference curve, III, is reached. If we connect the three consumer equilibrium points, E, E', and E'', we have what is called an income consumption curve. The *income consumption curve*

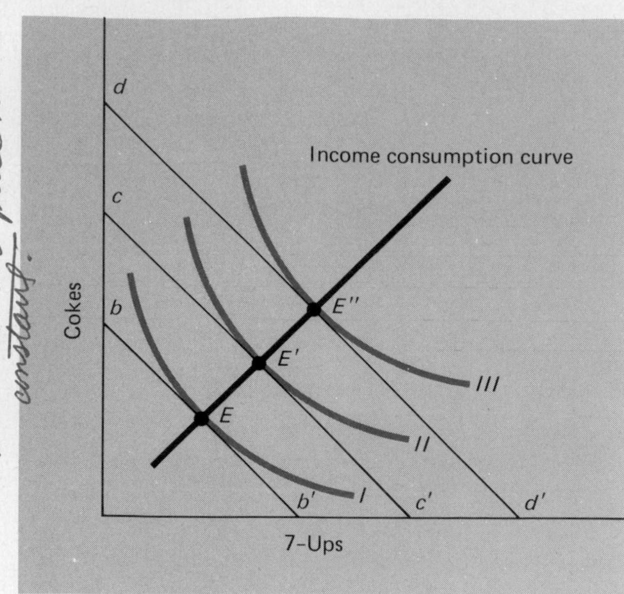

EXHIBIT C–7
The Income Consumption Curve. We start off with income sufficient to yield budget constraint *bb'*. The highest attainable indifference curve is *I*, which is just tangent to *bb'* at *E*. Next we increase income. The budget line moves outward to *cc'*, which is parallel to *bb'*. The new highest indifference curve is *II*, which is just tangent to *cc'* at *E'*. Finally, we increase income again, which is represented by a shift in the budget line to *dd'*. The new tangency point of the highest indifference curve, *III*, with *dd'*, is at point *E''*. When we connect these three points, we obtain the income consumption curve.

shows the equilibrium consumption points that would occur if income for that consumer were increased continuously, holding the prices of Cokes and 7-Ups constant.

NORMAL AND INFERIOR GOODS

We have shown in Exhibit C–7 that as income increases, the consumer purchases more of both Cokes and 7-Ups. This may not necessarily be the case. As income increases, the consumer could purchase more 7-Ups and fewer Cokes, or fewer 7-Ups and more Cokes. We show these possibilities in panels (a) and (b) of Exhibit C–8. In panel (a), we show that as income increases, the consumption of Cokes increases, but the consumption of 7-Ups decreases. In this situation, we call Cokes a normal good and 7-Ups an inferior good. The definition of a normal good is one for which quantity demanded increases as income increases. The definition of an inferior good is one for which quantity demanded decreases as income increases. In panel (b), we show the opposite situation. As income increases, fewer Cokes and more 7-Ups are consumed. Thus, Cokes become an inferior good, and 7-Ups become a normal good.

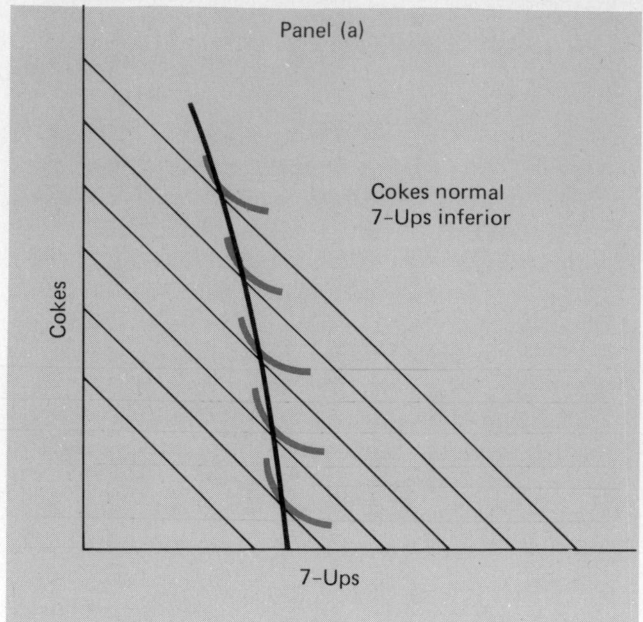

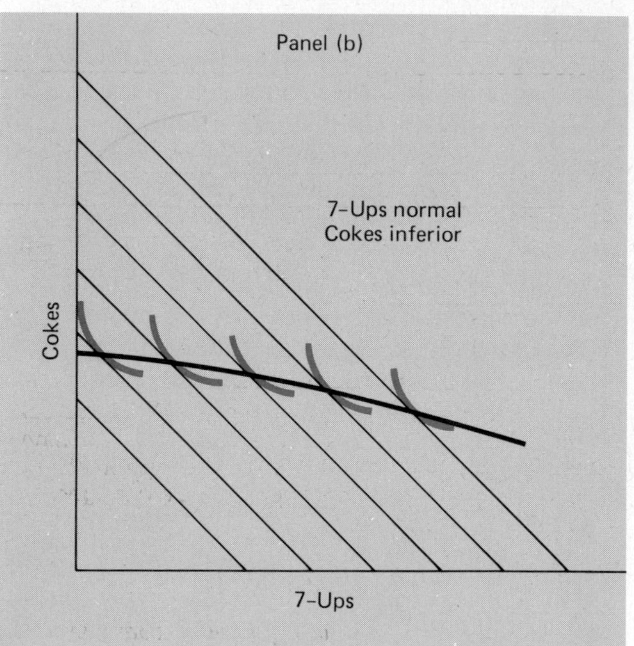

EXHIBIT C–8
Inferior and Normal Goods. We define an inferior good as one for which the quantity demanded decreases as income increases. We define a normal good as one for which the quantity demanded increases as income increases. In panel (a), we show that as income increases, the quantity of Cokes increases, while the quantity of 7-Ups decreases. In panel (a), Cokes are a normal good and 7-Ups are an inferior good. In panel (b), the quantity of Cokes decreases as the quantity of 7-Ups increases. In panel (b), Cokes are an inferior good and 7-Ups are a normal good.

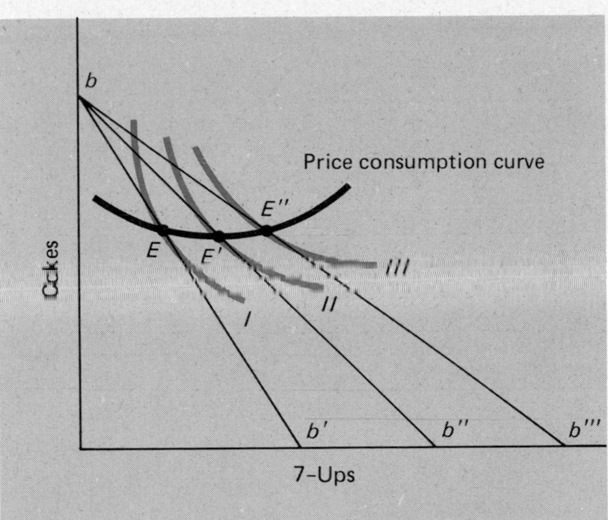

EXHIBIT C–9
Price Consumption Curve. In this experiment, we hold the price of Cokes constant, as well as money income. We keep lowering the price of 7-Ups. As we lower the price of 7-Ups, income measured in terms of 7-Ups increases. We show this by rotating the budget constraint from *bb′* to *bb″* and finally to *bb‴*. We then find the highest indifference curve that is attainable for each successive budget constraint (which is drawn with a lower and lower price of 7-Ups). For budget constraint *bb′*, the highest indifference curve is *I*, which is tangent to *bb′* at point *E*. We do this for the next two budget constraints. When we connect the equilibrium points, *E*, *E′*, and *E″*, we derive the price consumption curve, which shows the combinations of the two commodities that a consumer will purchase when money income and the price of one commodity remain constant while the other commodity's price changes.

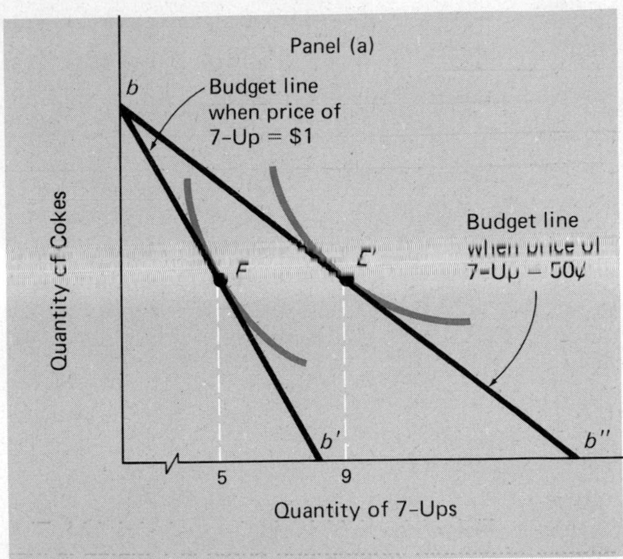

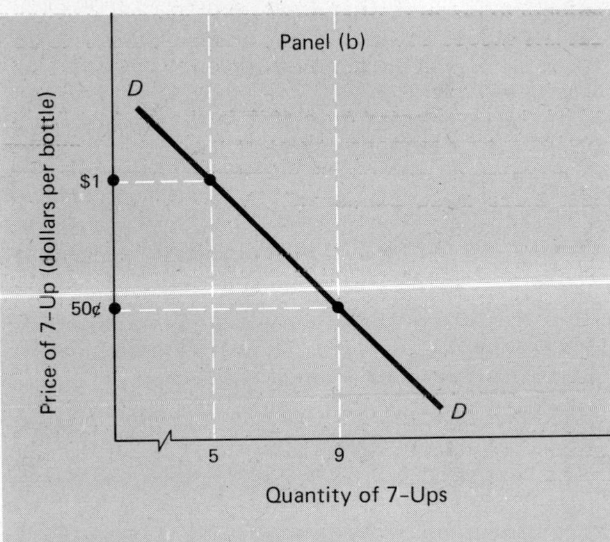

EXHIBIT C–10
Deriving the Demand Curve. In panel (a), we show the effects of a decrease in the price of 7-Up from $1 to 50¢. At a price of $1, the highest indifference curve touches the budget line *bb′* at point *E*. The quantity of 7-Ups consumed is five. We transfer this combination—the price of $1, quantity demanded five—down to panel (b). Next, we decrease the price of 7-Ups to 50¢. This generates a new budget line, or constraint, which is *bb″*. Consumer equilibrium is now at *E′*. The equilibrium quantity demanded of 7-Ups at a price of 50¢ is nine. We transfer this point—the price of 50¢, quantity demanded nine—down to panel (b). When we connect these two points, we have a demand curve, *DD*, for 7-Ups.

PRICE CONSUMPTION LINE

In Exhibit C-9, we hold money income and the price of Cokes constant while we change the price of 7-Up. Specifically, we keep lowering the price. As we keep lowering the price of 7-Up, the amount that could be purchased if all income were spent on 7-Up clearly increases; thus, the extreme points for the budget constraint keep moving outward to the right as the price of 7-Up falls. In other words, the budget line rotates outward from *bb′* to *bb″* and *bb‴*. Each time the price of 7-Up falls, a new budget line is thus formed. There has to be a new equilibrium point. We find it by locating on each new budget line the highest attainable indifference curve. This is shown at points *E*, *E′*, and *E″*. We see that as price decreases for 7-Up, the consumer purchases more and more 7-Up. We call the line connecting points *E*, *E′*, and *E″* the *price consumption curve.* It connects the tangency points of the budget constraints and indifference curves, thus showing the amounts of two goods that a consumer will buy when his or her income and the price of one commodity are held constant while the price of the remaining good changes.

Deriving the Demand Curve

We are now in a position to derive the demand curve from using indifference curve analysis. In panel (a) of Exhibit C–10, we show what happens when the price of 7-Up decreases, holding the price of Coke constant and income constant. If the price of 7-Up decreases, the budget line rotates from *bb′* to *bb″*. The two equilibrium points are given by the tangency at the highest indifference curve that just touches those two budget lines. This is at *E* and *E′*. But those two points give us two price-quantity pairs. At point *E,* the price of 7-Up is $1; the quantity demanded is five. Thus, we have one point that we can transfer to panel (b) of Exhibit C–10. At point *E′*, we have another price-quantity pair. The price has fallen to 50¢. The quantity demanded has increased to nine. We therefore transfer this other point to panel (b). When we connect these two points (and all the others in between), we derive the demand curve for 7-Ups. It is downward sloping.

8

Businesses and Their Costs

TOPICS FOR REVIEW

The topics listed below, which we have already analyzed, are applied in this chapter. You may find it worthwhile to review them. For your convenience each topic is followed by the number identifying its specific "Concepts in Brief."

a. Opportunity cost (1–2)

b. Supply (3–4)

c. Plant, firm, industry (5–1)

FOR PREVIEW AND STUDY

1. How does the economist's definition of profit differ from the accountant's?
2. What distinguishes the long run from the short run?
3. How does the law of diminishing returns account for an *eventually* increasing marginal cost curve for a firm in the short run?
4. Why is the average total cost (ATC) curve U-shaped?
5. How are the marginal cost (MC) and the average total cost (ATC) curves related?

In the last two chapters, the main focus was on the behavior of consumers and households. To fully analyze many economic questions concerning microeconomic behavior, a theory of how businesses work is also needed. Much of this chapter will deal with some of the tools needed to complete a model of the behavior of businesses. Since the object is to develop a model, the representation will be simplified. It may not be a 100 percent accurate representation of what actually goes on inside a working business. Be warned, therefore, that economics cannot be used to describe the actual way an owner operates a particular business. A businessperson may merely talk in terms of the cost of hiring Joe Smith or Mary Jones. In economics we will be more concerned about, say, marginal costs (which will be described below) of labor and how they affect output. Remember, we are not developing a model of how businesspersons think or the language they use in discussing their businesses.

The purpose of our theory, or model, of business behavior is to predict what costs will be, how costs will change, what a change in cost will do to production rates, and so on. If the government increases taxes on business profits, what will this do to the costs and revenues facing the business decision maker? Our model should help us predict this. We want to be able to predict what will happen if the government prevents firms from hiring college students for summer work at wages below the legal minimum. This chapter will equip us with the tools to analyze these questions.

Furthermore, in the preceding chapters, we have been looking at upward-sloping supply curves. At higher relative prices, suppliers are willing to provide more of their products for sale than they are at lower relative prices. We only vaguely referred to the reason why, and our vague explanation had something to do with businesses' costs of production. Here we will look into those costs of production in detail. Our examination of costs will then allow us to understand why supply curves generally slope upward.

Defining a Business

What is a business? Everybody knows that. It's the supermarket down the street, the dress shop around the corner, General Motors, Playboy Enterprises, American Telephone and Telegraph. The list will get very large indeed if we attempt to name every business in the United States. Everybody also knows that there is a difference between a corporate giant like General Motors and the local dress shop. In terms of our analysis, however, we will not usually make a distinction between these types of firms—except with regard to the market power they have—that is, the extent to which they control the prices of commodities they sell. The legal differences that exist among business organizations have already been covered in detail in Chapter 5, where we discussed proprietorships, partnerships, and corporations.

The Firm

We still haven't come up with a precise definition of what a business is, even though all of us have a pretty good idea. Let's define a business, or **firm,** as follows:

A firm is an organization that brings together different factors of production, such as labor, land, and capital, to produce a product or service which it is hoped can be sold for a profit.

A typical firm will have the following organizational structure: entrepreneur, managers, and workers. The entrepreneur is the person who takes the chances. Because of this, the entrepreneur is the one who will get any profits that are made. The entrepreneur also decides who to hire to run the firm. Some economists maintain that the true quality of an entrepreneur becomes evident when he or she can pick good managers. Managers, in turn, are the ones who decide who should be hired and fired and how the business should generally be set up. The workers are the ones who ultimately use the machines to produce the products or services that are being sold by the firm. Workers and managers are paid contractual wages. They receive a specified amount for a specified time period. Entrepreneurs are not paid contractual wages. They receive no specified "reward." Rather, they receive what is left over, if anything, after all expenses are paid. It is the entrepreneurs who make profits if there are any, for profits accrue to those who are willing to take risks.

PROFIT

Most people—businesspeople included—think of profit as the difference between the amount of money the business takes in and the amount it spends for wages, materials, and so on. In a bookkeeping sense, the following formula could be used:

accounting profits =
total revenues − total costs

The accounting definition of profits is appropriate when used by accountants, for example, to determine taxable income for a firm. Economists face a different problem; therefore, we use another concept of profit in which the *full opportunity cost* of *all* resources used is the cost figure that we subtract from revenues to obtain the economist's definition of profit. There are two areas of resource use and consequent accounting cost calculations where problems typically arise. The first resource is capital and the second resource is labor.

OPPORTUNITY COST OF CAPITAL

Firms enter or remain in an industry if they earn, at a minimum, a *normal rate of return* (NROR). By this term, we mean that people will not invest their wealth in a business unless they obtain a positive competitive rate of return, that is, unless their invested wealth pays off. Any business wishing to attract capital must expect to pay at least the same rate of return on that capital as all other businesses of similar risk are willing to pay. For example, if individuals can invest their wealth in almost any publishing firm and get a rate of return of 10 percent per year, then each firm in the publishing industry must *expect* to pay 10 percent as the normal rate of return to present and future investors. This 10 percent is a *cost to the firm.* This cost is called the **opportunity cost of capital.** The opportunity cost of capital is the amount of income, or yield, foregone by giving up an investment in another firm. Capital will therefore not stay in firms or industries where the expected rate of return falls below its opportunity cost.

FORGETTING THE OPPORTUNITY COST OF CERTAIN OTHER INPUTS

Often, single-owner proprietorships grossly exaggerate their profit rates because they forget about the opportunity cost of the time that the proprietor spends in the business. We are now referring to the opportunity cost of labor. For example, you may know people who run small grocery stores. These people, at the end of the year, will sit down and figure out what their "profits" are. They will add up all their sales and subtract what they had to pay to other workers, what they had to pay to their suppliers, what they had to pay in taxes, and so on. The end result they will call "profit." However, they will not have figured into their costs the salary that they could have made if they had worked for somebody else in a similar type of job. For somebody operating a grocery store, that salary might be equal to $6 an hour. If so, then $6 an hour is the opportunity cost of the grocery store owner's time. In many cases, people who run their own businesses lose money in an economic sense. That is, their profits, as they calculate them, may be less than the amount of labor income they *could* have earned had they spent the same amount of time working for someone else. Take a numerical example. If an entrepreneur can earn $6 per hour, it follows that the opportunity cost of his or her time is $6 × 40 hours × 52 weeks, or $12,480 per year. If this entrepreneur is making less than $12,480 per year in accounting profits, he or she is actually losing money. (This doesn't mean that such entrepreneurs are "stupid." They may be willing to pay for the nonpecuniary benefits of "being the boss.")

We have spoken only of the opportunity cost of capital and the opportunity cost of labor, but we could have spoken in general of the opportunity cost of all inputs. Whatever the input may be, its opportunity cost must be taken into account in order to figure out true economic profits.

ACCOUNTING PROFITS ≠ ECONOMIC PROFITS

You should have a good idea by now of the meaning of profits in economics.

The term *profits* in economics means the income that entrepreneurs earn, over and above their own opportunity cost of time, plus the opportunity cost of the capital they have invested in their business. Profits can be regarded as total revenues minus total costs—which is how the accountants think of them—but we must now include *all* costs. Our definition of economic profits will be the following:

economic profits = total revenues −
total opportunity cost of all inputs used

We indicate this relationship in Exhibit 8–1. We are assuming that the accountants' bookkeeping costs for all factors of production except capital are correct.

EXHIBIT 8–1
Simplified View of Economic and Accounting Profit. Here we see that on the right-hand side, total revenues are equal to accounting costs plus accounting profit. That is, accounting profit is the difference between total revenues and total accounting costs. On the other hand, we see in the left-hand column that economic profit is equal to total revenues minus economic costs. Economic costs are equal to accounting costs plus a normal rate of return (NROR) or normal profit on invested capital, which is the opportunity cost of capital.

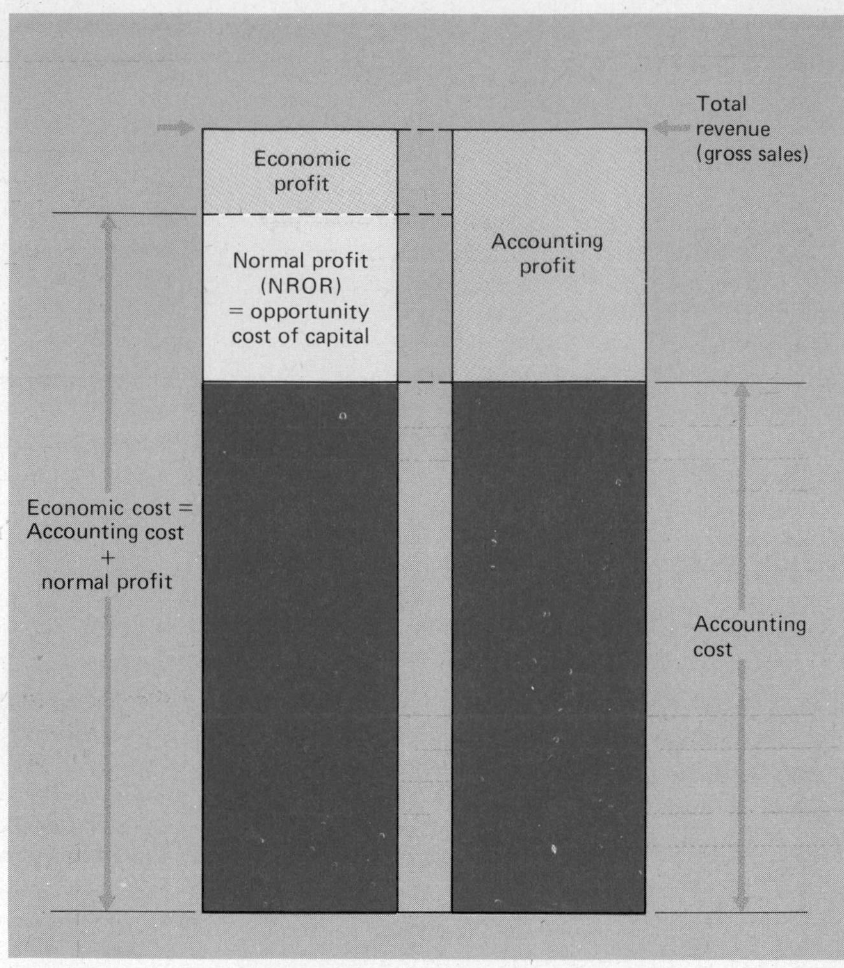

THE GOAL OF THE FIRM

In most instances we will use a model that is based on maximization of profits. In other words, the firm's goal is to maximize profit; it is expected to attempt to make the positive difference between total revenues and total cost as large as it can. We use a profit-maximizing model because it allows us to analyze a firm's behavior with respect to quantity supplied and the relationship between cost and output. Whenever this profit-maximizing model produces poor predictions, we will examine our initial assumption about profit maximization. We might have to conclude that the primary goal of some firms is not to maximize profits, but rather to maximize sales, the number of workers, the prestige of the owners, and so on.

Is this assumption of profit maximization realistic? If we are trying to explain business behavior, we don't actually have to assume that entrepreneurs consciously try to maximize profits. We hypothesize that their behavior is consistent with the maximization of profits. If a physicist wants to predict where a pool player will hit the cue ball in order to cause a particular ball to go into a pocket on the pool table, the physicist predicts the pool player's behavior by hypothesizing that the player knows the laws of physics. In virtually all cases, this may be an "unrealistic" assumption. If the physicist's predictions were consistently wrong, then he or she would have to go back and take a closer look at the model that was being used. As we stated above, if our model of the firm consistently makes poor predictions, economists will go back and build another model. Also, if an alternative model comes along that proves more usable in terms of how well it predicts businesses' behavior, that alternative will undoubtedly be adopted. Finally, even if the assumption of profit maximization does not work for all firms, as long as it works for many firms the model based on it may predict better than alternative models.

> ***Concepts in Brief 8-1***
>
> ■ A firm is an organization that brings together production inputs in order to produce a good or service that can be sold for a profit.
>
> ■ Accounting profits differ from economic profits.
>
> ■ Economic profits are defined as total revenues minus total costs, where costs include the full opportunity cost of all of the factors of production.
>
> ■ Single-owner proprietorships often fail to consider the opportunity cost of the labor services provided by the owner.
>
> ■ The full opportunity cost of capital invested in a business is generally not included as a cost when accounting profits are calculated. Thus, accounting profits overstate economic profits.

The Relationship Between Output and Inputs

A firm takes numerous inputs, combines them using a technological production process, and ends up with an output. There are, of course, many, many factors of production, or inputs. We classify production inputs into two broad categories (ignoring land)—labor and capital. The relationship between output and these two inputs is as follows:

output per unit time period = some function of capital and labor inputs[1]

SHORT VERSUS LONG RUN

The time period here is important. Throughout the rest of this chapter we will consider a "short" time period as opposed to a "long" time period. In other words, we are looking at *short-run* production relationships and short-run costs associated with production.

Any definition of the short run will, necessarily, be arbitrary. We cannot talk in terms of the short run being a specific time period such as a month, six months, or even a year. Rather, we must deal in terms of the short run having to do with the ability of the firm to alter the quantity of its inputs. For ease of understanding, we will simply define the short run as any time period when there is at least one factor of production that has a fixed cost. In the long run, therefore, all costs are variable. That is, all factors are variable.

In most short-run analyses, the factor that has a fixed cost, or is fixed in quantity, is capital. We therefore state that in our short-run model, capital is fixed and invariable. That is not unreasonable—in a typical firm, the number of machines *in place* will not change over several months, or even over a year. After all, the input that changes the most is labor. The production relationship that we use, therefore, holds capital constant, or given, and labor is variable.

THE PRODUCTION FUNCTION—A NUMERICAL EXAMPLE

The relationship between physical output and the quantity of capital and labor used in the production process is sometimes called a **production function.** The production function is given to the firm by the laws of physics, chemistry, and so on, that is, by production engineers not by economists, for it is a technological relationship between inputs and outputs. It depends on the available technology.

Look at panel (a) of Exhibit 8–2. Here we show a production function relating total output in column 2 to the quantity of labor measured in worker-weeks in column 1. When there are 0 worker-weeks of input, there is no output. When there are 5 worker-weeks of input (given the capital stock), there is a total output of 50 bushels per week. (Ignore for the moment the rest of that exhibit.) In panel (b) of Exhibit 8–2, we show this particular hypothetical production function graphically. Note, again, that it relates to the short run and that it is for an individual firm.

Exhibit 8–2(b) shows a total physical product curve, or the amount of physical output that is possible when we add successive units of labor while holding all other inputs constant. The graph of the production function in Exhibit 8–2(b) is not a straight line. In fact, it peaks at 7 worker-weeks and starts to go down. To understand why such a phenomenon occurs with an individual firm in the short run, we have to analyze in detail the **law of diminishing (marginal) returns.**

Diminishing Returns

The concept of diminishing marginal returns applies to many different situations. If you put one

[1] In simple mathematical formulation, the production relationship can be written as $Q = f(K,L)$, where Q = output per unit time period, K = capital, and L = labor.

EXHIBIT 8–2(a)

Diminishing Returns: A Hypothetical Case in Agriculture. In the first column, we measure the number of workers used per week on a given amount of land with a given amount of machinery and fertilizer and seed. In the second column, we give their total product—that is, the output that each specified number of workers can produce in terms of bushels of wheat. The last column gives the marginal product. The marginal product is the difference between the output possible with a given number of workers minus the output made possible with one less worker. For example, the marginal product of a fourth worker is 8 bushels of wheat. With 4 workers, 44 bushels are produced, but with 3 workers only 36 are produced; the difference is 8.

Input of Labor (no. of worker-weeks)	*Total Product (output in bushels of wheat per week)*	*Marginal Physical Product (in bushels of wheat per week)*
0	0	
		10
1	10	
		16
2	26	
		10
3	36	
		8
4	44	
		6
5	50	
		4
6	54	
		2
7	56	
		−1
8	55	

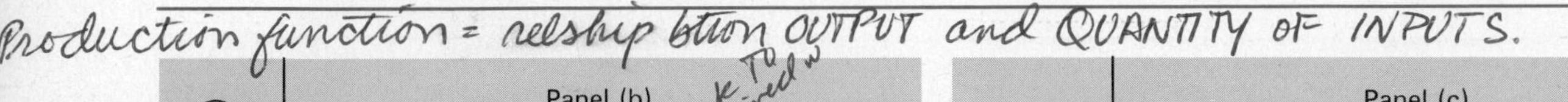

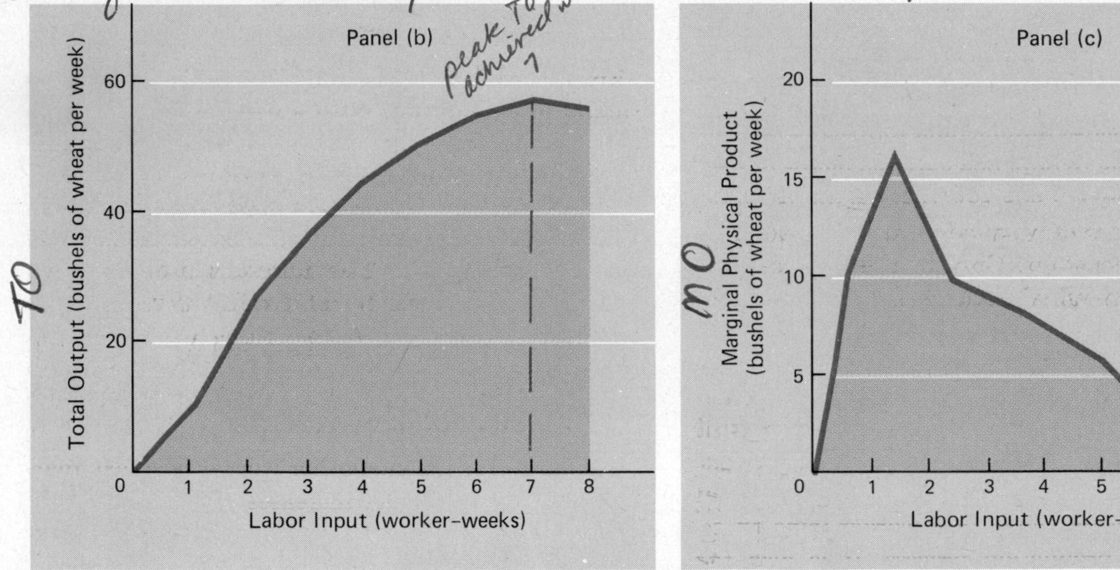

EXHIBIT 8–2(b)

A Production Function. A production function relates outputs to inputs. We have merely taken the numbers from columns 1 and 2 of panel (a) and presented them here.

EXHIBIT 8–2(c)

Marginal Product—Diminishing Marginal Return. On the horizontal axis, we plot the number of workers; starting from 0 and going to 8. On the vertical axis, we plot the marginal physical product in bushels of wheat. When we go from 0 workers to 1 worker, marginal product is 10. We show this at a point between 0 and 1 worker-weeks to indicate that marginal product relates to the change in the total product as we add additional workers. When we go from 1 worker to 2 workers, marginal product increases to 16. After 2 workers, marginal product declines. Therefore, after 2 workers, we are in the area of diminishing marginal physical returns. Since total product, or output, reaches its peak at 7 workers, we know that after 7 workers, marginal physical product is negative. In fact, when we move from 7 to 8 workers, marginal product becomes −1 bushel. (Note, again, that we have approximated the curve by using the *midpoints* between the number of worker-weeks; that is why the curve peaks between 1 and 2 worker-weeks rather than exactly at 2 worker-weeks.)

seat belt over your lap, a certain amount of additional safety is obtained. If you add another seat belt, some more safety is obtained, but less than when the first belt was secured. When you add a third seat belt, again the amount of *additional* safety obtained must be even smaller. In a similar way, Winston Churchill apparently believed that there were diminishing returns to dropping more and more bombs on German steel mills during World War II; later bombs, he felt, merely moved about the wreckage from prior bombs.

The same analysis holds for firms in their use of productive inputs. When the returns from hiring more workers are diminishing, it does not necessarily mean that more workers won't be hired. In fact, workers will be hired until the returns, in terms of the *value* of the extra output produced, are equal to the additional wages that have to be paid for those workers to produce the extra output. Before we get into that decision-making process, let's demonstrate that diminishing returns can be represented graphically and can be used in our analysis of the firm.

MEASURING DIMINISHING RETURNS

How do we measure diminishing returns? First, we limit the analysis to only one variable factor of production (or input). Let's say that factor is labor. Every other factor of production, such as machines, must be held constant. Only in this way can we calculate the marginal returns from using more workers and know when we reach the point of diminishing marginal returns.

Marginal returns for productive inputs are sometimes specifically referred to as the **marginal physical product.** The marginal physical product of a worker, for example, is the change in total product that occurs when that worker joins an already existing production process. It is also the *change* in total product that occurs when that worker quits or is laid off an already existing production process. The marginal productivity of labor therefore refers to the change in output caused by a one-unit change in the labor input.

The marginal productivity of labor may increase at the very beginning. That is, a firm starts with no workers, only machines. The firm then hires one worker, who finds it difficult to get the work started. When the firm hires more workers, however, each is able to *specialize,* and the marginal productivity of those additional workers may actually be greater than it was with the previous few workers. Beyond some point, however, diminishing returns must set in; each worker has (on average) fewer machines with which to work (remember, all other inputs are fixed). Eventually, the firm will become so crowded that workers will start running into each other and will become less productive. Managers will have to be hired to organize the workers.

Using these ideas, we can define the law of diminishing returns as follows:

As successive equal increases in a variable factor of production, such as labor, are added to other fixed factors of production, such as capital, there will be a point beyond which the extra or marginal product that can be attributed to each additional unit of the variable factor of production will decline.

Diminishing returns merely refer to a situation in which output rises less than in proportion to an increase in, say, the number of workers employed.

AN EXAMPLE

An example of the law of diminishing returns is found in agriculture. With a fixed amount of land, fertilizer, and tractors, the addition of more people eventually yields decreasing increases in output. A hypothetical set of numbers illustrating the law of diminishing marginal returns is presented in panel (a) of Exhibit 8–2. The numbers are presented graphically in panel (c) of Exhibit 8–2. Marginal productivity (returns from adding more workers) first increases, then decreases, and finally becomes negative. When one worker is hired, total output goes from 0 to 10. Thus, marginal physical product is equal to 10. When another worker is added, marginal physical product increases to 16. Then it begins to decrease. The point of diminishing marginal returns occurs after two workers are hired.

Concepts in Brief 8-2

- The technological relationship between output and input is called the production function. It relates output per unit time period to the several inputs, such as capital and labor.
- After some rate of output, the firm generally experiences diminishing marginal returns.
- The law of diminishing returns states that if all factors of production are held constant except one, equal increments in that one variable factor will eventually yield decreasing increments in output.

EXHIBIT 8–3
An Example of the Costs of Production.

Panel (a)

Total Output (Q/day) (1)	Total Fixed Costs (TFC) (2)	Total Variable Costs (TVC) (3)	Total Costs (TC) (4) = (2) + (3)	Average Fixed Costs (AFC) (5) = (2) ÷ (1)	Average Variable Costs (AVC) (6) = (3) ÷ (1)	Average Total Costs (ATC) (7) = (4) ÷ (1)	Total Costs (TC) (4)	Marginal Cost (MC) (8) = Change in (4) / Change in (1)
0	$10.00	0	$10.00	—	—	—	$10.00	
1	10.00	$5.00	15.00	$10.00	$5.00	$15.00	15.00	$5.00
2	10.00	8.00	18.00	5.00	4.00	9.00	18.00	3.00
3	10.00	10.00	20.00	3.33	3.33	6.67	20.00	2.00
4	10.00	11.00	21.00	2.50	2.75	5.25	21.00	1.00
5	10.00	13.00	23.00	2.00	2.60	4.60	23.00	2.00
6	10.00	16.00	26.00	1.67	2.67	4.33	26.00	3.00
7	10.00	20.00	30.00	1.43	2.86	4.28	30.00	4.00
8	10.00	25.00	35.00	1.25	3.13	4.38	35.00	5.00
9	10.00	31.00	41.00	1.11	3.44	4.56	41.00	6.00
10	10.00	38.00	48.00	1.00	3.80	4.80	48.00	7.00
11	10.00	46.00	56.00	.91	4.18	5.09	56.00	8.00

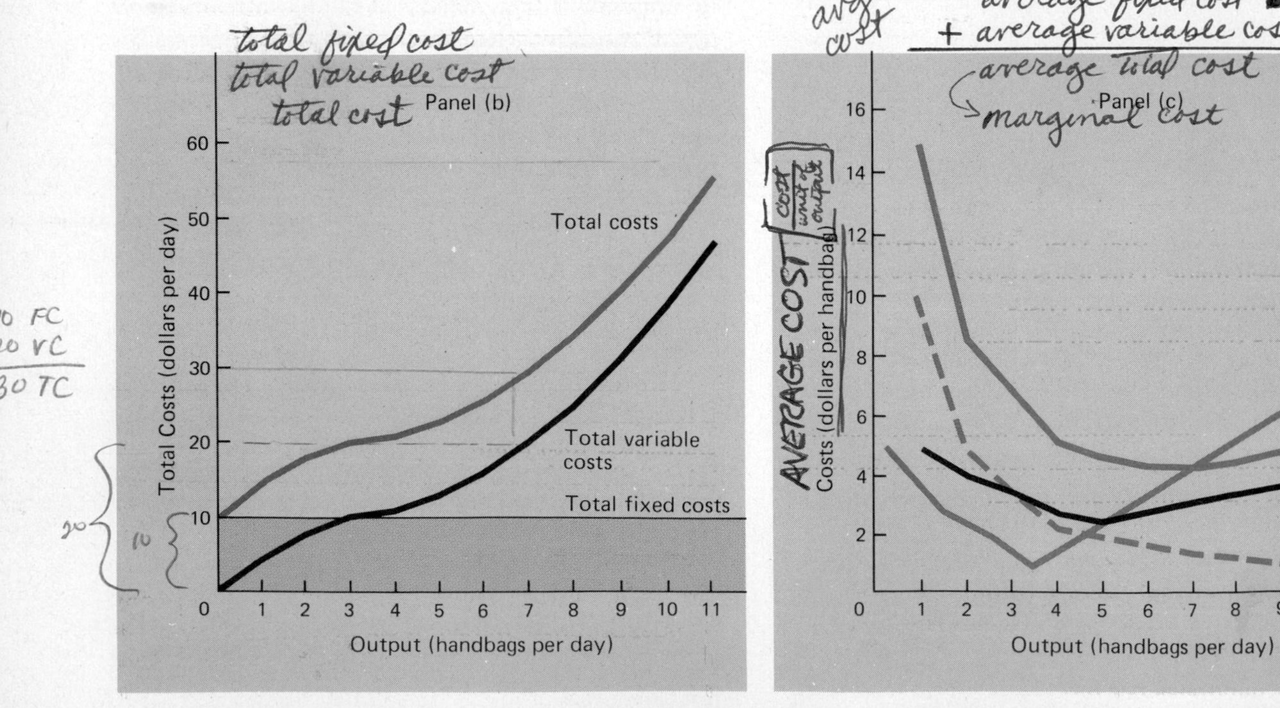

Short-Run Firm Costs

In the short run, a firm incurs certain types of costs. We label all costs incurred as **total costs.** Then we divide total costs into total fixed costs and total variable costs, which we explain below. The relationship, or identity, is, therefore:

total costs = total fixed costs + total variable costs

After we have looked at the elements of total costs, we will find out how to compute average and marginal costs.

TOTAL FIXED COSTS

Let's look at an ongoing business such as General Motors. The decision makers in that corporate giant can look around and see big machines, thousands of parts, huge buildings, and a multitude of other pieces of plant and equipment that are in place, that have already been bought. General Motors has to take account of the wear and tear and technological obsolescence of this equipment, no matter how many cars it produces. The payments on the loans taken out to buy the equipment will all be exactly the same. The opportunity costs of any land that General Motors owns will all be exactly the same.

We also have to point out that the opportunity cost (or normal rate of return) of capital must be included along with other fixed costs. Remember that we are dealing in the short run, where capital is fixed. Thus, if investors in General Motors have already put $10 million into a new factory addition, the opportunity cost of that capital invested is now, in essence, a fixed cost. Why? Because nothing can be done about that cost. The investment has already been made. This leads us to a very straightforward definition of fixed costs.

All costs that do not vary—that is, costs that do not depend on the rate of production—are called **fixed costs,** or *sunk* costs.

Let's take as an example the fixed costs incurred by a manufacturer of leather handbags. This firm's total fixed costs will equal the cost of the rent on its equipment and the insurance it has to pay. We see in panel (a) of Exhibit 8–3 that total fixed costs per day are $10. In panel (b) of Exhibit 8–3, these total fixed costs are represented by the horizontal line at $10 per day. They are invariant to changes in the output of handbags per day—no matter how many are produced, fixed costs will remain at $10 per day.

The difference between total costs and total fixed costs is total variable costs (total costs − total fixed costs = total variable costs).

TOTAL VARIABLE COSTS

Total **variable costs** are those costs whose magnitude varies with the rate of production. One obvious variable cost is wages paid. The more the firm produces, the more wages it has to pay. There are other variable costs, though. One is materials. In the production of leather handbags, for example, leather must be bought. The more handbags that are made, the more leather must be bought. Part of the rate of depreciation (the rate of wear and tear) on machines that are used in the production process can also be considered a variable cost, if depreciation depends partly on how long and how intensively the machines are used. Total variable costs are given in panel (a) of Exhibit 8–3 in column 3. These are translated into the total variable cost curve in panel (b) of Exhibit 8–3. Notice that the variable cost curve lies below the total cost curve by the vertical distance of $10. This vertical distance represents, of course, total fixed costs.

SHORT-RUN AVERAGE COST CURVES

In panel (b) of Exhibit 8–3, we see total costs, total variable costs, and total fixed costs. Now we want to look at average cost. The average cost concept is simply one in which we are measuring cost per unit of output. It is a matter of simple arithmetic to figure the averages of these three cost concepts. We can define them simply as follows:

$$\text{average total costs} = \frac{\text{total costs}}{\text{output}}$$

$$\text{average variable costs} = \frac{\text{total variable costs}}{\text{output}}$$

$$\text{average fixed costs} = \frac{\text{total fixed costs}}{\text{output}}$$

The arithmetic is done in columns 5, 6, and 7 in panel (a) of Exhibit 8–3. The numerical results are translated into graphical format in panel (c) of Exhibit 8–3. Let's see what we can observe about the three average cost curves on that graph.

Average Fixed Costs (AFC)

Average fixed costs continue to fall throughout the output range. In fact, if we were to continue the diagram farther to the right, we would find that average fixed costs would get closer and closer to the horizontal axis. That is because total fixed costs remain constant. As we divide this fixed number by a larger and larger number of units of output, the result, AFC, has to become smaller and smaller.

Average Variable Costs (AVC)

We assume a particular form of the **average variable cost** curve. The form that it takes is U-shaped: first it falls; then it starts to rise. It is certainly possible to have other shapes of the average variable cost curve.

Average Total Costs (ATC)

This curve has a shape similar to the average variable cost curve. However, it falls even more dramatically in the beginning and rises more slowly after it has reached a minimum point. It falls and then rises because ATC is the summation of the average fixed cost curve and the average variable cost curve. Thus, when AFC plus AVC are both falling, it is only logical that ATC would fall, too. At some point, however, AVC starts to increase while AFC continues to fall. Once the increase in the AVC curve outweighs the decrease in the AFC curve, the ATC curve will start to increase and will develop its familiar U shape.

MARGINAL COST

We have stated repeatedly in this text that the action is always on the margin—movement in economics is always determined at the margin. This dictum holds true within the firm also. Firms, according to the analysis we use to predict their behavior, are very interested in their **marginal costs.** Since the term *marginal* means additional or incremental, marginal costs refer to those costs that result from a one-unit change in the production rate. For example, if the production of 10 leather handbags per day costs a firm \$48 and the production of 11 leather handbags costs it \$56 per day, then the marginal cost of producing that eleventh leather handbag per day is \$8.

We find marginal cost by subtracting the total cost of producing all but the last unit from the total cost of producing all units, including the last one. Marginal costs can be measured, therefore, by using the formula:

$$\textbf{marginal cost} = \frac{\textbf{change in total cost}}{\textbf{change in output}}$$

We show the marginal costs of handbag production per day in column 8 of panel (a) in Exhibit 8–3, where marginal cost is defined as the change in total cost divided by the change in output. In our particular example, we have changed output by one unit every time, so we can ignore the denominator in that particular formula.

This marginal cost schedule is shown graphically in panel (c) of Exhibit 8–3. Just like average variable costs and average total costs, marginal costs first fall and then rise. It is interesting to look at the relationship between marginal costs and average costs.

THE RELATIONSHIP BETWEEN AVERAGE AND MARGINAL COSTS

There is always a definite relationship between averages and marginals. Consider the example of ten football players with an average weight of 200 pounds. An eleventh player is added. His weight is 250 pounds. That represents the marginal weight. What happens now to the average weight of the team? It must increase. Thus, when the marginal player weighs more than the average, the average must increase. Likewise, if the marginal player weighs less than 200 pounds, the average weight will decrease.

There is a similar relationship between average variable costs and marginal costs. When marginal costs are less than average costs, the latter are falling. Conversely, when marginal costs are greater than average costs, the latter are rising. When you think about it, the relationship is obvious. The only way for average variable costs to fall is for the extra cost of the marginal unit produced to be less than the average variable cost of all the preceding units. For example, if the average variable cost for two units of production is \$4 a unit, the only way for the average variable cost of three units to fall is for the variable costs attributable to the last unit—the marginal cost—to be less than the average of the past units. In this particular case, if average variable cost falls to \$3.33 a unit, then total variable cost for the three units would be three times \$3.33, or (to round it off) \$10. Total variable cost for two units is two times \$4, or \$8. The marginal cost is therefore \$10 minus \$8, or \$2, which is less than the average variable cost of \$3.33.

A similar type of computation can be carried out for rising average variable costs. The only way for average variable costs to rise is for the average variable cost of additional units to be more than that for units already produced. But the incremental cost is the marginal cost. Therefore, in this particular case, the marginal costs have to be higher than the average variable costs.

There is also a relationship between marginal

costs and average total costs. Remember that average total cost is equal to total cost divided by the number of units produced. Remember also that marginal cost does not include any fixed costs. Fixed costs are, by definition, fixed and cannot influence marginal costs. The above example can be repeated substituting the term *average total cost* for the term *average variable cost.*

In other words, the marginal cost curve is uniquely related to both the average total cost curve and the average variable cost curve because marginal cost is defined as the *change* in total cost. As we increase production, fixed costs do not change. Therefore, the average total cost curve is changing because of a change in variable costs. This means that the preceding discussion can be applied in terms of the relationship between marginal costs and average variable costs or marginal costs and average total costs. In other words, when marginal costs are less than either average total costs or average variable costs, the latter two are falling. Conversely, when marginal costs are greater than either average total costs or average variable costs, the latter two are rising. Finally, marginal cost will just equal both average total costs and average variable costs at their respective minimum points. These rising and falling relationships can be seen in Exhibit 8–3(c). You can also see there that MC intersects AVC and ATC at their respective minimum points.

FINDING MINIMUM COSTS

At what rate of output of leather handbags per day does our representative firm experience the minimum average total costs? Column 7 in panel (a) of Exhibit 8–3 shows that the minimum average total cost is $4.28, which occurs at an output rate of seven leather handbags per day. We can find this minimum cost also by finding the point in panel (c) of Exhibit 8–3 at which the marginal cost curve intersects the average total cost curve. This should not be surprising. When marginal cost is below average total cost, average total cost falls. When marginal cost is above average total cost, average total cost rises. At the point where average total costs are neither falling nor rising, marginal cost must then be equal to average total cost. When we represent this graphically, the marginal cost curve will intersect the average total cost curve at its minimum.

The same analysis applies to the intersection of the marginal cost curve and the average variable cost curve. When are average variable costs at a minimum? According to panel (a) of Exhibit 8–3, average variable costs are at a minimum of $2.60 at an output rate of five leather handbags per day. This is exactly where the marginal cost curve intersects the average variable cost curve in panel (c) of Exhibit 8–3.

The Relationship Between Costs and Production

There is a unique relationship between output and the shape of the various cost curves we have drawn. Let's consider specifically the relationship between marginal cost and the example of diminishing marginal physical returns in panel (a) of Exhibit 8–2. It turns out that (if wage rates are constant) the shape of the marginal cost curve is both a reflection and a consequence of the law of diminishing returns. Let's assume that each unit of labor can be purchased at a constant price. Further assume that labor is the only variable input. We see that as more workers are hired, marginal physical product first rises and then falls after the point where diminishing returns are encountered. Thus, the marginal cost of each extra unit of output will first fall as long as marginal physical product is rising, and then it will rise as long as marginal physical product is falling. Consider specifically panel (a) of Exhibit 8–2. Assume that a worker is paid $100 a week. When we go from zero labor input to one unit, output increases by 10 bushels of wheat. Thus, each of those 10 bushels of wheat has a marginal cost of $10. Now the second unit of labor is hired, and it, too, costs $100. Output increases by 16. Thus, the marginal cost is $100 ÷ 16 = $6.25. We continue the experiment. We see that the next unit of labor yields only 10 additional bushels of wheat, so that marginal cost starts to rise again back to $10. The following unit of labor increases marginal physical product by only 8, so that marginal cost becomes $100 ÷ 8 = $12.50.

Even though the above numerical example relates each additional output to some marginal unit of labor, remember that we are assuming that all labor is of equal quality. We assume that every worker is paid $100 a week, and we assume that every worker has exactly the same skills. Therefore, the additional output comes from a larger labor force as opposed to one specific worker who was just hired. The fact that we are actually dealing with a change in the entire labor force that the firm is using becomes important in later chapters when we discuss factor markets—the demand and supply of labor and capital.

> ***Concepts in Brief 8-3***
>
> ■ Total costs equal total fixed costs plus total variable costs.
>
> ■ Fixed costs are those that do not vary with the rate of production; variable costs are those that do vary with the rate of production.
>
> ■ Average total costs equal total costs divided by output, or ATC = TC ÷ Q.
>
> ■ Average variable costs equal total variable costs divided by output, or AVC = TVC ÷ Q.
>
> ■ Average fixed costs equal total fixed costs divided by output, or AFC = TFC ÷ Q.
>
> ■ Marginal cost equals the change in total cost divided by the change in output.
>
> ■ The marginal cost curve intersects the minimum point of the average total cost curve and the minimum point of the average variable cost curve.

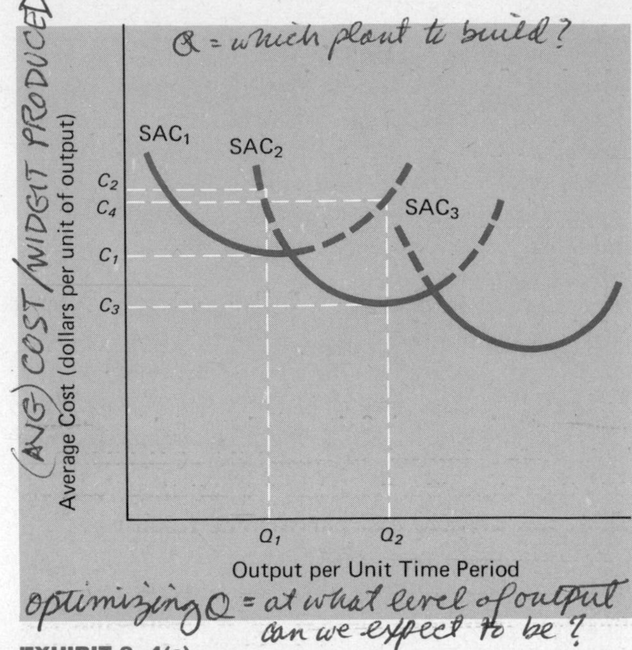

EXHIBIT 8–4(a)

A Preferable Plant Size. If the anticipated permanent rate of output per unit time period is Q_1, the optimal plant to build would be the one corresponding to SAC_1, because average costs are lower. However, if the permanent rate of output increases to Q_2, it will be more profitable to have a plant size corresponding to SAC_2. Unit costs fall to C_3.

Long-Run Cost Curves

The long run, as you will remember, is defined as a time period during which full adjustment can be made to any change in the economic environment. Thus, *in the long run, all factors of production are variable.* Long-run curves are sometimes called planning curves, and the long run is sometimes called the **planning horizon.**

We start out our analysis of long-run cost curves by considering a single firm contemplating the construction of a single plant. The firm has, let us say, three alternative plant sizes from which to choose on the planning horizon. Each particular plant size generates its own short-run average total cost curve. Now that we are talking about the difference between long- and short-run cost curves, we will label all short-run curves with an *S;* short-run average (total) costs will be labeled SAC, and all long-run average cost curves will be labeled LAC.

Look at panel (a) of Exhibit 8–4. Here we have shown three short-run average cost curves for three plant sizes that are successively larger. Which is the optimal plant size to build? That depends on the anticipated normal, sustained rate of output per unit time period. Assume for a moment that the anticipated normal, sustained rate is Q_1. If plant size 1 is built, the average costs will be C_1. If plant size 2 is built, we see on SAC_2 that the average costs will be C_2, which is greater than C_1. Thus, if the anticipated rate of output is Q_1, the appropriate plant size is the one from which SAC_1 was derived.

Note, however, that if the anticipated permanent rate of output per unit time period goes from Q_1 to Q_2, and plant size 1 had been decided upon, average costs would be C_4. However, if plant size 2 had been decided upon, average costs would be C_3, which are clearly less than C_4.

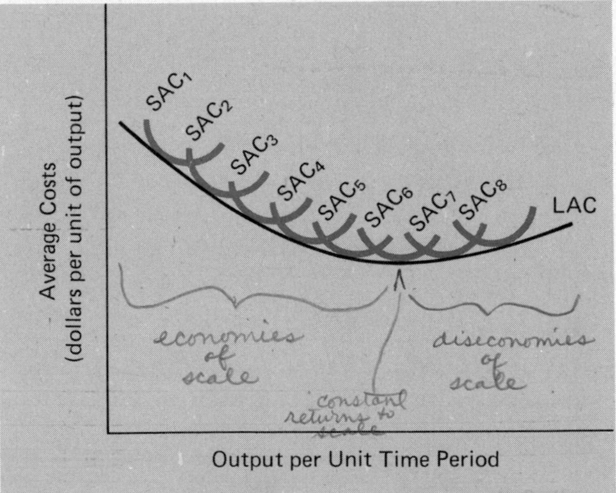

EXHIBIT 8–4(b)

Deriving the Long-run Average Cost Curve. If we draw all the possible short-run average cost curves that correspond to different plant sizes and then draw the envelope to these various curves, $SAC_1 \ldots SAC_8$, we obtain the long-run average cost curve, or the planning curve.

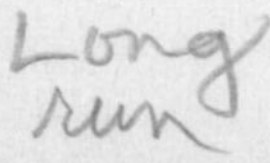

In choosing the appropriate plant size for a single-plant firm during the planning horizon, the firm will pick that plant size whose short-run average cost curve generates an average cost that is lowest for the expected rate of output.

LONG-RUN AVERAGE COST CURVE

If we make the further assumption that the entrepreneur is faced with an infinite number of choices of plant sizes in the long run, then we can conceive of an infinite number of SAC curves similar to the three in panel (a) of Exhibit 8–4. We are not able, of course, to draw an infinite number; we have drawn quite a few, however, in panel (b) of Exhibit 8–4. We then draw the "envelope" to all these various short-run average cost curves. The resulting envelope is the **long-run average cost curve (LAC).** This long-run average cost curve is sometimes called the **planning curve,** for it represents the various average costs attainable at the planning stage of the firm's decision making. It represents the locus (path) of points giving the least unit cost of producing any given rate of output. Note that the LAC curve is *not* tangent to each individual SAC curve at the latter's minimum point. This is only true at the minimum point of the LAC curve. Then and only then are minimum long-run average costs equal to minimum short-run average costs.

ECONOMIES OF SCALE, DISECONOMIES OF SCALE, AND CONSTANT RETURNS TO SCALE

We have been referring to long-run cost curves. Remember that in the long run, all factors of production are variable. Thus, we are talking about a change in the scale of a particular firm, where scale refers to a change in the amount of capital and labor. The long-run average cost curve of a firm, therefore, is a reflection of a changing scale. But the long-run average cost curve can slope down, be horizontal, or slope up. When it slopes down, it means that average costs decrease as output increases. Whenever this happens, the firm is experiencing **economies of scale.** If, on the other hand, the long-run average cost curve is sloping upward, the firm is incurring increases in average costs as output increases. That firm is said to be experiencing **diseconomies of scale.** Finally, if long-run average costs are invariant to changes in output, the firm is experiencing **constant returns to scale.** In Exhibit 8–5, we show three panels (a), (b), and (c). The first one is for a firm experiencing economies of scale; the second one, constant returns to scale; and the third one, diseconomies of scale.

Reasons Why We See Economies of Scale

Here we list several reasons why a firm might be expected to experience economies of scale. Of course, there are others.

Specialization

As a firm's scale of operation increases, the opportunities for specialization in the use of resource inputs also increase. This is sometimes called increased division of tasks, or operations. Gains from such division of labor or increased specialization are well known; see, for example, Adam Smith's famous

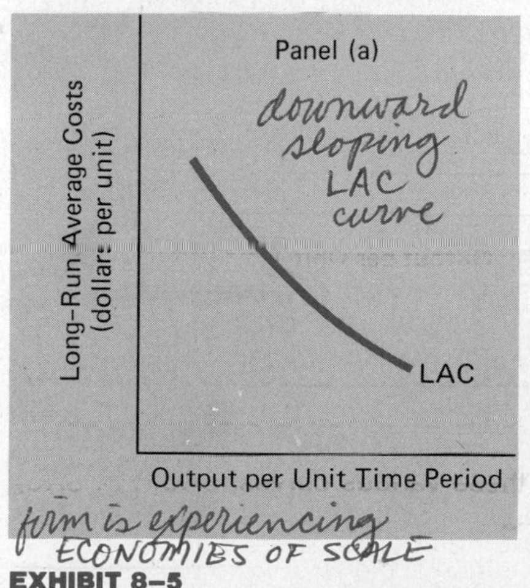

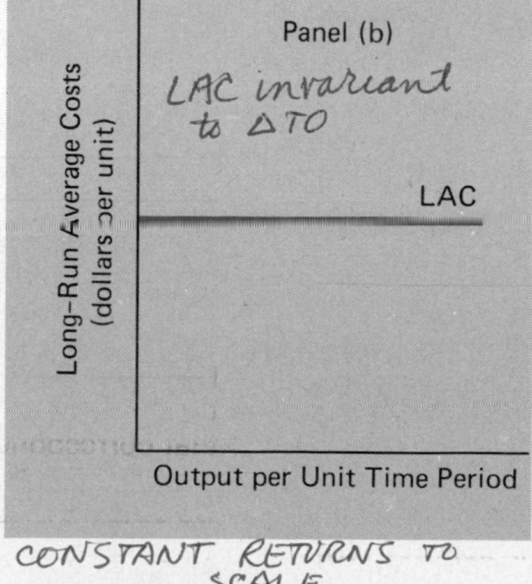

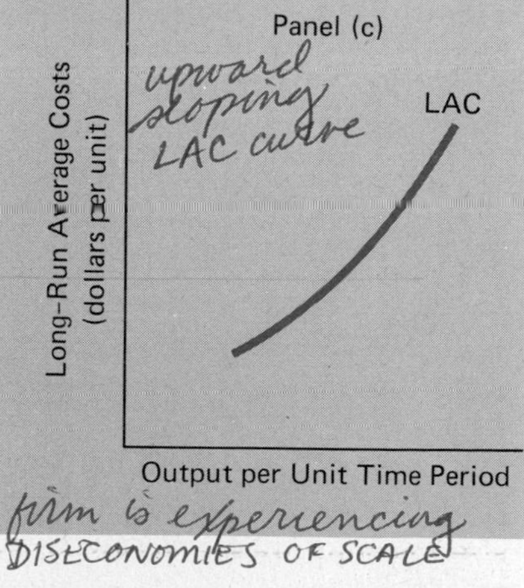

EXHIBIT 8–5

Economies of, Constant Returns to, and Diseconomies of Scale Shown with Long-run Average Cost Curves. Long-run average cost curves will fall when there are economies of scale, as shown in panel (a). They will be constant when the firm is experiencing constant returns to scale, as shown in panel (b). And, finally, long-run average costs will rise when the firm is experiencing diseconomies of scale, as shown in panel (c).

pin factory case.[2] When we consider managerial staffs, we also find that larger enterprises may be able to put together more highly specialized staffs. Larger enterprises may have the ability to tap better managerial technology.

Dimensional Factor

Large-scale firms often require proportionately less input per unit of output simply because certain inputs do not have to be physically doubled in order to double the output. Consider the cost of storage of, say, oil. The cost of storage is basically related to the cost of steel that goes into building the storage container; however, the amount of steel required goes up less than in proportion to the volume (storage capacity) of the container (because the volume of a sphere increases more than proportionately with its circumference).

Transportation Factor

The transportation cost per unit will fall as the market area increases. The market size increases by πr^2, which is the formula for the area of a circle where r is the radius. For example, transportation distance from the center of the circle to the perimeter is equal to r, the radius; doubling the transportation distance quadruples the market area.

Improved Productive Equipment

The larger the scale of the enterprise, the more the firm is able to take advantage of larger-volume (output capacity) types of machinery. Small-scale operations may not be able to use profitably large-volume machines.

WHY A FIRM MIGHT EXPERIENCE DISECONOMIES OF SCALE

One of the basic reasons that the firm can expect to run into diseconomies of scale is that there are limits to the efficient functioning of management. Moreover, as more workers are hired, a more-than-proportionate increase in managers may be needed, and this could cause increased costs per unit. For example, it might be possible to hire from one to ten workers and give them each a shovel to dig ditches; however, as soon as ten workers are hired, it may also be necessary to hire an overseer to coordinate their ditchdigging efforts. Thus, perhaps constant returns to scale will obtain until ten workers and ten shovels are employed; then decreasing returns to scale set in. As the layers of supervision grow, the costs of information and communication grow more than proportionately. Hence, the average per unit cost will start to increase.

ECONOMIES OF SCALE AT THE PLANT LEVEL

We have been referring to economies of scale for the firm. People often associate economies of scale with a large plant, such as a steel mill. There is a commonsense notion that average costs will fall as the rate of output per plant per day increases. There are certainly reasons for us to observe this. Larger plants can indeed take advantage of more specialized division of labor. In any event, to make the distinction clear, if we are referring to a single plant, we should state that we are interested in *plant level* economies of scale. For example, the downward-sloping portion of the LAC in Exhibit 8–4(b) is for a single plant that is changed in size as the scale of the plant increases. The downward sloping portion of that LAC would be a graphical representation of plant level economies of scale.

Concepts in Brief 8-4

- The long run is often called the planning horizon.
- The long-run average cost is the planning curve. It is found by drawing a line tangent to one point on a series of short-run average cost curves, each corresponding to a different plant size.
- The firm can experience economies of scale, diseconomies of scale, and constant returns to scale, all according to whether the long-run average cost curve slopes down, up, or is horizontal (flat). Economies of scale refer to what happens when all factors of production are increased.
- We observe economies of scale because of: (1) specialization; (2) improved productive equipment; (3) the dimensional factor, since large-scale firms require proportionately less input per unit of output; and (4) the transportation factor.
- The firm may experience diseconomies of scale because of limits to the efficient functioning of management.
- When we are observing what happens at a single plant, we are interested in plant level economies of scale.

[2] Adam Smith, *The Wealth of Nations [1776]* (Modern Library, Random House, New York, 1957), Book I, chap. 1, pp. 4–5.

ISSUES AND APPLICATIONS

How Do We Measure the Capacity of the Firm?

> ***Concepts Applied***
> ■ Short- and long-run marginal costs and average costs

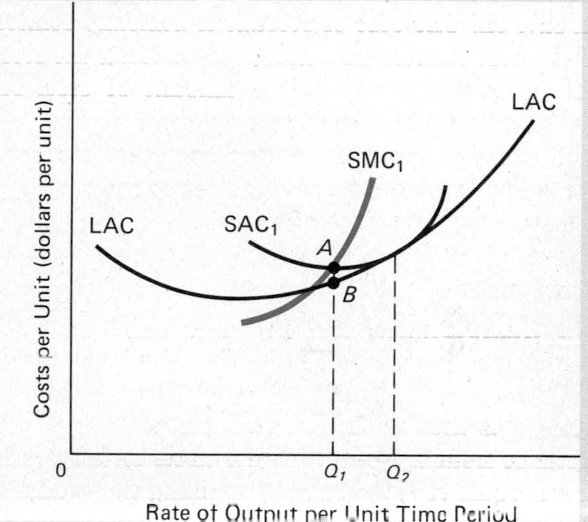

EXHIBIT 8–6
Defining Capacity. Capacity is often defined as the rate of output at which short-run average costs are at a minimum. One such output rate is Q_1, but at that output rate, the difference between short-run average costs and long-run average costs is the vertical distance between A and B. The firm would not, in the long run, keep that plant size if the expected output rate were permanently Q_1. If capacity is defined as the rate of output at which there is no incentive to alter the size of the plant, then output rate Q_2 is the measure of capacity because, at that output rate, short-run average costs are equal to long-run average costs.

One often reads that manufacturing is only producing at 60–80 percent of capacity. Or one often hears the phrase *at full capacity.* The notion of full capacity for a firm is an elusive one. Clearly, it must be a short-run concept, because in the long run the size of the plant and the number of plants are variable. Hence, the term *capacity* must refer to the use of a given capital stock. But it cannot refer to some physical notion of using plant and equipment to its ultimate limit. At a high enough price, just a little bit more output can always be obtained from a plant, even one already running 24 hours a day; but the marginal cost of obtaining that additional "bit" may be astronomical. Thus, the notion of capacity must in some way relate to unit cost.

Indeed, it is possible, but not appropriate, as we will see, to define capacity in terms of minimum average total cost. In fact, one suggested definition of capacity is the output at which short-run average costs are at a minimum. If this definition were used in Exhibit 8–6 for plant size 1, which yields short-run average cost curve SAC$_1$ (intercepted at its minimum point by SMC$_1$), capacity would be Q_1. But something seems wrong here. The long-run average cost curve is defined as the minimum unit cost of producing at every feasible rate of output. Average costs for output rate Q_1 in Exhibit 8–6 are represented by the vertical distance from point A, the minimum point on SAC$_1$, to the horizontal axis. However, if the firm expected to produce this rate of output indefinitely, it would not build so large a plant; it would build the smaller plant whose short-run average cost curve would be tangent to the LAC curve at point B. Average costs per unit would drop from AQ_1 to BQ_1.

This gives a hint of what the appropriate definition for capacity for a given size of plant might be. Capacity can be defined as the rate of output at which there is no incentive to alter the size of the plant if that rate of output is expected to be permanent. Thus, for plant size 1, as represented by SAC$_1$, the capacity would have to be at output rate Q_2 because here long-run average costs

"full capacity" for a firm: the rate of output at which there is no incentive to alter the size of the plant.

and short-run average costs are equal.

Thus, our notion of capacity, even though short-run in nature, relates to long-run considerations.

Questions

1. How was the LAC curve derived in Exhibit 8–6?
2. How does the notion of capacity relate to fixed capital?

How Does a Tax Affect a Firm's Cost Curves?

Concepts Applied

■ Marginal cost, average variable cost, and average total cost

It might be useful at this point to show how to represent the effects of a tax on a firm. Let's talk about a tax on each unit of production. This will be a unit tax. It is not based on the value of the output, but rather on the mere fact that output is being produced. What do you think happens to all of those curves in Exhibit 8–3(c)—which related to handbags—when a per unit tax is put on the production of handbags?

Let's ask ourselves what happens to fixed costs. The tax is incurred only if the firm produces handbags. If it produces nothing, it does not have to pay the tax. This means that fixed costs do not change; average fixed costs will remain the same also, so the AFC curve does not change. When it comes to the average variable costs, things do change. Each time a new unit is produced, the tax has to be paid. This means that the average variable cost curve will move up vertically by the amount of the tax. We show this in Exhibit 8–7. Since average variable cost moves up, so does the average total cost curve, and by the same amount.

What about marginal costs? Marginal costs will have to move up also. The marginal cost curve, MC, will move up vertically by the amount of the tax on each unit of production. After all, marginal cost is defined as the increment in costs. If the firm must pay a tax when it produces one more handbag, this means the marginal cost will go up by that tax also.

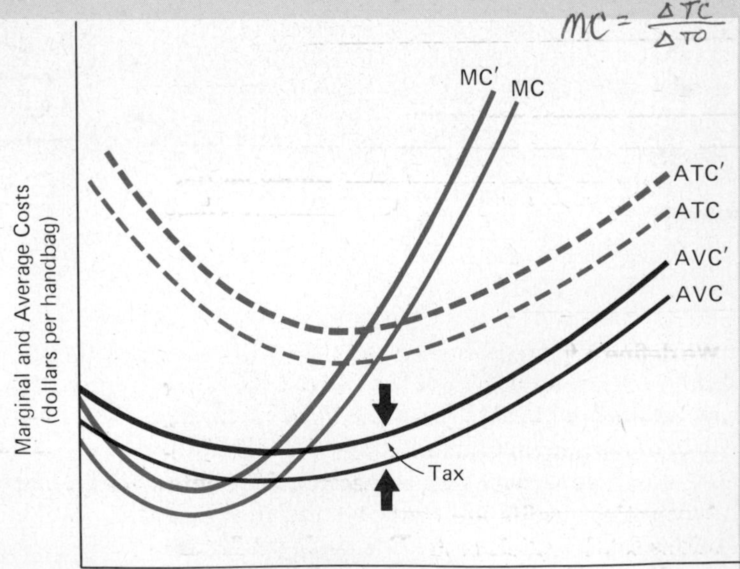

EXHIBIT 8–7
The Effects of a Per-Unit Tax. Here we redo Exhibit 8–3(a), but now we take into account the effects of a tax on each unit produced. The government, for example, charges 20¢ per handbag to the handbag manufacturer. This changes the handbag manufacturer's cost curves. The average variable cost curve moves up to AVC′, the heavy black line. It moves up by the vertical distance equal to the amount of the tax. After all, the tax is on each unit of production. That means that the marginal cost curve will move up also. It moves from MC to MC′. And finally, the average total curve, ATC, moves to ATC′.

Questions

1. What would a lump-sum tax on each firm do to each firm's marginal cost curves?
2. How does a lump-sum tax affect the average fixed cost curve?

Definition of Terms

Firm An organization that brings together different factors of production, such as labor, land, and capital, to produce a product or service that can be sold for a profit. A firm is usually made up of an entrepreneur, managers, and workers.

Opportunity cost of capital The normal rate of return or the amount that must be paid to an investor to induce her or him to invest in a business. Economists consider this a cost of production and it is included in our cost examples.

NROR

Production function The relationship between inputs and output. A production function is a technological, not an economic, relationship.

Law of diminishing (marginal) returns After some point, successive increases in a variable factor of production, such as labor, added to fixed factors of production, will result in less than a proportional increase in output.

Marginal physical product The physical output that is due to the addition of one more unit of a variable factor of production—that is, the change in total product occurring when a variable input is increased and all other inputs are held constant.

Total costs All the costs of a firm combined, including rent, payments to workers, interest on borrowed money, and so on.

Fixed costs Those costs that do not vary with output. Fixed costs include such things as rent on a building and the price of machinery. These costs are fixed for a certain period of time; in the long run they are variable.

Variable costs Those costs that vary with the rate of production. They include wages paid to workers, the costs of materials, and so on.

Average fixed costs Total fixed costs divided by the number of units produced.

Average variable costs Total variable costs divided by the number of units produced.

Average total costs Total costs divided by the number of units produced; sometimes called average per unit total costs.

$MC = \frac{\Delta TC}{\Delta TO}$

Marginal costs The change in total costs due to a change of one unit of production.

Planning horizon Another name for long-run cost curves. All inputs are variable during the planning period.

avg total

Long-run average cost curve (LAC) The locus of points representing the minimum unit cost of producing any given rate of output, given current technology and resource prices.

Planning curve Another name for the long-run average cost curve.

Economies of scale When output increases lead to decreases in long-run average costs.

Diseconomies of scale When output increases lead to increases in long-run average costs.

Constant returns to scale A situation in which the long-run average cost curve of a firm remains flat, or horizontal, as output increases.

Chapter Summary

1. We define a firm as a business organization that brings together factors of production in order to produce a product and sell it for a profit.
2. It is important in economics to distinguish between accounting profits and economic profits. Accounting profits are equal to total revenues minus total explicit costs. Economic profits are equal to total revenues minus total opportunity costs of all factors of production.
3. The technological relationship between inputs and output is called a production function.
4. When we hold constant all factors of production except one, an increase in that factor will lead to a change in total physical product. That is how we derive the total physical product curve.
5. The marginal physical product curve is derived from looking at the change in total physical product.
6. After some output rate, firms enter the region of diminishing marginal returns, or diminishing marginal physical product. In other words, af-

ter some point, each increment of the variable input will yield a smaller and smaller increment in total output.

7. Fixed costs are those that cannot be altered in the short run. Fixed costs are associated with assets which the firm owns that cannot be profitably transferred to another use.
8. Variable costs are associated with input costs that vary as the rate of output varies. The wage bill is a good example of a variable cost.
9. There are definitional relationships between average, total, and marginal costs. They are:

$$\text{ATC} = \frac{\text{TC}}{Q}$$

$$\text{AVC} = \frac{\text{TVC}}{Q}$$

$$\text{AFC} = \frac{\text{TFC}}{Q}$$

$$\text{MC} = \frac{\text{change in TC}}{\text{change in } Q}$$

10. When marginal costs are less than average costs, average costs are falling. When marginal costs are greater than average costs, average costs are rising.
11. The marginal cost curve intersects the average variable cost curve and the average total cost curve at their minimum points.
12. Given a constant wage rate, the marginal cost curve is the mirror image of the marginal physical product curve. Thus, because of the law of diminishing returns, marginal costs eventually will rise.
13. In the long run, all costs are variable, including the costs of plant and equipment, which can either be expanded or allowed to depreciate.
14. We derive the long-run average cost curve by connecting a smooth line to all of the short-run average cost curves. This long-run average cost curve is sometimes called the planning curve.
15. It is possible for a firm to experience increasing, constant, or decreasing returns to scale, in which case a proportionate increase in *all* inputs will be less than, the same as, or more than the increase in output.
16. Firms may experience increasing returns to scale because of: (a) specialization, (b) the dimensional factor, (c) the transportation factor, and (d) the ability to purchase improved productive equipment.
17. Firms may experience decreasing returns to scale because of the limitations of efficient management.
18. The long-run average cost curve will be downward sloping, horizontal, or upward sloping, depending on whether there are increasing, constant, or decreasing returns to scale.
19. We measure capacity as that rate of output at which there is no incentive to alter the size of the plant if the rate of output is expected to be permanent.
20. A per unit tax will shift up the MC, ATC, and AVC curves.

Selected References

Coase, Ronald H. "The Nature of the Firm." *Economica,* New Series, 4 (November 1936), pp. 386–405.

Kaish, Stanley. *Microeconomics: Logic, Tools, and Analysis.* New York: Harper & Row, 1976, chap. 6.

Leftwich, Richard H. *The Price System and Resource Allocation.* 7th ed. New York: Dryden Press, 1979, chaps. 8 and 9.

Watson, Donald S., and Malcolm Getz. *Price Theory and Its Uses.* 5th ed. Boston: Houghton Mifflin, 1981, chaps. 8–11.

Answers to Preview and Study Questions

1. How does the economist's definition of profit differ from the accountant's?

The accountant defines total profits as total revenues minus total costs; the economist defines total profits as total revenues minus total opportunity costs of all inputs used. In other words, the economist takes into account *implicit* as well as explicit costs; the economist's definition stresses that an opportunity cost exists for all inputs used in the production process. Specifically, the economist estimates the opportunity cost for invested capital, the owner's time, inventories on hand, and so on. Since the economist's definition of costs is more inclusive, accounting profits will always exceed economic profits; economic profits exist only when all the opportunity costs are taken into account.

2. What distinguishes the long run from the short run?

The short run is defined as any time period when there is at least one factor of production that a firm *cannot* vary; in the long run *all* factors of production can be varied by the firm. Since each industry is likely to be unique in its ability to vary all inputs, "the" long run differs from industry to industry. Presumably, the long run is a lot shorter (in absolute time periods) for firms in the carpentry or plumbing industry than for firms in the automobile or steel industry. In most economic models labor is usually assumed to be the variable input in the short run, while capital is considered to be fixed in the short run; this assumption is fairly descriptive of the "real world" situation.

3. How does the law of diminishing returns account for an *eventually* increasing marginal cost curve for a firm in the short run?

By definition, the short run is a period during which the firm can change output only by varying one input; the other inputs are fixed in the short run. As a consequence, the firm can produce more and more only by using more and more of that one input, say labor, other inputs being constant. *Eventually* the law of diminishing returns comes into play (previous to this point, specialization benefits might *increase* the marginal product of labor) and the marginal product of labor falls. That is, beyond the point of diminishing returns extra laborers contribute less to total product than do immediately preceding laborers, per unit of time. In effect this means that if output is to be increased by equal amounts (or equal "batches"), more and more labor time will be required—due to its lower marginal product. Later units of output, which are physically identical to earlier units of output, have more labor time embodied within them. If wages are constant then later units, which require more man-hours, have a higher marginal cost. If we ignore raw material costs, then marginal cost (MC) equals the given wage rate (W) divided by the marginal product of labor (MP_L);

$$MC = \frac{W}{MP_L}$$

We conclude that beyond the point of diminishing returns the marginal cost of output rises for the firm, in the short run. Prior to the point of diminishing returns the marginal cost curve falls, due to rising marginal product of labor.

4. Why is the average total cost (ATC) curve U-shaped?

ATC equals the sum of average fixed cost (AFC) and average variable cost (AVC); ATC = AFC + AVC. The AFC curve continuously falls since it is derived by dividing a constant number (total fixed cost) by larger and larger numbers (output levels). It falls rapidly at first, then slowly. The AVC curve falls during the early output stages because the benefits of specialization cause the marginal product of labor to rise and the marginal cost of output to fall; beyond the point of diminishing returns the marginal product of labor falls, eventually forcing marginal cost to rise above AVC, and therefore AVC rises too. As we go from zero output to higher and higher output levels per unit of time, AFC and AVC both initially fall; therefore, ATC falls too. Beyond the point of diminishing returns AVC rises and outweighs the now slowly falling AFC curve; the net result is that somewhere beyond the point of diminishing returns the ATC curve rises. Since the ATC curve falls at low output levels and rises at higher output levels we describe it as U-shaped.

5. How are the marginal cost (MC) and the average total cost (ATC) curves related?

To understand this relationship it is important to understand the relationship between marginal and average "anything"—batting averages, field goal percentages, foul shot averages, utility, propensities to consume—and labor outputs. The rule is that marginal "pulls and tugs" average; if marginal is *above* average (whether marginal is rising or falling), average will rise, and if marginal is *below* average (whether marginal is rising or falling), average will fall. Thus, if your marginal performance in anything is below average, your average will fall; if your marginal performance is above average your average will rise. Thus, whenever MC is below ATC, ATC will fall; whenever MC is above ATC, ATC will rise. It follows that when MC = ATC, ATC will neither rise nor fall, ATC will be at a minimum point. In summary, ATC and MC are both U-shaped; when ATC is falling MC is below it; when ATC is rising MC is above it; when ATC is at its minimum point (ATC is neither rising nor falling) it equals MC; hence, MC intersects ATC at ATC's minimum point.

Problems

(Answers at the back of the book)

1. What is wrong with the following reasoning: Now that I have paid off my van, it won't cost me anything except for the running expenses, such as gas, oil, and tune-ups, when I actually go somewhere in it.

2.

Units of Labor (per 8-hour day)	*Marginal Product of Labor (per 8-hour day)*
1	2
2	4
3	6
.	.
.	.
.	.
.	.
12	20
13	10
14	5
15	3
16	2

a. Suppose this firm, which is in the short run, wants to increase output in "batches" of 2; how much labor time is required to produce the first batch? The second and third batches? Do the fourth, fifth, and sixth batches of 2 require more or less labor time than the earlier batches of 2?

b. Suppose we move down our table to the point at which we have hired 11 laborers and *now* want to increase output in "batches" of 20. In order to produce the first batch of 20 (beyond the eleventh laborer) how many labor hours are required? What will the next batch of 20 cost, in labor hours? Do additional batches of 20 cost more or less than earlier batches (beyond the eleventh laborer)?

c. What do (a) and (b) imply about the relationship between the marginal product of labor and labor time embodied in equal increments of output?

3. Assume that wage rates equal $1 per 8-hour day:

a. By hiring the twelfth unit of labor, what was the cost to the firm of this first batch of 20?

b. What was the marginal cost of output in that range? (Hint: if 20 units cost $1, what did *one* unit cost?)
c. What will the next batch of 10 cost the firm?
d. What is the marginal cost of output over that range?
e. What is happening to the marginal cost of output?
f. How are the marginal product of labor and the marginal cost of output related?

4. Your school's basketball team had a foul shooting average of .800 (80 out of 100) before last night's game, during which they shot 5 for 10 at the foul line:
a. What was their marginal performance last night?
b. What happened to the team's foul shooting average?
c. Suppose their foul shooting in the next game is 6 for 10. What is happening to their marginal performance?
d. Now what is the team average foul shooting percentage?

5. The effects of a unit tax on the cost curves of Sunshinesea Surfboards can be seen by comparing the tables below. Plot the data in Table 2, then compare the results. What happens to the AFC curve? The AVC curve? The ATC curve? The MC curve?

a. Table 1: Sunshinesea Surfboards before the Unit Tax

TOTAL COSTS PER DAY				UNIT COSTS PER DAY			
(a) TP	(b) TFC	(c) TVC	(d) TC	(e) AFC	(f) AVC	(g) ATC	(h) MC
0	$50	$ 0	$ 50				
1	50	40	90	$50.00	$40.00	$90.00	$40
2	50	75	125	25.00	37.50	62.50	35
3	50	105	155	16.67	35.00	51.67	30
4	50	130	180	12.50	32.50	45.00	25
5	50	150	200	10.00	30.00	40.00	20
6	50	165	215	8.33	27.50	35.83	15
7	50	185	235	7.14	26.43	33.57	20
8	50	215	265	6.25	26.88	33.13	30
9	50	260	310	5.56	28.89	34.44	45
10	50	330	380	5.00	33.00	38.00	70

b. Complete the table.

Table 2: Sunshinesea Surfboards After the Unit Tax (Which Equals $5)

TOTAL COSTS PER DAY					UNIT COSTS PER DAY			
(a) TP	(b) TFC	(c) Tax Bill	(d) TVC	(e) TC	(f) AFC	(g) AVC	(h) ATC	(i) MC
0	50	0	0	50	..	..	..	45
1	50	5	45	95	50	45	90	
2								
•								
•								
•								
10								

9

The Firm in Competition

TOPICS FOR REVIEW

The topics listed below, which we have already analyzed, are applied in this chapter. You may find it worthwhile to review them. For your convenience each topic is followed by the number identifying the specific "Concepts in Brief."

a. Demand (3–1)

b. Supply, changes in supply versus changes in quantity supplied (3–4, 3–5)

c. Perfect price elasticity of demand (6–3)

d. Accounting versus economic profits (8–1)

e. Economies and diseconomies of scale (8–4)

FOR PREVIEW AND STUDY

1. What are the characteristics of the perfect competition market structure?

2. How much will a perfect competitor produce in the short run?

3. What is the perfectly competitive firm's short-run supply curve?

4. Can a perfectly competitive firm earn economic profits?

5. Why is the perfect competition market structure considered to be economically efficient?

In the preceding chapter, we looked at the cost curves of an individual firm. In the following several chapters, we will look at how individual firms set their prices (although not all firms can set their own prices) and how each firm decides the amount to produce. To do this, we must first have some information on the characteristics of firms. Firms in our economy can be grouped into two categories: competitive firms and monopoly firms. Of course, between these two categories lies an entire spectrum of possible degrees of competitiveness. Here we'll concentrate on a perfectly competitive market situation, or structure.

Characteristics of Perfect Competition as a Market Structure

In this chapter we are interested in studying how a firm acting within a perfectly competitive market structure makes decisions about how much to produce. Before we go ahead with this analysis, we want to give the characteristics of the market structure called *perfect competition.* These characteristics are:

1. *The product that is sold by the firms in the industry is homogeneous.* That means that the product sold by each firm in the industry is a perfect substitute for the product sold by each other firm. In other words, buyers are able to choose from a large number of sellers of a product that the buyers believe to be the same.
2. *Any firm can enter or exit the industry without serious impediments.* Resources must be able to move in and out of the industry without, for example, a government-mandated law that prevents such resource mobility to occur.
3. *There must be a large number of buyers and sellers.* When this is the case, no one buyer or one seller has any influence on price, and also when there are large numbers of buyers and sellers, they will be acting independently.
4. *There must be adequate information about prices, qualities, sources of supply, and so forth.*

Now that we have defined the characteristics of a perfectly competitive market structure, the definition of a **perfectly competitive firm** follows. It is one that is such a small part of the total industry in which it operates that it cannot significantly affect the price of the product in question. Since the perfectly competitive firm is a small part of the industry, that firm has no control over the price of the product. That means that each firm in the industry is a **price taker**—the firm takes price as given, as something that is determined *outside* the individual firm.

The price that is given to the firm is determined by the forces of market supply and market demand. That is to say, when all individual consumer's demands are added together into a market demand curve, and all the supply schedules of individual firms are added together into a market supply curve, the intersection of those two curves will give the market price, which the purely competitive or price-taking firm must accept.

This definition of a competitive firm is obviously idealized, for in one sense the individual firm *has* to set prices. How can we ever have a situation where firms regard prices as set by forces outside their control? The answer is that even though every firm, by definition, sets its own prices, a firm in a more or less perfectly competitive situation will find that it will eventually have no customers at all if it sets its price above the competitive price. Let us now see what the demand curve of an individual firm in a competitive industry looks like graphically.

Single-Firm Demand Curve

In Chapter 6, we talked about the characteristics of demand schedules. We pointed out that for completely elastic demand curves, if the individual firm raises the price one penny, it will lose all of its business. Well, this is how we characterize the demand schedule for a purely competitive firm—it is a horizontal line at the going market price. That is, it is completely elastic (see Chapter 6). And that going market price is determined by the market forces of supply and demand. Exhibit 9–1 is the hypothetical market demand schedule faced by an individual leather handbag producer who sells a very, very small part of the total leather handbag production in the industry. At the market price, this firm can sell all the output it wants. At the market price of $5 each, which is where the horizontal demand curve for the individual producer lies, people's demand for the leather handbags of that one producer is perfectly elastic. If the firm raises its price, they will buy from some other producer. (Why not worry about lowering the price?) We label the individual producer's demand curve *dd,* whereas the market demand curve is always labeled *DD.*

How Much Does the Perfect Competitor Produce?

As we have shown, a perfect competitor has to accept the given price of the product. If the firm raises its price, it sells nothing. If it lowers its price, it makes less money per unit sold than it otherwise could. The firm has only one decision variable left: How much should it produce? We will apply our model of the firm to this question to come up with an answer. We'll use the *profit maximization* model and assume that firms, whether competitive or monopolistic, will attempt to maximize their total profits—that is, the positive difference between total revenues and total costs.

TOTAL REVENUES

Every firm has to consider its **total revenues.** Total revenues are defined as the quantity sold multiplied by the price. (They are also the same as total receipts from the sale of output.) The perfect competitor must take the price as given.

Look at panel (a) of Exhibit 9–2. Much of the information comes from panel (a) of Exhibit 8–3, but we have added some essential columns for our analysis. Column 3 is the market price of $5 per handbag, which is also equal to average revenue (AR), since

$$AR = \frac{TR}{Q} = \frac{P \times Q}{Q} = P$$

Column 4 shows the total revenues, or TR, as equal to the market price, *P*, times the total output in sales per day, or *Q*. Thus, TR = $P \times Q$. We are assuming that the market supply and demand schedules intersect at a price of $5 and that this price holds for all the firm's production. We are also assuming that since our handbag maker is a small part of the market, it can sell all it produces at that price. Thus, panel (b) of Exhibit 9–2 shows the total revenue curve as a straight line. For every unit of sales, total revenue is increased by $5.

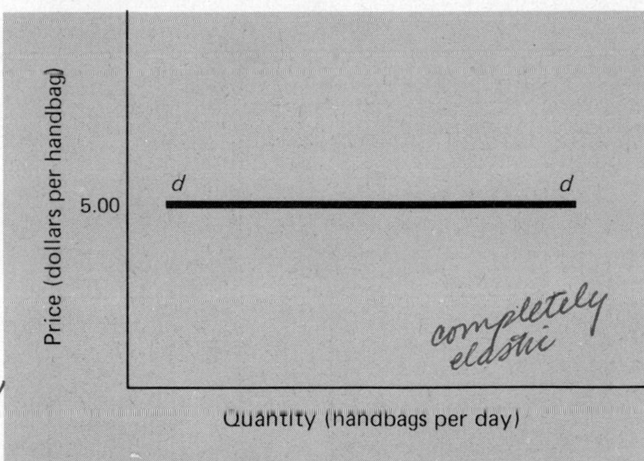

EXHIBIT 9–1
The Demand Curve for an Individual Leather Handbag Producer. We assume that the individual handbag producer is such a small part of the total market that he or she cannot influence the price. The firm accepts the price as given. At the going market price it faces a horizontal demand curve, *dd.* If it raises its price even one penny, it will sell no handbags. The firm would be foolish to lower its price below $5, because it can sell all that it can produce at a price of $5. The firm's demand curve is completely, or perfectly, elastic.

TOTAL COSTS

Revenues are only one side of the picture. Costs must also be considered. **Total costs** are given in column 2 in panel (a) of Exhibit 9–2. Notice that when we plot total costs on panel (b) of Exhibit 9–2, the curve is not a straight line but rather a wavy line that is first above the total revenue curve, then below it, and then above it again. When the total cost curve is above the total revenue curve, the firm is experiencing losses. When it is below the total revenue curve, the firm is making profits. (When we refer to profits, we will always mean economic profits.)

COMPARING TOTAL COSTS WITH TOTAL REVENUES

By comparing total costs with total revenues, we can figure out the number of leather handbags that the individual competitive firm should produce per day. Our analysis rests on the assumption that the firm will attempt to maximize total profits. In panel (a) of Exhibit 9–2, we see that total profits reach a maximum at a production rate of between seven and eight leather handbags per day. We can see this graphically in panel (b) of Exhibit 9–2. The firm will maximize profits at that place on the graph where the total revenue curve exceeds the total cost curve by the greatest amount. That occurs at a rate of output and sales of either seven or eight handbags per day; this rate is called the *profit-maximizing rate of production.*

We can also find this profit-maximizing rate of production for the individual competitive firm by looking at marginal revenues and marginal costs.

EXHIBIT 9–2(a)

The Costs of Production and the Revenues from the Sale of Output: Finding the Profit-Maximization Rate of Output and Sales. Profit maximization occurs at a rate of sales of either seven or eight handbags per day.

Total Output and Sales per Day (1)	Total Cost (TC) (2)	Market Price (P) (3)	Total Revenue (TR) (4) = (3) × (1)	Total Profit = (TR) − (TC) (5) = (4) − (2)	Average Total Cost (ATC) (6) = (2) ÷ (1)	Average Variable Cost (AVC)* (7)	Marginal Cost (MC) (8) = $\frac{\text{Change in (2)}}{\text{Change in (1)}}$	Marginal Revenue (MR) (9) = $\frac{\text{Change in (4)}}{\text{Change in (1)}}$
0	$10.00	$5.00	0	−$10.00	—	—		
							$5.00	$5.00
1	15.00	5.00	$ 5.00	− 10.00	$15.00	$5.00		
							3.00	5.00
2	18.00	5.00	10.00	− 8.00	9.00	4.00		
							2.00	5.00
3	20.00	5.00	15.00	− 5.00	6.67	3.33		
							1.00	5.00
4	21.00	5.00	20.00	− 1.00	5.25	2.75		
							2.00	5.00
5	23.00	5.00	25.00	2.00	4.60	2.60		
							3.00	5.00
6	26.00	5.00	30.00	4.00	4.33	2.67		
							4.00	5.00
7	30.00	5.00	35.00	5.00	4.28	2.86		
							5.00	5.00
8	35.00	5.00	40.00	5.00	4.38	3.12		
							6.00	5.00
9	41.00	5.00	45.00	4.00	4.56	3.44		
							7.00	5.00
10	48.00	5.00	50.00	2.00	4.80	3.80		
							8.00	5.00
11	56.00	5.00	55.00	−1.00	5.09	4.18		

* Taken from Exhibit 8–3.

EXHIBIT 9–2(b)

Finding Maximum Total Profits. Total revenues are represented by the straight line, showing that each handbag sells at $5. Total costs first exceed total revenues, then are less than total revenues, and then exceed them again. We find maximum profits where total revenues exceed total costs by the largest amount. This occurs at a rate of production and sales per day of seven or eight handbags.

EXHIBIT 9–2(c)

Profit Maximization Using Marginal Analysis. Profit maximization occurs where marginal revenue equals marginal cost. Marginal revenue is represented by the individual firm demand curve, *dd,* which is a horizontal line at $5. The marginal cost curve is represented by MC. It intersects the marginal revenue curve at a rate of output and sales of somewhere between seven and eight handbags per day.

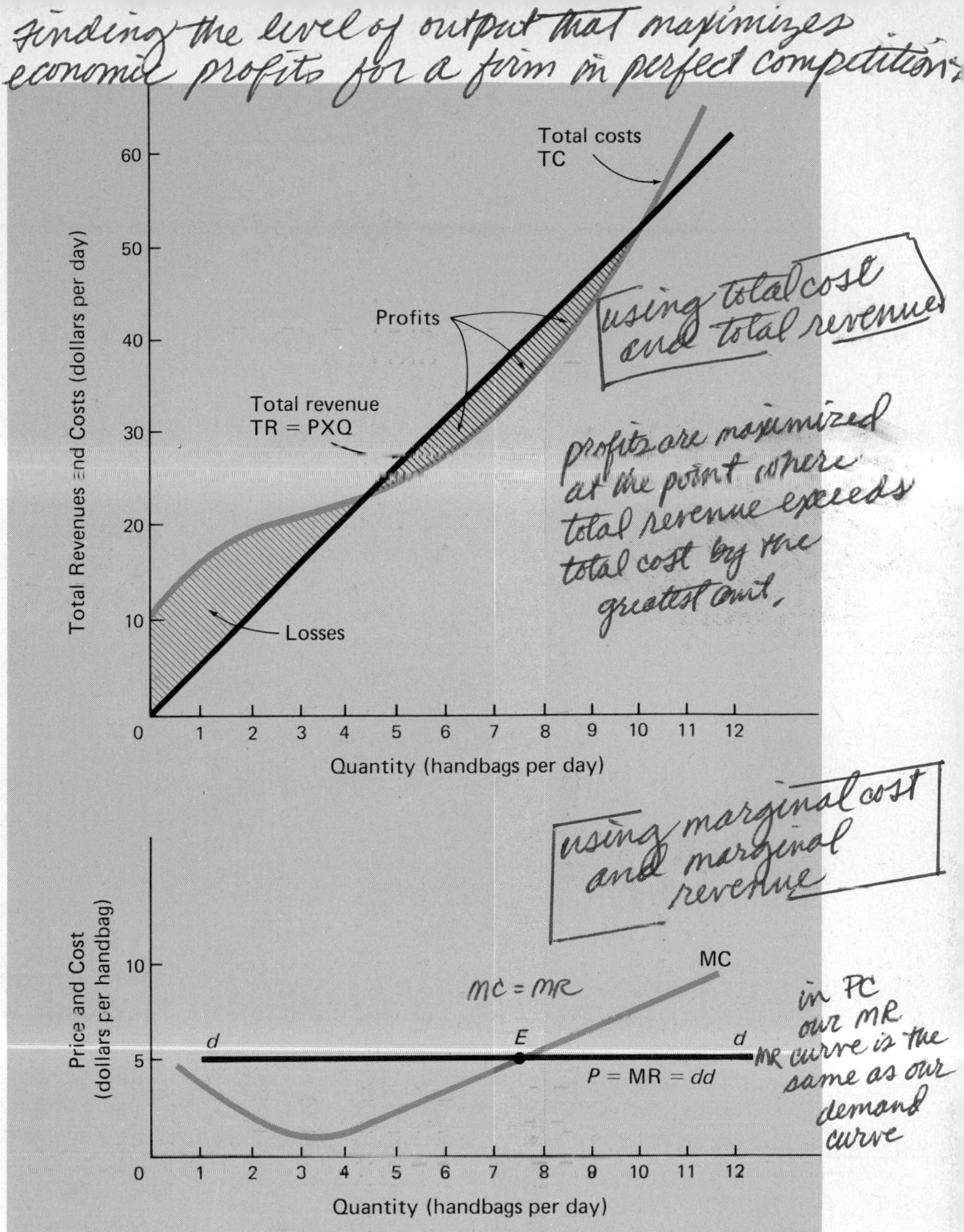

Using Marginal Analysis

Marginal cost was introduced in Chapter 8. It was defined as the change in total cost due to a one-unit change in production. This leaves only **marginal revenue** to be defined.

MARGINAL REVENUE

What amount can our individual handbag-making firm hope to receive each time it sells an additional (marginal) leather handbag? Since the firm is such a small part of the market and cannot influence the price, it must accept the price determined by the market forces of supply and demand. Therefore, the firm knows it will receive $5 for every handbag it sells in the market. So the additional revenue the firm will receive from selling one more handbag is equal to the market price of $5; marginal revenue, in this case, equals price.

Marginal revenue represents the increment in total revenues attributable to producing one additional unit of the product in question. Marginal revenue is also defined as the change in total revenue resulting from a one-unit change in output. Hence, a more formal definition of marginal revenue is:

$$\text{marginal revenue} = \frac{\text{change in total revenue}}{\text{change in output}}$$

In a perfectly competitive market, the marginal revenue curve is exactly equivalent to the price line—or, in other words, to the individual firm's demand curve, since the firm can sell all of its output (production) at the market price.

Thus, in Exhibit 9–1 the demand curve, *dd,* for the individual producer is at a price of $5—the price line is coincident with the demand curve. But so, too, is the marginal revenue curve, for marginal revenue in this case also equals $5.

The marginal revenue curve for our competitive

leather handbag producer is shown as a horizontal line at $5 in panel (c) of Exhibit 9–2. Notice again that the marginal revenue curve is equal to the price line, which is equal to the individual firm's demand curve, *dd*.

WHEN PROFITS ARE MAXIMIZED

Now we add the marginal cost curve, MC, taken from column 8 in panel (a) of Exhibit 9–2. As shown in panel (c) of Exhibit 9–2, the marginal cost curve first falls and then starts to rise, eventually intersecting the marginal revenue curve and then rising above it. Notice that the numbers for both the marginal cost schedule and the marginal revenue schedule in panel (a) of Exhibit 9–2 are printed *between* the figures that determine them. This indicates that we are looking at a change between one rate of output and the next.

In panel (c) of Exhibit 9–2, the marginal cost curve intersects the marginal revenue (or *dd*) curve somewhere between seven and eight handbags per day. Consider a rate of production that is less than that. At a production rate of, say, six handbags per day, marginal cost is clearly below marginal revenue. That is, the marginal cost curve at an output of six is below the marginal revenue curve at that output. Since it can receive $5 per handbag, and since marginal cost is less than this marginal revenue, the firm has an incentive to increase production. In fact, it has an incentive to produce and sell until the amount of the additional revenue received from selling one more handbag just equals the additional costs incurred from producing and selling that handbag. This is how it maximizes profit. Whenever marginal cost is less than marginal revenue, the firm will always make more profit by increasing production.

Now consider the possibility of producing at an output rate in excess of eight—say, at ten handbags per day. The marginal cost curve at that output rate is higher than the marginal revenue (or *dd*) curve. The individual producer would be spending more to produce that additional output than it would be receiving in revenues. The firm would be foolish to continue producing at this rate.

But where, then, should it produce? It should produce at point *E*, where the marginal cost curve intersects the marginal revenue curve from below.[1] Since the firm knows it can sell all the handbags it wants at the going market price, marginal revenue from selling an additional handbag will always equal the market price. Consequently, the firm should continue production until the cost of increasing output by one more unit is just equal to the revenues obtainable from that extra unit. *Profit maximization is always at the rate of output at which marginal revenue equals marginal cost.* (To be strictly correct, we should add: "and the MC curve cuts the MR curve from below.") For a perfectly competitive firm, this is at the intersection of the demand schedule, *dd*, and the marginal cost curve, MC. In our particular example, our profit-maximizing, perfectly competitive leather handbag producer will produce at a rate of between seven and eight handbags a day.

Notice that this same profit-maximizing rate of output is shown in both panel (b) of Exhibit 9–2, where the total revenue/total cost curve is drawn, and in panel (c) of Exhibit 9–2, where the marginal revenue/marginal cost curve is drawn. We can find the profit-maximizing output solution for the perfectly competitive firm by looking at either diagram.

[1] The marginal cost curve, MC, also cuts the marginal revenue curve *(dd)* from above at an output rate of less than one.

Concepts in Brief 9-1

- A perfectly competitive firm is a price taker. It takes price as given. It can sell all that it wants at the going market price.
- The demand curve facing a perfect competitor is a horizontal line at the going market price. The demand curve is also the perfect competitor's marginal revenue curve, since marginal revenue is defined as a change in total revenue due to a one-unit change in output.
- Profit is maximized at the rate of output where the positive difference between total revenues and total costs is the greatest. Using a marginal analysis, the perfectly competitive firm will produce at a rate of output where marginal revenue equals marginal cost. Marginal revenue, however, is equal to price. Therefore, the perfectly competitive firm produces at an output rate where marginal cost equals the price of the output.

Finding the Firm's Short-Run Profits

To find what our individual, competitive leather handbag producer is making in terms of profits in the short run, we have to add the average total cost curve to panel (c) of Exhibit 9–2. We take the infor-

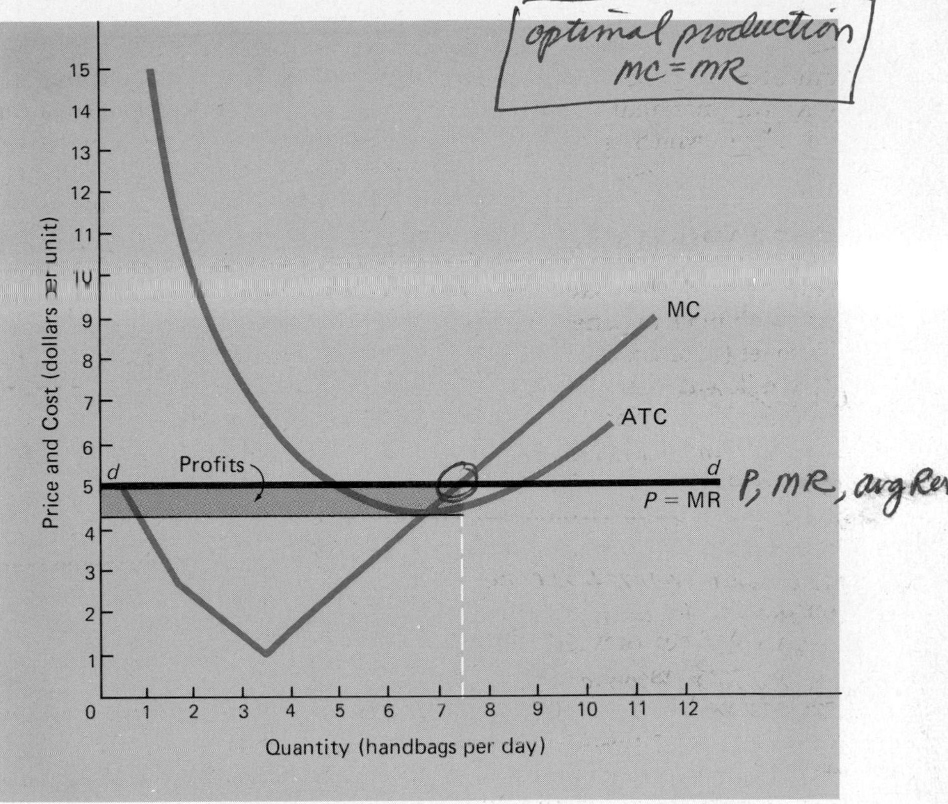

EXHIBIT 9–3
Measuring Total Profits. The profit-maximizing rate of output and sales is where marginal revenue equals marginal cost. Profits are the difference between total revenues and total cost. Total revenues will equal the rate of output and sales times the market price of $5. Total costs will equal the quantity produced and sold multiplied by average total cost (ATC). Profits are represented by the shaded area.

mation from column 6 in panel (a) of Exhibit 9–2 and add it to panel (c) of Exhibit 9–2 to get Exhibit 9–3. Again, the profit-maximizing rate of output is between seven and eight handbags per day. If we have production and sales of seven handbags per day, total revenues will be $35 a day. Total costs will be $30 a day, leaving a profit of $5 a day. If the rate of output in sales is eight handbags per day, total revenues will be $40 and total costs will be $35, again leaving a profit of $5 a day.

It is certainly possible, also, for the competitive firm to make short-run losses. We give an example in Exhibit 9–4. Here we show the firm's demand curve shifting from *dd* to *d'd'*. The going market price has fallen from $5 to $3 per handbag because of changes in market supply and/or demand conditions. The firm will always be better off by producing where marginal revenue equals marginal cost. We see in Exhibit 9–4 that the marginal revenue (or *d'd'*) curve intersects the marginal cost curve at an output rate of about $5\frac{1}{2}$ handbags per day. The firm is clearly not making profits, because average total costs at that output rate are greater than the price of $3 per handbag. The losses are shown in the shaded area. Here, by producing where marginal revenue equals marginal cost, the firm is minimizing its losses.

The Short-Run Shutdown Point

In Exhibit 9–4, the firm is making economic losses. Will it go out of business? Certainly in the long run it will, for the owners of the firm will not incur economic losses forever. But in the short run, the firm may not go out of business. So long as the loss from staying in business is less than the loss from going out of business, the firm will continue to produce. Now how can we tell when that is the case—when sustaining economic losses in the short run is still worthwhile? We must compare the cost of staying in business (with losses) with the cost of closing down. The cost of staying in business in the short run is given by the average variable cost curve, or AVC. As long as average variable costs are covered by revenues ($P \times Q$), the firm is better off staying in business. In other words, if average unit variable costs are exceeded even a little bit by the price of the product, then staying in business produces something that can be applied toward covering fixed costs.

A simple example will demonstrate this situation. Let the price of a product be $8. Let average total costs equal $9 at an output of 100. In this hypothetical example, average total costs are broken up into average variable costs of $7 and average

EXHIBIT 9–4
Minimizing Short-Run Losses. In cases where average total costs exceed the average revenue or price, profit maximization is equivalent to loss minimization. This again occurs where marginal cost equals marginal revenue. Losses are shown in the shaded area.

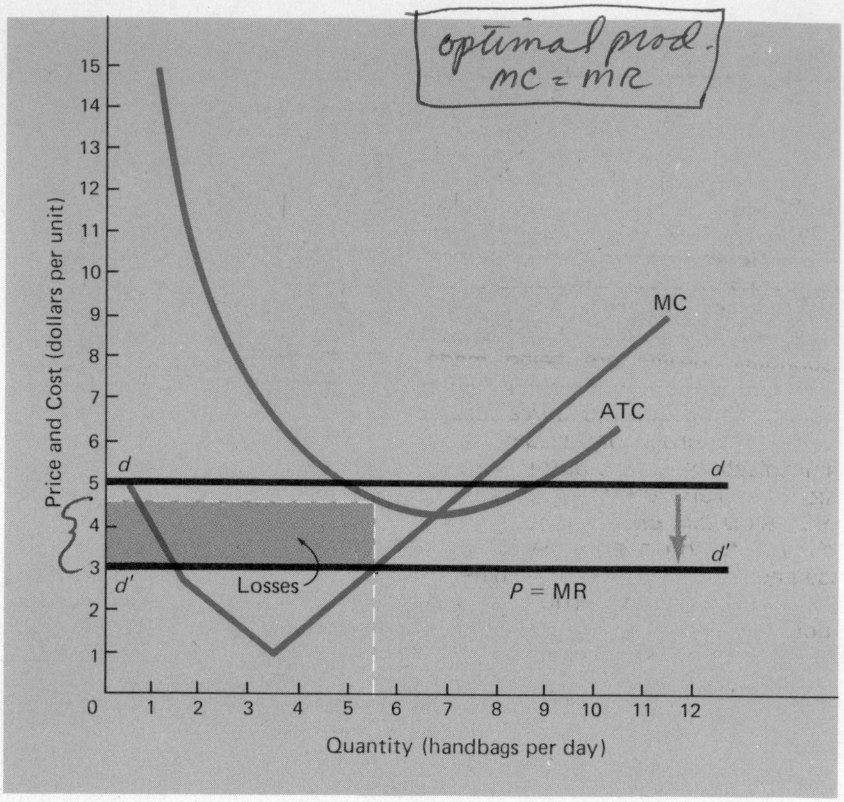

fixed costs of \$2. Total revenues, then, equal \$8 × 100, or \$800, and total costs equal \$9 × 100, or \$900. Total losses therefore equal \$100. However, this does not mean the firm will shut down. After all, if it does shut down, it still has fixed costs to pay. And in this case, since average fixed costs equal \$2 at an output of 100, the fixed costs are \$200. Thus, the firm has losses of \$100 if it continues to produce, but it has losses of \$200 (the fixed costs) if it shuts down. The logic is fairly straightforward: As long as the price per unit sold exceeds the average variable cost per unit produced, the firm will be paying for at least part of the opportunity cost of capital invested in the business. Although the price is below average total cost and the firm is not making a normal or competitive rate of return on its investment, at least it's making *some* return. A small rate of return on an investment is better than no rate of return at all.

If the firm continues to sustain economic losses, it will not replace any capital. In the long run, capital becomes a variable input. The reason capital becomes variable is that the firm can decide how much it should purchase and replace, given a long enough time period. In the long run, therefore, any cost associated with capital becomes a variable cost because the firm can decide how much it wants to purchase. Otherwise stated, in the long run, all costs are variable. Hence, in the above example, in the long run the firm will not be covering average variable costs and will therefore go out of business (if demand remains at *d′d′*).

THE SHORT-RUN BREAK-EVEN POINT

Let's look at demand curve *dd* in Exhibit 9–5. It just touches the minimum point of the average total cost curve, which, as you will remember, is exactly where the marginal cost curve intersects the average total cost curve. At that price, which is about \$4.30, the firm will be making exactly zero short-run economic profits. Thus, that particular price is called the short-run break-even price. And point *E* is therefore called the **short-run break-even point** for a competitive firm. It is the point at which marginal revenue = marginal cost = average total cost. The break-even price is the one that yields zero short-run profits or losses.

CALCULATING THE SHUTDOWN POINT

In order to calculate the firm's shutdown point, we must add the average variable cost (AVC) to our graph. In Exhibit 9–5, we have taken the AVC

EXHIBIT 9–5

Short-Run Shutdown and Break-Even Prices. We can find the short-run break-even price and the short-run shutdown price by comparing the price with average total costs and average variable costs. If the demand curve is *dd*, then profit maximization occurs at output *E*, where MC = marginal revenue (the *dd* curve). Since the ATC curve includes all relevant opportunity costs, point *E* is the short-run break-even point, and zero economic profits are being made. The firm is earning a normal rate of return. If the demand curve falls to *d′d′*, then profit maximization (loss minimization) occurs at the intersection of MC and MR (the *d′d′* curve) or *E′*. Below this price, it does not pay the firm to continue in operation, because its average variable costs are not covered by the price of the product.

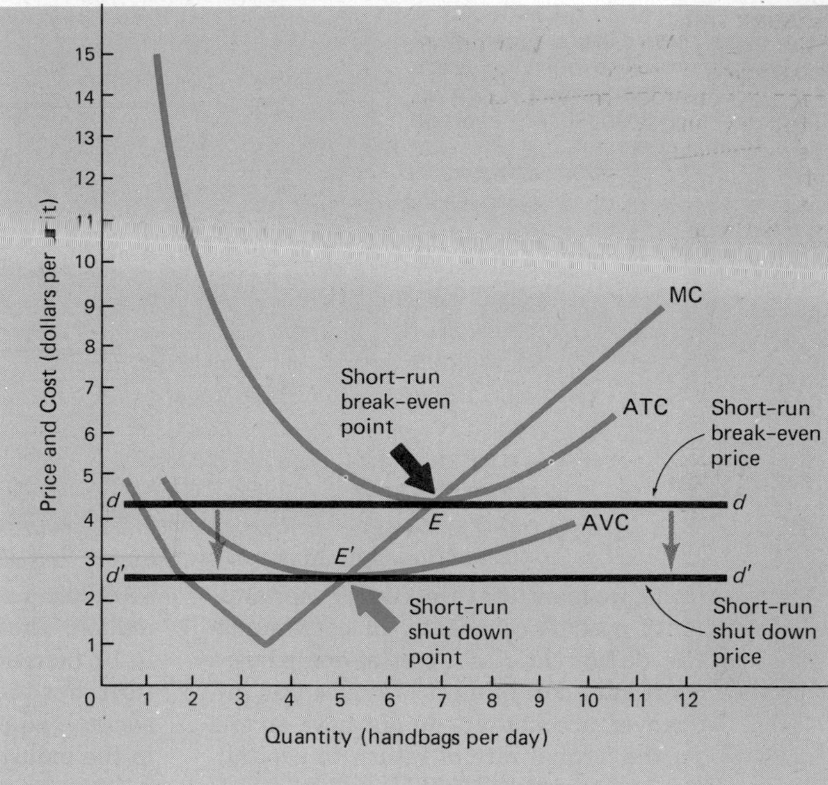

curve from column 7 in panel (a) of Exhibit 9–2. For the moment, consider two possible demand curves, *dd* and *d′d′*, which are also the firm's respective marginal revenue curves. Therefore, if demand is *dd*, the firm will produce at *E*, where that curve intersects the marginal cost curve. If demand falls to *d′d′*, the firm will produce at *E′*. The special feature about the hypothetical demand curve *d′d′* is that it just touches the average variable cost curve at the latter's minimum point, which is where the marginal cost curve intersects it also. This price is labeled the short-run shutdown price. Why? Below this price the firm is paying out more in variable costs than it is receiving in revenues from the sale of its product. On each unit it sells, it is adding to its losses. Clearly, the way to avoid incurring these additional losses, if price falls below the shutdown point, is in fact to shut down operations. (Of course, if price falls below the short-run shutdown price, a firm may still continue in business in the short run if it decides it can afford to wait until the price moves up again, and it can profitably reenter production.)

The intersection of the price line, the marginal cost curve, and the average variable cost is labeled *E′*. We called it the **short-run shutdown point.** This point is labeled short run because, of course, in the long run, the firm will not produce below a price that yields a normal rate of return and, hence, zero economic profits.

The Meaning of Zero Economic Profits

Perhaps the fact that we labeled point *E* in Exhibit 9–5 the break-even point may have disturbed you. At point *E*, price is just equal to average total cost. If this is the case, why would a firm continue to produce if it were making no profits whatsoever? If we again make the distinction between accounting profits and economic profits, then at that price the firm has zero economic profits but positive accounting profits.

ACCOUNTING VERSUS ECONOMIC PROFITS REVISITED

Think back to the last chapter when we talked about how an accountant must total up costs. The accountant adds up all of the expenses, subtracts them from all of the revenues, and calls the result profit. What is ignored is the reward offered to investors. Those who invest in the firm, whether they be proprietors or stockholders, must anticipate a rate of return that is at least as great as could be earned in similar investments of equal risk. Looking

> ***Concepts in Brief 9-2***
>
> - Short-run profits and losses are determined by comparing average total costs with price at the profit-maximizing rate of output. In the short run, the perfectly competitive firm can make economic profits or economic losses.
> - The competitive firm's short-run break-even output occurs at the minimum point on its average total cost curve, which is where the marginal cost curve intersects the average total cost curve.
> - The competitive firm's short-run shutdown output is at the minimum point on its average variable cost curve, which is also where the marginal cost curve intersects the average variable cost curve. Shutdown will occur if price falls below average variable cost.
> - The firm will continue production at a price that exceeds average variable costs even though the full opportunity cost of capital is not being met; at least some revenues are going toward paying some rate of return to capital.
> - At the short-run break-even point, the firm is making zero economic profits, which means that it is just making a normal rate of return in that industry.
> - The firm's short-run supply curve is that section of its marginal cost curve equal to or above minimum average variable costs.
> - The industry short-run supply curve is a horizontal summation of the individual firms' marginal cost curves above their respective minimum average variable costs.

Competitive Price Determination

How is the market, or "going," price established in a competitive market? This price is established by the interaction of all the firms and all the demanders. The market demand schedule *DD* in panel (a) of Exhibit 9–8 represents the demand schedule for the entire industry, and the supply schedule *SS* represents the supply schedule for the entire industry. Price P_e is established by the forces of supply and demand at the intersection of *SS* and *DD*. Even though each individual firm has no control or effect on the price of its product in a competitive industry, the interaction of all the producers determines the price at which the product will be sold. We say that the price P_e and the quantity Q_e in panel (a) of Exhibit 9–8 constitute the competitive solution to the pricing/quantity problem in that particular industry. It is the equilibrium where suppliers and demanders are both maximizing. The resulting individual firm demand curve *dd* is shown in panel (b) of Exhibit 9–8 at the price P_e.

The Long-Run Industry Situation—Exit and Entry

In the long run, we surmise that firms in perfect competition will tend to have average total cost curves that just touch the price = marginal revenue curve, or individual demand curve *dd*. That is, in the long run in a competitive situation, firms will be making zero economic profits. How does this occur? It is through an adjustment process that depends on economic profits and losses. We referred in Chapter 4 to changing prices and profits, signaling resource owners about where their resources should flow. Now we can be more precise about this process.

EXIT AND ENTRY OF FIRMS

Go back and look at Exhibits 9–3 and 9–4. The existence of either profits or losses is a signal to owners of capital within and outside the industry. If the industry is characterized by firms showing economic profits as represented in Exhibit 9–3, this will signal to owners of capital elsewhere in the economy that they, too, should enter this industry. If, on the other hand, there are firms in the industry that are like those suffering economic losses represented in Exhibit 9–4, this signals resource owners outside the industry to stay out. It also signals resource owners within the industry not to reinvest and if possible to leave the industry. It is in this sense that we say that profits direct resources to their highest valued use. Capital and labor will flow into industries where profitability is highest and will flow out of industries in the economy where profitability is lowest. In the price system, the allocation of capital is therefore directed by relative expected rates of return on investment.

In addition, when we say that in a competitive long-run equilibrium situation firms will be making zero economic profits, we must realize that at a particular point in time it would be pure coincidence for a firm to be making *exactly* zero economic profits. Real-world information is not as exact as the curves we use to simplify our analysis. Things

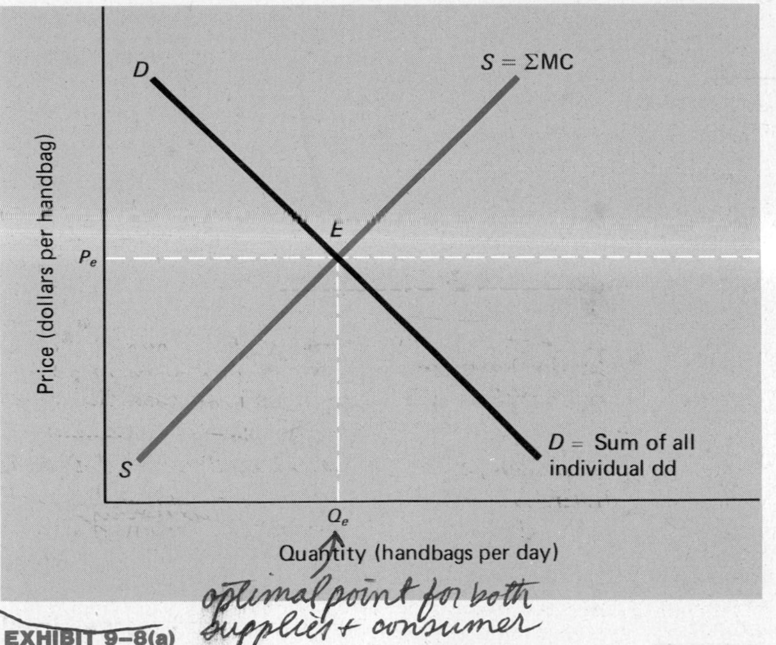

EXHIBIT 9–8(a)
The Industry Demand and Supply Curves. The industry demand curve is a representation of the demand curve for all potential consumers. It is represented by *DD*. The industry supply curve is the horizontal summation of all those sections of the marginal cost curves of the individual firms above their respective minimum average variable cost points. We show it as *SS* and mark it as equal to Σ MC. The intersection of the demand and supply curves at *E* determines the equilibrium or market price at P_e.

P_e d d

Quantity (handbags per day)

EXHIBIT 9–8(b)
Individual Firm Demand Curve. The individual firm demand curve is set at the going market price determined in panel (a). That is, the demand curve facing the individual firm is a horizontal line, *dd*, at price P_e.

change all the time in a dynamic world, and firms, even in a very competitive situation, may, for many reasons, not be making exactly zero economic profits. Remember, in any event, that the concept of long-run zero economic profits in a competitive industry is a long-run concept. We say that there is a *tendency* toward that equilibrium position, but firms are adjusting all the time to changes in their cost curves and in their (horizontal) *dd* curve.

LONG-RUN SUPPLY CURVES

In Exhibit 9–8(a), we drew the summation of all of the portions of the individual firm's marginal cost curve above each firm's respective minimum average variable costs as the upward-sloping supply curve of the entire industry. We should be aware, however, that a relatively steep upward-sloping supply curve may only be appropriate in the short run. After all, one of the prerequisites for a competitive industry is that there be no restrictions on entry. We expect, therefore, that if the consumer demand schedule shifts out to the right (there is increased demand for the product in question), eventually more firms will enter the market so that the quantity supplied can also be expanded. In fact, each time the demand curve shifts out to the right, the price can be expected to rise, other things being constant. But this means positive economic profits for the current producers. Therefore, existing firms will expand, and more producers will enter the market, thus eventually forcing the price down to its old equilibrium level—assuming costs in the industry remain constant.

Constant-, Increasing-, and Decreasing-Cost Industries

We have generally assumed that costs remain constant when the entire industry increases its rate of production. If this is the case, then the industry is a constant-cost industry. If, however, the average unit cost curve rises as the industry expands, we are dealing with an increasing-cost industry. And finally, if the unit cost curve falls when the industry expands output, it is a decreasing-cost industry. These three possibilities are shown by the slope of the long-run supply curve presented in panels (a), (b), and (c) of Exhibit 9–9.

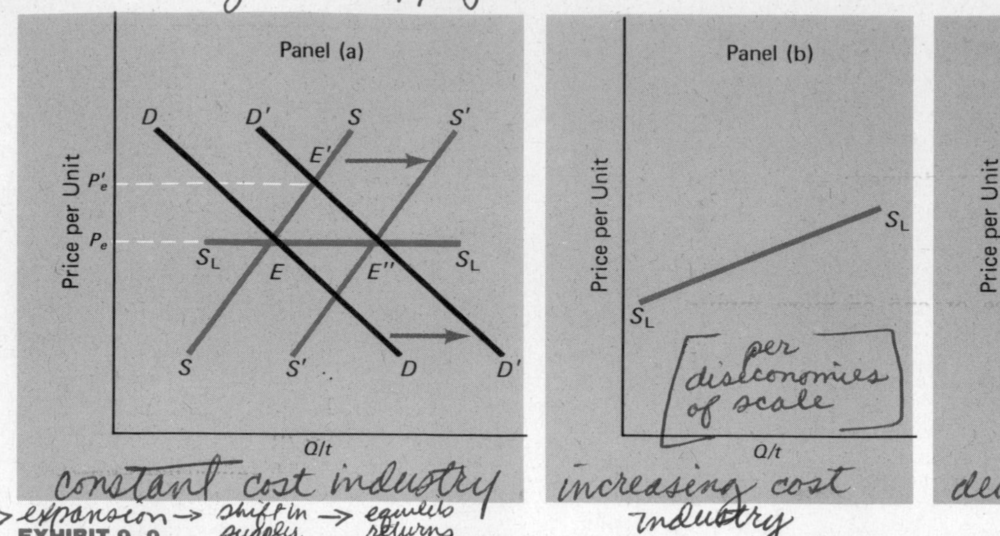

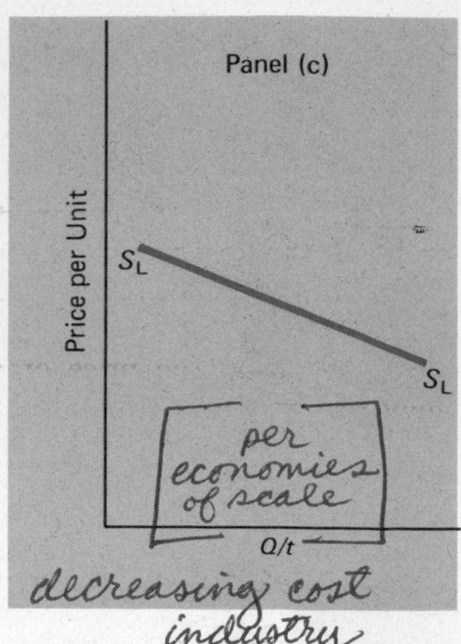

EXHIBIT 9–9

Constant-, Increasing-, and Decreasing-Cost Industries. In panel (a), we show a situation where the demand curve shifts from DD to $D'D'$. Price increases from P_e to P_e'; however, in time the supply curve shifts out to $S'S'$, and the new equilibrium shifts from E' to E''. The market clearing price is, again, P_e. If we connect points such as E and E'', we come up with the long-run supply curve S_LS_L. This is a constant-cost industry. In panel (b), costs are increasing for the industry, and therefore the long-run supply curve is upward sloping; in panel (c), costs are decreasing for the industry as it expands, and therefore the long-run supply curve is downward sloping.

We can work through the case in which constant costs prevail. We start out in panel (a) with demand curve DD and supply curve SS. The equilibrium price is P_e. There is a rightward shift in market demand to $D'D'$. In the short run, the supply curve remains stable. The equilibrium price rises to P_e'. This generates positive economic profits for existing firms in the industry. Such economic profits induce capital to flow into the industry. The existing firms expand and/or new firms enter. The supply curve shifts out to $S'S'$. The new intersection with the new demand curve is at E''. The new equilibrium price is again P_e. The long-run supply curve is obtained by connecting the intersections of the corresponding pairs of demand and supply curves, E and E''. It is labeled S_LS_L, and is horizontal. Its slope is zero. In a constant-cost industry, long-run supply is perfectly elastic. Any shift in demand is eventually met by an equal shift in supply, so that the long-run price is constant at P_e.

An increasing-cost industry is shown by the supply curve S_LS_L in panel (b); it is upward sloping. A decreasing-cost industry is shown in panel (c). We can define the long-run industry supply curve as the "path" of the industry's long-run equilibrium points as determined by the intersections of the short-run demand and supply curves, DD, $D'D'$, and SS, $S'S'$, in panels (a), (b), and (c) of Exhibit 9–9. [Can you draw them in panels (b) and (c)?]

Economies and Diseconomies of Scale

The reason that an industry can be other than a constant-cost industry is the presence of economies and diseconomies of scale. The former could generate the long-run supply curve in panel (c), and the latter could generate the long-run supply curve in panel (b) of Exhibit 9–9. We have already been introduced to the concept of economies and diseconomies of scale in Chapter 8.

Economies of scale were defined as a situation in which the long-run average cost curve sloped down. Economies of scale occur when an increase in the output of the entire industry allows suppliers to engage in increased specialization or innovative activities, which help lower their unit cost. This would cause the downward-sloping long-run curve shown in panel (c) of Exhibit 9–9. Take an example. One firm starts a business in a small residential area that has been set aside for offices and light industrial activity. This firm has photocopying needs but not enough to justify the purchase of its own equipment. The firm must take its originals to be photocopied some distance away. If, on the other hand, many firms move into the same area, it may become profitable for a photocopying firm to start business. There will at least be a reduction for the original firm in the time cost of having its photocopying done because it won't have to go so far. Additionally, the new photocopying firm may be able to use large, lower-cost-per-unit machines, which will additionally lower the monetary outlay involved in getting photocopies.

Diseconomies of scale were defined as a situation in which the long-run average cost curve sloped up. For example, an industry's expanding production may cause input prices to rise. If all firms expand simultaneously, the price of one or more inputs may rise and we will be in the presence of an increasing-cost industry, as depicted in panel (b) of Exhibit 9–9.

LONG-RUN INDUSTRY RESPONSE TO DECLINING OR INCREASING DEMAND

One of the reasons we attempt to develop a model of a market structure is to predict what will happen when there are changes in the economy. Exhibit 9–9 can be used to predict what will happen when there are changes in a perfectly competitive industry.

In the case of increasing demand, we first need to determine whether we are dealing with a constant-, increasing-, or decreasing-cost industry. Once we have determined that, we can then tell what will happen to price as industry demand increases. The simplest case is when we are dealing with the constant-cost perfectly competitive industry. This situation is, in fact, depicted in panel (a) of Exhibit 9–9. An increase in industry demand leads to a larger output being sold in the long run at a constant price, P_e. If, however, we are dealing with an increasing-cost industry, increasing demand will, in the long run, lead to increased production and also an increased price. Finally, if we are dealing with a decreasing-cost industry, in the long run, an increase in demand will lead to an increase in output and a *decrease* in price.

Our predictions can be made in a similar fashion if we are dealing with a declining perfectly competitive industry—one in which market demand is falling. If we are dealing with a constant-cost perfectly competitive industry, then in the long run, output will be reduced but price will remain constant at P_e, as in panel (a) of Exhibit 9–9. If we are dealing with an increasing-cost industry, a decline in industry demand will eventually lead to a reduction in output and a *reduction* in price. And, finally, if we are dealing with a decreasing-cost industry, a reduction in market demand will lead to a long-run reduction in output and an *increase* in price.

The Perfectly Competitive Firm in Long-Run Equilibrium

In the long run, the firm can change the scale of its plant. In the long run, the firm will adjust plant size in such a way that it has no further incentive to change. It will do so until profits are maximized. Exhibit 9–10 shows the long-run equilibrium of the perfectly competitive firm. Long-run average costs are at a minimum. So, too, are short-run average costs. Price is set equal to both marginal costs and minimum average costs. In other words, the long-run equilibrium position is where "everything is equal," which is at point E in Exhibit 9–10. There, *price* equals *marginal revenue* equals *marginal cost* equals *average cost* (minimum, short run, and long run).

PERFECT COMPETITION AND MINIMUM AVERAGE TOTAL COST

Look again at Exhibit 9–10. In long-run equilibrium, the perfectly competitive firm finds itself producing at output rate q_e. At that rate of output, the price is just equal to the minimum long-run average cost as well as the minimum short-run average cost. In this sense, perfect competition results in no

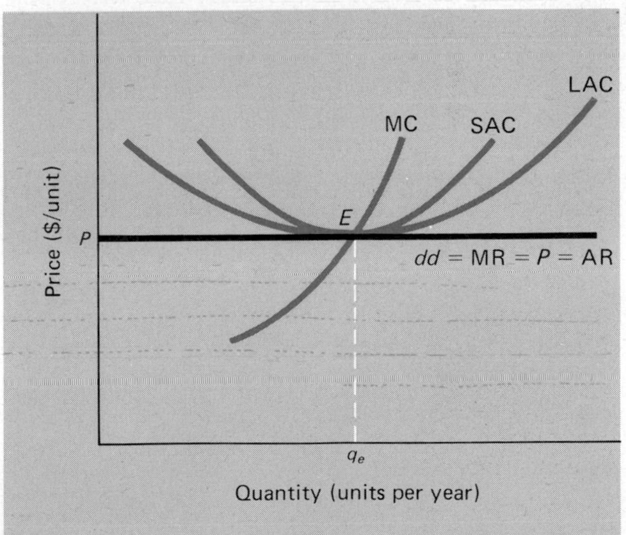

EXHIBIT 9–10
Long-Run Firm Competitive Equilibrium. In the long run, the firm operates where price equals marginal revenue equals marginal cost equals short-run minimum average cost equals long-run minimum average cost, or where "everything is equal." This is given at point *E*.

"waste" in the production system. Goods and services are produced using the least costly combination of resources. This is an important attribute of a perfectly competitive long-run equilibrium, particularly when we wish to compare the market structure of perfect competition with other market structures that are less than perfectly competitive. We examine these other market structures in later chapters.

Competitive Pricing Equals Marginal Cost Pricing

In a perfectly competitive industry, each firm produces where its marginal cost curve intersects its marginal revenue (or *dd*) curve from below. Thus, perfectly competitive firms always sell their goods at a price that just equals marginal cost. For many economists, this represents a "desirable" pricing situation because the price that consumers pay just reflects the opportunity cost to society of producing the good. In order to understand this, consider what marginal cost represents. It represents the cost of changing production by one incremental unit. Suppose a marginal cost curve shows that an increase in production from 10,000 leather handbags to 10,001 leather handbags will cost $1.50. That $1.50 represents the *opportunity cost* to society of producing one more leather handbag. Thus, the marginal cost curve gives a graphic representation of the opportunity cost of production.

The competitive firm produces up to the point where the market price just equals the marginal cost. Herein lies the element of the "desirability" of a competitive solution. It is called **marginal cost pricing.** The competitive firm sells its product at a price that just equals the cost to society—that is, the opportunity cost—for that is what the marginal cost curve represents.

When an individual pays a price equal to the marginal cost of production, then the cost to the user of that product is equal to the sacrifice or cost to society of producing that quantity of that good as opposed to more of some other good. (We are assuming that *all marginal social* costs are accounted for.) The competitive solution, then, is called *efficient.* It is efficient in the economic sense of the word. Economic efficiency means that it is impossible to increase the output of any good without lowering the total *value* of the output produced in the economy. No juggling of resources, such as labor and capital, will result in an output that is higher in value than the value of the goods and services already being produced. In an efficient situation, it is impossible to make one person better off without making someone else worse off. All resources are used in the most advantageous way possible. All goods and services are sold at their opportunity cost, and marginal cost pricing prevails throughout.

Is Perfect Competition Possible?

The analytic model presented here represents a situation that, by definition, can never be seen in reality. Perfect competition can exist only if information is also perfect. After all, the only way for a price to be uniform at every moment in time (corrected for quality changes and transportation costs) is for everybody to know what's happening everywhere at every moment in time. Obviously, information is never perfect. In fact, the cost of trying to achieve perfect information would be prohibitive and therefore undesired.

A profit-maximizing firm will produce at the point where the additional revenues obtained from producing more goods exactly cover the additional costs incurred (where marginal revenue equals marginal cost). Similarly, if we are wealth maximizing, we would never spend more than we get in return from improving information flows. That is, we would improve information in the marketplace only up to the point where the value of doing so is equal to the marginal cost. That is certainly at a point well below *perfect* information.

A purely competitive industry has been defined as one with many sellers. To satisfy the criterion of perfect competition where each seller has *no* control whatsoever over the price of his or her product, we would have to have a tremendous number of firms. There are many industries where the number of firms is not extremely large, and therefore individually each firm has, at least in the short run, some control over its price.[2] However, analyzing the industry in the long run, we might say that it was *tending* toward a competitive solution all the time because there was a sufficient number of firms *on*

[2] Actually, more advanced students would point out here that all we really require is constant returns to scale production functions and free entry, not a large number of firms.

the margin attempting to increase their total sales by undercutting the other firms. Notice we said that the industry might tend toward a competitive solution at all times. That is a dynamic process—which is to say that operates through time and it never ends. At any time, an investigation of the particular industry would reveal that the industry was tending toward a competitive solution, but the industry would probably never reach that point.

Even if an industry is not perfectly competitive, it does not necessarily follow that steps should be taken to make it more competitive so as to ensure efficiency. After all, it is not possible to change an industry's structure from noncompetitive to competitive without using resources. We will discuss some of the ways of doing this, such as legislation against noncompetitive business practices, regulation of noncompetitive industries, and others. Remember that legislation and regulation involve the use of resources that could be doing something else. That is, there is an opportunity cost involved in attempting to turn a noncompetitive industry into a competitive industry. Before engaging in such a campaign, we may want to be sure that the benefits of increased competition will outweigh the costs of getting the increased competition if we do not wish to waste resources.

The fact that we use the model of perfect competition in an economic analysis does not mean that we should accept perfect competition as the only type of industry structure to be tolerated. Sometimes, however, the competitive model predicts surprisingly well, even in noncompetitive industries, and you may not wish to seek out alternative theories.

Concepts in Brief 9-3

- The competitive price is determined by the intersection of the market demand curve with the market supply curve; the market supply curve is equal to the horizontal summation of those sections of the individual marginal cost curves above their respective minimum average variable costs.
- In the long run, competitive firms make zero economic profits because of entry and exit of firms into and out of the industry whenever there are industrywide economic profits or economic losses.
- Economic profits and losses are signals to resource owners.
- A constant-cost industry will have a horizontal long-run supply curve. An increasing-cost industry will have a rising long-run supply curve. A decreasing-cost industry will have a falling long-run supply curve.
- An increasing-cost industry may result from diseconomies of scale; a decreasing-cost industry may result from economies of scale.
- In the long run, a competitive firm produces where price equals marginal revenue equals marginal cost equals short-run minimum average cost equals long-run minimum average cost.
- Competitive pricing is essentially marginal cost pricing, and therefore the competitive solution is called efficient because marginal cost represents the social opportunity cost of producing one more unit of the good; when consumers are faced with a price equal to the full opportunity cost of the product they are buying, their purchasing decisions will lead to an efficient use of available resources.

ISSUES AND APPLICATIONS

Can People Get Rich Quick in the Stock Market?

Concepts Applied

- Long-run competitive process

A dream that many people have is to become rich. Some will be rich when they are older because they will inherit wealth. That is, they will inherit or be given stocks, bonds, real estate,

Because the stock market is a highly competitive market, your guess about what stocks to buy is as good as anyone else's. And the chances are that you won't get rich quick, but you will earn a normal rate of return in the long run.

valuable paintings, and other kinds of property that their parents or relatives own. Most people, however, are not so fortunate. For them to become rich, they must work hard and put their savings into wise investments.

A distinction must be made here between putting savings into investments that will pay a steady rate of return year after year and schemes into which someone puts savings in order to make a "killing" over the course of a few months or a year. The latter is the kind of investing that some individuals try as a means to get rich quick. Most people, however, do not gamble with their accumulated savings. Rather, they put their savings in a savings account, long-term bonds, a pension plan, and/or the stock market. Furthermore, they leave much of the money they invest for 20, 30, or even 40 years before taking it out to live on during retirement years.

There are, of course, many "get-rich-quick" schemes involving the stock market. One of the most popular "get-rich-quick" schemes involves picking the "right" stocks to buy at the "right" time. But what are the right stocks and when is the right time? Obviously, they are stocks whose price is low when bought and extremely high when sold.

Finding Out About the "Right" Stocks

Perhaps your parents or friends deal in the stock market—that is, they buy and sell stock, If so, you have probably heard some strange words about "the market" in their conversations. They may talk about "hot" tips, about reasons why the market might rise or fall, or about a broker's forecasts about stock prices.

When someone wants information about an illness, for example, he or she generally consults a doctor. The person may even go to a specialist. If one wants information about how to repair a car, he or she may go to another type of specialist—an automobile mechanic. Thus, when one wants information about the stock market, reason would seem to suggest that he or she should go to a stock specialist—a broker.

This reasoning is partly accurate. A stockbroker can provide information about how the stock market runs and about the costs of buying and selling stocks. The broker can also lead the investor away from very risky stocks that have a small chance of making a huge gain and a large chance of losing everything. The broker can give advice concerning the right combination of stocks and bonds and suggest different types of stocks for the investor's particular investment wants, in terms of security and income in the future. But the broker is generally *not* the person who can make the investor rich quick. The broker *cannot* tell the investor, with absolute certainty, the best way to invest his or her dollars in the market.

An experiment with a specialist. Look in the yellow pages of the telephone book under "Stock and Bond Brokers" and pick a name at random. If you were to call a brokerage firm, you would speak with a broker. (A broker is a salesperson, but he or she may have the title of "account executive.") The following is what would probably happen.

When you got the broker on the phone, you would tell him or her that you have $5,000 to invest, and ask for advice. Before the broker tells you anything, he or she will ask you what your goals are. Do you want steady income from your investment of $5,000? Do you want growth stocks that will provide a reasonable capital gain in the future?

After you tell the broker the strategy you want to take, he or she will probably advise you as to which stocks are the best to buy and will then predict (guess) whether the stock market will go up or down in the next few months. The broker's opinion will sound very informed and authoritative.

Nevertheless, strange as it may seem, the broker's advice on how to invest your money generally is not any better than anyone else's advice. In fact, *the chances of the broker's being right are no greater than the chances of your being right!* Does this sound improbable? Perhaps. Yet the fact remains that economists, statisticians, and investors have examined and tested this proposition from numerous angles. And all have reached the same conclusion.

Your guess is as good as anyone else's. You have probably never studied investing before. How can you guess about what the stock market will do? Or about how profitable a company may be in the future?

The stock market is one of the most competitive markets in the world. Competition among investors means that all investors try to do as well as they can. In doing so, each investor must compete with all other investors. Investors' efforts to gain higher profits are what make the stock market highly competitive. It is more competitive than most other markets because literally millions of investors trade in it. In addition, it is even more competitive because of the availability at relatively low cost of information about it.

Market Information

You can use almost any daily newspaper to find information about the price of stocks on the New York, American, and certain regional stock exchanges. Stock price quotations are published daily in the financial section of the newspaper. In addition, current stock price information is available from most brokerage firms. These firms have tickertape-type electronic machines that receive price changes for various stocks almost as fast as they are announced, even though the firm may be more than 3,000 miles from the stock exchange.

Information about a specific company also rapidly becomes widely known. As soon as a company announces its profits, literally millions of people learn about it. Such information is not as readily available as the prices of listed stocks, but it flows quite freely within the American economy.

The point is that by the time one investor reads about what a company, an industry, or, for that matter, the national economy is going to do, most other investors have also read it. The information is **public information**—available to anyone and everyone at very low cost. Public information cannot help you in your plan to get rich quick.

Public information. To understand why public information will not help, let us look at an example. Suppose a company in your neighborhood has discovered a substitute for gasoline. You read about the discovery in the newspaper. After reading the article, you decide the company's stock would be an excellent purchase because the company should make a great deal of money from its discovery.

But think about the idea more carefully. Will not everyone else think the same way? In fact, will not many people who learned about the discovery *before* you also realize that the company stands to make higher profits? Certainly they will. Some will already have bought stock in the company. As they bid against each other to buy stock, the price of the stock will start to rise. By the time you read about the discovery, competing investors will have *already* bid up the price of the stock to reflect the "new" information. Hence, by the time vital information becomes public, it is essentially useless to someone trying to get rich quick.

Inside information. The only useful information in a person's quest to get rich quick is information that is not yet public. This information, known only among a small group of people, is called **inside information.** Here is an example of how one might get inside information.

Suppose a lawyer meets with an executive of the International Chemical and Drug Company, in the executive's office. When the executive steps out of the office for a moment, the lawyer looks down in the wastebasket and sees a crumpled memo that reads, "Success! We've done it." Recently, the lawyer has noticed several news items about a miracle drug on which the company has been working. Now the lawyer has some inside information.

Assuming that the corporate officers at the International Chemical and Drug Company do not announce the discovery immediately, the lawyer has some very valuable information. No one outside the company knows about the discovery. If the lawyer were to buy as many shares of the International Chemical and Drug Company as he could, then he might be able to get rich quick. The probability is high that the stock would be bid up when the inside information became public and investors anticipated higher profits in the company.

A random walk. Suppose someone asked you to walk at random in a room. What would you do? You might close your eyes and walk in any direction, back and forth, diagonally, or around various objects in the room. If you have studied physics, you will recognize the similarity between such activity and the Brownian motion of molecules.

According to Brown's theory of motion, molecules jump at random. It is impossible to predict where a molecule might move next by knowing where it is or has been. In other words, when something follows a **random walk,** it takes directions that are totally unrelated to its past movements. Hence, no amount of information about the past is useful for predicting the future. Another example of a random walk is flipping a coin. It is impossible to predict whether a coin will come up heads or tails on the next flip by knowing what has happened on previous flips. The same is true for the toss of true (unloaded) dice. The past is not a predictor of the future in these cases.

Because the stock market is so highly competitive and because information about it flows so freely, it follows a random walk. The market as a whole has trends, such as the general upward trend from its beginning that reflects, among other things, the reinvestment of company earnings. The prices of specific stocks and the average of all stock prices, however, exhibit a random walk relative to the overall market trend. Any examination of past stock prices will not yield useful information for predicting future prices. Years of academic research have left little doubt that the stock market follows a random walk. If a person were to find out otherwise, he or she could get rich quickly.

Superior forecasting. Some individuals are superior forecasters of what will happen in the economy. They may have some special innate ability, or they may have developed a forecasting method that is superior to anyone else's. As long as the methods of forecasting used by these individuals do not become common knowledge, these individuals can indeed make higher-than-normal

EXHIBIT 9–11
The Dow Jones Industrial Stock Average. Here we have plotted the course of the stock market over the last half century or so. The ups and downs are tremendous, but the trend has been up. It would have been nice to buy during the low points and sell at the high points. Hindsight, however, is always more accurate than foresight.

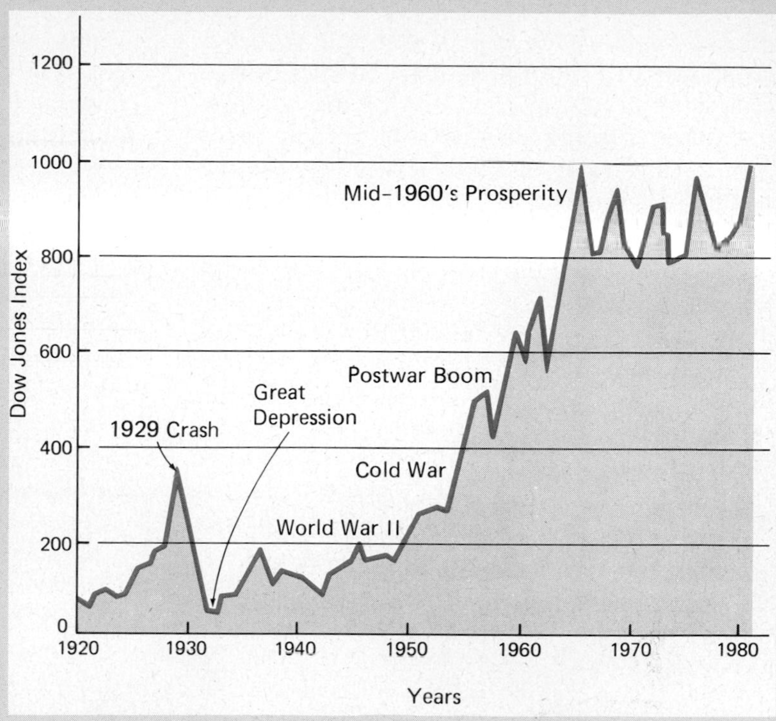

profits in the stock market. It is the ability to *interpret* public information (and inside information, also) that gives some individuals the edge in the stock market.

Is There No Way To Get Rich Quick?

Exhibit 9–11 shows the Dow Jones Industrial stock average for the years 1920 to 1981. The Dow Jones Industrial is an average of 30 large companies' stock prices. It is thus an indicator of stock prices in general.

Looking at the graph, you will see many movements up and down. (Stock market rates of return were negative during the Great Depression. They have been historically very low during the 1970s and 1980s, also.) But the general trend of stock prices is upward. Obviously, anybody who could buy stocks at the times when prices were low and sell them at the times when prices were high would become rich. But no one knows how to do that with any consistency.

Thus, when you have money to invest in the stock market, a wise course to follow might be to buy a random selection of stocks and hold the stocks for many years. The average annual return on such an investment, including both dividends and growth, has historically been between 8 and 15 percent. But for any given short period, it can be much less.

Most people find this difficult to accept. Many think they can outsmart the stock market. Yet the facts are irrefutable. In the words of economist Paul Samuelson, a Nobel Prize recipient:

> Even the best investors seem to find it hard to do better than the comprehensive common-stock averages, or better on the average than random selection among stocks of comparable variability.[3]

Questions

1. The stock market is highly competitive. Therefore, what average rate of return can you predict you will make by "wheeling and dealing" in the stock market?
2. Rates of return in the stock market during the 1970s were historically very low. Using the competitive model, what can you predict will happen to the amount of resources flowing into publicly owned companies listed on stock exchanges?

[3] Paul Samuelson, *The Bell Journal of Economics and Management Science,* Autumn 1973, Vol. 4, No. 2, pp. 369–374.

Definition of Terms

Perfectly competitive firm A firm that is such a small part of the total industry picture that it cannot affect the price of the product it sells.

Price taker Another definition of a competitive firm. A price taker is a firm that must take the price of its product as given. The firm cannot influence its price.

Total revenues The price per unit times the total quantity sold.

Total costs All costs added together.

Marginal Revenue The change in total revenues resulting from a change in output and sale of one unit of the product in question.

Short-run break-even point The point where a firm's total revenues equal its total costs. In economics the break-even point is where the firm is just making a normal rate of return.

Short-run shutdown point The point where the profit-maximizing price just covers average variable costs. This occurs just below the intersection of the marginal cost curve and the average variable cost curve.

Marginal cost pricing A system of pricing in which the price charged is equal to the opportunity cost to society of producing one more unit of the good or service in question. The opportunity cost is the marginal cost to society.

Public information Public information is any kind of information that is widely available to the public.

Inside information Inside information is any kind of information that is available only to a few people, such as the officers of a company.

Random walk The term *random walk* refers to the situation in which future behavior cannot be predicted from past behavior. Stock prices follow a random walk.

Chapter Summary

1. We define a competitive situation as one in which individual firms cannot affect the price of the product they produce. This is usually when the firm is very small relative to the entire industry. A firm in a perfectly competitive situation is called a price taker; it must take the price as given.
2. The firm therefore faces a completely elastic demand curve for its product. It can sell all it wants at the going market price. If it raises its price, it sells nothing. It will not lower its price, because it can sell all it wants at the market price.
3. The firm's total revenues will equal the price of the product times the quantity sold. Since the competitive firm can sell all it wants at the same price (the "going" price), total revenues just equal the going price times whatever the firm decides to sell.
4. The firm decides to produce and sell the output that maximizes profits. It maximizes profits when it maximizes the difference between total revenues and total costs. We can also find out where it maximizes profits by looking at its marginal cost curve.
5. The firm maximizes profits where marginal cost equals marginal revenue. The marginal revenue to the firm is represented by its own horizontal demand curve. This is because marginal revenue is defined as the change in total revenues due to a change in production by one unit. But the competitive firm can sell all it wants at the same market price; therefore, its marginal revenue will equal the price, which will equal its average revenue. The firm will always want to produce where marginal revenue equals marginal cost. If it produces a greater output, marginal cost will exceed marginal revenue. If it produces a smaller output, marginal cost is less than marginal revenue, and it could be making more profits if it expanded production.
6. A perfectly competitive firm ends up in the long run making zero economic profits. However, it still makes a normal or competitive rate of return, since that is the opportunity cost of capital. The competitive rate of return, or normal profits, are included in the costs as we have defined them for the firm. The point of maximum profits for the competitive firm is therefore also its break-even point; this is where total cost will equal total revenue. Businesspeople like to talk of a break-even point that does *not* include a normal rate of return as a cost. Note that this differs from the economist's notion of a break-even point.

7. The firm will always produce along its marginal cost curve unless the price falls below average variable costs; this would be the shutdown point. It occurs at the intersection of the average variable cost curve and the marginal cost curve. Below that price it is not profitable to stay in business, since variable costs will not be completely covered by revenues.
8. Economic profits are eliminated in a competitive situation because, in the long run, other firms will enter the industry if it is initially possible to make economic profits. These new firms increase the supply and lower the market price. Conversely, if there are economic losses (negative economic profits), firms will leave the industry, thereby decreasing the supply and causing a rise in the market price.
9. The supply curve of the firm is exactly equal to its marginal cost curve above the shutdown point. The supply curve of the industry is equal to the horizontal summation of all the supply curves of the individual firms. This is a short-run industry supply curve, and it is upward sloping.
10. The equilibrium, or market-clearing, price is determined by the intersection of the market demand curve and the industry supply curve. That is how we determine the going price in the market.
11. The competitive solution results in a situation where any change in the use of resources will result in a decrease in the economic value obtainable from a fixed amount of resources at any point in time. The competitive solution leads to what is called marginal cost pricing, where the price is set equal to the marginal cost, which is equal to the social opportunity cost of producing the good or service in question.
12. It is difficult to imagine many situations where perfect competition exists in the short run. However, we might say that in the long run there is a tendency toward a competitive solution, even if it will never be reached. That is because firms will constantly acquire new information and there will be entry and exit from the industry depending upon whether there are economic profits or economic losses.
13. The long-run supply curve will be upward sloping, horizontal, or downward sloping, depending on whether the industry is facing increasing, constant, or decreasing costs.
14. The industry may have an upward-sloping long-run supply curve if it faces diseconomies of scale or increasing costs. The industry may have a downward-sloping long-run supply curve if it faces economies of scale or decreasing costs.
15. In the long run, the perfectly competitive firm operates where price equals minimum long-run average cost equals minimum short-run average cost equals marginal cost.
16. Competition in the stock market implies that it is difficult, on average, to make higher-than-normal, or competitive, rates of return, unless, for example, you have inside information or a truly superior theory for interpreting that information.

Selected References

Knight, F. H. "Cost of Production and Price Over Long and Short Periods." *Journal of Political Economy,* 29 (April 1921), pp. 304–335.

Machlup, Fritz. *Economics of Sellers' Competition.* Baltimore: Johns Hopkins University Press, 1952, pp. 79–85, 116–125.

Malkiel, Burton C. *A Random Walk Down Wall Street.* 3rd ed. New York: Norton, 1980.

Thompson, Arthur A., Jr. *Economics of the Firm: Theory and Practice.* 2nd ed. Englewood Cliffs, N.J.: Prentice-Hall, 1977, chap. 10.

Answers to Preview and Study Questions

1. What are the characteristics of the perfect competition market structure?

The characteristics of the perfect competition market structure include: (a) a product for which each firm in the industry has a perfect substitute; (b) a large number of buyers or sellers, so that each transactor is a price taker; (c) adequate information about prices, qualities, and so forth; and (d) free entry and exit within the industry. Thus, a perfectly competitive firm is just one of many producers producing an identical product, none of which has any control over market price. The perfect competitor faces a perfectly elastic demand curve; it can sell all it wants at the market price, and none at any price above the market price.

2. How much will a perfect competitor produce in the short run?

A perfect competitor will produce at the profit-maximizing rate of output; it will maximize the positive difference between total revenues and total costs. Another way of viewing this process is through analyzing marginal revenue (MR) and marginal cost (MC). The firm can maximize total profits by producing all those outputs for which MR exceeds MC. Thus, if MR > MC, the firm will produce the unit in question; if MR < MC, the firm will not produce the unit in question. If MC > MR, the extra cost of producing that unit is greater than the extra revenue that the firm can earn by selling it; producing a unit for which MC > MR leads to a reduction in total profits or an increase in total losses. In short, the perfect competitor will produce up to the output rate at which MR = MC; by doing so it will have produced all those units for which MR > MC, and it will be maximizing total profits.

3. What is the perfectly competitive firm's short-run supply curve?

A supply curve indicates the various quantities that will be offered, voluntarily, at different prices per unit of time—other things being constant. Under perfect competition, price *(P)* equals marginal revenue (MR) and, since the profit-maximizing output occurs where *P* = MC, it follows that any price will induce output until MC is driven up to equal that price. Thus, the marginal cost curve *is* the firm's short-run supply schedule. We qualify this to note that since the firm has a shutdown point at the minimum average variable cost point, the technical short-run supply curve is the firm's short-run supply schedule *above* the minimum average variable cost point.

4. Can a perfectly competitive firm earn economic profits?

In the short run yes, in the long run no. While it is possible for a perfectly competitive firm to earn profits in the short run, our assumption of free (meaning unfettered, but not costless) entry forces us to conclude that any positive economic (abnormal) profits will be bid away. This will happen because excess profits induce entry into the industry, which amounts to an increase in industry supply. Given demand, an increase in supply will cause market price to fall—thereby shifting the individual firm's demand curve downward. This process continues until economic profits equal zero; free entry allows new entrants to compete away economic profits.

5. Why is the perfect competition market structure considered to be economically efficient?

The perfect competition market structure is considered to be economically efficient for two reasons: (1) in the long run economic profits are zero, and (2) price equals marginal cost. We discuss each in turn. Profits are a signal; if economic profits are positive, the signal is that society wants *more* of this good; if economic profits are negative, this means that society wants *less* of this good; when economic profits are zero, just the right quantity of resources is being allocated to the production of a good. Also, the marginal cost of a good represents the social opportunity cost of producing one more unit of that good; the price of a good represents society's marginal valuation of that commodity. When price equals marginal cost, the value to society of the last unit produced (its price) is just offset by what society had to give up in order to get it (its MC). Since under perfect competition long-run economic profits equal zero and price equals marginal cost, an efficient allocation of resources exists.

Problems

(Answers at the back of the book)

1. In the table below, we list cost figures for a hypothetical firm. We assume that the firm is selling in a perfectly competitive market. Fill in all of the columns that are left blank.

Output	*Fixed cost*	*AFC*	*Variable cost*	*AVC*	*Total cost*	*ATC*	*MC*
1	$100	______	$ 40	______	______	______	______
2	100	______	70	______	______	______	______
3	100	______	120	______	______	______	______
4	100	______	180	______	______	______	______
5	100	______	250	______	______	______	______
6	100	______	330	______	______	______	______

a. How low would the market price of its output have to go before the firm would shut down in the short run?
b. What is the price of its output at which the firm would just break even in the short run? (This is the same price below which the firm would go out of business in the long run.) What output would the firm produce at that price?
c. If the price of its output were $76, what rate of output would the firm produce and how much profit would it earn?

2. Consider the graph below and then answer the questions relating to it.

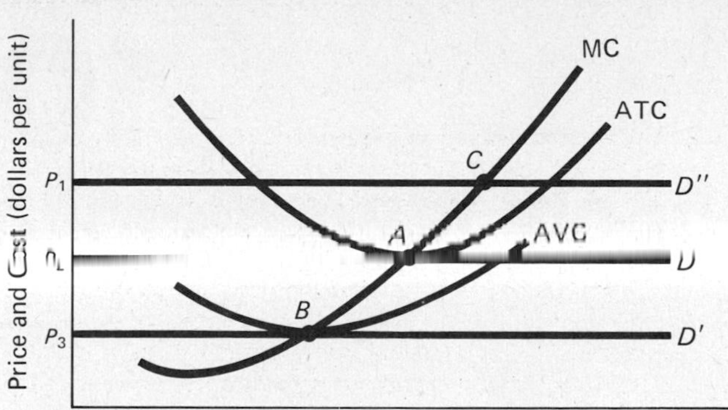

a. Which demand curve indicates that the firm is earning normal profits?
b. Which demand curve indicates that the firm is earning abnormal profits?
c. Which demand curve indicates that the firm is indifferent between shutting down and producing?
d. Which curve is the firm's supply curve?
e. Below which price will the firm shut down?

10

Monopoly Management

TOPICS FOR REVIEW

The topics listed below, which we have already analyzed, are applied in this chapter. You may find it worthwhile to review them. For your convenience, each topic is followed by the number identifying the specific "Concepts in Brief."

a. Total revenue and elasticity (6–2)

b. Perfectly elastic demand (6–3)

c. Long run (8–4)

d. Perfect competition model (9–1)

FOR PREVIEW AND STUDY

1. What is a monopolist, and how can a monopoly be formed?
2. For the monopolist, marginal revenue is less than selling price. Why?
3. What is the profit-maximizing rate of output for the monopolist?
4. What are some common misconceptions about a monopolist?
5. What is the cost to society of monopoly?

The world, of course, does not consist of *perfectly* competitive industries. In this chapter, we will present a model of a monopoly business and discuss how a monopolist decides what prices to charge and how much to produce. Most of the analytical tools needed here have already been introduced. In the Issues and Applications section, we will look at the creation of monopoly profits by restricting entry into the taxicab business and the conflict between author and publisher in the pricing of textbooks.

Definition of a Monopolist

The word *monopoly* or *monopolist* probably brings to mind a business that gouges the consumer, sells faulty products, gets rich, and any other bad thoughts that one can have about big business. If we are to succeed in analyzing and predicting the behavior of noncompetitive firms, however, we will have to be somewhat more objective in defining a monopolist. Although most actual monopolies in the United States are relatively large, our definition of monopoly will be equally applicable to small businesses. Thus, a **monopolist** is defined as a *single supplier*. (This is the Greek origin of the word.)

We must be careful of our definition of monopoly, for the more narrowly we define a product, the more easily we come up with a monopoly situation. Consider a small town with a single newspaper. By our definition of monopoly, the owner of the newspaper is a monopolist. He or she sells the only newspaper printed in town. What if we consider this product—the only newspaper in town—as part of the news media industry? Does a newspaper owner have a monopoly in all news media? Certainly not, for he or she is in competition with radio, television, magazines such as *Newsweek, Time,* and *U.S. News & World Report,* and newspapers from nearby towns, as well as national newspapers such as *The New York Times* and the *Wall Street Journal.*

As we shall see in this chapter, a seller prefers to have a monopoly rather than to face competition. In general, we think of monopoly prices as being higher than competitive prices, and of monopoly profits as being higher than competitive profits (which are merely equivalent to a normal rate of return). How does a firm obtain a monopoly in an industry? Basically, there must be **barriers to entry** that enable firms to receive monopoly profits in the long run. We define barriers to entry as restrictions on who can start a business or who can stay in a business.

Barriers to Entry

For monopoly power to continue to exist in the long run, there has to be some way in which the market is closed to entry. Either legal means or certain aspects of the industry's technical or cost structure must somehow prevent entry. Below, we will discuss several of the barriers to entry that have allowed firms to reap monopoly profits in the long run.

OWNERSHIP OF RESOURCES WITHOUT CLOSE SUBSTITUTES

Preventing a newcomer from entering an industry is often difficult. Indeed, there are some economists who contend that no monopoly acting without government support has been able to prevent entry into the industry unless that monopoly has had the control of some "essential" natural resource. Consider the possibility of one firm owning the entire supply of a raw material input that is essential to the production of a particular commodity. The exclusive ownership of such a vital resource input serves as a barrier to entry until an alternative source of the raw material input is found or an alternative technology not requiring the raw material in question is developed. A good example of control over a vital input is the Aluminum Company of America (Alcoa), a firm that prior to World War II controlled the world's bauxite, the essential raw material in the production of aluminum.

PROBLEM IN RAISING ADEQUATE CAPITAL

Certain industries require a large initial capital investment. The firms already in the industry can, according to some economists, obtain monopoly profits in the long run because no competitors can raise the large amount of capital needed to enter the industry. This is the "imperfect" capital market argument employed to explain long-run, relatively high rates of return in certain industries. These industries generally are ones in which large fixed costs must be incurred in order to merely start production. Their fixed costs generally are for expensive machines necessary in the production process.

Certainly, it is more difficult, at any given level of risk, to raise a larger rather than a smaller amount of capital. But a sufficiently high-risk premium can presumably be added to the anticipated rate of return from investing in the risky industry

monopoly

to enable a newcomer to raise the needed capital. It may be, of course, that the anticipated rate of return offered to investors in such an industry would have to be so high that it would not be profitable for an entrepreneur to undertake entry into the industry. It is not clear why such a situation is called an imperfect capital market or why it should be considered a barrier to entry any more than any other high-risk premium, but it often is.

Moreover, one must realize that it is not necessary to *purchase* all of the capital equipment required to enter an industry. Equipment can often be leased, and numerous components of the commodity to be sold can be purchased from outside suppliers. A few years ago, the Bricklin two-seater sports car venture did just that. Many of the components of the automobile were purchased from other automobile manufacturers. The company ultimately went into receivership after only a few thousand Bricklins were sold. Nonetheless, it had been able to raise sufficient amounts of capital to enter the industry but, as it turned out, not enough to sustain the initial production year's losses.

LICENSES, FRANCHISES, AND CERTIFICATES OF CONVENIENCE

In many industries it is illegal to enter without a governmentally provided license, or "certificate of convenience and public necessity." For example, you could not form an electrical utility to compete with the electric utility already operating in your area. You would first have to obtain a certificate of convenience and public necessity from the appropriate authority, which is usually the state's public utility commission. However, public utility commissions rarely, if ever, issue a certificate to a group of investors who want to compete directly in the same geographic area with an existing electric utility; hence, entry into the industry in a particular geographic area is prohibited, and long-run monopoly profits could conceivably be earned by the electric utility already serving the area.

In order to enter interstate (and also many intrastate) markets for pipelines, trucking, television and radio signals, the transmission of natural gas, and so on, it is necessary to obtain the equivalent of a certificate of convenience and public necessity. Since these franchises or licenses aren't given very often, long-run monopoly profits might be earned by those firms already in the industry. The logic behind issuing few certificates of convenience has to do with supposed economies of scale in the industries where they are required. If those industries do indeed experience large economies of scale, then allowing a large number of firms to compete would, it is reasoned, prevent consumers from benefiting from one firm being able to sell a large output with significantly reduced average costs.

Another example of a license that creates a monopoly has to do with taxicabs. In many major cities, it is illegal to operate a taxicab without first having obtained a permit to do so. We discuss this example in more detail in the Issues and Applications section of this chapter.

PATENTS

Closely related to the franchise required for entry is a patent. A patent is issued to an inventor to protect him or her from having the invention copied for a period of 17 years. Suppose I discover a new film for super-8 movie cameras that develops itself instantaneously so that the roll is ready for projection as soon as it is exposed. If I am successful (or my attorneys are) in obtaining a patent on this discovery, I can prevent other individuals from copying me. Note, however, that I must expend resources to prevent other individuals from imitating me even if I do have a watertight patent. Many resources are devoted by patent owners to enforcing their exclusive rights. Indeed, I can have a patent on a particular commodity or production process and end up having no monopoly profits at all, because the costs of policing are so high that I don't bother to protect my patent or, if I do, I end up spending so much on policing costs that I eat up all of my monopoly profits.

ECONOMIES OF SCALE

LAC

Sometimes it is not profitable for more than one firm to exist in an industry. Such a situation may arise because of a phenomenon we have already discussed known as economies of scale. When economies of scale exist, costs increase less than proportionately to the increase in output. That is, proportional increases in all factors of production yield proportionately smaller increases in total costs.

Economies of scale can create what is known as a *natural monopoly,* a topic sufficiently important that we devote much of Chapter 12 to it. It is generally clear that one electric utility and one natural gas distributor can provide the product at a lower average cost than if several firms attempt to provide electricity or natural gas. Economies of scale do exist and that means that at larger rates of output, one firm will face declining long-run average costs. The firm that is able to take advantage of the declining long-run average cost curve will indeed become the monopolist in the industry.

Concepts in Brief 10-1

- A monopolist is defined as a single seller of a product or a good for which there are no close substitutes.
- In order to maintain a monopoly, there must be barriers to entry. Barriers to entry include: (1) ownership of resources without close substitutes, (2) large capital requirements in order to enter the industry, (3) legally required licenses, franchises, and certificates of convenience, (4) patents, and (5) economies of scale.

The Demand Curve Facing a Monopolist

The term *true monopolist* refers to the original meaning of the word—single supplier of *one* product or good or service. A true monopolist faces a demand curve that is the demand curve for the entire market for the good. *The monopolist faces the industry demand curve because the monopolist is the entire industry.* A single corner drugstore in a small town is therefore just as much a monopolist as a corporate giant like American Telephone and Telegraph.

SOME EXAMPLES OF MONOPOLIES

Everyone is aware of at least some of the forms of pure monopoly that exist in our economy. When you turn on the light to read this text, you are purchasing the output of the local monopoly electric power company in your area. There is only one company to which you can go to buy electric power, right? How did it get to be a monopoly? A government franchise gave it monopoly power. That is, the government certifies a single electric power company to operate in a well-defined geographical area. You and your friends could not pool your money, buy a small generator, and solicit electricity customers in your neighborhood. That is illegal; government regulations do not allow it.

When you mail a letter at the post office, you are purchasing the services of a government monopoly. Although various groups have tested the legality of restricting first-class mail service to the U.S. Postal Service, for the moment first-class service is a government-controlled and owned monopoly (except for "urgent" letters shipped overnight). There is a single seller of first-class service, and that is the government. (First class does not, of course, necessarily refer here to high-quality service.)

When you dial a number on your telephone, you are using the services of a monopolist—probably your local chapter of the American Telephone and Telegraph system. And until recently, the phone you used was produced by a monopolist because the government did not allow just anybody to produce and install telephone equipment. That is no longer the case, but it is still true that telephone services are sold by one of the largest monopolists in the country.

Profit to Be Made from Increasing Production

How do competitors and monopolists profit from changing production levels? What happens to price in each case? We've already discussed the competitive situation.

PERFECT COMPETITOR'S MARGINAL REVENUE

Remember that a competitive firm has a horizontal demand curve. That is, the competitive firm is such a small part of the market that it cannot influence the price of its product. It is a price taker. If the forces of market supply and demand establish the price per bushel of wheat at $2, then the individual firm can sell all the wheat it wants to produce at $2 a bushel. The average revenue is $2, the price is $2, and the marginal revenue is also $2.

Let us again define marginal revenue:

Marginal revenue equals the change in total revenue due to a one-unit change in the quantity produced and sold.

In the case of a competitive industry, each time production is increased by one unit, total revenue increases by the going price, and price is always the same. Marginal revenue never changes; it always equals price, or average revenue. Average revenue was defined in the last chapter as total revenue divided by quantity demanded, or:

$$\text{average revenue} = \frac{TR}{Q} = \frac{P \times Q}{Q} = P$$

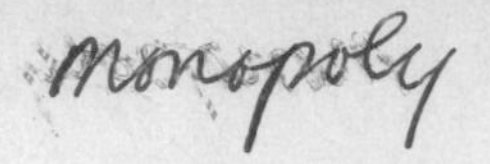

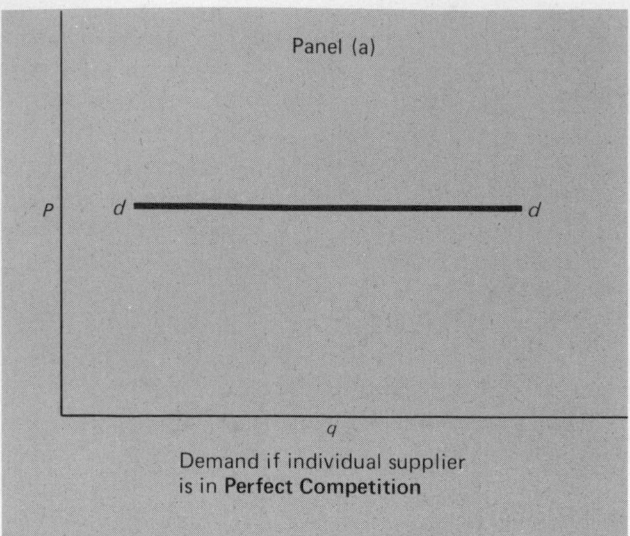

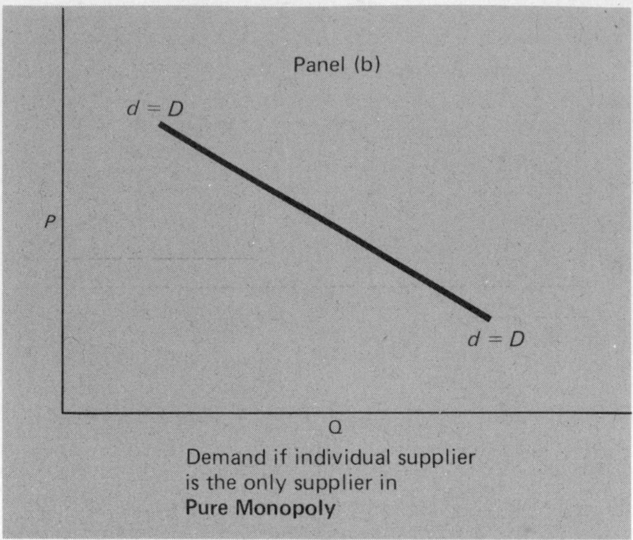

EXHIBIT 10–1

Comparison of the Perfect Competitor's and the Monopolist's Demand Curves. The perfect competitor faces a horizontal demand curve *dd* in panel (a). The monopolist faces the entire industry demand curve in panel (b), and it is downward sloping.

MONOPOLISTS' MARGINAL REVENUE

What about a monopoly firm? Since a monopoly is the entire industry, the monopoly firm faces the entire market demand curve. The market demand curve is downward sloping, just like the others that we have seen. Therefore, in order to sell more of a particular product given the industry demand curve, the monopoly firm must lower the price. Thus, the monopoly firm moves *down* the demand curve. If all buyers are to be charged the same price, the monopoly must lower the price on all units sold in order to sell more. It cannot just lower the price on the last unit sold in any given time period in order to sell a larger quantity.

It is sometimes useful to compare monopoly with competition. In a competitive situation, one firm takes away sales from other competing firms. In a monopoly situation, by definition, there are no other firms in the industry. Therefore, the monopolist takes away sales from the entire market of all other industries. That is to say, the only way the monopolist can increase sales is by getting consumers to spend more of their incomes on the monopolist's product and less on all other products combined. Thus, the monopolist is constrained by the entire market demand curve for its product. We see this in Exhibit 10–1, which compares the perfect competitor's and monopolist's demand curves.

Here we see the fundamental difference between the monopolist and the competitor. The competitor doesn't have to worry about lowering prices in order to sell more. In a purely competitive situation, the competitive firm sells such a small part of the market that it can sell its entire output, whatever that may be, at the same price. The monopolist cannot do this. The more the monopolist wants to sell, the lower the price it has to charge on the last unit (and on *all* units put on the market for sale). Obviously, the extra revenues the monopolist receives from selling one more unit are going to be smaller than the extra revenues received from selling the next-to-last unit. The monopolist has to lower the price on the last unit to sell it because it is facing a downward-sloping demand curve. The only way to move down the demand curve is to lower the price.

The monopolist's marginal revenue therefore is going to be falling. But it falls even more than one might think, because to sell one more unit the monopolist has to lower the price on *all* previous units, not just on the last unit produced and sold. This is because information flows freely; the monopolist will not usually be able to charge one consumer $2 and another consumer $3 for the same item. The consumer who could buy the product for $2 would buy lots of it and resell it to the one who was willing to pay $3 for a price of, say, $2.50. Unless the monopolist is successful in somehow separating (discriminating between) the different markets to prevent secondary transactions among the consumers in those markets, it will have to sell all goods at a uniform price. Therefore, when the monopolist increases production, it must charge a lower price on the last unit *and on all previous units.*

MARGINAL REVENUE IS ALWAYS LESS THAN PRICE

An essential point in the above discussion is that for the monopolist marginal revenue is always less than price. To understand why, look at Exhibit 10–2. Here we show a unit increase in sales due to a reduction in the price of, say, handbags from P_1 to P_2. After all, the only way that sales can increase, given a downward-sloping demand curve, is for price to fall. The price P_2 is the price received for the last unit. Thus, that price P_2 times the last unit sold represents what is received from the last unit sold. That would be equal to the horizontally gridded column showing the effects of a one-unit increase in sales. The area of that horizontally gridded column is one unit wide times P_2 high.

But the price times the last unit sold is not the addition to total revenues received from selling that last unit. Why? Because price was reduced on all previous units sold (0Q) in order to sell the larger quantity Q + 1. The reduction in price is represented by the vertical distance from P_1 to P_2 on the vertical axis. We must therefore subtract the vertically gridded row from the horizontally gridded column in order to come up with the *change* in total revenues due to a one-unit increase in sales. Clearly, the change in total revenues, i.e., marginal revenue, must be less than price, because marginal revenue is always the difference between the two gridded areas in Exhibit 10–2.

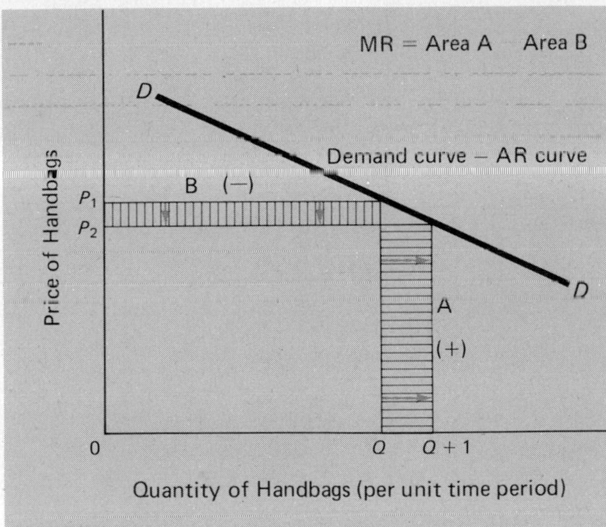

EXHIBIT 10–2
Marginal Revenue Is Always Less than Price. The only way to sell one more unit when facing a downward-sloping demand curve is to lower the price. The price received for the last unit is equal to P_2. The revenues received from selling this last unit are equal to P_2 times one unit, or the area of the horizontally crosshatched vertical column. However, if a single price is being charged for all units, total revenues do not go up by the amount of the area represented by that column. The price had to be reduced on all the previous 0Q units that were being sold at price P_1. Thus, we must subtract the vertically lined area [the rectangle (P_1 − P_2) high and 0Q wide] from the horizontally lined area in order to derive marginal revenue. Marginal revenue is therefore always less than price.

Elasticity and Total Revenues

The monopolist faces a downward-sloping demand curve. That means that it cannot charge just *any* price, (a common misconception) because, depending on the price charged, a different quantity will be demanded. In other words, there is a unique relationship between the price the monopolist charges and total revenues, which consist of price times quantity. Thus, there is a relationship between the total revenues and the price elasticity of the demand curve. We have already discussed this relationship, but it is worth going over again briefly. The demand curve of a monopolist has varying elasticities, depending on where we are on the demand curve. Remember that a straight-line demand curve has a price elasticity of demand that goes from infinity to zero as we move down the demand curve. Thus, it is not true that a monopolist faces an inelastic demand curve.

We earlier defined a monopolist as the single seller of a well-defined good or service with no *close* substitutes. That does not mean, however, that the demand curve facing a monopoly is vertical, or exhibits zero-price elasticity of demand. After all, consumers have limited incomes and alternative wants. The downward slope of a monopolist's demand curve occurs because individuals compare the marginal satisfaction they will receive to the cost of the commodity to be purchased. Take the example of telephone service. Assume that there is absolutely no substitute whatsoever for telephone service. The market demand curve will still slope down. At lower prices, people will add more phones and separate lines for different family members.

Additionally, the demand curve for telephone service slopes down because there are at least several *imperfect* substitutes, such as letters, telegrams, in-person conversations, and CB radios. Thus, even though we defined a monopolist as a single seller of a commodity with no *close* substi-

Monopoly

tutes, we can talk about the range of *imperfect* substitutes. The more such imperfect substitutes there are, the more elastic will be the demand curve facing the monopolist, all other things held constant.

EXHIBIT 10–3(a)

Elasticity of Demand and Total Revenues. Here we show the relationship between marginal revenue, the demand curve, and the elasticity of demand. From the point where marginal revenue equals zero—that is, point *A′*—demand is inelastic to the right and below and elastic to the left and above. At point *A′*, demand has unitary elasticity, or equals −1. To the right, the monopolist would find that if it lowered price, the quantity demanded would increase less than proportionally. To the left of *A′* as it raised price, the quantity demanded would fall more than proportionally.

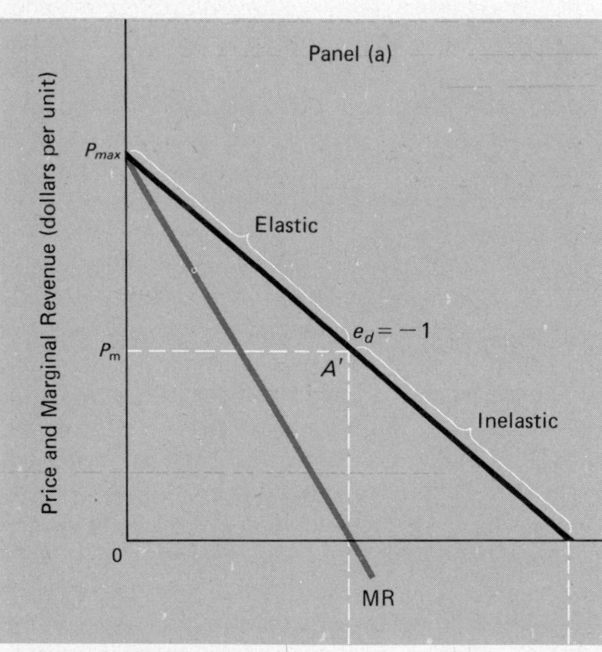

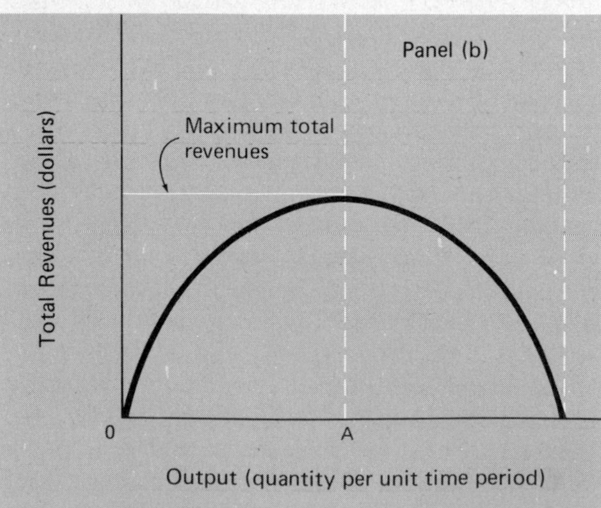

We can see the relationship now between the price elasticity of demand for a monopolist, marginal revenue, and total revenues. This relationship is presented in panels (a) and (b) of Exhibit 10–3. At point *A′* on the demand schedule, the point corresponding to zero marginal revenues, we have marked $e_d = -1$. That is, the elasticity of demand is such that a change in price elicits a proportional and opposite change in quantity demanded. That portion of the demand schedule to the right of point *A′* we have labeled *inelastic*. That is, to the right of point *A′*, a change in price elicits a proportionately smaller change in quantity demanded. That portion of the demand curve to the left and above point *A′* (above price P_m) we have labeled *elastic*. This means that to the left of *A′* a change in price will cause a proportionately larger change in quantity demanded.

We show the relationship between elasticity and total revenue graphically in panel (b) of Exhibit 10–3. Obviously, total revenues are zero at a zero price and at P_{max} where no units are sold. Between these points, total revenues rise and then fall. The maximum revenue is where the elasticity of demand is unity, as shown in panel (b) of Exhibit 10–3.

> *Concepts in Brief 10-2*
>
> - The demand curve facing a monopolist is downward sloping by definition.
> - The monopolist must look at its marginal revenue curve, where marginal revenue is defined as the change in total revenues due to a one-unit change in quantity sold.
> - For the perfect competitor, price equals marginal revenue equals average revenue. For the

EXHIBIT 10–3(b)

Total Revenues and the Demand Curve. Here we show the relationship between the demand curve, elasticity of demand, and total revenue. When the price is set at P_{max} in panel (a), the total revenues are, of course, zero. When the price is set at zero, total revenues are also zero. In between these two ends of the price possibilities scale, we will find some price that maximizes total revenues. That price happens to be where marginal revenue equals zero, or at point *A′* in panel (a). We have shown here that the maximum occurs at the output at which marginal revenue equals zero. If the monopolist had no variable costs at all, it would obviously want to produce at point *A* because that is where it would maximize its total revenues, which under *that* condition would maximize total profits.

monopolist, price is always greater than marginal revenue. Otherwise stated, for the monopolist, marginal revenue is always less than price because of the downward slope of the demand curve.

- The price elasticity of demand facing the monopolist depends on the number and closeness of substitutes. The more numerous and the closer the substitutes, the greater the price elasticity of demand of the monopolist's demand curve.
- The monopolist will never produce on the inelastic portion of its demand curve.

Costs and Short-Run Profit Maximization

In order to find out at what rate of output the perfect competitor would be maximizing profits, we had to add cost data. We will do the same thing now for the monopolist. We assume profit maximization is the goal of the pure monopolist, just as we assumed it was the goal of the perfect competitor. With the perfect competitor, however, we had only to decide on the profit-maximizing rate of output, because price was given. The competitor is a price taker. For the pure monopolist, we must seek a profit-maximizing *price-output combination.* The monopolist is a price maker. We can determine the profit-maximizing price-output combination in either of two ways—by looking at total revenues and total costs, or by looking at marginal revenues and marginal costs. Both approaches are given here.

TOTAL REVENUE–TOTAL COSTS APPROACH

We show hypothetical demand (rate of output and price per unit), revenues, costs, and so on in panel (a) of Exhibit 10–4. In column 3 we see total revenues for our hypothetical monopolist, and in column 4 we see total costs. We can transfer these two columns to panel (b). The only difference between this total revenue and total cost diagram [panel (b)] and the one we showed for a perfect competitor in the last chapter is that the total revenue line is no longer straight. Rather, it curves. For any given demand curve, in order to sell more, the monopolist must lower the price. The basic difference, therefore, between a monopolist and a perfect competitor has to do with the demand curve facing the two different types of firms. Fundamentally, the costs faced by the perfect competitor and the pure monopolist are the same. Monopoly market power is derived from facing a downward-sloping demand curve.

Profit maximization involves maximizing the positive difference between total revenues and total costs. This occurs at an output rate of about 10 units. We can also find this profit-maximizing rate of output by using the marginal revenue–marginal cost approach. The results will be the same.

MARGINAL REVENUE–MARGINAL COST APPROACH

Profit maximization will also occur where marginal revenue equals marginal cost. This is as true for a monopolist as it is for a perfect competitor (but the monopolist will charge a higher price). When we transfer marginal cost to marginal revenue information from columns 6 and 7 in panel (a) of Exhibit 10–4 to panel (c), we see that marginal revenue equals marginal cost at an output rate of about 10 units. Profit maximization occurs at the same output in panel (b).

Why Produce Where Marginal Revenue Equals Marginal Cost?

If the monopolist goes past the point where marginal revenue equals marginal cost (10 units of output), marginal cost will exceed marginal revenue. That is, the incremental cost of producing any more units will exceed the incremental revenue. It just wouldn't be worthwhile, as was true also in perfect competition. On the other hand, if the monopolist produces less than that, then it is not making maximum profits. Look at output rate Q_1 in Exhibit 10–5. Here the monopolist's marginal revenue is at *A*, but marginal cost is at *B*. Marginal revenue exceeds marginal cost on the last unit sold; the profit for that *particular* unit Q_1 is equal to the vertical difference between *A* and *B*, or the difference between marginal revenue and marginal cost. The monopolist would be foolish to stop at output rate Q_1, because if output is expanded, the marginal revenue will still exceed marginal cost and therefore total profits will rise. In fact, the profit-maximizing monopolist will continue to expand output and sales until marginal revenue equals marginal cost, which is at output rate Q_m. The monopolist won't produce at rate Q_2 because here we see that marginal costs are *C* and marginal revenues are *D*. The difference between *C* and *D* represents the reduction in total profits from producing that additional

EXHIBIT 10–4(a)
Monopoly Costs, Revenues, and Profits.

Rate of Output (1)	*Price per Unit (2)*	*Total Revenues [(2) × (1)] (3)*	*Total Costs (4)*	*Total Profit [(3) − (4)] (5)*	*Marginal Cost (6)*	*Marginal Revenue (7)*
0	8.00	0	10.00	−10.00		
					4.00	7.80
1	7.80	7.80	14.00	− 6.20		
					3.50	7.40
2	7.60	15.20	17.50	− 2.30		
					3.25	7.00
3	7.40	22.20	20.75	− 1.45		
					3.05	6.60
4	7.20	28.80	23.80	5.00		
					2.90	6.20
5	7.00	35.00	26.70	8.30		
					2.80	5.80
6	6.80	40.80	29.50	11.30		
					2.75	5.40
7	6.60	46.20	32.25	13.95		
					2.85	5.00
8	6.40	51.20	35.10	16.10		
					3.20	4.60
9	6.20	55.80	38.30	17.50		
					4.00	4.20
10	6.00	60.00	42.30	17.70		
					6.00	3.80
11	5.80	63.80	48.30	15.50		
					9.00	3.40
12	5.60	67.20	57.30	9.90		
					13.00	3.00
13	5.40	70.20	70.30	− 0.10		
					18.00	2.60
14	5.20	72.80	88.30	−15.50		
					24.00	2.20
15	5.00	75.00	112.30	−37.30		

unit. Total profits will rise as the monopolist reduces its rate of output back toward Q_m.

WHAT PRICE TO CHARGE FOR OUTPUT?

How does the monopolist set prices? We know the quantity is set at the point where marginal revenue equals marginal cost. The monopolist then finds out how much can be charged—that is, how much the market will bear—for that particular quantity, Q_m, in Exhibit 10–5. We know that the demand curve is defined as showing the *maximum* price for which a given quantity can be sold. That means that our monopolist knows that in order to sell Q_m it can only charge P_m, because that is the price at which that specific quantity, Q_m, is demanded. This price is found by drawing a vertical line from the quantity, Q_m, to the market demand curve. Where that line hits the market demand curve the price is determined. We find that price by drawing a horizontal line from the demand curve over to the price axis; that gives us the profit-maximizing price of P_m.

In our detailed numerical example, at a profit-maximizing rate of output of 10 in Exhibit 10–4, the firm can charge a maximum price of $6 and still sell all the goods produced.

The basic procedure for finding the profit-maximizing short-run price-quantity combination for the monopolist is first to determine the profit-maximizing rate of output, either by the total revenue–total cost method or the marginal revenue–marginal cost method, and then to determine

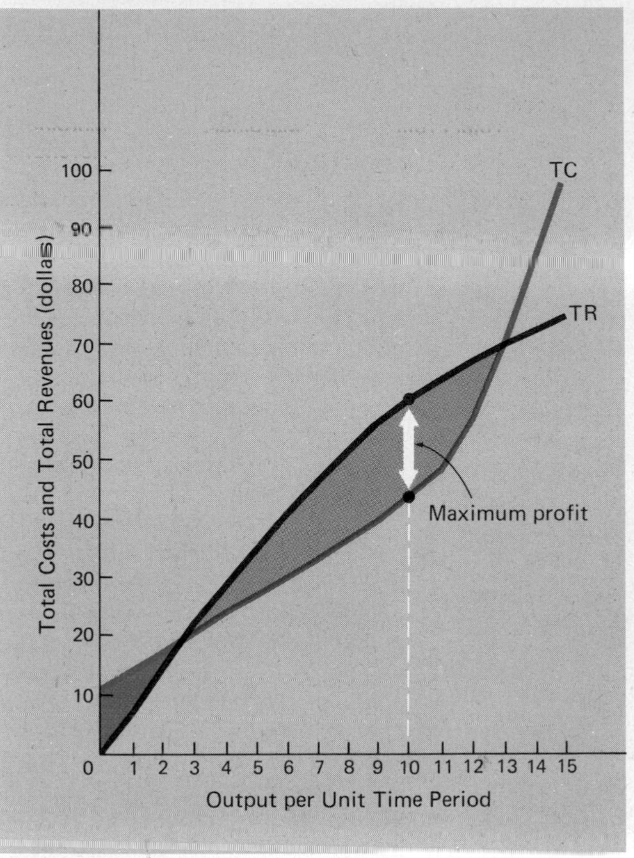

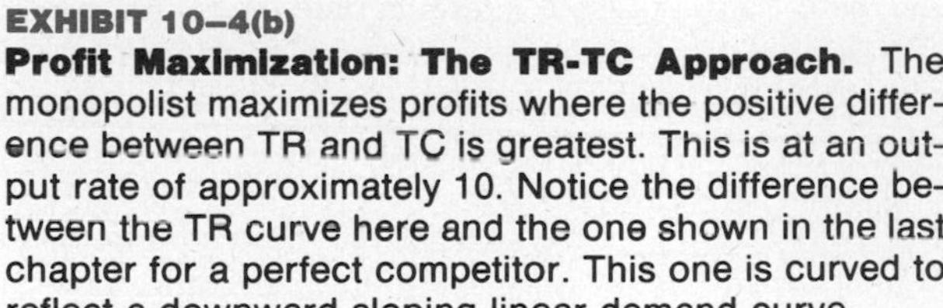
EXHIBIT 10–4(b)
Profit Maximization: The TR-TC Approach. The monopolist maximizes profits where the positive difference between TR and TC is greatest. This is at an output rate of approximately 10. Notice the difference between the TR curve here and the one shown in the last chapter for a perfect competitor. This one is curved to reflect a downward-sloping linear demand curve.

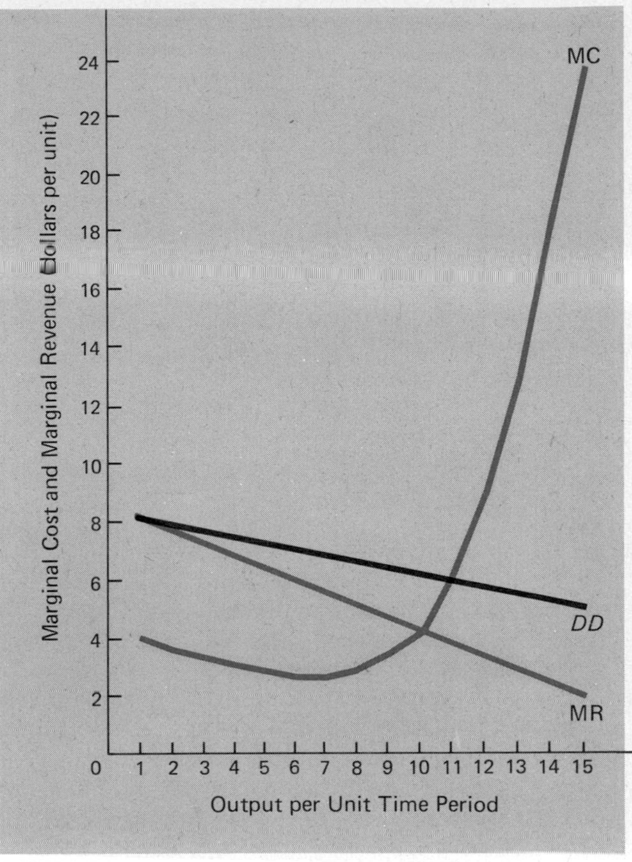

EXHIBIT 10–4(c)
Profit Maximization: The MR-MC Approach. Profit maximization occurs where marginal revenue equals marginal cost. This is at an output rate of approximately 10. (Also, the MC curve must cut the MR curve from below.)

by use of the demand curve *DD* the maximum price that can be charged to sell that output.

Short-Run Monopoly Profit

We have talked about the monopolist making profit, but we have yet to indicate how much profit the monopolist makes. We have actually shown total profits in column 5 of panel (a) in Exhibit 10–4. We can also find total profits by adding an average total cost curve to panel (c) of Exhibit 10–4. We do that in Exhibit 10–6. When we add the average total cost curve, we find that the profit that a monopolist makes is equal to the shaded area. Given the demand curve and a uniform pricing system, there is no way for a monopolist to make larger profits than those shown by the shaded area. The monopolist is maximizing profits where marginal cost equals marginal revenue. If the monopolist produces less than that, it will be forfeiting some profits. If the monopolist produces more than that, it will be forfeiting profits.

The same is true of a pure competitor. The competitor produces where marginal revenues equal marginal costs because it produces at the point where the marginal cost schedule intersects the horizontal *dd* curve. The horizontal *dd* curve represents the marginal revenue curve for the pure competitor, for the same average revenues are obtained on all the units sold. Pure competitors maximize profits at MR = MC, as do pure monopolists. But the pure competitor makes no true economic profits in the long run. Rather, all it makes is a normal competitive rate of return.

Monopoly

John Kenneth Galbraith

AMERICAN ECONOMIST (1908–)

ECONOMIC STATESMAN

John Kenneth Galbraith is perhaps the most popular American advocate of democratic socialism and state economic planning. In his distinguished career as a professor of economics, journalist, and public servant, and through his books—which include the best-selling *The Affluent Society* (1958), *The New Industrial State* (1967), and *The Age of Uncertainty* (1977)—the witty and urbane Galbraith has shown how the growth of monopoly and the power of advertising have irrevocably transformed the nature of modern economics.

Born in Canada, Galbraith was educated at the Ontario Agricultural College and the University of California, specializing in agricultural economics. He taught at the University of California, Harvard, and Princeton before moving, in 1941, to the Office of Price Administration. There, he was criticized for overzealously applying price controls to the largest corporations and for proposing that brand-name products be government graded for quality. Galbraith then worked as an editor at *Fortune* until 1948, when he joined the Harvard faculty, with which he remained affiliated until 1975.

Retirement from Harvard in no way subdued Galbraith's well-publicized career as advocate and critic. He has remained active, often crossing swords with the conservative William Buckley, a worthy foe, who once said that Galbraith acted as though he was on very short leave from Olympus where he conducts classes on divine standards.

Galbraith has always moved comfortably in the highest circles of the liberal Democratic establishment. He has been chairman of the Americans for Democratic Action and advised a string of Democratic presidential nominees. His former student, John Kennedy, considered him too controversial for appointment to a major economic policy post and instead named him ambassador to India. Galbraith served for over two years in that capacity, earning a reputation as an effective if unconventional emissary. For President Johnson, Galbraith helped plan the War on Poverty, but later criticized the way it was implemented.

Ever since he investigated the decline of farm prices during the 1930s depression, the overriding theme of Galbraith's writings has been the breakup of the free-market economy into a competitive sector and a relatively monopolistic one. Giant corporations, he contends, now dominate large segments of the market, deciding what is to be produced and channeling the needs of consumers to feed corporate interests. According to Galbraith, they have become so influential in state policy, yet so dependent on the state for contracts, research, and regulation of aggregate demand that the distinction between state and corporations is rapidly disappearing. But unlike many who see in these developments cause for antitrust action, Galbraith argues that nationalization is the only feasible solution. The danger to liberty, he says in *Economics and the Public Purpose* (1973), lies not in the great size of some corporations, but in their "monopoly of social purpose." Only by asserting its larger interests can the community put the industrial system in its proper place—subordinate to human needs instead of dominant over them.

Because of his interest in qualitative rather than quantitative economic analysis and because of his unorthodox political views, Galbraith has not always been well regarded by his colleagues. But Galbraith chides the economists of the mainstream for ignoring or mystifying the realities of political and economic power. He calls on them to confront the real issues of the day—inequality, planned economies, socialism, the environment. By simply fiddling with formulas of trivial matters, he says, they are condemning themselves to remain "socially more irrelevant than Keynes's dentist."

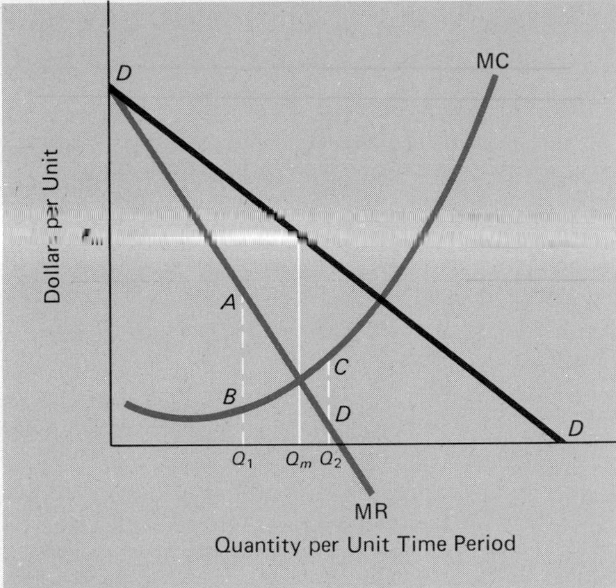

EXHIBIT 10–5

Maximizing Profits. Here we show the monopolist's demand curve, *DD*, as before and its marginal revenue curve, MR, with its marginal cost curve, MC. The monopolist will maximize profits where marginal revenue equals marginal cost; it will produce up to the point where MC equals MR and then will find the highest price at which it can sell that quantity. The profit-maximizing production rate is Q_m, and the profit-maximizing price is P_m. The monopolist would be unwise to produce at the rate Q_1, because here marginal revenue would be Q_1A and marginal costs would be Q_1B. Marginal revenue exceeds marginal cost. If production is increased by one unit, the monopolist will obviously be better off, because the extra revenues will more than cover the extra costs. It will keep producing until the point Q_m, where marginal revenue just equals marginal cost. It would be silly to produce at the rate Q_2, for here marginal cost exceeds marginal revenue. The benefits from selling the extra units here are outweighed by the additional costs. It behooves the monopolist to cut back production to Q_m.

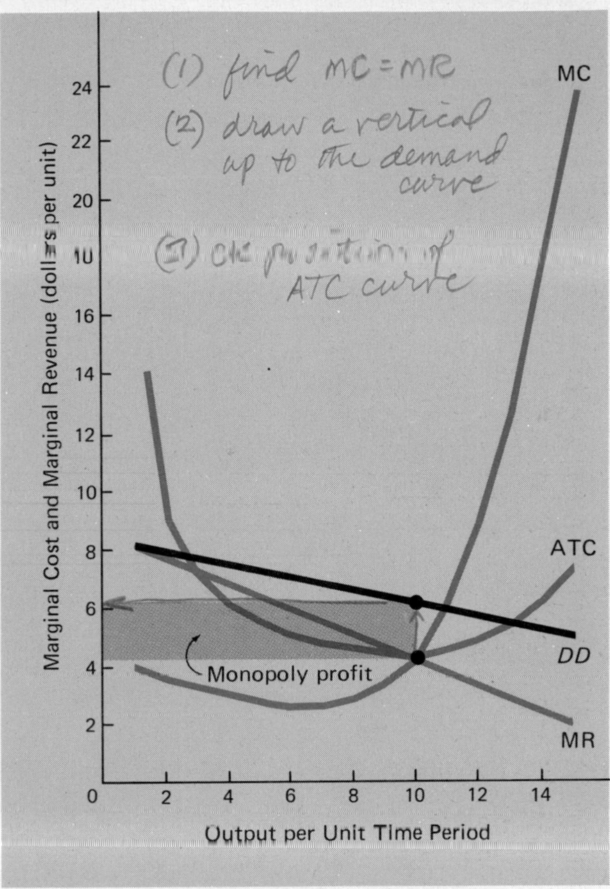

EXHIBIT 10–6

Monopoly Profit. We find monopoly profit by subtracting total costs from total revenues at an output rate of 10, which is approximately the profit-maximizing rate of output for the monopolist. Monopoly profit is given by the shaded area. This diagram is similar to panel (c) of Exhibit 10–4, except that we have added the short-run average total cost curve (ATC).

MONOPOLY DOESN'T NECESSARILY MEAN PROFITS

The term *monopoly* conjures up the notion of a greedy firm ripping off the public and making exorbitant profits. However, the mere existence of a monopoly does not guarantee high profits. Look at Exhibit 10–7. Here we show the demand curve facing the monopolist as *DD* and the resultant marginal revenue curve as MR. It does not matter at what rate of output this particular monopolist operates; total costs cannot be covered. Look at the position of the average total cost curve. It lies everywhere above *DD* (the average revenue curve). Thus, there is no price-output combination that will allow the monopolist even to cover costs, much less to earn monopoly profits. This monopolist will suffer economic losses. The diagram in Exhibit 10–7 depicts a situation for millions upon millions of typical monopolies that exist; they are called inventions. The owner of a patented invention or discovery has a pure legal monopoly, but the demand and cost curves may be such that it is not profitable to produce. Every year there are inventors' conventions where one can see many inventions that have never been put into production or innovated, having been deemed "uneconomic" by potential users.

monopoly

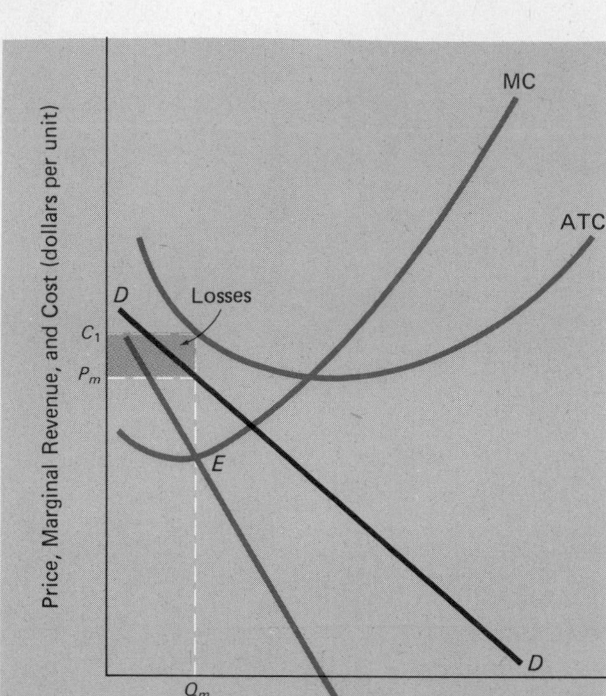

EXHIBIT 10–7
Monopolies Aren't Always Profitable. This diagram depicts the situation confronting some monopolists. The average total cost curve ATC is everywhere above the average revenue or demand curve *DD*. In the short run, the monopolist will produce where MC = MR at point *E*. Output Q_m will be sold at price P_m, but cost per unit is C_1. Losses are the shaded rectangle.

> ***Concepts in Brief 10-3***
>
> - The monopolist must choose the profit-maximizing price-output combination.
> - It is found by choosing that output where marginal revenue equals marginal cost and then charging the highest price possible as given by the demand curve for that particular output.
> - The basic difference between a monopolist and a perfect competitor is that a monopolist faces a downward-sloping demand curve and therefore marginal revenue is less than price.
> - Monopoly short-run profits are found by looking at average total costs compared to the price per unit. When this difference is multiplied by quantity, monopoly profit is determined.
> - A monopoly does not necessarily mean profit. One could have a monopoly, but if the average total cost curve lies everywhere above the monopoly demand curve, it will not pay to produce because there will be losses.

On Making Higher Profits—Price Discrimination

In our preceding discussion, we assumed that the monopolist sold all units at the same price. However, if the monopolist can somehow *price discriminate* according to the demand elasticities of different buyers, it can make even more profits. The monopolist then becomes a **price-discriminating monopolist.** It will charge those consumers who really desire the product a higher price than those consumers who have less desire for it. The monopolist will raise the price to those consumers with less elastic demand curves.

Do not get the impression that only a pure monopolist can price discriminate. Price discrimination is possible in practice even for firms with less than complete monopoly, or market, power, in an industry. In fact, we see price discrimination occurring in relatively competitive situations. We introduced the concept of price discrimination while discussing monopoly simply because under conditions of *perfect* competition, price discrimination is indeed impossible.

NECESSARY CONDITIONS FOR PRICE DISCRIMINATION TO EXIST

For price discrimination to be possible, there must first of all be at least two identifiable classes of buyers whose price elasticities of demand for the product are different; and the monopolist must know which class of buyers has the more price elastic demand. Furthermore, it is necessary to be able to separate these two or more identifiable classes of buyers at a reasonable cost. Additionally, the monopolist must be able to prevent, at least partially, the resale of the product by those buyers who paid a low price to those buyers who would be charged a higher price. Charging students a lower price for a movie than nonstudents can be done relatively easily. The cost of checking out student IDs is apparently not significant. Also, it is fairly easy to make sure that students do not resell their tickets to nonstudents.

Can you think of any other examples of price discrimination? What about discos that charge females less than males? It is easy to discriminate here, and it's pretty hard to transfer the service, right?

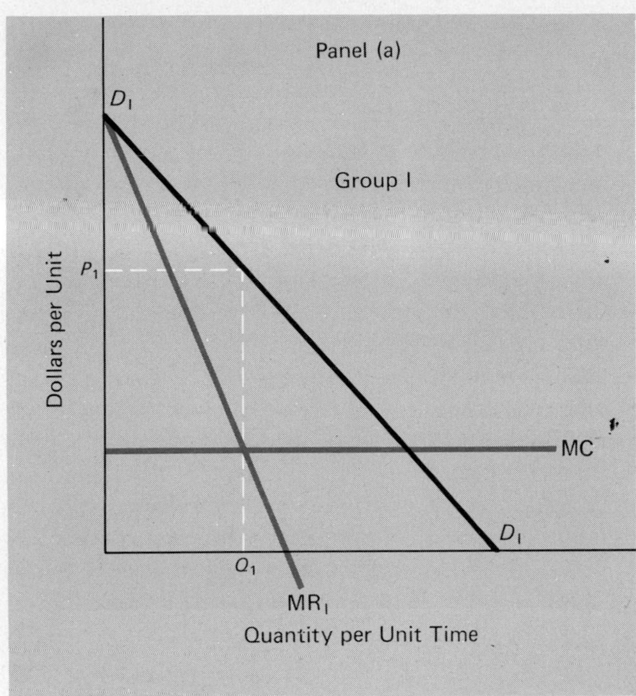

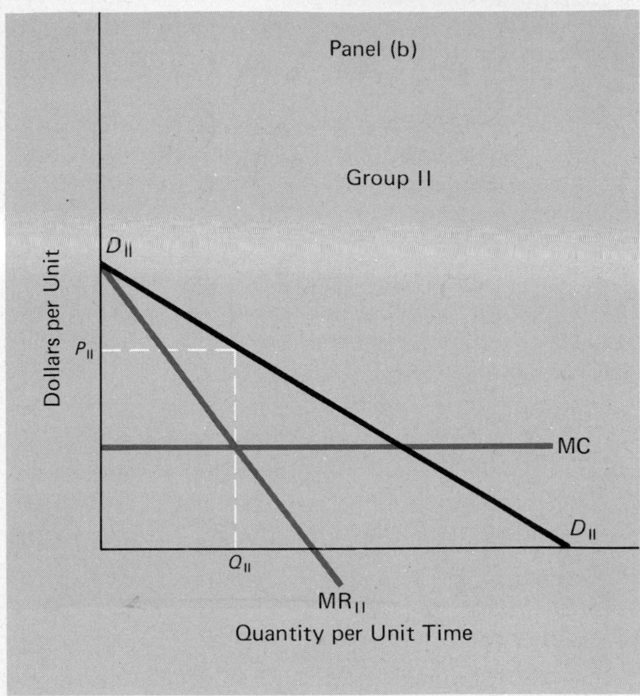

EXHIBIT 10–8
Price Discrimination. Here the smart monopolist has separated buyers into those with relatively less elastic demand curves (group I) and those with relatively more elastic demand curves (group II). Profit maximization occurs when marginal revenue equals marginal cost. Therefore, our monopolist sets marginal revenue equal to marginal cost in each individual category. We find that the monopolist sets a price of P_I for group I and a price of P_{II} for group II. Those with the relatively less elastic demand end up paying more than do those with the relatively more elastic demand for the same service. In such a situation, the monopolist earns a greater income than it would by charging a single price to all customers.

GRAPHIC ANALYSIS

We can see how a price-discriminating monopolist will act if there are two classes of buyers with identifiable differences in their demand curves. In panels (a) and (b) of Exhibit 10–8, we see group I and group II, the two classes of buyers. For simplicity, marginal cost for the monopolist is assumed to be constant. For profit to be at a maximum, we know that marginal revenue must equal marginal cost. We have a common marginal cost here, MC. We have two sets of marginal revenue curves, MR_I and MR_{II}. Thus, for profit maximization, $MR_I = MR_{II} = MC$. It is as if the goods sold to class I and class II were two *different* goods having exactly the same marginal cost of production. In other words, to maximize total profits, the monopolist wants to set marginal revenue equal to marginal cost in all markets in which it is selling. If marginal revenue in market I exceeded marginal cost, profits could be increased by expanding output (lowering price) in market I. The same holds for market II. On the other hand, if marginal revenue in market I (or market II) were less than marginal cost, profit could be increased by reducing output (raising price) in market I (or II).

We show this in Exhibit 10–8. Group I buyers are presented in panel (a), group II buyers in panel (b). We assume for simplicity's sake that the marginal costs for servicing both classes of consumers are both equal and constant. Marginal cost equals marginal revenue for group I at quantity Q_I. The price at which this quantity can be sold is P_I. On the other hand, for buyers in group II who have a more elastic demand curve (at *any* given P) than buyers in group I, the intersection of marginal cost with MR_{II} is at quantity Q_{II}. The price at which this quantity is sold is P_{II}, which is lower than P_I. In other words, the price-discriminating monopolist will sell that same product to the group of buyers having a relatively less elastic demand curve at a higher price than that charged to the other group of buyers having a relatively higher elasticity of demand.

monopoly

The Cost to Society of Monopolies

Let's run a little experiment. We will start with a purely competitive industry with numerous firms, each one unable to affect the price of the product. The supply curve of the industry is equal to the horizontal sum of the marginal cost curves of the individual producers above their respective minimum average variable costs. In panel (a) of Exhibit 10–9, we show the market demand curve and the market supply curve in a perfectly competitive situation. The competitive price in equilibrium is equal to P_e and the equilibrium quantity at that price is equal to Q_e. Each individual competitor faces a demand curve *dd* (which is not shown) that is coincident with the price line P_e. No individual supplier faces the market demand curve *DD*.

Now let's assume that a big monopolist comes in and buys up every single competitor in the industry. In so doing, *we'll assume that the monopolist does not affect any of the marginal cost curves.* We can therefore redraw *DD* and *SS* in the accompanying panel (b) of Exhibit 10–9. They are exactly the same as those in panel (a).

How does this monopolist decide how much to charge and how much to produce? If the monopolist is smart, it is going to look at the marginal revenue curve and produce at the output where marginal revenue equals marginal cost. But what is the marginal cost curve in panel (b) of Exhibit 10–9? It is merely *SS,* because we said that *SS* was equal to the horizontal sum of the portions of the individual marginal cost curves above each firm's respective minimum average variable cost. The monopolist therefore produces a quantity Q_m and sells it at a

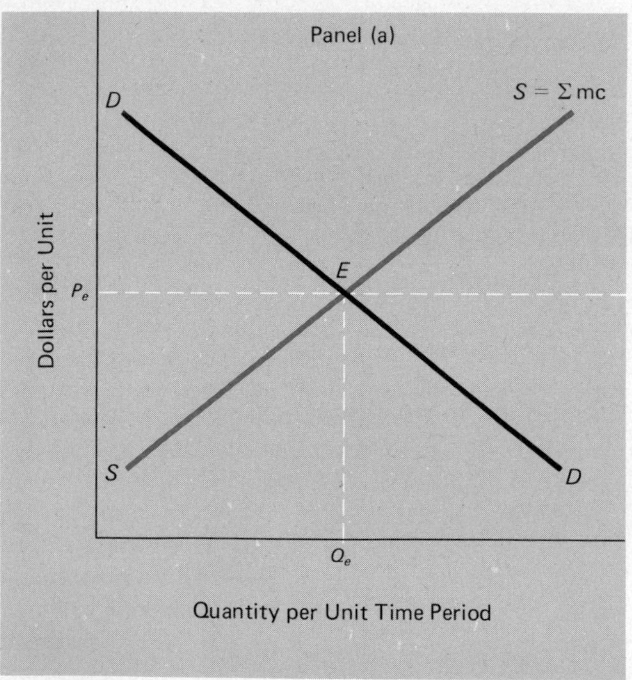

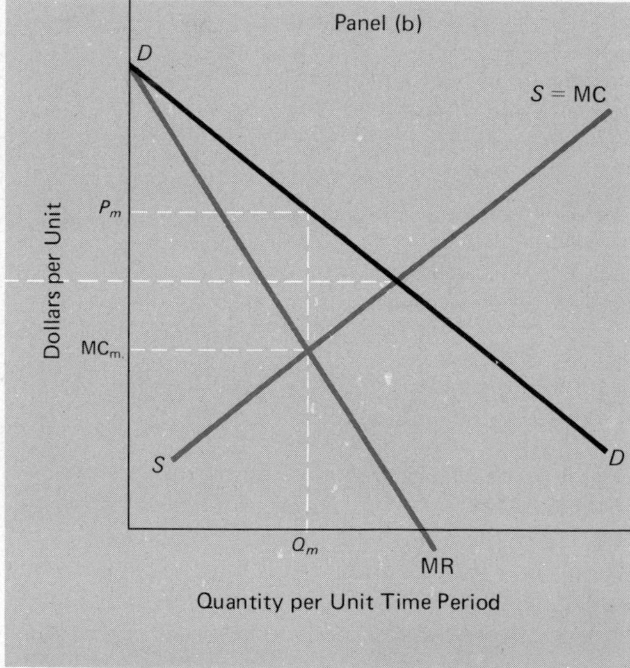

EXHIBIT 10–9

The Effects of Monopolizing an Industry. In panel (a), we show a competitive situation where *DD* is the market demand curve and *SS* is the market supply curve. The market supply curve is made up of the horizontal summation of all the individual firms' marginal cost curves above their respective minimum average variable costs. Equilibrium is established at the intersection of *DD* and *SS* at *E*. The equilibrium price would be P_e, and the equilibrium quantity supplied and demanded would be Q_e. Note that the demand curve *DD* is not the one facing each individual producer. Each individual competitive producer faces a demand curve that is a horizontal line at the market clearing price P_e. Nobody sees that industry demand curve *DD* except an observer looking from the outside at the entire industry. Now we assume that the industry is suddenly monopolized. We assume that the costs stay the same; the only thing that changes is that the monopolist now faces the entire downward-sloping demand curve. In panel (b), we draw the marginal revenue curve. The monopolist will produce at the point where marginal revenue equals marginal cost. Marginal cost is *SS* because that is the horizontal summation of all the individual marginal cost curves. The monopolist therefore produces at Q_m and charges a price P_m. P_m in panel (b) is higher than P_e in panel (a) and Q_m is less than Q_e. We see, then, that a monopolist charges a higher price and produces less than an industry in a competitive situation.

price P_m. Notice that Q_m is less than Q_e and P_m is greater than P_e. A monopolist therefore produces a smaller quantity and sells it at a higher price. This is the reason usually given when one attacks monopolists. Monopolists raise the price and restrict production, compared to a competitive situation. For a monopolist's product, consumers are forced to pay a price that exceeds the marginal cost of production. Resources are misallocated in such a situation—too few resources are being used in the monopolist's industry and too many are used elsewhere. As we have pointed out before, this difference between monopoly and competition arises not because of differences in costs, but rather because of differences in the demand curves facing the individual firms. The monopolist has monopoly power because it faces a downward-sloping demand curve. The individual perfect competitor does not have any market power.

Before we leave this topic concerning the cost to society of monopolies, we must repeat that our analysis is based on an heroic assumption. That assumption is that the monopolization of the perfectly competitive industry does not change the cost structure. If monopolization results in higher marginal cost, then the cost to society is even greater. On the other hand, if monopolization results in cost savings, then the cost, if any, to society of monopolies is less than we infer from our above analysis. Indeed, we could have presented a hypothetical example in which monopolization led to such a dramatic reduction in cost that society actually benefited. While we do not offer this as reality, it should be understood to be a possibility.

EXHIBIT 10–10

Where Monopoly Hurts Most. In these two panels, labeled (a) and (b), we show monopoly price distortions in two different industries. In panel (a), we show such distortions in the manufacturing industries, and in panel (b), we show similar distortions in regulated industries, including physicians' services, eyeglasses, transportation, airlines, and taxicabs. Interestingly, unregulated manufacturing industries show, according to at least one study, monopoly pricing distortions that range from 1.2 percent to 13.1 percent in terms of the percentage increase in price over what it would be in a perfectly competitive market. On the other hand, in panel (b), we see percentage increases in price over their competitive equivalent from a low of 16 percent, to a high of 66 percent in airlines prior to their deregulation.

Panel (a)		Panel (b)	
Industry	*Percentage Increase in Price*	*Industry*	*Percentage Increase in Price*
Bakery products	5.6	Physicians' services	40
Packaged foods	3.5	Eyeglasses	34
Knit goods	2.0	Motor carriers	62
Furniture	2.2	Airlines	66
Paints	3.4	Taxicabs	16
Wire and nails	1.2		
Scientific instruments	13.1		

Source:

Panel (a): Manufacturing industries: Arnold C. Harberger, "Monopoly and Resource Allocation," *American Economic Review* 44:77–87, May 1954.

Panel (b): Physicians' services: R. A. Kessel, "Higher Education and the Nation's Health: A Review of the Carnegie Commission Report on Medical Education." *Journal of Law and Economics* 15 (1972), p. 119.

Eyeglasses: L. Benham, "Price Structure and Professional Control of Information," mimeograph, University of Chicago Graduate School of Business, 1973, p. 19.

Motor carriers: Average of estimates in U.S. Department of Agriculture studies cited in T. G. Moore, *Freight Transportation Regulation* (Washington: American Enterprise Institute, 1972); and R. N. Farmer, "The Case for Unregulated Truck Transportation," *Journal of Farm Economics* 46 (1964), pp. 398–409.

Airlines: Average of estimates computed from R. E. Caves, *Air Transport and Its Regulators* (Cambridge: Harvard University Press, 1972), p. 372; W. A. Jordan, *Airline Regulation in America* (Baltimore: Johns Hopkins University Press, 1979), pp. 110–111, 124–125, and "Is Regulation Necessary? California Air Transportation and National Regulatory Policy," *Yale Law Journal* 74 (1965), pp. 1435–1436.

Taxicabs: Computed from estimates for Chicago presented in E. W. Kitch, M. Isaacson, and D. Kasper, "The Regulation of Taxicabs in Chicago," *Journal of Law and Economics* 14 (October 1971), p. 301.

Monopoly

Concepts in Brief 10-4

- A monopolist can make higher profits if it can price discriminate. Price discrimination requires that two or more identifiable classes of buyers exist whose price elasticities of demand for the product are different, and that these two classes of buyers can be cheaply separated.
- Monopoly results in a lower quantity being sold, because the price is higher compared to an ideal perfectly competitive industry in which the cost curves are essentially the same as those facing the monopolist.

How Much Does Monopoly Affect Price?

There have been relatively few attempts to estimate the true economic cost of noncompetitive behavior in the American economy. One researcher, Professor Arnold Harberger, attempted to measure the social cost of monopoly and came up with a relatively small number. In Exhibit 10–10, we show monopoly pricing distortions in manufacturing industries. In the second column we see the percentage increase in price due to noncompetitive behavior. The increase in price varies from a low of 1.2 percent to a high of 13.1 percent. Harberger looked only at manufacturing industries. Another researcher, Timothy Hannan, culled information from several researchers to determine that in certain government-regulated industries monopolylike distortions were relatively high. In Exhibit 10–10 we see that percentage price increases range from 16 percent for taxicabs to a high of 66 percent for airlines (prior to the deregulation of that industry in the last few years).

CONCLUSIONS

We cannot jump to conclusions on the basis of two researchers' studies of monopoly price distortions. If one were to believe the data just presented, however, one might tentatively predict that efforts at eliminating monopoly in the manufacturing sector would not yield tremendous increases in social welfare. On the other hand, attempts at improving competition in such regulated industries as medical care and transportation might yield significantly higher social benefits.

ISSUES AND APPLICATIONS

The Creation of Monopoly Profits, or How to Get Taken by a Taxicab

Concepts Applied

- Barriers to entry, monopoly profits, and competition

One way to attempt to obtain monopoly profits is to foreclose entry into the market by legal means. If a law can be passed that requires a license to be obtained in order to do business in a particular profession or industry, those in the industry prior to the licensing restriction (assuming there is a grandfather clause[1] in the law) will obtain monopoly profits. A clear-cut case can be seen if we examine the market for taxi services throughout the United States. In many, if not most cities, in order to operate a taxi a license must be obtained. In New York City, this license is called a medallion. Before 1937 in New York, the taxicab industry had free entry. The price of

[1] Under such clauses, everyone already in the industry is "grandfathered in" automatically when licensing is required. That is, existing firms obtain a license by virtue of already being in the industry.

taxi medallions was near zero, since they were given to anyone who wanted to operate a taxi. Little by little, the city began to restrict its issuance of new medallions. And little by little, anyone wishing to buy a medallion from the then-current owner had to pay a higher and higher price to purchase it. As the market price went up, those who obtained the medallions at lower than the market price were treated to increases in their net worth. By the end of the 1960s, the market price of a medallion reached $30,000.

What does this price represent? It represents the fully discounted present value of the expected stream of monopoly profits that can be obtained by owning a legal taxicab in New York City.

Owners who purchased or received the medallions in the late 1930s and early 1940s obtained "monopoly" profits. However, buyers *today* receive no more than a competitive rate of return on their labor and capital. Why? Because they have already paid the market price for their medallions, and the opportunity cost of that money capital has been added to their other costs. An elimination of the restrictions on entry into the New York taxicab market would immediately subject all the present owners of medallions to a large windfall loss. The emergence of "gypsy" cabs (whose owners don't have medallions) in New York City has already partially eroded the market value of medallions. Gypsies are cabs that have no *legal* right to pick up passengers for hire. Nonetheless, New York authorities have, for the most part, allowed these illegal cabs to operate in the city in recent years.

The taxicab industry in New York City is an example of how barriers to entry created a monopoly and monopoly profits.

We can understand this situation by looking at Exhibit 10–11. Here we show that the city of New York has issued a fixed number of medallions equal to Q_1. The supply curve of medallions is thus completely price inelastic at Q_1, and is represented by *SS*. As the city has grown and real income has increased, the demand curve for taxi services and hence for medallions has increased from *DD* to *D'D'*. The price of medallions has risen from P_1 to P_2. If free entry were allowed into the taxicab industry, the supply curve of medallions would shift to the right so as always to intersect the demand curve at a price of zero. (This is a point not lost on current owners!) In other words, the authorities would issue medallions to anyone who wanted them at a zero

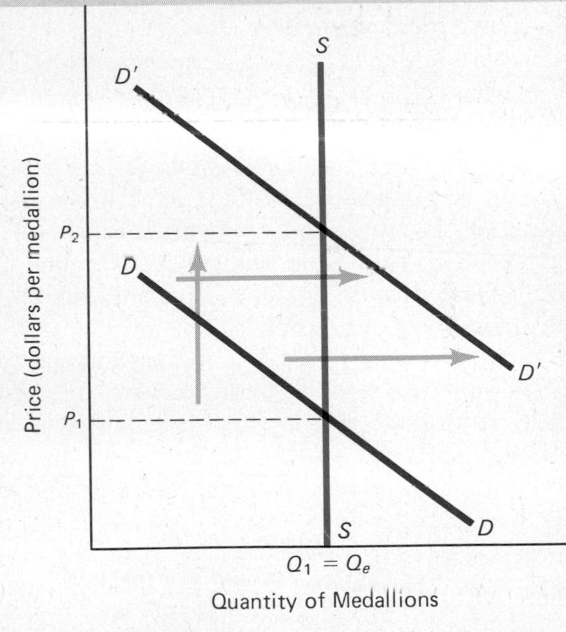

EXHIBIT 10–11
The Rise in Value of Medallions. If the city of New York sets the number of medallions at Q_1, then the supply curve is vertical, *SS*. If the demand curve a number of years ago was *DD*, then the going price was P_1. As population and real incomes rise, however, the demand curve shifts outward to the right to *D'D'*. The price or value of a medallion rises to P_2 because the quantity supplied is fixed.

price. Whatever the quantity demanded at that zero price, the quantity supplied would be equal—this would merely mean producing some more medallions that authorized the bearer to operate a taxi in New York City.

Questions

1. Who benefits from the licensing of taxicabs in New York City (or in other cities)?
2. How is it possible for a barrier to entry to remain in existence for such a long time?

Why This Book Is Priced Too High (From the Author's Point of View)

Concepts Applied

- Marginal revenue, marginal cost, and monopoly profit-maximizing price

You are reading a textbook that I wrote. The publisher, Harper & Row, decided on the net price. (Your bookstore set the list price that you were charged.) It used a complicated formula that included such expected costs as the price of paper, printing and binding, artwork, and so on. The price at which it arrived is most likely close to the prices of other competing books for principles of economics courses. The publisher knows, after all, that it cannot set the price significantly above competing books without reducing its potential sales significantly (the price elasticity of demand is not zero).

It would seem that the publisher and the author would be working jointly toward the same goal. After all, they both want to make the highest rate of return possible. It turns out, however, that there is a conflict between the best interests of the publisher and those of the author. Whatever the price at which the book is selling when you buy it, an author would be better off if it were sold at a lower price.

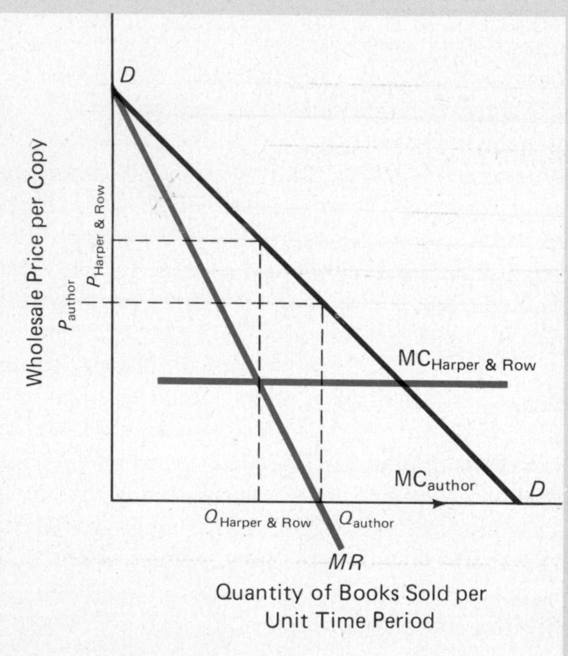

EXHIBIT 10–12
The Conflict Between Publisher and Author. Harper & Row faces a marginal revenue curve MR and a marginal cost curve $MC_{\text{Harper \& Row}}$. It would like to set the quantity produced of the textbook at $Q_{\text{Harper \& Row}}$ and sell that quantity at a price of $P_{\text{Harper \& Row}}$. The author, however, is paid a royalty based on a fixed percentage of total revenues from the book. The author's marginal cost curve is coincident with the horizontal axis because the author has no marginal costs once the book has been written. We know that total revenues are greatest when the price elasticity of demand equals -1 or at that rate of output at which marginal revenue equals zero. Thus, the author would prefer the larger output Q_{author} to be sold at the lower per unit price of P_{author}. That is also where $MR = MC_{\text{author}} = 0$. There is a conflict between author and publisher.

Two Profit-Maximizing Prices

Authors are typically paid a royalty that is a fixed percentage of the total revenues or receipts of wholesale sales obtained by the publisher. Authors want to have total sales revenues as high as possible because this will maximize their royalties. The cost to the author *once the book has been written* is equal to zero. Profit maximization from the author's point of view means maximizing total sales revenues. This is shown in Exhibit 10–12. Profit maximization occurs at the level of sales at which the marginal revenue curve intersects the horizontal axis (the author's marginal cost curve, which is so labeled), or where marginal revenue equals zero. This level of sales would be obtained if the price were set at P_{author}. At that price, the elasticity of demand is equal to -1.

However, consider the fact that the publisher does not have a marginal cost equal to zero. Rather, the publisher incurs additional paper, printing, and binding costs to produce one more unit of output. Thus, if we draw in the marginal cost curve $MC_{\text{Harper \& Row}}$ in Exhibit 10–12 for the publisher, we find that the publisher's profit-maximizing price $P_{\text{Harper \& Row}}$ is necessarily higher than the author's profit-maximizing price, which is labeled P_{author}. The textbook author is, therefore, constantly in conflict with his or her publisher. It is not surprising, then, that when queried, publishers often indicate that their authors frequently argue for a lower price. One observer of the publishing scene many years ago argued that this was because authors overestimate the price elasticity of demand and underestimate the cost of production. The latter point is irrelevant, however, to the author. Those costs are irrelevant because the author does not incur them. As long as the author believes that the publisher has set the price in the elastic region of the demand curve, the author will always find it in his or her best interests to argue for a lower price.

Questions

1. Would the analysis of the conflict between publisher and author be any different if the marginal cost curve for Harper & Row were upward sloping? (Hint: Redraw Exhibit 10–12.)
2. Will Harper & Row ever sell in the inelastic region of its demand curve? Will the demand elasticity be different if students, rather than professors, select their own books?

Definition of Terms

Monopolist The single supplier.

Barriers to entry Barriers that prevent new firms from entering an existing industry. Some barriers include government laws against entry and patents for research discoveries.

Price-discriminating monopolist A monopolist who discriminates among groups of demanders with different elasticities of demand. This person will charge a higher price to those with relatively less elastic demand than to those with relatively more elastic demand.

Chapter Summary

1. We formally define a monopolist as a single supplier. A monopolist faces the entire industry demand curve because it *is* the industry. There are not too many examples of pure monopolists. In general, they have a government franchise to operate so that they can remain pure monopolists. We cite as examples electric companies, the telephone system, and the post office. General Motors and U.S. Steel do not qualify as true monopolies under our restricted definition.
2. A monopolist can usually only remain a monopolist if there are barriers to entry—that is, if there is some reason why other firms cannot enter the industry and share in the monopoly profits. One of the most obvious barriers to entry is government restrictions. The government does not allow you to set up an alternative local telephone system or an alternative electric utility. Patents on a discovery can also be an effective barrier to entry.
3. A monopoly could arise because of returns to scale, which are defined as a situation where an increase in *all* inputs leads to a more than proportionate increase in output. If this were the case, then average total costs would be falling as production and all inputs were increased to produce an increased output. In a situation where true returns to scale exist, the first person to produce a great deal and take advantage of those returns to scale can conceivably take

advantage of the reduced average total cost by lowering price and driving everybody else out of the market.

4. The marginal revenue that a monopolist receives is defined in the same way as the marginal revenue that a competitor receives. However, there is one difference. Since the monopolist faces the industry demand curve, it must lower price to increase sales. It must lower price not only on the last unit sold but also on all the preceding units. The monopolist's marginal revenue therefore is equal to the price received on the last unit sold, minus the reduction in price on all the previous units, times the number of previous units sold.
5. The monopolist will produce where marginal revenue equals marginal cost. If the monopolist produces less than that, it is foregoing additional profits. Marginal revenue will exceed marginal cost; thus, it pays to continue production. If the monopolist produces at an output beyond where marginal revenue equals marginal cost, marginal cost will *exceed* marginal revenue. The benefits from producing more are less than the costs.
6. The profit-maximizing price that the monopolist charges is the maximum price that it can get away with while still selling everything produced up to the point where marginal revenue equals marginal cost. We find this price by extending a vertical line from the intersection of the marginal revenue curve and the marginal cost curve up to the demand curve and then over to the vertical axis, which measures price.
7. A straight-line demand curve can be separated into two sections. At the upper end is the elastic section; at the lower end is the inelastic section. Somewhere between is the point where elasticity is equal to -1, or unity. That can be found by extending a line vertically from the intersection of the marginal revenue curve and the horizontal axis. The quantity at which that line hits the demand curve is the quantity at which elasticity is unity. Price elasticity of demand is unity where marginal revenue equals zero. That is also the point where total revenues are maximized. If the monopolist had no variable costs at all, it would obviously want to produce where marginal revenue equals zero. That, in fact, is where such a monopolist would maximize profits, because it would be maximizing total revenues.
8. The monopolist's profits can be found easily. Profits are merely total revenues minus total costs. Total revenues are equal to the price of the product (the profit-maximizing price) times the quantity produced (the quantity found at the intersection of the marginal revenue and marginal cost curves). Total costs are equal to the quantity produced times average total costs. The difference between these total costs and total revenues is, as we stated, profits.
9. In general, it can be shown that a competitive industry, if monopolized, will end up with a higher price and a lower quantity supplied. That is why monopolies are "bad" in economic analysis. The monopolist will restrict production and increase price because it will look at the entire demand curve and realize that to sell more units of the product, the price must be lowered. The monopolist will look at the marginal revenue curve and produce where the marginal revenue curve intersects the marginal cost curve. Since the marginal revenue curve is below the demand schedule, we know it will produce less. Since the monopolist is producing less, it can obviously charge a higher price than can those in the competitive situation where more is produced.
10. If a monopolist can effectively separate different groups of demanders, grouping them according to their demand elasticities, it can become a price-discriminating monopolist. (But resale between groups charged different prices must be prevented.)
11. Restriction on entry into the taxicab industry generates monopoly profits for the original owners of the scarce licenses that legally allow a cab to be operated.
12. Once a book is produced, the publisher's profit-maximizing price is higher than the author's profit-maximizing price.

Selected References

Adams, Walter. *The Structure of American Industry.* 5th ed. New York: Macmillan, 1977, chap. 11.

Caves, Richard E. *American Industry: Structure, Conduct, and Performance.* 4th ed. Englewood Cliffs, N.J.: Prentice-Hall, 1977.

Kefauver, Estes. *In a Few Hands: Monopoly Power in America.* New York: Pantheon, 1965.

Schumpeter, Joseph A. *Capitalism, Socialism, and Democracy.* 3rd ed. New York: Harper & Row, 1950, chaps. 7 and 8.

Answers to Preview and Study Questions

1. What is a monopolist, and how can a monopoly be formed?

Technically, a monopoly is a market structure in which there is only one supplier in an industry; therefore, a monopolist is a single supplier. Of course, the incidence (or near incidence) of monopoly increases the more narrowly we define an industry. A monopoly can arise through one or more barriers to entry, such as: (a) ownership over a resource without close substitutes, (b) huge capital requirements, (c) government-granted licenses, (d) patents, and (e) economies of scale, which lead to a "natural" monopoly.

2. For the monopolist, marginal revenue is less than selling price. Why?

We have already noted that in the perfect competition model the firm's selling price equals its marginal revenue (MR); this is because the firm can sell all it wants to sell at the going market price. This is not the case for the monopolist, which is the sole supplier, and which consequently faces *the* (downward-sloping) demand curve for the product. Thus, the monopolist can only sell more by lowering price on all units sold per unit of time—assuming it can't price discriminate. Thus the monopolist's marginal revenue will equal price (which it gains from selling one more unit) *minus* the revenue that it loses from selling previously produced units at a lower price. In short, the monopolist's MR will be less than the price for which it can sell the next unit, since previous units must now be sold at the new (lower) price too.

3. What is the profit-maximizing rate of output for the monopolist?

As was true for the perfect competitor, a monopolist will produce up to the point where marginal cost (MC) equals marginal revenue (MR). And for the same reasons, assuming that the monopolist's marginal cost is rising, because such an output rate maximizes total profits. For example, if the output rate for the monopolist, at which MR = MC is 80,000 units per week, and MR is falling while MC is rising, any output beyond 80,000 units will have a MC > MR; to produce units beyond 80,000 units will lower total profits. To produce at a rate *less* than 80,000 units per week would mean that not all the outputs at which MR > MC will be produced; hence, total profits would not be maximized. Total profits are maximized at that output rate where MR = MC, since all those outputs for which MR > MC will be produced.

4. What are some common misconceptions about a monopolist?

Students (and most nonstudents too) often think that a monopolist charges the highest price possible. This is untrue; the monopolist tries to maximize total *profits,* not price. The monopolist produces where MR = MC and *then* charges the highest price consistent with that output rate. Note that a monopolist can't charge any price *and* sell any amount; it must choose a price and have the amount that it can sell be determined by the demand curve, or it must choose an output rate (where MR = MC) and have selling price determined by where that quantity intersects the demand curve. Another common misconception is that a monopolist must earn economic profits. This is not the case. To take an extreme example, if the monopolist's average cost curve lies above the demand curve (due to inefficiency) the monopolist will be suffering economic losses.

5. What is the cost to society of monopoly?

Since barriers to entry exist under monopoly, a monopolist could theoretically earn economic profits in the long run. Since profits are a signal that society wants more resources in that area, a misallocation of resources could exist; not enough resources flow to production of the monopolized commodity. Also, since the monopolist's selling price *(P)* exceeds its marginal revenue (MR), and since the profit-maximizing output rate is where MR = MC (marginal cost), the *P* > MR = MC. Or, simply *P* > MC (unlike under the perfect competition market structure where *P* = MC). The marginal cost of the commodity reflects what society had to give up in order to get the last unit produced, and price is what buyers have to pay in order to get it. Since *P* > *MC* under monopoly, then buyers must pay *more* to get this commodity than they must give up in order to get it; hence, not enough of this commodity is produced. In short, under monopoly, price is higher and output is less than under perfect competition.

Problems

(Answers at the back of the book)

1. a. Suppose the monopolist faces ATC_1. Define the rectangle that shows the monopolist's total costs at output rate *Q*. Also, define the rectangle showing total revenue. Is the monopolist showing an economic loss, a break-even (normal profit), or an economic profit situation? What is the significance of the MC = MR output?

b. Suppose the monopolist faces ATC_2. Define the rectangle that shows the monopolist's total costs. Also, define the rectangle showing total revenue. Is the monopolist showing an economic loss, a break-even (normal profit), or an economic profit situation? What is the significance of the MC = MR output?

c. Suppose the monopolist faces ATC_3. Define the rectangle that shows the monopolist's total costs. Also, define the rectangle showing total revenue. Is the monopolist

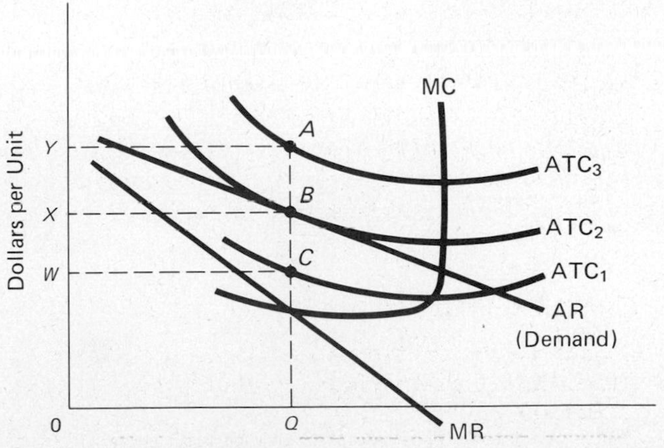

nopolist showing an economic loss, a break-even (normal profit), or an economic profit situation? What is the significance of the MC = MR output?

2. Suppose that a monopolist is faced with the following demand schedule. Compute marginal revenue.

Price	*Quantity demanded*	*Marginal revenue*
$1,000	1	$ ______
920	2	______
840	3	______
760	4	______
680	5	______
600	6	______
520	7	______
440	8	______
350	9	______
260	10	______

3. State the necessary conditions for price discrimination and then discuss how they might apply to the medical services of a physician.

4. In the text we indicated that a monopolist will produce at the rate of output where MR = MC and will then charge the highest price consistent with *that* output level. What conditions would exist if the monopolist charged a lower price? A higher price?

11

In Between Monopoly and Competition

TOPICS FOR REVIEW

The topics listed below, which we have already analyzed, are applied in this chapter. You may find it worthwhile to review them. For your convenience each topic is followed by the number identifying the specific "Concepts in Brief."

a. Perfect elasticity of demand (6–3)

b. Average total cost curve (8–3)

c. Perfect competition (9–1)

d. Monopoly, barriers to competition (10–1)

FOR PREVIEW AND STUDY

1. What are the characteristics of the monopolistic competition market structure?
2. How is the equilibrium price-output combination decided by the monopolistic competitor?
3. How does the monopolistic competition market structure differ from perfect competition?
4. What are the characteristics of the oligopoly market structure?
5. How do oligopolies compete?

Up to this point, we have discussed the two extremes in market structure—perfect competition and pure monopoly. In the perfectly competitive model, we assume that there are numerous firms that produce the same product and that have no influence over price—they are price takers. In the pure monopoly model, we assume that the firm is a single seller of a good to the entire market—the firm is a price maker. There are obviously market situations that fall between these two extremes. Indeed, almost all of the American economy is characterized by firms that are neither perfectly competitive nor purely monopolistic. After all, most firms have some control over price—that is, individually they do not face a perfectly elastic (horizontal) demand curve, but they really are not pure monopolists. In this chapter, we will look at market structures that lie in between competition and monopoly. The first model of such an "in-between" situation that we must look at is monopolistic competition—a situation where each seller has a small amount of market power but is in competition with a large number of others selling *almost* identical products.

Monopolistic Competition—Its Origin

Back in the 1920s and 1930s, economists became increasingly dissatisfied with the polar extremes of market structure mentioned above. There seemed to have been many industries around for which both the perfectly competitive model and the pure monopoly model did not apply and did not seem to yield very accurate predictions.

Theoretical and empirical research was instituted to develop some sort of middle ground. Two separately developed models of **monopolistic competition** resulted. At Harvard, Edward Chamberlin published *The Theory of Monopolistic Competition* in 1933. The same year, Britain's Joan Robinson published *The Economics of Imperfect Competition.* In this chapter, we will outline the theory as presented by Chamberlin.

THE CHARACTERISTICS OF MONOPOLISTIC COMPETITION

Chamberlin defined monopolistic competition as a market structure in which there are a relatively large number of producers offering similar but differentiated products. Monopolistic competition therefore has the following characteristics.

1. Significant numbers of sellers in a highly competitive market.
2. Differentiated products.
3. The existence of advertising.

We will treat these elements separately.

NUMBER OF FIRMS

In a perfectly competitive situation, there is an extremely large number of firms; in pure monopoly, there is only one. In monopolistic competition, there is a somewhat large number of firms, but not as many as in perfect competition.

There are several important implications of this fact concerning a monopolistically competitive industry.

1. **Small share of market.** With so many firms, each firm has a relatively small share of the total market. Thus, it has only a very small amount of control over the market clearing price.
2. **Collusion difficult.** With so many firms, it is very difficult for all of them to get together to collude—that is, to set a pure monopoly price (and output!). Rigging price in a monopolistically competitive industry is virtually impossible.
3. **Independence.** Since there are so many firms, each one acts independently of the others. That is to say, no firm attempts to take into account the reaction of all of its rival firms—that would be impossible with so many rivals. Rivals' reactions to output and price changes are largely ignored.

PRODUCT DIFFERENTIATION

Perhaps the most important feature of the monopolistically competitive market is product differentiation. In a sense, we can say that each individual manufacturer of a product has an absolute monopoly over its own product, which is slightly differentiated from other similar products. Consider the abundance of brand names for such things as toothpaste, soap, gasoline, vitamins, and shampoos. Should you buy Nature's Gate, Miss Clairol, Keratin, Prell, Body on Tap, Pert, or any of the numerous rival brands?

Indeed, it appears that product differentiation characterizes most, if not all, American markets.

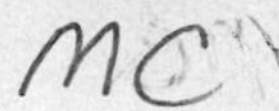

Joan Robinson

ENGLISH ECONOMIST (1903–)

HERETIC TO THE ORTHODOX

Joan Robinson is one of the world's leading contemporary economists. A professor emeritus at Cambridge University, England, where she taught for more than 40 years, Robinson has written and lectured widely on economic theory and made original contributions to the theories of imperfect competition and the accumulation of capital. She calls herself a "left-wing Keynesian," but she is versed in neoclassical economic theory as well as in Marxist thought. Eclectic in approach, but rigorous in analysis—"I don't know math," she once remarked, "so I am obliged to think"—she has drawn on the insights of history's great economists to develop critiques of modern capitalism and the current orthodox schools of economic thought.

Robinson is best known for developing a theory of "imperfect competition"—a way of making sense of the market in an age when many industries are dominated by a relatively few corporations. She first attempted to develop this alternative explanation of the behavior of large firms in *The Economics of Imperfect Competition,* published in 1933. In that same year the American economist Edward Chamberlin, working independently, came out with a similar text. Central to her findings (and to Chamberlin's) was that because of brand names, for example, firms can differentiate their products slightly from those of other firms producing in the same markets. Thus competition between these firms is partial.

Joan Robinson's interest in imperfect competition is also evident in much of her later works. In her book *Economic Heresies: Some Old-Fashioned Questions in Economic Theory* (1971), for instance, she analyzes how monopolistic corporations grow by "continuously expanding capacity, conquering new markets, producing new commodities, and exploiting new techniques." Though the growth of monopolies has tended to reduce competition within individual countries, she says, competition among the industries of different countries has increased. Now, "modern industry is a system not so much of monopolistic competition as of competitive monopolies." Robinson criticizes orthodox economists in the West for ignoring the social and moral issues inherent in their theories. The central assumption behind most economic thought since the time of Adam Smith is that individuals pursuing their self-interests will yield public good, and morality will therefore take care of itself. Although Keynes showed that the market does not necessarily provide a means for a harmonious reconciliation of conflicting interests, and the Great Depression gave ample evidence of the fallacy of this assumption, she contends it still pervades much contemporary economic thought.

According to Robinson, modern capitalism has failed to eliminate poverty in its own countries, failed to seriously aid the development of Third World nations, failed to be successful at all without an arms race, and perhaps is now making the planet uninhabitable ecologically. She argues: "It should be the duty of economists to do their best to enlighten the public about the economic aspects of these menacing problems. They are impeded by a theoretical scheme which (with whatever reservations and exceptions) represents the capitalist world as a kibbutz operated in a perfectly enlightened manner to maximize the welfare of all its members."

We are not obliged to buy just one type of television set, just one type of pantsuit, or just one type of automobile. There are usually a number of similar but differentiated products from which to choose. We note that the greater the success at product differentiation, the greater the monopoly power.

Real Versus Artificial Differentiation

Some economists like to distinguish between product differentiation that is "real" and that which is "artificial." Real product differentiation involves variations in physical characteristics, such as an actual chemical difference between two brands of

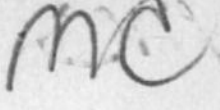

washing machine detergents. Artificial product differentiation would involve no significant differences in products but different packaging materials, brand names, and advertising outlays. The above examples of "real" and "artificial" product differentiation, of course, represent only the tip of an iceberg. Firms can also differentiate their products on the basis of location and service provided with the products sold. It is difficult to draw the line between real and artificial product differentiation.

Substitutes

However we wish to define product differentiation, the fact remains that each separate differentiated product has numerous close substitutes. This clearly has an impact on the price elasticity of demand facing the individual firm. Remember when we discussed the determination of the price elasticity of demand, we mentioned that one determinant was the availability of substitutes. The greater the number of substitutes available, other things being equal, the greater the price elasticity of demand. In other words, if the consumer has a vast array of alternatives that are just about as good as the product under study, a relatively small increase in the price of that product will lead consumers to switch to one of the many close substitutes. Thus, the ability of a firm to raise the price above the price of close substitutes is very small. In the extreme case, with perfect competition, the substitutes are perfect because we are dealing with only one particular undifferentiated product. In that case, remember that in pure competition the individual firm faces a horizontal, or perfectly elastic, demand curve.

Product Groups

Up until now we have defined an industry as a collection of firms producing a homogeneous commodity. However, it is difficult to maintain this definition of an industry when we talk in terms of differentiated products. Each firm has a distinct product and thus is itself an industry, and we could describe each industry as the differentiated product and the firm that produces it. Chamberlin sought to solve this problem by lumping together firms producing very closely related products. These are called product groups. Some product groups that come to mind are breakfast cereals, automobiles, toilet paper, and hand soap.

SALES PROMOTION—ADVERTISING

Monopolistic competition differs from perfect competition in that in the latter there is no sales promotion. No individual firm in a perfectly competitive market will advertise. A perfectly competitive firm, by definition, can sell all that it wants at the going market price anyway. Why, then, would it ever spend even one penny on advertising? Furthermore, by definition, the perfect competitor is selling a product that is identical to the product that all other firms in the industry are selling. Any advertisement that induces consumers to buy more of that product in effect will be helping all the competitors, too. We therefore would not expect the perfect competitor to incur any advertising costs.

But such is not the case for the monopolistic competitor. Since the monopolistic competitor has at least some monopoly power, advertising may result in increased profits. How much advertising should be undertaken? As much as is profitable. It should be carried to the point where the additional revenue from one more dollar of advertising just equals one dollar of marginal cost.

Shifting the Demand Curve

The goal of advertising is to shift the demand curve to the right. Advertising, it is hoped, will lead to a larger volume of business that more than covers the cost of the advertising. This is shown in Exhibit 11-1. In that exhibit, assume that the market clearing price is P_1. At that price with demand curve *dd,*

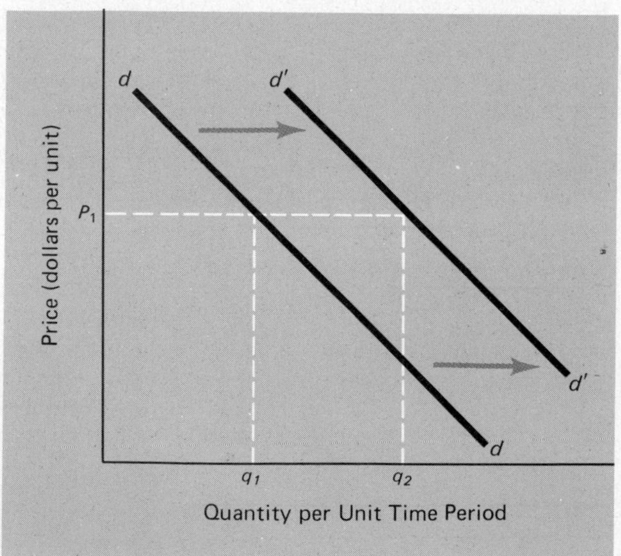

EXHIBIT 11–1
Advertising's Desired Effect. The firm that advertises hopes that the advertising will shift the demand schedule for its product to the right. In other words, before advertising, the demand schedule is at *dd;* after advertising takes place, the demand schedule should shift to *d′d′*.

the quantity sold will be q_1. If, however, advertising succeeds in shifting the demand curve over to $d'd'$, then at that same price the quantity q_2 will be sold.

It is possible, on the other hand, that advertising is necessary just to keep the demand curve at *dd*. Without advertising, the demand curve might shift inward to the left. This presumably is the case with competitive advertising. For example, cigarette manufacturers may have to expend large outlays on advertising just to keep the share of the market they now have. If they drop their advertising, they would lose ground to all the other companies that are engaged in heavy advertising.

Competitive Versus Informative Advertising

In the strictest model of monopolistic competition, advertising by one monopolistic competitor does not induce retaliatory action by others. That is to say, advertising is not undertaken as a reaction to encroachments of other firms on the particular market in question. Nonetheless, we generally observe advertising by all of the firms in a monopolistically competitive industry. Sometimes this advertising is called competitive or defensive, in the sense that it has no effect on *increasing* sales; rather, it is necessary for *keeping* sales at what they are and for preventing other firms from taking business away. Competitive advertising is sometimes contrasted with informative advertising, which actually imparts information that can be used by the consumer in deciding which product to buy. The distinction between competitive and informative advertising is murky; no meaningful definition has been offered to make that distinction clear in all cases.

Advertising and Economies of Scale

An alleged reason for advertising is that the subsequent increased sales can lead to economies of scale. This is possible only if the economies of scale outweigh the advertising costs. Look at Exhibit 11–2. Here we find that the hypothetical average total cost curve without advertising is ATC. With advertising, it is ATC′. If production is at q_1, then without advertising average total costs will be ATC_1. If advertising campaigns shift demand and increase the profit-maximizing output to q_2, then average total costs will fall to ATC_2. The reduction in average total costs will more than outweigh the increased expenses due to advertising. If the advertising campaign were not successful and demand and production remained where they were, then the firm would stop advertising. It would not be profitable to continue.

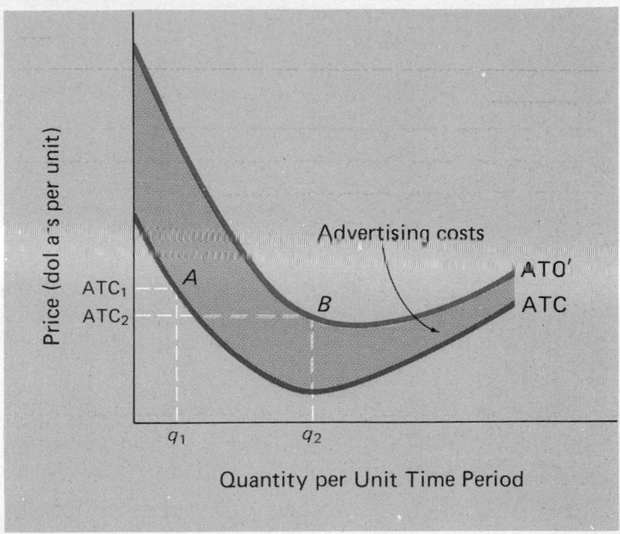

EXHIBIT 11–2

Another Desired Effect of Advertising. Advertising may be able to more-than-pay for itself. For example, in this diagram we start out on the average total cost curve ATC at point *A* with production of q_1. Here average total costs are ATC_1. Advertising is added, and the average total cost curve shifts up to ATC′. However, if we move out to point *B*, the quantity produced will be q_2 with an average total cost of only ATC_2, which is lower than ATC_1.

Arguments Against Advertising

Many critics of advertising do not accept the argument that expanded production through advertising makes for a lower unit cost. These critics contend that much advertising is self-canceling, as in the cigarette industry. Although each advertiser must continue to spend money on flashy billboards and magazine ads, the tobacco industry as a whole gets no additional customers with all members advertising at once. Moreover, if advertising can cause a firm to realize gains from mass production through increased growth, at some point the firm may incur diseconomies of scale.

Additionally, the critics of advertising point out that some of it attempts to impute a glamorous image to activities that are "undesirable." For example, billboard ads and magazine space advertising campaigns for cigarettes presumably are aimed at young people in an effort to portray smoking as glamorous and thereby induce additional customers to the industry.

Even though advertising accounts for less than 2 percent of national income, critics contend that advertising expenditures divert human and other resources away from much more pressing needs. Advertising, in short, gives rise to a misallocation of resources. The most telling argument along these lines is the claim that advertising causes people to consume more private goods and fewer "public" goods—such as schools, hospitals, better streets, and so on. Although the critics may be right, we should realize that private businesses are not the only ones who advertise. Look at the amount of advertising done by universities in need of funds; look at the amount of advertising that the government uses to "sell" its new programs.

Advertising has also been attacked as the means by which producers can create artificial wants. Numerous books have been written about how advertising subtly and not so subtly alters the ways we think and the things we desire to consume. Analyzing this particular contention is difficult because economics can say very little about the creation of wants. However, we do know that advertisers compete, and therefore it would seem to be quite difficult for one manufacturer to induce consumers to buy a product they didn't want when numerous other manufacturers were attempting to do exactly the same thing. Moreover, there is plenty of advertising for nonconsumption—that is, for savings. How many times do you see ads on TV and in the newspaper about new savings and loan associations wanting your money? And don't we see ads for U.S. savings bonds? The fact is that we find ads asking us to do everything imaginable with our income and our time. Thus, the question is whether some forms of advertising are more persuasive than others, and, if so, does one particular industry have a monopoly on that form of advertising? This is a question no one has yet answered.

Concepts in Brief 11-1

- Monopolistic competition is a market structure that lies in between pure monopoly and perfect competition.
- A monopolistically competitive market structure has (1) a large number of sellers, (2) differentiated products, and (3) advertising.
- Because of the large number of firms, each has a small share of the market and collusion is difficult; the firms are independent.
- The goal of advertising is to shift the demand curve outward to the right.
- Proponents of advertising argue that it leads to increased sales, which allow firms to take advantage of economies of scale.

Price and Output for the Monopolistic Competitor

Now that we have presented the assumptions underlying the monopolistic competition model, we can analyze the price and output behavior of each firm in a monopolistically competitive industry. We assume in the analysis that follows that the desired product type and quality have been chosen. Further, we assume that the budget and the type of promotional activity have already been chosen and do not change.

THE INDIVIDUAL FIRM'S DEMAND AND COST CURVES

Since the individual firm is not a perfect competitor, its demand curve is downward sloping, as is shown in panels (a), (b), and (c) of Exhibit 11-3. Thus, it faces a marginal revenue curve that is also downward sloping and below the demand curve. To find the profit-maximizing rate of output and the profit-maximizing price, we go to the output where the marginal cost curve intersects the marginal revenue curve from below. That gives us the profit-maximizing output rate. Then we draw a vertical line up to the demand schedule. That gives us the price that can be charged to sell exactly that quantity produced. This is what we have done in panels (a), (b), and (c) of Exhibit 11-3. In each of those panels, a marginal cost curve has been drawn in. It intersects the marginal revenue curve at E. The profit-maximizing rate of output is q_e, and the profit-maximizing price is P.

THE SHORT-RUN EQUILIBRIUM

In the short run, it is possible for a monopolistic competitor to make economic profits—that is, profits over and above the normal rate of return, or profits over and above what is necessary to keep that firm in that industry. In panel (a) of Exhibit 11-3, we show such a situation. The average total cost curve is drawn in below the demand curve *dd* at the profit-maximizing rate of output q_e. Economic profits are shown by the shaded rectangle in that panel.

Losses in the short run are clearly also possible. They are presented in panel (b) of Exhibit 11-3. Here the average total cost curve lies everywhere above the individual firm's demand curve *dd*. The losses are marked as the shaded rectangle.

Just as with any market structure or any firm, in

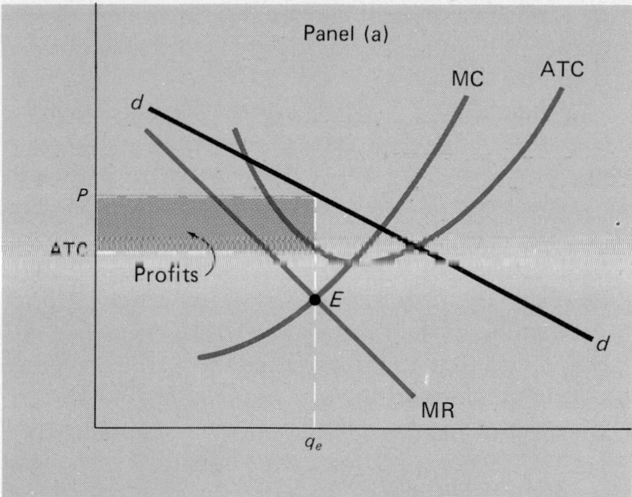

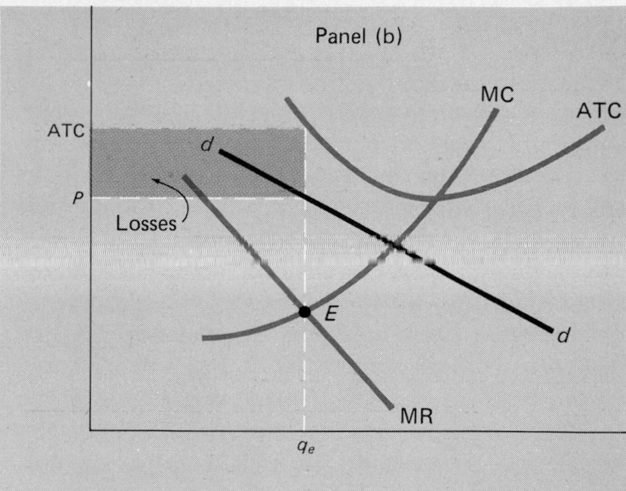

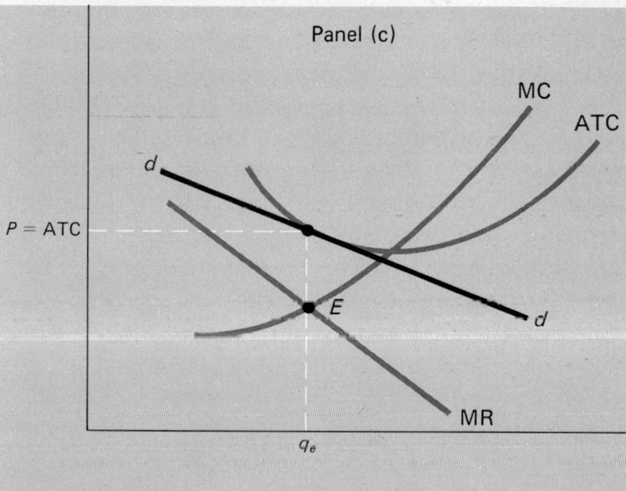

EXHIBIT 11–3

Long-Run Equilibrium with Monopolistic Competition. In panel (a), we show the typical monopolistic competitor making economic profits. If that were the situation, there would be entry into the industry, forcing the demand curve facing the individual monopolistic competitor leftward. Eventually firms would find themselves in the situation depicted in panel (c), where zero economic profits are being made. At the profit-maximizing rate of output, where marginal cost equals marginal revenue, price equals average total cost. In panel (b), we show a situation where the typical firm in a monopolistically competitive industry is making economic losses. If that were the case, firms would leave the industry. The demand curve would shift outward to the right. Eventually the average industry firm would find itself in the situation depicted in panel (c).

the short run it is possible to observe either economic profits or economic losses. In the long run, such is not the case with monopolistic competition, however.

THE LONG RUN—ZERO ECONOMIC PROFITS

The long run is where the similarity between perfect competition and monopolistic competition becomes more obvious. In the long run, since there are so many firms making substitutes for the product in question, any economic profits will be competed away. They will be competed away either through entry by new firms seeing a chance to make a higher rate of return than elsewhere, or by changes in product quality and advertising outlays by existing firms in the industry. (Profitable products will be imitated by other firms.) As for economic losses in the short run, they will disappear in the long run because those firms that suffer them will leave the industry. They will go into another business where the expected rate of return is at least normal. Thus, panels (a) and (b) of Exhibit 11–3 represent only short-run situations for a monopolistically competitive firm. In the long run, the average total cost curve will just touch the individual firm's demand curve *dd* at the particular price that is profit maximizing for that particular firm. This is shown in panel (c) of Exhibit 11–3.

A word of warning. This is an idealized, long-run equilibrium situation for each firm in the industry. That does not mean that even in the long run we will observe every single firm in a monopolistically competitive industry making *exactly* zero economic profits or *just* a normal rate of return. We live in a dynamic world. All we are saying is that if this model is correct, the rate of return will *tend* toward normal—that is, economic profits will tend toward zero.

Comparing Perfect Competition with Monopolistic Competition

If both the monopolistic competitor and the perfect competitor make zero economic profits in the long run, then how are they different? The answer lies in the fact that the demand curve facing the individual perfect competitor is horizontal—that is, the price elasticity of demand is infinity. Such is not the case for the individual monopolistic competitor. The demand curve has some slope to it. This firm has some control over price; it has some market power. Price elasticity of demand is not infinite. We see the two situations in panels (a) and (b) of Exhibit 11–4. Both show average total costs just touching the respective demand curves at the particular price at which the firm is selling the product. Notice, however, that the perfect competitor's average total costs are at a minimum. This is not the case with the monopolistic competitor. The equilibrium rate of output is to the left of the minimum point on the average total cost curve where price is greater than marginal cost. (The monopolistic competitor cannot expand output to the point of minimum costs without lowering price; and then marginal cost would exceed marginal revenue.)

It has been argued, therefore, that monopolistic competition involves waste because minimum average total costs are not achieved and price exceeds marginal cost. There are too many firms producing too little output. According to critics of monopolistic competition, society's resources are being wasted.

Chamberlin had an answer to this criticism. He contended that the difference between the average cost of production for a monopolistically competitive firm in an open market and the minimum average total cost represented what he called the cost of producing "differentness." In other words, Chamberlin did not label this difference in cost between prefect competition and monopolistic competition necessarily a waste. In fact, he argued that it is rational for consumers to have a taste for differentiation; consumers willingly accept the resultant increased production costs in return for choice and variety of output.

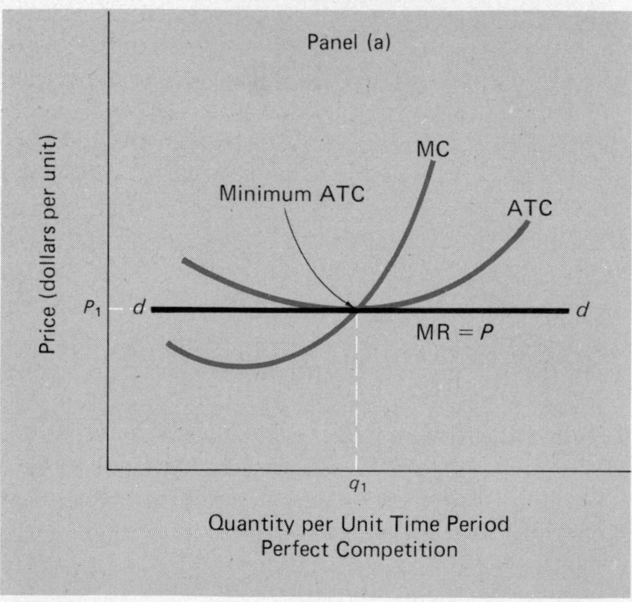

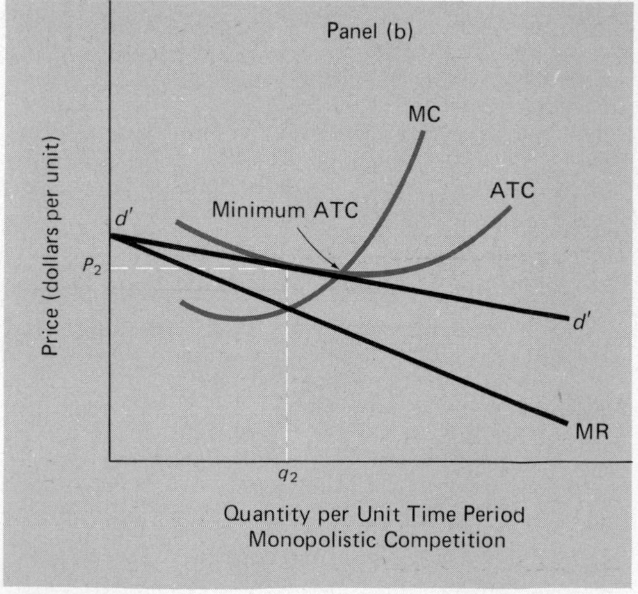

EXHIBIT 11–4

Comparison of the Perfect Competitor with the Monopolistic Competitor. In panel (a), the perfectly competitive firm has zero economic profits in the long run. Its long-run average total cost curve is tangent to the demand curve *dd* just at the point of intersection with the marginal cost curve. The price is set equal to marginal cost, and that price is P_1. There are zero economic profits. Also, its demand curve is just tangent to the minimum point on its average total cost curve, which means the firm is operating at its optimum rate of production. With the monopolistically competitive firm in panel (b), there are also zero economic profits in the long run, because the average total cost curve is tangent to the individual monopolistic competitor's demand curve, *d'd'*, at the output where production occurs. The price, however, is greater than marginal cost; the monopolistically competitive firm does not find itself at the minimum point on its average total cost curve. It is operating at a rate of output less than is optimal—that is, to the left of the minimum point on the ATC curve.

Concepts in Brief 11-2

- In the short run, it is possible for monopolistically competitive firms to make economic profits or economic losses.
- In the long run, monopolistically competitive firms will make zero economic profits—that is, they will make a normal rate of return.
- Because the monopolistic competitor faces a downward-sloping demand curve, it does not produce at the minimum point on its average total cost curve. Thus, we say that a monopolistic competitor has higher average total costs per unit than a perfect competitor would have. Some have called this a "waste."
- Chamberlin argues that the difference between the average costs of production for a monopolistically competitive firm and the minimum average total cost at which a competitive firm would produce is the cost of producing "differentness."

Oligopoly and Interdependence

There is another market structure that we have yet to discuss, and it is an important one indeed. It involves a situation where there are several large firms that dominate an entire industry. They are clearly not competitve in the sense that we have used the term; they are clearly not even monopolistically competitive. And since there isn't just one of them, a pure monopoly does not exist. We call such a situation an **oligopoly,** which means few sellers that are interdependent.

CHARACTERISTICS OF OLIGOPOLY

There are several characteristics of oligopoly that we can examine here.

Small Number of Firms

We have already mentioned that there is a small number of firms in an oligopolistic industry. Does that mean more than 2 but less than 100? The question is not easy to answer. Basically, though, we are interested in several firms dominating the entire industry so that these several firms really are able to set the price. By domination, we must be specific, however. We are referring to the percentage of total industry output accounted for by the few top firms.

You can probably think of quite a few examples of an oligopolistic market structure. The domestic automobile industry is dominated by three large firms: General Motors, Chrysler, and Ford. The steel industry has many firms, but the top four account each year for over 60 percent of the industry's ingot output.

Interdependence

When there are only a few large firms dominating the industry, they cannot act independently of each other. In other words, they recognize that there is mutual interdependence. Each firm will react to what the other firms do in terms of output and price, as well as to changes in quality and product differentiation. To specify a complete model of oligopoly, we would have to somehow specify the manner in which an oligopolist expects his or her rivals to react. Remember, in a perfectly competitive model each firm ignores the reactions of other firms because each firm can sell all that it wants at the going market price. In the pure monopoly model, the monopolist does not have to worry about the reaction of rivals, since, by definition, there are none.

We must stress here that the mutual interdependence results from the fewness of firms in the industry that produce the largest share of total industry output. In fact, we might state that in an oligopoly market structure, the firms must try to predict the reaction of rival firms. Otherwise, poor business decisions could be made that would spell lower profits.

Why Oligopoly Occurs

Why is it that some industries are dominated by a few large firms? What are the reasons that will cause an industry that might otherwise be competitive to tend toward oligopoly? We can present some partial answers here.

ECONOMIES OF SCALE

Perhaps the strongest reason that has been offered for the existence of oligopoly is economies of scale. Remember that economies of scale are defined as a production situation in which a doubling of output results is less than a doubling of the total costs. When economies of scale truly exist, the firm's average total cost curve will be downward sloping as it produces more and more output. That is, average total cost can be reduced by continuing to expand

Oligopoly

the scale of operation. Smaller firms will have a tendency in such a situation to be inefficient. That is, their average total costs will be greater than those incurred by a large firm. They will little by little go out of business (or be absorbed into the larger firm, which we discuss below). Historically, in many of the industries that have become oligopolistic in the United States, it has been technical progress that has made economies of scale obtainable. For example, consider the automobile business. When it started out, there were more than 60 firms in the industry. Today, in the United States, there are three major ones.

BARRIERS TO ENTRY

It is possible that certain barriers to entry have prevented more competition in oligopolistic industries. We mentioned what barriers to entry are in the last chapter. They include legal barriers, such as patents, control and ownership over critical supplies, and a few others. Indeed, we can look at the past and find periods where firms maintained market power because those firms were able not only to erect a barrier to entry but to keep it in place year after year. In principle, the chemical, electronics, and aluminum industries have been at one time or another either monopolistic or oligopolistic because of the ownership of patents and the control of strategic inputs by specific firms. The Aluminum Company of America (Alcoa) is a good example of how control of an input can be used. It was the sole manufacturer of aluminum ingots in the United States from the late nineteenth century until World War II. This monopoly (as opposed to oligopoly) position of the firm was at first maintained by the many patents that it had obtained for the different phases of the aluminum ingot production process. Later on, after these patents expired, one of the major ways in which Alcoa kept its monopoly position was by cornering sources of bauxite, the raw material necessary for making aluminum. It did this by signing long-term contracts with the companies owning rights to this essential raw material. The contract specified that those companies could not sell the essential ore to any other company. Furthermore, as early as 1895, Alcoa obtained electric energy from three power companies and signed contracts with each of them prohibiting those companies from selling or leasing power to anyone else for the manufacture of aluminum. (Such business tactics are now illegal.)

OLIGOPOLY BY MERGER

Another reason that we have seen oligopolistic market structures is that a number of firms have merged. A merger is the joining of two or more firms under a single ownership or control. There are two types of mergers—horizontal and vertical.

Horizontal Mergers

Horizontal mergers involve firms selling a similar product. If two shoe manufacturing firms merge, that is a horizontal merger. If a group of firms, all producing steel, merge into one, that is also a horizontal merger.

Vertical Mergers

Vertical mergers occur when one firm merges with either a firm from which it purchases an input or a firm to which it sells its output. Vertical mergers occur, for example, when a coal-using electrical utility purchases a coal-mining firm or when a shoe manufacturer purchases retail shoe outlets. (Obviously, vertical mergers do not create oligopoly as we have defined it.)

We have been talking about oligopoly in a theoretical manner up until now. It is time to look at the actual picture of oligopolies in the United States.

Industry Concentration

The definition of oligopoly is a situation in which very few interdependent firms control a large part of total output in an industry. This has been called industry concentration. Before we show the concentration statistics in the United States, we must describe the way in which industry concentration can be computed.

CONCENTRATION RATIO

The most popular way to compute industry concentration is to determine the percentage of total sales or production accounted for by, say, the top four or top eight firms in an industry. An example of an industry with 25 firms is given in Exhibit 11-5. We can see in that exhibit that the four largest firms account for almost 90 percent of total output in the hypothetical industry. That is an oligopoly situation.

EXHIBIT 11–5
Computing the Four-Firm Concentration Ratio.

	Annual Sales (in dollars)	
Firm 1	$150,000,000	= $400,000,000
Firm 2	100,000,000	
Firm 3	80,000,000	
Firm 4	70,000,000	
Firms 5–25	50,000,000	
Total	$450,000,000	
4-firm concentration ratio =	$400,000,000 / $450,000,000	= 88.9 percent

U.S. CONCENTRATION RATIOS

Now that we have explained what a concentration ratio is, we can look at what actual ratios are in the United States. Some are presented in Exhibit 11–6. We show the ratios for 1976, for both the largest four companies and the largest eight companies. Which industries out of those shown can we classify as oligopolistic? There is no definite answer. Some economists like to arbitrarily pick a four-firm concentration ratio of 50 percent as the cutoff point. Thus, in Exhibit 11–6, we would say that in 1976, the motor vehicles, primary copper, aircraft, and synthetic rubber industries were oligopolistic. Some economists like to pick the eight-firm concentration ratio. If we used the same 50 percent cutoff point, a larger number of those industries listed would be

~~when one cannot.~~

EXHIBIT 11–6
Concentration Ratios (Percent).

	SHARE OF VALUE OF SHIPMENTS IN 1976 ACCOUNTED FOR BY THE:	
	Largest Four Companies	*Largest Eight Companies*
Motor vehicles	93	99
Primary copper	72	*
Aircraft	66	86
Synthetic rubber	62	81
Blast furnaces and steel mills	45	65
Industrial trucks and tractors	50	66
Construction machinery	43	54
Petroleum	31	56
Paper mills	24	40
Meatpacking	22	37
Newspapers	17	28
Fluid milk	18	26

* Withheld by Commerce Department to avoid disclosing figures for individual companies.

Source: U.S. Department of Commerce

considered oligopolistic. As yet, no scientific procedure has been developed that tells us exactly when an industry can be classified as an oligopoly and when one cannot.

The concept of an "industry" is necessarily arbitrary. As a consequence, concentration ratios rise as we narrow the definition of an industry and fall as we broaden it. Thus, we must be certain that we are satisfied with the definition of the industry under study before we jump to conclusions about whether the "industry" is truly "too" concentrated, as evidenced by a high measured concentration ratio.

> ***Concepts in Brief 11-3***
>
> - Oligopoly means few sellers; an oligopoly is a market situation in which there are few interdependent sellers.
> - Oligopoly occurs because of: (1) returns to scale, (2) barriers to entry, and (3) mergers.
> - Horizontal mergers involve firms selling a similar product.
> - Vertical mergers involve the merging of one firm with either the supplier of an input or a firm to which it sells its output.
> - Industry concentration can be measured by the percentage of total sales accounted for by the top four or top eight firms.

Oligopoly Price and Output Determination

When we talked about perfect competition, pure monopoly, and monopolistic competition, we were able to explicitly present the profit-maximizing rate of output and price combination. In each case, we were able to draw a demand curve, a marginal revenue curve, and a marginal cost curve. For all three cases, profit maximization occurred when marginal revenue equaled marginal cost. (Remember that in the case of the perfect competitor, the demand curve and the marginal revenue curve are identical.) We cannot so easily do the same thing for oligopoly. Indeed, it is impossible for us to draw any one specific demand curve facing the oligopolist. Remember that we pointed out that each oligopolist had to take account of the reaction of other oligopolists. How can a demand curve be known or even guessed without specifying the way that the other oligopolists will react? The answer is, it cannot. In each oligopoly model, we must explicitly

Oligopoly

take account of other rivals' reactions. As you might expect, economists have come up with a multitude of oligopoly models, each one depending on a different type of reaction by rivals. We will look at two such models here, knowing full well that they represent only a small fraction of the possible models that exist.

No Collusion, Price Rigidity, and the Kinked Demand Curve

Let's assume that the decision makers in an oligopolistic firm assume that rivals will react in the following way: they will match all price *decreases* (in order not to be "undersold"), but not price *increases* (because they want to capture more business). The implications of this reaction function, as it were, are rigid prices and a kinked demand curve, which we will explain now.

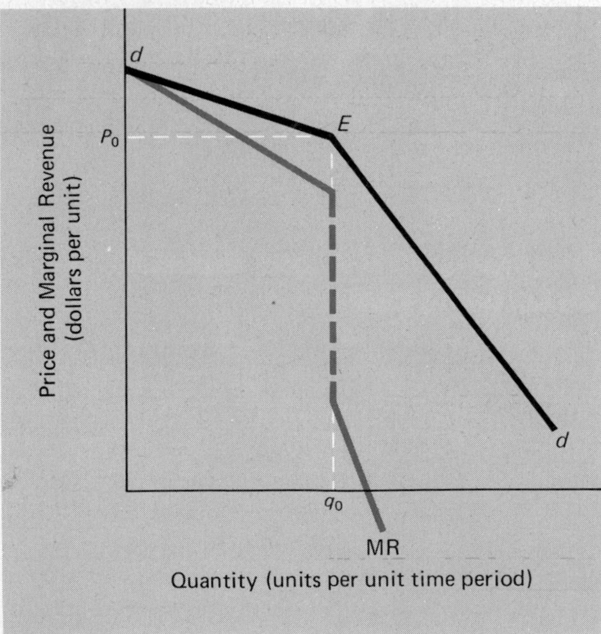

EXHIBIT 11–7

The Kinked Demand Curve. Start with the price P_0. The firm assumes that if it raises price, no firm (or at least, only a few firms) will follow. Its demand is relatively elastic, therefore, above P_0. However, if it lowers price, other oligopolists will follow. Its demand is much less elastic, therefore, below P_0. There is a kink at E. The kinked demand curve is *dd;* the marginal revenue curve is discontinuous at the output rate q_0 and is labeled MR.

THE NATURE OF THE KINKED DEMAND CURVE

In Exhibit 11–7, we draw a kinked demand curve, which is implicit in the assumption that oligopolists follow price decreases but not price increases. We start off at a given price of P_0 and assume that the quantity demanded at that price for this individual oligopolist is q_0. The oligopoly firm assumes that if it lowers its price, rivals will react by matching that reduction to avoid losing their respective shares of the market. Thus, the oligopolist that lowers its price will not increase its quantity demanded greatly. The portion of its demand curve to the right of and below point E in Exhibit 11–7 is much less elastic. On the other hand, if the oligopolist increases price, no rivals will follow suit. Thus, the quantity demanded at the higher price for this oligopolist will fall off dramatically. The demand schedule to the left of and above point E will be relatively elastic. This is the flatter part of the curve to the left of point E. Consequently, the demand curve facing the oligopolist is *dd,* which has a kink at E.

THE MARGINAL REVENUE CURVE

To draw a marginal revenue curve for the kinked demand curve in Exhibit 11–7, we first draw a marginal revenue curve out from the vertical axis for the elastic portion of the demand curve (from the upper d to a point directly below E). At quantity q_0, however, the demand curve abruptly changes slope and becomes steeper. The marginal revenue curve will have a discontinuous part in it that corresponds to the kink at quantity q_0 in the demand curve *dd.* To the left of that "step," marginal revenue is relatively high. This indicates that revenues will be lost rapidly if the firm moves up (raises price) the relatively elastic portion of its demand curve. To the right of the "step," on the other hand, marginal revenue is relatively lower. This indicates that little extra revenue can be obtained when the oligopolist moves down (lowers price) the relatively less elastic portion of the demand curve.

PRICE RIGIDITY

Over the discontinuous portion of the marginal revenue curve, the oligopolist does not react to changes in marginal cost (unless they are really large). Look, for example, at Exhibit 11–8. Assume that marginal cost is represented by *mc*. The profit-maximizing rate of output is q_0, which can be sold at a price of P_0. Now assume that the marginal cost curve rises to *mc′*. What will happen to the profit-maximizing rate of output? Nothing. Both quantity and price will remain the same for this oligopolist.

Remember that the profit-maximizing rate of output is where marginal revenue equals marginal cost. The shift in the marginal cost curve to *mc′* does not change the profit-maximizing rate of output, because *mc′* still "cuts" the marginal revenue curve in the latter's discontinuous portion. Thus, the equality between marginal revenue and marginal cost still holds at output rate q_0 even when the marginal cost curve shifts upward. What will happen when marginal cost falls to *mc″*? Nothing. This oligopolist will continue to produce at a rate of output q_0 and charge a price of P_0. Thus, whenever the marginal cost curve cuts the discontinuous portion of the marginal revenue curve, fluctuations (within limits) in marginal cost will not affect output or price, because the profit-maximizing condition MR = MC will hold. Thus, prices are seen to be rigid in oligopolistic industries if they react the way we assumed in this model.

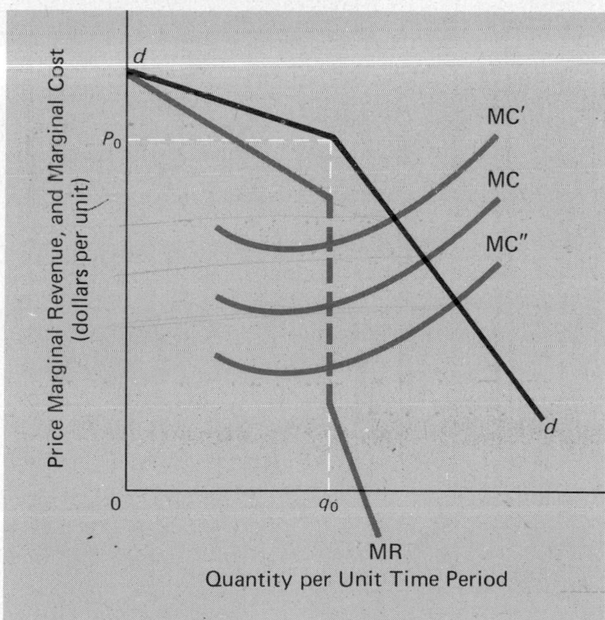

EXHIBIT 11–8
Changes in Cost May Not Alter the Profit-Maximizing Price and Output. As long as the marginal cost curve "intersects" the marginal revenue curve in the latter's discontinuous portion, the profit-maximizing price P_0 (and output q_0) will remain unchanged. (However, the firm's rate of profit will change.)

CRITICISMS AND EVIDENCE OF THE KINKED DEMAND CURVE

One of the criticisms that has been waged against the kinked demand curve is that we have no idea how the existing price, P_0, came into being. Seemingly, if every oligopolistic firm faced a kinked demand curve, it would not pay for it to change prices. The problem is that the kinked demand curve does not show us how supply and demand originally determine the going price of an oligopolist's product.

As far as the evidence goes, it is not encouraging. Several economists have compared the rigidity of prices in oligopolistic industries with prices in monopolistic industries. In Exhibit 11–9, we show the results of a study by Professor George J. Stigler. He looked at two monopolies—aluminum and nickel—during the period that spans virtually the entire Great Depression. He compared the price changes per month in those industries with the price changes in industries where there were 2, 6, and 8 firms. The number of price changes for the latter ranges from 5 to 46; for monopolies, from 0 to 2. Presumably, if the kinked demand curve is correct, oligopolies should be changing their prices much less often than monopolists who will react, in principle, to any change in demand and/or marginal cost.

A further test of the kinked demand curve and price rigidity within monopolies and oligopolies was carried out by economist Julian L. Simon. He looked at the quoted prices for trade magazine advertising. In each industry, there are one or more

EXHIBIT 11–9
A Test of Price Rigidity.

	No. of Firms	*No. of Monthly Price Changes*
Monopolies		
Nickel	1	0
Aluminum	1	2
Oligopolies		
Plows	6	25
Tires	8	36
Bananas	2	46
Grain Binders	2	5

Source: G. J. Stigler, "The Kinky Oligopoly Demand Curve and Rigid Prices," *Journal of Political Economy*, vol. 55 (1947), p. 443

magazines that discuss industry problems and prospects, and give advertising that is of interest to the firms of that industry. Simon compared advertising rates in magazines without a competitor—a monopoly situation—and magazines with competitors. He looked at two periods, 1955 to 1961 and 1961 to 1964. His findings suggest that there were fewer quoted price changes for advertising rates in monopoly magazines than in oligopoly groups. In other words, even though the kinked demand curve oligopoly theory predicts that oligopolists will change prices less often than firms in other types of market structures, the evidence in this study did not show that.

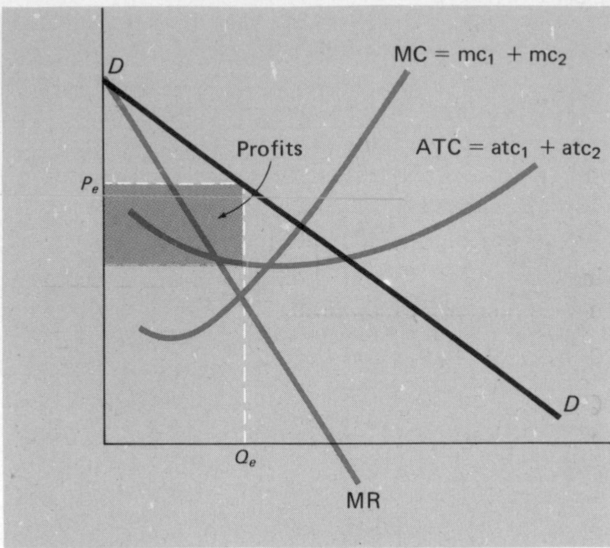

EXHIBIT 11–10

Joint Profit Maximization. If both firms jointly recognize that it is better to share monopoly profits, they will look at the combined industry demand curve *DD* and its marginal revenue curve MR. The industry marginal cost curve, or the horizontal summation of the two firms' marginal cost curves, is given by MC. The joint profit-maximizing rate of output is Q_e sold at price P_e. (The joint maximum profits are given by the shaded area.)

Joint Maximization

The other model of oligopoly that we will study in this chapter is one of joint profit maximization. It is associated with Edward Chamberlin of monopolistic competition fame. In Chamberlin's model, the assumption is that there are only two oligopoly firms in the market (although the analysis applies to more than two). Both firms recognize that each will react to the other's reduction in price by a further reduction in price. After this recognition takes place in both firms, the two firms jointly recognize that the best thing they can do is to share the monopoly profits. The solution is one of simple monopoly pricing, given in Exhibit 11–10. The profit-maximizing rate of output for the two firms taken together is the output at which marginal revenue intersects marginal cost. We are assuming here that the marginal cost curves for both firms are identical. The joint profit-maximizing output rate is Q_e, and the profit-maximizing price for the share of monopoly is P_e. Thus, each firm would produce exactly one-half of Q_e and sell at price P_e.

In essence, then, the Chamberlin solution to the oligopoly problem indicates that the oligopoly will act as if it were a monopoly. And it does this without any written or even verbal agreement that it will produce the monopoly profit-maximizing rate of output and therefore sell it at the monopoly price. To repeat, the two firms act as a monopoly because they both recognize that the other will match price cuts. Presumably, again without written or verbal agreement, they do not engage in any "cheating" by expanding output and lowering price.

Now let us turn to some general aspects of oligopoly.

Nonprice Competition

By their very nature, oligopolistic firms do not exhibit active price competition. Price wars do erupt occasionally, but these are only temporary. Therefore, competition for an increased percentage of total sales in the market must take some other form. The alternative form is what is generally called nonprice competition. Nonprice competition cannot be neatly subdivided into categories because it takes on a large number of aspects. The only thing that we can say about nonprice competition is that it is an attempt by one oligopolistic firm to attract customers by some means other than a price differential. Here we will consider only two types of product differentiation that we have explicitly or implicitly referred to when discussing monopolistic competition.

ADVERTISING

As we pointed out previously, the primary purpose of advertising is to shift the demand curve to the right. This allows the seller, whether it be an oligopolist, a monopolistic competitor, or a monopolist, to sell more at each and every price. Advertising may also have the effect of differentiating the product and of making the product's availability better known. A firm will advertise as a way of gaining a nonprice competitive advantage over other firms. Whatever can be said about advertising, its effect on the oligopolistic firm is certainly not completely predictable.

QUALITY VARIATIONS

Quality differentiation results in a division of one market into a number of submarkets. We talked earlier about differentiating product through quality variation when we discussed monopolistic competition. Now we can apply the same discussion to oligopoly. The prime example of product differentiation is the automobile industry. There are specific physically definable differences between different automobile models within one single firm. A Citation and a Seville are certainly not the same product. If we were to examine automobiles, we would see that competition among oligopolistic firms creates a continuous expansion and redefinition of the different models that are sold by any one company. There is competition to create new quality classes and thereby gain a competitive edge. Being the first in the market in a new quality class has often meant higher profits. Witness the phenomenal success of the original Mustang. The strategy doesn't always work, however: witness the dismal failure of Ford's Edsel prior to the introduction of the successful Mustang. Oligopolists are always looking for best-selling new models, though.

Comparing Market Structures

Now that we have looked at perfect competition, pure monopoly, monopolistic competition, and oligopoly, we are in a position to compare the attributes of these four different market structures. We do this in summary form in Exhibit 11–11, where we compare the number of sellers, their ability to set price, and whether product differentiation exists, and we give some examples of each of the four market structures covered in this unit.

Concepts in Brief 11-4

- The kinked demand curve facing an oligopolist arises if competing oligopolists match price decreases but not price increases.
- The marginal revenue curve corresponding to a kinked demand curve has a discontinuous section.
- The kinked demand curve theory predicts that small changes in marginal costs may lead to no change in output or price if the marginal cost curve intersects the discontinuous portion of the kinked demand curve's marginal revenue curve.
- One oligopoly model involves joint profit maximization in which the oligopolists look at the industry demand curve and the industry marginal cost curve. They set price where industry marginal revenue equals industry marginal cost, and they share the monopoly profits. No cheating takes place, by assumption.
- Oligopolists can engage in nonprice competition such as advertising and quality variations.

EXHIBIT 11–11
Comparing Market Structures.

Market Structure	*Number of Sellers*	*Unrestricted Entry and Exit*	*Ability to Set Price*	*Long-run Economic Profits Possible*	*Product Differentiation*	*Examples*
Perfect competition	Numerous	Yes	None	No	None No	Agriculture
Monopolistic competition	Many	Yes	Some	No	Considerable Yes	Toothpaste, toilet paper, soap, retail trade
Oligopoly	Few	Partial	Some	Yes	Frequently Yes	Automobiles, steel
Pure monopoly	One	No	Considerable	Yes	The product is unique	Electric company, telephone company

ISSUES AND APPLICATIONS

Why Do Producers Give "Cents Off" Coupons?

> *Concepts Applied*
> ■ Monopolistic competition, price elasticity of demand, and price discrimination

There are numerous producers of food and other products that are sold in the hundreds of thousands of retail food outlets in the United States. If these producers are so competitive, why do we see them using "cents off" coupons to attract customers? This practice is not consistent with a purely competitive model. However, this practice is consistent with a monopolistic competition model that allows for slight degrees of monopoly power by individual producers. Here we discuss how the use of "cents off" coupons is consistent with price discrimination.

The Price of the Product Includes Shopping Time

The full price of the product includes not only the monetary price but also the implicit opportunity cost of the time that went into searching out the product and purchasing it (and the time needed to consume it). We can assume that, all things being the same, the higher one values time released from shopping, the less one will engage in seeking out lower-cost shopping arrangements. In other words, a person who values time more relative to money income will substitute more money income in order to save shopping time. That person will use less time to discover lower prices. Therefore, the person whose time is valued more highly will exhibit a less elastic demand curve in a given store than the person who does not value time so highly.

Charging more to the "richer" person. Let us assume that there is a strong correlation between the value of time and the wealth of a person. We are assuming that richer people, on average, value their time more highly than do poorer people. It follows that a richer person's relative price elasticity of demand will be less than a poorer person's. Now the suppliers of the various products sold in retail food outlets are confronted with two classes of consumers. There are those with relatively less elastic demand and those with relatively more elastic demand. The supplier's problem is to separate these two classes and charge the richer customer a higher price than the poorer customer. One way that this can be and is done is to offer a rebate only to those customers who are willing to incur a time cost to obtain that rebate. The rebate is in the form of "cents off" coupons. They are obtainable only by those customers who take time to cut "cents off" coupons out of magazines, keep track of them if they are received in the mail, and find them through other means. These "cents off" coupons must be kept with the person, taken to the retail food outlet, and then exchanged at the cash register for a reduction in the price charged for the individual items. All of these activities require time. Thus, poorer people, whom we are assuming can be used as a proxy for the relatively more elastic demanders, do pay a lower money price for their food and other purchases in retail food outlets when they utilize their "cents off" coupons. The richer customers, with relatively less elastic demand, refuse to be bothered by "cents off" coupons because of the time cost involved. They get no discount at all.

Some implications. If the above "cents off" coupon model is useful, it presents us with some testable implications.

1. We predict that "cents off" coupons will be offered relatively less often in cases where the total value of a single purchase is large. In such instances, the receiver of the valuable

coupon for a large purchase incurs a relatively small time cost, that is, relative to the value of the "cents off" coupon. In other words, not enough differential time costs are imposed to discourage relatively low elasticity demanders from collecting the "cents off" coupons. This implication is consistent with the fact that "cents off" coupons are almost exclusively used for relatively low-priced items sold in retail food stores.

2. We predict that in cases where the commodity is personal service, relatively few "cents off" coupons will be used. The differentiation of quality of services rendered already accomplishes the price-discriminating goal; the "cents off" coupon is used only as a substitute for price discounting. This implication is consistent with the observation that beauty shops and barber shops typically do not *give* "cents off" coupons.

Questions

1. Why is monopolistic competition the appropriate model for food producers? Does it seem to be the appropriate model for other industries? Why or why not?
2. How does the use of "cents off" coupons allow the monopolistic competitor to price discriminate among customers with different price elasticities of demand?

International Collusion

Concepts Applied

■ Collusion, barriers to entry, and oligopoly/monopoly profits

We have pointed out that oligopolies may attempt to get together to jointly maximize profits. That is to say, in the long run they can all make higher profits if they somehow agree to the monopoly profit-maximizing rate of output. Once the agreement is reached, each must not exceed its share of the desired output. This may sound like an easy task, but it is not. There have been numerous attempts by firms to collude in order to form a cartel and act as a monopolist. A cartel is an association of producers in the same industry established to increase the cartel members' profits. The cartel members jointly establish monopoly quantities and prices. As long as the collusive arrangement works, higher overall profits can be earned relative to a situation in which there is competition among oligopolists. In this Issue, we wish to examine attempts at international collusion, or the setting up of international cartels. Attempts at forming cartels have involved international commodity associations.

The Organization of Petroleum Exporting Countries (OPEC) is a cartel which has had considerable impact on the entire world.

International Commodity Cartels

The most famous of these cartels is OPEC, the Organization of Petroleum Exporting Countries. So far, this cartel has had a relatively short but highly successful history. The cartel started back in 1960 but had limited impact on the world until the early 1970s. Since the Middle East 1973 War, OPEC has had a dramatic effect on the world supply and therefore the world price of oil. It has done this by cutting back the production of crude oil, thus allowing for large price increases. Remember that for a stable demand curve, the only way to raise prices, even if one is a pure monopolist, is to cut back on production. Thus, the OPEC members could have an effective cartel arrangement *only* if some or all of them cut back on production and sales. Since Saudi Arabia, which accounts for the bulk of oil production in the Middle East, did cut back greatly in 1973 and has continued to do so since then, the cartel arrangement has worked for a number of years.

Other cartels formed. Perhaps because of the success of OPEC, other cartels, involved with other commodities, have been formed.

Bauxite. Seven leading bauxite exporters have formed the International Bauxite Association (IBA). Immediately after its formation, Jamaica, one of the leading exporters of bauxite to aluminum producers in the United States, forced a sixfold increase in price. Other members followed suit and have since attempted to raise prices even further.

Copper. The Inter-Governmental Council of Copper-Exporting Countries (called, in French, CIPEC) has announced that it will attempt to market a greater share of world copper production. It has expanded its membership to increase market power.

Tin. The International Tin Agreement signatories have attempted to get a 42 percent increase in the guaranteed floor price maintained by their buffer stocks. This cartel has existed since before World War II.

Coffee. Leading coffee producers got together a few years ago through a series of interlocking marketing companies and stockpile-financing arrangements. They apparently seized control of world coffee prices.

Bananas. The Organization of Banana-Exporting Countries has started leveling sizable taxes on banana exports to increase their earnings.

Phosphate. Phosphate producers got together and agreed to triple their prices. Phosphate is an input to detergents and fertilizers.

Iron Ore, Mercury, Tea, Tropical Timber, Natural Rubber, Nickel, Cobalt, Tungsten, Columbium, Pepper, Tantalum, and Quinine. Producer cartels—such as the Association of Natural Rubber Producing Countries and the Asian Pepper Community—have been formed in all these commodities at one time or another.

Surprisingly, the U.S. State Department has entered the United States into numerous commodity agreements since 1973. The so-called commodity agreements are simply cartel pricing devices that members agree to uphold. For example, the International Sugar Organization attempts to keep the price of sugar higher than it would be otherwise. International commodity agreement organizations typically will keep "buffer" stocks as a way to "stabilize" prices. The product will be bought and added to the buffer stock in order to keep its price from falling and, presumably, part of the stock will be sold to keep the price from rising. The State Department's reason for joining and upholding international commodity agreements is that it claims that they are in our self-interest. The State Department argues that such pacts strengthen ties with Third World countries.

The question now is, "What are the necessary ingredients to a successful cartel arrangement?"

On Making A Successful Cartel

A cartel must meet four basic requirements if it is to be successful:

1. The cartel must control a large share of total output. It must not face substantial competition from outsiders.
2. Available substitutes must be limited. In other words, the price elasticity of demand for the product in question must be fairly low; that is, demand must be relatively inelastic over broad price ranges. Indeed, a cartel facing a highly elastic demand will never succeed.

We can further make the distinction between the short and the long run. If there is the possibility of long-run substitution for the product, then the long-run price elasticity of demand will be relatively high and the cartel will be destroyed. Thus:

3. The demand for the cartel's product must be relatively stable, regardless of business conditions. If this is not the case, then the amount sold at any given price will be greater during economic expansions than during recessions, and the cartel will find it difficult to maintain any given price and output combination for very long.
4. Producers must be willing and able to withhold sufficient amounts of their product to af-

fect the market. Each member must resist the temptation to cheat. As a corollary of this, consumers must not be able to have large stockpiles of the product on which to draw.

There are probably other conditions that would make a cartel's success probability even greater, but these can be considered the basic ones.

The Desire to Cheat

A big cause of cartel instability is cheating. When there are many firms or countries in a cartel arrangement, there will always be some that are unhappy with the situation. There will always be those who will want to cheat by charging a slightly lower price than the one stipulated by the cartel. If there are geographical allocations for sales for each member firm in the cartel, any change in regional demand patterns will cause those cartel members who lose sales to be unhappy. The unhappy members will either require a bribe on the part of the happy members or will cheat on the cartel by cutting prices and seeking customers outside their stipulated regions.

An individual cartel member is always tempted to cheat, to cut prices clandestinely. Any member who is producing a small percentage of the total output of the cartel essentially faces a very elastic demand curve if it cheats and no one else does. A small drop in price by the cheater will result in a very large increase in total revenues. The best analogy is the extreme case of the firm in a competitive industry. It can increase output without affecting the market price, since it is such a small part of the industry. The lure of such increases in revenues is probably too tempting for cartel members to allow a cartel to last forever.

There will always be cartel members who figure that it will pay them to cut prices, to break away from the cartel. Some firms will try to do this, thinking that the others will not do the same thing. Other firms may cheat, figuring that other firms are going to cheat anyway, so why not be the first? Obviously, though, when a sufficient number of firms in the cartel tries to cheat, the cartel breaks up. We would expect, therefore, that as long as the cartel is not maintained by legislation, there will be a constant threat to its very existence. Its members will have a large incentive to price-cut, and, once a couple of members do it, the rest might follow.

Indeed, cartel instability is not confined to business firms. Have you ever noticed how short-lived a homemakers' boycott of supermarkets is? There are so many members in that particular cartel that it is difficult for one of them not to "cheat" and actually go out and buy some food from the supermarket. It is impossible to police the large number of homemakers involved.

Consider another example, which is hypothetical. If you are in a class of 100 students who will be graded on a curve, how easily could all of you get together and agree to each cut down study time? Would your cartel be successful? The answer, of course, depends on each individual student's incentive to "cheat" by working harder. If only one student were to study longer than all the others, that student could get a higher grade than he or she would otherwise. But if enough students felt this way, then the cartel would break down.

Questions

1. What are the ways that OPEC members can lower the selling price of oil without actually posting a lower price? (Hint: Better credit terms, for example.)
2. Is there any way to prevent cartel members from cheating? Under what conditions is cheating less likely to be a problem?

Definition of Terms

Monopolistic competition A market situation where a large number of firms produce similar but not identical products. There is relatively easy entry into the industry.

Oligopoly A market situation where there are very few sellers. Each seller knows that the other sellers will react to its changes in prices and quantities.

Chapter Summary

1. Numerous market situations lie between the extremes of pure competition and pure monopoly. Monopolistic competition and oligopoly are two of these.
2. Monopolistic competition is a theory developed by Edward Chamberlin of Harvard University in 1933. It refers to a market situation composed of specific product groups in which the different companies involved have slight monopoly powers because each has a product slightly different from the others. Examples of product groups might include the toothpaste and soap industries. The monopolistic competitor ends up with zero economic profits because there is free entry into the industry. However, according to Chamberlin, the monopolistic competitor does not produce where price equals marginal costs, and therefore does not produce at the minimum point on the average total cost curve.
3. Advertising occurs in industries where the firms are not pure price takers. The basic goal of advertisers is to shift the demand curve for their product outward.
4. In the short run, it is possible for a monopolistic competitor to make economic profits or economic losses. In the long run, monopolistic competitors make zero economic profits (that is, they make just the normal rate of return).
5. When we compare monopolistic competition with perfect competition, we find that the monopolistic competitor does not produce where average total costs are at a minimum, whereas the perfect competitor does.
6. Oligopoly is a market situation where there are several firms. Each firm knows that its rivals will react to a change in price. Oligopolies are usually defined as those in which the four-firm concentration ratio is relatively high—for example, more than 70 or 80 percent. That means that we would classify as oligopolies all industries in which the leading four firms produce 70 percent or more of the value of the industry shipments each year.
7. Oligopolies are characterized by relatively high barriers to entry, interdependence, and growth through merger.
8. The kinked demand curve oligopoly model indicates that prices will be relatively rigid unless demand or cost conditions change substantially.
9. Firms advertise in order to make the demand curve shift outward to the right.
10. Producers give "cents off" coupons as a way to price discriminate in favor of those who place a low value on their time and against those who place a high value on their time.

Selected References

Adams, Walter. *The Structure of American Industry.* 5th ed. New York: Macmillan, 1977, chaps. 2, 3, 5, 7, 8, and 9.

Brozen, Yale, ed. *The Competitive Economy.* Morristown, N.J.: General Learning Press, 1975.

Chamberlin, Edward H. *The Theory of Monopolistic Competition.* 8th ed. Cambridge, Mass.: Harvard University Press, 1962.

Mansfield, Edwin, ed. *Monopoly Power and Economic Performance.* 4th ed. New York: Norton, 1978.

Robinson, Joan. *The Economics of Imperfect Competition.* New York: St. Martin's Press, 1969.

Weiss, Leonard W. *Case Studies in American Industry.* 3rd ed. New York: Wiley, 1979.

Answers to Preview and Study Questions

1. What are the characteristics of the monopolistic competition market structure?

The monopolistic competition market structure lies between the extremes of monopoly and perfect competition, but closer to the latter. Under monopolistic competition there exists a large number of sellers, each with a small market share, acting independently of one another, producing a differentiated product. This product differentiation is advertised; advertising emphasizes product differences or, on occasion, "creates" differences.

2. How is the equilibrium price-output combination decided by the monopolistic competitor?

The monopolistic competitor has some control over price; it faces a downward-sloping demand curve. As such, a monopolistic competitor must lower price in order to increase sales; the marginal revenue curve for the monopolistic competitor is therefore downward sloping. Equilibrium, the total profit-maximizing rate of output, will therefore be where the upward-sloping (increasing) marginal cost curve intersects the downward-sloping (decreasing) marginal revenue curve.

The output rate being thus established, price is set at the corresponding market clearing level. Of course any other output rate would lead to a reduction in total profits.

3. How does the monopolistic competition market structure differ from perfect competition?

Like the perfect competitor, the monopolistic competitor acts independently of its competitors and is able to earn economic profits only in the short run; severe competition from entrants eliminates long-run economic profits under both market structures. Yet an important difference exists in the two models: the perfect competitor faces a perfectly elastic (horizontal) demand curve, while the monopolistic competitor faces a downward-sloping demand curve. Since economic profits must equal zero in the long run, the demand (average revenue) curve must be tangent to the average total cost (ATC) under both models. Under perfect competition, a horizontal (zero-sloped) demand curve can only be tangent to a U-shaped ATC curve at the latter's minimum point (where its slope is zero). Under monopolistic competition the AR curve must be tangent to the firm's ATC somewhere to the *left* of the ATC's minimum point. Thus, under perfect competition long-run equilibrium will be at minimum ATC, whereas under monopolistic competition long-run equilibrium will be at a higher ATC—and a lower output rate.

4. What are the characteristics of the oligopoly market structure?

Like the monopolistic competition market structure, oligopoly lies between the extremes of perfect competition and monopoly. However, oligopoly is closer to being unique; under oligopoly a small number of firms dominate the market, and the firms cannot act independently. That is, an oligopolist must take into account the reactions of its rivals when it sets policy; this interdependence makes the oligopoly model unique. It also makes the price output decision a complex one for the oligopolists—and, therefore, for economists who analyze this market structure. It is believed by many that oligopolies emerge because great economies of scale, in conjunction with a limited market demand, allow the few largest to drive out competitors. Also, oligopolies may arise due to barriers to entry and mergers.

5. How do oligopolies compete?

Although the kinked demand curve analysis predicts that little price competition will exist among oligopolists "sharing" a market, empirical evidence exists to indicate that price competition does exist. Even this evidence probably understates the extent of price competition under oligopoly; in times of excess demand, oligopolists offer discounts below relatively constant *list* prices (which are more easily measured). Moreover, oligopolists compete through advertising and quality innovation—or by providing more and/or better service.

Problems

(Answers at the back of the book)

1. Suppose you own a monopolistically competitive firm that sells automobile tune-ups at a price of $25 each. You currently are selling 100 per week. You are the owner/operator and you initiate an ad campaign on a local AM radio station. You promise to smooth out any ill-running car at a price of $25. The result is that you end up tuning 140 cars per week. What is the "marginal revenue" of this ad campaign? What additional information do you need to determine whether your profits have risen?

2. In the graph below we depict long-run equilibrium for a monopolistic competitor.

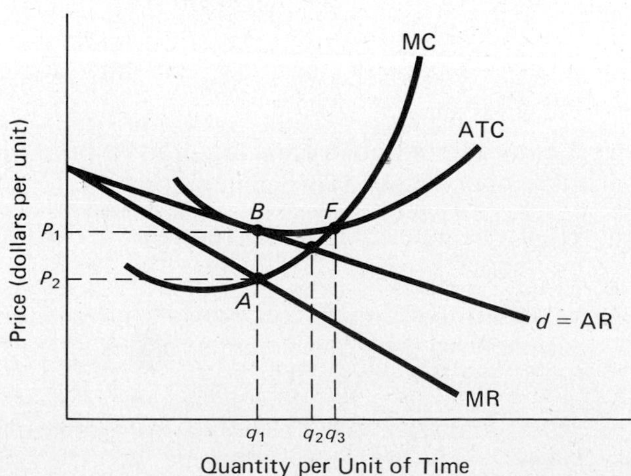

a. Which output rate represents equilibrium?
b. Which price represents equilibrium?
c. Which letter indicates that economic profits are zero?
d. Which letter indicates minimum ATC?
e. Is ATC at equilibrium higher than or equal to minimum ATC?
f. Is the equilibrium price greater than, less than, or equal to the marginal cost of producing the equilibrium output?

3. The table below indicates some information for Industry A.

	Annual sales (in dollars)
Firm 1	$200,000,000
Firm 2	150,000,000
Firm 3	100,000,000
Firm 4	75,000,000
Firms 5–30	300,000,000

a. What is the four-firm concentration ratio for this industry?
b. Assume that Industry A were the "steel industry." What would happen to the concentration index if we redefined Industry A as the "rolled steel industry"? As the "metal industry"?

12

Natural Monopolies, Regulation, and Antitrust

TOPICS FOR REVIEW

The topics listed below, which we have already analyzed, are applied in this chapter. You may find it worthwhile to review them. For your convenience each topic is followed by the number identifying the specific "Concepts in Brief."

a. Economies of scale (8–4)

b. Barriers to entry (10–1)

c. Price discrimination (10–4)

d. Concentration ratio (11–3)

FOR PREVIEW AND STUDY

1. What is a natural monopoly, and how could one arise?
2. If natural monopolies are required to price at marginal cost, what problem emerges?
3. What are some means to regulate a natural monopoly?
4. In recent years many economists have been reevaluating the government's role as an economic regulator. Why?
5. What industries are exempted from antitrust laws?

In our discussion of monopolies, we mentioned that there are relatively few examples of pure monopolies. There is a particular industry situation, however, that leads to what is called a **natural monopoly.** A natural monopoly is one that occurs because of the cost structure of the industry. The natural monopolist is the firm that first takes advantage of declining costs as output increases. The natural monopolist is able to undercut successfully its competitors and eventually force all of them out of the market. When such a situation occurs, government regulation often steps in to protect the consumer from the undesirable effect of monopoly—prices higher than marginal cost. In this chapter, we will look at government regulation of natural monopolies and also of other industries deemed so important to the public interest that they must be overseen.

The second topic we will undertake is antitrust legislation and theory. Antitrust legislation is a way of preventing monopolization in restraint of trade. Whereas regulation allows government to intervene directly into the decision-making processes of the regulated industries, antitrust legislation and enforcement seek to prevent monopolies from occurring in the first place, and therefore seek to obviate the need for regulation.

One Way for a Monopoly to Arise

In many industries, a tremendous amount of capital is required to produce a product or service. Think about how much money you would require to start an electric utility or a telephone company. Once you've started, however, the *marginal cost* of providing service is relatively small. Thus, in industries where large capital requirements are needed just to get started, long-run average fixed costs fall dramatically with higher and higher production rates. That is, the average total cost curve would be downward sloping throughout a very large range of production rates.

In Exhibit 12–1, we have drawn a downward-sloping long-run average total cost curve (LAC) for electricity. (A long-run cost curve is one that relates to a time span long enough for all inputs, including all fixed costs, to be freely variable.) Remember when we explained the relationship between marginal costs and average costs? We pointed out that when average costs are falling, marginal costs are less than average costs; and when average costs are rising, marginal costs are greater than average costs. We can apply the same analysis to the long run. Thus, when long-run average total costs are falling, the long-run marginal cost curve (LMC) is below the average total cost curve. In our example, long-run average costs are falling over such a large range of production rates (relative to demand) that we would expect that only one firm could survive in such an industry. That firm would be the natural monopolist. It would be the first one to take advantage of the decreasing average costs; that is, it would construct the large-scale facilities first. As its average total cost curve fell, it would lower prices and get increasingly larger shares of the market. Once that firm had driven all other firms out of the industry, it would set its price to maximize profits. Let's see what this price would be.

A monopolist will set the output rate where marginal revenue is equal to marginal cost. Let's draw in the market demand curve, *DD,* and the marginal revenue curve, MR, in panel (a) of Exhibit 12–2. The intersection of the marginal revenue curve and the marginal cost curve is at point *A*. The monopolist therefore would produce quantity Q_m and charge a price of P_m.

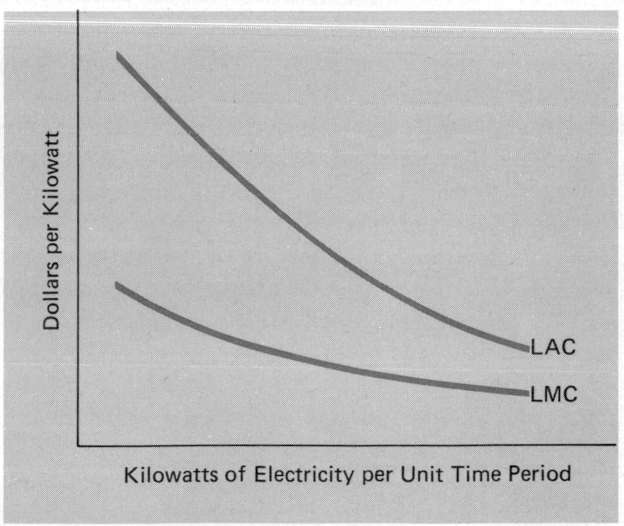

EXHIBIT 12–1
The Cost Curves that Might Lead to a Natural Monopoly. Here we show the long-run average total cost curve falling over a very large range of electricity production rates. The long-run marginal cost curve is, of course, below the average cost curve when the average cost curve is falling. A natural monopoly might arise in this situation. The first firm to establish the low unit cost capacity would be able to take advantage of the lower average total cost curve. This firm would drive out all rivals by charging a lower price than the others could sustain at their higher average total costs.

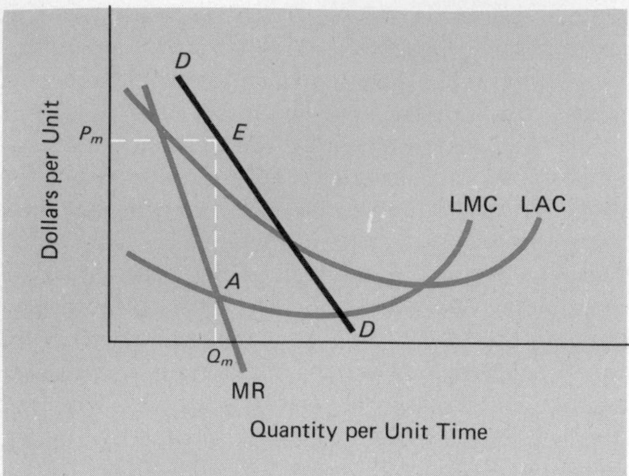

EXHIBIT 12–2(a)
Profit Maximization. The profit-maximizing natural monopolist here would produce at the point where marginal cost equals marginal revenue—that is, at point *A*, which gives the quantity of production Q_m. The price charged would be P_m.

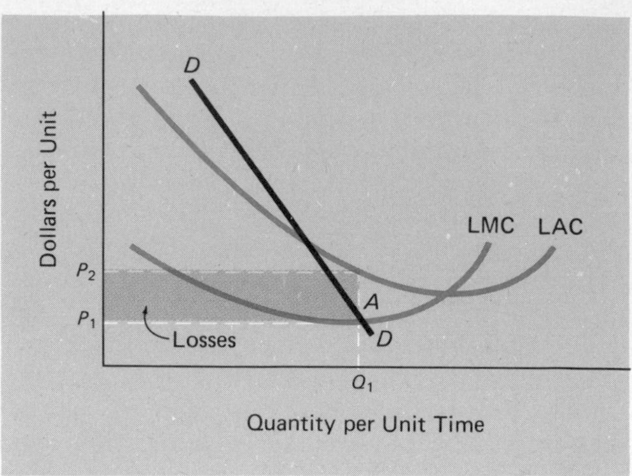

EXHIBIT 12–2(b)
Regulating Natural Monopolies—Marginal Cost Pricing. If the regulatory commission attempted to regulate natural monopolies so that a competitive situation would prevail, the commission would make the monopolist set production at the point where the marginal cost curve intersects the demand schedule, because the marginal cost schedule would be the competitive supply schedule. The quantity produced would be Q_1 and the price would be P_1. However, the average total costs at Q_1 are equal to P_2. Losses would ensue, equal to the shaded area. It would be self-defeating for a regulatory commission to force a natural monopolist to produce at a competitive solution without subsidizing some of its fixed costs, because losses would eventually drive the natural monopolist out of business.

What do we know about a monopolist's solution to the price-quantity question? When compared to a competitive situation, we know that consumers end up paying more for the product, and consequently they purchase less of it than they would purchase under competition. The monopoly solution is economically inefficient from society's point of view; the price charged for the product is higher than the opportunity cost to society, and consequently there is a misallocation of resources. That is, people are faced with a price that does not reflect the true marginal cost of producing the good because the true marginal cost is at the intersection *A*, not at price P_m. Look at panels (a) and (b) of Exhibit 10–9 in Chapter 10. Those figures demonstrate that if a competitive industry were suddenly monopolized, the output would be restricted and prices would be raised. Thus, in a monopoly situation, if we could somehow arrive at the price and quantity that would result from a competitive solution, prices would be lowered and the output would be increased. However, this will not occur with a natural monopoly, because costs are not similar to the competitive model.

REGULATING THE NATURAL MONOPOLIST

Let's assume that the government decides to make the natural monopolist produce as in a competitive situation. Where is that competitive solution in panel (b) of Exhibit 12–2? It is at the intersection of the marginal cost curve and the demand curve, or point *A*. Remember how we derived the competitive industry supply curve. We looked at all of the upward-sloping portions of actual and potential firms' marginal cost curves above their respective average variable costs. We then summed all of these portions of the firms' supply curves; that gave us the industry supply curve. Now the regulatory commission forces the natural monopolist to produce at quantity Q_1 and to sell the product at price P_1. How large will the monopolist's profits be? Profits, of course, are the positive difference between total revenues and total costs. In this case, total revenues equal P_1 times Q_1, and total costs equal average costs times the number of units produced. At Q_1, average cost is equal to P_2. Average costs are higher than the price that the regulatory commission forces our natural monopolist to charge. Profits turn out to be losses and are equal to the shaded area in panel (b) of Exhibit 12–2. Thus, regulation that forces a natural monopolist to produce and price as if it were in a competitive situation would also force that monopolist into negative profits, or losses. Obviously, the monopolist would rather go out of business than be subjected to such regulation, unless subsidized.

SUBSIDIZATION

How do we get out of such a dilemma? There are several possible answers. The first is to have the government force the natural monopolist to produce at the competitive price and then subsidize the monopolist. That is, the government could give the monopolist a subsidy that will allow the monopolist to break even (including a normal rate of return on investment). The subsidy per unit of output in this particular case would have to be equal to the difference between P_2 and P_1; it would have to match the natural monopolist's per unit losses. The government would have to pay the monopolist an amount $(P_2 - P_1)$ on every unit produced and sold to keep the monopolist producing. In practice such subsidization has rarely been used.

PRICE DISCRIMINATION

Another possible solution is to allow the monopolist to *price discriminate*. This means the monopolist could charge different prices to different customers who have different elasticities of demand for the product. The monopolist would charge a lower price to those who have very elastic demands and a higher price to those who have relatively less-elastic demands. Essentially, then, the demanders with relatively less-elastic curves would allow the monopolist to recover sufficient revenues to cover fixed costs. You might say that those with less-elastic demands would be subsidizing those with more elastic demands. (This would still be a misallocation of resources.)

As mentioned in previous chapters, any monopolist can earn higher profits if it can discriminate among the demanders of the product. Assume the monopolist is not discriminating but instead is charging everyone the same price. Now assume the monopolist begins to discriminate. First, the monopolist raises the price to less-elastic demanders and lowers the price to more elastic demanders. When the price to less-elastic demanders is raised, the total revenue received from them will rise because the fall in the quantity demanded is proportionately smaller than the increase in price. When the price to more elastic demanders is lowered, total revenues from them will rise also. The increase in the quantity demanded will be proportionately greater than the decrease in price. The monopolist therefore makes out in both areas, and total revenues rise. The telephone company, for example, price discriminates against businesses and in favor of residential customers. Essentially the same service costs more if a business wants it than if a household orders it.

Although allowing a natural monopolist to discriminate results in more production than would otherwise be the case, regulation in principle does not condone such discrimination. It is usually felt to be "unfair" if those with less-elastic demands are forced to pay more than those with more elastic demands; problems of equity arise. Many regulated utilities, however, do price discriminate. Electric utilities price discriminate, too, as does the U.S. Postal Service.

PRICE DISCRIMINATION IN THE SALE OF ELECTRICITY

It is usually true that industrial demand for electricity is more elastic than residential demand for electricity. After all, industrial concerns can, if the price becomes too high, generate their own electricity. Hence, a potential substitute called user-generated electricity exists. Residential consumers do not usually have this as a feasible option. Therefore, we find that residential rates are higher than industrial rates. It could be argued, of course, that the cost of servicing residents is higher than the cost of servicing industrial users, but the difference in cost does not seem to account for the entire difference in price. When prices to different people vary because of the different costs involved in servicing those people, the situation is called **price differentiation,** as opposed to price discrimination.

GRAPHIC ANALYSIS

Public utilities do use a form of price discrimination that they call **declining block pricing.** Look at Exhibit 12–3. If the electrical utility wanted to sell the quantity Q_3, it could do so by charging the same price of P_3 to everyone for each unit purchased. Its total revenues would be represented by the rectangle $0P_3CQ_3$. However, if it engages in declining block pricing or price discrimination, it might charge P_1 for the first Q_1 of kilowatts sold per month. It could charge P_2 for kilowatts sold between Q_1 and Q_2. And then finally it could charge P_3 for kilowatts sold between Q_2 and Q_3. The revenues it would receive would be the sum of the areas of the rectangles $0P_1AQ_1$ plus Q_1DBQ_2 plus Q_2ECQ_3, or $0P_1ADBECQ_3$. The sum of these three areas of the rectangles exceeds the area of the rectangle given by uniform pricing of P_3 times the quantity sold, Q_3.

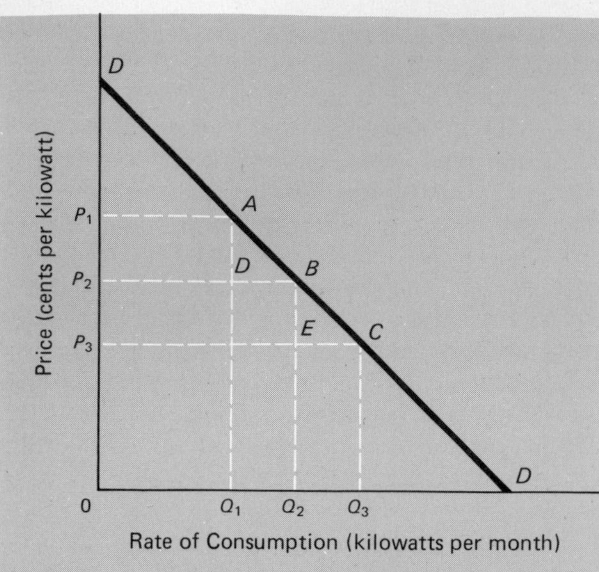

EXHIBIT 12–3
Declining Block Pricing. Public utilities often use declining block pricing in which separate "blocks" of electricity can be purchased at declining prices. If the electric utility charges a uniform price of P_3, its revenues will be $0P_3CQ_3$. If, however, it charges a price of P_1 for the first Q_1 kilowatts used, and then P_2 for the next "block" used up to quantity Q_2, and then price P_3 for the next "block" up to Q_3, its total revenues will equal $0P_1AQ_1 + Q_1DBQ_2 + Q_2ECQ_3 = 0P_1ADBECQ_3$.

Concepts in Brief 12-1

- A natural monopoly arises when the long-run average cost curve is downward sloping over a large range of outputs in relation to industry demand.
- The first firm to take advantage of the declining long-run average total cost can undercut all other sellers, forcing them out of business, thereby obtaining a natural monopoly.
- A natural monopolist allowed to profit maximize will set quantity where marginal revenue equals long-run marginal cost. Price is given from the demand curve for that quantity.
- If the natural monopolist is forced to set a price equal to long-run marginal cost, the natural monopolist will sustain losses. One way to compensate for the losses is to subsidize the natural monopolist.
- Another way for the natural monopolist to avoid losses is for it to be allowed to price discriminate.
- Price discrimination in the sale of electricity involves declining block pricing in which successive blocks of electricity are sold to buyers at lower and lower rates.

A Method of Regulating Monopolies

Since the government has decided to regulate the natural monopolies in our economy, it is faced with the problem of deciding how to regulate. There are many possible methods. We will discuss only one and then talk about the problems involved.

COST OF SERVICE

One way to regulate a monopoly is to keep a lid on prices—that is, to keep prices at the level that would prevail in a competitive situation. This is usually called **cost-of-service regulation.** The regulatory commission allows the regulated companies to charge only prices that are in accord with the actual *average* cost of providing the services to the customer. This was the standard practice for many years in the regulation of natural gas. Natural gas companies had to demonstrate exactly what their costs of service were, and it was on these costs that prices were based. It is not easy for any company, including regulated monopolies, to come up with an estimate of the costs involved for every service that they provide.

For example, there are certain costs that are common to several products or services sold by one business. We call these common costs joint costs of production. How does one allocate, or assign, **joint costs** to several products or services that may be sold? For example, the post office can put up a large building to handle incoming and outgoing mail. The post office sells various services: air mail, parcel post, first-, second-, third-, and fourth-class mail. All these different classes of mail service utilize in some way or another the services of the building that the post office constructed. How can the post office attribute, with precision, parts of the joint costs of the building to the various classes of services it provides? The answer is that it can't. The only way to allocate joint costs is to do so arbitrarily.

A reasonable expectation would be, therefore, that regulated monopolies that are forced to present costs of service in order to establish rate schedules would allocate more of the joint costs to services provided to less-elastic demanders. In other words, we would expect the regulated monopoly to attempt some form of price discrimination. If the monopoly is successful, quantity demanded would not be reduced very much and total revenues would rise.

CONTROLLING THE RATE OF RETURN ON INVESTMENT

Another method of regulation involves allowing the regulated companies to set prices that ensure a normal or competitive rate of return on the investment in the business—**rate-of-return regulation.** (The investment in the business is usually called its *equity.*) Assume that the rate of return on investing in a competitive industry with risks similar to those of the regulated monopoly is 12 percent per year. The regulatory agency will attempt to keep the rate of return on invested capital in the regulated monopoly also at 12 percent per year. Therefore, in requesting rate changes, the regulated monopoly must demonstrate to the regulatory commission that the proposed rate schedule will just allow investors in the company to obtain a 12 percent rate of return. To do this, the company has to establish what its costs are going to be. In many instances, the regulatory commissions will allow the company to base these on its costs in a historic test year. But some regulatory commissions will allow a company to predict what its costs will be in a future test year. In any event, the problem of allocating joint costs again arises, in addition to the problem of which costs should be included in the computations and which costs shouldn't. As you can imagine, the rate-making proceedings that are carried out before regulatory commissions are extremely complicated. One sometimes wonders if the regulators themselves even understand all the technical material presented to them.

It has also been pointed out by critics of regulation that when pecuniary, or money, profits are limited by regulation, unexploited monopoly profits may remain. How can the management take advantage of these unexploited profits? One way is to increase nonpecuniary gains. One can think of a thousand ways to do this. Managers can hire numerous secretaries, have lavish offices, do a lot of entertaining at the company's expense, work shorter hours, have innumerable underlings do every conceivable task for them, drive company cars that are large, roomy, and always new, and so on. In other words, regulated firms have less incentive to be efficient.

PROBLEMS WITH INFLATION

Regulation based on rate of return to investment will always run into problems in inflationary periods, particularly in cases where rate schedules are estimated on the basis of costs that occurred in a past year. If the costs of operating a regulated monopoly are rising along with all other prices in an inflationary economy, a rate schedule based on a previous year's costs will be insufficient in future years. That is, rates based on historic costs will turn out to yield a lower-than-normal rate of return in future years when costs will have risen. This has been particularly burdensome to the public utilities in the United States since 1965, when inflation began rising at rates that no one had been accustomed to. Until then, many regulated utilities had been asking for price *decreases* due to improved technology and economies of scale. After 1965, however, any increases in general productivity were swamped by the increases in costs due to the general inflation in the economy.

The utilities had to start asking for price increases. Regulatory commissions, which were used to granting price *decreases,* were against the idea of price *increases.* Many public utilities began to face serious capital problems by the beginning of the 1970s. They were faced not only with higher labor costs but with higher money capital costs and much higher fuel costs. Many of these companies had issued bonds in the past to get money for plant expansion at interest rates of 3 to 5 percent. Many of these bonds were coming due and had to be paid off. The utilities then had to replace them with bonds that cost 7 to 9 percent. Their money capital costs were therefore increasing along with their labor costs. The price of physical capital was going up, too. Expensive pollution equipment had to be added, also.

QUALITY OF SERVICE

A major problem with regulating monopolies concerns the quality of the service or product involved. Consider the many facets of telephone service: getting a dial tone, hearing other voices clearly, getting the operator to answer quickly, having out-of-order telephones repaired rapidly, putting through a long-distance call quickly and efficiently. The list goes on and on. But regulation of the telephone company usually deals with the prices charged for telephone service. Of course, regulators are concerned with the quality of service, but how can that be measured? Indeed, it cannot be measured very easily. Therefore, it is extremely difficult for any type of regulation to be successful in regulating the *price per constant-quality unit.* Certainly, it is possible to regulate the price per unit, but we don't really know that the quality remains unchanged when the price is not allowed to rise "enough." Thus, if regulation doesn't allow prices to rise, quality of service may be lowered, thereby raising the price per constant-quality unit.

LIMITS TO MONOPOLY POWER

We must not overestimate the monopoly power that an "obvious" monopolist has. Nothing has a completely inelastic demand schedule; rather, most things have substitutes in one form or another. For example, you can heat your house with gas, oil, electricity, or solar energy. You can cook with either gas or electricity. You can have a gas water heater or an electric water heater. And industrial users can generate their own electricity or avoid geographical areas with high electricity rates. There are perhaps fewer substitutes for telephone service, but there are still many: letters, person-to-person communication, and telegrams.

In some cases, a supposed natural monopoly is not a natural monopoly at all. The post office is a good example. There are numerous entrepreneurs just waiting for the legal opportunity to compete with the U.S. Postal Service. (We will analyze this topic in the Issues and Applications section of this chapter.)

Concepts in Brief 12-2

- There are basically two types of regulation: cost of service and rate of return.
- Cost-of-service regulation requires the allocation of joint costs over several products or services.
- Rate-of-return regulation requires deciding on the "appropriate" or permissible rate of return to the regulated monopoly.
- Even though it is possible to regulate the price of a particular good or service, it is difficult to regulate the quality; therefore, it is difficult to regulate the price per constant-quality unit.

The "New" Regulatory Analysis

Up to now, our discussion of regulation has been based on an underlying assumption, or premise—regulation is an attempt to prevent monopoly abuses, particularly in situations where a natural monopoly is in effect. Otherwise stated, regulation is, in principle, designed to create a competitive market structure when one would not otherwise occur. In either case, the "public good" is the underlying reason why economic regulation is supposed to occur.

The so-called new regulatory analysis of the last few years calls into question the effectiveness of regulation as a device to achieve efficiency. Increasing volumes of academic research have shown that the end result of regulation is different from the desired result. We have already been exposed to some of this evidence back in Chapter 10, where we showed that monopolylike price distortions were estimated to be higher in regulated industries than in manufacturing in general. The percentage increase in price over the competitive price ranged from a low of 16 percent for taxicabs to 62 percent for regulated motor carriers, up to 66 percent for airlines before deregulation. This evidence was compiled by economists and researchers who held a range of political philosophies that range from right to left. Thus, one cannot simply "write off" the "new" regulatory analysis as merely the outpouring of conservative economists who are basically anti-government.

THE CAPTURE THEORY

At the basis of the new regulatory analysis is the capture theory. This theory predicts that the regulated industry members themselves, sooner or later, are able to "capture" the regulatory bodies—the commissioners and their staff—who are supposed to be the ones making the decisions. Even if the regulated producers are not able to capture the regulatory commissioners, they are still, according to the new regulatory analysis, able to obtain legislative "favors." That is why, presumably, we find more monopolylike pricing distortions in regulated industries than in nonregulated industries.

THE CURRENT WAVE OF DEREGULATION

It is perhaps because of the tremendous amount of academic research that has been done, using the "new" regulatory analysis, that the current rage is for deregulation rather than for more regulation. It was therefore not so surprising that Dr. Alfred Kahn, respected economist and author of perhaps the leading reference volumes on regulatory economics, was able, almost singlehandedly, to deregulate the airline industry. Today, there are increased efforts at deregulating common motor carriers. And, certainly, in the communications field, AT&T and its subsidiary, Western Electric, have faced a massive amount of deregulation, which has impinged upon their monopoly position in the transmission of phone signals and in the manufacturing of phone equipment.

Whether the current rage of deregulation will continue is not yet clear. No full analysis of the effects of deregulation on consumer welfare will be completed for several years, but perhaps a majority of economists today seem to believe that economic regulation had, in the past, gone too far in the sense that it had become regulation to *prevent* competition, rather than to ensure it.

Antitrust Policy

It is the expressed aim of our government to foster competition in the economy. To this end, numerous attempts at legislating against business practices that seemingly destroy the competitive nature of the system have been made. This is the general idea behind antitrust legislation: If the courts can prevent collusion among sellers of a product, then monopoly prices will not result; there will be no restriction of output if the members of an industry are not allowed to join together in restraint of trade. Remember that the competitive solution to the price-quantity problem is one in which the price of the item produced is equal to its social opportunity cost. Also, no *economic* profits are made in the long run.

THE SHERMAN ACT

The first antitrust law in the United States was passed during the period of the greatest merger movement in American history. A large number of firms were monopolizing and merging with other firms. When a number of firms merged together, the business organizations were then called "trusts." A copper trust, a steel beam trust, an iron trust, a sugar trust, a coal trust, a paper bag trust, and the most famous of all, the Standard Oil trust, were formed. However, there was an increasing public outcry for legislation against these large trusts.

The Sherman Antitrust Act was passed in 1890. It was the first attempt by the federal government to control the growth of monopoly in the United States. The most important provisions of that act are:

Section 1: **Every contract, combination in the form of trust or otherwise, or conspiracy, in restraint of trade or commerce among the several states, or with foreign nations, is hereby declared to be illegal.**
Section 2: **Every person who shall monopolize, or attempt to monopolize, or combine or conspire with any other person or persons to monopolize any part of the trade or commerce . . . shall be guilty of a misdemeanor.**

Notice how vague this particular act really is. No definition is given for the terms *restraint of trade* or *monopolization.* Despite this vagueness, however, the act was used to prosecute the infamous Standard Oil trust of New Jersey. Standard Oil of New Jersey was charged with violations of Sections 1 and 2 of the Sherman Antitrust Act. This was in 1906, when Standard Oil controlled over 80 percent of the nation's oil-refining capacity. Among other things, Standard Oil was accused of both predatory price cutting to drive rivals out of business and of obtaining preferential price treatment from the railroads for transporting Standard Oil products, thus allowing Standard to sell at lower prices.

Standard Oil was convicted in a district court. The company then appealed to the Supreme Court, which ruled that Standard's control of and power over the oil market created "a *prima facie* presumption of intent and purpose to maintain dominancy . . . not as a result from normal methods of industrial development, but by means of combination." Here, the word *combination* meant taking over other businesses and obtaining preferential price treatment from railroads. The Supreme Court forced Standard Oil of New Jersey to break up into many smaller companies.

The ruling handed down in the Standard Oil case came about because the judges felt that Standard Oil had used "unreasonable" attempts at restraining trade. The court did not come out against monopoly per se. The fact that Standard Oil had a large share of the market did not seem to matter (it would today); rather, according to the Court, the problem was the way in which Standard acquired that large market share. In any event, antitrust legislation had been used to break up one of the largest trusts in United States business at that time.

THE CLAYTON ACT

The Sherman Act was so extremely vague that in 1914 a new law was passed to sharpen its antitrust provisions. This law was called the Clayton Act. It prohibited or limited a number of very specific business practices, which again were felt to be "unreasonable" attempts at restraining trade or commerce. Some of the more important sections of that act are listed here:

***Section 2:* [It is illegal to] discriminate in price between different purchasers [except in cases where the differences are due to differences in selling or transportation costs].**
***Section 3:* [Producers cannot sell] on the condition, agreement or understanding that the . . . purchaser thereof shall not use or deal in the goods . . . of a competitor or competitors of the seller.**
***Section 7:* [Corporations cannot hold stock in another company] where the effect . . . may be to substantially lessen competition.**

The activities mentioned in the Clayton Act above are not necessarily illegal. In the words of the law, they are illegal *only* when their effects "may be to substantially lessen competition or tend to create a monopoly." It takes the interpretation of the court to decide whether one of the activities mentioned actually has the effect of "substantially" lessening competition. On the other hand, there is an additional provision in the Clayton Act that represents a **per se violation**—one that is *always* illegal. This activity is interlocking directorates. It is illegal per se for the same individual to serve on two or more boards of directors of corporations that are competitive and have capital surplus and undivided profits in excess of $1 million. The existence of the interlock itself is enough to allow the government to prosecute.

THE FEDERAL TRADE COMMISSION ACT OF 1914

The Federal Trade Commission Act came about in order to prevent certain unfair competition. The act was designed to stipulate acceptable competitive behavior. In particular, it was supposed to prevent cutthroat pricing—that is, too aggressive competition, which would tend to eliminate too many competitors. One of the basic features of the act was the creation of the Federal Trade Commission (FTC). That commission is charged with the power to investigate unfair competitive practices. It can do so on its own or at the request of firms that feel they have been wronged. The commission can issue cease and desist orders where "unfair methods of competition in commerce" are discovered. In 1938, the Wheeler-Lea Act amended the 1914 Federal Trade Commission Act. The amendment expressly prohibits "unfair or deceptive acts or practices in commerce." Pursuant to that act, the FTC engages in what it sees as a battle against false or misleading advertising, as well as the misrepresentation of goods and services for sale in the marketplace.

THE ROBINSON-PATMAN ACT

In 1936, Section 2 of the Clayton Act was amended by the Robinson-Patman Act. The Robinson-Patman Act was aimed at preventing producers from driving out smaller competitors by means of selected discriminatory price cuts. The act has often been referred to as the "Chain Store Act" because it was meant to protect *independent* retailers and wholesalers from "unfair discrimination" by chain sellers.

The act was the natural outgrowth of increasing competition that independents faced when chain stores and mass distributors started to develop after World War I. The essential provisions of the act are as follows:

1. It was made illegal to pay brokerage fees unless there was an independent broker employed. Often chain stores would demand a brokerage fee as a form of discount when they purchased large quantities of their products directly from the manufacturer instead of going through a broker or wholesaler. Thus it was thought that the payment of a brokerage fee as a form of discount was a way that chain stores gained an unfair advantage over independents, who had to use a broker or wholesaler.
2. It was made illegal to offer concessions, such as discounts, free advertising, promotional allowances, and so on to one buyer of your product if you did not offer the same concessions to all buyers of your product. This provision was an attempt to stop large-scale buyers from obtaining special deals that would allow them to compete "unfairly" with small buyers.
3. Other forms of discrimination, such as quantity discounts, were also made illegal whenever they "substantially" lessened competition. Price discrimination as such was not made illegal if, in fact, price differences were due to differences in

costs or were "offered in good faith to meet an equally low price of a competitor."

4. It was made illegal to charge lower prices in one location than in another, or to sell at "unreasonably low prices" if such marketing techniques were designed to "destroy competition or eliminate a competitor." Thus, so-called predatory pricing was outlawed.

EXEMPTIONS TO THE ANTITRUST LAWS

There are numerous antitrust acts, many of which serve to exempt certain business practices from antitrust legislation. We will list a few here that have been prominent in the American industrial scene.

The Miller-Tydings Act and the McGuire Act

In 1937, the Miller-Tydings Act was passed as an amendment to Section 1 of the Sherman Act. The new act allowed individual states to permit so-called fair-trade agreements by which the manufacturer specified to all retailers a listed or fair-trade price below which they were prohibited from offering the product. Portions of this act were declared invalid by the Supreme Court in 1951. In 1952, Congress passed the McGuire Act, which restored those portions taken out by the Supreme Court the year before. In 1977, the McGuire Act was rescinded and resale price maintenance is, at least for the moment, no longer with us.

OTHER EXEMPTION LAWS

Other laws besides the Miller-Tydings Act and the McGuire Act exempt businesses from certain anticompetitive practices.

Small Businesses

Small businesses are allowed to engage in certain concerted activities without running afoul of the antitrust laws. This legislation started with the Small Business Act of 1953.

Oil Marketing

In 1935, the Interstate Oil Compact was passed. It allows states to determine quotas on oil that will be marketed in interstate commerce.

Foreign Trade

Under the provisions of the 1918 Webb-Pomerane Act, American exporters can engage in cooperative activity.

Labor and Agriculture

Labor and agricultural organizations are exempted from the Sherman Antitrust Act by Section 6 of the Clayton Act. Agriculture's exemption from antitrust legislation is further extended by the Capper-Volstead Act (passed in 1922), the Cooperative Marketing Act (passed in 1926), and certain provisions of the Robinson-Patman Act. Labor's exemption was strengthened by the Norris-LaGuardia Act of 1932.

The Court's View of Oligopoly

Go back and read Section 1 of the Sherman Act. Does it expressly prohibit oligopoly? No, it does not. With oligopoly, remember, there is no explicit contract or combination in restraint of trade. Of course, when there is explicit collusion, then violation of the law is clear. But otherwise, it is not clear at all.

OLIGOPOLY PRICING POLICIES

In an oligopoly in which a few sellers supply most of the sales, the pricing practices of the sellers in such markets have been called **conscious parallelism.** Such pricing policies are the result of the recognized interdependence of oligopolists. They know that there will be a reaction by the other oligopolists to a change in one's price. We discussed such reaction when we referred to the kinked demand curve. The result presumably is a tendency to avoid vigorous price competition. The question that has come before the courts is whether or not "conscious parallelism" that is a result of oligopolistic interdependence can properly be viewed as a form of agreement to fix prices in violation of Section 1 of the Sherman Antitrust Act. In a famous case argued before the Supreme Court, *Theater Enterprises* vs. *Paramount Film Distributing Corporation,* Supreme Court Justice Clark, speaking for the Court, noted:

> This court has never held that proof of parallel business behavior conclusively established agreement or, phrased differently, that such behavior itself constitutes a Sherman Act offense. Circumstantial evidence of consciously parallel behavior may have made heavy in-roads into the traditional judicial attitude toward conspiracy; but "conscious parallelism" has not yet read conspiracy out of the Sherman Act entirely.

In an important article, former Assistant U.S. Attorney General Donald F. Turner stated that oligopolistic pricing behavior is similar in nature to competitive pricing behavior. The difference is that rivals' responses have to be taken into account. Moreover, Turner pointed out that there is no effective remedy for oligopolistic interdependence. A court injunction that "prohibited each defendant from taking into account the probable price decisions of his competitors in determining his own price or output would demand such irrational behavior that full compliance would be virtually impossible." Turner went on further to point out that a court injunction would have to require that the defendants reduce price to marginal cost and that the enforcement of such a decree would involve the courts in public utility types of rate regulation for all oligopolists in the United States.

Turner therefore would not attempt to use the Sherman Act to prosecute oligopolists. Rather, he suggests as an appropriate remedy the breaking up of oligopolistic firms into smaller units either by special legislation or under Section 2 of the Sherman Act, which prohibits monopolization or attempts to monopolize. Turner thought it was appropriate to charge oligopolists with jointly monopolizing their markets.

Not all legal scholars agree with Turner's conclusions. Professor of Law Richard Posner, for example, points out that oligopoly (and monopoly) is a necessary condition of successful price fixing, but not a sufficient condition. He contends that there is no vital difference between formal cartels and tacit collusive agreements; the latter are simply easier to conceal. If Section 1 of the Sherman Act is to deter collusion by increasing the cost of colluding, then the tacit as well as the overt colluder should be, according to Posner, punished equally. Posner points out, however, that the most serious problem with his proposal—applying Section 1 against tacit collusion—is that of proving it.

The Enforcement of Antitrust Laws

The enforcement of antitrust laws has been rather uneven. Of course, there have been many spectacular cases brought and won by the government, such as the case against the electrical companies' conspiracy in the early 1960s. Use of the Sherman Act did allow the government to break up the Standard Oil trust, and the government also broke up the American Tobacco Company. Additionally, it can be argued that antitrust laws are effective in preventing the enforcement of collusive contracts. Hence, the existence of antitrust laws makes it hard to prevent cheating by cartel members. Governmental efforts to prevent problems of monopoly have been concentrated on preventing mergers. A merger occurs when two companies join together and become one legal entity. Today, large firms must first seek permission from the Justice Department before merging. The Justice Department will indicate whether it feels any antitrust laws would be violated if such mergers took place. Often, the Justice Department will deny the merger on the grounds that it will seriously lessen competition.

RECENT SUGGESTIONS FOR REDUCING ENFORCEMENT

It has been more than 90 years since the passage of the Sherman Antitrust Act. Surprisingly, some of the strongest supporters of an aggressive antitrust policy on the part of the U.S. government have recently come out in favor of reducing the amount of enforcement of antitrust laws. We are not talking about corporate executives, but, rather, about economists who have previously been staunch supporters of antimonopoly activities.

For example, Dr. Frederick M. Scherer of Northwestern University estimated a decade ago that gross national product would be as much as 6 percent higher if it had not been for so much monopoly in the economy. Scherer formerly was chief economist for the Federal Trade Commission. Now Scherer states that he would not place any credence on studies attempting to estimate the cost of monopoly in our economy, not even on his own 1971 estimate. Scherer now believes that economists have been ignoring for too long the benefit that could be obtained because of economies of scale. In other words, there is "some good to bigness in business."

Another example of a harsh critic of current antitrust activities is MIT economist Dr. Lester C. Thurow, known as one of the nation's leading liberal economists and certainly not one who could be accused of being a friend of business. Thurow is even urging that the government abandon almost its entire system of antitrust laws and enforcement mechanisms. He points out that the antitrust suit brought against International Business Machines Corporation (IBM) will require that it spend up to $1 billion fighting the lawsuit by the Justice Department. Says Thurow, "Such costs vastly exceed the benefits. Those dollars ought to be invested in production, not court cases."[1]

[1] *Business Week,* January 12, 1981, p. 92.

When to Prosecute?

Even if we accept the premise that monopolies should not be allowed, how can the government come up with a policy rule that will help determine which mergers should be stopped? How can the government decide which companies should be broken up into several companies? How can it know which business practices actually restrain trade? There have been numerous attempts by government officials and by interested academicians to derive specific policy rules. One of the most commonly mentioned rules states that the *concentration ratio* in a particular industry should not become too large. But does monopolization of the industry start when the four-firm concentration ratio becomes 50 percent, 60 percent, 70 percent, or 80 percent? Positive economic analysis cannot give us the answer.

ASSESSING WORLDWIDE CONCENTRATION

Furthermore, we must be concerned about which concentration ratio to look at. If we have a relatively open economy in which foreign products are allowed to compete with domestically produced products, then is a concentration ratio for domestic sales the right number to look at? For example, General Motors accounts for 64 percent of U.S. domestic auto production. It only accounts for about 45 percent of total sales because of foreign competition. Indeed, if we look at an index of concentration of *world* production in a number of commodities, we find that concentration has been declining since the 1950s. Look at Exhibit 12–4. Here we show an index of concentration of world production in several important commodities. In all cases, the index is falling. This has resulted from the entry of new

EXHIBIT 12–4
Declining Worldwide Concentration. In these six diagrams, we show the decline in worldwide concentration in the production of six different commodities—autos, aluminum, petroleum, pulp and paper, lead, and copper. We use an index of worldwide production developed by the Harvard Multinational Enterprise Project. For each commodity, the index is constructed in the same way and therefore the important fact is that the index of worldwide concentration is declining over the period 1950 to 1975.

Source: Harvard Multinational Enterprise Project.

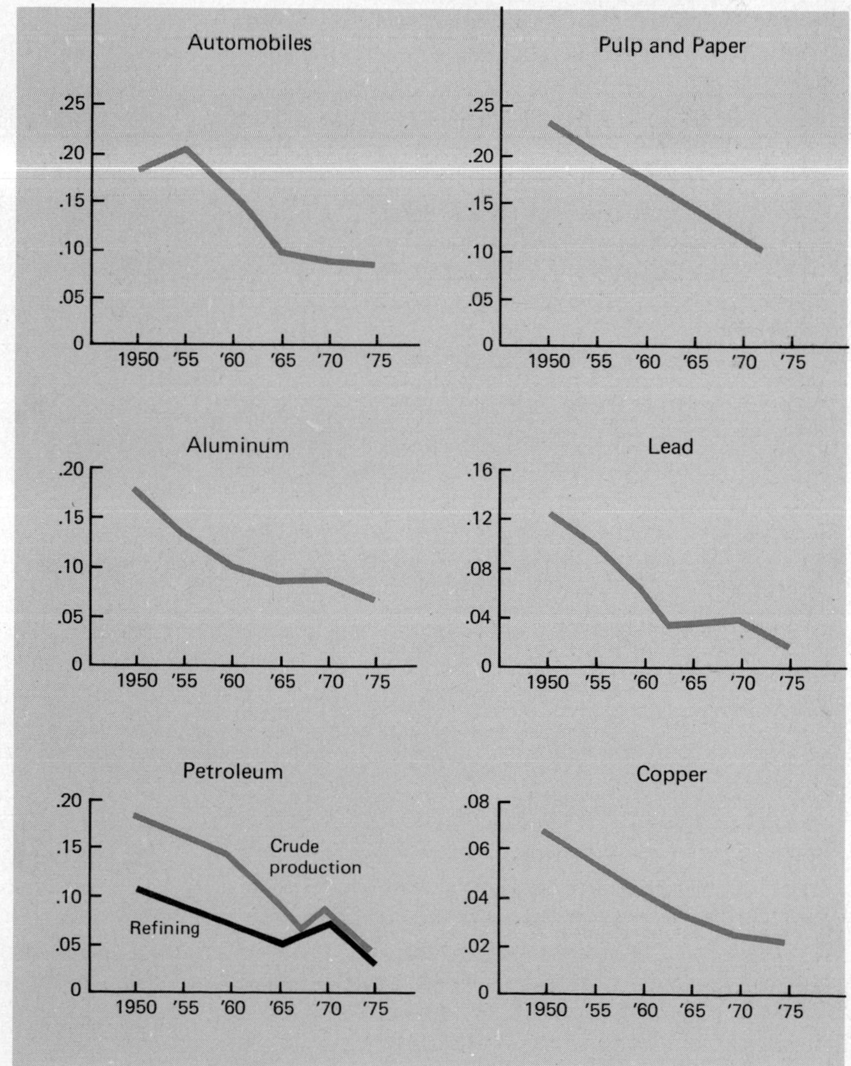

multinational and other companies into the markets concerned and, hence, a fall in the share of world output accounted for by the largest two or three firms.

Another way to assess the degree of a firm's monopoly power may be to look at its profits. If the profits are higher than the "normal" rate of return elsewhere, then that company may be making monopoly returns. (On the other hand, it may just be more efficient.) However, it is difficult to find out what those profits really represent. They are accounting profits and therefore do not include a return on invested capital adjusted for risk and inflation. Also, the empirical findings on profits are usually for very short periods of time and may not demonstrate that the industry is tending toward a zero economic profit. Suffice it to say that it is difficult to establish any readily observable statistical procedures for determining when antitrust enforcement should be attempted.

There is also a problem involved with attempting new legislation to increase competition in our economy. Even if the legislation is exactly what it should be for bettering our competitive system, by the time it goes through the legislative mill, it will be vastly different. Moreover, legislation that calls for increased enforcement of antitrust laws leads to increased costs on the part of government and the firms involved. Some maintain that only when we are fully convinced that the costs will be outweighed by the benefits should we proceed with our antitrust action.

Concepts in Brief 12-3

- The first national antitrust law was the Sherman Antitrust Act passed in 1890, which made illegal every contract and combination in the form of a trust in restraint of trade.
- The Clayton Act makes price discrimination and interlocking directorates illegal.
- The Federal Trade Commission Act of 1914 established the Federal Trade Commission. The Wheeler-Lea Act of 1938 amended the 1914 act to prohibit "unfair or deceptive acts or practices in commerce."
- The Robinson-Patman Act of 1936 was aimed at preventing large producers from driving out small competitors by means of selective discriminatory price cuts.
- There are numerous exemptions to the antitrust laws, including those for small businesses, oil marketing, and foreign trade, as well as for labor and agricultural organizations. These exemptions foster monopolization.
- The courts have taken a nebulous view of oligopoly. Oligopolies per se are not in violation of basic antitrust laws. Explicit collusive agreements in restraint of trade are illegal.

ISSUES AND APPLICATIONS

Antitrust Actions: The Case of a "Shared" Monopoly

Concepts Applied

- Antitrust law, monopoly power, concentration, normal rate of return to investment

Back in 1972 the staff of the Federal Trade Commission decided that breakfast cereal companies "shared" a monopoly. By 1981 the lawsuit against Kellogg, General Mills, and General Foods was still not settled. The FTC wanted those three companies to give away the use of their brand names.

The Breakfast Cereal Industry

The breakfast cereal industry is highly concentrated. Kellogg, at the beginning of this decade, has 42 percent of the market. The rest of the market is taken up by three other companies. Thus, by any measure of concentration, the industry does not appear competitive.

The breakfast cereal industry is supposedly an example of a 'shared' monopoly. A few large companies dominate the market.

Unfair methods of competition. The FTC has charged the industry with unfair methods of competition. The methods referred to involve the steady proliferation of new cereal brands as each major producer attempts to capture a share of the market. According to the staff of the FTC, this is simply a plan by major producers to corner scarce space on supermarket shelves.

Looking at profits. Assume for a moment that the FTC staff is correct in its charges against Kellogg and other companies. The end result presumably would be a higher-than-normal rate of return for those companies involved. Only Kellogg has what might be termed an enviable profit record. The other companies have earned profits, through the years, that are normal, or competitive. Therefore, if the FTC were effective in eliminating Kellogg's exclusive use of trademarks, the result to the consumer might only be one or two cents less per box of Rice Krispies, Fruit Loops, and Sugar Pops. On the other hand, Kellogg management contends that if Kellogg's geographically scattered manufacturing facilities were divided among several firms, the distance the average box of cereal would travel to market would rise sharply. This higher distribution cost to society would more than offset, according to Kellogg, any benefits to society in Kellogg's profit reduction.

Monopoly in Theory and Monopoly in Practice

The above case illustrates the difficulty of deciding which cases to prosecute. A monopoly in theory may turn out to be in practice one that does not yield a higher-than-normal rate of return to investment. If that is the case, the antitrust division of the Justice Department and the FTC may not greatly benefit consumers by attacking "monopolies." Critics of antitrust actions believe that more emphasis should be brought to bear on those monopoly situations that truly do raise prices to the consumer. Apparently, the shared monopoly of Kellogg et al. is not one such case.

Questions

1. If the top-selling breakfast cereal companies were exercising monopoly power, would you expect their rate of return to investment to be relatively high or low?
2. Is there such a thing as a "good" monopoly that should be exempt from antitrust laws?

Is the Post Office a Natural Monopoly?

> ***Concepts Applied***
> ■ Natural monopoly, economies of scale, competition, economic profits, and price discrimination

First-class mail service in the United States has been a government monopoly for more than 180 years. This monopoly has been partially in force by not allowing use of homeowners' mail boxes for any use other than the delivery of mail by U.S. Postal Service employees.

Recently, the U.S. Postal Service has come under fire. Competitors have attempted to take away the postal monopoly. Although the arguments both for and against the continued monopoly are varied and complex, the major points are actually relatively simple and fit well into the theoretical analysis presented in this chapter. What is at issue is the question of whether or not the mail service is a natural monopoly, which is a question of whether economies of scale actually exist.

The Natural Monopoly Argument

We defined a natural monopoly as a monopoly that arises from the existence of economies of scale, which is basically a long-run concept. The notion is that as output is expanded, long-run average total costs will continuously fall over a very wide range of outputs. Thus, the firm that expands output most rapidly will find its long-run average total costs falling most rapidly and will be able to undersell every other firm in the market and become the only profitable firm in the industry. This firm is the natural monopolist. The question is, Does the post office have a downward-sloping long-run average total cost curve over a large range of outputs, and (which is essentially the same thing) does the U.S. Postal Service experience large economies of scale?

The empirical evidence on the existence of economies of scale in the post office is indeed scanty. The President's Commission on Postal Organization accepted as "apparent" the existence of economies of scale and the waste that would result from competition in postal services. The academic studies that have been done, however, show either no evidence at all of economies of scale or only slight, statistically insignificant evidence.[2]

Furthermore, the actual technology of postal operations depends mostly on human beings, not machines. Eighty to 85 percent of all postal costs are still labor related, in spite of the post office's well-publicized attempts at mechanization. It is difficult to imagine such a labor-intensive industry exhibiting large economies of scale.

If we look at the evidence in terms of the possible profitability of competitors for the post office, we find that rather small companies can be formed and can compete—where they are allowed by law. This is another suggestion that economies of scale do not exist in the post office.

But let us look at the question from another point of view. Let us assume that the post office is indeed a natural monopoly. If it is, then is there any necessity for the U.S. Postal Service to hide under the law that gives it a monopoly? If the natural monopoly exists, laws aren't needed to uphold it; it will occur by its own force. Given that the U.S. Postal Service is already in existence, already has buildings and trucks and other capital equipment, it would seem that if indeed postal delivery is a natural monopoly, then the U.S. Postal Service would remain the monopolist, even without the law prohibiting competition for letter carrying.

Cream Skimming

The second argument in favor of government monopoly is based on the assertion that competition cannot be allowed because the most lucrative routes would be taken over by competitors, leaving the U.S. Postal Service with the crumbs. This is known as a **cream skimming** situation. Competitors will come in and skim off the cream. In a competitive situation, there is generally no cream to skim from a market. In fact, that is the whole basis of zero economic profits existing in a long-run competitive industry. As soon as economic profits exist, competitors enter the industry, depress price, and skim that cream away, leaving zero economic profits in the long run.

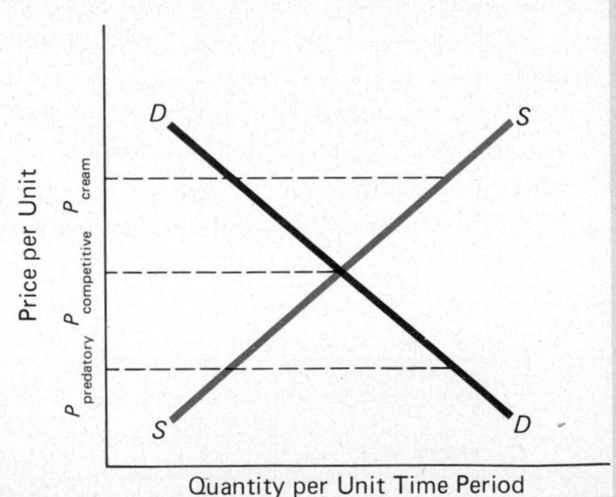

EXHIBIT 12–5
Skimming the Cream. Competitive price is given at $P_{competitive}$. If, however, price is set at P_{cream}, monopoly profits are being made. It is only in the case when monopoly profits are being made that there is any cream to skim off. The post office asserts that competitors would come in and set $P_{predatory}$, driving the post office out of business. However, it is more likely that the price would fall from P_{cream} to $P_{competitive}$, thus eliminating any monopoly profits.

[2] See, for example, Morton S. Baratz, *The Economics of the Postal Service* (Washington, D.C.: Public Affairs Press, 1962).

The only way for the U.S. Postal Service to contend that competitors would skim off the cream is for the cream to actually still exist. And it can exist only in a monopoly situation. We show the argument graphically in Exhibit 12–5.

Positive economic profits exist at a price of P_{cream} because that price is not above the competitive equilibrium price where the market supply curve intersects the market demand curve. If the U.S. Postal Service faced competition, competitors would come in and eventually force the price down from P_{cream} to $P_{competitive}$. The U.S. Postal Service no longer would be able to have any cream.

Price discrimination. Cream exists in the U.S. Postal Service because price discrimination has been utilized for many years. First-class mail has been charged a price that exceeds its cost. The extra revenues have been applied to subsidizing other services such as second-class mail, which consists mainly of magazines and periodicals. Moreover, there has been an implicit subsidy to certain types of mail service—in particular, mail service to rural customers who live in out-of-the-way places.

For many years, then, one class of mail users has been subsidizing other classes of mail users. Indeed, it would be true that if the U.S. Postal Service were no longer a legal monopolist in the carrying of first-class mail, it would no longer be able to obtain the additional revenues to subsidize second-class mail users and rural areas. It would be forced either to obtain a larger subsidy from the U.S. Treasury or to raise the rates on other classes of mail service.

Cream skimming already exists. To some extent, the exemptions to the Private Express Statutes have already allowed competitors to skim some of the cream from the postal system. In particular, by the early 1970s, the U.S. Postal Service faced major competition in the delivery of parcels, the home delivery of advertising material, and the delivery of bills by the companies sending them.

The most well known and perhaps the most successful competitor in the parcel area of postal service is United Parcel Service, or UPS. By 1974, UPS was already delivering more parcels than the U.S. Postal Service. Moreover, it was delivering them faster and with fewer "accidents." The U.S. Postal Service has constantly referred to UPS's activities as "cream skimming."[3]

For third-class mail—the home delivery of unaddressed advertising circulars—there are at least a dozen private mail delivery companies competing with the post office. Such names as American Postal System, Independent Postal Service of America, Private Postal Systems of America, and Rocket Manager Services are seen more and more throughout the country. By the beginning of the 1970s, the Independent Postal Service of America already had 53 offices in 19 states and one in Canada, almost 20,000 employees, and the ability to deliver materials to over 7 million homes.

Also, many companies are finding it cheaper to have their own employees deliver such things as bills to their customers. A number of large electric utilities, such as Virginia Electric and Power Company, found that it cost less to do it this way than to use the U.S. Postal Service.

What the Future Might Hold

What would happen if the U.S. Postal Service did lose its legal monopoly? For one thing, we would immediately have more cream skimming. Private competitors would enter the most lucrative postal service markets, those mainly involving first-class mail, which, as we mentioned, is now overpriced to allow the U.S. Postal Service to subsidize other classes of users. The U.S. Postal Service would have to do one of two things: (1) improve its efficiency—that is, lower costs—to such an extent that it could profitably compete with the private companies, or (2) raise its prices on all classes of service to reflect their true costs. Ultimately, we will probably see a rise in rural delivery rates and delivery rates for magazines and newspapers. This rise in rates, however, presupposes that the U.S. Postal Service will not be able to improve greatly its efficiency. This is not a foregone conclusion. If the U.S. Postal Service were in competition with many private companies, it might be forced to become as efficient as those competitors seem to be already.

We would also find out if the post office is

[3]See, for example, *Business Week,* July 18, 1970, p. 94.

indeed a natural monopoly. If it is, then it would be the only firm extant for certain types of mail services. Competitors would come and go because they could not compete with the natural monopolist.

Questions

1. Under what circumstances would you believe that delivering mail would involve economies of scale? (Hint: Consider capital costs.)
2. Why would a natural monopolist ever need to erect barriers to entry?

Definition of Terms

Natural monopoly A monopoly that arises from the peculiar production characteristics in the industry. Usually a natural monopoly arises when production of the service or product requires extremely large capital investments such that only one firm can profitably be supported by consumers. A natural monopoly arises when there are large economies of scale relative to the industry demand, and one firm can produce at a lower cost than can be achieved by multiple firms.

Price differentiation Differences in price that depend on differences in cost, as distinct from price discrimination, which is not a function of costs but rather a function of relative elasticities of demand.

Declining block pricing A system of price discrimination in which consumers are charged different prices per unit of electricity for each "block" of electricity that they buy. The per unit price for the first block is higher than the per unit price for the second block, which is higher than the per unit price for the third block.

Cost-of-service regulation A type of regulation based on allowing prices that reflect only the actual costs of production and do not include monopoly profits.

Joint costs Costs that are common to several of a firm's products. The post office, for example, could be using the same building to service first-, second-, third-, and fourth-class mail. It is difficult to allocate joint costs to the various separate services or products that use them.

Rate-of-return regulation Regulation that seeks to keep the rate of return in the industry at a competitive level by not allowing excessive prices to be charged.

Per se violation An activity that is specifically spelled out as a violation of the law. In antitrust law, whether or not competition is lessened does not have to be proven. A violation based on the facts only and not on the effects, which are taken as given.

Conscious parallelism Pricing behavior by oligopolists in which each presumably takes account of the other's potential reaction and therefore does not engage in vigorous price competition. No explicit collusive agreement is entered into, however.

Cream skimming Competing for the most profitable submarkets in a particular industry.

Chapter Summary

1. Traditionally, there have been two ways of regulating monopolies. One way is the actual regulation by some commission; the other way is by antitrust laws.
2. Regulation usually involves a natural monopoly that arises when, for example, the average total cost curve falls over a very large range of production rates. In such a situation, only one firm can survive. It will be the firm that can expand production and sales faster than the others to take advantage of the falling average total costs.
3. If regulation seeks to force the natural monopolist to produce at the point where the marginal cost curve (supply curve in the competitive case) intersects the demand curve, the natural monopolist will incur losses because when average total costs are falling, marginal costs are below average total costs. The regulators are faced with a dilemma. They can get out of this dilemma by (a) subsidizing the natural monopolist, or (b) allowing the regulators to price discriminate to prevent losses.
4. There are several ways of regulating monopolies, the most common ones being on a cost-of-service

basis or a rate-of-return basis. With a cost-of-service regulation, the regulated monopolies are allowed to charge prices that reflect only reasonable costs. With a rate-of-return regulation, the regulated monopolies are allowed to set rates so as to make a competitive rate of return for the equity shareholders. Supposedly, no monopoly profits can therefore be earned.

5. In any type of regulatory procedure, there is always a problem of keeping the quality of the product constant. If a price is regulated, it may be possible for the regulated monopoly to lower the quality of its product in order to raise effectively the price above that which the regulators desire to maintain.
6. Antitrust legislation is designed to obviate the need for regulation. The major antitrust acts are the Sherman, the Clayton, and the Robinson-Patman acts.
7. Although the legislation against monopolies may, in fact, be comprehensive, the enforcement of this legislation has been extremely erratic in the history of antitrust activities.
8. It has been suggested that the post office is a natural monopoly. If so, it does not need legislation that prevents competition with it.

Selected References

Bork, Robert H. *The Antitrust Paradox*. New York: Basic Books, 1978.

Kahn, Alfred E. *The Economics of Regulation,* Vols. 1 and 2. New York: Wiley, 1971.

MacAvoy, Paul W. *Regulated Industries and the Economy.* New York: Norton, 1979.

Needham, Douglas. *The Economics of Industrial Structure, Conduct and Performance.* New York: St. Martin's Press, 1978.

———. *Regulation: A Broader Perspective.* Cambridge, Mass.: Winthrop, 1981.

Shepherd, William G., ed. *Public Policies Toward Business.* Rev. ed. Homewood, Ill.: Irwin, 1979.

Stelzer, Irwin M. *Selected Antitrust Cases.* 5th ed. Homewood, Ill.: Irwin, 1976.

Weidenbaum, Murray. *Business, Government, and the Public.* 2nd ed. Englewood Cliffs, N.J.: Prentice-Hall, 1981.

Answers to Preview and Study Questions

1. What is a natural monopoly, and how could one arise?

A natural monopoly is a situation in which the long-run average cost curve falls persistently, as output expands. Thus, the natural monopolist is that firm which by expanding is able to charge a price lower than its competitors can—thereby eliminating them. A natural monopolist then aggressively expands firm size, and the resulting lower ATC allows it to drive out competitors by pricing below *their* costs. A natural monopolist arises due to tremendous economies of scale; by expanding output, ATC falls.

2. If natural monopolies are required to price at marginal cost, what problem emerges?

We have already noted, in previous chapters, that efficiency requires that people pay the marginal cost for a good or service. If regulators grant a firm monopoly privileges (recognizing it as a natural monopoly, and regulating it to "keep it in line") but force it to price at its marginal cost of production, a problem emerges. Since long-run ATC is persistently falling, it follows that long-run marginal cost must be below long-run ATC. Thus, forcing a firm to charge a price equal to marginal cost implies that average revenue = price = marginal cost < average total cost; in symbols $AR = P = MC < ATC$. It follows that $AR < ATC$ and, therefore, the regulated natural monopolist would experience *negative* economic profits. In that case it would shut down—unless subsidized. In short, forcing a regulated natural monopolist to price at marginal cost may be socially beneficial, but such a policy requires that the natural monopolist be subsidized to cover the resulting economic losses to the firm.

3. What are some means to regulate a natural monopoly?

Two important means of regulating a natural monopoly are (a) cost of service and (b) rate of return. We discuss each in turn. The cost-of-service regulation aims at requiring a natural monopolist to price at levels which would result from a more competitive situation. In effect, the natural monopolist is required to charge the average cost of providing the service in question—thereby assuring zero economic profits. The problem with this situation is that some costs are common to *several* products or services provided by the natural monopolist. Thus, the problem of assigning joint costs to several products or services arises; any assignment is bound to be arbitrary, thereby making the rule of charging the average cost difficult to interpret. The rate-of-return form of regulation, in effect, allows a natural monopolist to price at rates which permit it an *overall* "normal" rate of return. Since the natural monopolist will only remain in operation while it earns at least a normal return, this is a sensible idea. Yet, it is not without problems. The natural monopolist (and its managers) has an incentive to convert profits into "costs" via the accounting process. Thus, abnormal profits can *appear* to be normal if the cost base includes lavish buildings and offices, an overstaffed bureaucracy, extraordinary perquisites for management and employees, and many other such ruses. Thus a *given* amount of dollar profits yields a lower rate of return if expenses and overhead are overstated. Such practices are difficult to detect and eliminate. Also, rate-of-return regulation causes problems during periods of inflation, since such periods tend to overstate profits when fixed costs are valued at historic levels. The monopolist may appear to be earning normal profits, but *inflation-adjusted* profits may be subnormal. At such times the monopolist would be tempted to lower quality, thereby in reality raising price per constant-quantity units.

4. In recent years many economists have been re-evaluating the government's role as an economic regulator. Why?

Presumably, regulation is an attempt to prevent monopoly abuses and to simulate a competitive market structure where one would not otherwise exist. Yet, much academic research indicates that this is not the case; regulated industries apparently behave more like monopolies than does the overall manufacturing sector. Some have claimed that the regulated firms sooner or later "capture" the regulatory agencies; before long, regulated industries have the protection and sanction of the regulatory bodies! More and more economists are favoring deregulation—at least of the *older* variety, such as in the airline, common motor carrier, and communications industries. There seems to be less of a consensus favoring less regulation by the *newer* agencies such as the Environmental Protection Agency (EPA) and the Occupational Safety and Health Administration (OSHA).

5. What industries are exempted from antitrust laws?

Regulating natural monopolies is only one way of attempting to make U.S. industry simulate a more competitive model. Antitrust laws, which are legislative weapons against business practices that destroy competition, have also been put into effect in the United States. Such laws aim to prevent collusion among sellers in order to prevent them from fixing prices, or otherwise restraining trade or commerce. Yet, for one reason or another, certain exemptions from U.S. antitrust laws exist or have existed. The main exemptions have included: (a) manufacturers who are allowed to specify *minimum* prices charged by retailers via fair-trade laws; (b) labor unions, which are not subjected to laws restraining trade; (c) agricultural organizations; (d) small businesses; (e) state oil agencies, which are permitted to set quotas on oil marketed in interstate commerce; and (f) foreign exporters, who are permitted to cooperate overtly.

Problems

(Answers at the back of the book)

1. The graph at right depicts a situation for a natural monopolist.
   a. If this monopolist were required to price at marginal cost, what would the quantity and price be equal to?
   b. What rectangle would indicate total economic losses if this monopolist were required to price at marginal cost?

2. If a public electric utility used a declining block-pricing policy,
   a. Which group will pay higher prices per unit, small or large users?
   b. Which group, households or large businesses, is likely to purchase larger quantities of electricity?
   c. Which group is likely to have a higher elasticity of demand, households or large businesses.
   d. Does declining block-pricing policy in the public utility industry meet the requirements for price discrimination?

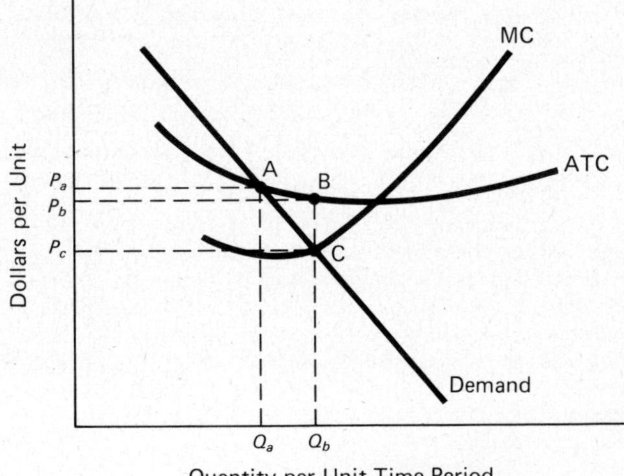

PART

III

DERIVED DEMAND, INCOME DISTRIBUTION, AND GENERAL EQUILIBRIUM

For 3d test: ch 13, 14, 15, 16, 18 +19

13

Resource Demand and Supply: The Case of Labor

TOPICS FOR REVIEW

The topics listed below, which we have already analyzed, are applied in this chapter. You may find it worthwhile to review them. For your convenience each topic is followed by the number identifying the specific "Concepts in Brief."

a. Determinants of elasticity (6–4)

b. Law of diminishing returns (8–2)

c. Profit maximization (9–1)

d. Monopolist's demand, marginal revenue less than price (10–2)

FOR PREVIEW AND STUDY

1. In hiring labor, what general rule will be followed by employers who wish to maximize profits?
2. What is the profit-maximizing rate of employment for a perfectly competitive firm?
3. What is the profit-maximizing rate of employment for an imperfectly competitive firm?
4. What is the shape of the supply of labor curve?
5. How is an industry wage rate determined?

When a firm decides to fire an employee, the employee usually suffers. The costs of unemployment are not insignificant in our economy. Conversely, when employers decide to hire new workers, the workers feel they are better off; otherwise, they probably would not have accepted the job. If employers are willing to pay higher wages to workers already employed, those workers are also obviously better off. If employers can get away with paying very low wages, then perhaps the employers will be better off, making higher profits. How much people are paid and the extent to which their labor resources are used are crucial issues in economics because they determine who is rich and who is poor. These factors determine what percentage of national income goes to wages and what percentage goes to interest, profits, and dividends.

Before analyzing the distribution of income, we first will develop a model that predicts the amount of a particular input that firms will demand and the price they will pay for it. In our discussion, we will consider only one variable factor of production: labor. We will assume that all other factors of production are fixed; in other words, the firm has a fixed number of machines but can hire or fire workers.

A firm's demand for inputs can be studied in much the same manner as we studied the demand for output in different types of market situations. Again, different types of market situations will be examined. Our analysis will always end with the same conclusion: A firm will hire employees up to the point where it isn't profitable to hire any more. It will hire employees to the point where the marginal benefit of hiring a worker will just equal the marginal cost. Basically, in every profit-maximizing situation, it is most profitable to carry out an activity up to the point where the marginal benefit equals the marginal cost. Remembering that guideline will help you in analyzing decision making at the firm level. We will start our analysis under the assumption that the market for input factors is perfectly competitive. We will further assume that the output market is perfectly competitive, also. This provides a benchmark against which to compare other situations where labor markets and/or product markets are not perfectly competitive.

A Competitive Market

Let's take as our example a prerecorded tape manufacturing firm that is in competition with many companies selling the same kind of product. Assume that the laborers hired by our tape manufacturing firm do not need any special skills. This firm sells its product in a perfectly competitive market and also buys its variable input—labor—in a perfectly competitive market. The firm can influence neither the price of its product nor the price that it must pay for its variable input; it can purchase all the labor it wants at the going market wage without affecting that wage. The "going" wage is established by the forces of supply and demand in the labor market. The total labor demand is the sum of all the individual firms' demands.

Marginal Physical Product

Look at panel (a) of Exhibit 13–1. In column 1, we show the number of worker-weeks that the firm can hire. In column 2, we show total physical product, or TPP, per week. In other words, column 2 shows the total *physical* production that different quantities of the labor input will generate in a week's time. In column 3, we show the additional output gained when a prerecorded tape manufacturing company adds additional workers to its existing manufacturing facility. You will notice that the third column, **marginal physical product (MPP),** represents the extra (additional) output attributed to employing additional units of the variable input factor, which in this case is labor. Thus, if this firm adds a seventh worker, the marginal physical product is 118. You will recall that the law of diminishing marginal returns predicts that additional units of a variable factor will, after some point, cause the marginal physical product to decline.

WHY DOES MARGINAL PHYSICAL PRODUCT DECLINE?

We are assuming that everything else is held constant. So if our tape manufacturing firm wants to add one more worker to an assembly line, it has to crowd all the existing workers a little closer together because it does not increase its capital stock (the assembly line equipment) at the same time that it increases the work force. Therefore, as we add more workers, each one has a smaller and smaller fraction of the available capital stock with which to work. If one worker uses one machine, adding another worker usually won't double the output, because the machine can run only so fast and for so many hours per day.

EXHIBIT 13–1(a)

The Value of Marginal Physical Product. In the first column is the number of workers. In the second column is Total Physical Product (≡TPP). The change in total physical product is given in column 3 and labeled Marginal Physical Product. When we add one worker to an already existing work force of eight workers, the marginal physical product falls from 111 tapes per week to 104 tapes per week. We find in the fourth column the value of the marginal physical product of each worker. We multiply the marginal physical product times the commodity price, which in our example is $3 per tape. Here we assume that the wage rate is $249 per week. In such a situation, the profit-maximizing employer will pay for only 12 worker-weeks, because then the value of marginal physical product is just equal to the wage rate or weekly salary.

(1) *Labor Input*	*(2)* *Total Physical Product (per week) ≡ TPP*	*(3)* *Marginal Physical Product ≡ MPP*	*(4)* *Price of Tape (P = $3) × Marginal Physical Product ≡ VMP ($ per additional worker)*	*(5)* *Wage Rate ($ per week) Marginal Factor Cost ≡ MFC ≡ change in total costs / change in labor*
6	882			
		118	354	249
7	1000			
		111	333	249
8	1111			
		104	312	249
9	1215			
		97	291	249
10	1312			
		90	270	249
11	1402			
		83	249	249
12	1485			
		76	228	249
13	1561			

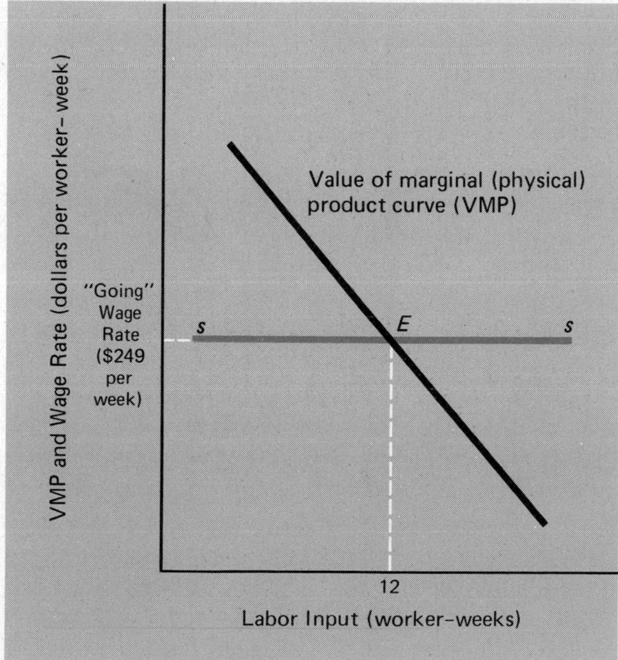

EXHIBIT 13–1(b)

Value of Marginal Physical Product Curve. Here we have plotted the value of marginal physical product curve from panel (a). On the horizontal axis is the number of workers hired. On the vertical axis is the value of marginal physical product and the wage rate ($249 per week in this figure). We find how many workers the firm will want to hire by observing the wage rate that is established by the forces of supply and demand in the entire labor market. The employer in a competitive situation takes this wage rate as given by the horizontal supply curve and hires workers up to the point where the value of marginal physical product equals the wage rate. In our case, it is 12 worker-weeks. We show that this employer is hiring labor in a perfectly competitive labor market and therefore faces a horizontal supply curve represented by *ss* at $249 per week. As in all other situations, we basically have a supply and demand model; in this example the demand curve is represented by VMP, and the supply curve is *ss*. Equilibrium occurs at their intersection.

All Workers Paid Same Wage

What additional information do we need to determine the number of workers to be employed? Since we have assumed that labor is employed in a competitive market, then every worker we employ is paid the same wage rate. Panel (b) of Exhibit 13–1 assumes that the wage rate is $249 per worker-week.

In addition, we need to know the price of the product. Since we have assumed pure competition, the hypothetical market equilibrium price established in Exhibit 13–1 is $3.[1] Our firm will employ workers up to the point where the marginal revenue, or benefit, of hiring a worker will equal the additional (marginal) cost.

The marginal cost of workers is the extra cost we incur in employing that factor of production. We call that cost the **marginal factor cost (MFC).** Otherwise stated,

$$\textbf{marginal factor cost} = \frac{\textbf{change in total cost}}{\textbf{change in amount of resource used}}$$

Marginal factor cost is relatively easy to determine when purchasing a resource in a competitive input market. In our example of labor, one additional worker can be hired at a constant cost of $249 per week, as shown in panel (b) of Exhibit 13–1.

VALUE OF MARGINAL PRODUCT

We now need to translate the physical product into a dollar value. This is done by multiplying the MPP by the market price of tapes. If the seventh worker's MPP is 118, and the market price is $3 per tape, then the **value of the marginal product (VMP)** is $354 (118 × $3). The value of the marginal product is shown in column 4 of panel (a) in Exhibit 13–1. *We call the worker's contribution to total revenues the value of marginal physical product,* or VMP.

Now in column 5 of panel (a) in Exhibit 13–1, we show the wage rate or marginal factor cost (MFC) of each worker. Since each worker is paid the same competitively determined wage of $249 per week, the MFC is the same for all workers.

Since the firm is buying labor in a perfectly competitive labor market, the wage rate of $249 per week really represents the supply curve of labor. It is, of course, the horizontal supply curve of labor, because that firm can purchase all labor at the same wage rate since, by definition, it is a minuscule part of the entire market purchasing labor. (Remember the definition of perfect competition.) We show this horizontal supply curve as *ss* in panel (b) of Exhibit 13–1.

RULE FOR HIRING

A general rule for the hiring decision of a firm is:

The firm hires workers up to the point where the additional cost associated with hiring the last worker is equal to the additional revenue generated by that worker.

In a perfectly competitive situation, this is the point where the wage rate just equals the value of marginal product (≡ VMP). If the firm hired more workers, the additional wages would not be sufficiently covered by additional increases in total revenue. If the firm hired fewer workers, it would be forfeiting the contributions that those workers could make to total profits.

Therefore, referring to columns 4 and 5 in Exhibit 13–1(a), we see that this firm would certainly employ the seventh worker, because the VMP is $354 while the MFC is only $249. The firm would continue to employ workers up to the point where MFC = VMP because as workers are added, they contribute more to revenue than to cost.

We can also use panel (b) of Exhibit 13–1 to find how many workers our firm should hire. First, we draw a straight line across from the going wage rate, which is determined by demand and supply on the labor market. The straight line is labeled *ss* to indicate that it is effectively the supply curve of labor facing the individual firm purchasing labor in a perfectly competitive labor market. In other words, that firm can purchase all the labor it wants of equal quality at $249 per worker-week.[2] This horizontal supply curve, *ss,* intersects the value of marginal physical product curve at 12 worker-weeks. At the intersection *E,* the wage rate is equal to the value of marginal physical product. This value of marginal physical product curve is also a *factor demand curve,* assuming only one variable factor of production and perfect competition in both the factor and product markets. In other words, equilibrium for the firm obtains when the firm's demand curve for labor, which turns out to be its VMP curve, intersects the firm's supply curve of labor, which is the horizontal line at the going

[1] To be more accurate, the price of the product, $3, is *net* of all other variable costs. For example, the $3 price of tapes is net of, say, the $3.50 price at which the tapes sell in the market, and the 50¢ cost of raw materials.

[2] The analysis is strictly equivalent to the perfectly competitive output market introduced in Chapter 9.

wage rate, and is labeled *ss*. This equilibrium occurs at their intersection *E*. The firm in our example would not hire the thirteenth worker who will only add $228 to revenue but $249 to cost. If the firm were to hire the thirteenth worker, its net income would be reduced by $21.

Derived Demand

This demand curve is *derived*—that is, it shows a **derived demand**—because the tape firm does not want to purchase the services of workers just for the services themselves. Factors of production are rented or purchased not because they give satisfaction per se but because they can be used to produce products that are expected to be sold at a profit. This is different from a consumer's desire to buy a product, for example. The product is bought because it will give satisfaction.

The value of marginal product curve, because it is derived, will shift whenever there is a change in the price of the final product that the workers are making. (Other changes will cause this curve to shift also, one of which we discuss below.) If, for example, the market price of tapes goes down, the value of marginal product curve will shift inward to the left to VMP′, as shown in Exhibit 13-2. If the market price of tapes goes up, the value of marginal product curve will shift outward to the right to VMP″. After all, we know that VMP = MPP × price of product. If output price falls, so, too, does the demand for labor; at the same going wage rate, the firm will require fewer workers. Conversely, if output price rises, the demand for labor will also rise, and the firm will want to hire more workers at each and every possible wage rate.

We just pointed out that value of marginal product ≡ MPP × price of product. Clearly, then, a change in marginal productivity, or the marginal physical product of labor, will shift the VMP curve. If the marginal productivity of labor decreases, the VMP curve, or demand curve, for labor will shift inward to the left. A lower quantity of labor will be demanded at every possible wage rate.

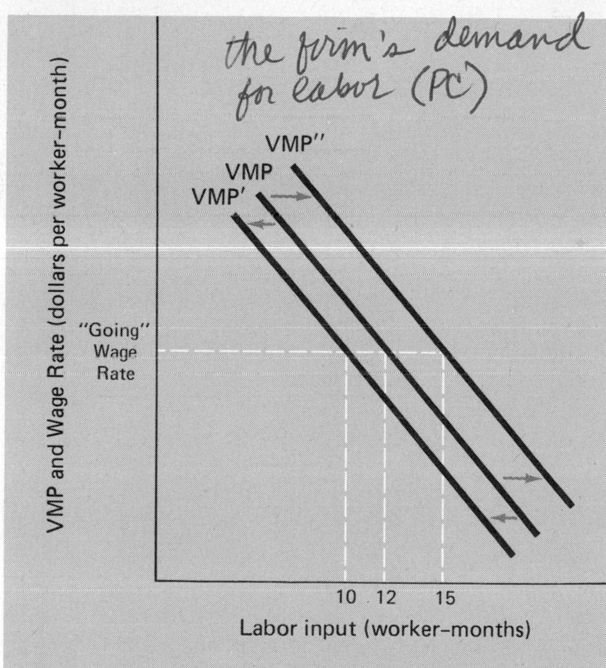

EXHIBIT 13-2
Demand for Labor, a Derived Demand. The demand for labor is a derived demand—derived from the demand for the final product being produced. Therefore, the value of marginal product curve will shift whenever the price of the product changes. If we start with the value of marginal product curve VMP, predicated on a price of tapes of $3 per reel, we know that at the going wage rate of $249 per week, 12 workers will be hired. If the price of tapes goes down, the value of marginal product curve will shift to VMP′ and the number of workers hired might fall to 10. If the price of tapes goes up, the value of marginal product curve will shift to VMP″ and the number of workers hired might increase to 15.

Input Demand Curve for All Firms Taken Together

An individual firm's value of marginal product curve is also its demand schedule for the variable factor of production—in our example, labor. Is it possible to add up these individual demand curves for labor—VMP curves—and come up with a market demand curve for labor? The answer is no, because this is a derived demand—derived from the demand for the final product being produced. Therefore, if all firms together react to a reduction in the price of labor (the wage rate) by hiring more workers and producing more of the good, the only way *all firms combined* will be able to sell that increased production is by lowering its output price.

Remember that while the *individual* firm's output demand curve is perfectly elastic (horizontal) at the going market price of the product, the demand curve for the entire *industry* is downward sloping. For a larger output to be sold, the price must fall (other things constant).

If the supply curve of the prerecorded tape industry shifts out to the right (due to a reduction in

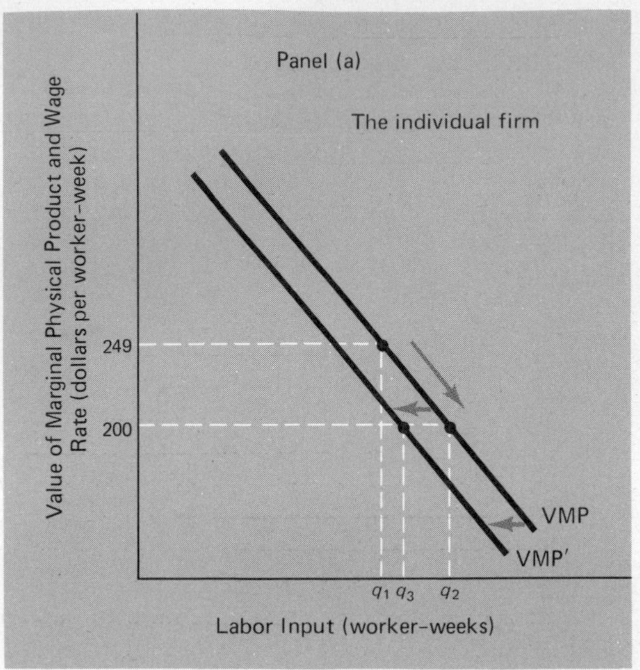

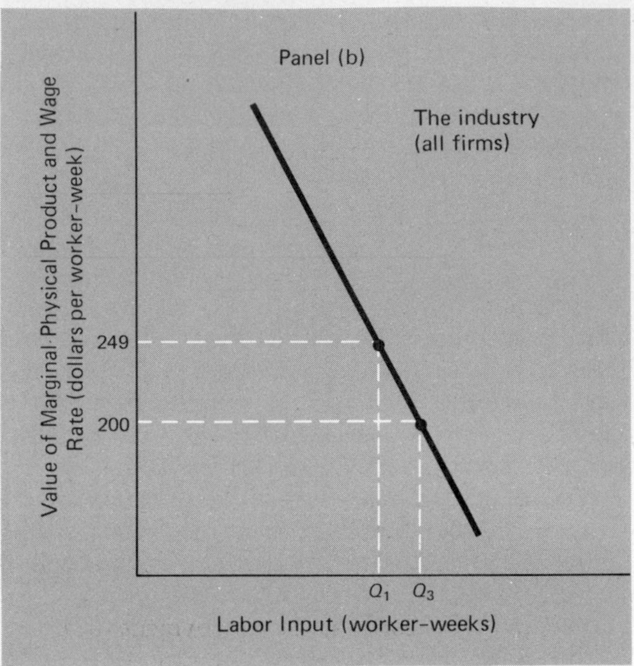

EXHIBIT 13–3

The Firm and Market Demand Curve for Labor. In panel (a) we draw the value of marginal product curve for the individual firm at VMP. The going wage rate is $249 per week. The total quantity of workers demanded by the firm is therefore q_1. We add up all the individual demands for workers at that wage rate and find it is equal to Q_1 in panel (b). Now the wage rate falls to $200 per week. The value of marginal product curve dictates that q_2 number of workers should be hired by the firm. But all firms do the same thing. Therefore, they all increase production and the price of the product has to fall in order to increase sales. This means that the value of marginal product curve will shift leftward to *VMP′*. At a wage rate of $200 per week, the quantity of workers demanded will fall from q_2 to q_3 for the firm. We add up all the q_3 quantities and find that the market quantity demanded of labor at a price of $200 per week is Q_3. Notice that the market demand curve for labor in panel (b) is less elastic than the individual firm's demand curve for labor in panel (a).

wage rates and therefore in marginal cost of output), the equilibrium price that will be established for tapes will be lower than it was before. If, for example, we go from a wage rate of $249 per week to $200 per week in the tape industry, we cannot simply look at how many more workers each individual firm wants to hire, because then we would be *overestimating* their total demand for labor. As firms hire more workers and expand production, the price of tapes will start to fall. This will shift the value of marginal product (VMP) curve inward to the left, which means that for the tape industry as a whole, the increased employment will be less than we would have predicted by looking at the original VMP curves for each firm. *The industry's price elasticity of demand for labor is less than the individual firm's price elasticity of demand for labor.* This is because the industry's price elasticity of demand is less than the firm's price elasticity of demand for the output.

We can see this more clearly in panel (a) of Exhibit 13–3. The original value of marginal product curve for the firm is VMP. At a wage rate of $249 a week, it demands quantity q_1 of workers. Let's now add together all the firms' VMP curves and put their total quantity demanded of workers at a wage rate of $249 per week on the accompanying graph in panel (b) of Exhibit 13–3. Total market quantity of workers demanded is Q_1. At a wage rate of $249 per week, the entire industry demands Q_1 workers.

Now we assume that the market wage rate falls to $200 per week. On the original VMP curve, our firm will desire q_2 workers. But when it hires more workers, it produces more; so, too, do *all* the other firms in the industry—that is, *all* other firms react to the lower wage rate. But all this increased production cannot be sold without lowering the price of the product. Therefore, we have to draw a new VMP curve, which we will call VMP′, and which is constructed using a *lower* price for the product.

Now the firm's equilibrium quantity of workers demanded is q_3 when the wage rate drops to \$200 per week. We find all the workers demanded at this lower wage rate and plot the number in panel (b) of Exhibit 13–3. It happens to be at quantity Q_3. Notice one important thing again: *The market elasticity of demand for an input is smaller than the individual firm's elasticity of demand for the same input at the market price for the input.* The firm's demand curve for labor is drawn assuming that product price is constant; the market's demand curve for labor must allow for changes in the product price since larger industry outputs can only be sold at a lower price. (Remember, the demand for labor is a derived demand.)

We don't know the exact elasticity of the demand for labor, but there are a few rules of thumb that can be followed for a general idea. It is important to know labor demand elasticity if we want, for example, to forecast the employment (or unemployment) effects of a new union contract in a specific occupation. So we should be aware of some of the determinants of this elasticity and not merely assume elasticity is the same for all industries and for all types of inputs.

Concepts in Brief 13-1

■ The change in total output due to a one-unit change in one variable input, holding all other inputs constant, is called the marginal physical product, or MPP.

■ When we multiply marginal physical product times the price per unit of output, we obtain the value of marginal product, or VMP. VMP, defined as $P \times$ MPP, applies *only* to perfect competition where a firm sells all output at a constant price per unit.

■ A (perfectly) competitive firm will hire workers up to the point where the additional cost of hiring one more worker is equal to the additional revenues generated. For the individual firm, therefore, its VMP curve is also its demand for labor curve.

■ The demand for labor is a derived demand, derived from the demand for final output. Therefore, if the price of final output changes, this will cause a shift in the VMP curve (which is also the firm's demand for labor curve).

■ The industry price elasticity of demand for labor is less than the individual firm's price elasticity of demand for labor.

Determinants of Demand Elasticity for Inputs

There are basically five determinants of the price elasticity of demand for an input:

1. The easier it is for a particular variable input to be substituted for by other inputs, the more price elastic the demand for that variable input will be.
2. The greater the price elasticity of demand for the final product, the greater the price elasticity of demand for the variable input.
3. The greater the price elasticity of supply of all other inputs, the greater the price elasticity of demand for a particular variable input.
4. The smaller the proportion of total costs accounted for by a particular variable input, the lower its price elasticity of demand.
5. The price elasticity of demand for a variable input will be greater in the long run than in the short run.

SUBSTITUTE FACTORS

The first determinant seems obvious. If one particular input can be substituted very easily for another, then an increase in the price of one input will lead to much more extensive use of the other. For example, sleeping bag manufacturers can use either plastic or metal zippers on their bags. Both are equally useful and equally productive in doing the same job. They are also equally expensive and are used, let's say, in equal proportions. If for some reason the price of plastic zippers rises by 20 percent, how many plastic zippers do you think a firm will use? Probably none; it will switch to metal zippers because they work just as well. On the other hand, thread is important for sewing the seams of the sleeping bags, and let's suppose that it cannot be easily replaced by anything else. We would expect the elasticity of demand for thread to be very low indeed. A rise in its price will not lead to a very large decrease in quantity demanded because few other inputs can be used as substitutes.

FINAL PRODUCT ELASTICITY

The second determinant of factor demand elasticity is the elasticity of demand for the final product. It is probably the easiest to understand because we have already seen that the demand for an input is a *derived* demand. Since it is derived from the demand for the final output, we would expect the elasticity of the derived demand to mirror the elasticity of the demand for the final product (all other things being held constant).

Assume the elasticity of demand for electricity is very low. If the wages of skilled workers in the electricity industry are forced up by a strong union, the companies will pass on part of the increase in costs to customers in the form of higher prices. But since the elasticity of demand for electricity is relatively low, customers will not reduce by very much the quantity of electricity demanded. The electricity companies will lay off very few workers. The low elasticity of demand for the final product leads to a low elasticity of demand for the factors of production, other things being held constant. The converse is also true.

SUPPLY ELASTICITY OF SUBSTITUTE FACTORS

The third determinant is the price elasticity of the supply of other inputs.[3] The greater the price elasticity of supply of other inputs, the greater the price elasticity of demand for the input under study. In other words, if firms in an industry can easily turn to a substitute input and obtain more of it by paying a very small increase in price, then the reduction in the quantity demanded of the input in question will be relatively great for any given increase in its price. Assume that aluminum and plastic are close substitutes for use in automobile grilles. If the supply elasticity of aluminum is very high—that is, increasing quantities can be purchased without significantly affecting the price of aluminum—then whenever the price of plastic goes up, automobile manufacturers can easily switch to aluminum. This switch will be accomplished without a significant increase in the unit price of the input for making grilles, since the supply elasticity of aluminum is assumed to be very high in this example. Thus, other things constant, the price elasticity of demand for the plastic input by automobile manufacturers will be higher than it would have been with a low price elasticity of aluminum.

[3] This is not the same thing as the first determinant, where we discussed the technological substitutability with other factors of production. Here we are taking as given the existence of technologically feasible substitutes. Now we look at their price elasticities of supply.

PROPORTION OF TOTAL INPUT COSTS

The fourth elasticity determinant is the proportion of total costs accounted for by the input under study. This determinant merely points out that if a factor of production accounts for only a very small part of the total cost of the product, any given price change will not affect total costs by much. Take the example of electricity as an input of manufacturing. On the average, the cost of electricity accounts for less than 1 percent of the total cost of manufactured goods. However, we'll assume that it accounts for exactly 1 percent. If electricity prices now double, only 1 percent more would be added to total costs. Hence, demand for electricity will not fall by very much. This may explain the relative amount of power that a union has in raising wage rates. If the labor input constitutes a very small percentage of the total cost of producing a commodity, then an increase in wages will not add very much to total cost. Presumably, in such situations, unions would be able to get their members higher wage rates than they would in situations where the labor input constituted a significantly greater percentage of total production costs.

LENGTH OF TIME ALLOWED FOR ADJUSTMENT

The fifth determinant concerns the difference between the short run and the long run. The long run is usually defined as the time period during which businesspersons adjust to a change in their business environment. As pointed out previously, the more time there is for adjustment, the more elastic both the supply and the demand curves will be. This assertion holds for *input* demand curves as well. The longer the time allowed for adjustment to take place, the more responsive firms will be to a change in the price of a factor of production. Particularly in the long run, firms can reorganize their production process to minimize the use of a factor of production that has become more expensive relative to other factors of production.

Consider one implication of this fifth determinant of the price elasticity of demand of an input. A union, for example, could succeed in raising workers' wage rates—the price of the labor input—considerably above what they are without immediately experiencing a substantial cutback in employment. The short-run price elasticity of demand for labor might be relatively small. If, however, time is allowed for adjustment, the union may find that the large increase in wage rates will result in significant cutbacks in employment—that is, in the quantity of the labor input demanded.

> ***Concepts in Brief 13-2***
>
> ■ The determinants of input price elasticity of demand are:
>
> 1. The easier it is to substitute other inputs for the input under study, the more price elastic will be that input's demand.
> 2. The greater the price elasticity of demand for the final product, the greater the price elasticity of demand for the variable input.
> 3. The greater the price elasticity of supply of substitutable inputs, the greater the price elasticity of demand for the variable input under study.
> 4. The smaller the proportion of total costs accounted for by the variable input under study, the lower its price elasticity of demand.
> 5. The greater the time allowed for adjustment, the greater the price elasticity of demand for an input.

The Supply of Labor

Having developed the demand curve for labor in a particular industry, let's turn to the labor supply curve. By adding supply to the analysis, we can come up with the equilibrium wage rate that work-

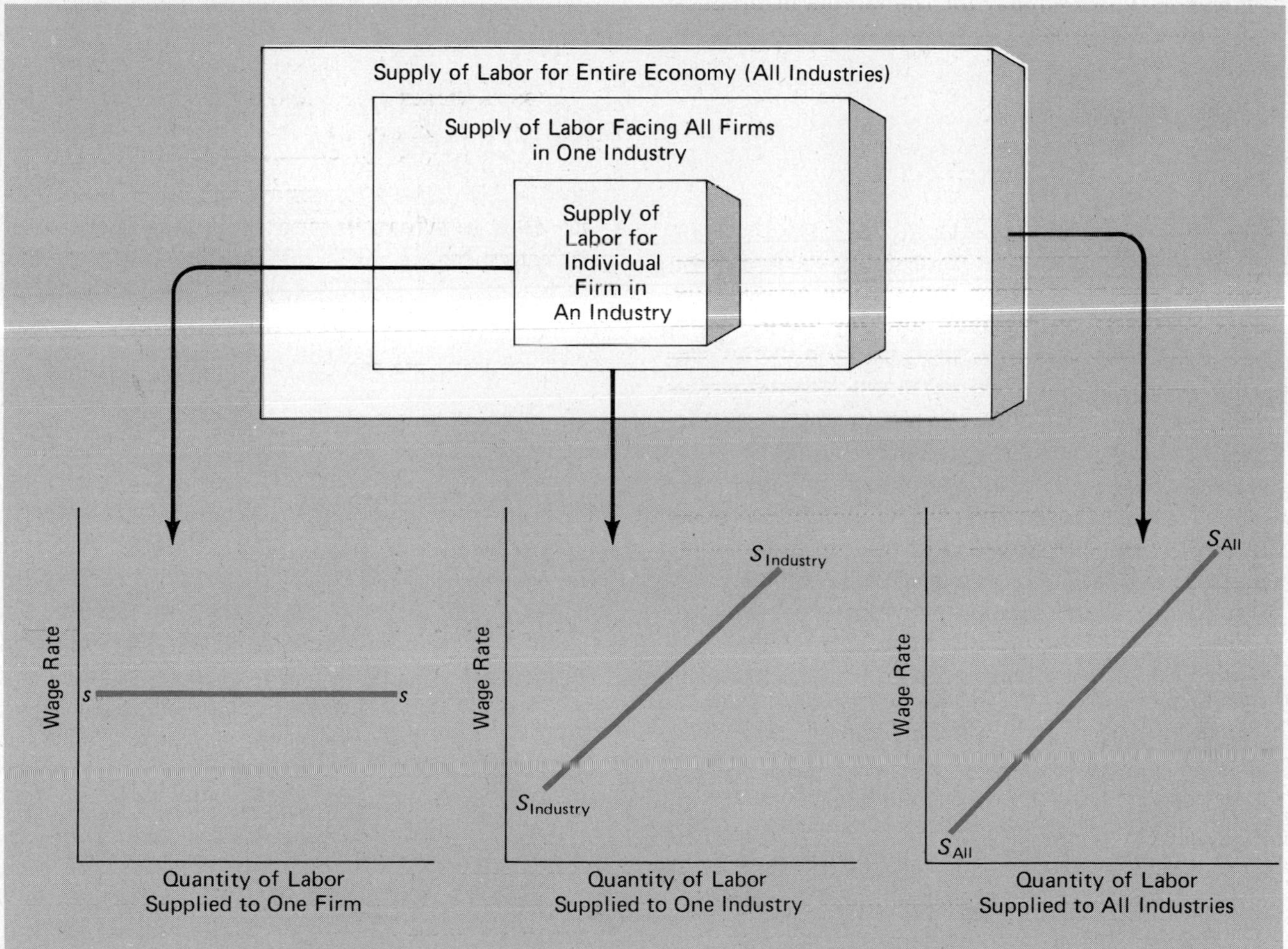

EXHIBIT 13–4

The Three Supply Curves of Labor. Here we see that the individual firm in an industry faces a perfectly horizontal supply curve at the going wage rate. Under the assumption of a perfectly competitive labor market, the industry faces an upward-sloping supply curve. So, too, does the entire economy. (We have labeled the supply curve facing the individual firm as *ss* to indicate that it is *not* the industry supply curve.)

ers earn in an industry. We can think in terms of a supply curve for labor that is upward sloping in a particular industry. At higher wage rates, more workers will want to enter that particular industry—in our example, tape manufacturing. The individual firm, however, does not face the entire *market* supply curve. Rather, in a perfectly competitive case, the individual firm is such a small part of the market that it can hire all the workers that it wants at the going wage rate. We say, therefore, that the industry faces an upward-sloping supply curve but that the individual *firm* faces a horizontal supply curve for labor.

There is also the *economywide* supply curve of labor. In Exhibit 13–4, we show all three supply curves of labor. Let us briefly look at why we expect more individuals to enter the labor force when wage rates go up. In other words, we want to look at economywide labor force participation by the population.

PARTICIPATION RATE

For the United States as a whole, at higher wage rates, people who are not in the labor force decide it is worth their while to enter it. In other words, as wages are raised, the **participation rate** increases, particularly for such groups as women, teenagers, and retired people. Exhibit 13–5 shows participation rates of different groups over time. There have been numerous studies attempting to explain phenomena such as why women enter the labor force during some phases of the business cycle but not during others. One of the main determinants of this phenomenon has been found to be higher wage rates during boom times and lower wage rates during recessions. We typically find higher participation rates during booms than during recessions. This is additional evidence that our labor supply schedule should slope upward from left to right.

From a purely psychological point of view, we would expect that most people put a positive value on their leisure time. Therefore, to induce them to work more hours, they have to be paid a higher wage rate. One would therefore expect that higher wage rates will induce more people to give up more of their leisure. Another way of looking at this leisure-labor choice is to consider the opportunity cost of *not* working. As defined earlier, opportunity cost is the value of a foregone alternative. In this case, it is the alternative use value of a person's time or resources. If the wage rate goes up from, say, $2 to $3 per hour, and you have the opportunity to work at the higher wage rate, your opportunity cost for *not* working is now considered to be at least $3 an hour.

THE LABOR SUPPLY CURVE FACING THE TAPE INDUSTRY

Now let us go back to one particular industry. We can draw in a hypothetical labor supply curve for the tape industry that is upward sloping. We transfer panel (b) of Exhibit 13–3 to Exhibit 13–6. We put in the upward-sloping supply curve *SS*. Now we are able to determine the wage rate in that industry.

THE EQUILIBRIUM WAGE RATE

When we put supply and demand of labor in the tape industry together on one graph, we find that the equilibrium wage rate of $249 a week is established at the intersection of the two curves. The quantity of workers both supplied and demanded at that rate is Q_1. If for some reason the wage rate

EXHIBIT 13–5

Labor Force Participation Rates by Race and Sex. The participation rates expressed here are percentages of the noninstitutionalized (age 16 and up) population actually in the labor force. Thus, in 1960, 59.2 percent of the noninstitutionalized (age 16 and up) population was actually in the U.S. labor force.

RACE AND SEX	PARTICIPATION RATES (PERCENT)				
	1960	*1965*	*1970*	*1975*	*1981*
Total	59.2	58.8	60.3	60.1	64.8
White	58.8	58.5	60.2	60.0	64.2
Male	82.6	80.4	79.7	79.4	80.1
Female	36.0	37.7	42.0	41.8	44.8
Black and other	63.0	62.1	61.1	61.4	61.0
Male	80.1	77.4	74.7	77.0	78.4
Female	47.2	48.1	48.9	47.4	50.0

Source: Department of Labor, Bureau of Labor Statistics.

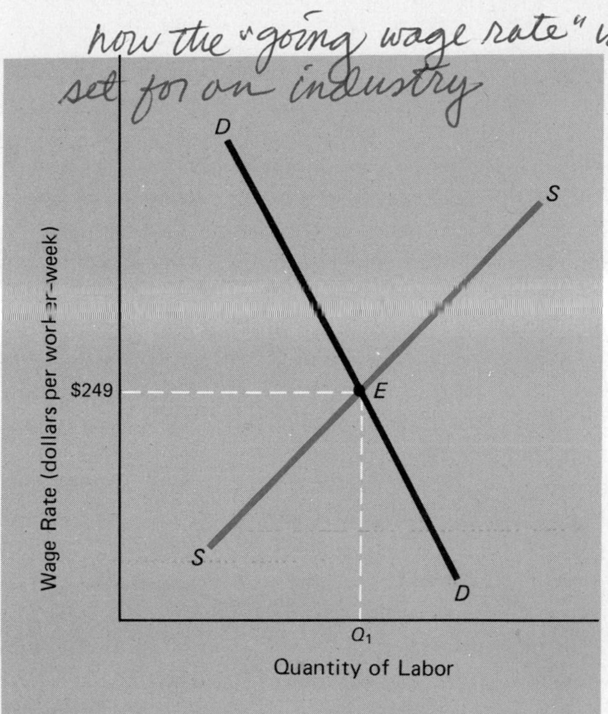

EXHIBIT 13–6
The Equilibrium Wage Rate and the Tape Industry. We take the industry demand curve for labor from panel (b) in Exhibit 13–3. We put in a hypothetical upward-sloping labor supply curve for the tape industry, *ss.* The intersection is at point *E,* giving an equilibrium wage rate of $249 per week, and an equilibrium quantity of labor demanded of Q_1. At a price above $249 per week, there will be an excess quantity supplied of workers. At a price below $249 per week, there will be an excess quantity demanded of workers.

fell to $200 a week, we would find in our hypothetical example that there was an excess quantity of workers demanded at that wage rate. Conversely, if the wage rate rose to $300 a week, there would be an excess quantity of workers supplied at that wage rate.

Remember that what we have just done is find the equilibrium wage rate for the entire tape industry. The individual firm must take that equilibrium wage rate as given in the competitive model used here; the individual firm is a very small part of the total demand for labor. Remember when we talked about perfect competition? We found the market demand curve by adding together the individual demand curves of the individual consumers. We found the market supply curve by adding together the marginal cost curves equal to and above their respective minimum average variable costs. This gave us market demand and market supply. The intersection gave us the market clearing price. Each individual perfect competitor took that price as given; all the output for each firm could be sold at the market clearing price. In the same way, the individual firm purchasing labor in a perfectly competitive market can purchase all of the input it wants at the going market price.

It is necessary to look at what happens to the demand for labor when we are looking at imperfectly competitive product markets. That is what we will do now.

Concepts in Brief 13-3

- The industry supply curve of labor is upward sloping. So, too, is the economy's supply curve of labor.
- However, the individual competitive firm faces a horizontal supply curve—it can buy all of the labor it wants at the going market wage rate.
- The economywide supply curve slopes up because the participation rate for different groups of individuals in the economy increases as the wage rate increases. That is to say, a larger percentage of available individuals join the labor force when wages increase.
- When we put on the same diagram an industrywide supply curve for labor and an industrywide demand curve for labor, we obtain the equilibrium wage rate in that industry.

Monopoly in the Product Market

Thus far, we've considered only a perfectly competitive situation, both in selling the final product and in buying factors of production. We will continue our assumption that the firm purchases its factors of production in a perfectly competitive factor market. Now, however, we will assume that the firm sells its product in an *imperfectly* competitive output market. In other words, we are considering an output market structure of monopoly, oligopoly, or monopolistic competition. In all such cases, the firm, whether it be a monopolist, oligopolist, or monopolistic competitor, faces a downward-sloping demand curve for its product. Throughout the rest of this chapter, we will simply refer to a monopoly output situation for ease of analysis. The analysis does, certainly, hold for all industry structures that are less-than-perfectly competitive. In any event, the fact that our firm now faces a downward-sloping demand curve for its product means that if it wants to sell more of its product (at a uniform price), it has to lower the price, *not only on the last unit, but on all preceding units.* The *marginal rev-*

enue received from selling an additional unit is continuously falling as the firm attempts to sell more and more. This is certainly different from our previous discussions in this chapter in which the firm could sell all that it wanted at a constant price. Why? Because the firm previously under discussion was a perfect competitor.

CONSTRUCTING THE MONOPOLIST'S INPUT DEMAND CURVE

Now, in reconstructing our demand schedule for an input, we must account for the facts that (1) the marginal *physical* product falls because of the law of diminishing returns as more workers are added, *and* (2) the price (and marginal revenue) received for the product sold also falls as more is produced and sold. That is, for the monopolist firm, we have to account for both the diminishing marginal physical product and the diminishing marginal revenue. In other words, marginal revenue is always less than price for the monopolist. The marginal revenue curve is always below the downward-sloping demand curve.

Marginal revenue for the perfect competitor is merely equal to the price of the product, since all units can be sold at the going market price. When we talked about tapes, we assumed that the perfect competitor could sell all it wanted at $3 per tape. A one-unit change in sales always led to a $3 change in total revenues. Hence, marginal revenue is always equal to $3 for that perfect competitor.

The monopolist, however, cannot simply calculate marginal revenue by looking at the price of the product.

CALCULATING MARGINAL REVENUE PRODUCT (MRP)

In order to describe the value of an additional unit of an input, we now have to come up with another term, because the monopolistic firm, in order to sell the additional output from an additional unit of input, has to cut prices on all previous units. Therefore, the firm does not get a payment that is equal to the value of the marginal product of the additional worker. Rather, the monopolist receives the **marginal revenue product (MRP).** It is defined as the change in total revenues due to a one-unit change in the variable input.

We should note here that the terminology, *value of marginal product* (VMP), and *marginal revenue product* (MRP), rests on convention in economics. The concept is, of course, exactly the same for both the perfect competitor and the monopolist. We are asking exactly the same question in both cases: "When an additional worker is hired, what is the benefit?" In either case, the benefit is obviously the change in total revenues due to the one-unit change in the variable input. In our discussion of the perfect competitor, instead of looking at the change in total revenues, we were able simply to look at the change in total physical product, or marginal physical product, and multiply it by the *constant* per unit price of the product. Why? Because the price of the product never changed. Now we are examining a monopolist (or any imperfect competitor, for that matter), and so we know that the price of the product must fall in order for the monopolist to sell more. Hence, we talk in terms of marginal revenue and refer to the benefit of hiring an additional worker as marginal revenue product.

Finally, an alternative definition for marginal revenue product is simply marginal revenue × marginal physical product, or

$$\text{MRP} \equiv \text{MR} \times \text{MPP}$$

That definition is very similar to the one for VMP; the only difference is that we are referring to MR instead of *P*, or price. To keep our example simple, in the following numerical example [Exhibit 13–7(a)], we merely calculate marginal revenue product as the change in total revenues due to a one-unit change in the labor input.

A NUMERICAL EXAMPLE

In panel (a) of Exhibit 13–7, we see what the change in total revenues is. This column is labeled marginal revenue product. This gives the monopolistic firm a quantitative notion of how profitable additional workers and additional production actually are. In panel (b) of Exhibit 13–7, the marginal revenue product curve has been plotted. Just as the VMP curve is the input demand curve for a competitor, the MRP curve is the input demand curve for a monopolist.

Why does the MRP curve represent the monopolist's input demand curve? Our profit-maximizing monopolist will continue to hire labor as long as additional profits result. Profits are made as long as the additional cost of more workers is outweighed by the additional revenues made from selling the

EXHIBIT 13–7(a)
Finding a Monopolist's Marginal Revenue Product. To find labor's marginal revenue product, we must calculate total revenue for the output provided by different rates of use of the labor input.

(1) Labor Input (worker-weeks)	(2) Total Physical Product (TPP)	(3) Marginal Physical Product (MPP)	(4) Price of Product (P)	(5) Total Revenue (2) × (4) = TR	(6) Marginal Revenue Product (MRP) = change in (5) / change in (1)
		118			
7	1,000		$4.00	$4,000.00	
		111			$332.90
8	1,111		3.90	4,332.90	
		104			284.10
9	1,215		3.80	4,617.00	
		97			237.40
10	1,312		3.70	4,854.40	
		90			192.80
11	1,402		3.60	5,047.20	
		83			150.30
12	1,485		3.50	5,197.50	
		76			109.90
13	1,561		3.40	5,307.40	

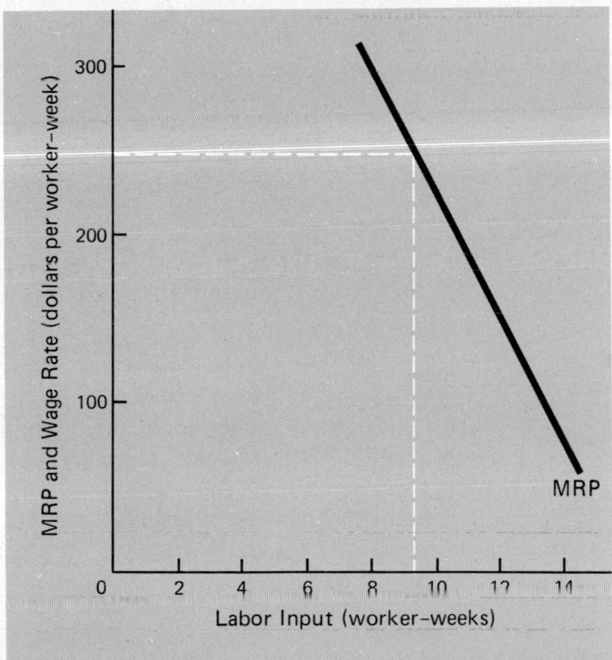

EXHIBIT 13–7(b)
Marginal Revenue Product. A Monopolist's Input Demand Curve. Here we plot the marginal revenue product curve, MRP, from panel (a). The monopolist hires just enough workers to make marginal revenue product equal to the going wage rate. If the going wage rate is $249 per week, the monopolist would want to hire somewhere between 9 and 10 worker-weeks. That is the profit-maximizing amount of labor.

output of those workers. When the wage rate equals these additional revenues, the monopolist stops hiring. That is, it stops hiring when the wage rate is equal to the marginal revenue product, since additional workers add more to cost than to revenue. (It stops hiring when MR = MC.)

When There Are Other Factors of Production

The analysis in this chapter has been given in terms of the demand for a variable input called "labor." However, exactly the same analysis holds for any other variable factor input. We could have talked about the demand for fertilizer or the demand for the services of tractors by a farmer, instead of the demand for labor, but we would have reached the same conclusions. The entrepreneur will hire or buy any variable input up to the point where its price equals its value of marginal physical product, or, in the case of a monopolist, where its price equals the marginal revenue product.

A further question remains. How much of each variable factor should the firm use when all the variable factors are combined to produce the product? We can answer this question by looking at either the profit-maximizing side of the question or the cost-minimizing side.

PROFIT MAXIMIZATION REVISITED

If a firm wants to maximize profits, how much of each factor should be hired (or bought)? As we just saw, the firm will never hire a factor of production unless the marginal benefit from hiring that factor is at least equal to the marginal cost. What is the marginal benefit? As we have pointed out previously in this chapter, the marginal benefit is the change in total revenues due to a one-unit change in use of the variable input. In order to follow convention, we have labeled this benefit as VMP in the case of the perfect competitor and MRP in the case of the monopolist (or any other imperfect competitor). What is the marginal cost? In the case of a firm buying in a competitive market, it is the price of the variable factor—or the wage rate if we are referring to labor.

The profit-maximizing combination of resources for the firm will be where, in a perfectly competitive situation:

VMP of labor = price of labor (wage rate)
VMP of land = price of land (rental rate per unit)
VMP of machines = price of machines (cost per unit of service)

The above formulas would change if the firm were selling its output in a monopolistic market. In all cases, we would replace VMP with MRP.

COST MINIMIZATION

From the cost-minimization point of view, how can the firm minimize its total costs for a given output? The answer should be obvious by now. Assume you are an entrepreneur attempting to minimize costs. Consider a hypothetical situation in which if you spend $1 more on labor, you would get, say, 20 more units of output, but if you spend $1 more on machines, you would get only 10 more units of output. What would you want to do in such a situation? Most likely, you would wish to hire more workers or sell off some of your machines, for you are not getting as much output per last dollar spent on machines as you are per last dollar spent on labor. In other words, you would want to employ relative amounts of every factor of production so that the marginal products per last dollar spent on each are equal. Thus, the least-cost, or cost-minimization, rule will be as follows:

To minimize total costs for a particular rate of production, the firm will hire factors of production up to the point where the marginal physical product per last dollar spent on each factor of production is equalized; or:

$$\frac{\text{marginal physical product of labor}}{\text{price of labor}} = \frac{\text{marginal physical product of machines}}{\text{price (rental value) of machines}} = \frac{\text{Marginal physical product of land}}{\text{price (rental rate per unit) of land}}$$

All we are saying here is that the profit-maximizing firm will always use *all* resources in *such combinations* that cost will be minimized for any given output rate. We are referring here to what is commonly called the *least-cost combination of resources.*

Concepts in Brief 13-4

- When a firm sells its output in a monopoly market, it must take account of marginal revenue, which is less than price.
- Marginal revenue product is the change in total revenues due to a one-unit change in the variable input.
- The MRP curve is the monopolist's input demand curve.
- For the perfect competitor, the profit-maximizing combination of factors will occur when each factor is hired up to the point where its VMP is equal to its unit price. For a less-than-perfectly competitive firm, the profit-maximizing combination of factors will occur where each factor is used up to the point where its MRP is equal to its unit price.
- In order to minimize total costs for a given output, the profit-maximizing firm will hire each factor of production up to the point where the marginal physical product per last dollar spent on each factor is equal to the marginal physical product per last dollar spent on each of the other factors of production.

ISSUES
AND APPLICATIONS

Establishing Minimum Wages

Concepts Applied

■ Demand for labor, value of marginal product, equilibrium wage rate, and short- and long-run elasticities

If you look at Exhibit 13–8, you can see that in an unrestricted labor market there will be an equilibrium wage rate at which equal quantities of labor are demanded and supplied. What if a legal **minimum wage** rate were set above the equilibrium wage rate? Who benefits and who loses from the imposition of a minimum wage rate above w_e?

We analyze the effects of a minimum wage in Exhibit 13–8. We start off in equilibrium with the equilibrium wage rate of w_e and the equilibrium quantity of labor demanded and supplied equal to Q_e. A minimum wage w_m, which is higher than w_e, is imposed. At w_m the quantity demanded for labor is reduced to Q_D, and some workers now become unemployed. Note that the reduction in employment from Q_e to Q_D, or the distance from B to A, is less than the excess quantity of labor supplied at wage rate w_m. This excess quantity supplied is the distance between A and C, or the distance between Q_D and Q_S. The reason the reduction in employment is smaller than the excess supply of labor at the minimum wage is that the latter *also* includes a second component that consists of the additional workers who would like to work more hours at the new higher minimum wage. Some of these workers may be unemployed, but others may be employed at a lower wage elsewhere in the noncovered sectors of the economy.

In the long run, some of the reduction in labor demanded will result from a reduction in the

EXHIBIT 13–8
The Effect of Minimum Wages. The market clearing wage rate is w_e. The market clearing quantity of employment is Q_e and is determined by the intersection of supply and demand at point E. A minimum wage equal to w_m is established. The quantity of labor demanded is reduced to Q_D; the reduction of employment from Q_e to Q_D is equal to the distance between B and A. That distance is smaller than the excess quantity of labor supplied at wage rate w_m. The distance between B and C is the increase in the quantity of labor supplied that results from the higher minimum wage rate.

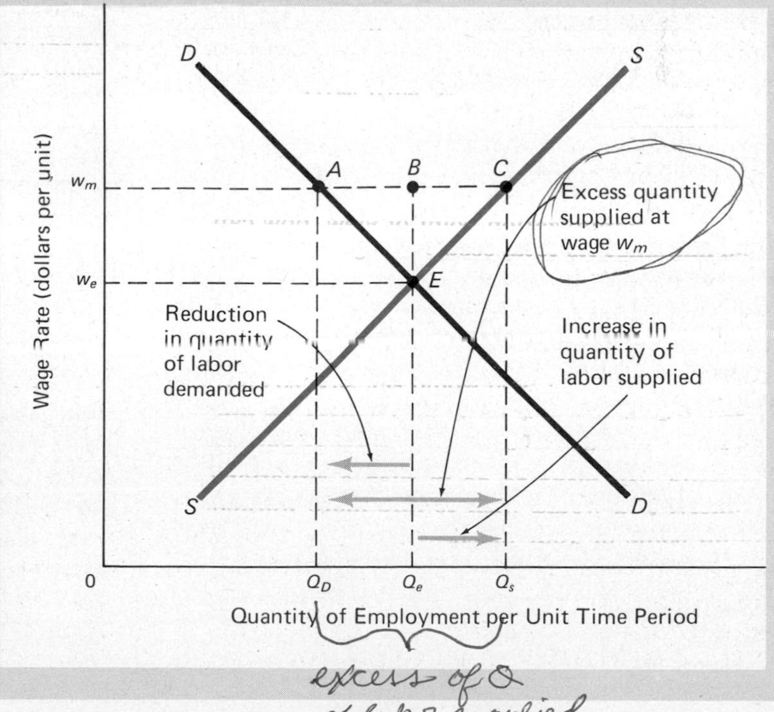

number of firms, and some will result from changes in the number of workers employed by each firm.[4]

Enforcement of the Law

The effects of a minimum wage law depend crucially upon whether or not it is enforced. If the law is not enforced, it may have no effect whatsoever. The analysis of minimum wages is identical with the analysis of price controls. Although it is easy to analyze the effects of minimum wage legislation because the law spells out specifically which kinds of labor are covered and what exemptions are allowed, it still does not always follow that the minimum wage is effective.

There are ways to get around minimum wage laws. In every instance where low-paid workers are receiving benefits in kind, such as below-cost lunches and free tickets to professional football games, there can be a substitution for benefits in kind by payment increases in money wages. For example, if a minimum wage forces money wages to go up, the employer can raise the price of lunches or charge for professional football tickets to make up the difference between the new minimum wage and the former lower wage rate paid to the workers. Furthermore, firms may require kickbacks from employees, establish company stores, or require workers to live in company-owned housing. The new price for company-store products or company-owned housing may now exceed its market value. This is a way of paying a lower wage. Thus, if a minimum wage is forced on the employer, the actual wage can still be kept below the legal minimum by use of these devices. Another method to avoid the minimum wage loss is to hire relatives. In many cases, relatives of employers, particularly close relatives, are not covered under minimum wage laws and/or are not monitored closely by the Department of Labor. This particular way to avoid minimum wage laws may be a clue to understanding how small neighborhood grocery stores and restaurants can successfully compete with larger, presumably more efficient competing enterprises in their area. Dry-cleaning establishments that are owned by retired couples apparently are competing very effectively with dry-cleaning chains, presumably because of the former's ability to avoid minimum wage legislation, since the workers in the firm—the retired couple—don't have to pay themselves any particular wage rate.

Teenage workers usually suffer more than adults because of minimum wage laws. Increases in minimum wage rates substantially reduces their full-time employment opportunities, forcing teenagers into part-time employment or unemployment.

Short and long-run price elasticity of demand. We also must be careful to distinguish between the short run and the long run. It is a general proposition that short-run curves tend to be less elastic than long-run curves. Hence, we would expect the minimum wage to have a much smaller effect in the short run than in the long run. What we would like to know (in order to assess its full impact on employment) is what happens in the long run.

Some Empirical Evidence

Quite a bit of empirical evidence has been gathered to demonstrate the unemployment effects of minimum wages on specific groups, such as teenagers. One study showed, for example, that there was a statistically significant reduction in the ratio of teenage/adult employment associated with increased minimum wage level or coverage.[5] The investigator estimated that a 1 percent increase in the effective minimum wage

[4] Since we are referring to a long-run analysis here, the reduction in labor demanded would be demonstrated by an eventual shift inward to the left of the demand curve, *DD*, in Exhibit 13–8.

[5] Finis Welch, "Minimum Wage Legislation in the United States," *Economic Inquiry*, Vol. 12, No. 3 (September 1974), p. 308.

reduces the teenage share of employment by .3 percent. Another investigator, Edward Gramlich, confirmed the above findings. Teenage workers in the low-wage category clearly lose as a result of an increase in minimum wage rates because high minimum wage rates substantially reduce full-time employment, forcing teenagers into part-time employment or unemployment. Those teenagers who become unemployed are further disadvantaged because they have a very low probability of qualifying for unemployment compensation. Gramlich found that adult males in the low-wage category break even or benefit slightly from minimum wage rates. Only low-wage adult women appear clearly to gain from the minimum wage according to his studies. They received, as a group, higher wages than they would have received in the absence of the minimum wage.

Other studies have shown that minimum wage legislation weakens the economic status of those at the bottom of the distribution of earnings. The apparent redistribution of income that occurs as a result of the minimum wage appears to be from some "have nots" to other "have nots." Additionally, low-wage workers who are the most skilled are the very ones who are not put out of work by increases in the minimum wage rate. The group with the greatest degree of poverty—those workers who are least productive—are the most likely to become unemployed due to minimum wage rate increases.

Questions

1. What effect does inflation have on our minimum wage analysis?
2. What are some of the ways that employers can avoid paying minimum wages?
3. Despite the above arguments, make the best case you can in favor of minimum wage legislation.

The Problem of Labor Market Shortages

Concepts Applied

■ Demand for labor, short- and long-run shifts in demand curve, and equilibrium wage rates

During the 1950s and the early 1960s, government officials proclaimed that a serious shortage of engineers existed in the United States. Ever since the end of World War II, there have been complaints of a shortage of professional nurses. No doubt we can discover at other times complaints of other labor market shortages. Is it possible for a shortage to persist in a labor market into which there is free entry? If we are willing to believe that specialized labor is in relatively fixed supply in the short run, then we can predict so-called shortages when there is an increase in the demand for a specific type of relatively specialized labor.

Let us consider what happened in the market for engineers and scientists in the late 1950s and early 1960s. That was a period when universities, government, and private industry were hiring an increased number of scientists and engineers in order to "win the space race." This situation can be depicted as in Exhibit 13–9. Here we show the supply curve of engineers as *SS*. The pre-space-race demand curve is *DD*. The wage rate is w_1 and the equilibrium quantity of engineers is Q_1 at that time before the space race.

Now the demand curve shifts out in the late 1950s and early 1960s to $D'D'$. There would be no shortage if the wage rate increased to w_2, because at w_2 the new demand curve intercepts the stable supply curve at E'. The equilibrium quantity of engineers would be Q_2.

But the wage rate does not rise instantaneously to its equilibrium rate. It moves up gradually, and during this period of transition, shortages do indeed exist at the lower-than-equilibrium wage rates. Take, for example, the wage rate w_3. Here the quantity demanded will be Q_3, but the quantity supplied will be only Q_4. The difference will be a shortage at wage w_3. Those organizations desiring to hire engineers during this period will experience what they call a "shortage." They will not be able to hire all the engineers they want *at the going wage rate.* A shortage of this sort can take many years to be eliminated when the demand curve continues to

EXHIBIT 13–9
Adjustments to Increases in Demand. We start out in equilibrium at point E, where the wage rate is w_1 and quantity of employment is Q_1. Assume demand increases to $D'D'$. The new market clearing equilibrium occurs at point E'. The wage rate would be w_2, and the amount of employment would be Q_2. However, because of lags in adjustment, the wage rate at first only rises to w_3. At that wage rate, the quantity demanded will be Q_3, but the quantity supplied will be Q_4. Firms will experience a "shortage" of labor at that wage rate.

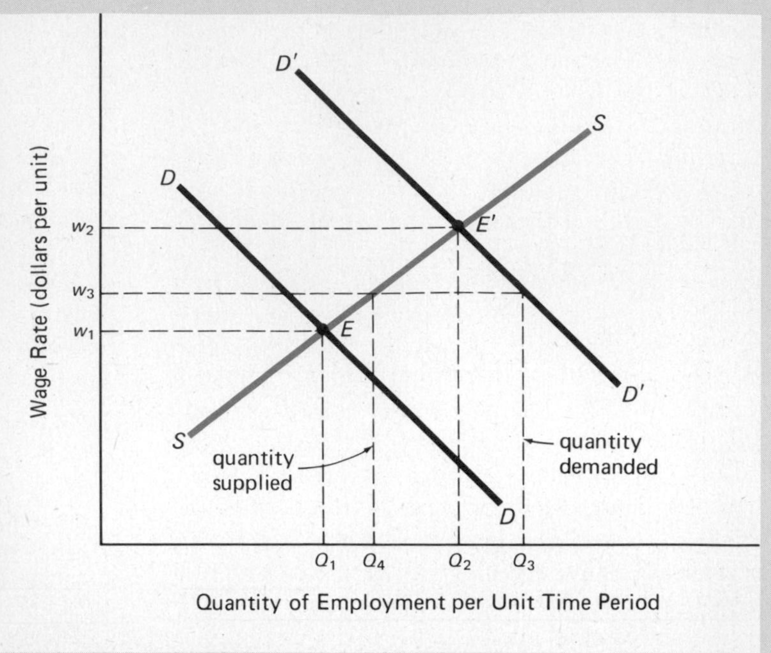

shift to the right faster than the wage rate adjusts.[6]

This application of supply and demand analysis serves to show that adjustments take time. All markets are, by comparison to our simplified models, imperfect. One cannot apply supply and demand analysis automatically without taking into account the imperfections in each market. In the case just studied, these imperfections had to do with the time needed for the labor market to adjust.

[6]This analysis is taken from K. Arrow and W. Capron, "Dynamic Shortages and Price Rises: The Engineer-Scientist Case," *Quarterly Journal of Economics,* May 1959. See also Donald E. Yett, "The Chronic Shortage of Nurses," in H. Klarman, ed., *Empirical Studies in Health Economics* (Baltimore: Johns Hopkins, 1970).

Questions

1. What forces prevent wage rates from rising quickly enough to eliminate shortages?
2. Why would a particular type of labor be in relatively fixed supply in the short run?

Sexism in the Labor Market

Concepts Applied

■ Demand and supply of labor, equilibrium wage rate, and marginal productivity

The Lord spoke to Moses saying: Speak to the Israelite people and say to them: When a man explicitly vows to the Lord the equivalent for a human being, the following scales shall apply: If it is a male from 20 to 60 years of age, the equivalent is 50 shekels of silver by the sanctuary weight; if it is female, the equivalent is 30 shekels.

–Leviticus, 27:1–4

Women's Wages

The Lord in the time of Moses, according to the *Five Books of Moses,* valued women at 60 percent of the going rate for men. In the job market today, things have not changed. In 1981, women earned about 60 percent of the median income for men. Women now constitute more than 45 percent of the total civilian labor force in the United States. Despite this fact, they earn far less than 45 percent of the total wage payments made to that labor force. How do we explain such a large disparity between the wages of men and women? Sex discrimination on the job is believed to be the culprit. "So widespread and pervasive are discriminatory practices against women that they have come to be regarded, more often than not, as normal"—so maintained the Presidential Task Force on Women's Rights and Responsibilities.

Tastes for Discrimination

One way to analyze the problem of discrimination against women is to assume, for the moment, that male employers have **tastes for discrimination.** This is merely a polite way to say, "Let's assume male employers are sexists." When a male employer has tastes for discrimination, he must be compensated before he will hire a female worker. The easiest way for him to be compensated is for the female to offer her services at wages that are below those demanded by her male counterparts (or to work more for the same pay). Sexist male employers essentially have two demand schedules for workers: one for women and one for men. In Exhibit 13–10, the upper line depicts the demand schedule for men, while the lower line depicts the demand schedule for women. This reflects the male employers' discriminatory preferences. For example, if one has to pay workers $4 per hour, this employer would be willing to hire 26 men but only 14 women. For the male employer to hire 26 women, he would have to be compensated; the women would have to work for $2.50 per hour. The differential in this particular example is assumed to be solely due to male employers' tastes for discrimination.

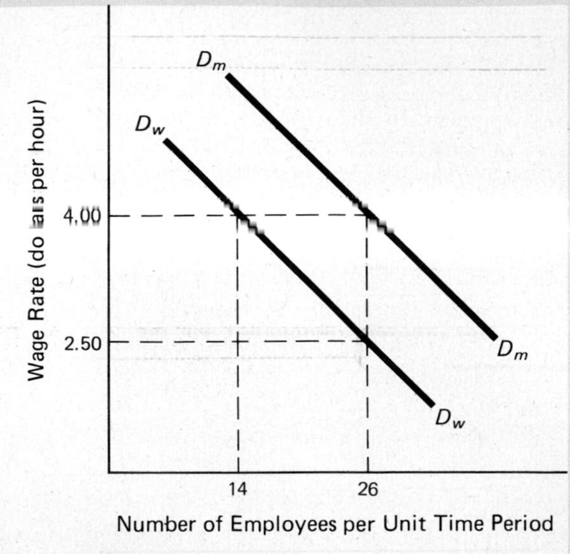

EXHIBIT 13–10
Tastes for Discrimination. The sexist employer essentially has two labor demand schedules: one for women and one for men. The one for men, D_mD_m, is higher and to the right of the one for women, D_wD_w. If the going wage rate for men is $4 per hour, our sexist employer would hire 26 men but only 14 women. To induce him to hire 26 women, women would have to accept a wage rate of only $2.50 per hour.

Other Explanations for Male-Female Wage Differences

The graphic analysis presented above *assumed* that all differences in wages between men and women were due to the sexist behavior of male employers. If we begin an analysis with the assumption that discrimination causes all wage differentials, then we can go no further, since we do not allow for the possibility that other factors may determine wage differences. Among the increasingly large number of economists who have devoted some of their research time to the sex discrimination problem, Professor Victor R. Fuchs of Stanford University has done a careful analysis of the 1960 Census of Population and Housing. His results shed a good deal of light on the causes of the sex differential in hourly earnings.[7]

Employer as chief sexist. One of the first things that Dr. Fuchs looked at was the theory that the male employer or supervisor is the principal source of discrimination against women. He reasoned that if this were the case, we should expect the male-female differential in earnings to be smaller for self-employed women because, by definition, no such discrimination could take place. We would also presume that the differential would be smaller in the private sector than in the government sector because we would assume that the pursuit of profit and survival would cause more "sex blindness" in private firms. This last statement probably needs a little clarification. If a private, profit-seeking firm is owned by a sexist, it will hire women only if the

[7] Victor R. Fuchs, "Differences in Hourly Earnings Between Men and Women," *Monthly Labor Review,* May 1971, pp. 9–15.

women compensate the firm by working for lower wages than a man would get. A firm run by a sexist and competing against nonsexist firms will eventually face higher labor costs because the nonsexist firm can hire women away from the sexist employer by paying them just a little more than the sexist pays, but still less than what a man gets. The nonsexist firms will get all the women in the labor force and thereby have lower labor costs than the sexist firms. Nonsexists will be able to cut prices and drive sexist firms out of business—or so goes the standard theory.

There is no such mechanism, however, in nonprofit institutions and government agencies. The sexists running the show in government should be able to get away with discriminating against women in the labor market because there are no competitive forces to drive any particularly sexist government agency out of business.

The data, however, refute the hypothesis of male-employer discrimination. On the one hand, the wages of self-employed females equal 41 percent of those of their male counterparts. On the other hand, females who work for others in the private sector earn wages equal to 58 percent of their male counterparts' wages. The hypothesis of male-employer discrimination, however, predicts the reverse will be true. Additionally, government-employed females earn 81 percent of what their male counterparts earn. This is further evidence to refute the proposition of employer discrimination. These results are not due to current civil rights laws, since the data were collected a year before that legislation was even introduced.

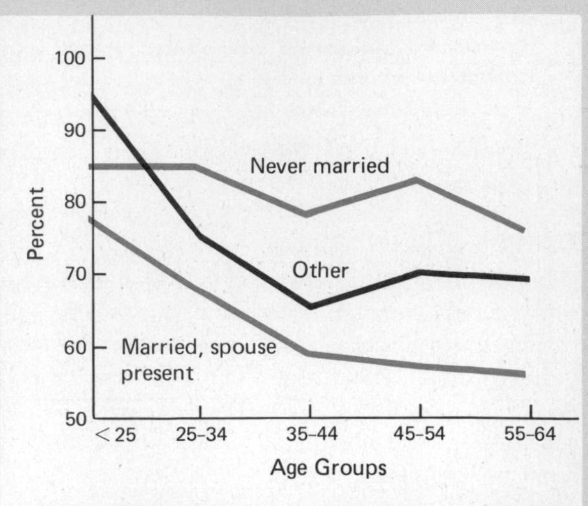

EXHIBIT 13–11
Women's Average Hourly Earnings Compared to Men's. Average hourly earnings of women, as a percentage of earnings and hours of men, by marital status and age group. (Whites only; adjusted for schooling, city size, class of workers, and length of trip to work.)

Customer discrimination. Fuchs points out that this particular pattern of earnings differentials and employment distribution is consistent with the hypothesis of **customer discrimination.** Customers may not want to have their sink fixed by a female plumber or their television repaired by a female electrician, regardless of her training and experience. Furthermore, restaurant customers may want to be served by a waiter instead of a waitress.

Marital status and age. Another important determinant of the differential in male-female wages seems to be marital status and age. Women who have never married and who are therefore much more likely to stay in the labor force have average hourly earnings that are 88 percent of those of their male counterparts; this percentage differs considerably from the general figure given for all women. In Exhibit 13–11, we plot Fuchs's findings for women who never marry and for women who are married, with the spouse present. The earnings differential increases for married women but remains fairly constant for those who never marry, even as they get older. This type of evidence is cited by Fuchs as support for the argument that much of the wage differential between men and women is due to economic factors. The variability of employment of single women in the labor force is much lower than that of married women, especially married women with a husband present. Single women who have been in the labor force a relatively long time stay in the labor force. Statistically, married women leave and reenter the labor force more often. Employers find it more profitable to hire workers who will stay on the job longer i.e., single women.

Role Differentiation

Dr. Fuchs presented his results as preliminary findings and certainly not as definitive ones. In any event, Fuchs concluded:

Most of the [differential] can be explained by the different *roles* assigned to men and women. Role differentiation, which begins in the cradle, affects the choice of occupation, labor force attachment, location of work, post-school investment, hours of work, and other variables that influence earnings. Role differentiation can, of course, result from discrimination. Given the changes that have been and are occurring in our society—such as the improvements in family planning and the shift from an industrial to a service economy—it appears to many [including Fuchs] that some reduction in role differentiation is desirable. Such reduction would require the combined efforts of men and women at home and in school, as well as the marketplace, and probably would result in a narrowing of earnings differences over the long run.

Evidence from other countries supports Fuchs's contention that role differentiation may be one of the reasons behind male-female wage differentials. We know in America that one reason women do not earn a percentage of total wage payments that equals the percentage of their participation in the labor force is that many of them are in low-paying, low-productivity work. Part of the reason why women are not in higher-paying jobs is probably due to our value system. In Germany, more than 12 percent of all executive positions are held by women; in France, the figure is at least 9 percent. In the United States, however, women executives represent only 2 percent of the total executive population.

Even in terms of physically demanding labor, role playing seems to be rampant in the United States. We don't find American women doing stevedoring. In many African countries, however, very heavy physical labor is regarded as "women's work." If you ever take a trip to the Soviet Union, you will see women sweeping the streets and using pneumatic drills to break up sidewalks. In Asia, you see women tilling the fields. Obviously, occupational distribution by sex is not strictly a function of the physical differences between men and women.

Questions

1. What happens when a law passes that requires equal pay for equal work?
2. How can women overcome job discrimination?

Definition of Terms

Marginal physical product (MPP) The output that the addition of one more worker produces. The marginal physical product of the worker is equal to the change in total output that can be accounted for by hiring the worker, holding all other factors of production constant.

Marginal factor cost (MFC) The cost of using an additional unit of an input. For example, if a firm can hire all the workers it wants at the "going" wage rate, the marginal factor cost is the wage rate.

Value of the marginal product (VMP) The marginal physical product (MPP) times the price at which the product can be sold in a competitive market. This definition applies to a firm in a perfectly competitive product market.

Derived demand Input factor demand derived from demand for the final product being produced.

Participation rate A group's percentage of the noninstitutionalized population in the labor force. We talk about labor force participation rates for females or for teenagers or for married males, for example.

Marginal revenue product (MRP) The change in total revenues that results from a unit change in the variable input; also equal to marginal physical product times marginal revenue, or MPP × MR.

Minimum wage A legal minimum wage rate below which employers cannot pay workers.

Tastes for discrimination Employers may hold certain values according to which, for example, they will not hire women at the same wage rate as men. These employers are said to have tastes for discrimination.

Customer discrimination Discrimination by customers against, for example, service by females.

Chapter Summary

1. In a competitive situation where the firm is a very small part of the entire product and labor market, the firm will want to hire workers up to the point where the value of their marginal physical product just equals their going wage rate.

2. The value of marginal physical product curve for the individual firm is equal to the input demand curve. The firm hires up to the point where the wage rate equals the VMP. The summation of all the value of marginal physical product curves does not equal the market demand curve for labor. The market demand curve for labor is less elastic because as more workers are hired, output is increased and the price of the product must fall, lowering the value of marginal physical product.
3. The demand for labor is a derived demand, derived from the demand for the product produced.
4. The elasticity of demand for an input is a function of several very obvious determinants, including the elasticity of demand for the final product and the elasticity of supply of other factors of production. Moreover, the price elasticity of demand for a variable input will usually be larger in the long run than it is in the short run because there is time for adjustment.
5. The supply curve facing the firm buying labor in a perfectly competitive labor market is horizontal at the going wage rate.
6. A supply curve facing the industry or the entire economy is upward sloping. Part of the reason that the economywide supply curve is upward sloping is that at higher wage rates, the labor force participation rate increases. The equilibrium wage rate occurs where the market demand curve for labor intersects the market supply curve of labor.
7. In a monopoly situation, the demand curve for labor is no longer the value of marginal physical product curve but the marginal revenue product curve, which is derived from the marginal physical product of workers times the marginal revenue. It slopes downward, just like the value of marginal physical product curve, but is usually steeper.
8. A firm minimizes total costs by equating the marginal physical product of labor divided by the price of labor with the marginal physical product of machines divided by the price of machines with all other such ratios for all the different factors of production.
9. A legislated minimum wage that is higher than a market clearing price will result in unemployed workers in the covered industries. Many of those workers will seek jobs in uncovered industries, thereby pushing down wages elsewhere.
10. Presumed "shortages" in the labor market may appear during periods of rapid shifts in supply and/or demand when there has not been enough time allowed for adjustment.
11. Differences in wage rates for men and women can be caused by tastes for discrimination, as well as by different marginal productivities.

Selected References

Becker, Gary. *The Economics of Discrimination.* Rev. 2nd ed. Chicago: University of Chicago Press, 1971.

Blaxall, Martha, and Barbara B. Reagan, eds. *Women and the Workplace: The Implications of Occupational Segregation.* Chicago: University of Chicago Press, 1976.

Fuchs, Victor R. "Differences in Hourly Earnings Between Men and Women." *Monthly Labor Review,* May 1971, pp. 9–15.

Gilman, C. P. *Women and Economics.* Boston: Maynard, 1898.

Kreps, Juanita M., et al. *Contemporary Labor Economics.* 3rd ed. Belmont, Calif.: Wadsworth, 1974.

Lloyd, C. B., and B. T. Meimi. *The Economics of Sex Differentials.* New York: Columbia University Press, 1980.

Answers to Preview and Study Questions

1. In hiring labor, what general rule will be followed by employers who wish to maximize profits?

Employers who wish to maximize total profits will hire labor (or any other factor of production) up to the point where the marginal cost of doing so equals the marginal benefit, MB. In that way, they will have used up all those instances in which the marginal benefit of hiring labor exceeds the marginal cost of hiring labor. If the MB > MC of hiring labor, they should hire more; if the MB < MC of hiring labor, they will hire less; when the MB = MC of hiring labor, they will be maximizing total profits.

2. What is the profit-maximizing rate of employment for a perfectly competitive firm?

A perfectly competitive firm will follow the general rule cited above. Since the perfectly competitive firm is a price taker in both the input and output markets, we can derive a simple profit-maximizing rule for it. This firm will accept prevailing wage rates; it can hire as much labor as it wishes at the going rate. It follows that the MC of hiring labor to the perfectly competitive firm is a constant, and equal to the prevailing wage rate; MC = *W*, where *W* is the market wage rate. The MB of hiring labor is the value of the marginal product of an additional unit of labor. In the short run, the law of diminishing returns indicates that eventually the marginal physical product of labor will fall. Since output price is given to our competitive firm, the value of the marginal product (VMP), which is defined as output price (*P*) times marginal physical product (MPP), falls as more and more laborers are hired. In short, the perfectly competitive firm will maximize total profits by hiring labor up to the point where it drives the VMP down to equal the constant wage rate; VMP = *W*.

3. What is the profit-maximizing rate of employment for an imperfectly competitive firm?

The imperfectly competitive firm will *also* follow the general rule cited in the answer to question 1 above. However, the *specifics* are different. Since our assumption is that our firm is imperfectly competitive in the output market, it follows that it faces a downward-sloping demand curve for its output. It inevitably follows that, for such a firm, $P > \text{MR}$. Thus, in the short run the marginal benefit of hiring additional units of labor falls for *two* reasons: (a) diminishing marginal physical product, due to the law of diminishing returns; and (b) in order to increase sales, price must fall—on previously produced units as well as the new one. Thus, the MB of hiring labor equals the *marginal revenue* times the marginal physical product of labor; MB = MRP = MR × MPP. Both marginal revenue and marginal physical product fall as the imperfect competitor hires more and more labor in order to produce higher and higher output rates. By assumption, our imperfectly competitive firm *is* a competitor in the input markets, so in hiring labor it (like the perfect competitor) faces a constant marginal cost equal to the going wage rate; MC = *W* for the imperfectly competitive firm too. What about the profit-maximizing rate of employment for the imperfectly competitive firm? It hires up to the point where it drives down the marginal revenue product of labor (MRP = MR × MPP) until it equals the going wage rate; MRP = *W* is the equilibrium condition in this model.

4. What is the shape of the supply of labor curve?

The supply of labor curve indicates the various quantities of labor that laborers will offer voluntarily, at different wage rates, per unit of time—other things being constant. We typically plot wage rates on the *y*-axis, and quantity of labor per unit of time on the *x*-axis. Now, for a perfectly competitive *firm* wage rates are constant; it can hire as much labor as it wants at the going wage rate. It follows that for such a firm the supply of labor curve is parallel to the *x*-axis, at the going or market wage rate. For the *industry,* however, things are different. In order to attract more laborers, a specific industry must compete with other industries; it must offer higher and higher wages (other things being constant) in order to entice laborers from other industries (or to retain them in its own). It follows that the supply curve for an industry is positively sloped; an industry must offer higher and higher wage rates (other things being constant) in order to get greater and greater quantities of labor per unit of time. The *economywide* supply schedule is still another matter. In order to get more and more laborers into the economy, all firms must entice people, as a group, to increase their participation rates. Thus, in order to get more people to *enter* the labor force, employers as a group are forced to pay higher and higher wage rates (other things being constant) in order to induce them to forego their leisure. It follows that the entire economy supply of labor schedule is also positively sloped; before participation rates will increase, wage rates must rise (other things being constant) to encourage people to forego leisure.

5. How is an industry wage rate determined?

Wage rates are a price; they are the price of labor. As such, wage rates are determined in a manner similar to that of *all* prices—by the forces of supply and demand. The market or industry wage rate will be determined by the point of intersection of the industry supply of labor and the industry demand for labor curves. At any wage rate *above* the point of intersection, the quantity of labor supplied will exceed the quantity of labor demanded—a surplus of labor (unemployment) will exist and laborers will be unable to realize their intentions. As a consequence, the unemployed will bid wage rates down toward the point of intersection. At any wage rate *below* the point of intersection, the quantity demanded for labor will exceed the quantity supplied of labor—a shortage of labor will exist. Buyers of labor will not be able to hire all they wish at that wage rate; their competition for laborers will drive wage rates up toward the point of intersection. At the point of intersection the quantity supplied of labor equals the quantity demanded for labor and equilibrium exists; both buyers and sellers are able to realize their intentions.

Problems

(Answers at the back of the book)

1.

Quantity of labor	*Total product per week*	*MPP*	*VMP*
1	250	______	______
2	450	______	______
3	600	______	______
4	700	______	______
5	750	______	______
6	750	______	______

Assume the above product sells for $2 per unit.

a. Use the information above to derive a demand curve for labor.

b. What is the most that this firm would be willing to pay each worker if five workers were hired?

c. If the going salary for this quality of labor is $200 per week, how many workers would be hired?

2. Below are some production function data for a firm in which the only variable input is capital; the labor input is fixed. First fill in the other columns. What quantity of capital will the firm use if the price of capital is $90 per machine-week? If the price of capital is $300 per machine-week, what quantity of capital will the firm use? Explain.

Quantity of capital (machine-weeks)	Total product (units/week)	Marginal product of capital (units/week)	Product price ($/unit)	VMP ($/week)
0	0	______	$10	______
1	25	______	10	______
2	45	______	10	______
3	60	______	10	______
4	70	______	10	______
5	75	______	10	______

3. The graph below indicates the supply and demand for labor in the construction industry.

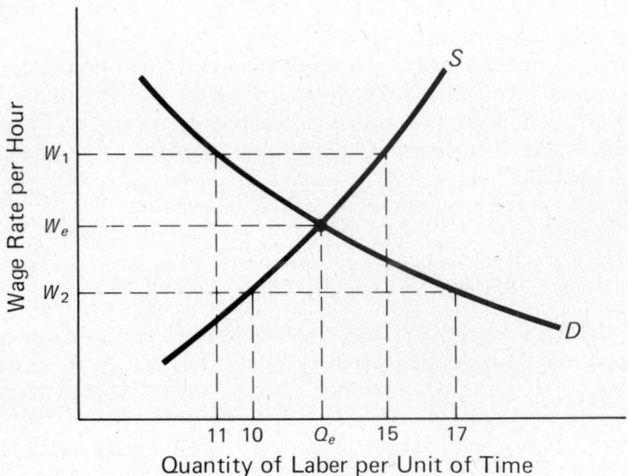

a. When wage rates are W_1 per hour, how much do laborers intend to offer per unit?
b. How much do businesses intend to buy at this wage rate?
c. Which group is able to realize its intentions and which can't?
d. What forces will be set in motion at wage rate W_1, given a free market for labor?

4. Using the graph in question 3 above, answer the following questions.

a. At wage rate W_2, how many labor hours do laborers intend to offer?
b. At W_2, how many labor hours do businesses intend to purchase?
c. Which group can realize its intentions and which can't?
d. What forces will be set in motion at W_2, if a free market for labor exists in this industry?
e. What will the equilibrium wage rate be?

14

Labor: Monopoly Supply, Monopoly Demand

TOPICS FOR REVIEW

The topics listed below, which we have already analyzed, are applied in this chapter. You may find it worthwhile to review them. For your convenience each topic is followed by the number identifying the specific "Concepts in Brief."

a. Monopolist's demand curve (10–2)

b. Value of marginal product (13–1)

c. Marginal revenue product (13–4)

FOR PREVIEW AND STUDY

1. What are the major types of unions?
2. What do unions maximize?
3. Do unions help laborers?
4. What is a monopsonist, and how does it go about deciding its profit-maximizing employment rate?
5. What is a bilateral monopoly?

So far, we have talked only in terms of a perfectly competitive labor supply situation. That is, we have assumed that employers compete to hire workers. We also have assumed that workers are actively competing in the sale of their labor services to employers. There are at least two situations in which these assumptions must be altered. The first one involves restraints on the competition among all workers for jobs. The one restraint that we examine in this chapter is union activities. Then we look at restraint among employers in their bidding for workers. Finally, in the Issues and Applications section, we apply the analysis of monopoly supply and demand for labor to the American Medical Association and to professional sports. Labor market restrictions exist in both "industries." We also look at the issue of the military draft.

EXHIBIT 14–1

Union Membership, 1830–1980. We see here that it wasn't until the twentieth century that union membership exceeded 3 percent of the United States labor force. In terms of percentage of the labor force, membership hit its peak in 1960. Since then it has slowly but steadily declined.

Year	*Union Membership (thousands)*	*U.S. Labor Force (thousands)*	*Percent Organized*
1830	26	4,200	.6
1860	5	11,110	.1
1870	300	12,930	2.3
1880	50	17,390	.3
1883	210	n/a	n/a
1886	1,010	n/a	n/a
1890	325	23,320	1.4
1900	791	29,070	2.7
1910	2,116	37,480	5.6
1920	5,034	41,610	12.1
1930	3,632	48,830	7.4
1935	8,728	52,600	16.6
1940	8,944	56,290	15.9
1945	14,796	65,600	22.6
1950	15,000	65,470	22.9
1960	18,117	74,060	24.5
1965	18,519	77,177	23.9
1970	20,589	85,903	24.1
1975	20,468	94,793	21.2
1980	22,829	104,719	21.8

Sources: L. Davis et al., *American Economic Growth* (New York: Harper & Row, 1972), p. 220, and U.S. Department of Labor, Bureau of Labor Statistics.

Union Power and the Labor Movement

The concept of **unions** goes back at least as far as the Middle Ages when guilds were formed. By the twelfth century, western European guilds were of four broad types: religious, frith (peace), merchant, and craft. Only the merchant and craft guilds had primarily economic goals. Although the merchant in a guild in England had unrestricted and monopolistic rights to regulate trade within his borough, this general guild category disappeared by the thirteenth century.

The medieval craft guilds were the original occupational associations, formed by the artisans in a particular field. Some strange partnerships resulted, however. For example, fourteenth-century Italian painters found themselves in the same guild as surgeon apothecaries. The English named these early union ancestors *mysteries,* which seems rather appropriate. The mysteries restricted membership by requiring an apprenticeship period before an artisan could become a journeyman. The journeyman was then required to provide proof of his technical competence (the "masterpiece") before he was judged a master craftsman.

AMERICAN LABOR MOVEMENT

The American labor movement started with local **craft unions.** These were groups of workers in individual trades, such as baking, shoemaking, or printing. Many of the efforts of the earlier craft unions were thwarted by unfavorable court judgments against them. In most cases, the conspiracy provisions of common law developed in England were used to squelch the beginning of any organization of trade workers. In Exhibit 14–1, we see that union membership remained small until the twentieth century.

The first permanent federation of labor on a national scale was the National Typographic Union, formed in Cincinnati in May 1852. It survives today in the form of the International Typographical Union and is still known as the most democratic of all the federations.

The Knights of Labor

From the period following the Civil War to Roosevelt's New Deal during the Depression, labor's struggle for the right to join together in collective bargaining was a hard and slow road upward. The trend was toward national labor organizations. In 1869, the Knights of Labor was formed. By 1886, the organization had reached a membership of approximately 800,000. Among its demands, the Knights of Labor asked for an 8-hour workday, equality of pay for men and women, and replacement of free enterprise with a socialist system. The organization was not very aggressive in carrying out its programs; in particular, the strike was to be used only after all other means of negotiation had failed. Apparently, many leaders within the organization were more militant than this and gradually left the union.

Public disdain for the Knights of Labor increased sharply after the famous Hay Market Riot in Chicago on May 4, 1886. On that day, approximately 100,000 workers demonstrated for their demands—the 8-hour workday being one. The demonstration was held in front of the McCormick Harvester Works at Hay Market Square. A group of anarchists decided to throw a bomb into the crowd, killing seven policemen and injuring scores of other demonstrating participants. Even though the news media disseminated the information concerning the anarchists' part in the bombing, the Knights of Labor in particular and organized labor in general were considered the cause of the "riot." The Knights of Labor slowly faded until it disappeared altogether in 1917.

The American Federation of Labor

About this time, at the end of the nineteenth century, a group of craft unions became increasingly dissatisfied with the Knights of Labor and formed their own group, which they named the American Federation of Labor (AFL). The AFL was formed in 1886 under the leadership of Samuel Gompers, who ran the organization until he died in 1924. By 1900, the AFL boasted a membership of over 1 million workers; by the start of World War I, the organization claimed that it was the voice of the majority of organized labor. The business community opposed the union movement. For much of the period preceding World War I, the government supported business opposition to the union by offering the use of police personnel to break strikes. The courts upheld many of these police actions, ruling that unions were in restraint of trade—that is, they were acting as a monopoly.

During World War I, there emerged an increasingly favorable climate of opinion toward unions; by 1920, membership had increased to over 5 million. But after the war, the growth of unionism suddenly stopped. The government decided to stop protecting labor's short-lived right to organize. Businesses refused to recognize labor unions, and membership began to fall. By the beginning of the Great Depression, union membership, as shown in Exhibit 14–1, had dropped to 3.6 million, or only 7.4 percent of the labor force.

THE GREAT DEPRESSION

Then came one of the worst periods of economic activity in the history of the United States. During the depths of the Great Depression, Franklin Delano Roosevelt was elected president. When he took office, the nation had seen output fall since 1929 by 36 percent. Roosevelt felt that the industrial depression could be reduced by raising prices back to their predepression levels and by getting rid of "wasteful, cutthroat competition." He wanted to allow management organizations to collude (get together to fix prices and quantities), and he also wanted organizations among workers to be encouraged. Roosevelt succeeded in passing the National Industrial Recovery Act in 1933. The act was originally intended to apply only to big industries, but the National Recovery Administration became ambitious and soon established a universally applied blanket code known as the President's Reemployment Agreement. The National Recovery Administration was supposed to grant "justice to the worker." A section in the National Industrial Recovery Act allowed for the right of labor to bargain collectively. This was in line with Roosevelt's belief that the way to cure the Great Depression was to increase wages. He and his advisers reasoned that if wages were increased, the income of labor would also be increased; thus, workers would be able to buy more goods and services. When workers buy more goods and services, overall aggregate demand increases and even more workers are needed.

THE WAGNER ACT—LABOR'S MAGNA CARTA

The National Industrial Recovery Act was declared unconstitutional. Section 7a, which gave workers the right to organize, was replaced by the National Labor Relations Act (NLRA), enacted in 1935 and otherwise known as the Wagner Act. The basis for the Wagner Act was the argument that the inequality in bargaining power between workers as individuals and large businesses depressed "the purchasing power of wage earners in industry" and prevented "stabilization of competitive wage rates and working conditions." Among other things, the NLRA guaranteed workers the right to start labor unions, to engage in **collective bargaining,** and to be members in any union that was started. The Wagner Act has been called labor's Magna Carta. It was declared constitutional by the Supreme Court in 1937; unions then grew.

THE CONGRESS OF INDUSTRIAL ORGANIZATIONS

At the time the Wagner Act was passed, several discontented leaders within the AFL decided that they did not like the restricted membership goals of that particular organization. Until then, the AFL was composed of various craft unions—that is, as we indicated before, unions with membership restricted to a particular skill or craft. John L. Lewis, the president of the United Mine Workers, was the head of the dissident group of union leaders. In 1938, he became president of the Congress of Industrial Organizations (CIO), composed of **industrial unions**—that is, unions with membership from an entire industry, such as steel or automobiles. Both the AFL and the CIO were able to make large gains in their membership until the end of World War II. Then, in November 1946, John L. Lewis's United Mine Workers apparently added the straw that broke the camel's back by defying a court order to go back to work after a long, violent strike. Even though the union and its leader were fined for contempt of court and the miners actually did go back to work, legislation against unions had already started in Congress.

THE TAFT-HARTLEY ACT

The Taft-Hartley Act of 1947, otherwise called the Labor Management Relations Act, has been termed by some union people the Slave Labor Act. Among other things, it allows individual states to pass their own **right-to-work laws.** A right-to-work law makes it illegal for union membership to be a requirement for continued employment in any establishment.

More specifically, the act makes a **closed shop** illegal; a closed shop requires union membership before employment can be obtained. A **union shop,** on the other hand, is legal; a union shop does not require membership as a prerequisite for employment but can, and usually does, require that workers join the union after a specified amount of time on the job. (Even a union shop is illegal in states with right-to-work laws.)

Jurisdictional disputes, sympathy strikes, and secondary boycotts are made illegal by this act as well. A jurisdictional dispute involves two or more unions fighting (and striking) over which should have control in a particular jurisdiction. For example, should a carpenter working for United States Steel be part of the steelworkers' union or the carpenters' union? A sympathy strike occurs when one union strikes in sympathy with another union's problems or another union's strike. For example, if the retail clerks' union in an area is striking grocery stores, teamsters may refuse to deliver products to those stores in sympathy with the retail clerks' demands for higher wages or better working conditions. A secondary boycott is the boycotting of a company that deals with a struck company. For example, if union workers strike a baking company, then the boycotting of grocery stores that continue to sell that company's products is a secondary boycott. The secondary boycott brings pressure against third parties to force them to stop dealing with an employer who is being struck.

In general, the Taft-Hartley Act outlawed unfair labor practices of unions, such as "make-work" rules and forcing unwilling workers to join a particular union. Perhaps the most famous aspect of the Taft-Hartley Act is its provision that the president can obtain a court injunction that will last for 80 days against a strike believed to imperil the national safety or health. Presidents have, on occasion, used this provision, much to the chagrin of the unions involved. For example, President Nixon applied the 80-day injunction order to striking longshoremen in 1971. President Eisenhower had done the same thing to striking steelworkers in 1959. And President Carter applied the injunction against striking coal miners in 1978.

THE MERGING OF THE AFL AND CIO

The AFL-CIO was formed in 1955 under the presidency of George Meany. Thus, years after the CIO—an industrial union—split from the AFL—a craft union—the two merged. Organized labor's failure to grow at a continuing rapid rate caused leaders in both unions to seek the merger. It was felt that a unified effort was needed to organize nonunion firms. The fact of the matter is, however, that the AFL-CIO merger has not caused a resurgence of organized labor as a percentage of the total labor force. There still remain arguments within the AFL-CIO about the issue of craft versus industrial unionism. Should union membership be restricted to members in one craft, such as printers or bricklayers, or should union membership encompass all types of workers in one industry, such as the automobile industry? Leadership rivalries have continued to exist. George Meany and Walter Reuther never seemed to be able to reach accord. Walter Reuther took his 1½ million member United Auto Workers out of the AFL-CIO in 1969. The UAW joined the maverick International Brotherhood of Teamsters, then under the control of James Hoffa. The merger of the UAW and the Teamsters started a federation that was called the Alliance for Labor Action.

THE LANDRUM-GRIFFIN ACT OF 1959

Internal union business procedures became more strictly regulated with the passage of the Landrum-Griffin Act (officially known as the Labor-Management Reporting and Disclosure Act), passed in 1959. The act regulates union elections. It requires that regularly scheduled elections of officers occur and that secret ballots be used. Ex-convicts and Communists are prohibited from holding union office. Moreover, union officials are made accountable for union property and funds. Any union officer who embezzles union funds violates a federal law. Certain rights of union members were laid out in the Landrum-Griffin Act. Workers have the right to attend and participate in union meetings, to nominate officers, and to vote in most union proceedings.

THE GROWTH IN PUBLIC-SECTOR UNIONS

Since 1965 the degree of unionization in the private sector has remained about constant. There has been, nonetheless, spectacular growth in the unionization of public employees. Membership in the three largest unions of government employees rose almost 40 percent from 1960 to 1981. Look at Exhibit 14–2. Here we show the number of members in the three largest public-employee unions.

EXHIBIT 14–2

The Growth in Public-Employee Unionism. Here we show the three largest public-employee unions. They have grown over 40 percent from 1960 to 1981.

Union Name	*1960*	*1981*
American Federation of State, County, and Municipal Employees	185,000	1,142,000
American Federation of Government Employees	70,000	300,000
American Federation of Teachers	56,000	580,000

Many important issues arise when one considers the implications of strikes by public-sector unions. The disruption due to a strike by police personnel or firefighters could be significant. The courts and legislators must grapple with this issue more and more often. In spite of the fact that several laws were passed at the federal, state, and local levels giving public employees more freedom to unionize, there are numerous strictures against strikes. However, it should be noted that penalties imposed on unions that defy such laws against strikes are frequently ignored. Indeed, the right to strike is one of the most controversial issues in public-sector bargaining.

Concepts in Brief 14-1

- The American labor movement started with local craft unions devoted to individual trades such as baking, shoemaking, and printing.
- The labor movement did not take hold during the period between the Civil War and Roosevelt's New Deal during the Great Depression in the 1930s.
- The American Federation of Labor (AFL)—composed of craft unions—was formed in 1886 under the leadership of Samuel Gompers. Membership increased until after World War I, at which time the government stopped protecting labor's right to organize.
- During the Great Depression, legislation was passed that allowed for collective bargaining. The National Labor Relations Act of 1935 guaranteed workers the right to start unions.
- The Congress of Industrial Organizations was composed of industrial unions. It was formed during the Great Depression. John L. Lewis, president of the United Mine Workers, took it over in 1938.
- The Taft-Hartley Act of 1947 allowed individual states to pass their own right-to-work laws and declared closed shops and secondary boycotts, among other things, illegal. The Taft-Hartley Act allows for an 80-day court injunction against strikes that will threaten national health or safety.
- In 1955, the AFL and CIO merged into one national organization, the AFL-CIO.
- Internal union business procedures became more uniformly regulated with the passage of the Landrum-Griffin Act (Labor-Management Reporting and Disclosure Act) in 1959.
- The largest growth in unionization in recent years has occurred in the public sector. Unionized public employees grew from 1 million in 1960 to 5 million in 1981.

Unions and Collective Bargaining Contracts

Unions can be looked at as setters of minimum wages. Through collective bargaining, unions establish minimum wages below which no individual worker can offer his or her services. Each year collective bargaining contracts covering wages as well as working conditions for about 7 million workers are negotiated. Union negotiators act as agents for all members of the bargaining unit. They bargain with management about the provisions of a labor contract. Thus, collective bargaining is collective in the sense that the union leaders bargain for all workers in the bargaining unit. No worker can individually offer to work at a different wage rate than is decided upon between union management and industry management.

Once union representatives believe that they have an acceptable collective contract, they will submit it to a vote of the union members. Once approved by the members, the contract establishes, in minute detail, times, wage rates, working conditions, fringe benefits, and so forth, usually for the next two or three years. Once the majority prevails, the individual union member cannot work for a lower than specified rate. Typically, collective bargaining contracts between management and the union apply also to nonunion members who are employed by the firm or the industry.

UNION SHOPS

Quite a few management-labor contracts contain a provision requiring all workers to join the union after a specified time of employment, such as 30 days. In this case, we have a union shop. Unions typically argue in favor of union shop provisions to make sure that all those who benefit from higher wages brought about by union bargaining pay dues to the union.

THE STRIKE—THE ULTIMATE BARGAINING TOOL

Whenever union-management negotiations "break down," union negotiators have the ultimate bargaining tool—the threat or the reality of a strike. Strikes make headlines; but in only 4 percent of all cases does a strike result before the contract is signed. The other 96 percent are signed without much ado.

The Purpose of a Strike

It is clear that the purpose of a strike is to impose costs on recalcitrant management, to force acceptance of proposed contract terms by the union. Strikes disrupt production and interfere with a company's or industry's ability to sell goods and services.

The impact of a strike is closely related to the ability of striking unions to prevent nonstriking (and perhaps nonunion) employees from continuing to work for the targeted company or industry. Therefore, steps are usually taken to prevent others from working for the employer. "Strike breakers" and "scabs" can effectively destroy whatever bargaining power rests behind a strike. We therefore observe all sorts of ways to prevent "scabs" from breaking the strike. Violence has not been unknown in the history of the labor movement, and that violence has almost always been associated with attempts to prevent any type of strikebreaking.

What Do Unions Maximize?

We have already pointed out that unions can be looked at as setters of minimum wages. In many situations, any wage rate set higher than a competitive market clearing wage rate will reduce total employment in that market. This can be seen in Exhibit 14–3. We have a competitive market for labor. The market demand curve is *DD*, and the market supply curve is *SS*. The market clearing wage rate will be w_e; the equilibrium quantity of labor will be Q_e. If the union establishes by collective bargaining a minimum wage rate that exceeds w_e, there will be an excess quantity of labor supplied (assuming no change in the demand schedule). For example, if the minimum wage established by collective bargaining is w_u, the quantity supplied would be Q_S; the quantity demanded would be Q_D. The difference is the excess quantity supplied, or "surplus." We see that one of the major roles of a union that establishes a wage rate above the market clearing price is to ration available jobs among the excessive number of workers who wish to work in unionized industries. The union may use a system of seniority, a lengthening of the apprenticeship period to discourage potential members from joining, and other such rationing methods. We see that there is a trade-off here that must be faced by any union's

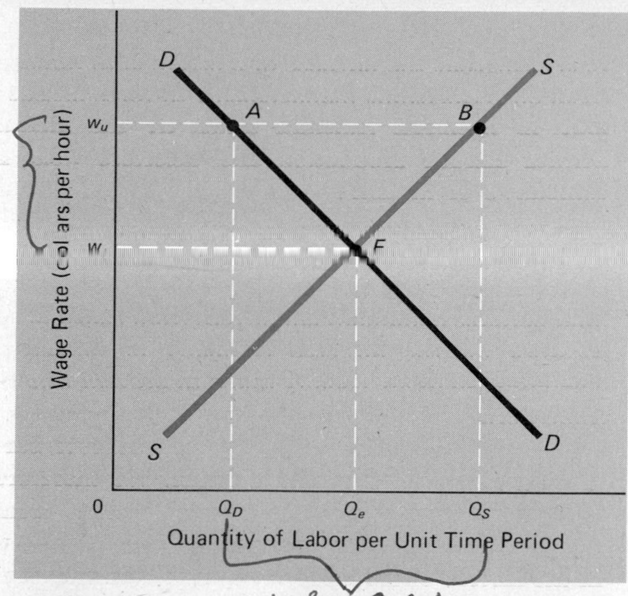

EXHIBIT 14–3
Unions Must Ration Jobs. If the union succeeds in obtaining wage rate w_u, the quantity of labor demanded will be Q_D, but the quantity of labor supplied will be Q_S. The union must ration a limited number of jobs to a greater number of workers.

leadership. Higher wages inevitably mean a reduction in total employment, as more persons are seeking a smaller number of positions. (Moreover, at higher wages, more workers will seek to enter the industry, thereby adding to the "surplus" that occurs because of the union contract.)

TYPES OF UNION BEHAVIOR, OR WHAT DO THEY MAXIMIZE?

The analysts of union objectives have considered three possibilities. We view a union here as a monopoly seller of a service, with different potential goals.

Employing All Members in the Union

Assume that the union has Q_1 workers. If it faces a demand curve such as DD in Exhibit 14–4, the only way it can "sell" all of those workers' services is to accept a wage rate of w_1.

Maximizing Total Wages

If the union is interested in maximizing the gross income of its members, it will not want a membership of Q_1 members. Rather, it will want a smaller membership of Q_2 workers, all employed and paid a wage rate of w_2. The aggregate income to all members of the union is represented by the wages of the ones who work. It is the area Q times wage rate w. That is a representation of the total revenues to the entire union. In Chapter 11, we showed that total revenues were maximized where the price elasticity of demand was numerically equal to 1. That also happened to occur where marginal revenue equaled zero. In Exhibit 14–4, marginal revenue equals zero at a quantity of labor Q_2. Thus, we know that if the union obtains a wage rate equal to w_2, and therefore Q_2 of workers are demanded, the total revenues to the union membership will be maximized. In other words, $Q_2 \times w_2$ will be greater than any other combination of wage rates and quantities of union workers demanded. It is, for example, greater than $Q_1 \times w_1$.

Note that in this situation, if the union started out with Q_1 members, there would be $Q_1 - Q_2$ members who would be out of *union* work at the wage rate w_2.

Maximizing Wage Rates for a Given Number of Workers

Assume that the union wants to maximize the wage rates for a part of the union's workers. This might

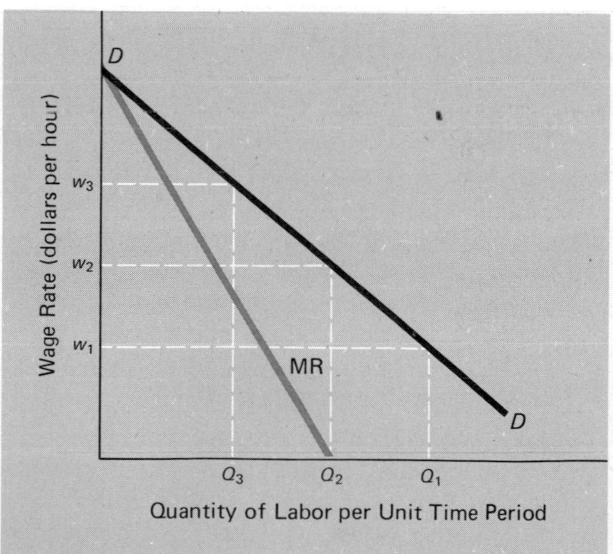

EXHIBIT 14–4
What Do Unions Maximize? Assume that the union wants to employ all its Q_1 members. It will attempt to get wage rate w_1. If the union wants to maximize total wage receipts, it will do so at wage rate w_2, where the elasticity of the demand for labor is equal to -1. If the union wants to maximize the wage rate for a given number of workers, say Q_3, it will set the wage rate at w_3.

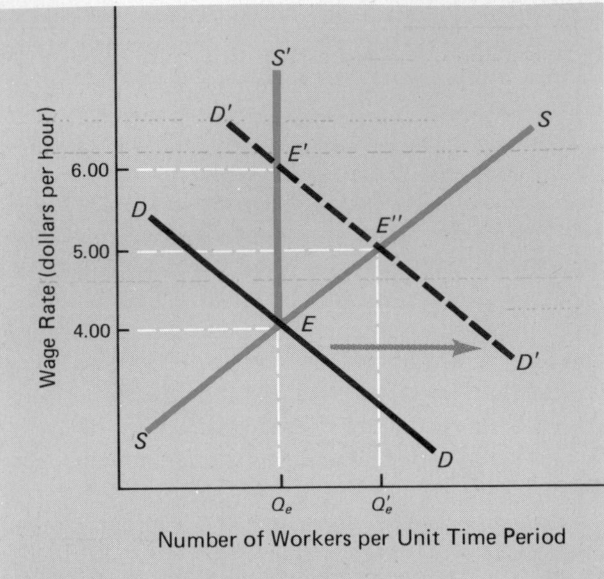

EXHIBIT 14–5
Restricting Supply over Time. When the union was formed, it didn't affect wage rates or employment, which remained at $4 and Q_e (the wage rate and equilibrium quantity). However, as demand increased—that is, as the demand schedule shifted out to $D'D'$ from DD—the union restricted membership to its original level of Q_e. The new supply curve is SS', which intersects $D'D'$ at E', or at a wage rate of $6. Without the union, equilibrium would be at E'' with a wage rate of $5 and employment of Q_e'.

be those with the most seniority. If it wanted to keep employed, say, Q_3 of workers, it would seek to obtain a wage rate of w_3. This would require deciding which workers should be unemployed and which workers should work and for how long each week or each year they should be employed.

A Pure Monopoly Approach

We could analyze unions as pure monopolies. If business monopolies behave as if they maximize profits, why don't we analyze unions in a similar manner? In other words, why don't we assume that they behave as if they maximize the equivalent of monopoly profits or members' wealth?

We could then say that unions would behave to maximize the difference between the total wage bill—the wage rate times the number of worker-hours—and the wage bill that is necessary to bid workers away from alternative employment or leisure. The problem with such an analysis is that it assumes that the unions are owned explicitly by individuals who are attempting to maximize profits. But unions are not like profit-making firms that have definite owners who receive the profits. Once we abandon the assumption of profit maximization for the union, it is difficult to continue our analogy with business monopolies.

LIMITING ENTRY OVER TIME

One hypothetical situation occurs when unions limit the size of their membership to the size of their employed work force when the union was first organized. No workers are put out of work at the time the union is formed. As demand for labor in the industry increases, these original members receive larger wage increases than otherwise would be the case. We see this in Exhibit 14–5. Union members freeze entry into their union, thereby obtaining a wage rate of $6 per hour instead of allowing a wage rate of $5 per hour with no restriction on labor supply.

Has the Labor Movement Helped Workers?

There should be some way that we can measure the effectiveness of the labor union movement. It would be a mistake to look merely at wage rates, for they were gradually increasing even before unions had many members in the United States, because of economywide increases in productivity. It would also be a mistake to look at money wages, because we would first want to eliminate the effects of inflation. If your wages go up from $2 to $4 an hour, but prices go up by 100 percent during the same time period, your real-wage rate has remained constant. We can define **real wages** as wages expressed in constant purchasing power (ignoring taxes)—or, in other words:

$$\text{real wages} = \frac{\text{money wages}}{\text{price index}}$$

One possible approach to establishing the effectiveness of unions is to look at the distribution of income in the United States. We want to examine the distribution between income that comes from labor services and income that comes from capital—that is, rents, profits, and interest. In Exhibit 14–6, we show the share of national income that has gone to labor over the past 49 years. It is relatively

EXHIBIT 14–6

Share of Total National Income Going to Workers. The percentage of national income paid as compensation to employees has remained between 64 and 76 percent since 1933. In less-developed countries this percentage is much smaller, for much of national income is paid in rents and interest to landowners.

Year	*Percentage of National Income as Compensation to Employees*
1933	73.2
1935	65.2
1940	64.2
1945	67.8
1947	64.8
1950	64.1
1955	67.8
1960	71.0
1965	69.8
1967	71.5
1968	72.1
1969	73.3
1970	74.9
1974	73.7
1975	76.4
1976	76.0
1981	75.4

Source: Department of Commerce, Office of Business Economics.

stable, hovering between 64 and 76 percent. On the basis of this type of evidence, one might conclude that unions have not been able to get a larger share of the total pie for all labor. But we really can't draw that conclusion without knowing what would have happened to labor's share of national income *in the absence of unions.* Moreover, the share of *all* labor's income going to *union* workers may have increased, thereby making union members better off.

Concepts in Brief 14-2

- When unions raise wage rates above market clearing prices, they are faced with the problem of rationing a restricted number of jobs to a more-than-willing supply of workers.
- A model of union behavior depends on what it is assumed they maximize.
- Unions may wish to: (1) employ all members in the union, or (2) maximize total wages for the union's workers, or (3) maximize wages for a *given* (small) number of workers.
- We cannot use a pure monopoly model to analyze union behavior, because unions are not profit-maximizing organizations that are owned by stockholders.
- In trying to assess whether labor unions have helped workers, we must look at real wages as opposed to nominal wages. Real wages in the economy will go up even without unions because of general increases in productivity.
- Labor's share of national income has remained relatively stable for the last 10 years. It is possible, however, that labor's share of national income would have dropped in the absence of unions.

Monopsony: A Buyer's Monopoly

Let's again assume that a firm is a perfect competitor in the product market. The firm cannot alter the price of the product it sells, and it faces a horizontal demand curve for its product. However, we will now assume that the firm is the only buyer of a particular input. Although this situation may not frequently occur, it is useful to consider. Let's think in terms of a "company town." There are examples of textile mills in the South, and there are numerous other examples in the mining industry. Let's assume that one company not only hires the miners but also owns the businesses in the community, owns the apartments that workers live in, and hires the clerks, waiters, paymaster, and all other personnel. This buyer of labor is called a **monopsonist,** which is Greek for "single buyer."

A monopsonist faces an *upward-sloping supply curve* for labor. The market supply curve has also generally been shown as upward sloping. However, firms don't usually face the market curve; most firms can buy all the workers they want at the going wage rate and thus usually face a fairly horizontal supply curve for each factor of production.

What does an upward-sloping supply curve mean to monopsonists in terms of the costs of hiring extra workers? It means that if they want to hire more workers, they have to offer higher wages. Only if they face a horizontal supply curve would things be otherwise. Our monopsonist firm cannot hire all the labor it wants at the going wage rate. If it wants to hire 10 percent more workers, it may have to raise wage rates 3 percent. Not only does it have to raise wage rates to attract new workers, but it also has to raise the wage rates of all its current workers. It therefore has to take account of these

EXHIBIT 14–7

Derivation of a Marginal Factor Cost Curve. The supply curve is taken from columns 1 and 2 of panel (a). The marginal factor cost curve (MFC) is taken from column 4. It is the increase in the total wage bill resulting from a one-unit increase in labor input.

Panel (a)

Quantity of Labor Supplied to Management (1)	*Required Wage Rate ($ per hour) (2)*	*Total Wage Bill [(1) × (2)] (3)*	*Marginal Factor Cost* $MFC = \frac{\text{change in (3)}}{\text{change in (1)}}$
0	—	—	
			$1.00
1	$1.00	$ 1.00	
			3.00
2	2.00	4.00	
			3.20
3	2.40	7.20	
			4.00
4	2.80	11.20	
			6.80
5	3.60	18.00	
			7.20
6	4.20	25.20	

Panel (b)

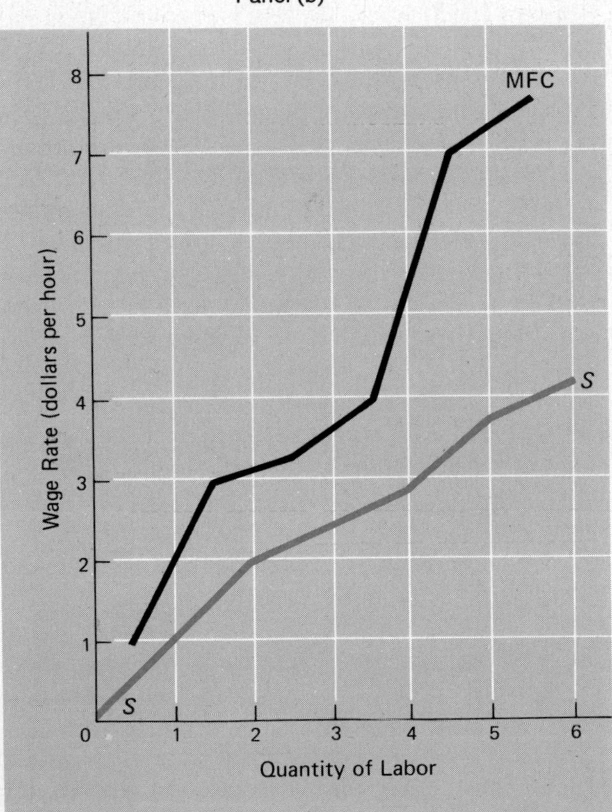

increased costs when deciding how many more workers to hire.

MARGINAL FACTOR COST

The monopsonist faces an upward-sloping supply curve of the input in question because, as the only buyer, it faces the entire supply curve. Each time the monopsonist buyer of labor, for example, wishes to hire more workers, it must raise wage rates. Thus, the marginal cost of another unit of labor is rising. In fact, the marginal cost of increasing its work force will always be greater than the wage rate. This is because in the situation where the monopsonist pays the same wage rate to everyone, in order to obtain another unit of labor, not only does the higher wage rate have to be offered to the last worker but it must be offered to *all* its other workers. We call the additional cost to the monopsonist of hiring one more worker the **marginal factor cost (MFC).** The marginal factor cost for the last worker is therefore his or her wages plus the increase in the wages of all other existing workers. As we pointed out in Chapter 13, marginal factor cost is equal to the change in total variable cost due to a one-unit change in the one variable factor of production, in this case, labor. In Chapter 13, marginal factor cost was simply the competitive wage rate, because the employer could hire all workers at the same wage rate.

Now we consider a numerical example of the marginal factor cost curve facing a monopsonist.

NUMERICAL EXAMPLE

Consider panel (a) of Exhibit 14–7. Here we show the quantity of labor purchased, the wage rate per hour, the total cost of the quantity of labor purchased per hour, and the marginal factor cost per hour for the additional labor bought.

We translate the columns from panel (a) to the graph in panel (b) of Exhibit 14–7. We show the supply curve as *SS*, which is taken from columns (1) and (2). (Note that the supply curve, *SS*, is the same thing as the *average* factor cost curve; thus, you can view Exhibit 14–7 as showing the relationship between average factor cost and marginal factor cost.) The marginal factor cost curve is MFC and is taken from columns (1) and (4). The marginal factor cost curve must be above the supply curve whenever the supply curve is upward sloping. If the supply curve is upward sloping, the firm must pay a higher wage rate in order to attract a larger supply of labor. This higher wage rate must be paid to all workers; thus, the increase in total costs due to an increase in the labor input will exceed the wage rate. Note that in a perfectly competitive input market, the supply curve is horizontal and the marginal factor cost curve is identical to the supply curve.

EMPLOYMENT AND WAGES WITH MONOPSONY

We still haven't found how the monopsonistic firm determines the number of workers it wants to hire. It does this by comparing its demand curve for labor with the marginal factor cost curve for labor. How does it get its demand curve? Since it is perfectly competitive in selling its product, its demand curve for labor is the value of its marginal physical product curve, VMP, in Exhibit 14–8. The intersection of the marginal factor cost curve and the demand curve for labor tells the monopsonist how many workers to hire, because this is the point at which the marginal cost of hiring a worker is exactly equal to the value of the marginal physical product produced by that additional worker.

How much is the firm going to pay these workers? In a nonmonopsonistic situation, it would be faced with a given wage rate in the labor market; but since it is a monopsonist, it faces the entire supply curve, *SS*. It therefore sets the wage rate so it will get exactly that quantity Q_m supplied to it by its "captive" labor force. We find that wage rate is W_m.

There is no reason to pay the workers any more than W_m because, at that wage rate, the firm can get exactly the quantity it demands. The quantity demanded is established at the intersection of the marginal factor cost curve and the demand curve for labor—that is, at the point where the marginal revenue from expanding employment just equals the marginal cost of doing so.

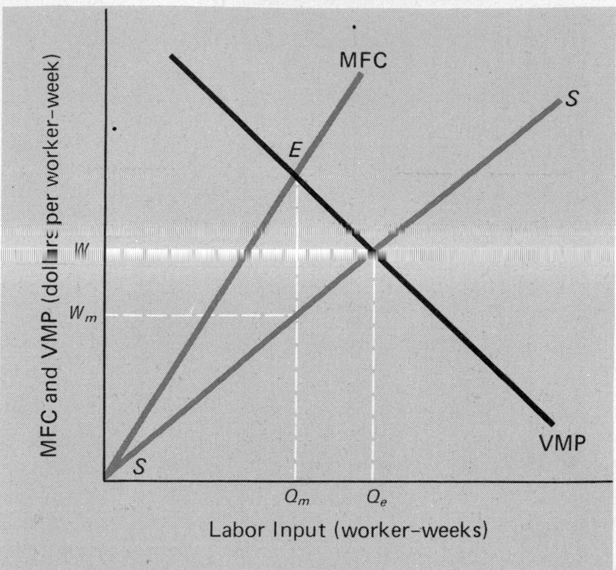

EXHIBIT 14–8
Marginal Factor Cost (MFC) Curve for a Monopsonist. The monopsonistic firm's demand curve for labor is its value of marginal product (VMP) curve—assuming it sells in a competitive product market. Since the firm is monopsonistic, it faces an upward-sloping supply curve instead of a horizontal one as in the previous situation. It therefore knows that to hire more workers it has to pay higher wage rates. It looks at a marginal factor cost curve, MFC, which slopes upward and is above its labor supply curve, *SS*. It finds how many workers to hire by seeing that marginal factor cost equals the value of marginal physical product at point *E*. It therefore hires Q_m workers and has to pay them only W_m in wages in order to attract them. Compare this solution with the competitive one in which the wage rate would be w_e and the quantity of labor would be Q_e.

The Monopsony Model and Minimum Wages

We discussed the effects of minimum wages in a competitive labor market in the Issues and Applications section of the last chapter. We now reexamine this argument in light of monopsony in the purchase of the labor input.

In Exhibit 14–9, the firm's demand for labor schedule has been drawn as its value of marginal physical product curve because we're considering that it is selling its product in a competitive market. We have also drawn in the supply curve of labor and the marginal factor cost curve that the monopsonistic firm actually faces because it is the only buyer of that labor supply. If it wants to get more labor, it has to raise wages, not only for the additional workers but also for all the preceding ones.

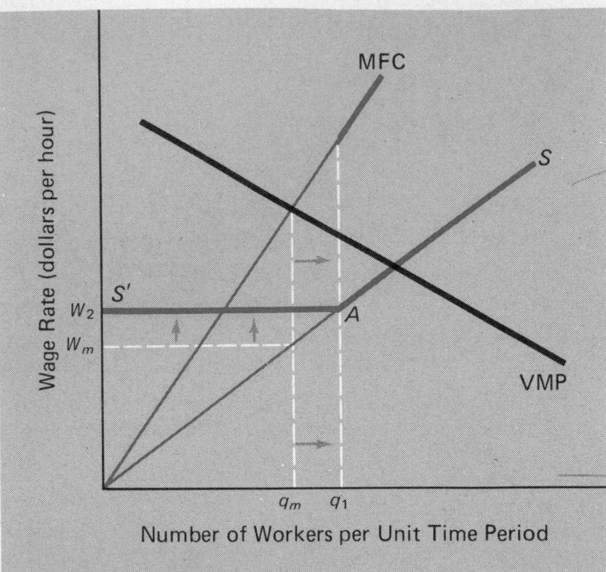

EXHIBIT 14–9
Minimum Wages and the Monopsony Model. A monopsonist looks at its marginal factor cost curve and, in the absence of restrictions, hires q_m workers and pays them a wage rate of W_m. However, if minimum wages are set, it is possible that we can get the monopsonist to hire more workers at a higher wage rate. Assume that the minimum wage rate is set at W_2. What is the effective supply curve now? It is equal to the horizontal line from W_2 to the old supply curve *SS*. The new supply curve, then, is *S'S*. What is the marginal factor cost curve for this situation? For the horizontal part of the supply curve, the marginal factor cost curve is exactly the same line. But when the supply curve starts to slope up at point *A*, the marginal factor cost curve jumps up to its original line. We have shown this as the heavily shaded part of MFC. How many workers does the monopsonist hire in this minimum wage situation? The monopsonist hires the number of workers that allows it to set marginal factor cost equal to value of marginal physical product. That's at q_1, where the marginal factor cost curve jumps up to its higher level. The minimum wage in this situation causes an increase in the quantity of workers hired from q_m to q_1.

The marginal factor cost curve is always above an upward-sloping supply curve. The desired level of employment from the monopsonist's profit-maximizing point of view is at the intersection of the marginal factor cost curve and the value of marginal (physical) product curve. That is, the monopsonist will desire q_m number of workers. To get q_m number of workers, it has to pay only W_m.

Now suppose a minimum wage is established at W_2. We draw a horizontal line at W_2. It extends to and then merges with the supply curve. The monopsonist now faces a new supply curve, *S'S* that starts at W_2, moves horizontally to the old supply curve, and then merges with it.

What is the new marginal factor cost curve? It is also the horizontal portion of the new supply curve—that is, the horizontal portion at the minimum wage rate, W_2. When the minimum wage rate line hits the old supply curve, we're also back to the old marginal factor cost curve. The new marginal factor cost curve therefore jumps up to coincide with the old one; as can be seen, it is discontinuous.

How do we figure out what quantity of workers the monopsonistic firm will demand when there is a minimum wage rate slapped on it that is higher than the wage rate it has been paying? Obviously, it will hire that amount of labor at which its marginal factor cost is just equal to the value of the marginal physical product of the additional workers. We find in Exhibit 14–9 that this happens to be where the new marginal factor cost curve—the horizontal line at W_2—jumps up to meet the old marginal factor cost curve. This is where marginal revenue (VMP) equals marginal cost (MFC) in hiring workers. Employment will now expand from the original level of q_m to q_1. Here is a situation where a rise in wages results in an increase in employment, contrary to the normal situation. The imposition of a minimum wage rate will cause employment to expand. The reason is that the monopsonist facing a minimum wage cannot gain by hiring less labor and thus reducing the wage rate that has to be paid to attract the smaller number of workers.

The monopsony argument for minimum wages might, in special circumstances, be applicable to a company town. However, it is difficult for us to imagine that a sufficient percentage of the labor force would actually be employed in company towns so that an increase in minimum wages throughout the nation would cause an increase in employment. Even if we take a very broad definition of a company town, we find that the fraction of the labor force employed in a monopsonistic situation is very small indeed. One researcher found that the fraction of counties in the United States where the 30 largest firms employed 50 percent of the labor force was extremely small.

Bilateral Monopoly

Now let's assume that in the labor market we have a single seller selling to a single buyer. In other

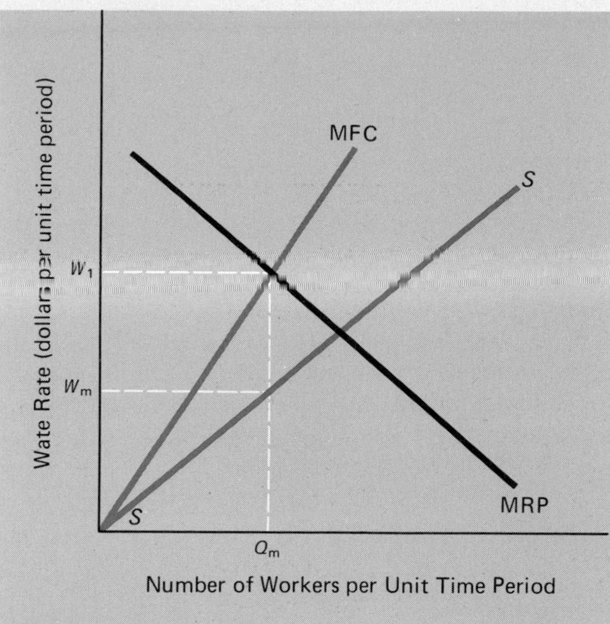

EXHIBIT 14–10

Bilateral Monopoly in the Labor Market. Here we show a monopsonist buying labor from a monopolistic seller of labor. The monopsonist might be a big company, and the monopolist seller of labor might be a union. The monopsonistic firm wants to hire Q_m workers, where the marginal factor cost curve intersects the marginal revenue product curve. It would like to pay a wage rate of W_m. However, the union will want a higher wage than W_m. If it is not willing to accept a decrease in employment below Q_m, it can exact a wage rate of W_1, at a maximum. This means that the range of wages will be between W_m and W_1. The bargaining process will, however, lead to an intermediate solution, with the wage rate certainly greater than W_m and probably less than W_1.

words, we have a monopolistic seller of labor (one who can exert an influence over wage rates) facing a monopsonistic employer (one who can also affect wage rates)—that is, we have a **bilateral monopoly.** This is an extreme example, but it does occur. For example, when the major league baseball club owners confront the major league Baseball Players Association, we have a bilateral monopoly situation. Often, large industrial unions will meet large industrial employers, and again we have a bilateral monopoly situation. We observe a bargaining process between them.

The bilateral monopoly is depicted in Exhibit 14–10. The monopsonistic firm (the employer) faces an upward-sloping supply curve of labor since it is the only buyer of this labor. It therefore looks at its marginal factor cost curve (which is above its supply curve) to determine how many workers it should hire. The intersection with its demand curve for labor, which is its marginal revenue product curve, is at Q_m. It would therefore like to hire Q_m workers and pay them just enough that they would be willing to work. That wage rate would be W_m. On the other hand, the monopolistic seller of labor, say a strong union, would presumably like to have a much higher wage rate. If we further assume that it would seek Q_m of employment, then the maximum wage would be W_1. We don't really know where the wage will be, but we can hypothesize that it will be somewhere between W_m and W_1, depending on the bargaining skills of the two sides and on what the union wants to maximize. (Note that at any wage between W_1 and W_m, the quantity of workers hired will be greater than Q_m.)

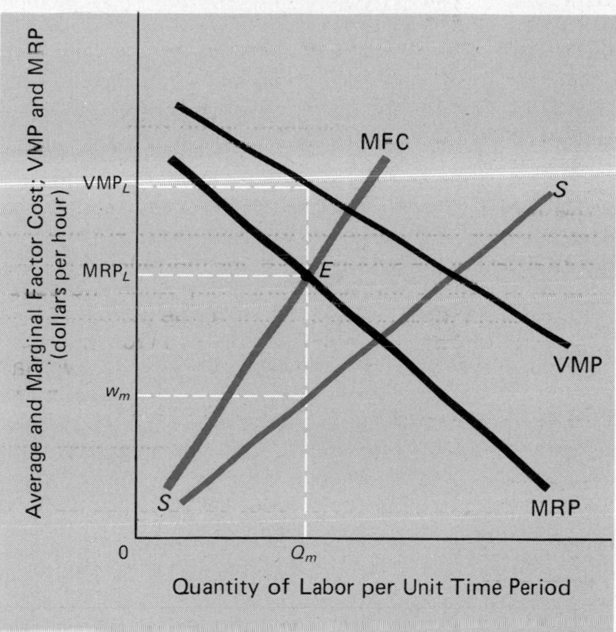

EXHIBIT 14–11

Exploitation. Exploitation may be defined as paying an input less than the value of its marginal product. In the situation depicted here, we have both monopoly and monopsony existing for one firm. The monopolist finds the profit-maximizing rate of employment of labor at the intersection of MFC and MRP, or point *E*. The profit-maximizing quantity of labor demanded will be Q_m, which will be paid a wage rate w_m. Monopoly exploitation equals ($VMP_L - MRP_L$). Monopsony exploitation equals ($MRP_L - w_m$). Total exploitation equals ($VMP_L - w_m$).

Exploitation

Exploitation may be defined as paying a resource less than its value. By one definition, labor exploitation would be equal to the difference between the wage rate and the value of marginal product of labor.

Let us consider the amount of exploitation that exists in a situation where a firm is *both* a monopolist and a monopsonist. This is depicted in Exhibit 14-11. The profit-maximizing monopolist/monopsonist will determine the quantity of labor demanded at the intersection of MFC and MRP, which is labeled E in Exhibit 14-11. It will pay a wage rate w_m for the quantity Q_m of labor. **Monopolistic exploitation** occurs because a monopoly firm looks at its MRP curve rather than its VMP curve, the latter of which would be relevant for a perfect competitor. **Monopsonistic exploitation** occurs because the monopsonist looks at the MFC curve rather than the supply curve, as does the buyer of labor in a perfectly competitive market.

In a situation of both monopoly and monopsony, exploitation can be summarized as follows:

$$\begin{aligned} \text{VMP}_L - \text{MRP}_L &= \text{monopolistic exploitation} \\ \text{MRP}_L - w_m &= \text{monopsonistic exploitation} \\ \text{VMP}_L - w_m &= \text{total exploitation} \end{aligned}$$

Concepts in Brief 14-3

- A monopsony is a single buyer. The monopsonist faces an upward-sloping supply curve of labor.
- Because the monopsonist faces an upward-sloping supply curve of labor, the marginal factor cost of increasing the labor input by one unit is greater than the wage rate. Thus, the marginal factor cost curve always lies above the supply curve.
- A monopsonist that is a competitor in the product market will hire workers up to the point where marginal factor cost equals value of marginal product. Then the monopsonist will find what minimal wage is necessary to attract that number of workers. This is taken from the supply curve.
- It is conceivable that minimum wages in the face of monopsony can raise wages *and* employment.
- Exploitation may be defined as paying a resource less than its value.
- Monopolistic exploitation is measured as the difference between the value of marginal product and the value of marginal revenue product.
- Monopsonistic exploitation is the difference between marginal revenue product and the wage rate.
- Total exploitation is the difference between the value of marginal product and the wage rate.

ISSUES AND APPLICATIONS

A Union Analysis of the AMA

Concepts Applied

- Demand and supply, shifts in curves, supply restrictions, and unions

Medical care consists of a number of items, including, but not limited to, the services of physicians, nurses, hospital staff, hospital facilities, maintenance of the facilities, medications, and drugs. We will limit our discussion in this Issue to what determines the supply of physicians' services.

The Production of Medical Doctors

In 1978-79, 34,969 people took the Medical College Admissions Test (MCAT); only 16,527 were accepted by medical schools. The number of applicants to Harvard's Medical School runs to almost 3,500, but the class size remains at less than 150. Some students apply to as many as 10 different medical schools, and when turned down, reapply two or three times. The number of students who don't apply because they know the odds are so much against them is probably two or three times the number who actually do take the chance. Why is there such a large discrepancy between those who want to go to medical school and those who are accepted? The reason for this discrepancy is not hard to find: the number of medical schools in the United States is severely restricted, and the number of entrants into those schools each year is similarly restricted.

Restrictions

Restricted by whom? In principle, restriction on the number of medical schools is due to state licensing requirements, which universally prohibit proprietary medical schools (schools run for profit). Also, it is difficult for a university that does not have a medical school suddenly to start one. Unless the medical school is accredited by the state, the graduates are not even allowed to take the licensing exam required for practicing medicine.

To understand why such restrictions have been put on medical schools, read the statements in Dr. John H. Knowles's article in *Saturday Review*, August 22, 1970:

> At the turn of the century, the AMA [American Medical Association] stood at the forefront of progressive thinking and socially responsible action. Its members had been leaders in forming much-needed public health departments in the states during the last half of the nineteenth century. It formed a Council on Medical Education in 1904 and immediately began an investigation of proprietary medical schools. Because of its success in exposing intolerable conditions in these schools, the Carnegie Foundation, at the AMA's request, commissioned Abraham Flexner to study the national scene. His report in 1910 drove proprietary interest out of medical education, established it as a full university function with standards for admission, curriculum development, and clinical teaching. Our present system of medical education, essentially unchanged since the Flexner (and AMA) revolution—and acknowledging its current defects—was accomplished through the work of the AMA. Surely this contribution was and is one of the finest in the public interest.

The Past

Looking back to the first decade in this century, we find that there were 192 medical schools. By 1944, that number had declined to 69. Today, there are 126. The number of physicians per 100,000 people dropped from 157 in 1900 to 132 in 1957. Perhaps the American Medical Association and the so-called Flexner Report lauded by Dr. Knowles were responsible for the reduction in the rate of growth of the supply of physicians. At least, this appears to be the case.

The AMA wins out. The American Medical Association was started in 1847. It represented then and still does represent existing practitioners in the field of medicine. From 1870 to 1910, there was a struggle between the AMA and medical educators over who should control the output of doctors—that is, who should control the number of doctors allowed to practice. This became a battle over who should control medical schools themselves. The American Medical Association won the battle. It essentially has complete control over medical education in the United States. For a medical school graduate to become licensed in any particular state, the graduate must have obtained a degree from a "certified" medical school. The certification is nominally done by the states themselves; however, in all cases the states follow exactly the certification lists of the American Medical Association.

The Flexner Report. The regulation and certification of medical schools was, in all probability, based on the outcome of the famous Flexner Report. As mentioned, in 1910 the prestigious Carnegie Foundation commissioned Abraham Flexner to inspect the existing medical education facilities in the United States. Flexner's recommendations resulted in the demise of half of the then-existing medical schools. It is interesting to note that Flexner had absolutely no qualifications himself for deciding which medical schools were to be rated class A. Flexner was not a physician; he was not a scientist; and he was never a medical educator. He had an undergraduate degree in arts and was the owner and operator of a for-profit preparatory school in Louisville, Kentucky. His method for deciding whether a medical school was qualified was to estimate how well it compared with the medical school at Johns Hopkins University.

It is also interesting to note that Flexner was examining the *inputs* and not the *outputs* of these particular schools. Instead of finding out

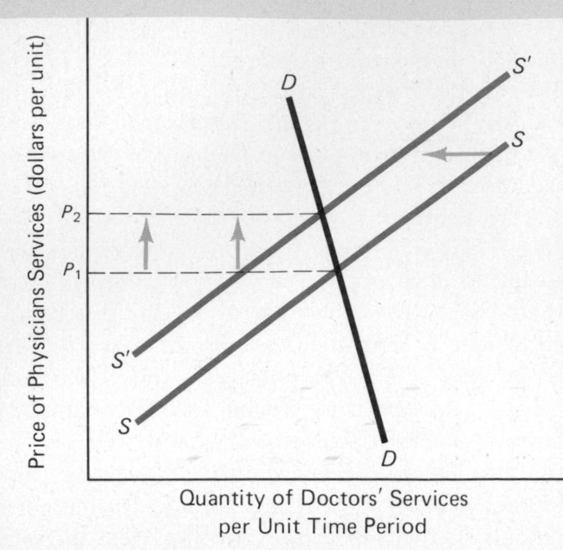

EXHIBIT 14–12
Restricting the Supply of Doctors. The AMA's successful attempt at restricting the supply of doctors shifted the supply schedule from *SS* to *S′S′*. Even with a stable demand schedule, the price of physicians's services goes up.

how well or how qualified the *graduates* of the different schools were, he looked at how they were taught.

Why Did the AMA Seek Control?

It is not hard to find the motive behind the AMA's desire to control medical schools. We need merely quote from the former head of the AMA's Council on Medical Education, Dr. Beven, who said in 1928:

> In this rapid elevation of the standard of medical education . . . the reduction of the number of medical schools from 160 to 80, there occurred a marked reduction in the number of medical students and medical graduates. We had anticipated this and felt that this was a desirable thing. We had . . . a great oversupply of poor mediocre practitioners.

Part of Dr. Beven's statement might be interpreted to mean that if the supply falls, the price will rise, whereas if the supply increases, the price will fall. Exhibit 14–12 shows that the reduction in the number of physicians during this period resulted in the supply curve of physicians shifting to the left. The demand curve was stable.[1] Therefore, the price of the physicians' services went up, thereby allowing them to make higher incomes.

The Future—A Doctor Surplus?

The Graduate Medical Education National Advisory Committee released a study in 1980 predicting that there would be a *surplus* of 70,000 doctors by 1990. What do you think the recommendations of this committee were? If you guessed that there should be increased restrictions on medical school enrollments, you would have been right. The exact recommendation was to slash medical school enrollments by 20 percent. Increased training not only of medical students but of most specialists, including cardiologists, obstetricians, allergists, ophthalmologists, and surgeons, was further recommended. A final recommendation was that sharp new restrictions on entry by graduates of foreign medical schools be instituted.

By now, you should be as suspicious of the concept of a "surplus" as you are of the concept of a "shortage." If medical schools continue to turn out M.D.s, and the demand for physicians' services does not increase accordingly, it is true that the relative price (yearly income) of all M.D.s will suffer on average. That means that physicians' salaries will not rise as rapidly as they would have. That is a far different analysis from one which states that we are facing a surplus of 70,000 doctors by 1990.

Questions

1. In what way is the AMA like a union?
2. Is the monopoly analysis of the AMA still useful if all members of the medical profession do not understand the concept of monopoly?

[1] Actually, the demand curve for all doctors could have shifted outward to the right if on average doctors were more reliable after medical schools were certified by the AMA.

Baseball Players—A Bilateral Monopoly Situation

Concepts Applied
- Demand and supply of labor, monopsony, monopoly, VMP, and MRP

Collusive agreements among potential monopolists and monopsonists are difficult to enforce. There is always an incentive to cheat. It turns out that with the help of Congress and the Supreme Court, professional sports teams have for many years limited wages. They have been able to engage in open collusive agreements to limit wages of their players. In this Issue, we will examine only the market for baseball players.

The Case Where Players Are Unorganized

We first assume that the players are unorganized and do not bargain collectively. The team owners, who operate a joint monopoly in the "output" market, however, have formed a monopsony and agree that no team will attempt to bid away any other team's players. They further agree not to raise wages. This is the simplest model that can be applied to the baseball situation.

The marginal revenue product curve of the baseball team owners, taken as a group, is represented by MRP in Exhibit 14-13. The marginal factor cost curve facing the team owners, taken as a whole, is MFC. The intersection of MRP and MFC is at *A*. The quantity demanded of baseball players is Q_m. The wage rate presented to baseball players is w_m. The amount of monopsony exploitation is the distance between *A* and *C*. The amount of monopolistic exploitation is the distance between *A* and *B*. Total exploitation is the vertical distance between *B* and *C*.

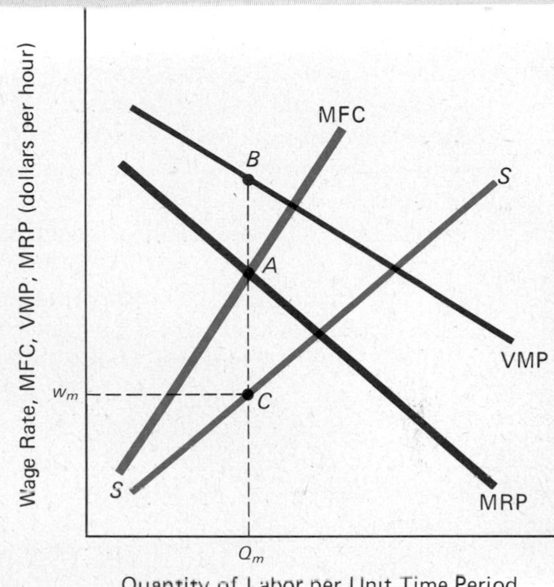

EXHIBIT 14–13
Monopsony and the Demand for Baseball Players. The baseball teams taken as a whole have an effective monopoly in the product market. Accordingly, they look to their MRP. They are also a monopsonist in the factor market. They hire workers to the point where MFC = MRP, which is at point *A*. They hire Q_m baseball players and pay a wage rate of w_m. The amount of monopolistic exploitation is the vertical distance between *A* and *B*, the amount of monopsonistic exploitation is the vertical distance between *A* and *C*; total exploitation is the vertical distance between *B* and *C*.

The Baseball Players Form a Union

Now, what happens when the baseball players band together and form a monopoly in the sale of their services? This situation is called a bilateral monopoly in the factor market. We show this in Exhibit 14-14. The marginal revenue product curve of the baseball team owners, taken as a whole, is represented by MRP. We draw a curve that is *marginal* to MRP and label it MR.[2] MR is, in effect, a marginal revenue curve, when we consider that MRP is the demand curve for baseball players' services by monopoly team

[2] Just consider the MRP curve as the demand curve. Then think in terms of drawing a marginal revenue curve to that demand curve. It will lie below the MRP curve, as we have shown in Exhibit 14-14.

owners. Thus, MR is no different from any other marginal revenue curve in a monopoly situation. The union of baseball players has a supply curve of *SS*. The curve marginal to that curve is called the marginal factor cost curve, or MFC. The baseball team owners would like to set a wage rate of w_m, because this is where the team owners could obtain the profit-maximizing number of players; it is determined by the intersection at point *A* of the marginal factor cost curve (MFC) and the marginal revenue product curve (MRP). However, the union, acting as the sole bargaining agent for all of the employees, would want, if it were maximizing the equivalent of monopoly profits, to set a wage rate of w_u. We determine the maximizing wage rate w_u by considering that the union is acting as a monopolist. Every monopolist will set output where MR = MC. What is marginal revenue in this case? It is the curve labeled MR, which is marginal to the demand curve (MRP) for baseball players by monopoly team owners. What is the marginal cost? It is given by the supply curve of baseball players, or *SS*. MR and *SS* intersect at point *B*. That amount of baseball players' services can be sold to the team owners at a price of w_u given by the team owners' demand curve MRP. What we can say is that, in a situation of bilateral monopoly, the agreed-upon wage rate will be between w_m and w_u. If we were to assume that the union is proprietary—for profit—we would state that the union would attempt to attain w_u because that is the wage rate that maximizes the difference between total wages paid to employed baseball players and the minimum amount of wages required to bring this quantity of labor into the baseball-playing market.

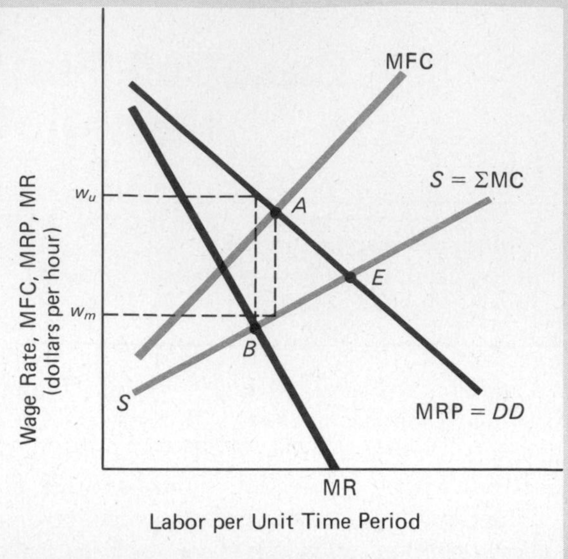

EXHIBIT 14–14

The Players' Union Versus the Team Owners—Bilateral Monopoly in the Factor Market. Baseball team owners would like to hire a quantity of labor where MFC = MRP; this occurs at point *A*. They would therefore want to set the wage rate at w_m. However, if the baseball players form a union, they want to sell the quantity of their product where MR = MC. Marginal revenue is given by the curve that is marginal to the MRP curve. This curve is labeled MR. The intersection, then, of marginal revenue and marginal cost, or *SS*, is at point *B*. Because the supply curve *SS* represents the summation of the individual marginal cost curves of the individual players, the players' union would like to set a wage rate of w_u.

Restricting Competition for Players

One of the ways that the team owners as a group have attempted to restrict the competition for players thereby destroying the monopsony power that they have by acting in unison, is the use of reserve clauses and drafts. A *reserve clause,* when in effect, has required any major league club wishing to acquire the services of another club's player to purchase his contract from the current owner. In this sense, once the player has signed a contract with a major league team, he has signed away part of the rights to his own baseball talent.

The reserve clause has in the past been coupled with the draft. With the draft system, the worst team in each league is given the first choice to select from ballplayers entering the profession, the next poorest team has the second choice, the third worst team has the third choice, and so on. The key provision to the past draft system has been that no team could bargain with a player who had been drafted by another team. Therefore, the draft system was used to eliminate the possibility that two or more teams would bid for the same athlete.

Question

1. When the World Hockey League came into existence to challenge the supremacy of the National Hockey League, hockey players' salaries increased. Is this consistent with the monopsony analysis just given? If so, why? If not, why not?

Bringing the Draft Back

Concepts Applied
■ Efficient allocation of resources, demand and supply of labor, opportunity cost

When the war in Vietnam ended, soon thereafter so did the draft. It was replaced with an all-volunteer army. It wasn't too many years later that headlines about the "failure of the volunteer armed forces" blossomed. Members of Congress cried out for a revival of the draft.

A Little Bit of History First

Before we can understand what is at issue, we have to look at the military conscription system that has been with us off and on for almost two centuries. It was first instituted during the War for Independence. Massachusetts and Virginia used conscription in 1777. On February 6, 1778, Congress recommended that the other colonies follow suit, but because France sent troops, it was unnecessary to initiate a general draft. During the War of 1812, Connecticut and Massachusetts apparently threatened to secede from the Union over the draft issue. In fact, when the draft almost became law in 1814, those two state legislatures were ready to guarantee the protection of their men from the federal government draft.

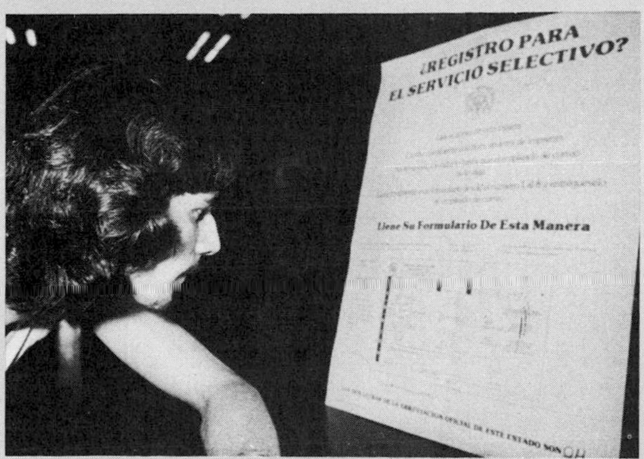

When the draft was discontinued after the Vietnam war, volunteers for the armed services seemingly failed to meet the labor power needs of the military. Congress succeeded in requiring Selective Service registration as a preparation for reinstituting the draft. Does the traditional system used in the past make the most efficient use of drafted personnel?

In April 1862, the Confederacy started universal conscription. By 1863, the North saw fit to pass the Enrollment Bill. Its passage started bloodshed and violence. Indeed, in 1863 police and militia battled antidraft mobs in the streets of New York for three days.[3] Even though there was a draft during the Civil War, men who were conscripted were allowed to "buy" someone else to go in their stead. Therefore, even though the method of conscription was arbitrary, the final determination of who would go to war was more flexible. For example, a lawyer who found himself conscripted had the option of paying someone else to replace him. As long as the price he paid was lower than the amount he could earn by remaining at work, both parties benefited financially from the arrangement. Since many workers did not earn as much as a lawyer could (that is, their opportunity costs were lower), it was not hard to find a replacement at a mutually agreeable price. Quite understandably, relatively few of the fighting men in the Civil War came from higher-paying civilian occupations. Since a man's contribution to the economy can be roughly indicated by his salary, it can be said in economists' terminology, that an efficient[4] allocation of resources resulted, since men worked (or fought) where their services were of most value.

Efficient allocation of resources. Let's detour for a moment into a more detailed discussion of this question of allocation of resources. Inefficiency exists whenever labor and machines are being used in such a manner that their full potential to the value of output of the economy is not being realized. A change from an inefficient to an efficient allocation therefore results, by

[3] Somewhat ironically, for at that same time only about 2 percent of the Union army were draftees.

[4] The term *efficient* as used in economics does not have any connotation of "good," "desirable," or "best," but merely refers to the most productive use of available resources.

definition, in an increase in the value of output. This does not mean that everyone will be better off. All changes in our economy carry certain costs, and those who incur these costs are worse off. But in theory, the increase in the value of output allows those who bear the costs of the change to be fully compensated, assuming, of course, that some institutional mechanism exists by means of which the compensating "side payment" can be carried out.

Employment Decisions in the Army

Costs that often go unnoticed are associated with any method of involuntary conscription. To simplify the explanation, let us analyze the military as though it were a business, referring to "managers" who hire and fire "workers" and who allocate part of their fixed yearly budget to pay for machines instead of men. When the Army obtains soldiers at a wage rate lower than that which would induce these men to join of their own free will, the military managers are obtaining incorrect information about the true costs of their operation. When labor is artificially underpriced (because of the draft), military management ends up using fewer machines and more men than it would otherwise have done. Why? The decision is made along the following lines: At a given price for men, the Army must consider the possibility of adding machinery either to aid the men or to replace them in certain jobs. If an additional adding machine will allow one man to do the work that two men would have done without the machine, management must look at the relative prices in order to decide rationally if the machine should be rented (or bought). If one man costs $100 a week and one adding machine rents for $25 per week, the machine will be used. But if the price for the man falls to $20 a week, it is not economically worthwhile to rent a machine for the purpose of saving labor costs. Because draftees are, in fact, paid far below their "going price" on the labor market, or the price that would induce them to volunteer, we know that the military is using "too many" men. We may say, then, that conscription results in a higher-than-optimal men-machine ratio in the military. As we will see later, this inevitably costs society more resources than are necessary for any desired level of national defense.

Additional costs of high turnover. Another cost results from the fact that conscription is typically for a period of only two years. In all likelihood, in a military composed entirely of volunteers obtained in the same way that firms hire their workers (adequate wages), the turnover time is longer than two years. In fact, since the volunteer Army must certainly pay much higher wages than those offered under a draft system, its management is making a relatively greater effort to ensure that turnover time is substantially longer.

Use of recruits when in the Army. In addition to the relatively high turnover costs associated with the draft, conscription also results in an inefficient allocation of men's talents once they are in the Army. In the civilian world one rarely sees college-trained men washing dishes and cleaning outhouses. Employers benefit from placing men where their training adds to productivity—that is, where they contribute most to the output of the firm. Not so in a draft Army.

All draftees are obtained at the same price, whether they are Ph.D.s or functional illiterates. As in business, an incentive probably exists for military management to use draftees most effectively, but the signals are not as apparent as in the civilian world where the highly differentiated salaries of workers of different quality are unmistakable. To hire a Ph.D., a business firm must pay more than it pays for an unschooled worker. It behooves the firm to get the most for its money by putting the Ph.D. to work at a task where he or she is most productive.

The Real Cost Is an Opportunity Cost

In addition to the above costs, the economy suffers an opportunity cost for every man drafted that is *totally independent of what draftees are paid.* The true cost to society of a draftee is what he could be earning as a civilian. When a man is paid $20,000 by an employer, we can usually assume that the employer is obtaining at least that amount in services; otherwise the arrangement would be terminated. If the same man is drafted, the economy is giving up about $20,000 worth of civilian productive services a year to obtain a much smaller amount in military services. *That* amount, and not the $6,500 in Army pay he might receive, is the true annual cost of his induction.

An implicit tax on draftees. Since a draft Army pays (via tax dollars) only a small fraction of the true opportunity cost of draftees, who, then, pays the rest? Obviously, the draftees themselves bear the burden of an implicit tax which roughly equals the difference between their civilian pay and their Army pay.[5] But all suffer somewhat, because the output of nonmilitary goods and services is lower and more expensive since these men are not working at their civilian jobs (unless, of course, all draftees are taken from the ranks of the unemployed).[6]

This hidden-tax aspect of the draft is certainly not new. Benjamin Franklin commented on it over 200 years ago in reviewing the court's opinion concerning the legality of impressment of American merchant seamen. He wrote:

> But if, as I suppose is often the case, the sailor who is pressed and obliged to serve for the defense of this trade at the rate of 25 shillings a month could have 3 pounds 15 shillings in the merchant service, you take from him 50 shillings a month; and if you have 100,000 in your service, you rob the honest part of society and their poor families of 250,000 pounds per month or three millions a year, and at the same time oblige them to hazard their lives in fighting for the defence of your trade.

Taxpayers Don't Want to Foot the Bill

One of the major complaints about an all-volunteer Army is that taxpayers do not want to pay the taxes to have the quantity and quality of armed forces desired by the military. That complaint is totally beside the point. Society pays for the Army whether or not the nation's youths are drafted. Additionally, it is not true that not enough volunteers have been found. Just because the final three months of 1978 showed enlistments at only 90 percent of desired enlistments does not mean our military strength is weaker. At the end of 1978, military power was 2,000 soldiers greater at the end of the year than had been budgeted for. The shortage in recruits had been more than made up by an excess of reenlistments. Only in specialized areas, such as medicine and the reserves, has there been any problem. Those shortfalls can be eliminated any time that Congress decides to pay the price to attract a desired number and quality of reservists and medical personnel.[7]

When we examine the data on quality, it is not at all clear what Congress means when it says that the all-volunteer Army has failed. When we had the draft in 1964, 68 percent of recruits were high school graduates. In 1979, almost 70 percent were high school graduates. In 1964, 1 of 7 recruits was classified in the lowest mental group eligible for recruitment. By 1979, the ratio had dropped to 1 in 20.

The clamor to revive the draft may grow louder in years to come; our analysis suggests that if it is revived, the quality of military labor power will not necessarily increase nor, certainly, will the full social cost of that manpower decrease.

The Supply of Military Personnel

Actually, there is a simple reason why the volunteer Army is "not working." That reason has to do with the lack of competitive wage rates offered by the military. Look at Exhibit 14–15. In it we show relative wage rates for the military, all industry, and government civilian workers. The average wages are expressed in 1980 dollars. When the all-volunteer Army was instituted, average real wages of the military approximated those in all of industry. Since 1972, however, the average real-wage rates have fallen significantly. It is not, therefore, surprising that the military is having a hard time filling its manpower quotas. It's not paying enough. You should be able to show in a simple supply and demand diagram of labor why the all-volunteer Army is "not working."

[5] To the Army pay should be added the benefits of training and education obtained while in the service, plus any consumption value received ("Join the Army and see the world").

[6] Some say we benefit because military service "makes men out of boys," good citizens out of bad, and community leaders out of juvenile delinquents. Of course, there may be cheaper ways of obtaining these "goods."

[7] One of the reasons there is such a demand for medical personnel is because the military services insist that uniformed personnel provide medical services to both enlisted personnel and their families wherever they are stationed. Presumably, the military could simply provide medical insurance as a fringe benefit rather than providing medical services directly.

EXHIBIT 14–15
Comparative Average Real Wages: Military Versus the Private Sector. Here we show comparative average real wages from 1939 through 1980. We see that the military has offered wages below those received in industry (and certainly those received in civilian government) most of the time. Only in 1972 were military and private industry wages comparable. Since then they have been falling. The result has been a "shortage" of volunteers for the military. (Average real wages are expressed in 1980 dollars.)

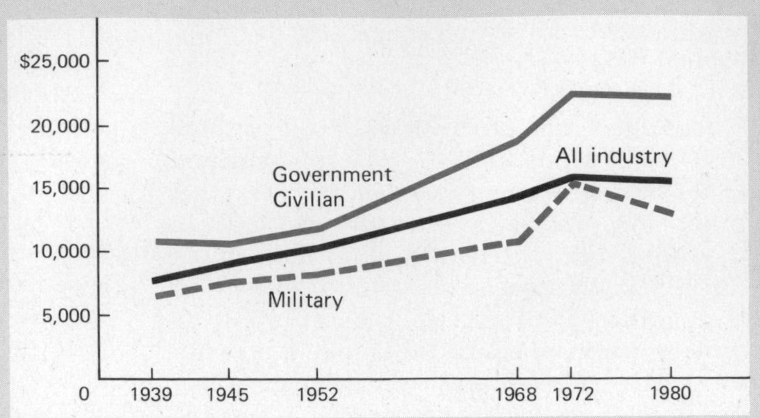

Additionally, the military today could reduce its labor costs by recruiting already trained civilian personnel for middle-level positions. This would mean recruiting individuals ages 30 to 50 to perform technical and management jobs for the military while remaining civilians. Today, the military basically draws all of its middle- and upper-level personnel from within the ranks. That means that it is forced to keep and train soldiers to staff important technical and management positions. Why can't it go out into the labor market and hire civilians, who remain civilians, to perform technical and management jobs? These are not individuals who would be operating "on the front," as it were, anyway. Do they really need to be soldiers?

Questions

1. How is it possible to have a "shortage" of military personnel?
2. Who benefits from the draft? Who loses?

Definition of Terms

Unions Organizations of workers that usually seek to secure economic improvements for their members.

Craft unions Labor unions composed of workers who engage in a particular trade or skill, such as baking, carpentry, or plumbing.

Collective bargaining Bargaining between management of a company or of a group of companies and management of a union or a group of unions for the purpose of setting a mutually agreeable contract on wages, fringe benefits, and working conditions for *all* employees in the union(s). Different from *individual* bargaining, where each employee strikes a bargain with his or her employer individually.

Industrial unions Labor unions that consist of workers from a particular industry, such as automobile manufacturing or steel manufacturing.

Right-to-work laws Laws that make it illegal to require union membership as a condition of continuing employment in a particular firm.

Closed shop A business enterprise in which an employee must belong to the union before he or she can be employed. That employee must remain in the union after he or she becomes employed.

Union shop A business enterprise that allows nonunion members to become employed, conditional upon their joining the union by some specified date after employment begins.

Real wages Money wages divided by a price index. Real wages are different from money or nominal wages because they represent the true purchasing power of the dollars paid to workers.

Monopsonist A single buyer.

Marginal factor cost (MFC) The change in total costs due to a one-unit increase in the variable input. The cost of using more of a factor of production.

Bilateral monopoly A situation in the labor market where a single seller of labor confronts a single buyer (monopsonist).

Exploitation Paying a resource less than its value (VMP).

Monopolistic exploitation Paying a resource its marginal revenue product instead of its value of marginal product. Thus, we measure monopolistic exploitation by the difference between VMP and MRP.

Monopsonistic exploitation Exploitation due to monopsony power. It leads to a price for the variable input that is less than its marginal revenue product. Thus, we measure monopsonistic exploitation by the difference between marginal revenue product and the wage rate.

Chapter Summary

1. The American labor movement started with local craft unions but was very small until the twentieth century. The history of labor in the United States involves the Knights of Labor, the American Federation of Labor, and the Congress of Industrial Organizations.
2. The Great Depression saw President Roosevelt get the National Industrial Recovery Act passed. This act allowed for the right of labor to bargain collectively. It was later supplanted by the Wagner Act, which is called labor's Magna Carta.
3. All fringe benefits must be included in the actual wages paid workers if we want to analyze the effects of unions. Fringe benefits include health insurance, better working conditions, life insurance, and so on.
4. In analyzing the effects of the labor movement, we must be careful to distinguish between money wages and real wages because it is the latter that represent the true purchasing power of money earned. Real wages are equal to money wages divided by a price index. For all labor taken together, the evidence is not overwhelming that the union movement has allowed workers to receive an increasing share of total national income. In fact, the share of national income going to labor has remained fairly constant for the last 47 years.
5. In a situation where there is only one buyer of a particular input, a monopsony arises. The single buyer faces an upward-sloping supply curve and therefore must pay higher wages to get more workers to work. The single buyer faces a marginal factor cost curve that is upward sloping and above the supply curve. The buyer hires workers up to the point where the value of marginal (physical) product equals the marginal factor cost. Then the buyer would find out how low a wage rate could be paid to get that many workers.
6. Often the monopsony model is used to justify a minimum wage, which in the monopsony situation may result in greater employment at higher wages.
7. Exploitation can be broken down into that due to monopoly power and that due to monopsony power. Monopolistic exploitation is the difference between value of marginal product and marginal revenue product; monopsonist exploitation is the difference between marginal revenue product and the wage rate. Total exploitation is the difference between the value of marginal product and the wage rate.
8. We can analyze the activities of the American Medical Association in restricting the supply of doctors as we would analyze any monopoly. The effect has been to prevent the supply from shifting out as fast as the demand curve has shifted out, thereby raising the wages of doctors.
9. When a professional players' union faces team owners who act as a monopsonist, we have a bilateral monopoly situation.
10. The military draft does not alter the social opportunity of supplying the Army with soldiers; it simply taxes draftees instead of all taxpayers.

Selected References

Demmert, H. G. *The Economics of Professional Team Sports*. Lexington, Mass.: Heath, 1973.

Mitchell, Daniel J. B. *Unions, Wages, and Inflation*. Washington, D.C.: The Brookings Institution, 1980.

Rees, Albert. *Economics of Trade Unions*. 2nd ed. Chicago: University of Chicago Press, 1977.

Rowan, Richard L., ed. *Readings in Labor Economics and Labor Relations*. 4th ed. Homewood, Ill.: Irwin, 1980.

Answers to Preview and Study Questions

1. What are the major types of unions?

The earliest, and one of the most important forms today, is the craft union, which is a collection of skilled laborers. Another major form of collectivized labor is the industrial union, in which all (or most) laborers (skilled or unskilled) in an industry unite—such as the steelworkers, or mineworkers, and so on. Union membership has increased and decreased in direct accordance with the degree of governmental protection provided. The 1935 Wagner Act was deliberately pro-union. However, since 1947 (the Taft-Hartley Act) and 1959 (the Landrum-Griffin Act) union power has been reduced somewhat. Since 1965 public-sector unions, which are organizations of public employees, have grown dramatically, while membership in nonpublic-employee unions has leveled off, or even fallen slightly.

2. What do unions maximize?

Unions do not have unlimited power; in the United States the "rules of the game" that have evolved declare that unions can set wage rates, *or* set the number of laborers who will be employed—they can't do both. As a consequence, a trade-off exists for union leaders; if they maximize wages, some members will become unemployed; if they maximize employment, wages will be relatively low. Union leaders often decide to maximize wages for a given number of workers—presumably the higher seniority workers; each union somehow reaches its own decision as to how the trade-off is to be resolved.

3. Do unions help laborers?

Surprisingly, the answer to this question is *not* a simple yes. If unions are to be considered effective, they must increase real-wage rates *above* productivity increases; after all, market forces will increase real wage rates at the rate of productivity change! Yet, if real wage rates *are* increased more rapidly than the rate of productivity increase, unions will create unemployment; hence, *some* laborers will be helped (those who retain their jobs at above-productivity levels) and some will be hurt (those who become unemployed). The evidence is that unions are neither a necessary nor sufficient condition for high real wages. That is, wages in the United States were relatively high *before* the U.S. labor movement, and countries with very strong unions (England, Italy, France) have relatively low real wages. Moreover, labor's *overall* share of national income has not changed significantly over the past five decades—although *union* labor's share may have increased relative to *nonunion* labor's share.

4. What is a monopsonist, and how does it go about deciding its profit-maximizing employment rate?

A monopsonist is a single buyer; in this chapter we consider a monopsonistic buyer of labor. How a monopsonist reaches the profit-maximizing employment rate is a familiar story; in general it hires labor up to the point where the marginal benefit of doing so equals the marginal cost of doing so. The specifics are a little trickier. Let's assume that our monopsonist is a perfect competitor (price taker) in the output market. As a consequence, the MB of hiring labor is labor's value of marginal product; MB = VMP of labor. The MC of hiring labor must reflect the fact that the monopsonist faces *the* industry labor supply schedule; as such the monopsonist must increase wage rates in order to hire more labor. But, of course, it must increase wage rates for *all* the labor that it hires—not just the marginal laborer. Thus, the MC of hiring labor for a monopsonist (the marginal factor cost, MFC) will be greater than the wage rate. Since the profit-maximizing employment rate is generally where MB = MC, the monopsonist will have labor up to the point where the VMP = MFC. It then pays the lowest wage rate required to attract that quantity of labor. This wage rate will be below the VMP of labor.

5. What is a bilateral monopoly?

As the name suggests, bilateral monopoly is a market situation in which one seller (a monopolist) faces one buyer (a monopsonist). While this situation might appear unlikely, in practice it is not. Such a situation exists in professional sports where team leagues face player unions, and is approached when industrywide bargaining takes place between management and union representatives.

Problem

(Answer at the back of the book)

1. The graph at right indicates a monopsonistic firm, which is a perfect competitor in the product market.
   a. Which curve is the monopsonistic firm's demand for labor curve?
   b. Which is the supply of labor curve?
   c. How many laborers will this firm voluntarily hire?
   d. Given the profit-maximizing employment rate, what is the lowest wage rate that this firm can offer in order to get this quantity of labor?
   e. To what extent are these laborers "exploited"?

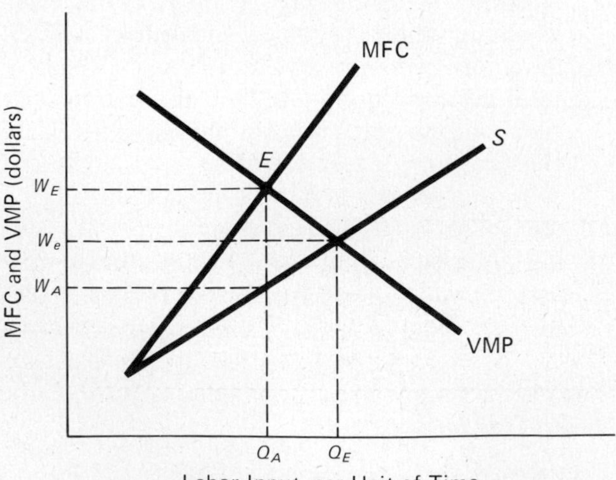

15
Rent, Interest, and Profits

TOPICS FOR REVIEW

The topics listed below, which we have already analyzed, are applied in this chapter. You may find it worthwhile to review them. For your convenience each topic is followed by the number identifying the specific "Concepts in Brief."

a. Trade-off between consumer and capital goods (2–3)

b. Profit as a resource allocator (4–3)

c. Elasticity of supply (6–5)

d. Accounting versus economic profits (8–1)

FOR PREVIEW AND STUDY

1. What is rent?
2. What criticisms can be made of a 100 percent tax on pure economic rents?
3. What is interest?
4. What is the economic function of interest rates?
5. What is the economic function of profits?

In Part I, we talked about four factors of production—labor, land, capital, and entrepreneurship. In this part, we have really discussed only the demand and supply of labor and the factor payments to labor—wages and salaries. The other three factors of production and their respective factor payments—rent, interest, and profits—are also important. In this chapter, we will look at the determination of each of these factor payments. In the Issues and Applications section, we will see what happens when there is legislation limiting interest rates.

Rent

Let us consider what the word *rent* has come to mean in economics. Economists originally used the term *rent* to designate the payment for the *use* of land in order to distinguish it from the payment for the use of capital equipment—buildings and machines. The distinguishing feature about land is that it is in completely inelastic supply (although there are exceptions that we will discuss below). Presumably, the supply of buildings and machines is, at least in the long run, not perfectly inelastic. Economists later discovered that there are other factors that are also in completely inelastic supply. Thus, the use of the word *rent* now applies to a payment to any resource that has a perfectly inelastic supply curve. In order to make the meaning of the term even clearer, we talk in terms of **pure economic rent.**

PURE ECONOMIC RENT

We define pure economic rent as a payment to any factor of production that is in completely inelastic supply. Remember that a supply curve that is completely inelastic is vertical: no matter what the prevailing market price for the resource, the quantity and quality supplied will remain the same. In other words, there is no responsiveness of quantity supplied to price. It is not surprising that the term *economic rent* has been associated with the payment for the use of land, for land seems to be the best example of a resource that is fixed in supply.

Determining Land Rent

One of the earliest writers on the topic of economic rent was David Ricardo. He assumed that the quantity of land in a country is fixed. The supply curve of land, then, is vertical and the price elasticity of supply of land is therefore zero. If the supply

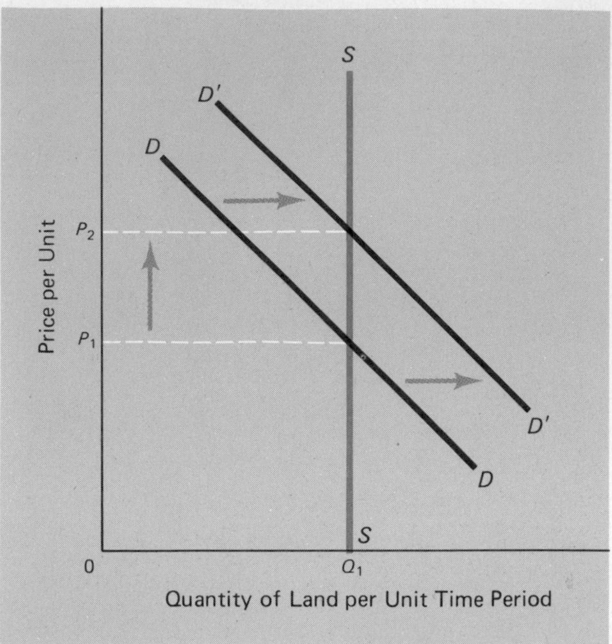

EXHIBIT 15–1
Pure Economic Rent. If indeed the supply curve of land were completely price inelastic in the long run, then it would be depicted by *SS*. At the quantity in existence, Q_1, any and all revenues are pure economic rent. If demand is *DD*, the price will be P_1; if demand is $D'D'$, price will rise to P_2. Economic rent would be $P_1 \times Q_1$ and $P_2 \times Q_1$, respectively.

of land is represented by *SS* in Exhibit 15–1 and the demand curve is *DD*, then the price of land would be P_1. If the demand curve for some reason shifts out to $D'D'$, then the price of land will rise to P_2. Nothing, however, would change the quantity of land supplied.

David Ricardo was looking at the *total* demand for land—that is, the demand for all land in existence. Therefore, there was no opportunity cost, he reasoned, to the economy of using that land, since it was fixed in supply. That is, no matter what the price of land, the same *total* quantity would remain in existence. Thus, the revenues (price × quantity) derived from the ownership of land were considered by David Ricardo to be a pure economic rent. In Exhibit 15–1, the demand curve is *DD*. Pure economic rent is equal to $P_1 \times Q_1$. If the demand curve shifts to $D'D'$, pure economic rent increases to $P_2 \times Q_1$.

Using Ricardo's analysis, even in the long run, the supply of all land will not change, no matter what its price. Thus, the notion of pure economic rent is long run. That is, in the long run, no matter what the price of the product, the available quantity of the resource in question will remain unchanged. Looking at pure economic rent in this light, we can redefine it thus:

Pure economic rent is the *rate* of payment to a resource over and above what is necessary to keep that resource in existence at its current level.

According to Ricardo's analysis, all payment to landowners was a pure economic rent because there was no alternative use for land if we consider the total supply. As we will see in another example, the concept of economic rent can be applied to human resources, also. A person can be paid more than is necessary to keep that person working in a particular occupation. cf OJ Simpson

IF LAND RENT IS A SURPLUS, THEN WHY NOT TAX ALL OF IT?

If land is indeed in perfectly inelastic supply, then the price of land (and hence pure economic rents) will not alter its allocation as a resource. Land is there and, taken as a whole, cannot be "reduced in supply" if its price falls. In other words, the price of land, given that it's a pure economic rent, performs no allocative function. Therefore, all payment to landowners has been labeled by some as a surplus—that is, a payment that is unnecessary in order to keep the resource in current use. One of the best-known proponents of this idea was Henry George, who wrote a book called *Progress and Poverty* in 1879. His idea was to eliminate this "surplus" by taxation. Furthermore, he felt that all *increases* in land value reduced the general economic growth. Hence, for George, they were "unearned" income.

The Single Tax on Land

George's idea came to be known as a single-tax movement. The idea was that except for a single tax on land all other taxes should be eliminated. Presumably, since the payment for land is a pure economic rent, all land payments can be taxed without reducing the availability of land, since we are considering the total supply, which is fixed. In the case of Exhibit 15-1, the government could, according to Henry George, make a tax equal to a fixed amount, say, one-half of the pure economic rent given by the rectangle $P_1 \times Q_1$. All the tax would be borne by the landowner rather than by consumers or manufacturers. The only thing in principle that the landowner could do is withdraw land from productive uses. But the landowner would not have an incentive to do that because there would be no rental income whatsoever. Presumably, so long as the single tax was less than 100 percent of all payments to land use, the land would still remain in use.

Criticism of the Single Tax

There have been numerous criticisms of Henry George's analysis that all payment for the use of land is a pure economic rent. Immediately, we can see that this cannot be the case for all units of land. After all, income payments for the use of land may reflect not only rent, but also interest, wages, and profits. Very little land is rented without having first been improved. Since the strict definition of land as a natural resource is that it has not been altered by man, then any alteration represents capital for which one expects to receive interest. It would be extremely difficult to disentangle the economic rent from the payments for capital improvements.

A second telling criticism is that at current levels of government spending—somewhere between 35 and 42 percent of national income—a land tax alone would not bring in enough revenue to cover all such government expenditures. Thus, a land tax cannot realistically be considered as a single tax, unless the size of government were to decrease dramatically.

ECONOMIC RENTS TO OTHER FACTORS OF PRODUCTION

So far, we have limited our discussion to the pure economic rent obtainable from a fixed supply of land. The analysis, however, is equally applicable to any other factor of production that is fixed in supply. Let's consider the economic rents accruing to those individuals possessing scarce natural talents. Remember that pure economic rent is defined as any payment over and above what is necessary to maintain a factor of production in its current activity. Natural talents that human beings possess will be more significant in some occupations than in others. They seem to be particularly important in athletics, acting, music, and other entertainment endeavors. In some cases, pure economic rents can explain a great part of the difference between the extraordinary earnings of highly successful musicians, for example, and the average musician. At least part of the wages of "superstars" like the Bee Gees, Linda Ronstadt, or the Doobie Brothers consists of economic rents. In other words, they would be willing to work just about as hard as they do now for less pay. The question then becomes, Why do they get paid so much if they are really willing to work for less? The answer is in the following discussion, where we see that economic rent may be described as a surplus, although it still serves a rationing or allocative function.

Joan Baez's Curious Habit

During the 1960s and for part of the 1970s, a female folk singer was extremely popular. Her name is Joan Baez. She was a major participant in the anti-Vietnam War movement and has offered political-type folk songs for years. At the height of her career, she decided to put into practice her egalitarian ideas. She determined that ticket prices for her musical performances were too "high." Consequently, when she gave a concert, she insisted in her contract that all tickets be sold at the same price—say, $5. Assume that she gave five concerts a year, that each concert hall had 20,000 seats, and that 20,000 tickets were available at a price of $5. Thus, 100,000 individuals per year were allowed to hear Ms. Baez. This is represented by point *A* in Exhibit 15–2.

Baez was, by assumption, still receiving economic rents, because we hypothesized that her supply curve of concerts was vertical at 100,000 concert seats per year. At $5 a ticket, however, the annual quantity of seats demanded was 150,000, represented by point *B*. The difference between *A* and *B* was the excess quantity of tickets demanded at the below market clearing price of $5 a seat. The *additional* economic rent that she could have earned by charging the market clearing price of, say, $15 per seat, would serve as the rationing device that would make the quantity demanded equal to the quantity supplied.

Part of the rent that she *could* have earned was dissipated—it was captured, for example, by radio station owners in the form of promotional gains if they were allowed to give away a certain number of tickets on the air (even if they had to pay $5 per ticket, since the tickets were worth $15). Ticket scalpers (who resell tickets at higher prices) also captured a part of the rents. Conceivably, at 100,000 seats Ms. Baez could have charged the market clearing price ($15 per ticket) and given away to her favorite charity the portion of these rents ($10 per ticket) that was being dissipated. In that manner, she could have made sure that the recipients of the rents were "worthy" in her own estimation. Presumably, she had no special desire to increase the net worth position of scalpers and corporations that own radio stations.[1]

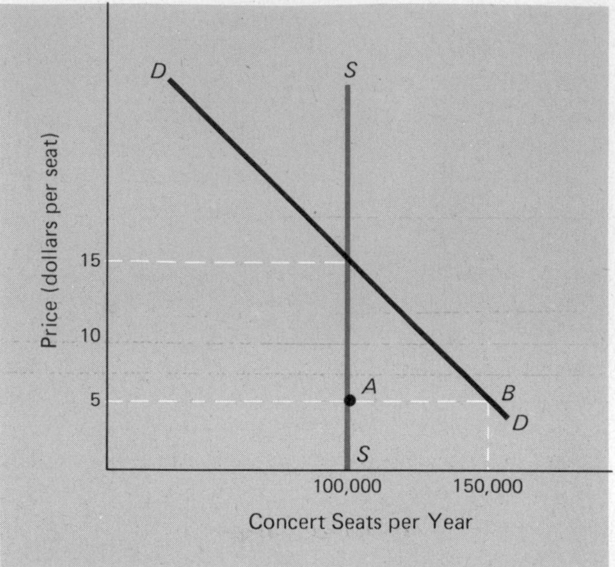

EXHIBIT 15–2

The Allocative Function of Rent—the Case of Joan Baez's Concerts. If Joan Baez agreed to give five concerts a year at any price, and assuming that there were 20,000 seats in each concert hall, then her supply curve of concerts *SS* was vertical at 100,000 seats per year. The demand curve is given by *DD*. She wanted only a price of $5 to be charged. At that price, the quantity of seats demanded per year was 150,000. The excess quantity demanded was equal to the horizontal distance between point *A* and point *B*, or 50,000 seats per year.

> ***Concepts in Brief 15-1***
>
> ■ Pure economic rent is defined as any payment to a factor of production that is completely inelastic in supply.
>
> ■ Pure economic rent is a payment to a resource over and above what is necessary to keep that resource in existence at its current level.
>
> ■ The payment for the use of land was considered a surplus by Henry George, who suggested that this surplus be taxed away by a single tax.
>
> ■ Factors of production other than land can earn pure economic rents if their supply is completely price inelastic.

[1] It is interesting to note that Muhammad Ali understood this argument. In the beginning of his fighting career, he was interested in low-priced tickets so that "his general public fans" could see him fight. They seldom did, however, since the actual price of a ticket exceeded the printed price. He then changed his behavior and started charging market clearing prices and contributing enormous sums to hospitals and other charitable outlets.

Interest

Interest as a factor payment is related to the use of capital. It is also related to the payment that must be made to obtain credit.

INTEREST AND CREDIT

Interest takes on the form of a payment for the use of money. When you obtain credit, you actually obtain money to have command over resources today. We can say, then, that interest is the payment for current rather than future command over resources. Thus, interest is the payment for obtaining credit. If you borrow $100 from me, you have command over $100 worth of goods and services today. I no longer have that command. You promise to pay me back $100 plus interest at some future date. The interest that you pay is usually expressed as a percentage of the total loan calculated on an annual basis. Thus, if at the end of one year, you pay me back $110, the annual interest is $10 ÷ $100, or 10 percent. When you go out into the marketplace to obtain credit, you will find that the interest rate charged differs greatly. A loan to buy a house (this type of loan is called a mortgage) may cost you 10–17 percent annual interest. An installment loan to buy an automobile may cost you 10–20 percent annual interest. The federal government, when it wishes to obtain credit (issues U.S. Treasury securities), may have to pay only 7–13 percent annual interest. Variations in the rate of annual interest that must be paid for credit depend on the following factors:

Length of Loan

In some (but not all) cases, the longer the loan will be outstanding, other things being equal, the greater will be the interest rate charged.

Risk

The greater the risk of nonrepayment of the loan, other things being equal, the greater the interest rate charged. Risk is assessed on the basis of the credit worthiness of the borrower. It is also assessed on the basis of whether the borrower provides collateral for the loan. Collateral consists of any asset that will automatically become the property of the lender should the borrower fail to comply with the loan agreement. Typically, when you borrow to purchase a car, the car itself is collateral for the loan. Should you default on payments to the lending institution, it can, in most cases, repossess the car, sell it, and pay off the loan that way. The more and the better the collateral offered for a loan, the lower the rate of interest charged, other things being equal.

Handling Charges

It takes resources to set up a loan. Papers have to be filled out and filed, credit references have to be checked out, collateral has to be examined, and so on. It turns out that the larger the amount of the loan, the smaller will be the handling (or administrative) charges as a percentage of the total loan. Therefore, we would predict that, other things being equal, the larger the loan, the lower the interest rate.

Loans are taken out both by consumers and by businesses. It is useful for us to separate the motives underlying the demand for loans by these two groups of individuals. We therefore will treat consumption loans and investment loans separately.

CONSUMPTION LOANS

Consumption loans are taken out by consumers in order to purchase goods and services today, to be paid for in the future. When you borrow, you generally will not be able to consume as much in the future, for that is when you will be paying for your loan. Borrowing—consumer loans—can be looked at as a form of dissaving.

You can save until you have enough saved to buy the things you want, such as consumer durables like cars and houses and washing machines; but if you do that, you will be concentrating all your purchases at a point in time in the future. However, by borrowing you can spread out your purchases more evenly during your lifetime. Therefore, borrowing (consumption loans) can be viewed both as a form of dissaving and also as a form of obtaining optimal consumption over your lifetime.

Often one's current income temporarily falls below the average income level that one expects to earn over, say, the next few years. People sometimes borrow whenever they perceive a temporary dip in their current income, assuming they expect their income to go back up to "normal" later on.

Your credit worthiness is usually based upon the probability that you will be able to pay off your loan as it comes due. Obviously, you could have an extremely high discount rate (be very impatient) and not be able to borrow much because the prospects of your paying the loan back might be very low. Few would want to lend you money, which is usually the case with students. You want to borrow—buy on credit—but have difficulty doing so because you have no credit rating, no job, and so on (although you might get a government-backed loan or get your parents to guarantee that a regular loan will be repaid).

Demand for Consumption Loans

The demand curve for consumption loans will be like any other demand curve; it will be downward sloping. We show it as *DD* in Exhibit 15-3. At lower rates of interest, a larger quantity of credit will be demanded by consumers for the purpose of consuming today rather than waiting. At higher rates of interest, the quantity demanded of credit will be less, other things being constant.

The Supply of Credit, or Loanable Funds

The demand side is only one part of the picture. We must also look to the supply side in order to find the equilibrium rate of interest in the consumption loan market. The supply of loanable funds depends on individuals' willingness to save. When you save, you exchange rights to current consumption for rights to future consumption. The more current consumption you give up, the more valuable a marginal unit is in comparison with future consumption.

Remember our discussion of diminishing marginal utility? We said that the more of something you have, the less you value an additional unit. Conversely, the less of something you have, the more you value an additional unit. Thus, when you give up current consumption of a good—that is, have less of it—you value an additional unit more. In other words, the more that you save today, the more utility you attach to your last unit of consumption. Thus, in order to be induced to save more—that is, to consume less—you have to be offered a bigger and bigger reward to match the marginal utility of current consumption that you will have lost by saving. To induce people to save more, one must offer a higher rate of interest. Thus, we expect that the supply curve of loanable funds will be upward sloping. At higher rates of interest, savers will be willing to offer more current consumption to borrowers, other things constant.[2]

[2] Actually, to give a complete discussion of the *supply* of loanable funds would require a more detailed analysis of the banking system and monetary policy. Such a discussion would be found in a course on macroeconomics.

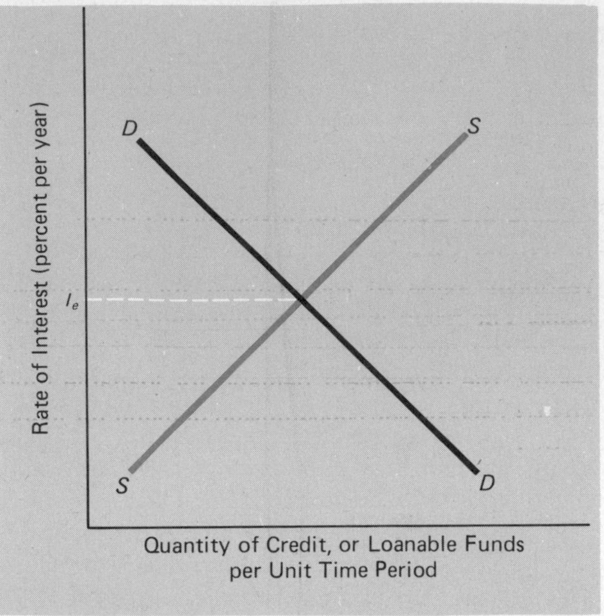

EXHIBIT 15-3
The Supply and Demand of Consumption Loans. We draw *DD* as the demand curve for consumption loans by households. It is downward sloping. *SS* is the supply curve of credit, or loanable funds. It is upward sloping. The intersection of *SS* and *DD* gives the equilibrium interest rate, which is i_e.

Equilibrium Rate of Interest

We can see in Exhibit 15-3 that the equilibrium rate of interest is established at the intersection of the supply curve and the demand curve for loanable funds. This equilibrium rate of interest is labeled i_e.

Now we turn to investment loans.

INVESTMENT LOANS

Why do businesses wish to use the loanable funds made available by savers? The answer is: to invest in capital equipment—such as more machines or more buildings—or in more improvements to land. We therefore call such loans **investment loans.** Any time a firm believes that by using more physical capital in its production process it can increase the revenues (net of other costs) by more than the cost of the capital, it will enter the loanable funds market, obtain credit, and make the investment. The price paid for the use of loanable funds is called interest. So, too, is the market return earned by the capital. If a machine that costs $100,000 earns $10,000 a year, we say that the capital earns 10 percent interest. (The $10,000 is *not* profit as we have defined profit.) Businesses compare the interest rate they must pay in the loanable funds market with the interest rate they think they can earn by investing in capital; this comparison helps them decide whether to invest.

Adding the Demand for Investment Loans

In Exhibit 15–4, we have added the demand for investment loans to the demand for consumption loans. The result is a new equilibrium rate of interest in the loanable funds (or credit) market. (In reality, the investment demand for loanable funds greatly exceeds the consumption demand for loans.)

In Exhibit 15–4, we see that when we consider both consumer loans and investment loans, the new equilibrium rate of interest is i_e'. This is the rate that equates the quantity of credit supplied with the quantity of credit (or loans) demanded. Remember that $D'D'$ consists of both types of loan demand—consumption and investment.

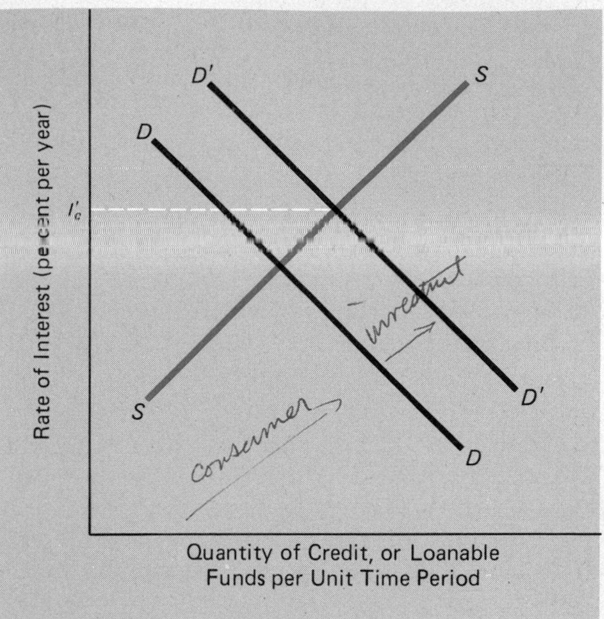

EXHIBIT 15–4
Adding the Demand for Investment Loans. We add the demand curve for investment loans to the demand curve for consumption loans, which is *DD*. The result is *D'D'*. The intersection of *D'D'* with *SS*, the supply curve of loanable funds, gives us the new equilibrium level of interest in the economy, i_e'.

THE ALLOCATIVE ROLE OF INTEREST

Back in Chapter 4, we talked about the price system and the role that prices played in the allocation of resources. Interest is a price that allocates loanable funds (credit) to consumers and to businesses. Within the business sector, interest allocates loanable funds to different firms and therefore to different investment projects. Those investment, or capital, projects whose rates of return are higher than the market rate of interest in the credit market will be undertaken, given an unrestricted market for loanable funds. For example, if the expected rate of return on the purchase of a new factory in some industry is 20 percent and loanable funds can be acquired for 15 percent, then the investment project may take place. If, on the other hand, that same project had only an expected rate of return of 9 percent, it would not be undertaken. In sum, the interest rate allocates loanable funds to those industries where resources will be the most productive.

It is important to realize that the interest rate performs the function of allocating money capital—loanable funds—but that what this ultimately does is allocate real physical capital to various firms for investment projects. Often, noneconomists view the movement of loanable funds (credit) simply as something that has to do with "money" and not with the "real" world of machines and factories.

CALCULATING THE RETURN TO CAPITAL

We started out this analysis explaining that interest was considered a return to capital. The way we would calculate the return to capital would be as follows: We would take the total receipts from the production and sale of the firm's commodities. We call that total revenues, or TR. We then subtract all costs for raw materials and purchased intermediate goods. We call that C_R. Then we subtract labor costs (C_L). We must also subtract out any depreciation costs for the capital equipment (C_D). And, finally, we have to subtract out the full opportunity cost of any owner-manager's contributed talents if they are not explicitly included in salaries paid for workers (C_O). Finally, we have to worry about the government, because there will be taxes (T) to pay.

If we subtract out all of the costs mentioned above from total revenues, we will get what is known as the **gross return to capital,** or:

$$\text{gross return to capital} = \text{TR} - (C_R + C_L + C_D + C_O + T)$$

The gross return to capital can be used to pay interest on borrowed money capital, or loanable funds, and to pay a profit to entrepreneurs. We discuss profit in the next section.

Part of the gross return to capital is what is known as the **pure return to capital** and that is simply the opportunity cost of capital, which we have always referred to as a cost of doing business.

We now turn to profits, the payment to the factor of production called entrepreneurship.

Concepts in Brief 15-2

- Interest is a factor payment for the use of capital.
- However, interest payments normally take the form of payments for the use of money. Interest is really the payment for current command over resources (credit). The interest that must be paid for borrowing depends on: (1) length of loan, (2) risk, and (3) handling charges.
- The total private demand for loans consists of the demand for consumption loans and the demand for investment loans. The former are loans by households; the latter are loans by businesses.
- The supply of credit (or loanable funds) is upward sloping.
- The intersection of the total demand for credit with the supply of credit yields the equilibrium rate of interest.
- The interest rate represents the price of current consumption. It serves as the allocating signal to consumers and businesses.

Profits

We earlier called entrepreneurship, or entrepreneurial talent, the fourth factor of production. Profit is the reward that this factor earns. You may recall that entrepreneurship involves engagement in the risk of starting new businesses. In a sense, then, nothing can be produced without an input of entrepreneurial skills.

Until now in this part, we have been able to talk about the demand and the supply of labor, land, and capital. We can't as easily talk about the demand and supply of entrepreneurship. For one thing, we have no way to quantify entrepreneurship. What measure should we use? No one knows. We do know that entrepreneurship exists. We cannot, however, easily present a supply and demand analysis to show the market clearing price per unit of entrepreneurship. We must use a different approach. What we will do is first point out what profit is *not.* Then we will examine the sources of true, or economic, profit. Finally, we will look at the functions of profits in a market system.

DISTINGUISHING BETWEEN ECONOMIC PROFITS AND BUSINESS, OR ACCOUNTING, PROFITS

When we started out the discussion of rent, we had to make a distinction between the common notions of rent and what the economist means by pure economic rent. We must do the same thing when we refer to profit. We have to distinguish between **economic profit** and **accounting profit.** The accountant calculates profit for a business as the difference between total explicit revenues and total explicit costs. Consider an extreme example. You are given a large farm as part of your inheritance. All of the land, fertilizer, seed, machinery, and tools are fully paid for. You take over the farm and work on it diligently with half a dozen laborers. At the end of the year, you sell the output for, say, $1 million. Your accountant then subtracts your *explicit* expenses.

The difference is called profit, but it is not economic profit. Why? Because no accounting was taken of the implicit (as opposed to the explicit) costs of using the land, seed, tools, and machinery. The only explicit cost that was considered was the laborers' wages. As long as the land could be rented out, the seed could be sold, and the tools and machinery could be leased, there was an opportunity cost of using them. To derive the economic profits that you might have earned last year from the farm, you must subtract from total revenues the full opportunity cost of all factors of production used (which will include both implicit and explicit costs).

As a summary, then, accounting profits' main use is the definition of taxable income and, as such, includes returns to both owner's labor and capital. Economic profit, on the other hand, represents a return over and above the opportunity cost of both resources.

When viewed in this light, it is possible for economic profits to be negative, even if accounting profits are positive. Using the farming case again, what if the opportunity cost of using all of the resources turned out to be $1.1 million? Then the economic profits would have been $-\$100,000$. You would have suffered economic losses.

In sum, the businessperson's accounting definition and the economist's economic definition of profits usually do not coincide. Economic profits are a residual. They are whatever remains after *all* economic, or opportunity, costs are taken into account.

THEORIES OF WHY PROFITS EXIST

When goods and services are sold, the owners of labor, land, and capital receive wages, rents, and interest. The question now remains, Why doesn't the summation of payments to the owners of labor, land, and capital just equal the revenues received from the sale of products? Why should there ever be anything left over? Otherwise stated, why should there ever be profits, which are the residual after all costs are taken into account? In order to answer this question, we must come up with a theory of why profits exist. Unfortunately, there is no one accepted (or acceptable) theory that we can give. Here we present three possible reasons why profits exist. These theories have to do with risk taking, disequilibrium, and monopoly power. We treat them in that order.

Risk Taking

One theory of profit contends that profits are the reward for bearing risk. Every person who undertakes a new business opportunity is subjecting himself or herself to the risk of failure, or to the risk of earning less in that venture than in another. Individuals who engage in contractual labor avoid, to a large extent, such a risk. They can sign long-term contracts that guarantee a specified wage rate. Owners of land (or natural resources) can do the same thing. But the owner of a business does not have a contract with some "higher power" that guarantees that revenues will exceed cost. If the business fails, it is the owner who explicitly suffers a reduction in wealth, or net worth. And businesses do fail. Some estimates show that two out of three new small businesses fail. Clearly, in order to get entrepreneurs to take a risk, greater-than-normal accounting profits must be expected. That is to say, potential economic profits must be lurking in the future, if indeed the business venture will be undertaken.

The reason that individuals must be rewarded or compensated for undertaking risk is that most people seem to dislike risk. Consider an example. You are offered a business proposition. You must contribute \$1,000. The chances of losing the whole \$1,000 are 50 percent. On the other hand, the chances of earning \$1,000 are also 50 percent. Would you go into this business? Probably not. You have to be better rewarded for taking the risk of losing all your money.

Some businesses fail and others don't. When we average out the losses and the profits, we find that, on average, positive economic profits are made. The reason they are made, according to the risk theory of profit, is to compensate entrepreneurs for undertaking the risk of failure.

Disequilibrium

Another theory of profits concerns the possibility of markets being out of equilibrium. A market is in disequilibrium when higher- or lower-than-normal rates of return are being earned. Remember that the long-run equilibrium of a perfectly competitive situation is one in which zero economic profits are earned. We are constantly moving *toward* long-run equilibrium; thus, in the short run we are normally in disequilibrium. Consider an example where there is an abrupt increase in demand for a particular product. The first entrepreneurs to perceive this increase in demand will be able to enter the market. Their production and sales plans can be adjusted before others catch on. They will be rewarded for catching this momentary disequilibrium by higher-than-normal profits. That is, they will receive economic profits.

The same analysis may hold with respect to the supply side. Certain entrepreneurs who realize that a newly available method of production could earn them higher profits may attempt to take advantage of that knowledge. They put the new production technique into effect and do indeed temporarily earn economic profits.

Notice here that economic profits are temporary. In the long run, under this disequilibrium theory of profits, all economic profits are competed away. Only a normal (accounting) rate of return can be earned.

Imperfect Competition

A third theory of profits concerns monopoly power. We have already shown that a profit-maximizing monopolist will reduce output and raise prices. The monopolist *may* then earn monopoly profits. So long as the monopolist can prevent entry into the industry, monopoly profits can prevail even in the long run. Thus, this is not a disequilibrium theory of profits.

Critics of the monopoly theory of profits contend that such profits can exist only in the short run (although this may be many years). After all, it is difficult to prevent permanently entry into an industry, even by legislative means. Monopolists must, by their very position in the market, expend resources to protect their monopoly position. Those resources may eventually eat away at the monopoly profits. Thus, to the critics of the monopoly theory of profits, such profits are akin to disequilibrium economic profits because they are only a temporary phenomenon.

All Three Theories Not Rivals

We have just given three theories of monopoly, or economic, profit. They are not necessarily rivals. They may each have some explanatory power in telling us why economic profits exist.

THE FUNCTION OF PROFIT

In a market economy, the expectation of profits induces firms to discover new products, new production techniques, and new marketing techniques—literally all the new ways to make higher profits. Profits in this sense spur innovation and investment.

Additionally, as we pointed out in Chapter 4, profits cause resources to move from lower-valued to higher-valued uses. Prices and sales are dictated by the consumer. If the demand curve is close to the origin, then there will be few sales and few, if any, profits. The lack of profits therefore means that there is insufficient demand to cover the opportunity cost of production. In the quest for higher profits, businesses will take resources out of areas where either accounting losses or lower-than-normal rates of return are being made and put them into areas where there is an expectation of higher profits. The profit reward is an inducement for an industry to expand when demand and supply conditions warrant it. The existence of economic losses, on the other hand, indicates that resources in the particular industry are not as valued as they might be elsewhere. These resources therefore move out of that industry or, at a minimum, no further resources are invested in it. Therefore, resources follow the businessperson's quest for higher profits. They allocate resources.

Income Shares in the United States

We have now discussed the four factors of production and their payments. It is interesting to see what percentage of national income is accounted for by these various factor payments. We cannot, however, obtain data on exactly the same categories that we have discussed in this part. We see in Exhibit 15-5 five different categories for which data are available. Those categories are (1) wages and salaries, (2) proprietors' income, (3) corporate profits, (4) interest, and (5) rent.

Wages and salaries correspond to factor pay-

EXHIBIT 15-5
Relative Income Shares over Time.

	(1) Wages and Salaries (percent)	*(2) Proprietors' Income (percent)*	*(3) Corporate Profits (percent)*	*(4) Interest (percent)*	*(5) Rent (percent)*
1900–1909	55.0	23.7	6.8	5.5	9.0
1910–1919	53.6	23.8	9.1	5.4	8.1
1920–1929	60.0	17.5	7.8	6.2	7.7
1930–1939	67.5	14.8	4.0	8.7	5.0
1939–1948	64.6	17.2	11.9	3.1	3.3
1949–1958	67.3	13.9	12.5	2.9	3.4
1954–1963	69.9	11.9	11.2	4.0	3.0
1963–1968	71.6	9.6	12.1	3.5	3.2
1969–1977	76.7	7.9	8.0	5.1	2.3
1976–1980	74.9	6.2	8.5	8.5	1.9

Source: Irving Kravis, "Income Distribution: Functional Share," *International Encyclopedia of Social Sciences* (New York: Macmillan, 1968), Vol. 7, p. 134. Updated data from the Department of Commerce and the Bureau of Labor Statistics.

ments to labor. However, part of those factor payments are also included in what is called proprietors' income, which represents the accounting profits of unincorporated businesses. Economically, this represents the opportunity cost of capital, owners' labor, and some element of economic profit. The columns marked "Corporate Profits" and "Interest" do not correspond at all well to the terms *profit* and *interest* as used in this chapter. Finally, the column marked "Rent" includes more than pure economic rent.

Nonetheless, it is instructive to see what has happened to the relative shares of national income since 1900. We see that wages and salaries account for about three-fourths of national income today. In 1900, they accounted for only 55 percent. This means that labor income has grown in importance in our economy. On the other hand, income from the ownership of land and capital is falling.

Concepts in Brief 15-3

- Profit is the reward to entrepreneurial talent, the fourth factor of production.
- It is necessary to distinguish between accounting profits and economic profits.
- Accounting profits are measured by the difference between total revenues and all explicit costs.
- Economic profits are measured by the difference between total revenues and the total of all opportunity costs of all factors of production.
- There are numerous theories of why profits exist. These include the notions that profits are: (1) a reward to risk taking, (2) a result of disequilibrium in the marketplace, and (3) a result of imperfect competition.
- The function of profits in a market economy is to allocate scarce resources. Resources will flow to where profits are highest.

ISSUES AND APPLICATIONS

Who Is Helped by Usury Laws?

Concepts Applied

- Supply, demand, consumer loans, and equilibrium rate of interest

Savers and Borrowers Getting Together

When individuals save—that is, when they do not consume—they usually seek to obtain a positive rate of return on their savings. A positive rate of return often (but not always) can be obtained by investing in the stock market or by lending money to corporations or to the government by buying their bonds. Alternatively, individuals can put money in savings and loan associations and receive interest on those savings. There are many savings vehicles where the wealth of individuals increases because of interest earned or a positive rate of return obtained.

On the other side of the picture is the process of dissaving, or borrowing. We know that since the total quantity of resources in the economy is fixed at any point in time, for every borrower there must be a saver, at least in dollar terms. The amount borrowed cannot exceed the amount saved. The market where savers and borrowers get together is called the *credit market.* In this Issue, we won't go into the operation of the credit market in great detail; rather, we'll look at what happens when restrictions are placed on the prices that can prevail in the credit market. Moreover, we will not deal with how monetary policy affects the amount of credit available in our economy.

Usury Laws

The price charged in the credit market for borrowing money is called the *interest rate.* When ceilings are put on interest rates, we say that **usury laws** have been applied—**usury** meaning

When banks and credit card companies are forced to lower their interest rates, people will demand a larger quantity of credit; but the supplier will want to supply a smaller quantity. Usury laws thereby create an excess quantity demanded.

lending money at "unreasonable rates." The history of usury laws is long indeed.

Babylonians permitted credit but restricted the rate of interest. The Bible (Deuteronomy 23:19–20) tells us that "Unto a stranger thou mayest lend upon usury; but unto thy brother thou shalt not lend upon usury." In Luke 6:35 of the New Testament, we are told that we must "lend freely, hoping nothing thereby."

One of the earliest writers on economics, Aristotle, considered money to be sterile. The "breeding" of money from money was unnatural and justly to be hated. During the Roman republic, no interest charges were permitted; but by the time of the Roman Empire, this restriction was relaxed.

During the Middle Ages, the Catholic Church had very specific rules against lending money at interest. Such a pursuit of wealth was considered "unnatural" and sinful because humility and charity were considered the greatest virtues that could be obtained. Secular legislation responded to the Church's influence at that time, and interest and usury were regarded as synonymous.

In the United States, most usury laws were inherited from the British during the Colonial days. It is interesting to note that most of these usury laws still remain in force in the United States, but Great Britain repealed them in 1854.

Let's take a look at a specific instance where a usury law was passed in a state.

The Case of Washington State

Prior to 1968, interest rates on consumer loans from the credit card companies—VISA, MasterCard, and so on—as well as revolving credit loans from the big stores—Sears and others—were generally 18 percent per year, or 1.5 percent per month, in the state of Washington. Many consumer advocates and concerned citizens felt that this rate of interest was much too high. At that time, commercial bank loans to some customers were going for as low as 9 percent per year. It was felt that poor people were the ones being discriminated against because they could not "afford" the high interest charge. They therefore had to forego the benefits of being able to buy on time. A movement was started to pass legislation against such usurious interest rates.

In 1968, a motion was put on the ballot to set the maximum legal interest rate on consumer loans at 12 percent instead of 18 percent. It was felt that lowering the interest rate would benefit those who could not afford the higher rate.

The measure passed quite successfully, and all the credit card companies and stores in the state were forced to lower their rates to 1 percent per month, or 12 percent per year. We should be able to analyze and predict what happens after such legislation is enacted.

Supply and demand analysis. Let's simplify our analysis and assume that the only money market that existed in the state of Washington was the consumer credit market represented by the major credit card companies and the individual stores that offered their own revolving credit cards. Let's further assume that, during the period under study, there is no technological change in the credit card business. That is, no new computerized technique lowers the cost of being able to process bills and so on.

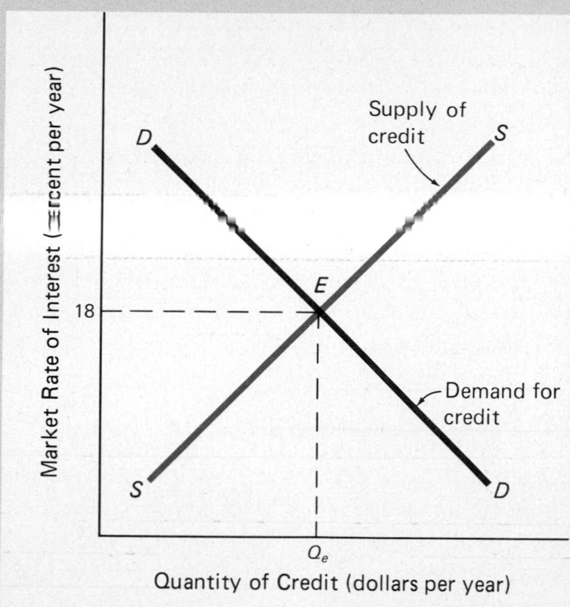

EXHIBIT 15–6
The Demand and Supply of Credit. At a lower price, more credit will be demanded. At higher interest rates, more credit will be supplied. The equilibrium is established at the intersection of the demand and supply curves, *E*. The quantity supplied and demanded at the equilibrium interest rate of 18 percent is Q_e.

Exhibit 15–6 shows the demand and supply of credit in the state of Washington. At higher interest rates, credit card institutions will be willing to lend more money. At lower interest rates they will want to lend less money. Obviously, the reverse relationship holds for the demand side. If the price of credit falls, more credit is demanded, and we move down our downward-sloping demand schedule (*DD*). Here we see that the supply and demand schedules intersect at an interest rate of 18 percent per year. This is the equilibrium, or market clearing, rate. Now obviously it is true that at 18 percent, some people will feel they cannot "afford" credit. These people will not partake in obtaining command over goods and services today by promising to pay back the principal and an interest rate in future days. They will consume only when they have enough current income to do so. Many people who feel they cannot afford to borrow are indeed less wealthy than most of those who do borrow.

If we assume that the supply schedule presented in Exhibit 15–6 is representative of the actual situation, then the equilibrium price of 18 percent for credit represents the lowest price possible in Washington state, if all credit demands are to be satisfied, given the then-current technology and the willingness of savers to forego present consumption.

Setting the maximum rate below the equilibrium rate. Now a new law sets the maximum rate below the market clearing equilibrium rate: only 12 percent per year, or 1 percent per month, can be charged on loans. We see in Exhibit 15–7 that at 12 percent, there is an excess quantity of credit demanded equal to the difference between Q_d and Q_s. At an interest rate of 12 percent, suppliers of credit are willing to give out only Q_s in loans, but demanders want much more. How are things resolved?

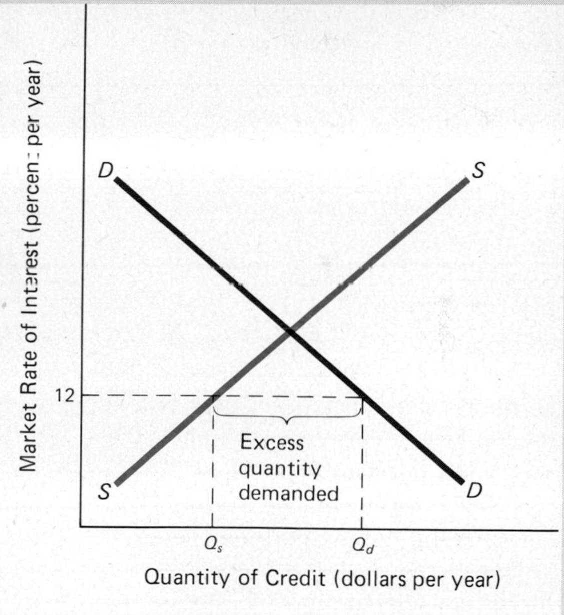

EXHIBIT 15–7
The Effects of a Usury Law. When a legal maximum interest rate of 12 percent is imposed on credit cards, the quantity demanded will be Q_d but the quantity supplied will be Q_s. The difference will be an excess quantity demanded. How is this "shortage" taken care of? Credit companies will find out how to charge higher prices for credit, and some borrowers will seek out other sources of credit that will cost more—such as the friendly local finance company.

The first thing that happens is that those who lend money seek out ways to get around the legal limit. Many companies that were formerly not imposing a service charge on small amounts of borrowed money start doing so. Companies also begin to set other rules. Some start charging a fee for opening an account, for example. There are numerous methods of skirting the law. But insofar as these methods are not fully effective, at a rate of 12 percent lenders eventually find that their profits aren't as high as before. If we assume that the equilibrium was at 18 percent before the legislation, a credit price of 12 percent means that the less efficient firms in the business of lending now earn less than the normal, or competitive, rate of return. Their costs are now high relative to the revenues made from lending money elsewhere. These companies, and some of the others too, attempt to find ways to cut their costs. One way to do this is to eliminate some of the bad (potential and actual) accounts—the ones that are less likely to pay what is owed. But how do companies decide which are the bad accounts when people come to apply for loans? They look at past behavior and at future earnings possibilities. Who do you think are the people denied credit at 12 percent?

The poor lose out again. Obviously, the people who have the worst credit rating are the ones denied credit at 12 percent. Welfare mothers, people with records of unstable employment, easily identifiable "minority" groups (such as blacks and Hispanics), students, and very old people fall into this category. The fact is that this list includes just about every group of people that the legislation was originally supposed to help.

Who benefits? Surprise! The people who benefit from lower interest rates on consumer credit are the ones who are the most credit worthy. They are the ones with the most money, the best jobs, and the highest probability of being able to pay off. These are the people who gain, and the poor are once again left out.

The Lesson to Be Learned

Usury laws have pernicious long-run effects. Our simplified example of the state of Washington ignored all the other credit markets available to high-risk borrowers. If, for example, these high-risk borrowers are refused credit from MasterCard, they can go to their local finance company or, worse, to the local loan shark, where interest rates are not restricted. The borrowers end up effectively paying a much higher price. This means that many people will go to finance companies and other credit institutions and end up paying more than they would have paid if the legal maximum had not been set.

Questions

1. What would happen if the legal maximum rate of interest were set above the market clearing rate of interest?
2. Aristotle considered that money was "sterile." Analyze his argument.

Definition of Terms

Pure economic rent The payment to any resource that is in completely inelastic supply. The payment to any resource over and above what is necessary to keep the resource in supply at its current level.

Interest The payment for current rather than future command over resources; the cost of obtaining credit. Also, the return paid to owners of capital.

Consumption loans Loans taken out by households for the purpose of purchasing goods and services.

Investment loans Loans taken out by businesses for the purpose of investing in physical capital.

Gross return to capital The amount left over after the costs of raw materials, intermediate goods, depreciation, the opportunity cost of owner-manager's contributed talents, and taxes are deducted from total revenues. The gross return to capital represents the total amount available for payments to owners of capital and includes a pure, or opportunity cost, return to capital, as well as economic profits.

Pure return to capital The opportunity cost of capital, or what capital could earn in an alternative investment.

Accounting profit The difference between total revenues and total explicit costs.

Economic profit The difference between total revenues and the opportunity cost of all factors of production.

Usury laws Laws prohibiting the charging of an interest rate in excess of a statutory maximum percentage; usually set by the individual states and varying with the type of loan (that is, the use to which the borrowed money will be put).

Usury The lending of money at an exorbitant interest rate or one that exceeds the legal maximum.

Chapter Summary

1. Resources that have a fixed supply are paid economic rent. We therefore define economic rent as the payment over and above what is necessary to keep a resource in supply at its current level.
2. Henry George felt that a single tax on land would be appropriate in place of all other taxes, since land rent was considered a pure economic rent.
3. Resource owners (including labor owners) earn economic rent because of competition among potential users of those resources.
4. Interest can be defined as the payment for command over resources today rather than in the future. Interest is typically seen as the payment for credit, but it can also be considered the payment for the use of capital.
5. Interest charged depends on: (a) length of loan, (b) risk, and (c) handling charges.
6. The demand for loans consists of consumption demand by consumers and investment demand by businesses. The equilibrium rate of interest is where the aggregate demand curve for credit intersects the aggregate supply curve.
7. Profits occur because of: (a) risk taking, (b) disequilibrium, and (c) imperfect competition.
8. Usury laws that limit the maximum interest charged on loans can create an excess quantity demanded at the maximum interest rate.
9. When usury laws are effectively enforced, those who are poor credit risks will be turned down for credit more often.

Selected References

Arrow, Kenneth J. "The Limitations of the Profit Motive," *Challenge,* Sept./Oct., 1979.

Nell, Edward J. *Growth, Profits, and Property.* Cambridge, England: Cambridge University Press, 1980.

Watson, Donald S., and Malcolm Getz. *Price Theory and Its Uses.* 5th ed. Boston: Houghton Mifflin, 1981, chap. 21.

Whipple, John. *The Usury Debate After Adam Smith.* New York: Arno Press, 1972.

Answers to Preview and Study Questions

1. What is rent?

Rent is a payment for the use of land. Economists have long played with the notion that land is completely inelastic in supply—although this is a debatable issue and depends on various definitions. Modern economists now refer to a payment to *any* factor of production that is in completely inelastic supply as pure economic rent. For instance, from society's point of view, the total supply of land is fixed. Also, athletes and entertainers presumably earn pure economic rents: beyond some "normal" income the opportunity cost to superstars for performing is zero; hence, abnormal income is not necessary to induce them to perform. Note that we usually discuss positively sloped supply schedules indicating that higher relative prices are necessary to induce increased quantity supplied. This is *not* the case for pure economic rents.

2. What criticisms can be made of a 100 percent tax on pure economic rents?

Since land, as a whole, and "superstar" performances (beyond some income level) are perfectly inelastic in supply, it is suggested that a near 100 percent tax on these pure economic rents could and should be levied. Such a tax would create problems however. For one thing, much land has been improved and, as such, possesses elements of man-made capital. Is it possible to separate the rent from the interest components on the payment for the use of "land"? Similarly, some superstars have made human capital investments in training; is it possible to separate *this* return from pure economic rent? Would it be "fair" to tax *improvements* on land or human talent? Secondly, it must be remembered that rent, as is true for any price, performs an allocative function. Even if *all* land is fixed in supply, nevertheless a 100 percent tax on land would, in effect, leave us with an allocation problem. How can we be assured that *specific* parcels of land will be allocated to their highest-valued use—since there is no incentive for landowners to offer them to the highest bidders (who presumably will be those who will put land to its highest-valued use)? Similarly, if economic rents are bid away from superstars, how do we allocate their performances? There will be no incentive for individual superstars to go to those places where earnings are highest (since it will be taxed away), so how will this talent be allocated? Note that those who are willing to forego the most in *other* goods and services *cannot* bid superstars' performances away from others, if pure economic rents are taxed away from the superstars.

3. What is Interest?

On the most obvious level, interest takes on the form of a payment for the use of money. On another level, interest can be considered as payment for obtaining credit; by borrowing, people (consumers or businesses) obtain command over resources *currently,* rather than in the future. Those who wish to make purchases now, instead of later, are allowed to make these expenditures even if they do not currently have purchasing power. They do so by borrowing, and interest is the price they must pay for the privilege of making expenditures now instead of later.

4. What is the economic function of interest rates?

Interest rates are the price of credit, and like all prices, interest rates play an allocative role. That is, interest is a rationing device—as are wages, rents, the price of carrots and beans, and so on. We have said that interest is the price of credit; as such this credit is allocated to those households and businesses that are willing to pay the highest price (interest rate). Such is the rationing function of credit. At a more fundamental level we can see that something other than scarce loanable funds is allocated. After all, businesses don't borrow money for the privilege of paying interest! The key to understanding what *physical* resources are being allocated is to follow the money: on what do businesses spend this borrowed money? The answer is capital goods—mostly. Thus, the interest rate plays the crucial role of allocating scarce capital goods; those firms that are willing to pay the highest interest rates will be those that will be able to purchase the scarce capital goods. Presumably, the most profitable firms will be able to pay the highest interest rates (and be most acceptable to lenders) and will therefore receive disproportionately greater quantities of capital; the less profitable firms will be forced to contract as the most profitable firms expand. Interest rates help bring about this capital rationing scheme in a market economy.

5. What is the economic function of profits?

Profit is the return to entrepreneurial talent or the price paid to risk takers. Profits also play a rationing role in society. Profits (in conjunction with interest rates) perform the all-important function of deciding which industries (and which firms *within* an industry) expand—and which are forced to contract. Profitable firms can reinvest profits (and offer to pay higher interest rates), while unprofitable firms are forced to contract or go bankrupt. In short, businesses' quests for profits assure that scarce resources flow from less-profitable to more-profitable uses; profits help society decide which firms are to expand, and which are to contract.

Problems

(Answers at the back of the book)

1. "All revenues obtained by the Italian government from Renaissance art museums are pure economic rent." Is this statement true or false, and why?
2. Some people argue that the extraordinary earnings of entertainment and sports "superstars" are not pure economic rents at all, but merely the cost of ensuring that a steady stream of would-be stars and starlets continues to flow into the sports and entertainment fields. How would the argument go?

16
The Distribution of Income and Wealth

TOPICS FOR REVIEW

The topics listed below, which we have already analyzed, are applied in this chapter. You may find it worthwhile to review them. For your convenience each topic is followed by the number identifying the specific "Concepts in Brief."

a. Positive versus normative economics (1–5)

b. Exploitation (14–3)

FOR PREVIEW AND STUDY

1. What is a Lorenz curve, and what does it measure?

2. What has been happening to the distribution of income in the United States?

3. What is the difference between income and wealth?

4. Why do people earn different incomes?

5. What is the best distribution of income?

Everyone knows there are a lot of rich people around, and everyone knows there are a lot of poor people, too. However, not many of us know why some people earn more income than others. Why is the **distribution of income** the way it is? Economists have devised different theories to explain this distribution. In this chapter, we will present some of these theories. In addition, we will present some of the more obvious institutional reasons why income is not distributed evenly in the United States.

We will see that there is a difference between wealth and income. For the moment, let's just talk about income.

The Lorenz Curve

We can graphically represent the distribution of money income by the use of what is called the **Lorenz curve.** The Lorenz curve shows what portion of total money income is accounted for by different proportions of the nation's families. Look at Exhibit 16–1. On the horizontal axis, we measure the *cumulative* percentage of families. Starting on the left-hand corner, there are zero families; on the right-hand corner, we have 100 percent of the families; and in the middle, we have 50 percent of the families. The vertical axis represents the *accumulated* percentage of money income. The 45-degree line represents perfect equality, which means 50 percent of the families obtain 50 percent of total income. Then 60 percent of the families would obtain 60 percent of total income, and so on. Of course, in no real-world situation is there such perfect equality of income; no actual Lorenz curve would be a straight line. Rather, it would be some curved line, such as that which is labeled "actual income distribution" in Exhibit 16–1. For example, the bottom 50 percent of families in the United States receive something less than 30 percent of total money income.

In Exhibit 16–2, we again show the actual money income distribution Lorenz curve, and we also compare it to the distribution of money income in 1929. Since that year, the Lorenz curve has become less bowed; that is, it has moved closer to the line of perfect equality. It might be interesting to compare the United States today with other countries in the world. We see in Exhibit 16–3 that the Lorenz curve for Sweden is closer to the straight line than

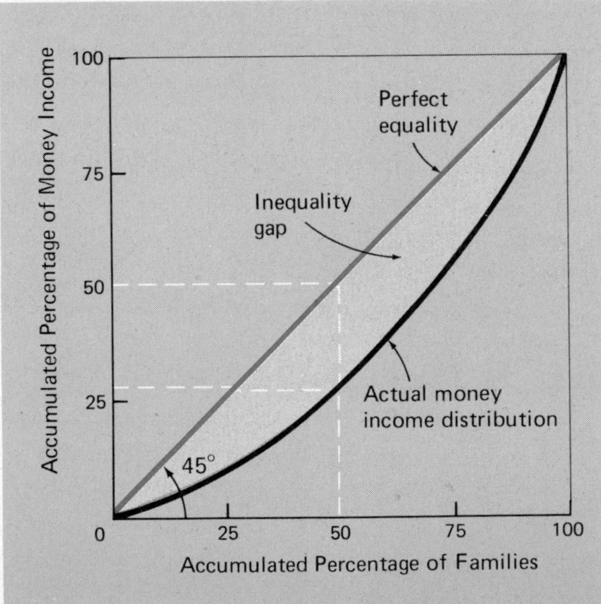

EXHIBIT 16–1

The Lorenz Curve. The horizontal axis measures the accumulated percentage of families from 0 to 100 percent. The vertical axis measures the accumulated percentage of money income from 0 to 100. A straight line at a 45-degree angle cuts the box in half and represents a line of perfect income equality, where 25 percent of the families get 25 percent of the money income, 50 percent get 50 percent, and so on. The Lorenz curve, showing actual money income distribution, is not a straight line but, rather, a curved line as shown. The difference between perfect money income equality and the Lorenz curve is the inequality gap.

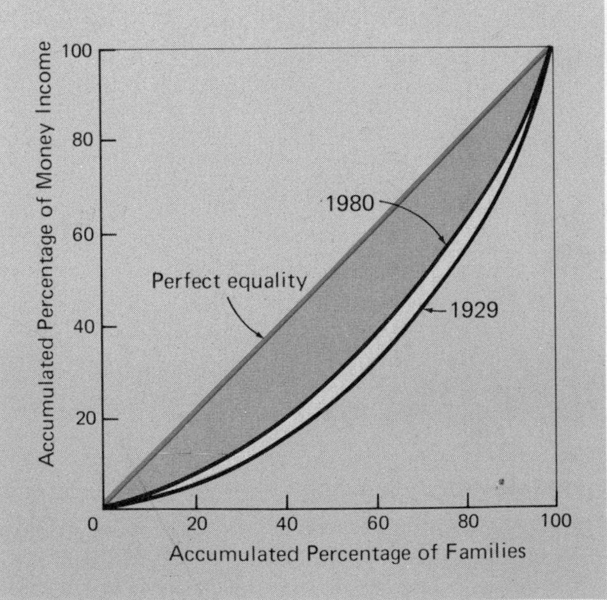

EXHIBIT 16–2

Lorenz Curves of Income Distribution, 1929 and 1980. We notice that since 1929 the Lorenz curve has moved slightly inward toward the straight line of perfect income equality.

Source: U.S. Department of Commerce.

is the curve for the United States. Sweden has a more equal distribution of income than we do. This has been accomplished in Sweden by a tax system that is extremely progressive. On the other hand, we see that the distribution of income in Thailand is much more unequal than in the United States. The bottom 80 percent of families receive less than 40 percent of all income, whereas the top 10 percent of families receive more than 40 percent of all income.

As an aside, it might be noted that the more industrialized a nation becomes, the larger is the percentage of national income that is paid in wages. In less-developed countries, much of the national income goes to rent, interest, and profits. In countries such as the United States, Britain, France, Germany, Sweden, and the rest of Western Europe, the majority of national income does not originate from capital but rather from labor services, as we saw in Chapter 15. In the United States today, for example, over three-fourths of national income is paid in wages; less than one-fourth is paid as returns to investment in land, buildings, companies, and so on.

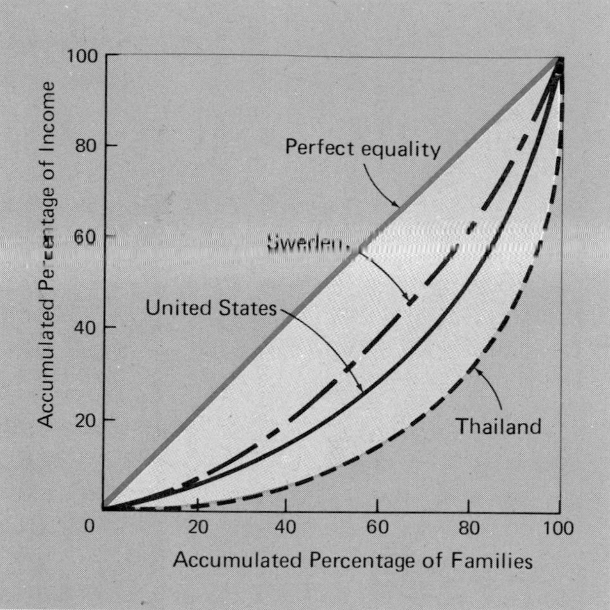

EXHIBIT 16–3
International Comparisons of Income Distribution. Here we show the Lorenz curves for the United States, Sweden, and Thailand. As can be expected, Sweden has a Lorenz curve that is closer to the straight line of perfect income equality than that of the United States. Sweden has a much more progressive income tax system. Thailand, on the other hand, has a much more unequal distribution of income.

Sources: United States data from U.S. Department of Commerce. Data for Thailand from *Statistical Yearbook of Thailand*, 1977. Data for Sweden from *Statistical Abstract of Sweden*, 1978.

CRITICISMS OF THE LORENZ CURVE

In the past few years, economists have placed less and less emphasis on the shape of the Lorenz curve as an indication of the degree of income inequality in any country. There are five basic reasons why the Lorenz curve has been criticized:

1. The Lorenz curve is typically presented in terms of the distribution of *money* income only. It does not include income in kind, such as government-provided food stamps, housing aid, and the like.
2. The Lorenz curve does not account for differences in family size and effort. A family, whether there are two or three or four wage earners, is compared to a family of one wage earner.
3. It does not account for age in income differences. Even if all families in the United States had exactly the same *lifetime* incomes, young families would have lower incomes, middle-aged families would have relatively high incomes, and retired families would again have low incomes. Since the Lorenz curve is drawn at a moment in time, it could never tell us anything about the inequality of *lifetime* income.
4. The Lorenz curve typically is given for money income before taxes.
5. It does not measure the income from the "underground economy," a substantial and rising portion of income for many individuals.

Measuring the Degree of Income Inequality

One measure of the degree of income inequality is the *Gini coefficient of inequality*. A diagram showing a Lorenz curve, such as the one in Exhibit 16–1, can also demonstrate the concept of the Gini coefficient. We compare the area between the 45-degree line and the Lorenz curve of actual income distribution to the entire area under the diagonal—that is, to the triangle that represents one-half of the box in Exhibit 16–1. In other words:

$$\text{Gini coefficient of inequality} = \frac{\text{area between diagonal and Lorenz curve of actual income distribution}}{\text{triangular area under diagonal line}}$$

What does this mean? It means that the Gini coefficient will range from 0 to 1. If we had perfect equality, the Gini coefficient would obviously be 0 because there would be no area between the diagonal line, or curve of absolute equality, and the curve of actual distribution of income. The greater that area becomes, however, the greater becomes the Gini coefficient and, hence, the measure of inequality.

Can you imagine what the Lorenz curve would look like if the Gini coefficient were 1?

INCOME DISTRIBUTION IN THE UNITED STATES—PAST AND PRESENT

We could talk about the percentage of income earners within specific income classes—say, those earning between $5,000 and $6,000 per year, those earning between $6,000 and $7,000 per year, and so on. The problem with this type of analysis is that we are a growing economy. Income is going up all the time. If we wish to make comparisons about the relative share of total income going to different income classes, we cannot look at specific amounts of money income. Rather, we talk about a distribution of income over, say, five groups. Then we can talk about how much the bottom fifth makes compared to the top fifth, and so on. In Exhibit 16–4, we see the percentage share of income for families before direct taxes. The table groups families according to whether they are in the lowest 20 percent of the income distribution, the second lowest 20 percent, and so on. We see that in 1979, the lowest 20 percent had a combined money income of 5.8 percent of the total money income of the entire population. This is about the same as the lowest 20 percent had at the end of World War II. Accordingly, the conclusion has been drawn that there have been only slight changes in the distribution of money income. Indeed, considering that the definition of money income used by the U.S. Bureau of the Census includes only wage and salary income, income from self-employment, interest and dividends, and such government cash-transfer payments as Social Security and unemployment compensation, we have to agree that the distribution of money income has not changed. *Money* income, however, is not *total* income for individuals who receive *in-kind* transfers from the government in the form of food stamps, public housing, and so on.

EXHIBIT 16–4
Percentage Share of Money Income for Families Before Direct Taxes.

Income Group	*1979*	*1973*	*1960**	*1947**
Lowest fifth	5.8	5.5	4.8	5.1
Second fifth	13.1	11.9	12.2	11.8
Third fifth	17.1	17.5	17.8	16.7
Fourth fifth	24.8	24.0	24.0	23.2
Highest fifth	39.2	41.1	41.3	43.3

* *Total does not equal 100 percent due to rounding.*

Source: U.S. Bureau of the Census. "Money Income in 1973 of Families and Persons in the United States." *Current Population Reports,* ser. P-60, no. 97 (1975), table 22, plus various issues.

THE DISTRIBUTION OF TOTAL INCOME

If we include in-kind transfers in estimating the distribution of total income, we find a very different picture of what has happened to the poor in the United States since World War II. In 1973, there were 23 million people officially regarded as poor. However, those 23 million people received $18.8 billion of such in-kind transfers as food stamps, health care, and public housing. The lowest-fifth income group in 1960 was estimated to have 4.8 percent of the nation's money income. In terms of total income, it had 5 percent. In 1973, it was estimated (as shown in Exhibit 16–4) that this lowest fifth obtained only 5.5 percent of total money income. However, when in-kind transfers are added to the money income figure for 1973, the estimated share of the first quintile (fifth) reaches about 12 percent.[1] Indeed, when these noncash forms of income are included, the relative position of the poorest fifth of families has improved by over 100 percent between 1960 and 1973.

Wealth and Income Not the Same

We have been referring to the distribution of income in the United States. We must realize that income can be viewed as a return to wealth, both human and nonhuman. Individuals receive income basically as a return to renting out their labor services. Hence, wages are a return to the use of human wealth. Individuals also receive a return for the ownership of land. We have called this rent. Individuals receive income as a return to the ownership of capital. We have called this interest. And, finally, entrepreneurs receive economic profits as a return to entrepreneurial ability, again a form of human wealth. Income is a flow received year in and year out. It is the flow received from wealth, which is a stock of both human and nonhuman capital.

Therefore, the discussion of the distribution of

[1] Edgar K. Browning, "How Much More Equality Can We Afford?" *The Public Interest,* Spring 1976, pp. 90–110.

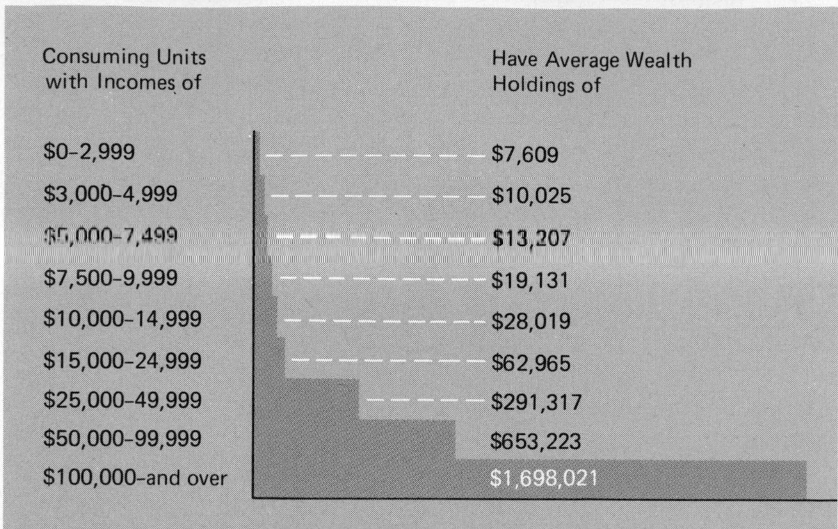

EXHIBIT 16–5
Average Amount of Wealth Held by Income Groups. The largest amount of wealth is held by the 700,000 consuming units with yearly incomes of $25,000 or more. A great amount of wealth is held by consuming units with incomes of over $100,000. Even individuals with incomes of less than $3,000 when this survey was done had wealth holdings of almost $8,000. However, many individuals in this category are retired, with little or no current income. They have a life savings upon which they are drawing.

income in the United States is not the same thing as a discussion of the distribution of wealth. A complete concept of wealth would include tangible objects, such as buildings, machinery, land, cars, and houses—nonhuman wealth—as well as people who have skills, knowledge, initiative, talents, and so on—human wealth. The total of *human* and nonhuman wealth in the United States gives us our nation's capital stock. (Note that the terms *wealth* and *capital* are often used *only* with reference to nonhuman wealth.) The capital stock refers to anything that can generate utility to individuals in the future. A fresh ripe tomato is not part of our capital stock. It has to be eaten before it turns rotten, and after it is eaten it can no longer generate satisfaction. The nonhuman aspect of our capital stock has a market value of about $5 trillion. (The human aspect of our capital stock is difficult to estimate.) Just looking at the distribution of nonhuman wealth alone, we find that the bulk of wealth is held by the households with yearly incomes of $25,000 or over, as can be seen in Exhibit 16–5.

HOW TO OBTAIN WEALTH

Let's say that you have no wealth at all except your own human wealth. You decide to get a job. You start making income. How do you acquire nonhuman wealth? If you spend everything that you make on consumption goods, you won't be able to get any nonhuman wealth at all. That is, if you consume everything, nothing is left over with which to acquire nonhuman wealth, like houses, stocks and bonds, and so on. Thus, the most common way to obtain wealth is to save—that is, not to spend all your income. (Of course, you can also obtain wealth either by inheritance or by theft.) The larger the percentage of your income that you decide to save, the larger your wealth will be in the future, other things being equal.

STOCKS AND FLOWS

The wealth that you have is a **stock.** (Note here that we are not talking just about stock in a company, shares of which are sold on, say, the New York Stock Exchange.) Lots of other things are stocks, too, such as a building that you might own. Stocks are defined independently of time, although they are assessed at a point in time. A car dealer can have a stock or inventory of cars that may be worth $500,000. A timber company may have five acres of trees worth $3,000; this is a stock of trees.

On the other hand, the income you make is a flow. Remember, a **flow** is an ongoing concept, a stream of things through time. It is a certain number of things per time period. You receive so many dollars per week or so many dollars per month or so many dollars per year. The number of cars that a car dealer sells per week is a flow; the inventory of cars on the lot is a stock. Flows, in other words, are defined as occurring over a given *period* of time; stocks are defined at a *point* in time.

If you want to add to your stock of wealth or capital, you must save. That is, you must not consume part of your income. The act of saving is a flow that makes your stock of wealth larger. You should not confuse the act of saving with how much you have in savings. "Savings" is a stock concept akin to wealth, as we have defined it. If you have $5,000 in a savings account, you have a stock of $5,000 of accumulated savings. If you want to increase that stock, you have to save more. You have to add a flow of saving to your stock of savings.

There is a big difference, for example, between a millionaire and someone who makes $1 million a year. The person who makes $1 million a year is probably much richer than the former. The millionaire has a stock of wealth worth $1 million; however, individuals who make $1 million a year have a flow of income equal to $1 million per year—year in and year out. They could easily save a big chunk of that $1 million each year to add to their wealth or savings so that in time they would be much more than mere millionaires. They could become multimillionaires in very short order.

People build up their wealth positions by saving. Savings outlets include holdings of cash (not such a good idea with so much current inflation), stocks, bonds, businesses, precious metals, as well as consumer durable goods. The purchase of a house, for example, adds to one's accumulated savings, or wealth.

For the next several sections of this chapter, we will concentrate on the determinants of differences in income. Then we will briefly look at ways to increase your human wealth.

Concepts in Brief 16-1

- The Lorenz curve graphically represents the distribution of income. If it is a straight line, there is perfect equality of income. The more it is bowed, the more inequality of income exists.
- The degree of income inequality can be measured by the Gini coefficient of inequality.
- The Gini coefficient ranges from zero to one. For perfect equality, the Gini coefficient would be zero because there would be no area between the diagonal line, or curve of absolute equality, and the curve of actual distribution of income.
- There has been relatively little change in the entire distribution of total *money* income in the United States since World War II.
- There has been a significant change in the distribution of *total* income, including in-kind transfers, such as food stamps. When we consider total income, the bottom 20 percent of income earners received about 5 percent in 1947, but today receive about 12 percent.
- Wealth is not the same thing as income. Wealth is a stock concept, such as your accumulated savings at a point in time.
- Stocks must be distinguished from flows; flows are measured over time. You have a flow of sav*ing*, which might be so many dollars per month that you put into your saving*s* account.

Determinants of Income Differences

There are a multitude of determinants of income differences. They have to do with age, talent, education, productivity, and the like. We will discuss each of those determinants now.

THE AGE-EARNINGS CYCLE

Within every class of income earners, there seem to be regular cycles of earning behavior. Most people earn more when they are middle-aged than when they are younger or older. This is called the **age-earnings cycle.** Every occupation has its own age-earnings cycle, and every individual will probably experience some variation from the average. Nonetheless, we can characterize the typical age-earnings cycle graphically in Exhibit 16–6. Here we see that at age 18 income is relatively low. Income gradually rises until it peaks at about age 45 to 50. Then it falls until retirement, when it becomes zero—that is, currently earned income becomes zero, although retirement payments may then commence. The answer as to why there is such a regular cycle in earnings is fairly straightforward.

When individuals start working at a young age, they typically have no work-related experience. Their ability to produce is lower than that of more experienced workers. That is, their productivity is lower. As they become older, they attain more training and more experience. Their productivity rises, and they are therefore paid more. Moreover, they start to work longer hours, in general. At the age of 45 or 50, the productivity of individual workers usually peaks. So, too, do the number of hours per week that are worked. After this peak in the age-earnings cycle, the detrimental effects of aging usually outweigh any increases in training or experience. Moreover, hours worked usually start to fall for older people. Finally, as a person reaches retirement age, his or her productivity and hours worked fall rather drastically relative to, say, 15 or 20 years earlier.

Note that general increases in overall productivity for the entire work force will result in an upward shift in the typical age-earnings profile given in Exhibit 16–6. Thus, even at the end of the age-earnings cycle, when the worker is just about to retire, he or she would not receive a really "low" real wage compared with what he or she started out with 45 years earlier. The wage would be much higher due to factors that contribute to rising real

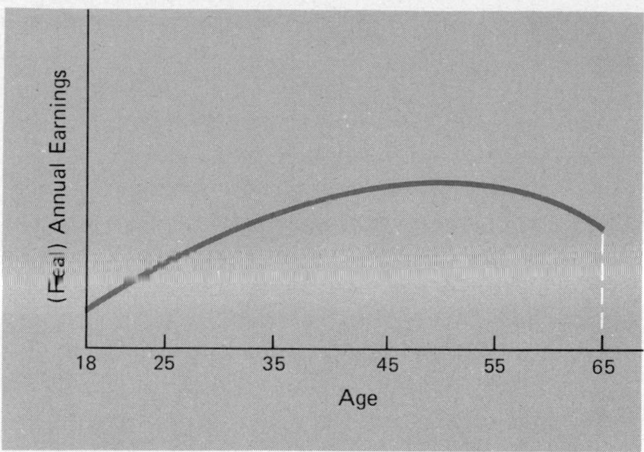

EXHIBIT 16–6

Typical Age-Earnings Profile. Within every class of income earners, there is usually a typical age-earnings profile. Earnings are lowest when starting work at age 18, reach their peak at around age 45–50, then taper off until retirement at around age 65, when they become zero for most people. The rise in earnings up to age 45 to 50 is usually due to increased experience, longer working hours, and better training and schooling. (We abstract from economywide productivity changes that would shift the entire curve.)

wages for everyone, regardless of where they are in their age-earnings cycle.

Now we have some idea why specific individuals earn different incomes at different times in their lives, but we have yet to explain why different people are paid different amounts of money for their individual labors. One way to explain this is to recall the marginal productivity theory developed in Chapter 13.

Marginal Productivity Theory

When trying to determine how many workers a firm would hire, we had to construct a value of marginal product curve. We found that as more workers were hired, the value of marginal product fell due to diminishing marginal returns. If the forces of supply and demand established a certain wage rate, workers would be hired until the value of their marginal physical product was equal to the going wage rate. Then the hiring would stop. This analysis suggests what *all* workers can expect to be paid in the labor market. *They can each expect to be paid the value of their marginal product*—assuming, of course, that there are low-cost information flows and that the labor and product markets are competitive.

PROCESS OF COMPETITION

In most situations, the value of marginal product theory gives us a rough idea of what workers will be paid. In a competitive situation, with mobility of labor resources (at least on the margin), workers who are being paid less than the value of their marginal product will be bid away to better employment opportunities. Either they will seek better employment themselves or employers, in an attempt to lower labor costs, will try to find workers who are being paid below the value of their marginal physical product. This process will continue until each worker is paid his or her value of marginal product. In general, employers will not want to keep workers if those workers' wage rates are greater than their VMPs. In such a situation, it would pay an entrepreneur to fire or lay off those workers who are being paid more than the worth of their contribution to total output. It would be unusual, then, to find situations where large numbers of workers were being employed at wages exceeding their VMPs.

FULL ADJUSTMENT IS NEVER OBTAINED

You may balk at the suggestion that people are paid the value of their marginal physical product, because you may personally know individuals whose value of marginal product is more or less than they are being paid. Such a situation may, in fact, exist because we do not live in a world of perfect information, or in a world with perfectly competitive input and output markets. Employers cannot always seek out the most productive employees available. It takes resources to research the past records of potential employees, their training, their education, and their abilities. You may know musicians, artists, photographers, singers, and other talented people who are being paid much less than more well-known, publicized "stars." But this does not mean that marginal product theory is invalid. It merely indicates that information is costly. It is not always possible for talent scouts to find out exactly who the next superstars are going to be, which means that many potential stars never fulfill their dreams. Furthermore, we must distinguish carefully between the *market* evaluations of an individual worker's worth and *subjective* evaluations. You may subjectively believe that the output of a particular artist is extremely high. Unfortunately for the artist and perhaps for your sense of fairness, few other people may share your subjective evaluation. Therefore, the artist is unable to sell his or her work very easily or at very high prices. Finally, the marginal productivity theory of wages applies in the large—that is, on average. It is not necessarily meant to explain every single individual case.

If we accept marginal productivity theory, then we have a way to find out how people can, in fact, earn higher incomes. If they can manage to increase the value of their marginal physical product, they can expect to be paid more. Some of the determinants of marginal product are innate intelligence, schooling, experience, and training. Most of these are means by which marginal product can be increased. Let's examine them in greater detail.

Innate Abilities and Attributes

These factors are obviously the easiest to explain and the hardest to acquire if you don't have them. Innate abilities and attributes can be very strong, if not overwhelming, determinants of a person's potential productivity. Strength, good looks, coordination, mental alertness, and so on are all facets of nonacquired human capital and, thus, have some bearing on one's ability to earn income. If one is born extremely tall, one has a better chance of being a basketball player than someone else who is born short. If one is born with a relatively superior talent for abstract thinking, then one has a better chance of making a relatively higher income as, say, a mathematician or philosopher, than someone who is not born with that talent. The list of innate abilities and attributes that gives some people an "edge" on other people is long indeed.

Education

Schooling is usually placed under the heading of "investment in human capital," a topic we will discuss later. For the moment, suffice it to say that schooling or education improves one's productivity by increasing the human capital one has available for use in the labor market. If you have been taught to read, write, work with mathematics, understand scientific problems, do engineering or drafting, lay out advertisements, design clothes, or edit manuscripts, you obviously are of more value to a potential employer than a person who is illiterate and unknowledgeable about anything except manual labor. Schooling usually allows an individual to be more versatile in the things he or she can do.

Experience

Additional experience at particular tasks is another way to increase one's productivity. Experience can be linked to the well-known *learning curve* that occurs when the same task is done over and over. Take an example of a person going to work on an assembly line at General Motors. At first, he or she is able to screw on only three bolts every two minutes. Then the worker becomes more adept and can screw on four bolts in the same time plus insert a rubber guard on the bumper. After a few more weeks, even another task can be added. Experience allows this individual to improve his or her productivity. The better that people learn to do something, the quicker they can do it and the more efficient they are. Hence, we would expect experience to lead to higher rates of productivity. And we would expect people with more experience to be paid more than those with less experience. More experience, however, does not guarantee a higher wage rate. The *demand* for one's services must also exist. Spending a long time to become a first-rate archer in modern society will probably add very little to the income of the person who becomes an archer. As another example, a more experienced pianist in a primitive society may earn the same as an inexperienced pianist, for they both may earn virtually nothing at all, since there is little demand for their talents. Experience only has value if the output is demanded by society.

Training

Training is similar to experience but is more formal. Much of a person's increased productivity is due to on-the-job training. Many companies have training programs for new workers. They learn to operate machinery, fill out forms, and do other things required for the new job. On-the-job training is perhaps responsible for as much of an increase in productivity as is formal schooling beyond grade school.

EXPLOITATION AND DISCRIMINATION

Exploitation and discrimination also affect the distribution of income. Even with equal educational achievement, both in quality and quantity, certain disadvantaged groups may not and empirically do not receive incomes equal to those of other groups. We know, for example, that urban nonwhite males earn approximately 40 percent less than urban white males. We know that, on the average, blacks obtain lower rates of return from investing in a college education than do whites. Are minority groups, and especially blacks, being exploited? Are minority groups being discriminated against in the labor market?

Exploitation

The economist's definition of **exploitation** is somewhat more restrictive than the common one. We have said that a factor of production is being exploited if it is being paid less than the value of its marginal product. (We are distinguishing here between low pay and pay that is less than the value of marginal product. By our definition of exploitation, a person can be receiving a relatively low wage rate without being exploited if that person's wage rate accurately reflects the individual's VMP.) The definition of exploitation given here is, to be sure, subjective. It is in the realm of normative economic analysis—because, in providing this definition, we are implicitly assuming that wages that are equal to the value of marginal product in an unrestricted market are the "proper" wage rates. Other definitions do exist for exploitation.

How can exploitation exist in the labor market? Lack of information can allow it. If employees (on the margin) are ignorant of better job opportunities, they may be exploited by employers. Also, if laborers experience restricted entry into an industry, they may be exploited. Professional sports leagues, for example, try to prevent the entry of competing leagues into the system because the price of professional athletes would be bid up. We say that a player may be exploited because of the monopsony power of the employers in the single existing major league. Another possible cause of exploitation is restricted mobility. If a lawyer is prevented from practicing in states other than the one where he or she now works, he or she may be exploited because of the impossibility of going where the value of his or her services to society and, therefore, potential income are the highest.

Note, however, that we have talked about the possibility but not the certainty of exploitation. Stress should be placed on the possibility, because the lack of information, the lack of free entry, and the lack of mobility do not offer *prima facie* evidence of exploitation. More evidence is needed.

Discrimination

Discrimination is usually defined in almost the same way as exploitation, but it may also include not being able to find a job and not being able to buy certain products, such as housing in particular neighborhoods. Usually we say that employers have "tastes for discrimination" when they act as if there were nonmonetary costs associated with the hiring of blacks or other minority group members or women. This type of behavior leads to lower incomes for blacks or women than they would receive otherwise. In fact, there is quite a bit of evidence of discrimination in the labor market, particularly in restricted situations such as those caused by union activities. We have already discussed discrimination against women in the Issues and Applications section of Chapter 13. Here we will look at discrimination against blacks.

In a theoretical and empirical study of discrimination against blacks, Professor Gary S. Becker found that discrimination was related to a number of readily observable variables.[2] In the study, discrimination is defined by wage differentials not accounted for by different VMPs between whites and blacks in similar job situations. Becker found the following relationships:

1. Discrimination is positively related to the relative number of blacks and whites. For a given-sized city, the larger the proportion of blacks, the more discrimination there will be. This is sometimes called the "propinquity" theorem. Further, discrimination is more prevalent when large numbers of blacks are involved in nonmarket activities such as attaining a formal education. This means that the larger the number of blacks relative to whites, the more discrimination we would expect to see.
2. Discrimination is less evident against those seeking temporary as opposed to permanent work.
3. Discrimination is greater against those who are older and better educated.
4. Discrimination has deterred blacks from entering professions such as law because of their competitive disadvantage in arguing before white juries.

Becker also found that black incomes were reduced by 16 percent as a result of discrimination.

There appears to be quite a bit of discrimination against blacks and other minorities in the acquisition of human capital. That is, the amount and quality of schooling offered blacks has been inferior to that offered to whites. We find that even if minorities attend school as long as whites, their scholastic achievement is usually less because they typically are allotted more meager school resources than their white counterparts. Analysis of census

[2] Gary S. Becker, *The Economics of Discrimination,* rev. ed. (Chicago: University of Chicago Press, 1971).

data revealed that a large portion of white/nonwhite income differentials resulted from differences in both the quantity of education received and in scholastic achievement, which is more or less a function of the quality of education received. One study showed that nonwhite urban males receive between 23 and 27 percent less income than white urban males because of lower-quality education. This would mean that even if employment discrimination were substantially reduced, we would still expect to see a difference between white and nonwhite incomes because of the low quality of schooling received by the nonwhites and the resulting lower level of productivity. We say, therefore, that among other things, blacks and certain other minority groups, such as Chicanos, suffer from too small an investment in human capital. Even when this difference in human capital is taken into account, however, there still appears to be an income differential that cannot be explained. The unexplained income differential between whites and blacks is often attributed to discrimination in the labor market. Since no better explanation is offered, we will stick with the notion that discrimination in the labor market does indeed exist.

DISTRIBUTION OF INCOME AND OTHER FACTORS OF PRODUCTION

We have restricted most of our analysis in this chapter to the determination of the distribution of personal income. We point out here that, in particular, the marginal productivity theory that we have just presented applies equally to *all* factors of production, including land, capital, and entrepreneurial talents.

Concepts in Brief 16-2

- There are numerous determinants of income differences.
- Most people follow an age-earnings cycle in which they earn relatively small incomes when they first start working, increase their incomes until about age 45 to 50, then slowly experience a decrease in their real incomes as they approach retirement.
- If we accept the marginal productivity theory of wages, workers can expect to be paid the value of their marginal product. Note, however, that full adjustment is never obtained, so that some workers may be paid more or less than the value of their marginal product. The marginal productivity theory of wages applies in the large; it is not necessarily able to explain every single individual case.
- Marginal productivity depends on: (1) innate abilities and attributes, (2) education, (3) experience, and (4) training.
- We say that a person has been exploited if he or she is being paid less than the value of his or her labor services to an employer. Exploitation can occur because of monopsony and monopoly.
- Discrimination is difficult to define but appears to relate to exploitation plus one's inability to find a job or to buy certain products, such as housing in particular neighborhoods.

Investment in Human Capital

Investment in human capital is just like investment in any other thing. If you invest in a building, you expect to realize a profit later on by receiving a rate of return for your investment. You expect to receive some reward for not consuming all your income today. The same is true for investment in human capital. If you invest in yourself by going to college, rather than going to work after high school and spending more income, you presumably will be rewarded in the future by a higher income and/or a more interesting job. This is exactly the motivation that usually underlies the decision of many college-bound students to obtain a formal higher education. Undoubtedly, there would be students going to school even if the rate of return to formal education were zero or negative. After all, college is fun, right? (And it's certainly better than going to work.) But we do expect that the higher the rate of return on investing in oneself, the more investment there will be. And we find that the investment in a college education does pay off. Exhibit 16–7 shows the age-earnings cycle of grade school graduates, high school graduates, and college graduates. The age-earnings cycle jumps up for each increase in formal education. The investment in human capital does pay off.

As we pointed out in Chapter 1, to figure out the rate of return on an investment in a college education, we first have to figure out the costs of going to school. The main cost is not what you have to pay for books, fees, and tuition, but, rather, the income you forego. *The main cost of education is the income foregone or the opportunity cost of not working.* That may amount to as much as $10,000 a year. In addition, of course, you have to pay for the direct expenses of college (or rather, your parents do in many cases). Of course, not all students forego all income during their college years. Many people

EXHIBIT 16–7
Age-Earnings Profile for Selected Degree Holders. The age-earnings cycle jumps up for each increase in formal education. It is obvious that the investment in human capital eventually "pays off."

Source: U.S. Department of Commerce, Consumer Income, ser. P-60, no 74

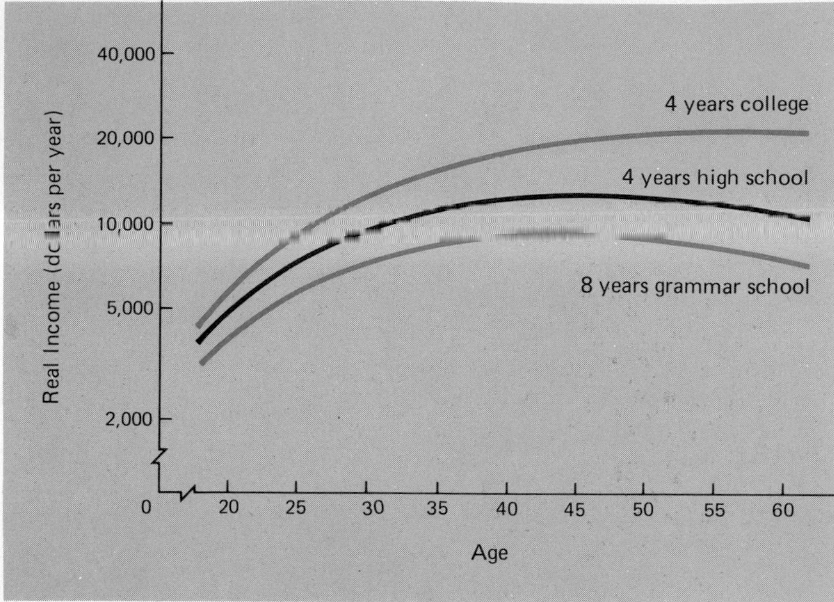

work part-time. Taking account of those who work part-time and those who are supported by state tuition grants and other scholarships, the average rate of return of going to college is somewhere between 8 and 12 percent. This is not a bad rate of return. Of course, this type of computation does leave out all the consumption benefits you get from attending college. College is not *all* pain. Also omitted from the calculations is the change in one's personality after going to college. You undoubtedly come out a different person, for better or for worse. Most people who go through college think they better themselves both culturally and intellectually, as well as increase their marginal physical product so they can make more income. How does one measure the benefit from expanding one's horizons and one's desire to experience different things in life? Certainly this is not easy to measure, and such nonpecuniary benefits from investing in human capital are not included in our normal calculations.

Theories of Income Distribution

We have talked about the factors affecting the distribution of income, but we have not yet mentioned the normative issue of how income *ought* to be distributed. This, of course, requires a value judgment. We are talking about the problem of economic justice. We can never completely resolve such a problem because there are always going to be conflicting interests. It is impossible to give everyone what he or she thinks is just. Nonetheless, there are three particular normative standards for the distribution of income that have been popular with social philosophers, economists, and politicians. These normative standards are income distribution based on (1) need, (2) equality, and (3) productivity.

NEED

"To each according to his needs." So goes the distributive principle of pure Communism, associated most often with Karl Marx. Although this principle, or standard, of income distribution certainly has little to do with how income is distributed in this country, it does apply roughly to the way income is distributed within a family unit, and also to the way income is distributed within a geographical area during wartime or other periods of emergency. There is little doubt that this distribution standard has a great appeal to many individuals. However, its implementation poses a number of extremely thorny problems. The most difficult problem, perhaps, is the establishment of an unbiased objective, an operational mechanism for measuring "need." In general, the only way we can determine need is by using subjective judgment. It is very difficult for us to establish just what is a necessity for each individual.

EQUALITY

The egalitarian principle of income distribution can be simply stated as "To each exactly the same." In other words, everyone would have exactly the same amount of income. This criterion of distribution has been debated as far back as biblical times. Just as with the need criterion, the equality criterion has problems.

If there were an equal distribution of income, *the incentive of rewards would be eliminated.* What would motivate people to develop and apply their skills and capacities to the most productive uses? What incentive would there be for individuals to use economic resources efficiently? If we used the equality principle in the distribution of income, this nation would probably suffer a decline in economic growth. However, this does not necessarily mean that the equality criterion should be eliminated—the benefits from equalizing income may still outweigh the costs.

PRODUCTIVITY

The productivity standard for the distribution of income can be stated simply as "To each according to what he or she produces." This is also called a *contributive* standard, because it is based on the principle of rewarding according to the contribution to society's total output. It is also sometimes referred to as a merit standard and is one of the oldest concepts of justice known. People are rewarded according to merit, and merit is judged by one's ability to produce what is considered useful by society.

However, just as the other two standards are value judgments, so is the contributive or productivity standard. The productivity standard is rooted in the capitalist ethic, though, and has been attacked vigorously by some economists and philosophers, including Karl Marx who, as we pointed out, felt that people should be rewarded according to need and not according to productivity. Those who believe in equality will often reject the productivity standard by saying that a person's "true worth," and hence claim on income, depends on his or her decency, warmth, political attitudes, and other human qualities unrelated to one's productivity.

We measure one's productive contribution in a capitalist system by the market value of one's output. We have already referred to this as the marginal productivity theory of wage determination.

Do not immediately jump to the conclusion that in a world of income distribution determined by productivity, society will necessarily allow the aged, the infirm, and the disabled to die from starvation because they are unproductive. In the United States today, the productivity standard is mixed with the need standard so that the aged, the disabled, the involuntarily unemployed, the very young, and other unproductive (in the market sense of the word) members of the economy are provided for.

Concepts in Brief 16-3

- Going to school and receiving on-the-job training can be considered an investment in human capital.
- The main cost of education is the opportunity cost of not working.
- There are at least three normative standards for income distribution: income distribution based on (1) need, (2) equality, and (3) productivity.

ISSUES AND APPLICATIONS

Can Poverty Be Eliminated?

Concepts Applied

- Distribution of income, marginal productivity theory, equality and efficiency

Throughout the history of the world, mass poverty has been an accepted inevitability. However, this nation and others, particularly in the Western world, have sustained enough economic growth in the last several hundred years so that *mass* poverty can no longer be said to be a problem for these fortunate countries. As a matter of fact, the residual of poverty in the United States appears bizarre—an anomaly. How is it that

Poverty: As long as we strive for economic efficiency, there will be unequal distribution of income. And as long as the distribution of income is not perfectly equal, there will always be relative poverty.

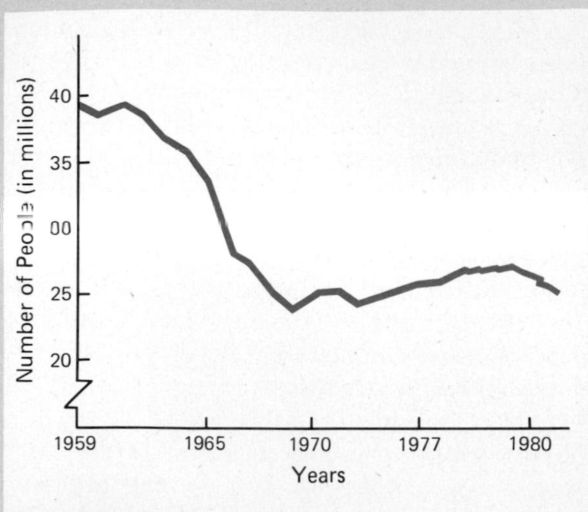

EXHIBIT 16–8
The Official Number of Poor in the United States. The number of individuals classified as poor fell steadily from 1959 through 1969. But since then there has been little change in the absolute number classified as poor.

Source: U.S. Department of Labor.

there can still be so much poverty in a nation of so much abundance? Having talked about the determinants of the distribution of income, we now have at least some ideas of why some people are destined to remain low-income earners throughout their lives.

There are methods of transferring income from the relatively well-to-do to the relatively poor, and as a nation, we have begun using them. Today we have a vast array of welfare programs set up for the purpose of redistributing income and for that purpose alone. However, we know that these programs have not been entirely successful. Are there alternatives to our current welfare system? Is there a better method of helping the poor? Before we answer these questions, let's look at the concept of poverty in more detail and at the characteristics of the poor.

The Low-Income Population

We see in Exhibit 16–8 that the number of individuals classified as poor fell rather steadily from 1959 to 1969. For a while, the number of poor leveled off, although in the last few years the total number of officially designated poor people has increased.

Defining poverty. The threshold income level, which is used to determine who falls into the poverty category, was originally based on the cost of a nutritionally adequate food plan designed by the Department of Agriculture for emergency or temporary use. The threshold was determined by multiplying the food plan cost times 3, on the assumption that food expenses comprise approximately one-third of a poor family's income. In 1969, a federal interagency committee looked at the calculations of the threshold and decided to set new standards. Until then, annual revisions of the threshold level were based purely on price changes in the food budget only. After 1969, the adjustments were made on the basis of changes in the Consumer Price Index.

The low-income threshold thus represents an absolute measure of income needed to maintain a specified standard of living as of 1963, with the real-dollar value, or the purchasing power value, increased year by year in relation to the general increase in prices. For 1981, for example, the low-income threshold budget for a nonfarm family of four was $8,410. By the time you read this book, it will have gone up by whatever the change in the Consumer Price Index has been during the period. (It varies for families of different size.)

Absolute poverty. Since the low-income threshold is an absolute measure, we know that if it never changes in real terms, we will reduce poverty even if we do nothing. How can that be? The reasoning is rather straightforward. Real incomes in the United States have been growing at a compounded annual rate of about 1.5 percent per capita for the last 100 or more years, and at about 2.5 percent since World War II. If we define the poverty line at a specified real level, more and more individuals will make incomes that exceed that poverty line. Thus, in absolute terms we will eliminate poverty (assuming continued per capita growth).

Relative poverty. One should be careful with this analysis, however. Poverty has generally been defined in relative terms; that is, it is defined in terms of the income levels of individuals or families relative to what exists in the rest of the population. As long as there is a distribution of income that is not perfectly equal, there will always be some people who make less income than others and some people who have a relatively low income—even if that relatively low income is high by historical standards. Thus, in a relative sense, the problem of poverty will always exist, although it can be reduced.

Who Are the Poor?

Individuals who are classified as poor share some general characteristics. They usually fall into one or more of the following classifications.

Minority groups. Minority groups—blacks, Hispanics, and so on—have a relatively high incidence of poverty. It is interesting to note that the poverty rate among black families is more than three times that of white families. This is also true—even more so—for Native Americans and Chicanos.

The elderly. Family units headed by individuals over 65 years of age often have very low levels of income also. Of every five poor families, one is headed by an elderly person. (Note, however, that their situation is often mitigated by the fact that they own their own homes and therefore don't need income for housing. They have other wealth, too.)

The young. The young, especially black teenagers, usually suffer high rates of unemployment. As indicated earlier, the minimum wage law further aggravates this situation. The younger members of society are generally not as educated or experienced as the older groups, and therefore they are not as productive. Hence, their value is often not sufficient to induce employers to pay the statutory minimum wage to hire them.

Rural population. Poverty is far more common among families living in rural areas than among those living in a city or in an urban area. Poverty rates among families living on farms are almost twice as high as among those in urban areas. (Note, however, that rural families often grow much of their own food and therefore do not require as much money income.)

Households headed by women. Nearly 40 percent of all women heading a household and providing for their children are defined as poor. If we look at the nonwhite population of fatherless families, this figure rises to nearly 60 percent.

Now that we have some idea as to how individuals are classified as poor or nonpoor, and who those individuals are, let's look at some current means of helping low-income families.

Attacks on Poverty—Major Income-Maintenance Programs

There are a variety of income-maintenance programs designed to help the poor. We examine a few of them here.

Social insurance. For the retired and unemployed, certain social insurance programs exist that provide income payments in prescribed situations. The best known is Social Security, which includes what has been called old age, survivors, disability, and health insurance—or OASDHI. This is essentially a program of compulsory saving financed from compulsory payroll taxes levied on both employers and employees. Workers pay for Social Security while working and receive the benefits later after retirement. The benefit payments are usually made to those reaching retirement age. When the insured worker dies, benefits accrue to the survivors, including widows and children. There are also special benefits that provide for disabled workers. Over 90 percent of all employed persons in the United States are covered by OASDHI. Social Security was originally designed as a social insurance program that workers paid for themselves and received benefits that varied with the size of past contributions. In reality today, it is simply an intergenerational income transfer that, at best, is roughly associated with past earnings. In other words, Social Security is a system in which income is transferred from those who work—the young—to those who do not work—older retired persons.

In 1981, there were more than 30 million people receiving OASDHI checks averaging about $365 a month. Benefit payments from OASDHI redistribute income to some degree. However, benefit payments are not based on the recipient's need. Participants' contributions give them the right to benefits even if they would be financially secure without them. In fact, Social Security appears to be a system whereby the relatively young subsidize the relatively old. One pays in when one is younger and receives payment when one is older. Social Security is not really an insurance program, however, because people are not guaranteed that the benefits they receive will be in line with the contributions they have made. It is not a personal savings account. The benefits are legislated by Congress. In the future, Congress may not be as sympathetic toward older people as it is today. It could legislate for lower real levels of benefits instead of higher ones.

Supplemental security income (SSI) and aid to families with dependent children (AFDC). There is a large number of persons who are poor and who do not qualify for Social Security benefits. They are assisted through other programs. Starting in 1974, a federally financed and administered Supplemental Security Income (SSI) program was instituted. The purpose of SSI is to establish a nationwide minimum income for the aged, the blind, and the disabled.

The Aid to Families with Dependent Children (AFDC) is a state-administered program, partially financed by federal grants. This program provides aid to families in which dependent children do not have the financial support of the father because of desertion, disability, or death.

Food stamps. In 1964, 367,000 Americans were receiving food stamps. By 1981, there were over 17 million recipients. The annual cost jumped from $860,000 to more than $11 billion. The eligibility requirements for the program in 1977 were such that a family of four with an income of $300 a month could obtain $170 worth of food stamps by paying $83. Individuals who find themselves on strike and also many college students are eligible for the food stamp program.

A congressional committee found that in 1975, one in every 14 persons was estimated to be using food stamps. The food stamp program has become a major part of the welfare system in the United States. It was started in 1964 and, in retrospect, seems to have been used mainly to shore up the nation's agricultural sector by distributing "surplus" food through retail channels. In addition, of course, the food stamp program was and continues to be a method of supporting better nutrition among the poor.

Welfare programs and implicit tax rates. One major problem with any welfare program is its impact on the incentive for individuals to obtain gainful taxable employment. If someone is currently receiving any type of welfare benefit which will be lost or reduced if that person goes to work, there is an implied, or implicit, tax involved in going back to work. Consider a simple example: A person is receiving welfare benefits equal to $400 a month, all of which is untaxed. In the most extreme example, assume that the individual loses $1 of welfare benefits for every dollar earned. Ignoring any taxes paid on the dollar earned, the marginal tax rate clearly is 100 percent. The individual is no better off by working until he or she earns $401. If we take account of the fact that most earnings are taxed by the federal government and some state governments, then the effective marginal tax rate in our example is *greater* than 100 percent.

Two economists at the University of Southern California have put together a table showing the actual effects of income and taxes on family spendable income from wages and welfare benefits. This table is reproduced as Exhibit 16–9. The table is calculated for an inner-city family of four in Los Angeles. It is assumed to be comprised of two adults, one of whom is either unemployed or disabled. The family is assumed to obtain maximum city, county, state, and federal welfare benefits to which it is entitled. Look at the column labeled "Actual Marginal Tax Rate." That is the implicit marginal tax rate that this family of four is paying when one of the members goes to work. The lowest marginal tax rate

EXHIBIT 16–9

The Effects of Income and Taxes on Family Spendable Income from the Total of Welfare Benefits and Wages. This table shows the effects of welfare benefits and taxes on spendable income in California for 1980. In column 1, we show monthly gross wages, which include the employment taxes paid by employers. In column 2, we show net family spendable income after all taxes and welfare benefits, both from the federal government and the state, are included. That is why we label column 2 "Net Family Spendable Income." In column 3, we show the increase in spendable income as gross monthly wages from working increase from 0 to $1,000. For example, if a typical California family is making $200 a month and works enough to make $300 a month, spendable income will go up by only $30.04, even though gross monthly wages increase by $100. In column 4, the actual marginal tax rate is calculated. In the example we just discussed, since gross monthly wages increase by $100 but spendable income by only $30, the actual, or implicit, marginal tax rate is 70 percent.

(1) Monthly Gross Wages	(2) Net Family Spendable Income	(3) Increase in Spendable Income	(4) Actual Marginal Tax Rate (percent)
0	$718.33	n.a.	n.a.
100	759.43	$41.10	58.9
200	780.53	21.10	78.9
300	810.57	30.04	70.0
400	815.80	5.23	94.5
500	794.58	−21.22	121.2
600	794.58	none	100.0
700	794.58	none	100.0
800	809.92	15.34	84.7
900	832.49	22.57	77.4
1000	858.58	26.09	73.9

Source: Arthur B. Laffer and Christopher R. Petruzzi, University of Southern California.

is 58.9 percent; the highest is 121.2 percent. That means that if the family decides to earn $500 instead of $400, it is *worse off by $21.22.*

Although this example may seem exaggerated, it does drive home the point that welfare programs by their very nature must involve a high implicit marginal tax rate. Individuals may respond to these high marginal tax rates by avoiding gainful employment, by taking longer to look for a job, or by joining the cash, or underground (nonreported), economy.

Some Alternative Ways to Eliminate Poverty

A couple of the most popular alternatives to the current morass of welfare programs are a guaranteed annual income and negative income taxes which we discuss in order.

Guaranteed annual income. For many years now, a number of economists, sociologists, and social workers have been suggesting that a guaranteed annual income be instituted so that all families under the "poverty line" obtain a straight cash payment, varying perhaps according to the size of the family. As the family's income rose, the payments would of course be reduced.

Under this system, although families are still not as well off as they would be if they were working, there is a significant disincentive to work. After all, if the gain from working were small because of the consequent loss in guaranteed annual income, there would be fewer people who would be willing to work. This would not have much effect on those making substantially higher than poverty-line incomes, but it certainly would have an effect on those making incomes around and below the poverty line. There are also a number of critics who maintain that it smacks of government "paternalism."

Negative taxes. The other suggested alternatives to welfare programs involves the individual income tax. Through a system of negative taxation, the actual income of poor families could be raised to the income that society stipulates as the poverty line. The money would be paid directly out of the federal Treasury according to a schedule based on family size, actual income earned, and other attributes. Notice that we're talking not about setting up a new system but of extending an already existing, fully computerized income taxation setup.

With a **negative income tax,** a family of four, for example, making an income of $1,000, might be said to have a *poverty income gap* of $2,000. Their income is $2,000 below a poverty line of $3,000. The $1,000 of earned income also falls below the total of personal tax exemptions for a family of four allowed under current income tax laws. Under current laws, each person is allowed a $1,000 exemption for each member of the family. For a family of four, total exemptions would be $4,000. In this particular situation, with an income of only $1,000, there would be $3,000 of unused exemptions. This is the negative base to which one would apply a tax rate to compute a negative tax. In this particular example, the negative tax base would be $3,000. If the negative tax rate were 50 percent, then the family of four would receive a check for $1,500.

Advantages of the negative income tax. Proponents of the negative income tax point out that it has many advantages—particularly in relation to a guaranteed annual income. In the first place, it could be administered very efficiently by using the Internal Revenue Service. Secondly, there would be no problem of determining who were the "worthy" poor. The decision would be based purely on income. (This does not mean that some individuals wouldn't cheat by accepting income only in cash—and then not reporting it.) Lastly, there would be more incentive to work, because the payment scheme from the government would decrease gradually, not abruptly as would the guaranteed annual income.

Disadvantages of the negative income tax. Critics of the negative income tax point out that it would be extremely costly. Perhaps more importantly, there would be criticisms from lower middle-income groups who would receive no benefits. These groups would probably resent paying taxes to subsidize the incomes of families who, for example, earned only a few hundred dollars less than they did. In other words, equity problems would undoubtedly emerge.

The trade-off between equality and efficiency. The philosophy underlying redistributing income in general and helping the poor specifically is strongly associated with egalitarianism, or equality for all. The notions of liberty, justice, and equality are strong underlying sentiments in this country. They pervade our political and social institutions. On the other hand, our economic institutions in a price (or market) system have resulted in significant income and wealth differences. To many, this is a conflict in our society. Forcing more equality onto the economic system conflicts with economic efficiency. A fundamental trade-off is therefore confronting policymakers. It was best described by a former member of the President's Council of Economic Advisers, the late Arthur M. Okun:

> The contrasts among American families in living standards and in material wealth reflect a system of rewards and penalties that is intended to encourage effort and to channel it into socially productive activity. To the extent that the [market] system succeeds, it generates an efficient economy. But that pursuit of efficiency necessarily creates inequalities. And hence society faces a trade-off between equality and efficiency.[3]

This big trade-off will be confronting policymakers forever. The more equality that is sought, the less productive efficiency will prevail. How much economic efficiency can we sacrifice in order to obtain more equality? That is not an easy question to answer, but it must be asked.

Questions

1. Why does there have to be a trade-off between efficiency and equality?
2. What is a work disincentive effect? Are there any income transfer programs that you can think of that do not have a work disincentive effect?

[3] Arthur M. Okun, *Equality and Efficiency: The Big Trade-off* (Washington, D.C.: The Brookings Institution, 1975), p. 1.

Definition of Terms

Distribution of income The way income is distributed among the population. For example, a perfectly equal distribution of income would result in the lowest 20 percent of income earners receiving 20 percent of national income and the top 20 percent also receiving 20 percent of national income. The middle 60 percent of income earners would receive 60 percent of national income.

Lorenz curve A geometric representation of the distribution of income. A Lorenz curve that is perfectly straight represents perfect income equality. The more bowed a Lorenz curve, the more unequally income is distributed.

Stock The quantity of something at a point in time. An inventory of goods is a stock. A bank account at a point in time is a stock. Stocks are defined independently of time although they are assessed at a point in time; different from a flow. Savings is a stock.

Flow Something that is defined per unit time period. Income is a flow that occurs per week, per month, or per year. Consumption is a flow. So is saving.

Age-earnings cycle The regular earnings profile of an individual throughout his or her lifetime. The age-earnings cycle usually starts with a low income, builds gradually to a peak at around age 45 to 50, and then gradually curves down until it approaches zero at retirement age.

Exploitation The payment to a factor of production that is less than its value of marginal product.

Negative income tax A system of transferring income to the relatively poor by taxing them negatively—that is, giving them an income subsidy that varies depending upon how far below a "target" income their earned income lies.

Chapter Summary

1. The distribution of money income in the United States has remained fairly constant since World War II. The lowest fifth of income earners still receive only about 5 percent of total money income, while the top fifth of income earners receive over 40 percent.
2. We can represent the distribution of income graphically with a Lorenz curve. The extent to which the line is bowed from a straight line shows how unequal the distribution of income is.
3. Most individuals face a particular age-earnings cycle or profile. Earnings are lowest when starting out to work at age 18 to 24. They gradually rise and peak at about age 45 to 50, then fall until retirement age. They go up usually because of increased experience, increased training, and longer working hours.
4. The marginal productivity theory of the distribution of income indicates that workers can expect to be paid the value of their marginal product. For this theory to be exactly correct, we must have competition in labor and product markets with fairly minimal information costs. Otherwise there will always be people who are being paid more or less than the value of their marginal product.
5. The value of marginal product is usually determined by innate intelligence, schooling, experience, and training.
6. Exploitation can be defined as a situation in which a worker is paid less than his or her value of marginal product. Exploitation may occur in situations where monopoly or monopsony power exists on the part of the employer, where information is restricted, or where entry into the industry is also restricted.
7. Discrimination is usually defined as a situation in which a certain group is paid a lower wage than other groups for the same work.
8. One way to invest in your own human capital is by going to college. The investment usually pays off, for the rate of return is somewhere between 8 and 12 percent.
9. The number of individuals officially classified as poor dropped dramatically from 1959 to 1969 and then leveled off.
10. A definition of poverty made in relative terms means that there will always be poor in our society, since the distribution of income will never be exactly equal.
11. The major income maintenance programs are Social Security (OASDHI), Aid to Families with Dependent Children (AFDC), and Supplemental Security Income (SSI).
12. As an alternative to existing programs, policymakers could institute a guaranteed annual income or a negative income tax.
13. There is often a trade-off between equality and productive efficiency.

Selected References

Easterlin, Richard E. *Birth and Fortune: The Impact of Numbers on Personal Welfare.* New York: Basic Books, 1980.

Harrington, Michael. *The Other America: Poverty in the United States.* Rev. ed. New York: Macmillan, 1970.

Okun, Arthur M. *Equality and Efficiency: The Big Tradeoff.* Washington, D.C.: The Brookings Institution, 1975.

Robins, P. K., et. al., eds. *A Guaranteed Annual Income,* 2 vols. New York: Academic Press, 1980.

Thurow, Lester C. *Generating Inequality: Mechanisms of Distribution in The U.S. Economy.* New York: Basic Books, 1975.

Van Driel, G. J. *Limits to the Welfare State.* Boston: Martinus Nijhoff, 1980.

Williamson, J. G., and P. H. Lindest. *American Inequality.* New York: Academic Press, 1980.

Answers to Preview and Study Questions

1. What is a Lorenz curve, and what does it measure?

A Lorenz curve plots the accumulated percentage of money income on the *y*-axis, and the accumulated percentage of families on the *x*-axis; it is a curve indicating the portion of total money income accounted for by given proportions of a nation's families. It is one measure of income inequality, and as such it is not without its critics. Two major problems with using the Lorenz curve to measure income equality are: (a) it typically does not take into account "income in kind," such as food stamps, housing aid, and so on; (b) it does not account for differences in family size (and effort) or age. Adjustments for these would undoubtedly reduce the degree of measured income inequality in the United States.

2. What has been happening to the distribution of income in the United States?

Since World War II the distribution of *money* income has not changed significantly. On the other hand, the distribution of *total* income—which includes "in-kind" government transfers—has changed significantly in recent years. Since the 1960s *total* income inequality has been reduced significantly. The fact that more income equality has been achieved in the United States in recent years is of tremendous importance, yet few people seem to be aware of this fact.

3. What is the difference between income and wealth?

Income is a flow concept and, as such, is measured per unit of time; one usually states that a person's income is "*X* dollars *per year*." On the other hand, wealth is a stock concept; as such it is measured at a given point in time. One usually says that a person's wealth is $200,000 or $1 million. Note that, if people save out of a given income, it is possible for their wealth to be rising—while their income is constant. Technically a person's wealth may be defined as the value of his or her assets (human and nonhuman) minus his or her liabilities (wealth is equivalent to net worth) at some point in time.

4. Why do people earn different incomes?

The major theory to account for income differentials (at least in market economies) is the marginal productivity theory. This theory says that laborers (as well as other resources) tend to be paid the value of their marginal product. Laborers who are paid less than their value of marginal product will go to other employers who will gladly pay them more (it will be profitable for them to do so); laborers who are being paid more than their marginal product may well lose their jobs (at least in the private sector). Thus, productivity differences due to age, innate talent (intelligence, skills, coordination), experience, and training can account for income differences. Of course, imperfect markets can potentially lead to income differences, *given productivity,* due to exploitation and discrimination. Income differences can also be accounted for by differences in nonhuman wealth—individuals can earn income on their property holdings.

5. What is the best distribution of income?

Clearly the best distribution of income is ultimately dependent on one's tastes. Value judgments are required to determine whether one distribution of income is "better" than another; there is no objective way to decide that a more even distribution of income is preferable to a less-even one. Three main normative theories of what the income distribution "ought" to be are: (a) to each according to his or her need (this is the distributive principle of Communism and has obvious measurement problems; what is "need"?), (b) to each exactly the same (incentive problems obviously emerge here), and (c) to each according to what he or she produces (this theory suggests that income differences due to differences in people's value of marginal product are "fair"). Each of these is a normative statement.

Problems

(Answers at the back of the book)

1. It is often observed that blacks, on average, earn less than whites. What are some possible reasons for these differences?

2. The graph at right represents Lorenz curves for two countries.
   a. Which line indicates perfect equality of income?
   b. Which line indicates the most income inequality?
   c. Assume a country's "income inequality" were described by line *B*. Suppose this country's income were adjusted for age and other variables such that "income" on the *y*-axis reflects *lifetime* income instead of income in a given year. Would the new, adjusted Lorenz curve move inward toward *A*, or outward toward *C*?

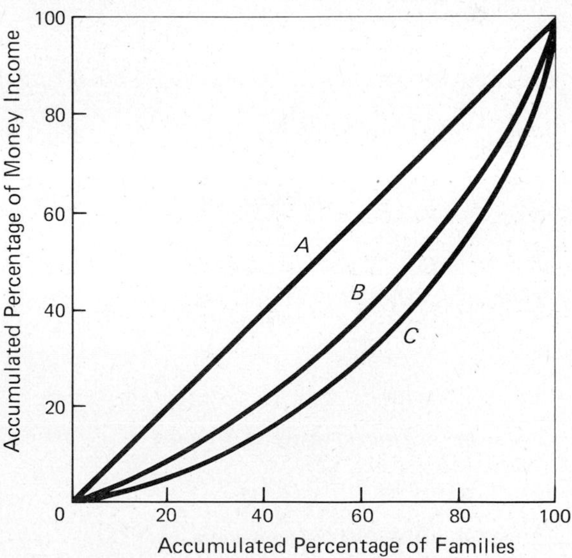

17

Putting It All Together: General Equilibrium Analysis

TOPICS FOR REVIEW

The topics listed below, which we have already analyzed, are applied in this chapter. You may find it worthwhile to review them. For your convenience each topic is followed by the number identifying the specific "Concepts in Brief."

a. Other things being constant (3–2)

b. Consumer sovereignty (4–4)

c. Consumer maximization (7–2)

d. Long-run equilibrium, perfect competition (8–4, 9–3)

e. Value of marginal product (13–1)

f. Minimum cost conditions (13–4)

FOR PREVIEW AND STUDY

1. What are stable and unstable market equilibrium situations?
2. Is an unstable market equilibrium situation likely?
3. What is dynamic equilibrium analyis?
4. What is the difference between partial and general equilibrium analysis?
5. Why is a perfectly competitive price system considered to be economically efficient?

Within the market system, we have looked at three parts of our price system: (1) the household sector and the demand for goods and services; (2) the production sector and the supply and pricing of goods and services; and (3) the labor market with its demand for labor by firms and the supply of labor from households. We have treated each sector of the economy separately, but in reality they all interact. The world is one in which all things depend on all other things. In this chapter, we will look at this interdependence in more detail. In the Issues and Applications section, a specific example of an economic model with definite interdependence among sectors is presented.

Equilibrium Revisited

We have defined equilibrium at several points throughout the text. Equilibrium prevails when opposing forces are in balance. A market is in equilibrium when the quantity supplied is equal to the quantity demanded. Such an equilibrium occurs when the price in the marketplace is equal to the equilibrium price, or the market clearing price. But what happens (given supply and demand) if there is a shock that disturbs the equilibrium? Are there self-corrective forces that automatically push the disequilibrium back to the original equilibrium price and quantity? The answer is yes for most markets at most times. There are, however, cases in which a shock will more than temporarily keep the price and quantity out of equilibrium. The two possible situations can be labeled stable and unstable equilibria.

STABLE AND UNSTABLE EQUILIBRIA

When we refer to a **stable equilibrium,** we mean that if there is a movement away from the equilibrium price or quantity, there will be forces pushing price and/or quantity back to equilibrium. An **unstable equilibrium** is one in which, if there is a movement away from the equilibrium, there are forces that push price and/or quantity even further away from equilibrium (or at least do not push price and quantity back toward the equilibrium level or rate). The difference between a stable and an unstable equilibrium can be illustrated by looking at two balls: one made of hard rubber, the other made of soft, moist Play-Doh. If you were to squeeze the rubber ball out of shape, it would bounce back to its original form. However, if you were to squeeze the Play-Doh ball out of shape, it would remain out of shape. With respect to the shape of the two balls made out of different materials, the former illustrates a stable equilibrium and the latter an unstable equilibrium.

Stable Equilibrium in Graphic Form

Look at panel (a) of Exhibit 17–1. Here we show an equilibrium price of P_e. What if the price is P_1 (which is more than P_e)? Then the quantity supplied will exceed the quantity demanded at that price. The result will be an excess quantity supplied at price P_1, or a "surplus." However, given *DD* and *SS,* there will be forces pushing the price back down toward P_e. Suppliers will attempt to reduce their inventories by cutting prices and reducing output, and/or demanders will offer to purchase more at lower prices. The reason that suppliers will want to reduce inventories is that the latter will be above their optimal level; that is, there will be an excess over what the firm believes to be the profit-maximizing stock of inventories. After all, inventories are costly to hold. Their cost is, at minimum, the opportunity cost of the capital tied up in them. On the other hand, demanders may find out about such excess inventories and see the possibility of obtaining increased quantities of the good in question at a reduced price. It behooves demanders to attempt to obtain a good at a lower price, and they will therefore try to do so. If the two forces of supply and demand are unrestricted, they will bring the price back to P_e. (For the moment, we will ignore restrictions in the marketplace that might prevent the forces of supply and demand from changing price.)

What if the price is for some reason at P_2? At this price, the quantity demanded exceeds the quantity supplied. There is an excess quantity demanded at P_2, or a "shortage." Forces will cause the price to rise. Demanders will bid up the price, and/or suppliers will raise the price and increase output, whether explicitly or implicitly.

The point is that any disequilibrium situation automatically brings into action correcting forces that will cause a movement back toward equilibrium. The equilibrium price and quantity will be maintained as long as demand and supply do not change (that is, as long as the nonprice determinants of supply and demand do not change).

Unstable Equilibrium in Graphic Form

Look at panel (b) of Exhibit 17–1. Here we show the supply curve at *SS*. It is downward sloping, just like the demand curve *DD*. We start out in equilibrium with price P_0 and quantity Q_0. Now let's assume there's a shock to the system. The price tem-

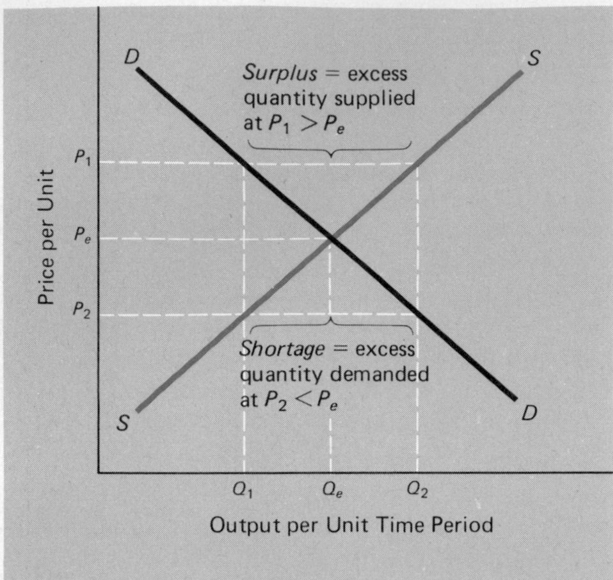

EXHIBIT 17–1(a)
Equilibrium Price, Shortages, and Surpluses. At a price of P_e, the quantity demanded equals the quantity supplied. At price P_1, the quantity supplied exceeds the quantity demanded. The difference is the excess quantity supplied at price P_1. It is sometimes called a surplus. At price P_2, the quantity demanded exceeds the quantity supplied. There is an excess quantity demanded at P_2. It is sometimes called a shortage. In both cases, forces will push the price toward P_e and the quantity sold to Q_e.

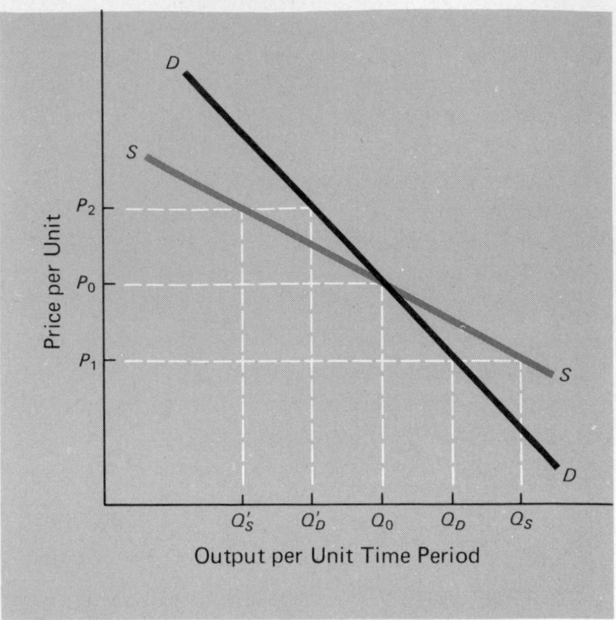

EXHIBIT 17–1(b)
Unstable Equilibrium. Here we start off at a price of P_0, which is an unstable equilibrium price. If price is, for whatever reason, "shocked" down to P_1, the quantity supplied will be Q_s and the quantity demanded will be Q_D. When the quantity supplied is greater than the quantity demanded, the price will continue to fall rather than go back up to P_0. If the price is "shocked" up to P_2, the quantity supplied will decrease to Q_s' and the quantity demanded to Q_D'. The quantity demanded exceeds the quantity supplied, and the price will continue to rise.

porarily falls to P_1. What happens? The quantity supplied increases to Q_S, and the quantity demanded increases to Q_D. At price P_1, there is an excess quantity supplied. Whenever there is an excess quantity supplied (a surplus), the price will continue to fall. Thus, it will continue to decline rather than go back to its initial position of P_0. Look at another possible shock in panel (b) of Exhibit 17–1. The price is, for whatever reason, temporarily at P_2. At that price, the quantity demanded will be Q_D', and the quantity supplied will be Q_S'. In other words, there is an excess quantity demanded (a shortage). Such situations elicit an increase in price; hence, price will continue to move away from rather than back toward its initial position of P_0.

DO WE NEED TO WORRY ABOUT UNSTABLE EQUILIBRIA?

Panel (b) of Exhibit 17–1 presents a situation of unstable equilibrium. Clearly, if such an unstable equilibrium represented a large percentage of market situations in our economy, we would not have much faith in the ability of markets to be self-correcting and adjusting. But empirically, we do not observe "exploding" market situations. That is to say, shocks to different markets in our economy do not cause prices to plummet toward zero or to skyrocket toward infinity. Therefore, it is reasonable to assume that a stable equilibrium situation will prevail in markets that are allowed to clear. Thus, shocks to different markets in our economy will not cause those markets with upward-sloping supply curves to be permanently out of equilibrium. And most short-run supply curves are upward sloping as in panel (a) of Exhibit 17–1.

The Movement of Prices and Quantities—The Cobweb Theorem

The prices and outputs of some commodities show cyclical movements over long periods of time. As prices move up and down in waves, quantities pro-

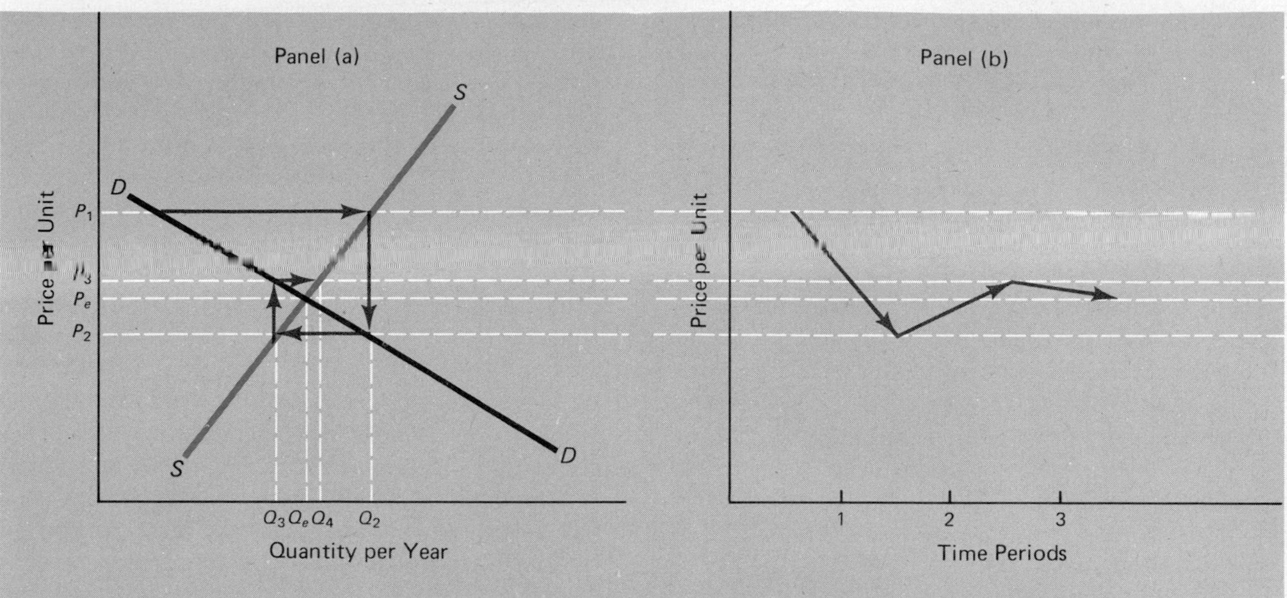

EXHIBIT 17–2

A Dynamic Model of Corn Production, Sales, and Prices. In this model, we assume that the amount of corn planted this period depends on the price this period, so that the amount of corn offered for sale next period depends on prices this period. In panel (a), we start off at price P_1, which calls forth a quantity supplied next period of Q_2. The only way Q_2 can be sold, however, is for the price to fall to P_2. But this price P_2 calls forth a quantity for sale next period of only Q_3. The sellers of corn can raise their price to P_3 and still sell all that they have produced during the previous period. At the new higher price P_3, there will be offered for sale during the following period the quantity Q_4. This diagram takes on the appearance of a cobweb being spun clockwise closing in on the center. In panel (b), we see that the price moves toward the eventual long-run equilibrium price of P_e.

duced seem to move up and down in counterwaves. One explanation for such cycles in prices and output in certain industries is the so-called cobweb theorem. The name *cobweb* comes from the appearance of the diagrams. We can discuss one case in which a long-run equilibrium price will prevail in such a market structure. Let's look at Exhibit 17–2 which depicts the cobweb model.

Let's assume that the price of corn today happens to be P_1. In other words, the price in period 1 is P_1. Corn farmers—the suppliers—look at that price P_1 and decide to plant now Q_2 of corn that they expect to sell at that price when the corn is grown and ready for market next year. We see in panel (a) of Exhibit 17–2 an arrow moving from price P_1 horizontally over to the supply curve. Follow that arrow now to see what happens to corn production and price. Next year comes around and the farmers find out that the only way to get rid of Q_2 of the corn that they have produced is to sell it to consumers at price P_2. You can see this by the arrow that is now vertical and goes down to the demand curve. The lower price comes to pass. Farmers in period 2 look at the price P_2 and decide at that price to produce only quantity Q_3. When that smaller quantity comes to market in period 3, farmers find they can charge a price of P_3 and still sell all of it. That higher price induces farmers to produce quantity Q_4. This cycle continues, but the price movements, as you can see in panel (b) of Exhibit 17–2, get smaller and smaller. The price will hone in on the long-run equilibrium price of P_e, which is given at the intersection of *DD* and *SS*.

DYNAMIC EQUILIBRIUM

We have just dealt with a dynamic model of the production and sale of corn. The assumption here is that the amount of corn offered for sale in period 2 depends on the production of corn in period 1, which depends on the price that corn fetches in the marketplace today. Thus, the time factor is explicitly taken into account. Any dynamic model is one in which economic activities are analyzed by relating them to preceding (or anticipated succeeding) events.

Up until now, we have spoken only of static models that involve the study of economic phenomena without reference to time—that is, without reference to preceding or succeeding events.

General Versus Partial Equilibrium Analysis

You have been presented almost exclusively with what is called **partial equilibrium analysis.** The meaning of partial equilibrium analysis can best be expressed by a particular qualifying statement that we have tacked on to most of our "laws" and theories. That particular statement is: "other things being equal." In partial equilibrium analysis, it is assumed that, aside from whatever else we are analyzing, just about everything else is held constant. Not *all* other things are constant, because then there would be no change possible. In essence, partial equilibrium analysis allows us to focus on a single market and view it in isolation. For analytical purposes, the market is viewed as independent and self-contained. That is, it is independent of all other markets. Consider an example. What would happen if there were a new 10¢ tax per pound of salt legislated by Congress? We could do our analysis in terms of the demand and supply curves for salt. We would say that the cost of production would increase by 10¢ per pound, assuming that the government required the salt producers to remit 10¢ for every pound put on the market. Would we talk about the effect of this salt tax on the steel industry? On national unemployment? The answer is probably no. We would safely assume that the salt industry is such a small part of the total economy that it could be analyzed in isolation for most situations. We could safely assume other things being equal throughout our partial equilibrium analysis. It is not the case that the other factors do not change. They do, but the feedbacks from these changes are so small that we can successfully ask what happens if one factor changes and the others remain constant. In other words, we can *ignore* all other factors.

GENERAL EQUILIBRIUM ANALYSIS

General equilibrium analysis regards all sectors as important. General equilibrium analysis recognizes the important fact that everything depends on everything else. It takes account of the interrelationships among prices and quantities of various goods and services. It is a more precise analysis than partial equilibrium analysis, but also a more difficult one to undertake. Just as partial equilibrium analysis does not require that *all* other things be held constant, general equilibrium analysis does not permit *all* other things to vary. There is a limit to how many markets can be taken into account in any analysis. That limit is reached either by the cerebral limits of the economist doing the analysis or by the capacity of the computer that he or she is utilizing. When economists talk of general equilibrium analysis in dealing with practical problems, they are referring to taking account of *several markets* and the relationships among them. If the goal of the economist is to predict what will happen when the economic environment changes, his or her choice of general equilibrium analysis depends on (1) the question being asked, and (2) the degree to which the answer will change if several markets are *not* considered. One would want to use general equilibrium analysis when analyzing the effects of, say, a new law requiring the producers of steel to pay a 300 percent tax on the value of all steel produced. There would be important interrelationships among the steel industry, the automobile industry, and the labor markets involved in both industries, as well as effects on and from a multitude of other industries in the economy.

Let's now look at the simplest general equilibrium model. We will go back to the world of guns and butter discussed in Chapter 1.

> ***Concepts in Brief 17-1***
>
> ■ There are two types of equilibrium—stable and unstable.
>
> ■ A stable equilibrium is one in which a disturbance from the equilibrium price or quantity will be met by forces pushing price or quantity back to the equilibrium level or rate.
>
> ■ An unstable equilibrium is one in which, if there is a movement away from the equilibrium, forces will push the price and/or quantity further away from equilibrium.
>
> ■ In a dynamic model of corn production, we can have the quantity supplied this year depending on the price last year. Such a model takes on the form of a cobweb. In one cobweb model, price eventually settles down to a long-run equilibrium.
>
> ■ Partial equilibrium analysis is one that does not take account of interrelationships among markets.
>
> ■ General equilibrium analysis attempts to take into account the interrelationships among different markets.

The Circular Flow in a Two-Good World

Assume that there are only two goods available—guns and butter. Nothing else is produced, nothing else is consumed. All income is spent on either guns or butter. Thus, there are two industries. We show the circular flow of income and product in Exhibit 17-1. This is merely an expanded version of Exhibit 2-3. We have broken the factor markets and the product markets into two industries—guns and butter. We have also assumed that there is only one factor of production—labor. (Of course, there have to be others, but we want to make the model simple to show the interrelationships involved.) Let's start off in equilibrium in both labor markets and both product markets. The equilibrium prices and quantities of guns and butter are P_G, P_B, Q_G, and Q_B, respectively. The equilibrium wage rates and quantities of labor are W_G, W_B, L_G, and L_B, respectively.

Now, to show how the interrelationships work, we will assume an increase in the demand for guns. This is shown by a shift in the demand schedule in the product market from D_GD_G to $D'_GD'_G$. The short-run equilibrium price, given the supply curve of S_GS_G, will rise from P_G to P'_G. What will this mean? It will mean that firms in this industry will be making higher than normal profits. (We assume they were in equilibrium before; thus, they were making normal profits, or a competitive rate of return.) That is why output expands to Q'_G.

THE LABOR MARKET

There is only one way for firms in the gun industry to expand, however. More resources must be obtained. Considering labor alone, the demand curve for labor in the gun industry must shift from d_Gd_G to $d'_Gd'_G$. It will shift outward to the right because, as you will remember, the demand for labor is a derived demand. Now that output (guns) can be sold at a higher price (P'_G), the value of marginal product curve shifts outward to the right, and so too does the demand curve for labor in the gun industry. The only way the industry can attract more workers is for the wage rate to increase. That is why we show an upward-sloping labor supply curve of s_Gs_G. The wage rate rises to W'_G.

What About the Butter Industry?

The opposite short-run adjustments will occur in the butter industry. The product demand curve will shift leftward from D_BD_B to $D'_BD'_B$. This is so because we are living in a two-good, full-employment world. The only way for the population to demand and consume more guns is to reduce its demand for butter. Given the supply curve S_BS_B, the short-run equilibrium price will fall in the butter industry to P'_B. Looking at the labor market, since the demand for labor is a derived demand, the demand curve will shift leftward from d_Bd_B to $d'_Bd'_B$. The market clearing wage rate will fall to W'_B, and labor will leave the butter industry and enter the gun industry.

GENERAL EQUILIBRIUM IN THE LONG RUN

What we have done is trace the short-run adjustments to a shift in demand in favor of guns and away from butter. This is only a short-run situation because at the new equilibrium, economic profits are being made in the gun industry while economic losses are being made in the butter industry. Resources will flow out of the butter industry into the gun industry. That is to say, firms may go out of business in the butter industry; they or others will quickly see a place to make higher profits and move into the gun industry even before bankruptcy threatens. Thus, the supply curve in the gun industry will shift outward from S_GS_G to $S'_GS'_G$. Simultaneously, the supply curve will shift inward in the butter industry. A new long-run equilibrium price will prevail in both industries. It will fall in the long run from P'_G to P''_G in the gun industry. In the butter industry, it will rise from P'_B to P''_B.

There will be long-run adjustments also taking place in the resource markets. Workers will shift out of the butter industry and into the gun industry. The supply curve in the former will shift leftward while simultaneously the supply curve in the latter will shift rightward. The new equilibrium rate in the long run will fall slightly in the gun labor market from W'_G to W''_G. It will simultaneously rise in the butter labor market to W''_B.

FURTHER ADJUSTMENTS

The process doesn't end there, for the demand curve for labor in both markets will have to shift again. Remember, the demand for labor is a derived demand. When the price of guns and the price of butter change again to P''_G and P''_B, this will cause the value of marginal product to change also. We don't show these further changes, but they will continue with the demand and supply curves shifting

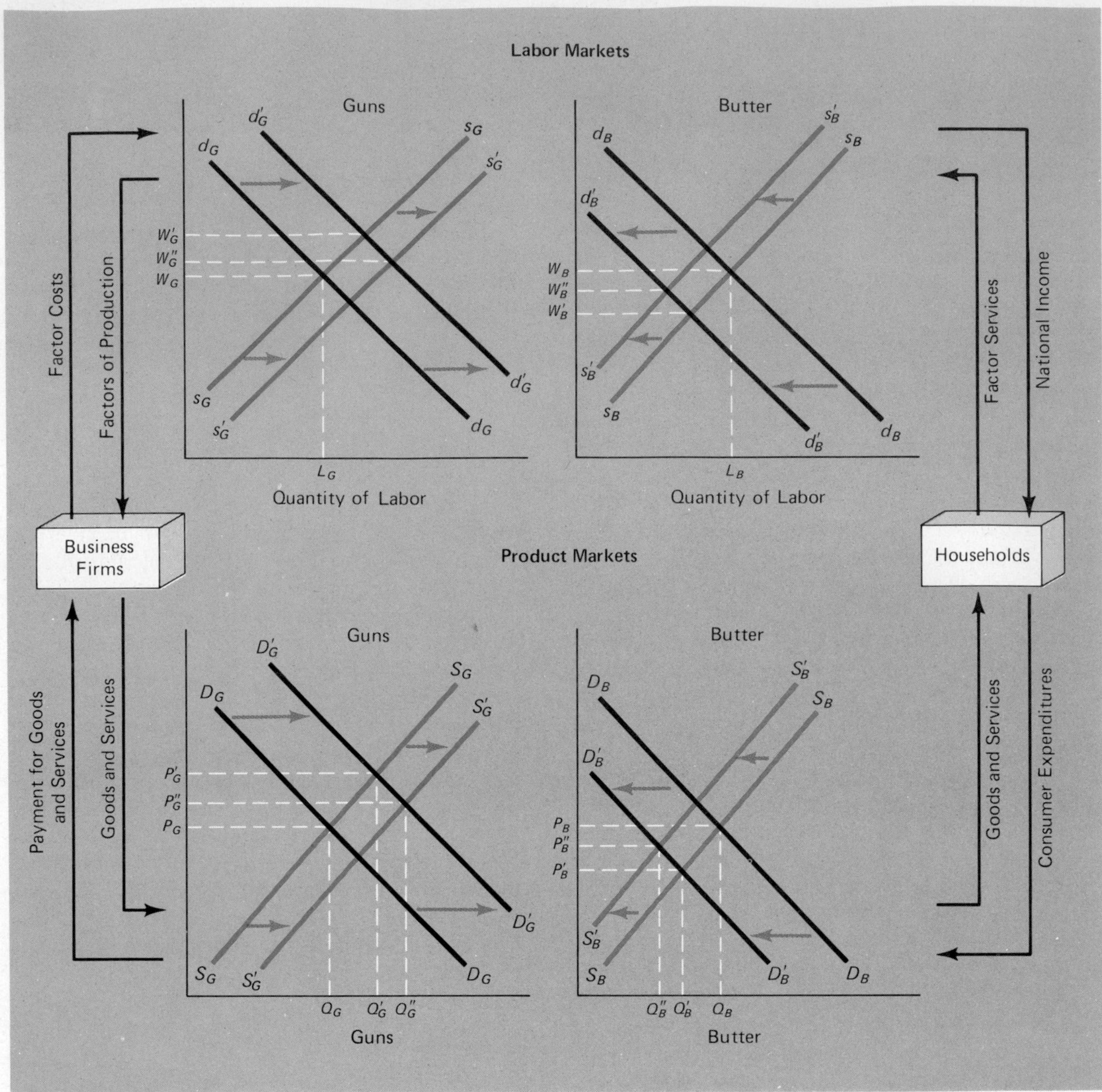

EXHIBIT 17–3

A Simplified General Equilibrium Model: Guns and Butter. We assume that there are only two goods in the world—guns and butter. All income is spent on them. All labor is used in manufacturing either guns or butter. We see a simplified circular flow diagram here in which business firms purchase resources in the labor market and sell goods and services in the product market. Households sell factor services to the labor market and receive national income as factor payments. Households purchase goods and services in the product market and make consumer expenditures. We assume that there is a shift in tastes in favor of guns. In the above diagrams we use lowercase *d*'s and *s*'s for the demand and supply curves in the labor markets and upper case *D*'s and *S*'s for the demand and supply curves in the product markets. The demand curve for guns shifts out to $D'_G D'_G$. The price increases to P'_G. This causes the derived demand curve for labor in the gun industry to shift outward to $d'_G d'_G$. Wage rates in the gun industry increase to W'_G. Concurrently, the demand curve for butter shifts inward to $D'_B D'_B$. The price of butter falls to P'_B. The derived demand for labor in the butter industry decreases to $d'_B d'_B$. Wage rates fall in the butter industry to W'_B. In the long run, further shifts occur. Labor and resources flow into the gun industry so that the supply curve shifts outward. The supply curve in the butter industry shifts inward. Prices move to P''_G in the gun industry and to P''_B in the butter industry. Workers move into the gun industry so that its supply curve of labor shifts outward. The supply curve of labor shifts inward in the butter industry. The equilibrium wage rate in the gun industry goes to W''_G. The equilibrium wage rate in the butter industry goes to W''_B. There are further adjustments that then take place, which we do not show.

until the long-run equilibrium is established in both the labor markets and the product markets. If we were to consider the possibility of other markets existing—that is, a world in which there were more than two goods—we would also take into account shifts in the demand for other goods due to a change in the price of guns and of butter. We would then have to find out what would happen to the resources used in other industries. A true general equilibrium analysis would take account of every relevant market.

The Correspondence Between Perfect Competition and Economic Efficiency

In this chapter, we have described a general equilibrium system. Underlying the description was a perfectly competitive economy. It turns out that the perfectly competitive price system has a very special quality. There is a correspondence between an efficient allocation of resources and the results of the allocation from a perfectly competitive price system. Indeed, this correspondence is exact. Every perfectly competitive allocation in long-run equilibrium yields an economically efficient allocation of resources. Remember the definition of economic efficiency: it is a situation in which the economy is deriving maximum economic value from the economy's given resources. Once we have attained a position of economic efficiency, it is impossible to make any person better off without making another person worse off.

THE MEANING OF A PERFECTLY COMPETITIVE PRICE SYSTEM

Let's be specific about what we mean by a perfectly competitive price system. In such a system, each good has an equilibrium price that is established by the interaction of supply and demand. The equilibrium price clears each market; the quantities demanded and supplied of each good are equal.

Consumers take the prices of the goods and services they buy as given. Subject to their budget constraints, they adjust their behavior to maximize satisfaction, or utility. Firms, of which there are a large number, each operate to maximize profits. Under these conditions, three things happen:

1. Profit-maximizing competitive firms produce at an output rate at which price equals marginal cost. Price reflects the worth to consumers, because they are willing to pay the price of a product. Marginal cost reflects the social opportunity cost of the resources needed in production. Thus, when price is set equal to marginal cost, the extra value placed on goods and services by consumers is just equal to the extra social opportunity cost of producing those goods and services. We say, then, that the optional output of each commodity gets produced.
2. Perfect competition results in each good or service being produced at minimum long-run average total cost. Thus, there is no "waste" in the system. Goods and services are produced using the least costly combinations of resources. Specifically, for each industry, the last dollar spent on each factor input generates the same marginal physical product. Additionally, perfect competition results in every factor of production being paid its value of marginal product (VMP).
3. Consumers will choose in competitive markets so that the distribution of output will maximize consumer satisfaction, or utility. That is to say, each consumer will buy goods and services in such amounts that the last dollar spent on each good or service yields the same amount of extra satisfaction, or marginal utility.

The following formulae summarize these points:

1. $P = \text{MC}$

2. $$\frac{\text{MPP of labor}}{\text{price of labor}} = \frac{\text{MPP of land}}{\text{price of land}} = \frac{\text{MPP of capital}}{\text{price of capital}} = \frac{\text{MPP of entrepreneurship}}{\text{price of entrepreneurship}}$$

3. $$\frac{\text{MU}_x}{\text{price of } x} = \frac{\text{MU}_y}{P_y} = \frac{\text{MU}_z}{P_z} = \cdots$$

The three conditions above describe an economi-

The three conditions above describe an economically efficient situation. They also describe what occurs in a perfectly competitive system. Hence, there is an exact correspondence between perfect competition and economic efficiency.

THE REAL WORLD

Just because we have just demonstrated (very loosely) that perfect competition leads to economic efficiency does not mean that perfect competition is "desirable." Nothing in the analysis relates to desirability, because that is in the realm of normative, or value-laden, economics. You may not accept economic efficiency as a worthwhile goal and may therefore not accept perfect competition as a goal. For example, an economically efficient economy could still have large numbers of individuals starving, for nothing is said about the distribution of income in the above analysis. Moreover, the real world does not provide us with a perfectly competitive price system. The model of perfect competition may nonetheless be useful for analysis and prediction.

Concepts in Brief 17-2

- A change in the demand for one good will elicit changes in the demand for another good and also cause changes in the corresponding factor markets.
- It is possible to show that there is a correspondence between perfect competition and economic efficiency.
- In perfect competition: (1) price equals marginal cost, (2) the marginal physical products per last dollar spent on each input are equal, and (3) the marginal utilities for the last dollar spent on each good by consumers are equal.

ISSUES AND APPLICATIONS

A Case Study in Economic Interdependence—Input-Output Analysis

Concepts Applied

- General equilibrium

In the nineteenth century, a French economist named Leon Walras was apparently the first to construct a general equilibrium model of an economy.[1] In subsequent years that model was modified, but the formulation remains much the same as it was more than 100 years ago. Improvements have been made and the model has been extended. One of the major applications of general equilibrium analysis was first developed by Harvard's Nobel laureate, Wassily Leontief.[2]

Input-output analysis is an empirical study of the interdependence among the various sectors in an economy. By interdependence we mean that the sectors depend on each other rather than being independent, because production in one sector utilizes inputs that other sectors produce. The manufacture of a bicycle requires inputs from such industries as fabricated metal, machinery, rubber products, chemical products, and the like. A change in the output of the bicycle industry therefore will require a change in the output of related industries. These changes may in turn require other changes in the outputs of still other industries.

Statisticians and economists have applied input-output analysis to a variety of problems. If one has a final output target, for example, input-output analysis can help determine the production of the various sectors of the economy required to obtain that final output. The analysis has also been used to predict what employment, demand, and investment in a region or a country will be in the future. Economists have used it extensively in planning economic development. Indeed, its uses have been many in the last 25 years.

Assumptions

In order to employ general equilibrium analysis, input-output analysis must make a number of

[1] Leon Walras, *Elements of Pure Economics,* trans. William Jaffe (Homewood, Ill.: Irwin, 1954). The original French version was published in 1874.

[2] Wassily Leontief, *The Structure of the American Economy* (New York: Oxford University Press, 1951).

The output from fabricated metal industries, such as steel, serves as the input to many other industries, such as the automobile, shipbuilding, and construction industries.

simplifying assumptions. The first assumption we use is that the quantities demanded by consumers are taken as given, or are determined outside of the system. In other words, we ignore for the moment the law of demand that smaller quantities will be demanded at higher prices and larger quantities will be demanded at lower prices. Thus, input-output analysis generally ignores price as a determinant of the quantity demanded.

The second assumption is that inputs are used in fixed proportions and that there are constant returns to scale. This assumption is crucial to Leontief's input-output system. From it we know that a given change in the output of a sector will require a proportionate change in all individual inputs used by that sector.

A simple input-output model. We consider a hypothetical economy composed of manufacturing, service, and agricultural sectors plus the household sector. The annual flow of input in billions of dollars among these sectors is presented in Exhibit 17–4.

The columns show which sector is a purchaser of output from other sectors and from itself. For example, if we read down the service column, we find that the service sector purchased $104.8 billion of output from its own sector, $500.9 billion from the manufacturing sector, $120 billion from the agricultural sector, and $307.9 billion from the household sector (capital and labor). Reading across the service sector row, we find that the sector produced $1,033.6 billion of total output. Note that the next-to-the-last column represents purchases by the household sector.

The rows show what each sector does as a supplier or producer. For example, the first row shows that the service industry provided $104.8 billion of output to itself, $478.7 billion of output to the manufacturing sector, $100.1 billion of output to agriculture, and $350 billion of output to the household sector.

The total sales column, which is the last one in Exhibit 17–4, gives us the sum of the purchases by the three intermediate sectors, as well as the purchases by the household sector. As can be seen in input-output analysis, all outputs are also inputs. The difference between total sales and total intermediate purchases represents each of the first three sectors' payments to households for their capital and labor services (or value added). For example, the difference between the service sector's total output of $1,033.6 billion and total intermediate purchases of $725.7 billion is $307.9 billion, which represents payments to the household sector for the use of their capital and labor in that industry. Similar calculations can be made for the other sectors.

Technical Coefficients

We now show Exhibit 17–5, which is a listing of the **technical coefficients** that are derived from

EXHIBIT 17–4
The Annual Flow of Inputs and Outputs (in Billions of Dollars per Year).

	SECTOR PURCHASING				
Sector Producing	*Service*	*Manufacturing*	*Agriculture*	*Household Sector*	*Total Sales*
Service	104.8	478.7	100.1	350	1,033.6
Manufacturing	500.9	704.8	310.7	400	1,916.4
Agriculture	120.0	190.3	94.1	200	604.4
Household sector	307.9	542.6	99.5	—	950.0
Total production	1,033.6	1,916.4	604.4	950	4,504.4

EXHIBIT 17–5
The Structural Matrix.

	SECTOR PURCHASING			
Sector Producing	*Service*	*Manufacturing*	*Agriculture*	*Household*
Service	.1014	.2498	.1656	.3684
Manufacturing	.4846	.3678	.5141	.4211
Agriculture	.1161	.0993	.1557	.2105
Household	.2979	.2831	.1646	
Total	1.0000	1.0000	1.0000	1.0000

the data in Exhibit 17–4. These are sometimes called production coefficients or input coefficients. In order to understand how we derive the coefficients in Exhibit 17–5, look at the services column in Exhibit 17–4. Total output for the service sector is $1,033.6 billion. To obtain the technical coefficients for the service sector, we divide each of the entries in the service column by the value of total gross output, or:

$$\frac{104.8}{1033.6} = .1014$$

$$\frac{500.9}{1033.6} = .4846$$

$$\frac{120.0}{1033.6} = .1161$$

$$\frac{307.9}{1033.6} = .2979$$

Each column entry in Exhibit 17–5 lends itself to an economic interpretation. The technical coefficients give us the fraction of a dollar's value of input used in producing a dollar's value of output from each sector. For example, in the service sector column, we can state that in order to produce a dollar's worth of service output, 10.14 cents of service inputs, 48.46 cents of manufacturing inputs, 11.61 cents of agricultural inputs, and 29.79 cents of capital and labor inputs must be used.

We can also see by viewing the structural matrix, Exhibit 17–5, which sectors are quantitatively "more important" in the production of any particular output. Furthermore, we can determine the total amount of output required from each sector to accommodate a particular final demand "requirement." (We have rounded off to the nearest 4 decimal places.)

Empirical Estimates of the Input-Output Structure

The U.S. Department of Commerce has available estimates of technical coefficients for the United States economy for the years 1947, 1958, and 1963. The November 1969 issue of the *Survey of Current Business* presents estimates for almost 370 separate industries. The interested student can look at pages 16–47 in that periodical for the results of the aggregated 1963 study in which the 370 separate categories have been reduced to 86. You can see by scanning those 30 pages that the task involved in constructing a large-scale input-output table is not a simple one.

Questions

1. If input-output analysis ignores price as a determining factor of the quantity demanded, under what circumstances would you have confidence in predictions based on the results of such analysis?
2. Look at Exhibit 17-5. For every dollar spent on producing a manufactured product, how much input (in cents) is spent on each of the four sectors shown?

Definition of Terms

Stable equilibrium An equilibrium situation in which a movement away from the equilibrium price or quantity will put into play forces that push price and/or quantity back toward the equilibrium level or rate.

Unstable equilibrium An equilibrium situation in which, if there is a movement away from equilibrium, there are forces that push price and/or quantity further away from equilibrium, or at least do not push them back toward the equilibrium level or rate.

Partial equilibrium analysis A way of analyzing a market in isolation without taking account of the interrelationships among markets.

General equilibrium analysis Economic analysis that takes account of the interrelationships among markets; to be contrasted with partial equilibrium analysis, which does not.

Input-output analysis The empirical study of the interdependence among the various sectors in the economy.

Technical coefficients Coefficients in input-output analysis that indicate the dollar value of inputs used in producing a dollar's value of output from a particular industry or sector. Also called production or input coefficients.

Chapter Summary

1. There are basically two types of equilibrium: stable and unstable.
2. A stable equilibrium is one in which any movement away from the equilibrium price or quantity will be met by forces pushing price or quantity back toward the equilibrium level. An unstable equilibrium will see price and quantity being pushed further and further away from equilibrium once there is a shock to the system.
3. If production today of a farm commodity such as corn depends on prices today, then the amount available for sales in the next period will be a function of this period's prices. If we plot the movement of prices and quantities in each period, we may come up with a "cobweb" diagram that gives a dynamic model of corn production, sales, and prices.
4. When we deal with partial equilibrium analysis, we assume that other things are held constant. In many situations, it is necessary to take account of other sectors. Then we enter the realm of general equilibrium analysis.
5. In even the most simplified general equilibrium model, the shift in the demand for one good will lead to a shift in the demand for another good, which will simultaneously lead to shifts in the demands for and eventually the supplies of inputs into the production of the goods.
6. A perfectly competitive system is one in which, for all commodities: (a) price equals the marginal cost, (b) marginal physical product of each factor of production per last dollar spent on that factor is equal to the marginal physical product of every other factor of production per last dollar spent on it, and (c) marginal utility per last dollar spent on each good is equal to the marginal utility per last dollar spent on every other good. Such a system is also one that is economically efficient.
7. We can use general equilibrium analysis to determine input-output tables for the economy or any sector within it.

Selected References

Barrett, Nancy Smith. *The Theory of Microeconomic Policy.* Lexington, Mass.: Heath, 1973.
Miernyk, William H. *The Elements of Input-Output Analysis.* New York: Random House, 1965.
Zeuthen, F. *Economic Theory and Method.* Cambridge, Mass.: Harvard University Press, 1955, chap. 11.

Answers to Preview and Study Questions

1. What are stable and unstable market equilibrium situations?

We have noted that when a market is in equilibrium, price is set at a level where the quantity supplied equals the quantity demanded (per unit of time) and that both sellers and buyers are realizing their intentions—hence, neither has an incentive to change behavior. The question at hand now is: What happens when *changes* in price occur, *given* these supply and demand curves? If price movements away from the equilibrium price set forces in motion which drive price back toward the equilibrium price, we refer to this as a stable equilibrium situation. If price movements away from the equilibrium price set forces in motion which drive price further away (in the same direction) from the equilibrium price, we refer to this as an unstable equilibrium situation. Viewed from another perspective, if price rises above equilibrium and a surplus occurs, a stable equilibrium exists; if a shortage exists, an unstable equilibrium exists. Similarly, if price falls below equilibrium and a shortage exists, equilibrium is stable; if a surplus exists, equilibrium is unstable.

2. Is an unstable market equilibrium situation likely?

No. For a stable equilibrium situation to exist demand must be downward sloping (relative price and quantity demanded are inversely related) and supply must be upward sloping (relative price and quantity supplied are directly related). It is difficult to imagine instances in which demand curves are not downward sloping, and equally unlikely that short-run supply schedules will not be upward sloping. Hence, equilibrium will almost always be stable.

3. What is dynamic equilibrium analysis?

Dynamic equilibrium analysis is a technique which explicitly takes time into account. Thus, a dynamic model is one in which economic activities are analyzed by relating them to preceding events or succeeding events. Thus dynamic models indicate that a person's consumption today might be related to his or her previous income (or consumption) levels, as well as expected future income levels. As noted in the text (the cobweb theorem), it is possible that farmers might plant a quantity of crops today based on today's prices, but this crop won't be offered for sale until a later period. Thus, the amount of a crop offered for sale at a later date depends on the production in the present, which itself could depend on present price.

4. What is the difference between partial and general equilibrium analysis?

Almost all of the analysis used in this text is partial equilibrium analysis, which focuses on a single market and views it in isolation from other markets. Aside from the one market in question, all other things are held constant. This analysis is useful when analyzing relatively small markets, which are not likely to affect other markets. On the other hand, general equilibrium analysis is broader in conception; it recognizes that some markets are so large or so interrelated with other markets that partial equilibrium analysis would result in misleading predictions. For instance, events which cause steel prices to rise will affect the automobile, construction, and metal industries, as well as factor markets. General equilibrium analysis, therefore, takes into account the interrelationships among prices and quantities (in both output and factor markets) of various goods and services. Of course, allowing *all* other things to vary is a complex, if not impossible task; thus, general equilibrium analysis is simply more inclusive than partial equilibrium analysis. Each method is useful and the selection of one or the other is a practical consideration.

5. Why is a perfectly competitive price system considered to be economically efficient?

Under a perfectly competitive price system all firms in all markets (factor or product) are price takers, and all prices in all markets are allowed to equate quantity supplied with quantity demanded. Such a market system is said to be efficient in (a) production, (b) consumption, and (c) resource allocation. If all producers are maximizing and all face the same factor prices, each firm will hire inputs up until the marginal product per dollar's worth of each is equated (MPP of labor ÷ wage rate = MPP of capital ÷ rental price of capital, and so on). This results if each factor is paid its VMP, and it assures that each quantity of output is produced using the least-cost combination of inputs. Secondly, if each consumer maximizes his or her total utility and faces the same set of prices, for each consumer the marginal utility per dollar's worth of each good consumed is equated (MU of good A ÷ price of good *A* = MU of good *B* ÷ price of good B, and so on). This assures that no consumer can be made better off unless another is made worse off. Finally, since price equals marginal cost for all goods, at the margin consumers will be giving up (in other goods and services foregone) just what they receive in extra benefits. This assures that just enough resources will be allocated to the production of each good or service and consumer sovereignty will exist. It should be noted that the perfect competition price system is not without its detractors. Some feel that consumer sovereignty is not "good"; all agree that such a price system may not lead to the socially optimal distribution of income. Moreover, as we shall see in the next part, sometimes even a perfectly competitive market system leads to a misallocation of resources.

Problems

(Answers at the back of the book)

1. The graph below indicates a theoretical supply and demand situation for some commodity.

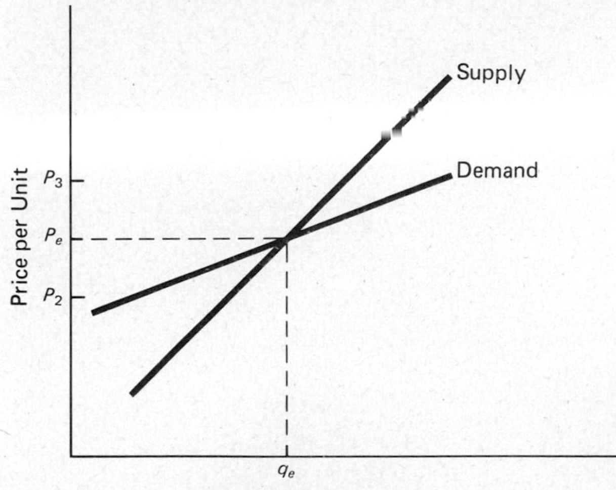

a. Which price is the equilibrium price?
b. What condition exists at P_3?
c. What condition exists at P_2?
d. Is this a stable or an unstable equilibrium situation? Why?

2. Write "partial equilibrium analysis" and "general equilibrium analysis" on the top line of a piece of paper and list each of the following events under the model where it could be better understood.

a. Wage rates rise in the automobile industry.
b. A tariff is placed on steel imports.
c. Consumers increase their demand for chewing gum.
d. The demand for hula-hoops falls.
e. Legal minimum wage rates are increased.
f. U.S. consumers change tastes in favor of smaller autos.

PART

IV

ECOLOGY, POPULATION, AND FOOD

18

Social Costs, Ecology, and Externalities

TOPICS FOR REVIEW

The topics listed below, which we have already analyzed, are applied in this chapter. You may find it worthwhile to review them. For your convenience each topic is followed by the number identifying the specific "Concepts in Brief."

a. Opportunity costs, trade-off (1–2)

b. Normative versus positive economics (1–5)

FOR PREVIEW AND STUDY

1. What is a negative externality?
2. How can indefinite property rights create negative externalities?
3. If property rights are indefinite, *must* negative externalities arise?
4. What is the optimal quantity of pollution?
5. What is a positive externality?

Today there seems to be an annoying amount of air, water, noise, olfactory (smell), and visual pollution. At first glance, it seems that the market solution to the problem of allocating scarce resources has gone awry. In fact, as pollution increases, so too do people's fears that the free working of supply and demand will bring about the ultimate destruction of the world as we know it. Perhaps there is a way we can alter some of the existing signals in our market economy so as to bring about a more socially acceptable use of resources and a less-polluted environment. We will see in this chapter that some fairly straightforward changes, which might bring about the desired reduction in pollution, could be made in the institutional setup in our economy. In the Issues and Applications section, we will look at a classic problem in social costs related to the production of honey and fruit. Finally, we will look at the question of marketing the right to pollute.

We begin our study of the ecology by establishing why some individuals and business firms have been permitted to harm our environment without paying for the consequences.

Private Versus Social Costs

For the most part, we've been dealing with situations where the costs of an individual's actions are borne directly by the individual. When a business firm has to pay wages to workers, it knows exactly what its labor costs are. When it has to buy materials or build a plant, it knows quite well what these will cost. When an individual has to pay for car repairs, or shoe repairs, or for a theater ticket, he or she knows exactly what the cost will be. These costs are what we term **private costs.** Private costs are those borne solely by the individuals who incur them. They are *internal* in the sense that the firm or household must explicitly take account of them.

SOCIAL COSTS

What about a situation where a business firm dumps the waste products from its production process into a nearby river? Or where an individual litters a public park or beach? Obviously, a cost is involved in these actions. When the business firm pollutes the water, people downstream suffer the consequences. They may not want to drink the polluted water or swim and bathe in it. They may also be unable to catch as many fish as before because of the pollution. In the case of littering, the people who come along after our litterer has cluttered the park or the beach are the ones who bear the costs. The scenery certainly will be less attractive. The cost of these actions is borne by people other than those who commit the actions. That is, the creator of the cost is not the sole bearer. The costs are not internalized by the individual or firm; they are external. When we add *external* costs to *internal,* or private, costs, we get **social costs.** Pollution problems and, indeed, all problems pertaining to the environment may be viewed as situations where social costs are greater than private costs. Since some economic agents don't pay the full social costs of their actions, but rather only the smaller private costs, their actions are socially "unacceptable." In such situations where there is a divergence between social and private costs, we therefore see "too much" steel production, automobile driving, and beach littering, to pick only a few of the many examples that exist.

POLLUTED AIR

Why is the air in cities so polluted from automobile exhaust fumes? When automobile drivers step into their cars, they bear only the private costs of driving. That is, they must pay for the gas, maintenance, depreciation, and insurance on their automobiles. However, they cause an additional cost—that of air pollution—which they are not forced to take account of when they make the decision to drive. The air pollution created by automobile exhaust is a cost that, as yet, individual operators of automobiles do not bear *directly.* The social cost of driving includes all the private costs plus the cost of air pollution, which society bears. Decisions made only on the basis of private costs lead to too much automobile driving or, alternatively, to too little money spent on the reduction of automobile pollution for a given amount of driving.

Consider the example of lights in hotel rooms. Paying guests know that they will not pay any more on any single occasion if they leave their lights on in the hotel room. Of course, the more frequently the guests leave their lights on, the higher will be the cost of running the hotel and the higher will be the average room charge. But for the individual guest at any one point in time, there is no direct cost to being "wasteful" with energy used for lights. We predict, therefore, that people will leave lights on more often in hotel rooms than they will in their own houses and apartments. We can look at another example and consider clean air as the scarce resource offered to automobile drivers free of charge. The same analysis will hold—they will use more of it than they would if they had to pay the full social costs.

Externalities

When private costs differ from social costs, we usually term the situation a problem of **externalities,** because individual decision makers are not internalizing *all* the costs. Rather, some of these costs are remaining external to the decision-making process. Remember that the full cost of using a scarce resource is borne one way or another by others who live in the society. That is, society must pay the full opportunity cost of any activity that uses scarce resources. The individual decision maker is the firm or the customer, and external costs and benefits will *not* enter into that individual's or firm's decision-making processes.

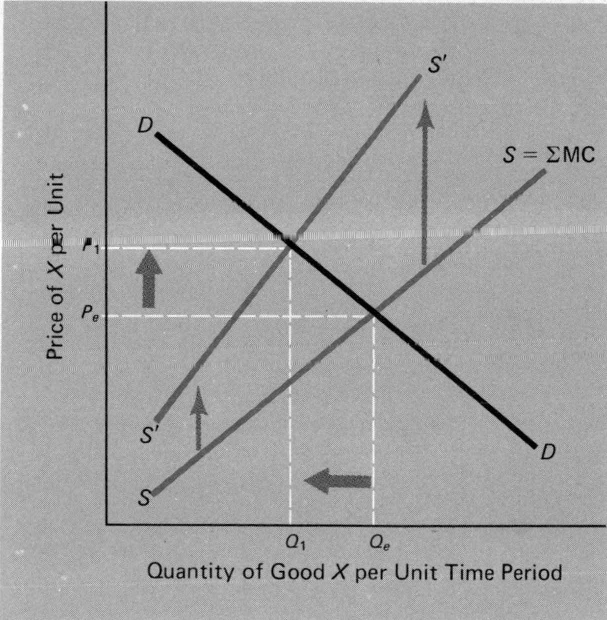

EXHIBIT 18–1

Reckoning with Full Social Costs. Here we show the demand for good X as DD. The supply curve, SS, is equal to the horizontal summation of the individual marginal cost curves above the respective minimum average variable costs of all the firms producing that good. These individual marginal cost curves include only internal, or private, costs; they do not include any external costs such as pollution of the air or water. If the external costs were included and added to the private costs then we would have social costs. The supply curve would shift left to $S'S'$. In the uncorrected situation, the equilibrium price would be P_e and the equilibrium quantity would be Q_e. In the corrected situation, the equilibrium price would rise to P_1 and the equilibrium quantity would fall to Q_1.

We might want to view the problem as it is presented in Exhibit 18–1. Here we have the market demand curve, DD, for product X and the supply curve, SS, for product X. The supply curve includes only internal, or private, costs. The intersection of the demand and supply curves as drawn will be at price P_e and quantity Q_e. However, we will assume that the production of good X involves externalities that the private business firms did not take into account. Those externalities could be air pollution or water pollution or scenery destruction or anything of that nature.

We know that the social costs of producing X exceed the private costs. We show this by drawing the supply curve $S'S'$. It is left of the original supply curve SS because it includes the externalities, or the full social costs of producing the product. Now the "correct" market equilibrium price is P_1, and the equilibrium quantity is Q_1. The inclusion of external costs in the decision-making process leads to a higher-priced product and a decline in quantity produced. We can say, therefore, that in an unrestricted situation where social costs are not being fully borne by the creators of those costs, the quantity produced is "excessive."

Correcting the Signals (In Theory, at Least)

We can see here an "easy" method of reducing the amount of pollution and environmental degradation that exists. Somehow the signals in the economy must be changed so that decision makers will take into account *all* the costs of their actions. In the case of automobile pollution, we might want to devise some method whereby motorists are taxed according to the amount of pollution they cause. In the case of a firm, we might want to devise a system whereby businesses are taxed according to the amount of pollution for which they are responsible. In this manner, they would have an incentive to install pollution-abatement equipment.

We see, then, that there are two choices open to the polluter who is faced with a higher price for pollution: (1) there can be a change in the production method, thereby reducing pollution, or (2) there can be a reduction in the amount of activity that causes the pollution. In most cases, both techniques for reducing pollution will be used. The relative costs and benefits of each will determine for each polluter which will be undertaken and in what quantities.

However, it may not be appropriate to levy a *uniform* tax according to physical quantities of pollution. After all, we're talking about social costs. Such costs are not necessarily the same everywhere in the United States for the same action. If you drive your smelly, belching car in the middle of the Mojave Desert, you will inflict little damage on anyone else. No one will be there to complain; the natural cleansing action of the large body of air around you will eliminate the pollution you generate to such an extent that it creates little or no economic or environmental harm. If a business firm pollutes the water in a lake that is used by no other parties and the lake is, in fact, inaccessible to everyone else, the external economic damages created by this pollution may be negligible.

Essentially, we must establish the size of the *economic damages* rather than the size of the physical amount of pollution. A polluting electric plant in New York City will cause much more damage than the same plant in, say, Nowhere, Montana. This is because the concentration of people in New York City is much higher than in Nowhere. There are already innumerable demands on the air in New York City, so that the pollution from smokestacks will not naturally be cleansed away. There are millions of people who will breathe that smelly air and thereby incur the costs of sore throats, sickness, emphysema, and even early death. There are many, many buildings that will become dirtier faster because of the pollution, and many cars and clothes that will also become dirtier faster. The list goes on and on, but it should be obvious that a given quantity of pollution will cause more harm in concentrated urban environments than it will in less-dense rural environments. If we were to establish some form of taxation to align private costs with social costs and to force people to internalize externalities, we would have to somehow come up with a measure of *economic* costs instead of *physical* quantities. But the tax, in any event, would fall on the private sector and modify private-sector economic agents' behavior.[1]

[1] Therefore, since the economic cost for the same physical quantity of pollution would be different in different locations according to population density, to the natural formation of mountains and rivers, and so forth, so-called optimal taxes of pollution would vary from location to location. Nonetheless, a uniform tax might make sense where administrative costs, particularly the cost of ascertaining the actual economic costs, are relatively high.

Concepts in Brief 18-1

- Private costs are those explicit costs that are borne directly by consumers and producers when they engage in any resource-using activity.
- Social costs include private costs plus any other costs that are external to the decision maker. For example, the social cost of driving includes all the private costs plus any pollution and congestion caused.
- When private costs differ from social costs, the situation is one of externalities, because individual decision makers are not internalizing all the costs that society is bearing.
- When social costs exceed private costs, environmental problems may ensue, such as excessive pollution of air and water. These are problems of externalities.
- One way to make private costs equal social costs is to impose taxes on pollution-causing activities.
- The taxes imposed would be set equal to the economic damages, or externalities, caused by the pollution-creating activity.

The Optimal Amount of Pollution

When asked how much pollution there should be in the economy, many will respond, "none." Is that a correct answer? In effect, there is no correct—positive economic—answer because when we ask how much pollution there *should* be, we are entering the realm of normative economics. We are asking people to express their values. There is no way to scientifically disprove somebody's value system. One way we can approach a discussion of the "correct" amount of pollution that can be allowed is to consider a basic fact—pollution is intimately tied up with the concept of scarcity.

POLLUTION IS A SCARCITY PROBLEM

What is at issue here? Is it that there is too little pollution to go around? Certainly not. The scarce resource is the environment's capacity to absorb or disperse pollution so that the pollution will have no economic effect—that is, the environment's capacity to cleanse itself of pollution is the resource of which we do not have "enough." Otherwise stated, the waste-disposing capacity of our ecosystem is a scarce resource. That capacity has specific limits. After the natural limits are reached, we have in-

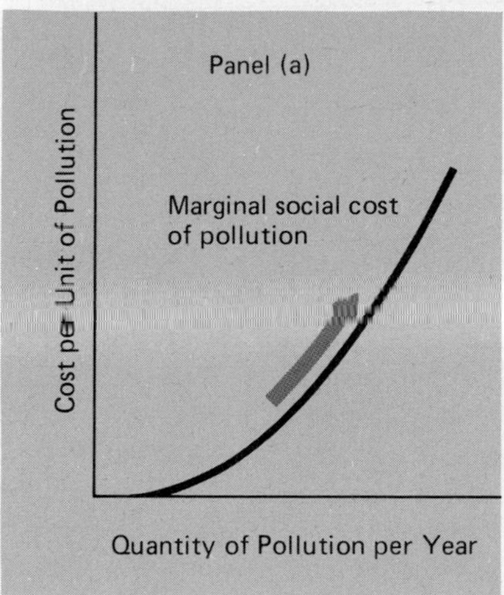

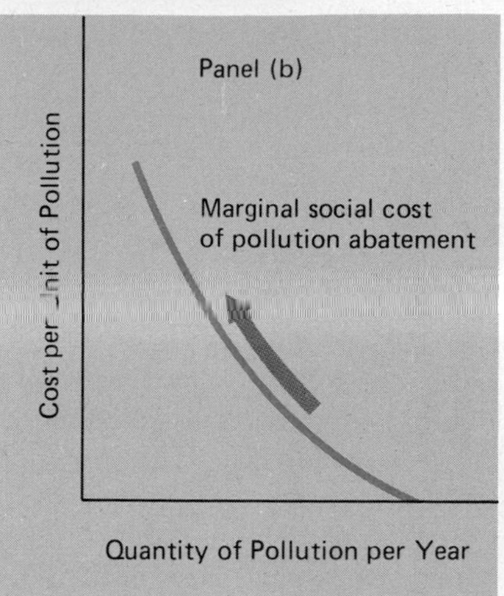

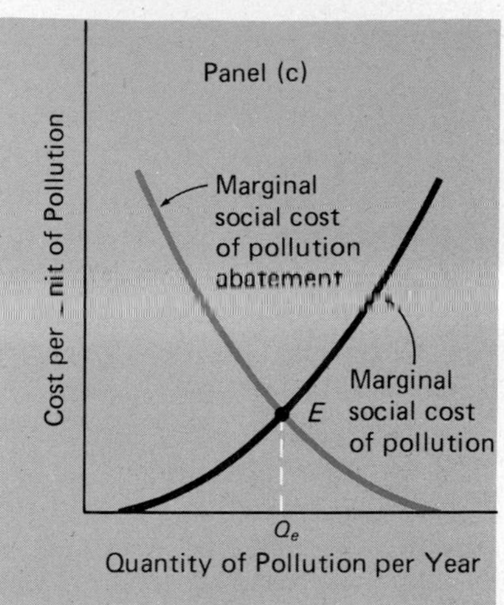

EXHIBIT 18–2

Finding the Optimal Level of Pollution. In panel (a) we show the marginal social cost of pollution. That cost is relatively small or nonexistent when there is only a small quantity of pollution admitted into the environment. This is because of the natural cleansing activities in our environment. As the quantity of pollution increases, however, the marginal social cost increases also, and at an increasing rate. Thus, we see that the marginal social cost of pollution curve is upward sloping. In panel (b) we show the marginal social cost of pollution abatement. If we are willing to accept a large amount of pollution and we want to reduce only a few units, the marginal social cost of that pollution abatement is very small. As we attempt to get a cleaner and cleaner environment, however, the marginal social cost of pollution abatement becomes greater. Thus, we find a negative relationship between the quantity of pollution allowed in the economy and the cost of reducing a few more units. Finally, in panel (c), we put together the marginal social cost of pollution abatement curve and the marginal social cost of pollution curve. Their intersection gives the optimal quantity of pollution, which is labeled Q_e. At that quantity, the marginal social cost of pollution abatement just equals the marginal social cost of pollution.

creasing amounts of pollution as we produce and consume more. Since pollution abatement requires the use of scarce resources, to answer the question "What is the optimal level of pollution that can be allowed?" requires us to compare the cost of eliminating pollution with the benefits of doing so. What we must do now is look at the social cost of pollution and the social cost of getting rid of pollution.

THE SOCIAL COST OF POLLUTION

When sulphur oxides are spewed out into the atmosphere, individuals may suffer more respiratory diseases, feel worse, work less efficiently, and so on. People incur a cost from that pollution. When chemicals are dumped into waterways, the fish population may suffer and swimmers may have to avoid the water, which may be unfit to drink. Let us think in terms of the marginal social cost of pollution, which we define as the cost that all members of society will bear when there is one more unit of pollution. If you lived in a society with 100 members, and if each of you would suffer damages equivalent to 1¢ more per year if one more unit of pollution occurred, then the marginal social cost of pollution in your small economy would be 1¢ per year × 100 = $1 per year.

We hypothesize that for a given locale, the marginal social cost of pollution rises as the quantity of pollution increases. In this sense, the marginal social cost of pollution is quite similar to the marginal cost curves that we have used throughout this book.

Previously we stated that we were interested in a measure of economic cost as opposed to physical quantities of pollution. For simplicity, we are assuming that the economic cost—marginal social cost—of pollution is somehow positively related to the quantity of pollution, but certainly not identical with the quantity of pollution.

In panel (a) of Exhibit 18–2, we show an upward-sloping marginal social cost of pollution curve. Notice that the curve starts from the horizontal axis at a quantity of pollution per year greater than zero. This means that there is some natural capacity of the environment to absorb pollution—the environment can handle certain quantities of pollution without there being any marginal social costs imposed on the economy's members.

Now let us turn to pollution abatement.

THE SOCIAL COST OF POLLUTION ABATEMENT

In order to reduce the effects of pollution, we must use scarce resources. If we reduce air pollution emissions from smokestacks, we might have to use "air-scrubbing" systems. These are costly. If we wish to reduce thermal pollution around nuclear power plants, resources must be used for cooling towers. And last, but not least, as an example, reducing pollution from internal combustion engines has added significantly to the cost of new cars. Also, curbing one type of pollution may bring about other unintended forms of pollution.

Now we can talk about the marginal social cost of pollution abatement. It is clearly cheapest to reduce the most easily abatable types of pollution. That is to say, when we first start to eliminate pollution from our environment, it is relatively inexpensive to remove the first few units of pollution. As we attempt to reduce more and more units of pollution, we will have to incur higher and higher marginal costs. It follows that the less pollution we are willing to endure, the higher the cost of eliminating the additional units. Thus, we expect an *inverse* relationship between the quantity of pollution in the environment and the marginal cost of pollution abatement. The less pollution we are willing to accept, the higher the marginal cost of getting rid of a little bit more. In Exhibit 18–2(b), we see this inverse relationship between the cost per unit of pollution abatement and the quantity of pollution per year. The marginal social cost curve of pollution abatement slopes upward as we move from a lot of pollution to very little.

Consider an example. The cost of eliminating, say, 20 percent of the pollutants emitted by internal combustion engines may be relatively small per unit of pollution removal. The cost of eliminating the next 20 percent will certainly rise. Finally, as we get to the upper limits of pollution removal of the emissions from internal combustion engines, we find that the elimination of one more percent of the amount of pollutants becomes astronomically expensive. In other words, to go from a 20 percent clean-up rate to a 21 percent clean-up rate might cost very little for the marginal unit, but to go from a 97 percent clean-up rate to a 98 percent clean-up rate could involve a marginal cost that is 100 times greater than going from a 20 to 21 percent clean-up. The same empirical, real-world results occur when dirty rivers and lakes are cleaned up.

Now we are in a position to ascertain analytically the optimal quantity of pollution we "should" allow.

THE OPTIMAL QUANTITY OF POLLUTION

If we combine panels (a) and (b) of Exhibit 18–2 into one diagram shown in panel (c), we can derive the optimal quantity of pollution, which is defined as that level of pollution where the marginal social cost of pollution abatement is just equal to the marginal social cost of pollution. This occurs where the two curves intersect in panel (c) at point E. The optimal quantity of pollution is given as Q_e. Why is it optimal? Because if we reduce pollution by one more unit (to the *left* of Q_e), the marginal social cost of pollution abatement will exceed the marginal social cost of pollution. In other words, we will be paying more than it is worth to reduce pollution by one more unit.

At Q_e the benefit of reducing one more unit of pollution is equal to the marginal social cost of one unit of pollution, for that is what society will suffer if that one unit is allowed to exist. Essentially, then, we are eliminating pollution only up to the point where the marginal cost equals the marginal benefit, where here the marginal cost is called the marginal social cost of pollution abatement and the marginal benefit is the mirror image of the marginal social cost of pollution. (Of course, in a world where pollution abatement was costless, the optimal amount of pollution *would* be zero.)

SHOULD THE OPTIMAL QUANTITY OF POLLUTION BE ZERO?

Now, what can be said about the statement that the level of pollution should be zero? Looking at Exhibit 18–2(c), we find that at a zero quantity of pollution, the marginal social cost of pollution abatement greatly exceeds the marginal social cost of pollution. In other words, if we have too much pollution abatement, we are wasting resources. The benefits of reducing the effects of the last unit of pollution are far exceeded by the social marginal costs of pollution abatement. In other words, resources are being used in pollution abatement that would have a higher value elsewhere in society.

Remember, we live in a world of scarce resources. If the value we receive from spending one more dollar on cleaning up the environment is less than the value we *would* receive by spending that dollar on something else—say, cancer research—then we are not efficiently allocating our resources if we still choose to spend that dollar on pollution abatement.

In a sense, then, the trade-off is between pollution abatement and alternative uses of resources. As we use resources to reduce the quantity of pollution, we reduce the quantity of resources available to produce other goods and services in society.

Pollution of the air, water, and environment is not the only "ill" that we endure. We also endure automobile accidents and diseases. Both of these "ills" could be reduced if we wished to spend more of our scarce resources on preventing accidents and sickness. Moreover, different individuals attach different costs to the same type and level of pollution. In other words, when we talk of the marginal cost of pollution, we are really allowing value judgments to be embedded into our analysis. An extreme antipollution individual could indicate that any pollution at all would have an almost infinite "cost" to him or her. Clearly, in a world of scarce resources, we must balance the subjective valuations that individuals place on enduring a given level of pollution against the actual resource cost of reducing that level of pollution.

Concepts in Brief 18-2

- In order to find the optimal level of pollution, we must compare the costs of pollution abatement with the benefits.
- The marginal social cost of pollution abatement increases as we attempt to rid our environment of more and more pollution.
- The marginal social cost of pollution is at first very small because only a few people are affected, or many people are affected in insignificant ways. Then, the marginal cost of pollution to society starts increasing.
- In order to find the optimal level of pollution that we "should" allow, we go to the point where the marginal social cost of pollution abatement just equals the marginal social cost of pollution. Otherwise stated, we go to the point where the marginal benefit of reducing the effects of one more unit of pollution just equals the marginal cost of doing so.
- Pollution abatement is a trade-off. We trade off less of other goods and services for cleaner air and water.

Property Rights

Now let's find out why there will be a divergence between social costs and private costs. Why do certain situations create externalities while others do not? For an example, consider some of the things you own. Suppose you own a bicycle. If someone comes along and alters it unfavorably by slashing the tires or bending the spokes, you can, in principle, press civil charges and recover damages. The damages you might recover would at least be equal to the reduction in the market value of your bike.[2] The same goes for your car or any other property you own. Anyone damaging your property is liable for those damages. The courts will uphold your right to compensation.

We have just discussed, therefore, situations in which externalities do not exist—that is, in which private costs are equal to social costs. In other words, an externality will not typically occur in a situation in which a person's rights to the use of resources are well defined and upheld by our legal system. In contrast, we would expect situations in which individuals' rights to specific resources are not well defined, or are costly to enforce, to create externalities and, indeed, that is what often happens.

Common Property

Suppose you live next to a smelly steel factory. The air around you—which is something that you have to use—is damaged. You, in turn, are damaged by breathing it. However, you do not necessarily have grounds for stopping the air pollution or for obtaining compensation for the destruction of the air around you. In most cases, you do not have *private property rights* in the air surrounding you, nor does anyone else. Air is a **common property** resource. Herein lies the crux of the problem: Whenever private property rights are indefinite or nonexistent, social costs may be different from private costs, particularly in the situations we will outline below. This is as you would expect. When no one owns a particular resource, people do not have any incentive (conscience aside) to consider their particular despoliation of that resource. If one person decides not to pollute the air, there will be no significant effect on the total level of pollution. If one person decides not to pollute the ocean, there will still be approximately the same amount of ocean pollution—provided, of course, that the individual is responsible for only a small part of the total amount of ocean pollution.

[2] A judge might also award "punitive" damages over and above the reduction in the value of your bicycle.

Basically, then, we have pollution only where we have no well-defined private property rights, such as in air and common bodies of water. We do not, for example, have a pollution problem in people's backyards that no one else can see into. That is their own property, which they choose to keep as clean as they want—given their preferences for cleanliness weighed against the costs of keeping the backyard looking nice.

When private property rights are in existence, individuals have legal recourse to any damages sustained through the misuse of their property. When private property rights are well defined, the use of property—that is, the use of resources—will generally involve contracting between the owners of those resources. If you own any land, you might contract with another person who wants to use your land for raising cows. The contract would most likely be written in the form of a lease agreement.

THE RELATION BETWEEN PRIVATE COSTS AND SOCIAL COSTS

Surprisingly enough, even when private property rights do not exist, it is sometimes possible for private costs to equal social costs. In such situations, there is no misallocation of resources. Let's take a simple example. Suppose you live in a house with a nice view of a lake. The people living below you plant a tree. Over the years the tree grows larger and larger, and eventually it cuts off your view. In most cities, nobody has property rights to views, and therefore you usually cannot go to the courts for relief. You cannot file suit against your downhill neighbors for obstructing your view. Nor can you go to the courts to force your downhill neighbors to take account of the social costs of their actions. They are taking account only of the private costs, which involve any expenses for watering, fertilizing, and maintaining the tree. Clearly, though, you are suffering economic damages when the tree grows to a height that obstructs your view. Thus, the social cost of your downhill neighbors' tree-planting action equals the private cost—water, fertilizer, and care—plus the cost *you* incur because of an obstructed view.

Contracting

You do have an alternative, however. You can, as it were, bribe your neighbors (contract with them) to top their tree (make it shorter). What kind of bribe would you offer them? You could start with a small money figure and keep going up until either they agree or you reach your limit. Your limit will be equal to the value you place on having an unobstructed view of the lake. The neighbors will be willing to top their tree if the payment is at least equal to the reduction in their (implicit) property value due to a stunted tree. In this manner, you make them aware of the social cost of their action. The social cost of their action, we can repeat here, is equal to the private cost—the care of the trees—plus the cost suffered by you from an impeded view of the lake. You inform your neighbors of the social cost of their growing a large tree that blocks your view and thereby lowers the value of your property. But you do this in a rather odd way—essentially, you bribe them. Nonetheless, they are still informed of the true cost of their actions. Alternatively, your neighbors could come to you and ask you how much you would be willing to pay to have them top their tree.

Now suppose property rights were actually vested in views. If the property right to your view were vested in you, anybody destroying your view would have to pay the consequences. In this particular case, the downhill landowner would have to pay you to be able to let the tree grow higher than you would want. The payment to you would have to be at least equal to the reduction in the value of your property because of an obstructed view. (This will, of course, be a measure of the value of the view itself.) If the downhill landowner doesn't offer a high enough payment, he or she will have to top the tree because you will not go for the deal. Again, social costs will have to be taken into account in the downhill landowner's decision-making process. At a minimum, the social cost will be equal to the private costs of taking care of the tree plus the reduction in your property value because of an obstructed view. Since the downhill landowner must contract with you, there will be no divergence between private and social costs.[3]

Opportunity Costs

Now let's change the situation. Assume that the downhill landowners have the property right in your view—a strange situation indeed, but actually equivalent to the example where *no one* had the property right. If your neighbors have the property right in your view, will the assets called "view" and "tree" be used differently from when *you* had the property right? If you think so, you're wrong. Just

[3]This is a modified formulation of what has been called the Coase theorem, named after Ronald Coase who wrote the seminal article in this field, entitled "The Problem of Social Costs," *Journal of Law and Economics,* October 1960, pp. 1–44.

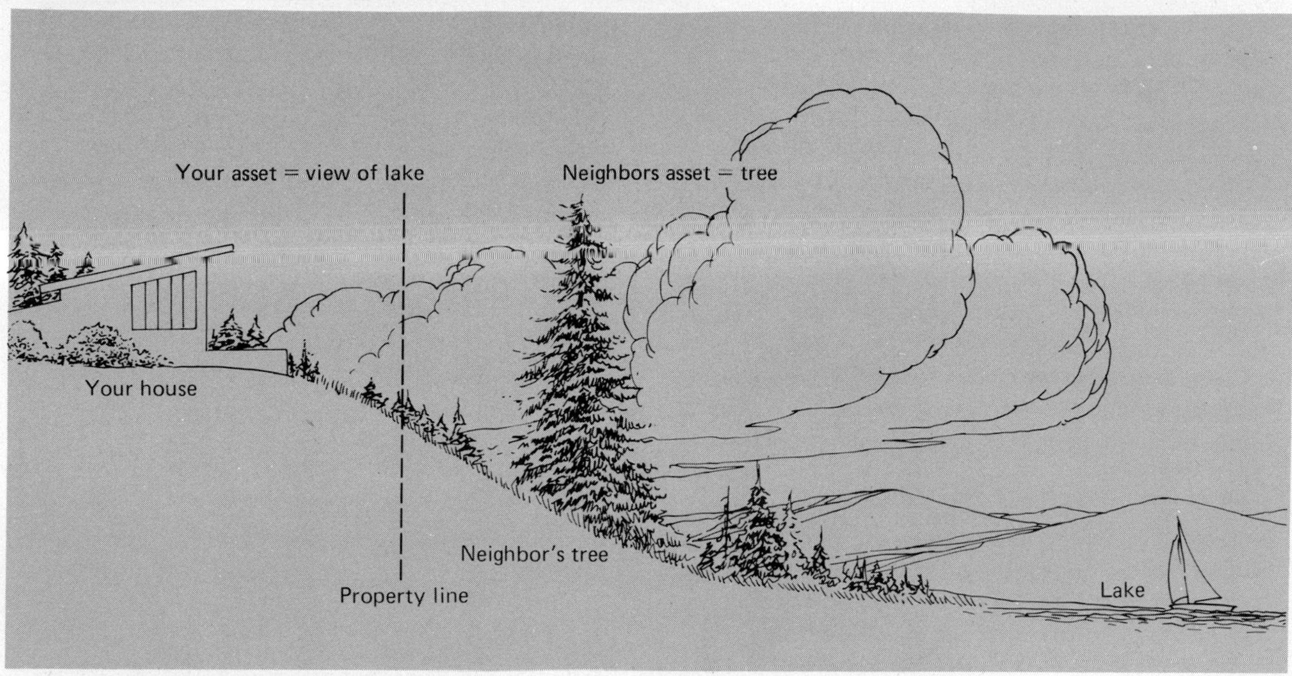

EXHIBIT 18–3
Effect of Changing Property Rights.

	Nobody Has Property Rights to Views	*You Have Property Rights to View of Lake*	*Neighbor Has Property Right to Your View*
Your Situation	You can suffer a reduction in your property value due to the tree blocking your view, or you can pay your neighbor to top the tree.	You can always require that your downhill neighbor top his or her tree. However, you can accept a payment from your downhill neighbor in exchange for allowing the tree to grow, thereby blocking your view. The payment from your neighbor must exceed the reduction in your land value because of the blocked view.	If you wish to have the tree topped, you must offer a payment to the downhill neighbor. Your payment will never exceed the value that you place on having a view of the lake.
Your Neighbor's Situation	Your neighbor's property value will increase as the tree gets larger. The neighbor can, however, accept a payment from you in exchange for topping the tree so that you have a better view of the lake.	The tree must be topped unless your neighbor offers a payment to you that is at least sufficient to compensate you for a reduction in your property value.	The tree may grow as tall as possible. However, a payment from you may be sufficient to justify topping the tree. As long as the payment exceeds your neighbor's satisfaction from the higher tree, the tree will be topped.

because your neighbors now own the view does not mean they will ignore the cost they are imposing on you. After all, your neighbors would be giving up the opportunity of perhaps making some money in a deal with you. Your neighbors could gingerly walk to your house and ask you how much you would be willing to pay to have the tree topped. If you were willing to pay enough, they would do so. If not, they would leave it as is.

In other words, your neighbors would take account of the *opportunity cost* of the tall tree. This is the key to understanding why private costs equal social costs in all three of the above situations—in the first instance where there were no property rights, in the second case where property rights were given to the uphill landowner, and in the third case where property rights were given to the downhill landowner. In each situation, opportunity costs exist and will be taken into account. The contracting involved is relatively simple: Only two parties are concerned and agreements can be made relatively easily. We summarize what happens in Exhibit 18–3. These particular examples lead us to a strange but nonetheless correct conclusion: When transactions costs are minimal, the allocation of resources does not depend on who has the property rights in the resources in question. They will be used in exactly the same way no matter who owns them. Whenever contracting becomes exceedingly expensive or difficult, social and private costs will tend to diverge. Whenever contracting is relatively costless, social costs and private costs will end up being one and the same thing, as we will see. In fact, this is why externalities are only problems in certain areas of activity in our society. We don't worry about social and private costs with the majority of activities that occur in our economy, because almost all of what occurs involves contracting among individuals and the transference (whether temporary or permanent) of property rights.

Wealth Distribution

Note also in this example that the distribution of wealth differs, depending on the assignment of private property rights. *The person who gets the property rights to some resource that was formerly common property will obviously be better off because that person's wealth will now be greater.* If a large untopped tree is more valuable than the view of the uphill landowner, the tree will not be topped. Think about this. In the case where the uphill landowner has the property right in the view, the uphill landowner will accept a bribe that is at least equal to the reduction in the property value due to the large tree. The downhill landowners will offer a sum that does not exceed the increase in their property value due to an untouched tree. If the view is more valuable than the untouched tree, they will not be able to bribe the uphill landowner; they will have to top the tree.

On the other hand, if the downhill landowners have the property rights in the view, they will have to be bribed to top the tree. If the increased value of the unobstructed view leads the uphill landowner to offer a sum that is greater than the value of the untouched tree to the downhill landowners, the downhill landowners will accept the bribe and top the tree. In either case, the two resources—the view and the tree—will be used such that they generate the highest economic value.

When Transactions Costs Are High

Our example so far is pretty simple. It involves only two parties, the contracting or transactions costs are small, and we have ignored changes in wealth distribution. What about a case where the transactions costs aren't as small? Take the example of a factory polluting a city of several million people. It would be difficult for the several million people to get together to somehow bribe the factory into reducing its pollution. The transactions costs here would be extremely high. Therefore, we cannot predict that private costs will equal social costs for the factory. This is probably true with many environmental problems.

There are indefinite property rights that in and of themselves are not always a problem if contracting can be done easily. However, when multiple parties are involved, contracting is difficult, and in many instances, the creators of those costs are difficult to identify. If ships are spilling excess oil into the ocean, how do we police them to find out which ones are doing it? The costs of such policing may be high. This discussion of property rights leads us to another possible solution to our environmental problems.

Pinpointing Property Rights

Instead of attempting to tax polluters in proportion to the economic damages caused by their pollution, we could define property rights more precisely so that contracting would have to take place. In the example of the view of the lake, it did not really matter who had property rights in the view. In fact, indefinite property rights were inconsequential to the outcome of the situation except, of course, with reference to the wealth positions of the individuals. This is not the case with other environmental problems. For example, we might want to make factories liable for the pollution that they create. When we do that, we are implicitly vesting surrounding landowners and passersby with property rights to the common property resources of water and air surrounding the factories. The individuals living nearby will implicitly be the owners of that air and water. The factory will therefore be liable for its use of water and air if its use imposes costs on others.

In a sense, this is not really "fair." After all, a common property resource is, by definition, owned by everyone. We would be arbitrary in assigning property rights in a common property resource to the homeowners, just as we would be arbitrary in assigning the property rights to the factory. But because it is "easier" to make the individual factory owner pay, we still might want to go ahead with this arbitrary assignment of property rights to the adjacent homeowners.

Another way of viewing the pollution problem is to argue that property rights are "sacred" and that there are property rights in every resource that exists. We can then say that each individual does not have the right to act on anything that is not his or her property. Hence, no individual has the right to pollute, because that is using property that the individual does not specifically own.

We can view all of the above discussion as ways to fill the gap between private costs and true social costs in situations where we have to make up somehow for the fact that property rights are not well defined and/or assigned. The three ways to fill the private/social costs gap are (1) taxation, (2) subsidization, and (3) regulation. Government is involved in all three. Unfortunately, government does not have perfect information and may not pick the appropriate tax, subsidy, or type of regulation. We also have to consider cases where taxes are hard to enforce or subsidies are difficult to give out to the "worthy" recipients. In such cases, outright prohibition of the polluting activity may be the "best" solution to a particular pollution problem. For example, if it is difficult to monitor the level of a particular type of pollution that even in small quantities can cause certain environmental damages, then outright prohibition of such pollution may be the only alternative.

> ***Concepts in Brief 18-3***
>
> ■ A common property resource is one that no one owns—or otherwise stated, that everyone owns.
>
> ■ Common property exists when property rights are indefinite or nonexistent.
>
> ■ When no property rights exist, pollution occurs because no one individual or firm has a sufficient economic incentive to care for the common property in question, be it air, water, or scenery.
>
> ■ Private costs will not equal social costs when common property is at issue, unless only a few individuals are involved and they are able to contract among themselves.
>
> ■ When transactions costs are minimal, the allocation of resources does not depend on who has the property rights of the resource under study.
>
> ■ Those who obtain the property rights to formerly common property will be wealthier.
>
> ■ The assignment of property rights, particularly for common property resources such as air, water, and scenery, involves legal and moral issues.

What About External Benefits?

So far, we've discussed external costs that were not internalized by individual decision makers. We should note that there are also situations with **external benefits.** Examples of external benefits include the pleasure passersby receive from looking at well manicured lawns, the freedom from disease that individuals in the community receive from mass inoculation programs (even if some do not participate), and the satisfaction that a neighbor might receive from listening to someone else's high-quality stereo system played very loudly. In cases where the social benefits of an action exceed the private benefits, we would expect that individual decision makers would do too little of such an action from society's point of view. In fact, it is often argued that many endeavors involve large social benefits that are not internalized. It is further argued that government subsidization or provision of such activity is in order. This is often the argument used to justify public education. An educated citizenry, some will argue, votes more wisely, commits less crime, and so on. Therefore, it behooves society to furnish public education priced below its marginal cost.

In many cases, the mere fact that an external benefit exists does not economically justify government subsidization of the activity. A well-dressed, attractive person generates a considerable amount of external benefits. Does that mean that we are underproducing attractive persons? Should the government subsidize attractive clothes so that more persons can generate more external benefits? Well-developed males and females also generate external benefits; should the government therefore subsidize gyms? When someone has a beautiful garden, passersby benefit from that garden, yet do not pay anything. Does that mean that we should subsidize beautiful gardens so that there will be more of them?

The key to understanding when an external benefit is relevant is in finding out whether those people who are benefiting from the externality would be willing to pay, on the margin, for one more unit. For example, it is argued that when electric wires are put underground, more people than just the property owners benefit. People driving or walking in a neighborhood that has no overhead wires benefit because they are looking at a more beautiful neighborhood. That does not necessarily mean, however, that underground electric wires should be subsidized (paid for by the government instead of the property owners). We would somehow have to find out if people who do not live in the area but who enjoy walking, bicycling, and driving through it would nonetheless be willing to pay something for the privilege of seeing the neighborhood without electric wires. If they are unwilling, then in this particular situation it is probably not economically meaningful to consider the externality problem as a real problem.

External Benefits and Nonpayers

When external benefits exist, we usually find that those who obtain those external benefits cannot be excluded from obtaining them. The producers want to charge, but for a variety of reasons can't. Otherwise, the benefits wouldn't be external; they would be internal. A theater could generate external benefits if, in fact, there were no way to exclude viewers. After all, once the picture is being shown, everybody can benefit from the picture as long as there is sufficient space. But since theater owners like to capture profits, they construct walls and doors to exclude nonpayers. The exclusion of nonpayers is important to making sure that all benefits from an action are internalized.

This is not the case in all situations. Consider, for example, fireworks displays. They can be seen for many, many blocks, and it is difficult to exclude nonpayers. Here is a case where social or external benefits actually exist because nonpayers will not be excluded and can get value from the production of a fireworks display. However, business firms in general are quite ingenious at finding ways to exclude nonpayers. To the extent that they are successful, we need not worry about external benefits. Football stadiums have high walls, theaters have closed doors, and so on.

There are situations, however, where, even if it is relatively costless to exclude nonpayers, it might be socially beneficial if no one were excluded.

Public Goods

This is the case for goods that economists have labeled **public goods.** With such goods, the amount that one individual uses of the good or service does not take away from the amount that any other individual can use of the good, *once it has already been produced.* If a dam is put up, your ability to be protected from flood does not reduce the ability of anyone else in that immediate area to be protected. If you are protected by national defense, the benefits you receive from that protection do not detract from anyone else's benefits. The marginal cost, once the good or service is produced, is zero. Indeed, pricing on the basis of marginal cost, we would see that once the good is produced there is no price! This is the situation with television and radio signals. Once they are produced, they are public goods. Anyone who wants to use them can do so without taking away from any other person's ability to use them. Furthermore, the marginal cost to the television or radio generating station is zero when a new person decides to use the waves. The marginal cost of providing TV or radio programs, once they are produced, is zero, and in that sense, the price would be zero in a purely competitive world. However, if the price were zero, then you would not expect much to be produced, would you? Entrepreneurs usually don't produce goods that sell at a zero price.

In such cases, and for most public goods, there has to be some way to transform the public good into a private good. Otherwise, the government would have to provide the good itself. In the case of television, we have a *semi*public good because TV stations allow advertisers to buy time. The advertising pays for the production of the signals. You pay for the TV programs you watch when you buy the products that are advertised. If you buy none of the products advertised on television, then in essence you are being subsidized by those people who do. In the case of national defense, another classic public good, government has taken on the responsibility for the service. (With that particular public good, it would be very expensive to exclude nonpayers from the benefits.)[4]

Sometimes there are ways of transforming a public good into a private good by setting up a system that will exclude nonpayers. That's exactly what cable or pay television is all about. People who do not pay do not obtain the TV signal, or if they do, it is scrambled. In this case, we do not have to see commercials on television because we

[4] Note that there is a difference between a government *providing* the good and *producing* that good. The two concepts involve separate decisions. If a government chooses to provide national defense or garbage collection, it does not mean that the government must directly provide the service; it can choose only to finance it through revenues received from taxes. It can then hire mercenaries and private garbage collectors.

pay directly for the service; TV becomes a private good.

The classic case of a public good is a lighthouse. Once it is built, the marginal cost of providing its services to ships is close to zero, and it appears impossible to make ships pay because of the problems of identifying which ships go by it and of enforcing payment. But in England, lighthouses were for many years private. In fact, the number of private lighthouses increased from the years 1700 to 1834. While it may seem that enforcement costs were high, they were not high enough to prevent entrepreneurs from collecting enough revenues to continue building more lighthouses.

The area of public goods is new in economics and not very well defined. At this point, we can say that it is inappropriate to blindly carry over the principles we have laid out for private goods to public goods. We have, however, established a fairly comprehensive theory in this chapter that we can apply to various ecological and social issues. We shall turn to these issues next.

Concepts in Brief 18-4

- When external benefits occur, it is possible that individual decision makers will engage in too little of the socially beneficial action.
- The existence of external benefits does not automatically justify government subsidization; consumers must be willing, at least in principle, to pay something in order to have one additional unit of the external benefit.
- External benefits are often associated with public goods, defined as those goods whose marginal cost is zero once they have been produced.
- It is difficult to prevent nonpayers from consuming public goods.
- Profit-maximizing firms will seek ways to transform public goods into private goods. For example, theater owners will put walls around the theater to prevent nonpayers from viewing. Outdoor band concerts will have fences to prevent nonpayers from being able to see and hear the musicians clearly.

ISSUES AND APPLICATIONS

Externalities and Honeybees

Concepts Applied

- Social versus private costs, social versus private benefits, and common versus private property

The classic case of external benefits is the production of honey and apples. You can buy apple blossom honey, blueberry blossom honey, alfalfa honey, red clover honey, fireweed honey, mint honey, sage honey, orange honey, and even cabbage honey. We all know how honey is made. Bees extract the nectar of various blossoms and transform it, via one of nature's mysterious processes, into the honey you buy in the store.

Beekeepers and bees work throughout the year. During part of the year, usually from spring to fall, the colonies of bees hatch continuously. The infants are raised on pollen, and they remain in the brood for about three weeks of their working lives, helping to clean and repair the wax cells in the brood. For the remainder of their lives, usually two or three more weeks, they look for pollen and nectar.

External Benefits

Bees are at their busiest in the spring, when they are pollinating fruit trees and the infant bees must be fed with nectar and pollen. Fruit tree owners benefit from having honeybees nearby: they will enjoy a larger yield per acre because of the pollination services the bees provide. Here we have a classic situation that in the economic literature has been labeled as an external benefit. In a classic 1952 article, the economist J. E. Meade presented a colorful example: applying more labor, land, and capital to apple farming will not only increase the output of apples, but

Bees feed off nearby fruit trees—an external benefit for the beekeeper. In feeding off the trees, the bees pollinate the fruit blossoms—an external benefit for the fruit tree farmer.

will also provide more food for the bees. Meade called this a case "of an unpaid factor, because the situation is due simply and solely to the fact that the apple farmer cannot charge the beekeeper for the bees' food."[5]

We can look at the situation from the other side of the coin. The apple trees may provide food for the bees, but the bees also fertilize the apple blossoms. If the beekeeper in the vicinity of the apple trees increases the size of the colony, he or she presumably foresees the increased benefit as the additional revenues that will be received from selling a larger quantity of honey. At the same time, though, the apple farmer will receive a benefit in the form of a higher pollination rate of his or her apple blossoms at the end of the season. Again we appear to have a situation of an unpaid factor or an externality. There are benefits external to both the decision made by the apple farmer and the decision made by the beekeeper.

In economic analysis, an externality is a market failure. That is, the private market fails to allocate resources in an efficient manner—it fails to generate the appropriate price signals. The apple and bee example has been used in economics for many years now to demonstrate an externality where the government should step in and correct the relative prices by appropriate taxes and subsidies in order to take account of benefits that the apple farmer and the beekeeper apparently do not perceive, or at least cannot charge for.

Contracting Occurs

Only recently did an economist take the time to find out if the quaint apple farmer-beekeeper example is real. Besides the fact that apple blossoms yield little or no honey, apparently both beekeepers and fruit growers do understand that bees provide valuable pollination services. More-

[5] J. E. Meade, "External Economies and Diseconomies in a Competitive Situation," *Economic Journal,* March 1952, pp. 56–57.

EXHIBIT 18–4
Bee-Related Plants Investigated in the State of Washington, 1971.

Plants	Number of Beekeepers	Pollination Services Rendered	Surplus Honey Expected	Approximate Season	Number of Hives per Acre (range)
Fruits and nuts					
Apple and soft fruits*	7	Yes	No	Mid April–Mid May	.4–2
Blueberry (with maple)	1	Yes	Yes	May	2
Cherry (early)	1	Yes	No	March–Early April	.5–2
Cherry	2	Yes	No	April	.5–2
Cranberry	2	Yes	Negligible	June	1.5
Almond (Calif.)	2	Yes	No	February–March	2
Legumes					
Alfalfa	5	Yes and no†	Yes	June–September	.3–3
Red clover	4	Yes and no	Yes	June–September	.5–5
Sweet clover	1	No‡	Yes	June–September	.5–1
Pasture§	4	No	Yes	Late May–September	.3–1
Other plants					
Cabbage	1	Yes	Yes	Early April–May	1
Fireweed	2	No	Yes	July–September	n.a.
Mint	3	No	Yes	July–September	.4–1

* Soft fruits include pears, apricots, and peaches.
† Pollination services are rendered for alfalfa and the clovers if their seeds are intended to be harvested. When they are grown only for hay, hives will still be employed for nectar extraction.
‡ Sweet clover may also require pollination services, but such a case is not covered by this investigation.
§ Pasture includes a mixture of plants, notably the legumes and other wild flowers such as dandelions.

Source: S. N. S. Cheung, "The Fable of the Bees: An Economic Investigation," *Journal of Law and Economics,* April 1973, Table 1.

over, beekeepers and fruit growers realize that plants will provide valuable honey crops. Once it is understood by at least one of the parties in question that a valuable external benefit occurs as a result of that party's or the other's action, we would expect that some attempt would be made to take advantage of this knowledge. That attempt would translate itself into a contractual arrangement between the fruit grower and the beekeeper. We all know of certain types of contracts—for example, the kind made with a bank in order to borrow money. But contracts are not limited to such obvious endeavors. In fact, contracts exist, either explicitly or implicitly, for an incredibly large number of economic and even noneconomic transactions. We can cite a marriage contract, an employment contract, and an educational contract; there are contracts for just about every action known. The beekeepers and the fruit and plant growers therefore might be expected to reach an agreement that would take account of the so-called externalities involved in each one's behavior. After all, if the beekeepers don't like the deals made, they can move their beehives elsewhere.

We find conclusive evidence that both nectar and pollination services are indeed bought and sold in the marketplace. In many cases, all we have to do is look in the Yellow Pages. We find there an entry for "pollination services." Economists for many years thought that the apple farmer could not charge the beekeeper for the bees' food and the beekeeper could not charge the apple farmer for the bees' pollination services, but this is not the case. Not only can the parties charge for the services they render each other, but they actually do so; and some of them make a very good business of it. In a study in the state of Washington,[6] it was found that about 60 beekeepers each owned 100 or more colonies. During the peak season, the colonies' total strength was about 90,000 bees. Beekeepers relo-

[6]Steven N. S. Cheung, "The Fable of the Bees: An Economic Investigation," *Journal of Law and Economics,* April 1973.

cate hives from farm to farm by truck. Beekeepers not only render pollination services to different fruit and plant owners at different times of the year, but extract different types of honey at different times of the year as well. On the average, the Washington hives take care of $2\frac{1}{2}$ crops a year. Exhibit 18–4 shows that beekeepers sometimes provided pollination services and sometimes didn't; sometimes plant owners provided honey services and sometimes they didn't.

When we look at what beekeepers charge for pollination services, we find an interesting but not wholly unexpected phenomenon. The greater the expected honey yield, the smaller the pollination fee. Essentially, then, the beekeeper is paid partly in honey for the pollination services that are rendered to the plant owner. Moreover, the more effort per pint of honey yield the beekeeper puts into dispersing hives throughout the orchard, the more he or she charges for this service, because pollination improves with increased dispersal of hives.

So here we have a situation where a seemingly elusive resource, a flying insect, renders services to the owner of another resource. A very specific type of contract has been drawn up for these circumstances in order to take account of any benefits obtained. These contracts take both oral and written forms. In the state of Washington, a printed one is issued by the Association of Beekeepers. A contract need not be in writing, however, to be enforceable in a court of law. In any event, oral contracts are not generally broken when information about who broke one travels quickly. This is exactly the situation in the world of beekeepers and farmers, in which everyone knows everyone else's reputation. A glance at the written pollination contracts reveals stipulations concerning the number and strength of the colonies, the time of delivery of the hives and the time of their removal, what will be done to protect the bees from pesticides, how the hives should be placed, and the cost of the hives' services.

Whenever there are expected gains to be made from contracting among different parties in an economic system, and as long as the cost of making and enforcing the contract is less than the expected gains, we generally observe the making of written or oral contracts. This is even true where natural resources are concerned. Thus, the economist's classic example of what was once considered an externality in theory turns out to have been largely internalized in practice. It does provide us, however, with valuable clues to when and where externalities will exist. In the case of the bees, contracting was profitable for the parties concerned; in the cases of automobile pollution, destruction of scenic beauty, and fishing rights in the ocean, the costs of negotiating and enforcing contracts clearly exceed the potential gains. This is so because we do not yet have any cheap (efficient) way to define, measure, and enforce property rights to the clean air, scenic beauty, and the fish swimming in the ocean.

Questions

1. Can you think of other examples of so-called unpaid factors of production?
2. Are contracts relevant in everyday life?

Should We Market the Right to Pollute?

Concepts Applied

■ Property rights, pollution abatement, demand and supply for pollution

The Environmental Protection Agency has for several years attempted to create a marketplace for the buying and selling of rights to pollute. A crazy idea? Perhaps, but it is one that might lead to a more efficient use of resources. Before we explain the plan itself, let us first examine why such a plan is needed. To understand the situation, we must understand the Federal Clean Air Act.

The Federal Clean Air Act

The Federal Clean Air Act was passed in 1963, in an attempt to force a reduction in pollution, particularly in metropolitan areas in the United States. Through rules and regulations of the EPA, the Clean Air Act presents localities with specified permitted pollution levels. These so-called National Air Quality Standards must be met in most major metropolitan areas. In many metropolitan areas, however, air quality is already poor. Thus, a company that wishes to build a plant in such metropolitan areas is theoretically barred from doing so because of its detrimental impact on air quality. If held to its strictest guidelines, this would mean no further industrial growth in many urban areas.

The Offset Policy

The Environmental Protection Agency approved an offset policy to get around this problem. It requires a company that wants to build a plant to work out a corresponding reduction in pollution at some existing plant. For example, when Volkswagen wanted to build a plant in New Stanton, Pennsylvania, the state of Pennsylvania agreed to reduce pollutants from its highway-paving operations. This reduction would offset the Volkswagen plant's additional pollution.

The problems with the offset policy. One major problem with the offset policy involves the difficulty in finding an offset partner. In other words, each time a firm wants to build a new plant in an already polluted area, it must seek, on an individual basis, an offset partner that agrees to reduce pollution (usually after a payment from the other company). This is where the idea of a bank for the buying and selling of pollution rights comes into play.

Creating the Pollution Rights Bank

Rather than seeking individual offset partners, the EPA suggests that a bank for pollution rights be started. It would be a clearinghouse that identifies, records, and stores the credits earned by any company that reduces its pollution beyond the legal requirements. Such credits would be expressed, probably, in terms of the amount of pollutants removed (from some hypothetical level), such as so many pounds of sulphur dioxide per day. The company requiring an offset in order to build a new plant could buy directly from the company that deposited the pollution rights credit. Alternatively, the depositor might use the credit itself later on. The system would probably work best if carried out at the state level, with supervision by the Environmental Protection Agency.

The incentives involved. Clearly there would be economic incentives to reduce pollution levels below those required by law if such a bank existed. Any firm that believed it could cheaply reduce pollutants further would know that at some point another firm would pay it for such reduction in order to build a plant in that area. Presumably, such a marketplace for the right to pollute would encourage further research and development in pollution-reduction techniques than now exist. Today, many standards are set on an absolute physical basis, offering companies no additional incentive to reduce pollution below the air quality standard.

Questions

1. Does marketing the right to pollute mean that we are allowing too much destruction of our environment?
2. Who implicitly has property rights in the air if a pollution bank is set up and the right to pollute is sold to the highest bidder?

Definition of Terms

Private costs Those costs incurred by individuals when they engage in using scarce resources. For example, the private cost of running an automobile is equal to the gas, oil, insurance, maintenance, and depreciation costs. Also called explicit costs.

Social costs The full cost that society bears when a resource-using action occurs. For example, the social cost of driving a car is equal to all of the private costs plus any additional cost that society bears, including air pollution and traffic congestion.

Externality A situation in which a private cost diverges from a social cost. A situation in which the costs or benefits of an action are not fully borne by the two parties engaged in exchanges or by an individual engaging in a scarce resource-using activity.

Common property Property that is owned by everyone and therefore owned by no one. Examples of common property resources which have historically been owned in common are air and water.

External benefit A benefit received by a third party for which no specific payment was made. You receive an external benefit from well-manicured lawns when you drive by them. Your pleasure or benefit may have been external to the decision-making process of the person who mowed the lawn or had it mowed.

Public goods Goods for which the marginal cost of an additional person using them, once they have been produced, is zero. National defense is a good example of a public good.

Chapter Summary

1. Up until this chapter, we had been dealing implicitly with situations where the costs of individual actions are fully recognized. These are called private costs, and they are borne privately by people making voluntary exchanges in the economy. In some sense, they are internal to the firm or the household and must explicitly be taken account of. Most individuals and firms only consider private costs of their actions.
2. In some situations, there are social costs that do not equal private costs. That is, there are costs to society that exceed the cost to the individual. These costs may include such things as air and water pollution, for which private individuals do not have to pay. Society, however, does bear the costs of these externalities. Few individuals or firms *voluntarily* consider social costs.
3. One way to analyze the problem of pollution is to look at it in terms of an externality situation. Individual decision makers do not take account of the negative externalities they impose on the rest of society. In such a situation, they produce "too much" pollution and "too many" polluting goods.
4. It might be possible to ameliorate the situation by imposing a tax on polluters. The tax, however, should be dependent upon the extent of the economic damages created rather than upon the physical amounts of pollution. This tax therefore will be different for the same level of physical pollution in different parts of the country because the economic damages differ, depending upon the location and the density of the population and on other factors.
5. Another way of looking at the externality problem is to realize that it involves the lack of definite property rights. We are talking about common property resources such as air and water. No one owns them, and therefore no one takes account of the long-run pernicious effects of excessive pollution.
6. In situations where transactions costs are minimal, the same allocation of resources will result whether the property in question is commonly or privately owned. The distribution of wealth, however, will change depending on who is able to appropriate what, until now, have been common property rights.
7. External benefits arise when individual actions generate benefits to other individuals without those other individuals having to pay for them. It is often thought that whenever external benefits exist, subsidization is desirable in order to achieve a socially optimal rate of production. Such may not be the case if people are unwilling to pay for one more unit of the good in question.
8. In economics we have a body of theory devoted to public goods. These are defined as goods for which the cost of providing service to an additional individual is zero, once the good has already been produced. National defense and radio and TV signals are examples of public goods. There are ways to make public goods into private goods.
9. Honeybees have been characterized as an "elusive" resource, the pollinating benefits of which do not carry a price tag. Nonetheless, beekeepers can and do charge for helping to pollinate fruit orchards.

Selected References

Commoner, Barry. *The Closing Circle: Nature, Man and Technology.* New York: Knopf, 1971.

Kneese, A. V., and C. L. Schultze. *Pollution, Prices, and Public Policy.* Washington, D.C.: The Brookings Institution, 1979.

McKean, Roland M. *Public Spending.* New York: McGraw-Hill, 1968, pp. 67–75.

Seneca, Joseph, and Michael R. Taussig. *Environmental Economics.* 2nd ed. Englewood Cliffs, N.J.: Prentice-Hall, 1979.

Thurow, Lester C. *The Zero-Sum Society.* New York: Basic Books, 1980.

Answers to Preview and Study Questions

1. What is a negative externality?

A negative externality exists if the social costs exceed the private costs of some activity; if third parties outside a two-party transaction are adversely (negatively) affected, negative externalities are said to exist. Pollution is considered to be an example of a negative externality; transactions between automobile producers and users impose costs (pollution) on third parties (people who neither produce nor consume the autos).

2. How can indefinite property rights create negative externalities?

Indefinite property rights—or unenforced nominal property rights—create a situation in which no one has the incentive to use a resource efficiently. The atmosphere, oceans, lakes, rivers, and forests all possess certain self-cleansing properties. Nature's ability to self-cleanse can be considered a scarce resource, and, as such, it behooves society to use this resource efficiently. However, if everyone owns these resources, then, in effect, *no one* owns them. As a consequence people will use these resources (as dumping grounds for consumer and producer waste) as though they were free. Of course, excessive use of these resources eventually impairs nature's ability to self-cleanse; enter the concept of pollution (a collection of unwanted matter). Now the marginal cost to *private* polluters is still zero (or nearly zero), whereas the cost to society of using this (now) scarce resource is positive. In short, third parties are adversely affected when pollution results from the production and consumption of goods that lead to waste—which creates pollution. These third parties cannot drink, swim, or otherwise recreate in the bodies of water, and they suffer the ill effects of polluted air. Note that if some businesses voluntarily impose pollution-treatment devices on themselves they will incur extra costs of production and put themselves at a market disadvantage with respect to their competitors; they will probably be forced out of the marketplace.

3. If property rights are indefinite, *must* negative externalities arise?

No. If contracting costs are small, and enforcement is relatively easy, voluntary contracts will arise and the full opportunity costs of actions will be accounted for. That is, when transacting costs are small, private and social costs will converge, and externalities will disappear. What is interesting is that regardless of how property rights are assigned, resources will be allocated in the same way. Of course, the specific assignment of property rights *does* affect the distribution of wealth, even though resource allocation is independent of the specific property right assignment; what is important for efficient resource allocation is that *someone* have property rights. It should be noted that, unfortunately, the main externalities, such as air and water pollution, are very complex, contracting costs are very high, and enforcement is difficult. As a consequence, free-market solutions are not likely to emerge—indeed, they have not.

4. What is the optimal quantity of pollution?

As is usually the case in economic analysis, the optimal quantity of just about anything is where marginal cost equals marginal benefit. That is, the optimal quantity of pollution occurs at the point where the marginal cost of reducing (or abating) pollution is just equal to the marginal benefit of doing so. The marginal cost of pollution abatement rises as more and more abatement is achieved (as the environment becomes cleaner and cleaner, the *extra* cost of cleansing rises). The state of technology is such that early units of pollution abatement are easily achieved (at low cost), but attaining higher and higher levels of environmental quality becomes progressively more difficult (as the extra cost rises to prohibitive levels). On the other hand, the marginal benefit of a cleaner and cleaner environment falls; the marginal benefit of pollution abatement falls as a cleaner and cleaner environment moves from human to nonhuman life-support requirements, to recreation, to beauty, to a perfectly pure environment. The point at which the increasing marginal cost curve of pollution abatement intersects the decreasing marginal benefit curve of pollution abatement defines the (theoretical) optimal quantity of pollution. Recognizing that the "optimal" quantity of pollution is not zero becomes easier when one realizes that it takes scarce resources to reduce pollution. It follows that a trade-off exists between a cleaner environment and the production of *other* goods and services. In that sense nature's ability to self-cleanse is a resource that can be analyzed like any other resource, and a cleaner environment must take its place with other societal wants.

5. What is a positive externality?

A positive externality exists when the social benefits exceed the private benefits of some activity; when two-party transactions generate benefits to third parties, positive externalities exist. Education, the arts, and so-called public goods are alleged to be examples of positive externalities. It should be stressed that true positive externalities exist only when third parties would willingly *pay* for the privilege of the two-party transactions. The problem is that it is difficult to force third parties to pay; again, property rights are muddled. Nevertheless, it still is true that, *in principle,* third parties must be willing to pay for the "positive externalities." The fact that enforcement of property rights is difficult, or that voluntary payment is not likely to be forthcoming, does not violate this ultimate test for the *existence* of a positive externality.

Problems

(Answers at the back of the book)

1. Construct a typical supply-demand diagram. Show the initial equilibrium price and quantity. Assume that the good causes negative externalities—external costs—on third parties (persons not involved in the transactions). Adjust the diagram to compensate for that fact. How does the "adjusted" situation compare with the original?
2. Construct a second supply-demand diagram for any product. Show the equilibrium price and quantity. Assuming that the good generates external benefits, modify the diagram to allow for them. Show the new equilibrium price and quantity. How does the "adjusted" situation compare with the original?
3. Suppose that polluters were charged by governmental agencies for the privilege of polluting.
   a. How should the price be set?
   b. Which firms will treat waste, and which will pay to pollute?
   c. Is it possible that some firms will be forced to close down because they now have to pay to pollute? Why might this result be "good"?
   d. If producers are charged to pollute, they will pass this cost on to buyers in the form of higher prices. Why might this be "good"?
4. Why has the free market not developed contractual arrangements to eliminate excess air pollution in major U.S. cities?

19
Conservation and Energy

TOPICS FOR REVIEW

The topics listed below, which we have already analyzed, are applied in this chapter. You may find it worthwhile to review them. For your convenience each topic is followed by the number identifying the specific "Concepts in Brief."

a. Capital stock and economic growth (2–3)

b. Disadvantages of specialization and dependence (2–4)

c. Shortages (3–7)

d. Nominal versus relative prices (4–2)

e. Price elasticity of demand (6–1, 6–4)

FOR PREVIEW AND STUDY

1. How do economists define conservation?
2. Do economists analyze resources differently if the resources are nonrenewable?
3. It was widely believed that during the 1973–1974 energy crisis (in the United States and elsewhere), shortages existed because the world was running out of energy sources. Is there an alternative explanation to that period's shortages?
4. What are proven reserves?
5. Is the world running out of crude oil?

We live in a world of scarce resources. And because population and per capita incomes are expanding, we are using up larger amounts of our limited resources. To many people that means that "something" must be done. The energy crisis of 1973–1974 convinced a segment of the population, both here and abroad, that drastic conservation measures must be undertaken. In this chapter, we will look at what conservation of natural resources is all about. Then we will grapple with some of the specific energy questions facing us today.

The Debate

Conservation is a loaded word. The first head of the U.S. Forest Service, Gifford Pinchot, felt that "conservation means the greatest good for the greatest numbers, and that for the longest time." Let's look carefully at Gifford Pinchot's quotation. We should ask whether this is really an operational definition of conservation. Is this really what conservationists believe should be the *modus operandi* of the government in conserving our natural resources? The answer is probably no.

LIMITED RESOURCES

We know that *at any particular moment,* the total amount of resources in the United States is fixed. Therefore, with the exception of public goods, whatever you use of a resource, your friends cannot use. Whatever your friends use, you cannot use. This makes it difficult to talk about the greatest good for the greatest number, and this is what economists refer to as an erroneous and impossible double maximization. It is like saying that you want the best for the least. Either you seek out the highest-quality product you can buy for a given price, or for a given quality you seek out the lowest-priced brand. The same holds for conservation at any particular moment in time. It is impossible to have the greatest good for the greatest number because (for most goods) what one person has, another person can't have.

Also consider the clause, "and that for the longest time." What does this mean? What could it possibly lead to in terms of the use of resources? Doesn't it imply that no resources should be used at all today and forever after? That, of course, is how we use our resources for the longest time—by never using them at all! We can keep coal in the ground from now to eternity by never taking any out. But does conservation mean that we should limit the amount of resources we use so that they will last the longest? If so, we should stop consuming resources today. Then our grandchildren and their grandchildren and their grandchildren will inherit the largest amount of natural resources.

AN OPERATIONAL DEFINITION

Another definition of conservation must be found if we are to have a rational, objective standard by which to judge current actions involving our natural resources. Let's take the simple example of one acre of land with some trees on it. Suppose you are the owner of that land. How would you decide whether to cut the trees or let them grow? If you decide to cut the trees, when should you cut them and how many should you cut? Should you cut one tree, two trees, or all the trees?

Let's make the problem simple and assume that the trees are located in an area that no one ever sees. We will assume you get no pleasure from the mere fact of owning trees. You are a wealth maximizer and look only at the monetary return on the piece of property that you own. If you wanted to maximize wealth, you would decide how to use your trees by looking at how profitable it would be either to cut them or let them grow. It's a hard decision but really no different from the decisions facing any property owner. You must decide the optimal use of your resources over time. With natural resources, this also involves the optimal *timing* of the use of the resource.

If you thought you could build a road to your stand of trees and charge campers a certain amount of money to use the area, you would consider this alternative. Or you could cut down the trees today, sell them on the open market, and receive a certain price per unit of lumber rendered. If you waited another year, you could sell them on the open market and perhaps receive a better price. Since the trees would have grown during that time, there would be more board feet of lumber to sell. If you thought the price was going to rise in the future and the trees were going to grow bigger with no corresponding increase in the cost of cutting them, you might wait to cut them. But obviously you shouldn't wait forever. At some point, you will maximize your net wealth position by cutting the trees or, if camping becomes very lucrative, by making your tree stand into a private campground. The point is that you must compare the benefits of cutting the trees now with the costs of not cutting the trees now. One benefit of not cutting is the fact that they could be used as a campground. Moreover, if you do not cut now, you might get a higher price for them in the future.

Your costs of cutting the trees include the opportunity costs of not cutting the trees and selling them for what you could get. If, for example, you could sell them for $1 million this year and invest that money in a government bond yielding a 10 percent rate of return, the opportunity cost of not cutting the trees is going to equal 10 percent of $1 million, or $100,000. The combined benefits of not cutting the trees—that is, the benefits of a potentially higher price in the future with bigger trees to sell—must at least equal the $100,000. Otherwise, you would cut the trees right away. (You also have the alternative of cutting now and then replanting. You might want to sell the timberland with small young trees on it.)

Discounting

To maximize the value of a piece of property that has natural resources on it, you should time your use of those resources so as to maximize their *discounted* value. If you get a dollar today, it's worth a dollar; but if you get a dollar one year from now, in today's terms, it is not worth $1. It is worth less even if we assume no inflation. You must discount tomorrow's dollar back to today to find out what it is really worth to you. After all, today's dollars could be put in a savings and loan association to earn interest. If somebody said you had to pay them $1 one year from now, you could probably put 92¢ in the bank today and earn interest so that in one year, you would be able to pay the dollar. Thus, in **discounting,** *costs that are a given amount to be borne in the future are less of a burden than those that must be paid today, even assuming no inflation.*

The same is true of benefits. In this particular case, the benefits will be the income received from cutting the timber. Money that will be forthcoming a year from now is worth less than money today. Even if you didn't want to invest the money you have today, you would be better off having it today than in the future, even assuming no inflation, because this way you have the opportunity to invest it or spend it during the interim if you desire to do so.

Given benefits are worth less the further away they are in the future. If you had one acre of trees, you could estimate how much money you would receive for each possible time profile of cutting them. (You could sell the land and trees, too.)

A time profile of cutting gives the percentage of the total available trees that you could cut each year over a long period of time. You might cut 10 percent this year, 10 percent next year, 30 percent the next year, and so on. That is one time profile of cutting. You might cut 80 percent this year and nothing for five years, then cut 2 percent every year for 10 years. That is another time profile. It could be that you should never cut them if the money you could make from turning the acre into a private campground exceeded the money you could make from cutting the trees.

DISCOUNTING AND SOCIETY'S OPPORTUNITY COST

The above discussion may give the impression that discounting reflects only private opportunity costs. But consider the following analysis:

We have a choice. We can consume today. Or we can use our productive resources not for consumption, but rather to produce capital equipment or education, which will lead to more goods and services in the future. Hence, the rate of return on money put in the bank is not just an artifact of the banking system; rather, it reflects a trade-off in resources across time for a society as a whole.

So when you ask the question whether the owner of trees in our above example will pick the correct—from society's point of view—time profile for cutting the trees, the answer is normally yes. There is no other time path of production levels that could make someone (either a consumer or owner of a firm) better off without making someone else worse off.

For those of you who have never been introduced to discounting before, a short appendix on this subject can be found at the end of this chapter.

Conservation Defined

Conservation now takes on a very definite meaning. The definition we will use is *conservation is the optimal timing of the use of our known reserves of resources based upon present and anticipated technology and preferences.* What does optimal timing involve? It involves utilizing resources in such a way that the present value of the streams of net benefits from those resources is maximized. In a moment, we will apply this definition to many of the problems of conserving our natural resources.

> ***Concepts in Brief 19-1***
>
> ■ Conservation involves the "correct" timing of the use of scarce resources.
>
> ■ In order to assess the value of future resources, we must discount dollars of any future costs and any future benefits back to today. A dollar one year from now is worth less than a dollar today, even assuming no inflation, as long as interest rates are positive.
>
> ■ A dollar in costs that is borne in the future is less of a burden than a dollar in costs that must be paid today.
>
> ■ A dollar in benefits in the future is worth less than a dollar in benefits today.
>
> ■ An operationally meaningful definition of conservation is that it involves the optimal timing of the use of our known reserves of resources based upon present and anticipated technology and preferences.

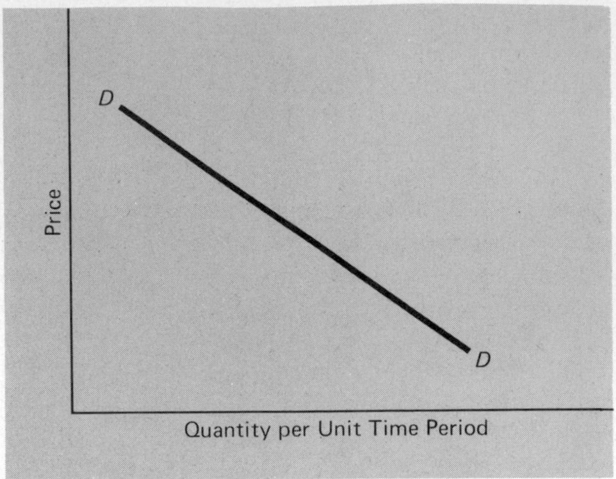

EXHIBIT 19–1
The Demand Curve for Natural Gas. Here we show the demand curve for natural gas. The inverse relationship between price and quantity demanded is a reflection of the fact that an increase in price of natural gas causes people to seek alternative, cheaper sources of energy or substitutes. That means that during all following time periods, as the price rises, the economy will find itself at higher and higher points on the demand curve, *DD*, and the result will be a lower quantity of natural gas demanded.

Depletion of Nonrenewable Resources

There is much concern about using up all the natural gas under the earth. There's also much concern about using up the iron ore, coal, oil, and other nonrenewable (or renewable) minerals and resources found in the earth. Many conservationists believe that because certain resources cannot be renewed, their use should be limited. Using our newly found definition of conservation, we can agree that the use of such resources should indeed be limited.

The question really is: *How fast* should we use our coal? or how fast should we use our natural gas? We will eventually run out of many of our natural resources if we consume them indefinitely at some constant rate. Any constant rate of use of finite nonrenewable resources will deplete the stock of those resources. Thus, the slower we use them, the longer they'll last. But how do we decide the rate at which we should actually use these resources?

CORRECT TIMING

Again, we can go back to a wealth-maximizing situation and assume that it is the wealth of the entire world that is important. Here we can use the same criterion. The value from nonrenewable resources is maximized if they are used at different periods in time so that the net present value of these resources is highest. You might immediately scream "bloody murder" at this criterion because it leads to an eventual depletion of the kinds of resources with which you are familiar. Let's take the case of natural gas. We may indeed eventually run out of natural gas if we continue using it. We will not, however, continue to use natural gas at the same rate if the price rises, reflecting increases in *relative* scarcity. Exhibit 19–1 shows the demand curve for natural gas. As the price of natural gas becomes higher, people will seek alternative, cheaper sources of energy or substitutes. This phenomenon is reflected by the inverse relationship between price and quantity demanded. Consider the demand curve *DD* in Exhibit 19–1 for each future time period for the economy as a whole. As the price of natural gas rises to reflect its increasing relative scarcity, the economy will find itself at a higher point on the demand curve, *DD,* in each period. (And *DD* will shift outward over time.) Hence, less natural gas will be used in each period in the future.

One key to understanding why there is an economic limit to how much of a nonrenewable natural resource we will use can be stated here: After a certain point, the resource becomes so expensive relative to other energy sources that few will use it. In that sense, we will never "run out" of natural gas.

USING SUBSTITUTES

The use of substitutes is another key to understanding why it might be better to consume some of our natural resources in the present rather than to limit their use today. If we do not use natural gas, for example, we will use oil, coal, or some other form of energy. If we restrict the production and consumption of any one of our natural resources, we can be sure that some others will be used more intensively or other substitutes will be developed.[1] This means that other substitute resources will be used up faster than otherwise. It is impossible to conserve *everything,* because that means that we would have to cease to produce and consume. It is also somewhat naive to talk in terms of conserving only one or a selected few natural resources, because then other resources will be used up more quickly. If, in fact, we want to maximize the benefits from our available resources, we would be wise to use up the cheapest ones first and then go on to the more inaccessible and less readily available ones. This can perhaps be best illustrated by another example.

USING TOO LITTLE MAY MEAN LESS FOR THE FUTURE

In some situations, "conserving" resources may not help future generations. To see why, consider two hypothetical examples involving the government. Let's say that the government has $1 million to invest in the economy, and let's say that it invests the $1 million in a project that yields a 25 percent rate of return. If the rate of return in the private sector is 10 percent, then clearly future generations will be better off because of the government investment. Now consider the opposite example.

Assume the government has $1 million to invest in the economy. If the government decides to invest the $1 million in a project that yields a 5 percent rate of return, and the rate of return in the private (nongovernmental) sector is 10 percent, future generations will not be better off by the government investment. They would inherit a larger capital stock, that is, more wealth, if the government had not used the $1 million—which it got from the private sector in the first place—and had allowed the private sector to use it in private investment, where it would have yielded a 10 percent rate of return. The same goes for the use of natural resources.

If we decide to use a combination of natural resources that has a higher cost than some other combination where the return will be less than what it could be, we will be cheating future generations, not helping them, because they would have had more if we had used the lower-cost combination. It may be that if we decide to use less natural gas and, hence, more of other energy sources, the wealth that future generations will inherit will be less than it would be otherwise. We will be doing future generations a disfavor by being "conservationist-minded." Admittedly, this is a hard concept to accept because it means allowing nonrenewable resources to be depleted if this is in fact the cheapest way to provide consumption and investment for the present generation. But acting in any other way would leave future generations worse off, contrary to the notion of most conservationists. Again, *conservation does not mean limiting the use of our resources; it means maximizing the present value of net benefits from our limited resources.*

Resource Depletion, Destruction, and Property Rights

Whether we are referring to a renewable or a nonrenewable resource, the question of who owns the resources under study is important. More specifically, we have to know what the property rights structure is to determine what types of problems we can expect to encounter. Take a serious conservation problem concerning the destruction of whales throughout the world. There is an official International Whaling Commission that attempts to restrict the number of whales killed of each species each year so that no existing species will be totally wiped out. The International Whaling Commission has had less-than-phenomenal success in carrying out its task. Why? Because we have *indefinite* property rights in whales. No one nation owns them. If, however, one or more nations did own specific species of whales and could track and protect those species throughout the year at a low enough cost, then the owner nations would not allow the species to be destroyed by overharvesting.

Numerous conservation problems relating to en-

[1]Some people argue that we should cut back on our use of *all* natural resources. The way we would do this would be by living the "simple" life without so many material goods.

dangered species occur simply because no one has property rights in the species that is endangered. Of course, there are other important contributing factors in many special cases where species are endangered, but if we were willing to invest certain groups with property rights in certain endangered species, it would be to their advantage to prevent the destruction of the species.

In effect, today we are partially solving the "overfishing" problem in the ocean's waters throughout the world by having each nation extend its so-called economic limits to 200 miles from its shoreline. The United States is spending much larger sums of money on its Coast Guard to police U.S. fishing waters now that the 200-mile economic limit has become law.

> ***Concepts in Brief 19-2***
>
> - When a resource is exhaustible, we must ask the question: At what rate should we use this nonrenewable resource?
> - Using up nonrenewable resources efficiently involves correct timing; thus, our definition of conservation also applies to nonrenewable resources.
> - At any level of income, if we decide to "conserve" on the use of one resource, we will use substitutes for that resource.
> - If we conserve on relatively cheap resources and therefore use up more expensive resources, we will be leaving future generations less wealth.

The Energy Question

The basic analysis in this chapter is applicable to all resources. However, there is an additional aspect to the resource called *energy*. Many people believe that an energy "crisis" has occurred (or will soon occur). Energy can be obtained from many sources: fossil fuels, nuclear fission and fusion, the sun, rivers, tides, wind, and so forth. For now, we will combine these alternative sources and refer to them all simply as "energy."

THE ENERGY CRISIS OF 1973–1974 AND OPEC

In the last few years, we have seen a series of "crises" caused by the "insufficient" amount of energy in various forms that was available to the consuming public, at least in the United States. In 1973 and 1974, the energy crisis mainly affected automobile gasoline consumption and, to a lesser extent, heating-oil consumption. There were also sporadic problems with electric utilities not having enough fuel for their generating systems. In 1973 and 1974, the sudden increase in the relative scarcity of petroleum products was due to an embargo on crude oil shipped from countries that form part of the Organization of Petroleum Exporting Countries (OPEC). There was immediate talk at that time about the need to conserve energy because we were "using it up" at a faster rate than we could supply it.

To understand how all this happened back in 1973–1974, we must understand the formation of one of the most successful cartels of all times—the Organization of Petroleum Exporting Countries, or OPEC. This cartel so far has had a highly successful history.

A HISTORY OF OPEC

In 1960, OPEC started as an organization designed to benefit the oil-exporting countries. By 1970, it included Abu Dhabi, Algeria, Indonesia, Iran, Iraq, Kuwait, Libya, Nigeria, Qatar, Saudi Arabia, and Venezuela. Then a few other countries, such as Ecuador, joined the group. When OPEC came into existence, its purpose was to maximize the benefits of owning oil. During the 1960s, its success was limited because an ever-expanding supply of oil kept just ahead of demand at prevailing prices. As demand grew, new discoveries expanded the supplies so fast that wellhead prices for crude oil actually fell slightly from 1960 to 1970. In 1970 and 1971, the rate of growth of the demand for crude oil tapered off. Also in 1970, Libya, which had become a major supplier of crude oil to Western European markets, had a revolution. The new regime cut output sharply in a partly political move against the concessions that the oil companies had been granted by the previous regime. Libya's cutback made sizable price increases possible in 1971 despite the lowering of the rate of growth of demand. These increases were ratified by the other members in agreements drawn up in Tripoli and Teheran. Much of the success of this rise in price was attributed to OPEC, but some observers contend that Libya alone was responsible and had little help from OPEC.

Contrary to worldwide trends, there was an upsurge in demand in the United States, in Western

Europe, and especially in Japan. For example, the United States increased its imports of crude oil from 1.5 to 3.5 million barrels a day from 1970 to 1973. The main reason for this increase in imports was the relaxation of the import quota system that had previously been in force, in which import quotas restricted the amount of relatively cheap foreign crude oil that could be brought into this country.

THE YOM KIPPUR WAR

But the main ingredient in OPEC's success was the outbreak of war in the Middle East in 1973. In the wake of this war, Saudi Arabia, Kuwait, and a few smaller Arab countries agreed to cut back greatly their production of crude oil, thus allowing for large price increases. Remember that the only way to raise price, even if one is a pure monopolist, is to cut back on production and quantity sold. (The law of demand holds for oil, too.) Thus, the OPEC members are able to have an effective cartel arrangement only if most or all of them cut back on production and quantity sold. Since Saudi Arabia, which accounts for the bulk of the oil production in the Middle East, did cut back greatly in 1973, the cartel arrangement worked, as it has since. The total profits for the oil-exporting countries have increased greatly as a result.

Effects of OPEC

The effect of OPEC cartelization activities on world oil prices was dramatic. On January 1, 1973, one could buy Saudi Arabian crude oil at $2.12 a barrel. It should be noted that most of this amount—$1.52—was being taken by the Saudi Arabian government. Thus, only $.60 per barrel was left to cover private oil companies' costs of operation and profits. Within one year, the price of crude oil had risen to $7.61 per barrel. Practically all of this was taken by the Saudi Arabian government—$7.01 per barrel. By 1975, the Saudi Arabian government was taking $10.12 a barrel out of the $10.50 at which it was selling the crude oil. By 1981, the price had risen to $32.54.

Higher Oil Prices Lead to Cries for Conservation

Subsequent to the 1973–1974 energy crisis and the continuing rise in oil prices, there has been continuing talk about conservation of energy. Presumably there is a need to conserve energy because we are

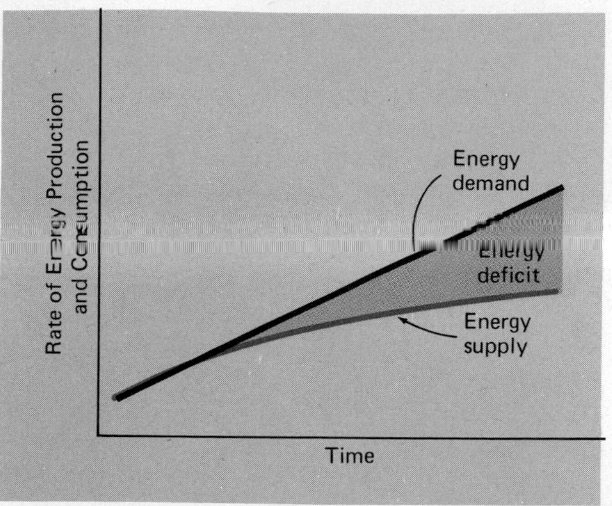

EXHIBIT 19–2

The Energy Deficit. If we put time on the horizontal axis and rate of energy production and consumption on the vertical axis, we can look at projected quantities of energy supplied and demanded. In the typical scenario, there is a line called "Energy Supply" below the line called "Energy Demand." In other words, the energy supply grows over time at a smaller rate than energy demand. The difference is the "Energy Deficit."

"using it up" at a faster rate than producers can supply it.

Generally, the argument is presented in the following manner. We see in Exhibit 19–2 the two lines "Energy Demand" and "Energy Supply." The difference between these two lines is the "Energy Deficit." Basically, the lines are obtained by using the historical rate of growth of the quantity of energy demanded projected into the future, and the future increase in the quantity of the energy supplied, taking into account OPEC production cutbacks. A projected energy deficit clearly exists. But this analysis is deficient.

Relative Prices

If we look at the energy question from the long-run point of view, however, we might have a difficult time accepting the reasoning behind Exhibit 19–2. It does not take into account changing *relative* prices. We have seen throughout this text that in unrestricted situations, relative prices will change so as to bring into equality the quantity of any particular good or service demanded and the quantity supplied. Since energy, in principle, is no different from any other resource, in a long-run unrestricted situation we would expect that the relative price of

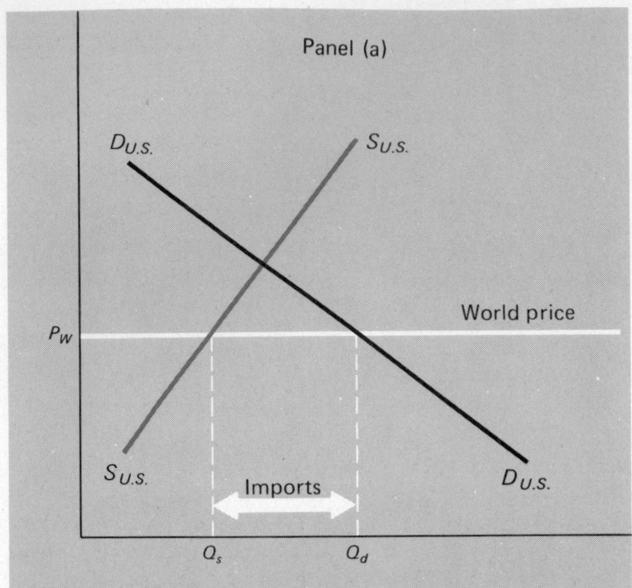

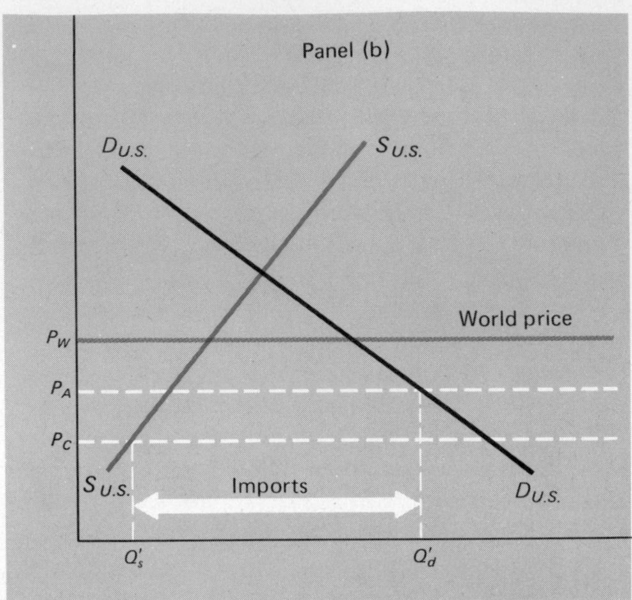

EXHIBIT 19–3

The Effect of Price Controls on Energy Sources and Imports. In panel (a) we show the domestic demand for oil as $D_{US}D_{US}$. We show the domestic supply of oil as $S_{US}S_{US}$. We assume that the United States forms a small part of the entire world's supply and demand for oil. That means that the world price of oil, represented as P_W, is the price at which the United States can purchase all of the oil it wants. In effect, then, the price line, P_W, in panel (a) is the horizontal supply curve facing the United States. That price, P_W, is determined by the world demand and world supply of oil, of which by assumption the United States forms only a part. Now, at that price, P_W, the quantity demanded in the United States is Q_d, but the quantity supplied will be Q_s. The difference is made up by imports. In panel (b) we show a situation where *domestic* price controls are imposed. Since the government has used many types of price controls, we assume for convenience that the government simply sets the price that domestic producers can *receive* for *domestically* produced oil at P_c. The quantity of oil supplied domestically is therefore Q'_s. Remember, though, that oil is still imported at a price of P_W. What we have to assume is that the government allows the U.S. price to consumers to be the average of the world price of oil, P_W, and the domestically controlled price of oil, P_c. For convenience, we just assume that the average price, P_A, is equal to $[(P_W + P_c)/2)]$. The quantity demanded at price P_A is Q'_D. The difference between Q'_d and Q'_s is imports. The result of price controls is: (1) greater domestic consumption, since Q'_d is greater than Q_d in panal (a); (2) lower domestic production, since Q'_s is less than Q_s; and (3) greater reliance on imports.

energy (or more specifically, of the various components of total energy consumption) would change so as to bring total quantity supplied into accord with total quantity demanded. If, in fact, a "deficit" were developing, the relative price of energy would rise so that the quantity demanded would fall. At the same time, this rise in the relative price of energy would bring additional investment, and eventually additional supplies, to that particular area. In other words, the price system automatically works to equalize supply and demand for oil, gas, and electricity.

We should note, however, that the price system does so only if the prices of various energy sources are allowed to rise and fall in response to shifts in supply and demand.

THE EFFECTS OF PRICE CONTROLS ON ENERGY SOURCES

Using economic analysis, we know immediately that there can be no long-run situation of either "surplus" or "shortage" without there being some types of controls on production, distribution or prices. Effectively, in the 1970s, there were price controls of one sort or another on most aspects of producing and selling oil. We can show in typical supply-demand fashion the effects of price controls on oil products.

In panel (a) of Exhibit 19–3, we show the domestic demand curve in the United States as $D_{US}D_{US}$. This represents the demand for oil products by Americans living in the United States. The supply curve for the United States is represented by $S_{US}S_{US}$. We assume, however, that the United States represents a small part of the world. It therefore can obtain all of the oil imports it wants at the going world price. (Obviously, the world price is established by the interaction of world supply and world demand of oil.) We give the world price as P_W. It intersects the U.S. demand curve at a quantity Q_d. But, clearly, at that low price, domestic producers will only supply Q_s. The difference can be made up by imports from the rest of the world. Panel (a) represents a situation where there are no price controls on neither domestic nor imported oil.

Now look at the situation with domestic price controls (after all, we cannot control the price of oil in the rest of the world). This is somewhat more complicated because the government has often used many types of price controls. We assume that the government sets the price that domestic producers can receive for domestically produced oil at P_c. That generates a quantity Q_s'. However, oil is imported at the price P_W. Through price controls and allocation systems, the government is assumed to allow an average price, P_A, of world and domestic oil to be charged to users of oil $[(P_W + P_c)/2]$. Thus, users pay P_A and demand a quantity, Q_d'. The difference $(Q_d' - Q_s')$ must be made up by imports. *In the situation described here, price controls lead to greater domestic consumption, lower domestic production, and greater reliance on imports.* This greater reliance on imports has often caused concerned politicians and laypersons alike to cry out for severe cutbacks in the use of energy. Typically physical formulae are used in which energy "needs" are shown to be less than what we are actually using. In economics, however, it is difficult to talk in terms of "need" when we use a demand schedule, because a demand schedule shows that the quantity "needed" of any commodity or resource depends on the relative price. At higher relative prices of gasoline, for example, consumers of gasoline consume less. They consume less by reducing their use of the resource. They voluntarily reduce the number of trips they take, increase the number of car tune-ups, reduce the horsepower and size of their cars, and alter the manner in which they drive. They may also voluntarily switch to public transportation, ride in car pools, and the like. In other words, the analysis of the demand for gasoline is no different, in principle, from the analysis of the demand for any other commodity. Changing the relative price of gasoline elicits changing relative intensities of use by consumers. The price elasticity of demand for gas is greater than zero.

Empirical Estimates of Demand Elasticity

We do have some estimates of the price elasticity of demand of different sources of energy. Let's consider what happened when the price of oil from OPEC members went up during 1973 and 1974. In Holland and Belgium, 1974 consumption of oil was down from 1973 by over 14 percent. During the same period, it dropped by 10 percent in West Germany and Spain, almost 4 percent in the United States, and 2 percent in Italy and Japan. Given that the growth in demand had been 4 percent per year in the United States, for example, prior to 1973–1974, this drop in consumption represented a significant reaction to OPEC's raising of oil prices.

Consider what happened after the revolution in Iran in 1979. At that time, Iran severely reduced the production of oil from its wells. Previously, Iran had been the second-largest exporter of oil (after Saudi Arabia) in the world. By 1980, the Iranians were exporting almost nothing. World crude oil prices more than doubled. In the United States, the average price of gasoline went from 65¢ per gallon in 1978 to $1.25 per gallon in 1980.[2] Drivers in this country not only stopped the steady increase in gasoline use, but actually cut back their purchases of gasoline by 10 percent during this period (from 7.4 million barrels of oil per day in 1978 to 6.65 million barrels of oil per day in 1980). Simultaneously, heating oil prices rose from 49.4¢ per gallon in 1978 to 94.9¢ per gallon in 1980. People cut their purchases by 15 percent during this time.

Professor Joe Kalt of Harvard University has estimated that in the long run, the price elasticity of demand for gasoline is actually .51. That means that in the long run, a 1 percent increase in the price of gasoline leads to a .51 percent reduction in the quantity of gasoline demanded. He has further estimated that the long-run price elasticity of demand for distillate fuel, such as heating oil, is .26. In other words, a 1 percent increase in the price of heating oil ultimately leads to a .26 percent decrease in the quantity demanded. That tells us that the demand for gasoline is more flexible (price sensitive) than for distillate fuel, such as heating oil.

The basic point is that the law of demand holds even for energy in all of its forms. At a higher relative price, a lower quantity will be demanded, other things being equal.

[2] This is the average price for all grades computed by the Bureau of Labor Statistics.

EXHIBIT 19–4(a)

Oil- and Gas-Drilling Rigs in Operation. Here we show the number of United States oil- and gas-drilling rigs in operation. They reached a low point in 1970 and have been rising ever since. Indeed, there are more oil- and gas-drilling rigs in operation than ever before.

Source: Hughes Tool Company.

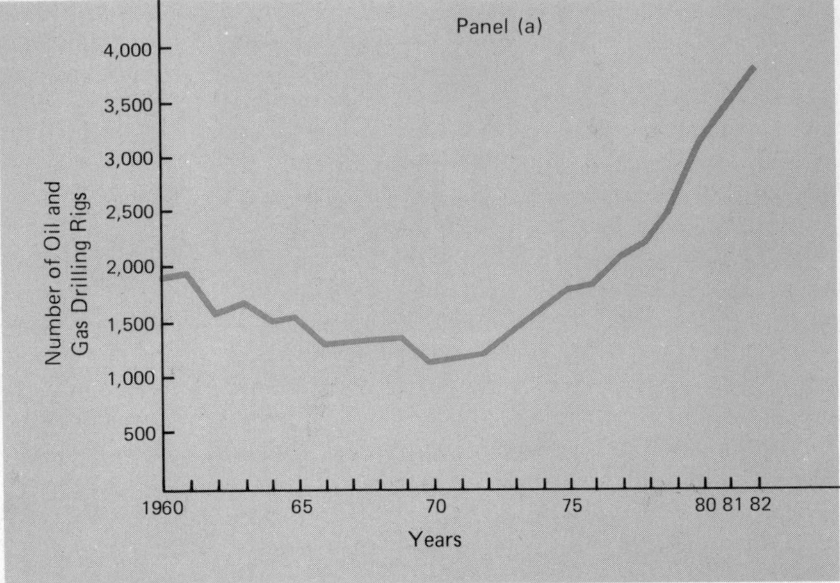

EXHIBIT 19–4(b)

U.S. Proven Reserves of Crude Oil. Proven reserves of crude oil reached a low in 1979 and have risen ever since.

Source: Department of Energy. 1982 is an estimate.

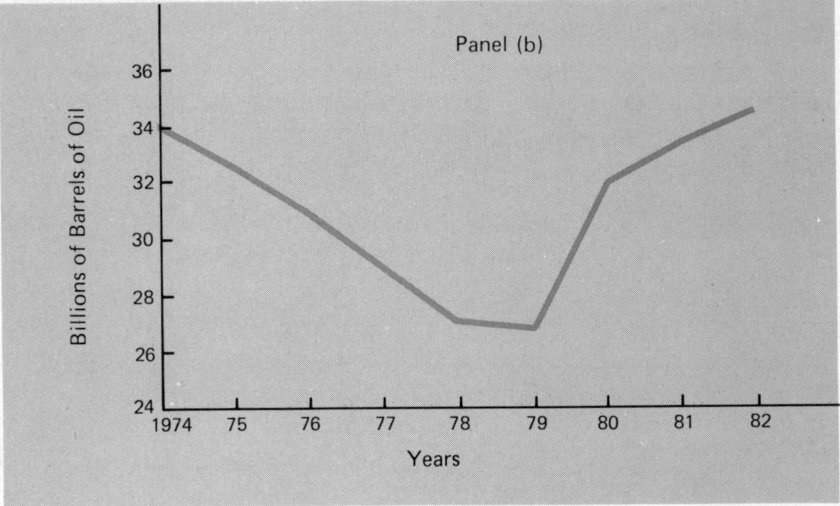

THE THORNY QUESTION OF PROVEN RESERVES

On the supply side of the oil picture, we often read that proven reserves are so low that we have only 5, 10, or 20 years of oil left to use. We must realize that even an engineer's definition of proven reserves depends on economic factors. Proven reserves are those known reserves that can be *profitably* taken out of the ground. When the market price of oil goes up, even with no improvement in technology, we necessarily will have more proven reserves because oil that is harder to find or extract now becomes worthwhile to look for and to produce. Consider the number of oil- and gas-drilling rigs in operation in the United States. In Exhibit 19–4(a), we show that there has been a big upsurge since the so-called oil crisis of 1973. In 1980, the estimate of drilling rigs in use was over three times the number in operation in 1960, and the highest ever for the United States.

Not surprisingly, the Department of Energy's latest available estimate of U.S. proven reserves of crude oil has risen from its low point in 1979 as seen in Exhibit 19–4(b). What that tells us is that indeed oil is like other commodities—a higher relative price leads to a greater quantity supplied. Additionally, this gives us some evidence of the so-called second law of supply—the longer the time allowed for adjustment, the greater the price elasticity of supply. Otherwise stated, long-run supply curves are more elastic than short-run supply curves.

THE PROBLEM OF DEPENDENCY

Although the economic analysis may tell us that energy should not be treated in any special manner, we still may be faced with a *political* aspect of the issue that is beyond the realm of economic analysis. Specifically, if we depend on foreign nations for significant amounts of energy sources,[3] then we are vulnerable to short-run disruptions in our sources of energy. Understandably, some people would prefer that the United States not have to depend on crude oil for so much of its energy needs. If the danger is one of brief disruptions, apparently the "best" policy may be to build a stockpile of supplies to use in an emergency. However, the more we import, the larger is the stockpile that we need to yield any level of protection.

How Do We Reduce the Quantity of Imports?

A frequently discussed policy is the forced conservation of gasoline by government "rationing" or other mandatory requirement schemes. The nation's current policy toward possible supply disruptions is a stand-by gasoline rationing system, which will be implemented during the next disruption. The Department of Energy has estimated that this plan will cost $2 billion to implement and run for six months. Furthermore, some studies show that even the nation's current plan will not eliminate gasoline lines when it is implemented.

Another, more efficient alternative is a tax, such as the 1975 tax on the import of petroleum products. It reduces imports and raises the price that domestic oil companies can charge for their own crude oil products (unless a domestic excise tax is also added), thus stimulating greater production of domestic oil; at the same time, the relatively higher price causes oil to be conserved in all its uses, not just in some—as would be the case with a gasoline rationing system.

FURTHER ENERGY CONSIDERATIONS

Political considerations would have to be brought into our analysis if we were to get a complete picture of the energy problem. We would have to know the foreign policy implications of various energy policies; we would have to know which groups would be hurt and which groups would be favored by different energy policies. The list becomes long indeed.

[3] Particularly crude oil, where imports have been from 30 to 50 percent of our use during the 1970s.

The Income Effect of Energy Policies

We have just mentioned one important political consideration concerning energy policies—the income effect. If the price of energy is always allowed to rise whenever there is a relative increase in scarcity, how will certain income groups be affected? In particular, there is much concern about the effect of higher energy prices on the living standards of the relatively poor in our society. More specifically, can policymakers allow poor individuals to suffer adversely because heating-oil costs have skyrocketed? Actually, this very concern lies at the heart of much of the resistance to allowing the price system to ration available supplies of energy. One possibility, when the low-income population is the point of concern, is to issue "energy stamps" to those same people who qualify for food stamps. Although policymakers are not all uniformly ecstatic about the results of the food stamp program, a similar energy stamp program would eliminate many of the political roadblocks set up to prevent the price system from always performing its rationing function in the energy markets.

There is also an "income" problem with the supply side of energy. When OPEC members, particularly Saudi Arabia, started restricting production of crude oil back in 1973, the result was a worldwide increase in the price of crude oil. To some extent, policymakers, and certainly many laypersons, did not like the idea that shareholders in oil companies would reap benefits due to the higher world price of crude oil. In other words, there was and continues to be concern about "unjust" enrichment of petroleum companies' stockholders. Hence, we see another political reason why policymakers were, for almost a decade, reluctant to allow the price system to work unimpeded in the energy markets.

It is extremely easy to look only at the supply and demand relationships for the different sources of energy and ignore all these other questions. As we said, if we do the former, we find that energy, particularly in the long run, is no different from any other resource and, from a policy point of view, does not necessarily have to be treated differently. But politicians live in the short run and must contend with short-run problems, such as an oil embargo from oil-exporting nations. And although economic analysis is a useful basis for policy considerations, policymakers must look at all other aspects of the energy problem as well. The federal Department of Energy is not just thinking about economics.

Concepts in Brief 19–3

- The energy crisis in 1973–1974 was precipitated by a restriction on the importation of petroleum originating in the Middle East.
- The Organization of Petroleum Exporting Countries (OPEC) has successfully maintained a cartel in which the quantity of oil produced has been restricted in order to raise the price of oil and increase profits.
- Pursuant to the energy problem in 1973–1974, predictions of continued energy "deficits" have been made. Some rely on mechanically projecting "supply" into the future and doing the same for energy "need." Such a projection ignores people's reactions to changes in relative prices.
- When energy becomes relatively scarcer, its price relative to other goods will rise, thereby inducing energy consumers to use less and seek substitutes, and inducing energy producers to produce more and seek alternatives.
- It is possible that we do not wish to import large quantities of oil from Middle Eastern countries because such dependency could be a problem during a war or during a future embargo from OPEC members. One way to reduce dependency on foreign oil is to impose a tax on imported oil. Another way is to store large quantities to provide for future emergencies.

ISSUES AND APPLICATIONS

Are We Running Out of Everything?

Concepts Applied

- Supply, demand, price elasticity of supply and demand, and long versus short run

Americans have grown used to enjoying one of the highest living standards in the entire world. But perhaps our way of life has become too wasteful and we can no longer take its preservation for granted. We are in an era of supposed shortages, and scarcity seems to plague not only the American economic landscape but also that of just about every other country today.

The Shortage Society

The number of items considered in "short" supply began to grow rapidly after the first couple of years in the 1970s.[4] By 1974, large companies were seeking alternatives for practically everything. General Foods was looking for a sugar substitute, Clorox was looking for a soda ash replacement to use in bleach, Alcoa decided to stop producing household aluminum foil, and Del Monte Corporation could not purchase enough glass for jars, fiberboard for boxes, or tinplate for cans.

The energy shortage that started it all. People first became acutely aware of serious shortages throughout our economic system when the Persian Gulf oil-producing nations decided to boycott the United States in the fall of 1973. At the time, it was feared that the shortfall of petroleum products—mainly gasoline and heating-fuel oil—would greatly disrupt our economy. Indeed, some politicians and many concerned scientists told us that because we had been wasteful in the use of energy in the past, we now had to pay for our sins. Many spokespersons assumed that the increased scarcity of petroleum products would last indefinitely, even after the embargo was lifted, so they prescribed expensive long-run policies for research and development to make the United States self-sufficient in energy by 1980. They also exhorted the American people to change their basic life-style in order to

[4] Remember, however, that an economic definition of shortage applies to situations where the price is less than the market clearing, or equilibrium, price. In other words, we can only speak of an excess quantity demanded at a particular price. All of the shortages in the 1970s were related to the Nixon price-wage freeze. The freeze was removed (except on oil and natural gas) in 1974 and the shortages "mysteriously" disappeared (except for oil and natural gas).

During the energy crisis of the 1970s, people learned to make adjustments to deal with the shortages.

EXHIBIT 19–5

When Will the Day of Reckoning Arrive for Natural Resources? By using a projection based on an ever-increasing rate of growth of consumption of nonrenewable natural resources, it is possible to predict how many years we have left before we exhaust today's known global reserves of these resources. This prediction was made for the year 1973.

Resource	*When Known Worldwide Reserves Will Run Out*
Aluminum	31 years
Copper	21 years
Lead	21 years
Manganese	46 years
Mercury	13 years
Natural Gas	22 years
Petroleum	20 years
Silver	13 years
Tin	15 years
Zinc	18 years

Sources: U.S. Bureau of Mines, *Mineral Facts and Problems* (Washington, D.C.: Government Printing Office, 1970), and D. L. Meadows et al., *Dynamics of Growth in a Finite World* (Cambridge, Mass.: Wright-Allen Press, 1974).

conserve precious energy resources. In fact, some observers went so far as to state that the energy crisis suffered by Americans was "good." Why? Simply because it brought us to our senses, made us aware of our dependence on foreign sources for a vital resource, and showed us how wasteful our life-style had become.

Our dwindling mineral resources. When we look at mineral resources, we find the same perplexing scenario—increasing shortages. Just look at Exhibit 19–5. Here we list some of the better-known and critical nonrenewable natural resources and the approximate number of years it will take to use up known worldwide reserves at current rates of consumption. Assuming no recycling, it is clear that we will one day run out of nonrenewable natural resources, no matter how slowly we use them. The problem, according to many, is that we are going to run out of critical natural resources in the very near future. Hence, we will be faced with increasingly disruptive shortages throughout the world economy, as well as in our own.

Some Proposed Solutions to Shortages

What can be done about the shortages that have been observed in the last few years? We have already touched on some long-term proposals for the energy crisis, including increased research and development for new energy sources and policies that would change our energy-consuming life-style. There are also numerous proposals for fixing limits on the amount of energy each person can use. These limits might come in the form of an allotment per individual or per family. Each family might, for example, be allotted a certain number of gallons of gasoline per month and would not be allowed to consume any more. This process is generally known as **rationing.** It was used during World War II for gasoline and other commodities. At that time, ration coupons were given out and had to be used (in addition to money) to purchase gas. (Such a system should be contrasted with rationing via the price system.)

With respect to nonrenewable natural resources, numerous conservation schemes have been suggested. These include limiting the extraction of certain nonrenewable resources so that we can lengthen the amount of time during which they will be available. Such a rationing, or allocation, procedure presumably would guarantee our grandchildren a continuing supply of such resources as natural gas and copper.

At issue, then, is really the question of whether we can continue our current American life-style—that is, whether we can keep consuming large quantities of many items that have been or threaten to be in very short supply. Americans represent only 6 percent of the world's population but consume more than 30 percent of the world's nonrenewable resources. The implication is clear: unless we are superbly successful in improving technology so that we can simultaneously use fewer resources and increase the output of others, we will have to reduce our standard of material well-being.

ANOTHER VIEW OF ENERGY SHORTAGES

When the supply of petroleum was temporarily reduced a few years ago, there was great expectation of chaos. Many commentators predicted freezing homes and automobiles abandoned for want of gas. There were indeed problems for motorists who, in some sections of the country, had to wait hours in line to get their gasoline. But in many other sections of the country, motorists did not have to wait at all. The heating-fuel situation, too, was bleak but not catastrophic. The Denver schools had to close for lack of fuel oil, and some houses did not have enough heat, but massive freezing did not occur. In fact, at the end of the so-called crisis, the amount of fuel oil in inventories of oil companies was greater than at any other time in the history of the United States. How could that have occurred during such a crisis? To be sure, appeals from high-level politicians for the American public to conserve all energy sources did have an impact. But there was another, perhaps even more powerful force that was causing consumers of fuel oil to lower their thermostats, to close their windows, and to take all sorts of measures to reduce their total heating bills. That powerful force was a gradual but nonetheless significant rise in the relative price of heating oil.

At that time, the Federal Energy Office (later called the Federal Energy Administration and now the Department of Energy) was allowing the price of fuel oil to be raised several cents a month. Several cents does not sound like much, but after a number of months, the price to consumers of fuel oil had risen approximately 50 to 70 percent over levels that had prevailed the previous year. At the higher relative price, consumers voluntarily conserved fuel oil. (The publicity campaign waged by government officials to get Americans to use less fuel may also have had an effect.)

What we found out was that the "required" amount of fuel oil was related, at least partially, to how much consumers had to pay for it. When they had to pay more, they decided that they could live in a house at 68 degrees Fahrenheit instead of 72 degrees, thereby freeing income that would otherwise have gone to pay higher fuel bills. The same thing happened with gasoline, but not as dramatically. In the first place, the Federal Energy Office did not allow the retail price of gasoline to rise as sharply as the price of fuel oil. Nonetheless, within less than a year, the price of gas at the pump had risen, and consumers had reacted—by cutting their consumption of gasoline by almost 8 percent. (Again, it could be argued that exhortations from government officials to Americans to drive less and to obey gas-saving lower speed limits were at work here. Speed limits, however, may only have been obeyed where there were effective enforcement efforts.)

The other view of shortages and increased scarcity indicates that after a while shortages may work themselves out because the products in short supply will sooner or later end up costing more and consumers will decide to conserve on those relatively more expensive items. Those who provide the items—the suppliers—will also react to the higher prices, but in the opposite direction. They will be willing to expend more effort and money to find ways to produce more in order to benefit from such higher prices. An understanding of how consumers and producers react when the cost of short-supply items rises is basic to understanding world natural resource markets.

World mineral supplies. Refer back to Exhibit 19–5. The second column is based on the assump-

EXHIBIT 19–6

The Amount of Minerals Contained in 1 Cubic Kilometer of Average Crustal Rock. The physical quantity of minerals contained in the earth's crust is indeed staggering and gives some idea of the extent of resources physically available.

Resource	*Amount of Minerals Contained*
Aluminum	2,000,000,000 tons
Iron	1,000,000,000 tons
Zinc	800,000 tons
Copper	200,000 tons

Source: D. B. Brooks and P. W. Andrews, "Mineral Resources, Economic Growth, and World Population," *Science,* Vol. 185, no. 4145 (July 1974), p. 13.

EXHIBIT 19–7

Estimates of Supply Availabilities of Various Elements and Compounds. In this table, we show the years to exhaustion and current usage rates estimated in 1968 for several compounds found in nature which are essential to our current economic system. These compounds and elements would be difficult to produce synthetically. Hydrocarbons—coal, oil, and gas—are indeed relatively scarce. But it will be some while before we physically run out of hydrocarbons.

Resource	*Years to Exhaustion at Current Usage Rates (1968)*
Hydrocarbons (which are extractable from coal, oil, gas)	2,500 years
Carbon	4,000,000 years
Silicon	5,000,000 years
Hydrogen	4,000,000 years
Iron ore	4,500,000 years
Phosphorous	1,300 years
Aluminum from ores	200,000,000 years
Tin	30,000,000 years
Nickel	1,400,000 years

Source: Oak Ridge National Laboratories.

tion that known global reserves will run out simply because we will consume them all. But what do known global reserves really mean? Those reserve figures are based on the amounts that would be taken out of the earth, given the current state of the art (that is technology) and given the current profitability of mining those amounts. But that current profitability certainly must, in part, be related to the relative price that those minerals can bring in the marketplace. Look at Exhibit 19–6. Here we show how many tons of some important minerals are contained in a single cubic kilometer of average crustal rock. If we were to multiply the numbers included in Exhibit 19–6 by the surface area of the earth that would, on the average, contain those amounts of minerals, we would come up with quantities of physical reserves many, many times those listed in any tables of "available" minerals. The reason we do not use those numbers is that at today's prices it would not be economically feasible to mine them, for, at today's prices, only "proven" reserves, by definition, are profitable to mine. We might expect, and indeed we have seen, that as the relative price of a mineral goes up, the amount of proven reserves goes up also. Witness what happened with petroleum. We have more proven reserves today than we had in 1930, even though we have consumed an enormous quantity of petroleum over the 50 years since.

Will We Ever Run Out?

The question of whether we could actually run out of any of our important natural resources has been examined by two researchers at Oak Ridge National Laboratories. They looked at many of the elements, compounds, and resources found in nature that are difficult to produce synthetically and that are essential to our current economic system. They compared our current rates of use to what is potentially available (using the current state of science, but regardless of how high the cost would be). Exhibit 19–7 indicates some of the results of their analysis. It does appear that the fossil fuels (e.g., coal, oil, and gas) with which we are so familiar and upon which modern society is so dependent, are actually some of our scarcer resources. However, the danger of simply running out appears to be remote.

The real problem, then, is that there is a limited supply of any one of these resources that we are able to extract at any given cost. Extracting any one of these resources and preparing it for use requires the expenditure of human effort, capital investment, and numerous other materials—all of which have alternative uses that would also produce goods and services for society. As we use up the cheap sources, the cost and, hence, the price will rise for the resource. This gives the consumers the choice whether to expand their own control over resources, that is, their money income, in an effort to extract more of nature's unreplaceable resources, or whether to put our current efforts into other uses.

The example of petroleum. Petroleum offers a good example. No one prior to World War II thought it possible to drill a mile down into the ground for oil. Within the last few years, dozens of wells have been drilled several miles down into the earth's crust, probing for oil. This oil comes from a more expensive source—it was not considered a potential resource until the rise in oil prices led to the development of more modern drilling techniques. One day, we may well run out of oil that can be extracted at today's prices. In fact, several researchers at the Rand Corporation (a Los Angeles think tank) have tried to estimate the amount of crude oil currently in the ground that might be extracted by conventional techniques at a cost of no more than $50 per barrel (only a little above today's prices). Their estimate is only 73 times our current rate of use. We are truly running out of *cheap* oil, but not out of oil.

Who Is Right?

Are we facing a shortage society? Must we suffer an inevitable decline in the quality of life, or will things work themselves out? In other words, will Americans respond to inevitable higher prices of items in short supply by consuming less, and will industry respond to those higher prices by finding better ways to produce and by finding substitutes for the items in short supply?

The answer depends on the long-run price elasticity of demand and the long-run price elasticity of supply. Additionally, we must realize that the old "Mother Hubbard" model of the world is highly inaccurate. We do not suddenly go to the cupboard and find it bare of natural resources. Many, if not most, resources have owners. Owners of resources have an incentive to "conserve" them, particularly if they expect prices to rise. (Also, these resource owners have an incentive to search for new supplies and for alternatives.)

When resources are kept off the market, prices will indeed start to rise, even before we might actually start running out of particular resources. The increase in price will cause us to allocate the available resources differently over time. That is, we will now take account of the increased relative scarcity of certain resources and use fewer today so that we will have more tomorrow.

Questions

1. How do shortages arise?
2. Why have predictions about dwindling natural resource supplies almost always proved inaccurate?

Definition of Terms

Conservation Operationally defined as choosing the best timing in the use of resources so as to maximize the total (present) value placed on all resources.

Discounting A method by which we take account of the lower value of a dollar in the future, compared to a dollar in hand today. Discounting is necessary even after we adjust for inflation because of the trade-off between having more goods tomorrow if we consume less today.

Rationing The lay term that relates to the government using some imposed method of deciding who gets what. Typical government rationing schemes use ration coupons.

Chapter Summary

1. Since we live in a world of limited resources, conservation cannot mean the greatest good for the greatest number and that for the longest period of time.
2. When we conserve on one resource, we use more substitutes.
3. Conservation involves the optimal timing in the use of available resources. When we compare the benefits and costs of future activities, we must discount these future dollars back to the present.
4. A dollar in cost today is more of a burden than a dollar in cost to be paid a year from now; a dollar in benefits today is worth more than a

dollar in benefits to be received a year from now.

5. The definition of conservation that involves the optimal timing of resource use applies equally well to both nonrenewable and renewable resources.
6. If we invest in activities that yield a lower rate of return than alternative activities, we will pass down a smaller capital stock—that is, less wealth—to future generations.
7. The success of the Organization of Petroleum Exporting Countries (OPEC) is attested to by the dramatic rise in the price of petroleum products since 1973.
8. It is generally incorrect to project future energy "demands" and "supplies" on the basis of their past growth rates. Changes in the relative prices of energy sources will affect both the quantity demanded and the quantity supplied in the future.
9. The price elasticity of demand for gas is not zero.
10. There is a problem in being dependent on foreign sources for critical materials such as oil. This is the reason some people offer to justify taxation of imports or restrictions on energy use domestically.
11. Some observers contend that we have entered the era of the "shortage" society.
12. Projections of when we will run out of resources typically have been wildly incorrect. When relative prices increase, producers of those resources seek better methods of extracting them and users of those resources seek more economical ways of using them, or they search out substitutes.

Selected References

Ehrlich, Paul R., and Anne H. Ehrlich. *Population, Resources, Environment.* 2nd ed. San Francisco: Freeman, 1972.
Energy: The Next Twenty Years. Resources for the Future. New York: Ballinger, 1979.
Miller, Roger LeRoy. *The Economics of Energy: What Went Wrong?* Glen Ridge, N.J.: Horton, 1974.
Nash, H., ed. *Energy Controversy.* Friends of the Earth, 1980.
Rifkin, J. *Entropy: A New World View.* New York: Viking Press, 1980.
Simon, Julian L. *The Ultimate Shortage.* Princeton, N.J.: Princeton University Press, 1980.

Answers to Preview and Study Questions

1. How do economists define conservation?

To an economist, conservation refers to the optimal timing of the use of our known reserves—based upon present and anticipated technology and preferences. That is, conservation involves the "correct" timing of the use of scarce resources. In particular, a resource is being conserved when it is used at a rate that maximizes the present value of the future streams of net benefits accruing from its use. Conservation could take place by maximizing a resource's use in the present (if the group is extremely present-oriented and interest rates are very high) or by minimizing its use in the present (if the group is very future-oriented and interest rates are very low)—or any rate in between these extremes. Thus, unless present and future tastes are considered, "conservation" as usually understood ("use less now") biases resource use inefficiently toward the future.

2. Do economists analyze resources differently if the resources are nonrenewable?

No. Just because a resource is nonrenewable does not mean that it should be used less in the present. Knowing that a resource is exhaustible does not help in deciding *when* it should be used. Exhaustible resources are conserved in the same manner as renewable resources: use them at a rate that maximizes the present value of the future streams of net benefits accruing from their use. After all, if we use less of a given nonrenewable resource, to maintain a given living standard we must substitute more of *other* nonrenewable resources—or more renewable resources.

3. It was widely believed that during the 1973–1974 energy crisis (in the United States and elsewhere), shortages existed because the world was running out of energy sources. Is there an alternative explanation to that period's shortages?

Yes. Many economists analyze the shortages during that period as the result of a combination of events. First, the OPEC cartel placed an embargo on oil shipments to the United States (and other nations) and radically curtailed oil production. This, by itself, would not have created a shortage of oil distillates (gasoline, heating oil, kerosene); prices of these distillates would have increased relative to other goods, quantity demanded would have decreased, and quantity supplied would have increased. However, as fate would have it, the U.S. government had frozen prices and wages in 1971; therefore, oil distillates were not allowed to rise to market clearing levels (to reflect reduced supply). Thus, since relative price did not rise, quantity demanded did not fall and quantity supplied did not increase. The shortages of these goods reflected the reduced supply of crude oil and the inability of the price of crude oil and its distillates to rise due to price controls. The shortages did *not* necessarily reflect the fact that the world was running out of crude oil or other energy sources. The widespread shortages of *non* oil-related goods in the United

States during that same period can also be traced directly to the price-wage controls. After all, the controls were lifted after 1974 on everything except oil (at every phase of production) and natural gas; shortages disappeared for all other goods, but continued to appear periodically for these.

4. What are proven reserves?

People often become alarmed when they discover that proven reserves indicate that we have only about a 20-year supply of oil left. Actually, we have had only between 15 and 30 years of oil left for about a century now. The point is that proven reserves are *not* an indicator of the remaining supply of oil—or of any other resource. Proven reserves merely represent known reserves that can be extracted profitably. It costs firms resources to prove reserves; therefore, firms will try to optimize (not maximize) the reserves they prove. Moreover, when the relative price of the resource rises, so will proven reserves, since firms will increase exploration and drilling and tap sources previously not economically feasible. Technological improvements in extraction will arise also when the resource's relative price increases.

5. Is the world running out of crude oil?

Worldwide proven crude oil reserves have not fallen over the last decade; they are likely to rise in the near future in response to the relatively higher price of crude oil. It is unlikely that the world will "run out" of oil in our lifetime. Why? As crude oil becomes scarcer, its relative price will rise. This will encourage users to seek substitutes—of which there are many. Moreover, more exploration and technological advances will occur, thereby increasing supplies. But, you ask, what about that far-off future date when no more oil can be found? Crude oil does exist in finite amounts, right? Right. But, at that time the relative price will be so high that users will use it very sparingly; substitutes for crude oil (some of which we are not even aware of yet) will be used, and oil's role will decrease. That is, the percentage of overall energy use resulting from crude oil will have fallen dramatically, and oil will no longer be "king."

Problems

(Answers at the back of the book)

1. The present value (P) of future income streams depends on the *net* (revenues minus costs) revenues and the discount (interest) rate i. The equation is

Present Value =

$$P = \frac{A_1}{(1+i)} + \frac{A_2}{(1+i)^2} + \cdots + \frac{A_t}{(1+i)^t}$$

where A_1 represents the net revenue at the end of the year 1, A_2 the net revenue at the end of year 2, and so on to year t.

a. What is the present value of $1 one year from now?

b. Two years from now?

c. t-years from now?

d. What happens to the value today of $1 further and further into the future?

e. The value of a given revenue stream does what (rises or falls) as the discount rate rises?

f. Does this equation allow us to compare the value of revenue streams of different time lengths?

2. It is often said that we in the United States "need" gasoline, which presumably means that we must buy the same quantity of gasoline regardless of how high price rises. What are some ways in which people could use less gas as its relative price rises?

APPENDIX

D

Discounting and Present Value

You have been introduced to the concept of discounting in this chapter. In this short appendix we show you in more detail how you can discount future costs and benefits in order to get an idea of what they are valued at today.

What is the present value of $110 to be received one year from now? That depends on the market rate of interest, or the rate of interest you could earn in some appropriate savings institution, such as a money market mutual fund. To make the arithmetic simple, let's presume that the rate of interest is 10 percent. Now you can figure out the present value, as it were, of $110 to be received one year from now. You figure it out by asking the question, "How much money must I put aside today in a money market mutual fund at the market rate of interest of 10 percent to receive $110 one year from now?" Mathematically we represent this question by the following:

$$(1 + .10)\,P_1 = \$110$$

where P_1 is the sum that you must set aside now.

Let's solve this simple equation to obtain P_1:

$$P_1 = \$110 \div 1.10 = \$100$$

That is to say, $100 will accumulate to $110 at the end of one year with a market rate of interest of 10 percent. Thus, the present value of $110 one year from now, using a rate of interest of 10 percent, is $100. The formula for present value of any sums to be received one year from now thus becomes:

$$P_1 = \frac{A_1}{(1 + i)}$$

where

P_1 = present value of a sum one year hence
A_1 = future sum of money paid or received one year hence
i = market rate of interest

Present Values for More Distant Periods

The present-value formula for figuring out today's worth of dollars to be received at a future date can now be seen easily. How much would have to be put in the same money market mutual fund today to have \$110 two years from now if the account pays a rate of 10 percent per year compounded annually.

After one year, the sum that would have to be set aside, which we will call P_2, would have grown to P_2 (1.10). This amount during the *second year* would increase to $[P_2 (1.10)] \times 1.10$, or $P_2 \times (1.10)^2$. To find the P_2 that would grow to \$110 over two years, let:

$$P_2 (1.10)^2 = \$110$$

and solve for P_2, or:

$$P_2 = \frac{\$110}{(1.10)^2}$$

which becomes:

$$P_2 = \$90.91$$

Thus, the present value of \$110 to be paid or received two years hence, discounted at an interest rate of 10 percent per year compounded annually, is equal to \$90.91. In other words, \$90.91 put into a money market mutual fund yielding 10 percent per year compounded interest would accumulate to \$110 in two years.

The general formula for discounting. The general formula for discounting becomes:

$$P_t = \frac{A_t}{(1 + i)^t}$$

where the exponent t refers to the number of years in the future the money is to be paid or received.

Exhibit D–1 gives the present value of \$1 to be received in future years for various interest rates. The interest rates that were used to derive the present value are sometimes called the rate of discount, or the *discount rate*.

EXHIBIT D–1

Present Value Table: Present Values of a Future Dollar. Each column shows how much a dollar received at the end of a certain number of years in the future (identified on the extreme left-hand or right-hand column) is worth today. For example, at 5 percent a year, a dollar to be received 20 years in the future is only worth 37.7¢. At the end of 50 years, it isn't even worth a dime today. To find out how much \$10,000 would be worth a certain number of years from now, just multiply the figures in the columns by 10,000. For example, \$10,000 received at the end of ten years discounted at a 5 percent rate of interest would have a present value of \$6,140.

Year	*3%*	*4%*	*5%*	*6%*	*8%*	*10%*	*20%*	*Year*
1	.971	.962	.952	.943	.926	.909	.833	1
2	.943	.925	.907	.890	.857	.826	.694	2
3	.915	.890	.864	.839	.794	.751	.578	3
4	.889	.855	.823	.792	.735	.683	.482	4
5	.863	.823	.784	.747	.681	.620	.402	5
6	.838	.790	.746	.705	.630	.564	.335	6
7	.813	.760	.711	.665	.583	.513	.279	7
8	.789	.731	.677	.627	.540	.466	.233	8
9	.766	.703	.645	.591	.500	.424	.194	9
10	.744	.676	.614	.558	.463	.385	.162	10
11	.722	.650	.585	.526	.429	.350	.134	11
12	.701	.625	.557	.497	.397	.318	.112	12
13	.681	.601	.530	.468	.368	.289	.0935	13
14	.661	.577	.505	.442	.340	.263	.0779	14
15	.642	.555	.481	.417	.315	.239	.0649	15
16	.623	.534	.458	.393	.292	.217	.0541	16
17	.605	.513	.436	.371	.270	.197	.0451	17
18	.587	.494	.416	.350	.250	.179	.0376	18
19	.570	.475	.396	.330	.232	.163	.0313	19
20	.554	.456	.377	.311	.215	.148	.0261	20
25	.478	.375	.295	.232	.146	.0923	.0105	25
30	.412	.308	.231	.174	.0994	.0573	.00421	30
40	.307	.208	.142	.0972	.0460	.0221	.000680	40
50	.228	.141	.087	.0543	.0213	.00852	.000109	50

20
Population Economics

TOPICS FOR REVIEW

The topics listed below, which we have already analyzed, are applied in this chapter. You may find it worthwhile to review them. For your convenience each topic is followed by the number identifying the specific "Concepts in Brief."

a. Opportunity cost (1–2)

b. Specialization (1–4)

FOR PREVIEW AND STUDY

1. What are the basic arithmetic tools of population analysis?
2. What has been happening to the doubling time of world population?
3. Are *all* countries concerned about overpopulation?
4. What are the typical stages of population growth?
5. It is often said that population and pollution are directly related. Are they?

It seems like every few decades or so, there is an increased discussion about a population explosion. In the United States, the last wave of such discussions occurred in the 1960s. At that time, numerous books and articles, including some multimillion bestsellers, told us that the world would come to an end if we didn't cut back on the growth of population. And at that time a new movement for zero population growth (ZPG) was started.

Today, the fervor over the so-called population explosion has not died out completely, but it is certainly less in evidence. In order to understand any of the arguments concerning population, you need to understand first the arithmetic of population economics. That's where we'll start our study of population. We'll see how demographers—those people who study population—measure trends in population growth. We'll also look at the economic variables that determine fertility and mortality. By so doing, we will be better equipped to analyze the arguments presented by those who advocate zero population growth. Although today few writers are arguing for ZPG, it is still an important topic.

EXHIBIT 20–1

Birth and Death Rates and the Rate of Increase of Population for Selected Countries. Column 2 shows the crude birth rate per 1,000 people per year in each of these countries. Column 3 shows the crude death rate, per 1,000 people per year. Column 4 is the difference between the crude birth rate and the crude death rate, divided by 10. It represents the percentage annual rate of change per year of population (ignoring migration).

Country	*Crude Birth Rate (1000/yr)*	*Crude Death Rate (1000/yr)*	*Rate of Increase (percent/yr)*
United States	13.2	9.2	.40
Canada	14.1	7.5	.66
Denmark	14.2	10.2	.40
France	14.7	10.6	.41
Germany— East	11.9	13.0	−.11
Iceland	20.0	7.1	1.29
Israel	26.1	7.4	1.87
Japan	11.1	6.7	.44
Mexico	37.2	8.8	2.84
Pakistan	48.4	17.1	3.13
Poland	16.4	7.9	.85
Sweden	12.4	10.2	.22
U.S.S.R.	17.2	9.9	.73
Venezuela	38.4	7.6	3.08

Source: Statistical Office of the United Nations, 1980.

The Arithmetic of Population Growth

Demographers look at the difference between birth rates and death rates. They calculate for a given country and a given year what is called the **crude birth rate**—the number of babies born per 1,000 people in the population per year. Then they look at the **crude death rate,** which is the number of deaths per 1,000 people in the population per year. When we subtract the crude death rate from the crude birth rate, we obtain the net change in population per 1,000 people for that year. If we divide that by 10, we get the result as a percentage, and we have the annual **rate of population growth** (assuming net immigration equals zero). Let's look at a few examples. In Exhibit 20–1, we list the crude death rates and the crude birth rates for several countries. When the difference is divided by 10, we find that the rate of increase of population in these countries varies from a high of 3.13 percent per year in Pakistan to a low of −.11 percent per year in East Germany.

DOUBLING TIME

Population experts translate rates of population growth per year into what is called the **doubling time.** To take a specific example, if the population of Denmark is growing at .4 percent a year, how many years will it take for the population to double? In the case of Denmark, it would take almost 175 years!

In Exhibit 20–2, we see the doubling time at current rates of growth for the populations of the countries in Exhibit 20–1. A good rule of thumb to use to estimate the doubling time is the *rule of 72.* If you divide the annual rate of increase in population into 72 percent, you get an approximate doubling time. In our example of Denmark, the growth rate of population is .4 percent a year. Thus, 72 percent divided by .4 equals 180 years, just about the figure we got before.

Doubling times are fascinating (and often misleading) numbers because if we extend them indefinitely into the future, we find that the population of even very small Latin American countries will increase until there are so many people there will no longer be a place to walk. The countries literally will be covered with people. Even if the doubling time is 175 years, as in Denmark, if you extend that rate of growth far enough into the future, the result is one horrendously large number. Confining our analysis or our projections only to arithmetic, like

EXHIBIT 20–2
The Doubling Time for Selected Countries' Populations. Here we show how many years it takes for each country's population to double at current growth rates (ignoring migration). The range is enormous, from Pakistan's 23 years to Sweden's 327 years.

Country	*Doubling Time*
United States	180
Canada	109
Denmark	180
France	176
Iceland	56
Israel	38
Japan	164
Mexico	25
Pakistan	23
Poland	85
Sweden	327
U.S.S.R.	99
Venezuela	23

Source: Statistical Office of the United Nations, 1980.

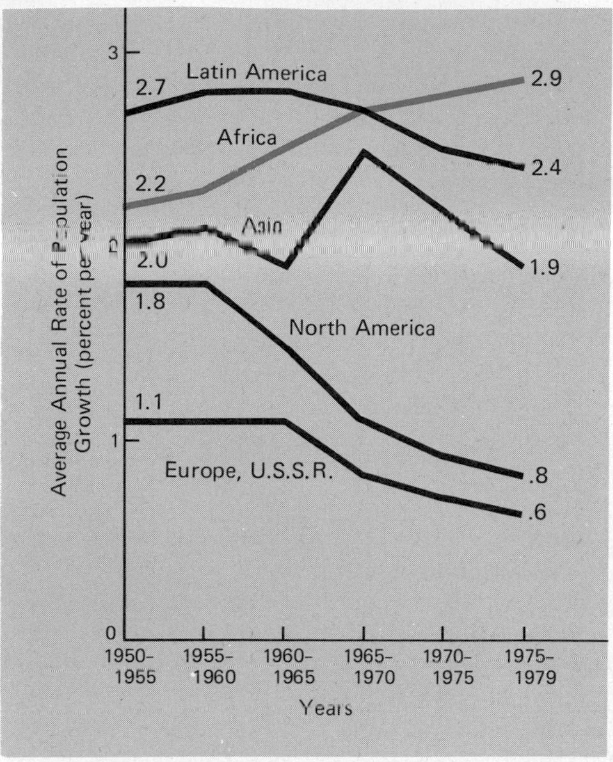

EXHIBIT 20–3
Annual Average Rates of Population Growth. In this diagram, we show that the annual average rates of population growth for most of the world have fallen since the 1950s. The only continent that has not seen this occurring is Africa, where average population growth rates have increased from 2.2 percent per year to 2.9 percent per year over a two-decade period. This represents over a 30 percent increase in the rate of growth of population.

Source: United Nations.

doubling times, is often misleading. We tend to overlook the fact that things will usually occur to prevent sustained catastrophic increases in population in specific countries. Nonetheless, simple projections using doubling times have caused large numbers of people to be concerned about the future population size in this country and elsewhere. For example, those who favor zero population growth are adamant about the necessity of limiting the number of births, not only in countries where the populations are unbelievably dense, as in Hong Kong, but also in countries where population is much less dense.

NET REPRODUCTION RATE

Demographers also talk in terms of the **net reproduction rate.** This rate is calculated on the basis of the total number of female children born to every thousand mothers during their childbearing years. If the average mother has exactly one daughter in her lifetime (1,000 have 1,000), then the net reproduction rate will be exactly 1. What do you think will happen to the population? It will eventually stabilize (assuming life expectancy doesn't change). If mothers tend to have more than one daughter throughout their childbearing years, then the net reproduction rate will be in excess of 1 and the population will grow.

The Population Bomb's Fuse Is Burning at a Slower Rate

If we look at population growth statistics throughout the world, we find that in many countries population growth rates have slowed. Indeed, from the middle of the last decade to the beginning of this decade, population in Switzerland, West Germany, Austria, and Great Britain actually fell. In Belgium, Denmark, Sweden, and France, it did not even rise 2 percent from the beginning to the end of that period. What has happened is that birth rates have fallen. Look at Exhibit 20–3. Here we see that population growth rates in Latin America, North America, Europe, and the U.S.S.R. have fallen from

1950 to the present. Even in Asia, where there was an abrupt increase in the 1960s, the population growth rate at the end of the 1970s was less than it was at the beginning of the 1950s. Only Africa has shown a consistent increase in its population growth rate.

SOCIOECONOMIC PROBLEMS OF FALLING BIRTH RATES

Strange as it may seem, falling birth rates, and hence actual or projected reductions in population, have created concerns in those countries about their economic, social, and military future. Some of these concerns are:

1. Fewer workers will be available to support a greater number of retirees.
2. Industries catering to children will lose their customers.
3. Declining school enrollments will provide fewer teaching jobs.
4. The military force will not have "sufficient" young personnel.

Concepts in Brief 20-1

- The crude birth rate is the number of babies born per 1,000 people per year.
- The crude death rate is the number of deaths per 1,000 people per year.
- The annual percentage rate of population growth is the arithmetic difference between the crude death rate and the crude birth rate divided by 10.
- The arithmetic doubling time for a nation's population is approximately equal to the annual percentage rate of population growth divided into 72 percent.
- The net reproduction rate is based on the lifetime number of female babies born to every 1,000 average mothers throughout their childbearing years. When the net reproduction rate is 1 (1,000 female babies for 1,000 mothers), the annual percentage rate of population growth will be zero. When the net reproduction rate is below 1, the population will eventually decline.
- The annual average rates of population growth throughout the world have dropped rather dramatically since the 1950s. The only exception is Africa, where the annual rate of population growth has increased by 30 percent in two decades.

Where the People Are

Until recently, most population growth has occurred in relatively dense urban environments. In other words, even if we were witnessing rapid population growth, that would not mean that the countrysides were filling in with people. Rather, the urban areas would tend to become more crowded. Historically, we find that people have moved to where the jobs were. Jobs were usually in ports or locations with many natural resources. After transportation became relatively cheap, other geographical locations became centers of economic activity. One factor that determines where people will move to, even when transportation becomes cheap, is income. And individuals working in cities earn higher incomes than those working in rural areas. Hence, population has tended *until the 1970s* to increase in our major urban centers. Recently population has shifted out of the Northeast to the South and to the West. The South and the West have more agreeable climates.

If people did not benefit from living in large cities, there would probably be a much more even population distribution throughout our entire land area. Presumably, if this were the case, there would be less concern over population explosion. Indeed, one need only take a cross-country drive or plane trip to realize how sparsely populated these United States really are. This is not to say that we should or should *not* do something about population growth. The paucity of people in certain areas merely demonstrates that overpopulation in the United States is really only a problem in overcrowded urban environments.[1] And this problem may be slowly correcting itself.

The Population Curve

If we were to examine population growth in other animal species, we would find that there are natural limits to the total population of a particular species. An experiment can be run with a pair of willing fruit flies in a small enclosure. At first, the population grows by leaps and bounds. It increases at a geometric rate: first 2, then 4, then 8, then 16, and so on. If this geometric progression of the fruit

[1] This last statement is *not true* for most of Asia, however. Also, some Africans consider their continent underpopulated even though they have high and increasing birth rates.

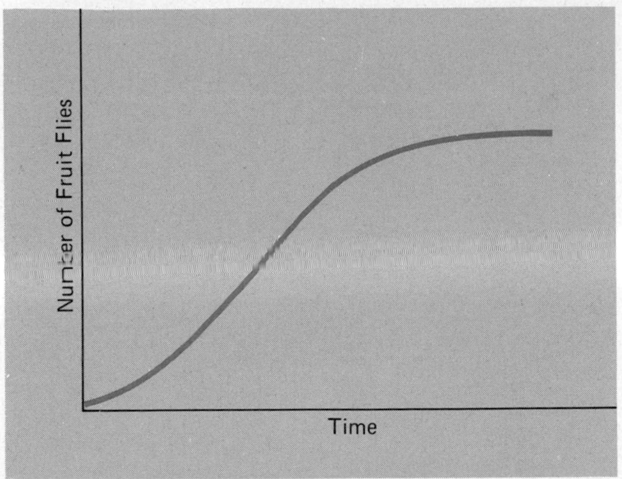

EXHIBIT 20–4
Curve for Fruit Fly Population. The population of fruit flies in a container might grow very rapidly at first, but it will level off and reach its natural limit at some specific number. The growth in population looks like an S-curve, as depicted in this diagram.

fly population were extended way into the future, we would find that their mass would eventually overcome the earth. However, this geometric growth rate does not continue indefinitely. Eventually the growth rate diminishes because there aren't enough resources to sustain it.

In our particular example, one resource that holds the fruit flies back is the size of the container. For other populations, it might be the food supply. In any event, reproduction slows down, and at some point a ceiling is reached. The growth curve for the fruit fly population in our container can be plotted as an S, as shown in Exhibit 20–4. The ceiling is called the *natural population limit.* It is determined by the supply of the resources that are needed for survival.

Can the S-curve presented in Exhibit 20–4 be considered an accurate representation of what will happen to population in the world? During the 1960s and 1970s, numerous studies attempted to show that the S-curve had gone awry. It was simply continuing to rise rather than flatten out as is shown in the right-hand part of Exhibit 20–4. It is true that doubling time for the world has fallen from 2,000 years to 1,000 years to 500 years. But in the 1960s, it was 35 years. In the beginning of the 1980s, it was up to over 40 years. In other words, population growth has slowed.

Moreover, we know that there has to be a ceiling somewhere. One famous economist characterized the earth as a spaceship. It can hold only so many people because it has a fixed amount of space and a fixed number of resources. Population obviously cannot continue to grow forever (unless we migrate to other planets). It has only been since the 1700s that world population has grown at a much more rapid pace than it did on average during the previous thousands and thousands of years.

In any event, recent evidence about world population growth does seem to give hope that we are reaching a natural limit, as it were, and that the population bomb will indeed not explode. Go back and look at Exhibit 20–3. There you see that only the African countries, on average, are experiencing an increase in the rate of population growth. Practically everywhere else in the world, there have been significant decreases in the annual percentage rate of growth of the population.

A MODEL OF POPULATION TRANSITION

In this section we would like to present a simple model of population transition in which a society experiences a movement from a very low level of population to a relatively high and stable level of population. There are three phases of population growth, each characterized by different crude birth rates and different crude death rates.

Phase 1

In the underdeveloped or preindustrial society, both crude birth rates and crude death rates are very high. But since they are both high, the rate of population growth remains relatively low.

Phase 2

As a society experiences economic development, per capita income starts rising. The World Health Organization (WHO) attributes phase 2 to the availability, use, and low cost of certain vaccines, and to the development of mass low-cost techniques used for the elimination of major diseases, such as malaria, that do *not* depend on individual education, literacy, or personal hygiene. After all, notions of medical care, nutrition, and hygiene are *culturally* rooted and are not necessarily the same as those used in most Western countries. For example, after World War II, WHO developed a program to eradicate certain diseases. The eradication of those dis-

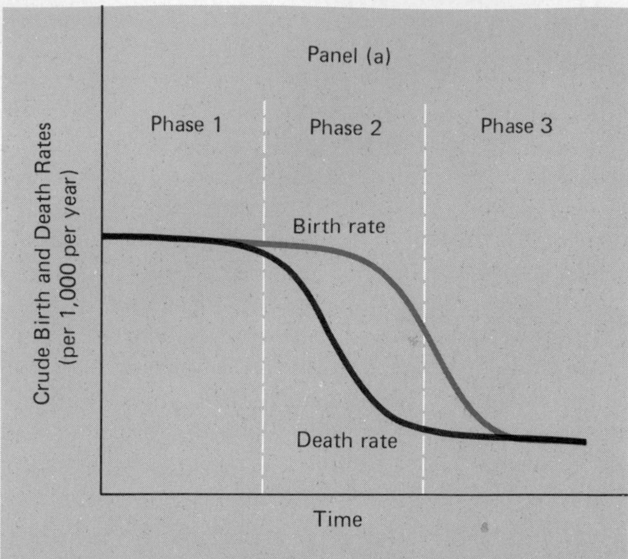

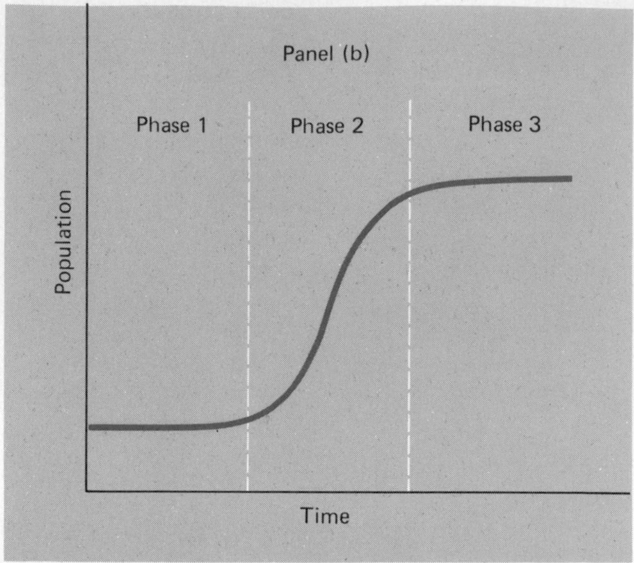

EXHIBIT 20–5

The Stages of Population Growth. In panel (a), we show the crude birth and death rates. In phase 1 for underdeveloped countries, the crude birth rate is extremely high, but so, too, is the crude death rate. Therefore, we see in panel (b) that population remains stable during phase 1. During phase 2, because of medical advances and increases in knowledge about health and nutrition, the crude death rate falls, but the crude birth rate remains relatively high. Thus, we see in panel (b) that the population grows rapidly during phase 2. Finally, we stabilize when birth rates fall to match death rates. This is shown in phase 3 in both panels (a) and (b). In panel (b), population stabilizes again but at a higher level.

eases has been correlated with the "population boom."

In any event, the result of a reduction in crude death rates does nothing to alter the crude birth rate. Hence, the difference between the crude birth rate and the crude death rate widens. The result is a relatively high rate of population growth that may last for many years.

Phase 3

When a country becomes highly developed and/or concerned about population growth, it may expend resources on controlling the population. This has occurred, for example, with great success in Japan. And, households may desire fewer children because of a lowered mortality rate for them. Also, as income rises, people decide to have fewer children because, for one thing, the opportunity cost of time spent raising children rises. Furthermore, the opportunity cost of spending time with your children may also involve foregone consumption, since the richer a household is, the more consumption possibilities there are, such as travel and entertainment. Time spent with children takes away from time that can be spent on travel and entertainment. Now the crude birth rate falls to a level more in line with the crude death rate. The rate of population growth slows down. In principle, it could even be lower than it was in phase 1 (or negative), depending on how effective birth control is.

Graphic Analysis

In panels (a) and (b) of Exhibit 20–5, we see the hypothetical phases of population growth. Phase 1 is where the crude death rate is high and so is the crude birth rate. This results in no population growth, so that in panel (b) we see a flat population size during phase 1. Phase 2 is where the crude death rate falls dramatically but the crude birth rate doesn't fall as rapidly. This results in a dramatic jump in the population size, as seen in panel (b). Finally, in phase 3, the crude birth rate comes down in line with the crude death rate. Population size stabilizes in our example, as shown in panel (b). To be sure, Exhibit 20–5 is an oversimplification. It does show, however, the effects of "death" and birth control when they are introduced at different times or with different degrees of success. Phase 3 in Exhibit 20–5(b) could point steadily down if birth control were even more effective than shown.

Concepts in Brief 20-2

- Most population growth, at least in Western countries, has been in large urban centers (though this is now changing).
- If we plot the population growth of animal species in a particular geographic region, we find that population at first grows by leaps and bounds and then slows down, eventually remaining stable. This has been called the population S-curve because of its shape.
- The ceiling on the population S-curve is called the natural population limit.
- Until about the seventeenth century, the world rate of population growth was relatively small. Since that time we have moved up the S-curve. Recently, though, the rate of population growth has slowed down.
- One of the main reasons that population growth rates had increased in the world has been our success at reducing the crude death rate without reducing birth rates.
- There are three population phases: (1) a stable population when crude birth rates are high but so, too, are crude death rates; (2) a rapid increase in population because modern medicine and health knowledge reduce the crude death rate while the crude birth rate continues at a relatively high level; and (3) a stable population when, through birth control techniques, the crude birth rate falls to a level in line with the crude death rate.

Birth Control

Even before the advent of modern birth control techniques, couples had ways to determine the number of children they would have. Also, when marriage occurs at a later age, the birth rate will be lower. Celibacy, of course, is always an effective method of birth control, and it doesn't require modern techniques.

In any event, economists have found that fertility rates or birth rates can be explained by a number of economic variables. This is especially true in Western countries, where birth control is widely practiced and relatively inexpensive. The more inexpensive birth control methods become, the fewer unwanted babies there will be. We might discover how couples decide how many offspring they want by looking at children from an economic vantage point.

Investing in Children

If we treat children as an investment, the rate of return on that investment will most likely be an important determinant of how many children are desired. This is especially true for agricultural societies where children become productive members of the family at a very young age. In the past, it was not uncommon for 5- and 6-year-old children to be picking cotton, olives, grapes, or strawberries on the family farm (or elsewhere for hire). Most probably, the higher the relative price of the farm products, the more farm babies were desired, because the rate of return on children would have been higher—that is, the value of their marginal physical product would have been higher.

It is not quite so appropriate now, however, to consider children as an investment (at least in the United States). Some parents do, nonetheless, get a return on their "investment" later in life when their retirement is supplemented by their chilren. This is increasingly rare, however, because of Social Security and other retirement plans.

CHILDREN AS CONSUMPTION

It might be more appropriate to consider children as a consumption good. We would expect, therefore, that the normal determinants of the quantity demanded would prevail. What are those determinants? In the main, they are the price of the good and the income of the demander. As with other commodities that people value, the demand curve will have a negative slope—the higher the price of raising children, the lower the quantity demanded.

Although the income elasticity of demand will be positive, it may be less than unity. As real incomes go up, the quantity of children demanded may or may not go up in proportion. In any event, we can estimate the cost of raising children, and this is exactly what the Insurance Institute of America has done.

COST OF CHILDREN

Surprising as it may seem, the cost of raising children through college has risen to over $100,000 per child (undiscounted). This means that over $100,000 in income that the parents could have used in other ways will be used instead to raise the child. This does not indicate the total cost of raising children, however, as any parent can testify.

There is a tremendous time cost involved. The higher the wage rate that a parent makes, the higher the opportunity cost of time devoted to a child. This is perhaps where the term *a millionaire's family* comes from. The millionaire's family is one boy and one girl—only two children. It becomes very expensive in terms of opportunity cost for the high-income individual to have more children. The opportunity cost of spending time with one's children—playing baseball, going to the movies—is the amount of income one could have earned using this time to work. Alternatively, instead of spending time taking care of one's children, one can engage in other consumption activities. Richer individuals have more income to spend on consumption activities, such as travel and entertainment. Therefore, the opportunity cost of spending time with children for richer individuals is greater than for poorer individuals.

Given the rapidly rising cost of higher education and the larger and larger portion of young people attending college, one would expect that, other things being equal, the number of children desired would fall. For this and for some other reasons, the net reproduction rate in the United States has done just that. In the long run, our current reproduction trend may lead to below ZPG.

The Economic and Social Consequences of ZPG

Zero population growth advocates believe that the only way to prevent increasing amounts of pollution (and perhaps stave off resource depletion) is to check our rapidly growing population. In fact, some maintain that the underlying cause of pollution is too large a population. In a ZPG ad appearing in a major magazine, the assertion was made that if we stabilize our population we will have "Clear skies. Clean water." There is a problem with this line of reasoning. It is possible to have the same or greater levels of pollution even with a smaller population. Consider the following world:

1. Pollution is a constant function of output.
2. The population has decreased.
3. Total output increases, that is, per capita output rises faster than the number of "capitas" falls (we get richer and richer).

In such a hypothetical situation, assuming no change in our current set of institutions—property laws, pricing systems, and so on—we could conceivably experience the same or even higher levels of pollution, depending on how much total output there was. This leads us to conclude that the problems of despoiling our environment are not uniquely tied up with the problems of overpopulation, although certainly less population could help reduce future pollution levels. Much of the problem of pollution is due to the fact that no individual clearly owns natural resources such as air and water. In other words, there is a common property problem. It is perhaps misguided, then, to think that without solving the common property problem, or the problem of equating social costs and private costs, the reduction in population growth will somehow create a cleaner environment. In fact, we would imagine that if property rights became more indefinite, we could have more pollution with a smaller population, even if income fell. (Of course, if property rights and real output remain unchanged and the population continues to grow, we will likely have more pollution.)

CROWDING

One of the inevitable consequences of the population explosion is overcrowding. In fact, all you need do is try to get to work on the subway at 8 A.M. in New York City to find out what crowding is, or travel to Hong Kong to see how closely people can pack themselves into a restricted space. But are these really the problems of overpopulation looked at alone?

The population density per square mile in the United States is quite small relative to other countries. Does the United States, then, face a problem of overcrowding due to a population explosion? No. The United States faces a problem of too many people in too concentrated an area. That is, we find that 96 percent of the people live on only 2 percent of the available land. We know, of course, that lots of the land in the United States is "uninhabitable." But still, much land is left that generally does not have people living on it. Perhaps, instead of attempting to control the population, we should consider attempting to control its location to reduce overcrowding in big cities.

Big cities are crowded despite the supposed horrendous distresses created by them. Of course, when you think about it, it should not be too surprising. *Specialization is a function of the size of the market.* How many baseball teams, football teams, operas, symphonies, and playhouses can be supported in small rural towns? Even when you go to a relatively large city, you cannot always find what you want in terms of entertainment and cultural activity. Seattle is one of the largest cities in the United States, but the variety of cultural activities available to its inhabitants is small relative to what is available in, say, New York City. This may explain why people like to live in New York City despite the tremendous cost of doing so. The benefits are also tremendous—thousands of restaurants, hundreds of theaters, and everything else imaginable that one might want to do.

AN UNEXPECTED RESULT OF ZPG —A GERIATRIC POPULATION

If we accept the premises of zero population growth advocates, then our population should indeed stabilize. If we accept some of the more radical suggestions, such as the one that Paul Ehrlich made in a *Playboy* magazine interview some years back, then we should have a net reproduction rate of less than 1 so that population will decline to about 50 million people in the United States. A transitional consequence of either course on the age structure of the population is a little-talked-about and less-understood aspect of population control. It is important, nonetheless.

Right now, the median age in the United States is 30. As the population growth rate increases, the median age falls, as you would expect. However, if we were to go to a stable population, the median age would jump by about 10 years. That is, it would lie somewhere around 40. Some demographers estimate that it would be 37. There would be an aging of the population, and if we were to go from our current 200 million plus to Ehrlich's desired 50 million, the age distribution of the population would be skewed dramatically toward older people. That is, for several decades, the median age would go from its current 30 to 37 to 47 or even to 57, depending upon how fast we reached the magic number of 50 million. The thought of a geriatric population may be somewhat discomforting to you, but, of course, that is a noneconomic problem. In any event, we would find that there would be less chance for rapid advancement in the job market. There would be very few young people who would move up the corporate ladder as rapidly as they do now, and there would be almost no presidents of corporations in their 30s, as there are now. Everything would become much more stabilized in terms of job advancement. Perhaps the benefits from population stabilization or reduction would be worth the costs. But in any event, the costs would be there, and there would be no way to avoid them. The age structure of the population must change; it's an arithmetic certainty if we stabilize the population.

DEPOPULATION

While the United States concerns itself with limiting population growth, other countries in the world concern themselves with how to *increase* population growth. Believe it or not, populating—adding more people—is a problem in certain countries of the world, such as France, East Germany, Israel, and Canada.

France has had a population "problem" for many years. Various methods have been tried to increase average family size and prevent France's total population from declining. The government has even given special family allowances to encourage larger families. Family size increased for a few years after World War II and after incentives were presented to French families, but then it started to go down again. The government increased family allotments and used other monetary methods to encourage larger families. For most countries, it is frightening for many concerned citizens to think that their population size is actually getting smaller (except, of course, in India, Pakistan, and some other non-Western nations where overpopulation is truly a problem).

In any event, France's methods for increasing family size should give us a hint as to what might be done in the United States to encourage *smaller* families, if indeed that is what we want to do. Currently in the United States, there is an incentive to have larger families—a $1,000 annual exemption per dependent when paying federal income taxes. For every child in the family, the parent is allowed to exempt $1,000 from gross income before computing taxes. Obviously, eliminating this deduction would raise the price of having children.[2] And we would expect (at least on the margin) that there

[2] In general, the elimination of any subsidy given to families with children will have the same effect. For example, eliminating "free" public education would raise the cost of having children. Some might respond (on the margin) by choosing to have fewer children.

Thomas Robert Malthus

ENGLISH ECONOMIST (1766–1834)

OF POPULATION AND POVERTY

The Reverend Thomas Robert Malthus was Britain's first professional political economist. The son of well-to-do parents, Malthus was a man of the cloth for a brief period but spent most of his career as a professor at the East India Company College. He mingled with the leading English economists James Mill and David Ricardo, wrote an important text, *Principles of Political Economy* (1820), and made the first attempt to sketch a theory of effective demand, which Keynes would develop a century later.

Malthus's real significance for economic thought, however, rests on a pamphlet, first published anonymously in 1798, in which he summarized his disagreement with his father over the possibility of a society free from want. In *An Essay on the Principle of Population as It Affects the Future Improvement of Society,* Malthus argued that not utopia but continual misery would be the lot of much of civilization. Population rose at a geometric rate, he said, but the food supply increased merely arithmetically, because cultivatable land could only be slowly added to. Thus, more and more people, if not killed by the "vices of mankind" (murder, war, and the like) or by plague and pestilence, would simply starve to death.

Because poverty was essentially a problem of nature, Malthus went on to argue, the upper classes were not responsible for the lot of the poor, and, therefore, the poor had no claim on them for relief. Providing relief or granting higher wages would only encourage the poor to breed more, increasing their misery, and thus would not be in their own or in society's best interests. Instead, mortality among the poorer classes should actually be encouraged.

The poor were doomed, according to Malthus, and could only ameliorate their misery by practicing "moral restraint" (abstinence). Malthus opposed all other forms of birth control. "I should particularly reprobate any artificial and unnatural modes of checking population," he wrote in the 1817 edition of his essay, "both on account of their immorality and their tendency to remove a necessary stimulus to industry." Like many others of his day, Malthus believed misery a necessary goad to hard labor; if the poor restricted their numbers too much, they could command higher wages and might become indolent from lack of misery, undercutting the business profits of their more comfortable brethren.

Many readers have found Malthus's views on relief as abhorrent as they have feared the truth of his prophecies about population and food supply. But so far those prophecies, at least for the industrialized West, have turned out to be ill-founded. Population has grown at a slower rate than Malthus projected. Rising living standards associated with the Industrial Revolution have caused birth rates to drop (not rise, as Malthus assumed); individuals marry later, practice more birth control, and have fewer children. Malthus also didn't recognize that the agricultural yield of land could be increased many times over by modern methods of farming. Thus, many critics of Malthus have argued that present-day famine is not a consequence of overpopulation but of maldistribution, because the wealthy "control" the technology and enough food resources to feed everyone. Still, the specter of population outrunning food supply on a world scale is hard to dispel completely. With Malthus, the English essayist Thomas Carlyle remarked after reading his work, economics had become "the dismal science."

would be fewer children born because of the increase. Perhaps zero population growth sympathizers might suggest this as a start toward finding out what the natural population growth rate in the United States would be without any special inducements. It may turn out that there is no need to worry about a population explosion because the natural net reproduction rate is 1.

Concepts in Brief 20-3

- It is possible to view the decision to have children from an economic perspective. If we treat children as an investment, the net rate of return (after all costs are considered) will be a determinant of how many children are desired. In agricultural societies, children can be viewed as an investment because they start to work at a very young age.
- In modern industrial societies, children are perhaps better viewed as a consumption good.
- As with any consumption good, other things being equal, the greater the price, the lower the quantity demanded.
- One important cost of raising children is the opportunity cost of time spent parenting. As families become richer, the opportunity cost to the parents rises and, hence, other things being equal, fewer children will be desired.
- It is often argued that zero population growth would lead to less pollution. Other things being equal, this is true; but given our current set of legal institutions and property rights, pollution may be more a function of how much we produce and consume.
- Population concentration has its benefits, for specialization is a function of the size of the market. Individuals living in densely populated cities can choose from a larger array of consumer goods and entertainment possibilities than those living in small towns.

ISSUES AND APPLICATIONS

Was Malthus Right?

Concepts Applied

- Diminishing marginal returns, crude birth rate, crude death rate, and natural rate of population growth

In 1798, a little-known English minister named Thomas Robert Malthus published *An Essay on the Principle of Population, as It Affects the Future Improvement of Society*. The uncomfortable and, indeed, depressing conclusion of that 50,000-word treatise was that "population, when unchecked, goes on doubling every 24 years or increases in the geometric ratio," while, according to Reverend Malthus, food production—or more generally, the means of subsistence—only increases at an arithmetic ratio. We can see what Malthus meant about geometric as opposed to arithmetic rates by looking at Exhibit 20–6. Here the white line represents something—say, population—rising at a geometric rate. Notice that it starts slowly and then gradually gets steeper and steeper. Compare this with the black line, which represents, say, food growing at an arithmetic rate. It remains equally steep throughout its path.

In 1803, Malthus put out a second edition of his now famous essay on population. Instead of talking about population increasing at a geometric ratio, he indicated that the human species was destined to poverty and a life of misery unless the rate of population growth was retarded by **positive checks** and/or **preventive checks.** He listed as preventives such things as late marriages or no marriage at all, sexual abstinence, and moral restraint. Malthus put much more faith in such "positive" checks as wars, pestilence, and famine. (Preventive checks decrease the birth rate, and positive checks increase the death rate.)

As you can imagine, Malthus was criticized severely. His fellow clergymen thought he was crazy; politicians and journalists called him a heretic. But others, especially a famous economist of the time named David Ricardo, made much use of the Malthusian theory. Let's delve a little more deeply into why Malthus came up with such heretical ideas. We will see that although his theories didn't describe the industrial society of his own time very well, they did do a great job of describing preindustrial Europe (and perhaps certain less-developed countries today).

In some parts of the world Malthus' predictions were fairly accurate.

A Product of Traditional Europe

Although the Reverend Malthus grew up during the Industrial Revolution, he was a product of traditional Europe—that is, preindustrial, pregrowth society. He believed that economic life depended on the productivity of land, so that ultimately it was the land that determined the level of existence.

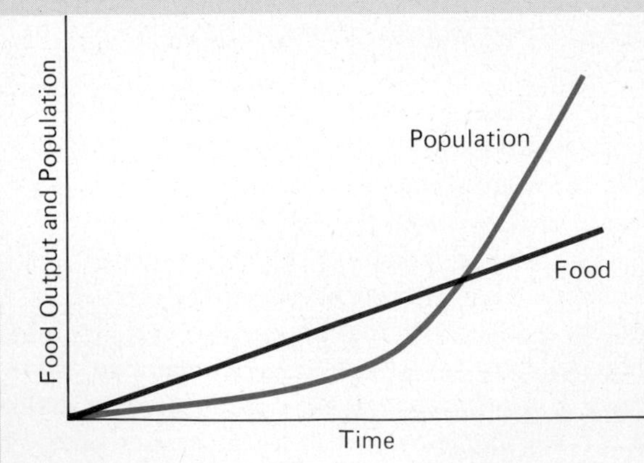

EXHIBIT 20–6
The Malthusian Dilemma. Population increases at an exponential or geometrically increasing rate, as evidenced by the blue line, whereas food production increases only linearly or arithmetically. Eventually population outstrips the food supply.

Positive checks. Malthus was convinced that the "passion between sexes" would cause men and women to breed, and as long as there was enough food around to feed a growing family, the family size would increase. We depict the Malthusian cycle, as it is called, graphically in Exhibit 20–7. Here we show the population size on the horizontal axis and the real-wage rate per family on the vertical axis. Notice here the emphasis on the word *real.* The real-wage rate is essentially the wage rate expressed in purchasing power over real goods and services. Real-wage rates—wage rates expressed in terms of purchasing power—are therefore an indication of a family's ability to purchase the things it wants. By using real-wage rates, we don't have to worry about problems of inflation, or rather, general changes in the price level. Notice that we have drawn in a heavy black line that we call subsistence. This is the so-called subsistence level of income, or real wages—the amount necessary for a family to survive. Presumably, if the family does not obtain at least this level of income, some of the children will die because the parents cannot feed or clothe them. Real wages first increase, but after diminishing returns set in, they fall. Once they fall below point *D*, widespread famines occur and there are numerous deaths in the society, according to the Malthusian doctrine. This was the period of "positive" checks—disease, famine, and wars—plus a preventive check, such as an increase in vice (including birth control!) that, according to Malthus, was degrading but resulted in fewer births.

Key assumption. The key assumption that Malthus made was that there was a fixed technology. As we said before, Malthus grew up in the Industrial Revolution, when this assumption certainly did not hold, but he was a product of an era when technology in fact had not changed very quickly. This was certainly true with agricultural societies, when technological changes were very slow. For example, English crop rotation and fertilization methods were only slowly adopted during the commercial revolution. This

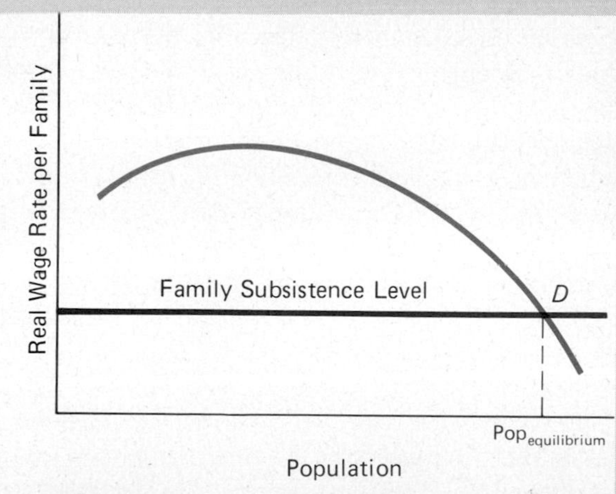

EXHIBIT 20–7
The Malthusian Cycle. Population is on the horizontal axis, and the real-wage rate, or standard of living, is on the vertical axis. The heavy horizontal line indicates the subsistence level of real wages that the family must receive to survive. Real wages per family will first increase, but after diminishing returns set in, they will fall until point *D*. Then positive checks come into account: famines, pestilence, and the like.

is one of the reasons that Malthus viewed agricultural output as growing at an arithmetic rate, instead of at a geometric rate like the population. But, according to Malthus, even if there were some once-and-for-all increase in the food base of a society, it would only lead to inexorable pressure of the population on the increased resources. He felt that when everything got sorted out, the average level of living would be just as low as it was before the great increase in the food base.

What Went Wrong?

What was wrong with Malthus's thesis was that he assumed, as we mentioned, a fixed technology. He also assumed that population size was a function only of real income, and in fact that survival rates were a function of the income level. As to the first assumption, we know that starting in the seventeenth and eighteenth centuries the technological capacity of society increased; whether it was due to the Industrial Revolution, to increased schooling of the population, or to other determinants, it did increase.

Malthus also ignored the possibility that the real wage curve in Exhibit 20–7 could rise. Look at Exhibit 20–8. Here we show three separate curves, each with a different productivity of the population. The increases in productivity that are indicated are a result of increases in technology. The real per capita income of the population can rise even though the population is growing, if the curves shift up fast enough. In this particular simplified model, there need never be a Malthusian positive check as long as the curve keeps shifting upward.

Additionally, in many situations, as real income rises, the survival rate of children may increase, but the demand for children may fall, or at least may not rise as fast as income does. Stable populations are not unknown in the world today—witness, for example, Japan. However, we do still find the Malthusian cycle acting in various less-developed countries today.

"Passion between the sexes" not the reason. Remember that Malthus maintained that passion between the sexes produced population growth at a geometric rate, whereas food production would grow only at an arithmetic rate. This isn't what has really happened in less-developed countries. In fact, the developed nations may be

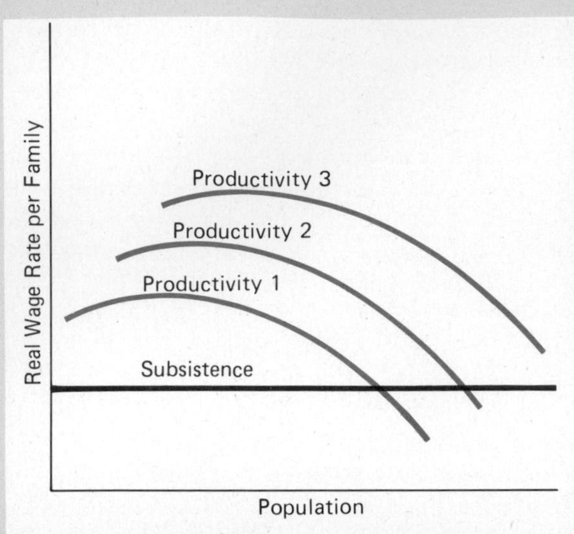

EXHIBIT 20–8
Possibility of Improved Technology. In this diagram, the curves move to the right as technology improves productivity. We labeled these curves successively Productivity 1, 2, and 3. If productivity rises fast enough, the population can grow without real wages falling to subsistence levels.

more at fault for the rapid population rise in these countries than the countries themselves. For example, in Exhibit 20–9, look at the birth rates in three selected underdeveloped countries: Mexico, Mauritius, and Barbados. The implications are clear.

The birth rate in Mexico has been steady; the one in Mauritius has started to fall, as it has in Barbados. However, the big change has been in the death rate. It has fallen dramatically and persistently since the 1930s. Obviously, if the birth rate remains fairly constant and the death rate falls, the rate of population growth is going to rise dramatically, just as it has done. Population increases of 1 percent a year were considered fairly high in years past, but today in countries like Costa Rica, Mexico, Pakistan, and Venezuela, growth rates of 3 and 4 percent a year are not uncommon. It all has to do with the improved chances of people to live a longer and healthier life. Crude death rates in some developing countries are lower than in European countries. And in a number of these developing countries, life expectancies have risen by one year or more per year for a decade. In Taiwan, for example, the life expectancy is well over 60 years for men and women. In Puerto Rico, it is over 70 for women and not much less for men! Mortality and morbidity have decreased so rapidly because public health knowledge has been imported into the Third World to eradicate disease and pestilence. Also, developed countries have exported their knowledge of nutrition.

Falling mortality rate a mixed blessing. In other words, developed countries have transmitted their health technology to less-developed countries. Consequently, less-developed countries now have more healthful living environments and better medical treatment for those in need of it. Fewer babies die at birth, and fewer individuals die at an early age in less-developed countries now. The crude death rate therefore has fallen because of our humanitarian assistance to these countries. The result, given little reduction in birth rates, is a population boom in many of these countries. In other words, a falling mortality rate due to improved health and medical conditions has been a mixed blessing to these countries.

Breaking Out of the Malthusian Cycle

There is no question as to what developing countries must do to raise the per capita standard of living at a faster rate than currently. (Since population is growing just as fast as output in *some* of these countries, the real per capita income is essentially standing still.) We can hardly suggest that crude death rates be allowed to rise again, so there is only one variable left to change, and that is the birth rate. Fertility among underdeveloped populations must fall. We are all aware of how this can be accomplished: later marriages, more widespread use of birth control techniques, subsidizing legalized abortion—in short, whatever available birth reduction techniques a country is willing to use. The results of such techniques are indeed amazing. In Hong Kong and Singapore, crude birth rates per 1,000 fell from 36 and 38.7 respectively in 1960 to 24.9 and 29.9 in 1966. That is an amazing reduction, probably unprecedented in the history of modern times. Another country that has been successful in reducing its birth rate is Japan. At the moment, the net reproduction rate in Japan is less than unity. In other words, eventually, if nothing changes in that society, its population will contract.

The conclusion: Reducing birth rates and,

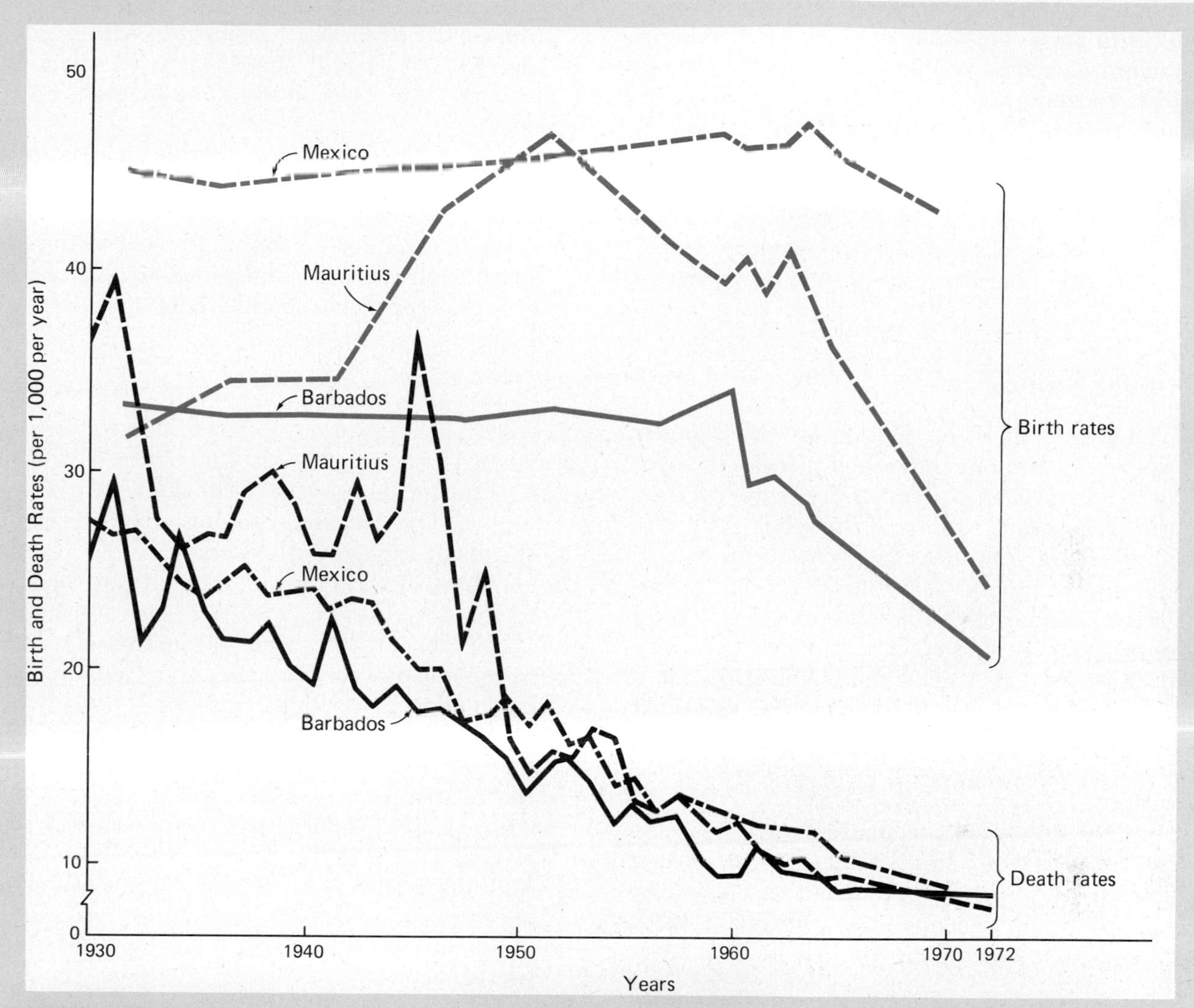

EXHIBIT 20–9

Death Rates Fall Dramatically in Three Selected Underdeveloped Countries. Although the birth rates in Mexico, Mauritius, and Barbados have remained constant or fallen slightly, the dramatic change has been in death rates, which have fallen since the 1930s in all these countries. This has caused a widening gap between birth and death rates, and thus higher rates of growth in population.

Source: Statistical Office of the United Nations.

hence, reducing the population growth rate is medically and technically possible now for many, if not all, developing nations. The implementation of the necessary policies is up to them. Cultural and religious convictions may, however, impede progress in this area.

Questions

1. What does the concept of diminishing returns have to do with the Malthusian theory of population growth?
2. If a tax were put on children, would this have any effect on the rate of population growth?

Definition of Terms

Crude birth rate The number of births per 1,000 people in the population per year.

Crude death rate The number of deaths per 1,000 people in the population per year.

Rate of population growth The crude birth rate minus the crude death rate divided by 10.

Doubling time The number of years it takes a quantity, such as population, to double, assuming a constant rate of increase. We calculate the approximate doubling time by using the rule of 72, or doubling time = 72 percent ÷ rate of growth.

Net reproduction rate The long-run growth rate of population measured as the average number of daughters born to each female over her lifetime.

Positive checks According to Malthus, these were the necessary checks on population growth that came about whenever the subsistence level of living was reached. These included famines, plagues, and other things that increase death rates.

Preventive checks These, according to Malthus, involved abstinence, late marriage, and other actions that would prevent population from outstripping the food supply. Preventive checks lower birth rates. If enough preventive checks were taken, positive checks would not occur.

Chapter Summary

1. The arithmetic of population growth is rather simple. To find out the rate of increase in population per year in percentage terms, we subtract the crude death rate from the crude birth rate and divide by 10. We can translate the rate of increase in population into a doubling time, which is equal to the number of years it takes the population to double.
2. The easiest way to find the doubling time of a population is to use the rule of 72. We divide the annual percentage rate of increase of population into 72 percent and get an approximate doubling time.
3. Another important population statistic is the net reproduction rate. When it is equal to 1, it means that, on average, one mother has one female child and the population will remain stable.
4. Although population growth used to be greatest in major cities, in the last decade smaller cities have been growing faster.
5. Although animal species reach a natural population limit, human beings apparently have not reached one yet. The S-curve of population growth has turned out to be an incorrect predictor of human population. One of the reasons is the drastic increase in technology which prevents the premature death of human beings.
6. We might explain fertility rates using economic variables. The children in agricultural societies can be looked at as an investment because by the age of 5 or 6 they become productive. However, in an industrial society such as ours, children are much more a consumption item.
7. Like any other consumption item, the demand for children should be a function of income and the relative cost of raising them. The relative cost of raising children has been increasing rapidly.
8. Malthus predicted that food supply would be outstripped by population because the latter grows geometrically while the former grows arithmetically.
9. Changing technology, however, has caused the population to be more productive; thus, for many countries, population growth has not been outstripping food production.

Selected References

Brown, Lester R. *In the Human Interest: A Strategy to Stabilize World Population.* Elmsford, N.Y.: Pergamon Press, 1976.

Easterlin, Richard A., ed. *Population and Economic Change in Developing Countries.* Chicago: University of Chicago Press, 1980.

Simon, Julian L. *The Economics of Population Growth.* Princeton, N.J.: Princeton University Press, 1977.

———, ed. *Research in Population Economics,* Vol. 2. New Haven, Connecticut: JAI Press, 1980.

Answers to Preview and Study Questions

1. What are the basic arithmetic tools of population analysis?

The basic arithmetic tools used by demographers include the crude birth rate (the number of babies born per 1,000 people per year), the crude death rate (the number of deaths per 1,000 people per year), the rate of population growth (crude birth rate minus crude death rate divided by 10, assuming zero net immigration), and the net reproduction rate (the number of female children born per 1,000 mothers over their child-bearing years).

2. What has been happening to the doubling time of world population?

World doubling time has shrunk dramatically (that is, population growth has increased dramatically) over the past few centuries. It has fallen from 2,000 years to 1,000 years to 500 years. In the 1960s it fell to 35 years! However, in the early 1980s this trend may be reversing; doubling time is now slightly over 40 years. The dramatic shortening of doubling time has been due primarily to reductions in the crude death rate resulting from improved living standards and health care. It is believed that in recent years crude birth rates have been declining to match this phenomenon.

3. Are *all* countries concerned about overpopulation?

Surprisingly, the world goes through periodic waves of concern about overpopulation *and* underpopulation! Even today, some nations are concerned with populations that are too large—while other nations fear underpopulation. For instance, France, Canada, Israel, East and West Germany, some Arab nations, and many African nations are concerned about underpopulation. Their reasons are diverse, but they include fears about sufficient military personnel, labor shortages (skilled *and* unskilled), shrinking labor markets to support retirees, and so on.

4. What are the typical stages of population growth?

There is much evidence on the population curve—for human and nonhuman species. For humans three distinct phases have been observed. In phase 1, exhibited in underdeveloped or preindustrial societies, *both* crude birth and crude death rates are high; hence, population does not grow rapidly. In phase 2, economic development leads to higher living standards and better health care, which dramatically reduce crude death rates—but leave crude birth rates relatively unaltered. The result is rapid population growth. In phase 3, nations attempt to reduce birth rates, or birth rates fall naturally as high income people in industrialized societies discover that children have changed from assets to liabilities, and the opportunity costs of raising children rise dramatically. At any rate, both crude birth *and* crude death rates are relatively low; hence, population is stabilized in economically developed nations.

5. It is often said that population and pollution are directly related. Are they?

Yes, *other things being constant.* But, it should be noted that "other things" are important, and therefore the relationship between population and pollution is complex. For instance, population could be stabilized or falling, while pollution problems could be increasing—if property rights become more muddled, or if *per capita* incomes are rising. Similarly, population could be rising, while pollution is falling—if property rights for "nature" become better defined, if technological advances in pollution treatment occur, or if per capita incomes fall.

Problem

(Answer at the back of the book)

1. Assume that 100 people move to some deserted island; 50 of the people are women, and 50 are men. The first generation, therefore, has a population of 100. Suppose each of these women has one daughter and 10 sons over her lifetime.

a. What is the population of the second generation?

b. What is the net reproduction rate for the island?

c. Suppose the net reproduction pattern remains the same; what will be the population of the third generation?

d. Is the island's population (generation by generation) rising, falling, or remaining constant?

21
Food and the Agricultural Sector

TOPICS FOR REVIEW

The topics listed below, which we have already analyzed, are applied in this chapter. You may find it worthwhile to review them. For your convenience each topic is followed by the number identifying the specific "Concepts in Brief."

a. Surpluses (3–7)

b. Law of diminishing returns (8–2)

c. Total revenue and price elasticity of demand (6–2)

d. Price elasticity of supply (6–5)

FOR PREVIEW AND STUDY

1. What is the farm problem?
2. How does the concept of elasticity help explain part of the farm problem?
3. How can price supports be maintained above market clearing levels?
4. How do the soil bank and acreage restriction plans help eliminate surpluses?
5. What is a target price, and how does it differ from other price support programs?

One of the basic problems that has faced civilization since its beginning concerns food. We live in a world in which some countries produce enormous quantities of food, while others do not. In the United States, we have rarely in modern times been faced with the serious prospect of food shortages. Rather, during the last three decades, the farming sector has produced (often embarrassing) surpluses of agricultural products. We need to understand how the United States can generate food surpluses in eras when part of the world's population is on the verge of starvation. We first look at the situation facing today's individual farmer, then we examine the agricultural sector in general. Finally, we look at government programs designed to aid American farmers. In the Issues and Applications section, we ask the very important question, "Is there an impending world food crisis?"

Poor Farmers

Many farmers can be considered rather poor. In the early 1980s, per capita farming income was only $11,800 compared to $13,000 for the nonfarm population. Today there are more than 800,000 farms with annual product sales of less than $2,500 each. In fact, those 800,000 farms produce only 2 percent of the total output of the farming industry. Exhibit 21–1 indicates the nature of the farming situation.

The farm problem is quite perplexing to some people. The agricultural sector is frequently referred to as the industry where technological progress has been more effective than anywhere else. Productivity has grown faster in agriculture than in any other major economic sector. Nonetheless, in terms of the percentage of the population engaged in farming, the agricultural sector is a declining industry. In Exhibit 21–2, we see the number of farms in the United States through the years. By 1964, the number of farms was less than the number existing before the turn of the century. Today the figure is even smaller.

EXHIBIT 21–1

Distribution of Total Farm Sales. The smallest 34 percent of farms produce about 2 percent of total farm sales, while the largest 8 percent of farms produce about 54 percent. These agribusiness firms have annual sales of $100,000 or more.

Annual Sales	*1980 Percentage of Total Farm Sales*	*Percentage of Total Number of Farms*
$100,000 and over	54	8
40–100	24	16
20–40	9	13
10–20	4	11
5–10	4	10
2.5–5	3	10
Less than $2,500	2	34

Source: Economic Research Service, USDA, 1981.

EXHIBIT 21–2

The Number of Farms in the United States. The number of farms in the United States rose from 1.4 million in 1850 to a high of 6.8 million in 1935. Today there are fewer than 3 million farms.

Year	*Millions of Farms*	*Year*	*Millions of Farms*
1850	1.4	1950	5.4
1870	2.7	1959	3.7
1900	5.7	1964	3.2
1920	6.5	1972	2.9
1930	6.3	1976	2.8
1935	6.8	1980	2.4
1940	6.1		

Source: U.S. Bureau of the Census.

The Growth in Demand for Farm Products

It is actually not surprising that the agricultural sector should decline as a proportion of the total economy. For one thing, productivity increases have been so great that more and more can be produced on farms by fewer and fewer people.

Also consider that there is a limit to how much food people can eat. Even if they can "afford" to buy huge quantities, they will not do so. We expect, therefore, that as households get richer, the percentage of their budget spent on food will fall. This occurs because the income elasticity of demand for food is less than 1. We have previously defined income elasticity of demand as follows:

$$\text{income elasticity} = \frac{\text{percentage change in amount of good purchased}}{\text{percentage change in income}}$$

If the income elasticity of demand for agricultural products is less than 1, for every 1 percent increase in income there will be a *less*-than-1 percent increase in quantity demanded, other things being constant. Look at Exhibit 21–3, where we show the income elasticity for food products in var-

EXHIBIT 21–3
Income Elasticity for Food Products. The income elasticity of demand for food is defined as being equal to the percentage change in the quantity demanded divided by the percentage change in real income. This income elasticity is quite low for the richer nations in the world.

Richer Nations	*Elasticity*	*Poorer Nations*	*Elasticity*
United States	0.08	Ireland	0.23
Canada	0.15	Italy	0.42
Britain	0.24	Greece	0.49
Germany	0.25	Spain	0.56
France	0.25	Portugal	0.60

Source: Charles L. Schultze, *The Distribution of Farm Subsidies: Who Gets the Benefits?* (Washington, D.C.: The Brookings Institution, 1971).

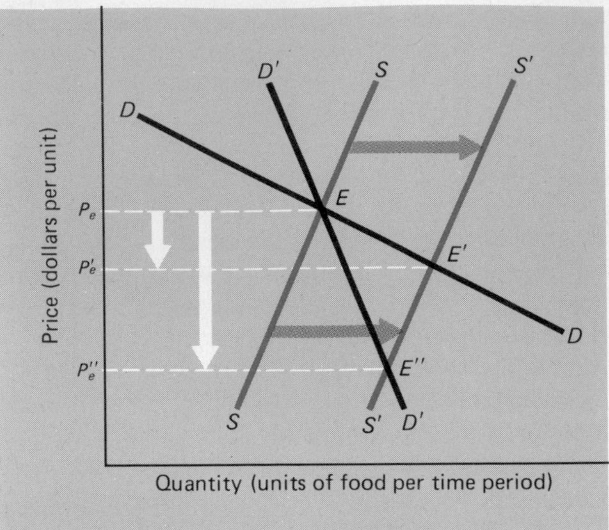

EXHIBIT 21–4
Consequences of a Relatively Inelastic Demand. The quantity of food produced per time period is on the horizontal axis and the price per unit on the vertical axis. Assume that the original supply curve is *SS*—relatively inelastic supply in the short run. If the demand curve facing farmers is *DD*, a shift in the supply curve from *SS* to *S'S'* due to a good year of weather will lower the equilibrium price from P_e to P_e'. But if the demand curve is instead *D'D'*, when the supply curve shifts to *S'S'*, the new equilibrium price falls to P_e''. This accounts for the large variability in incomes of farmers in different years.

ious countries. We see that income elasticity is quite low for the richer nations in the world. In fact, the richer the nation, the lower the income elasticity of demand for agricultural products. All nations seem to exhibit income elasticities for food products that are less than 1. Therefore, we predict that agriculture will be of declining importance in all nations as each becomes richer. (We are ignoring the possibility of *exports* of food becoming more and more important. If that were to happen because of increased world demand, the agricultural sector could conceivably even grow as a nation became richer.)

Low Price Elasticity of Demand

Not only is the income elasticity of demand for agricultural products low; so too is the price elasticity. Whereas the low-income elasticity was important for explaining the long-run downward trend in the farm sector, the low-price elasticity of demand is important for understanding the high variability of farmers' incomes in the short run.

Let's consider the change in price that results from an increase in supply due to abnormally good weather conditions. In Exhibit 21–4, we show the supply schedule shifting from *SS* to *S'S'*. It has shifted out to the right, indicating a large increase in production. Notice that the supply schedule here is fairly vertical, indicating that the *price elasticity of supply* in the short-run period under consideration is also quite small (at *E*). After all, once the farmers have planted and cultivated their crops, they can supply no more and no less—unless, of course, they decide to store or destroy the crops.

What if the demand schedule is in addition very elastic, such as *DD* (at *E*)? The new equilibrium price in this case will be set at the intersection of the new supply curve *S'S'* and the demand curve *DD*, or at point *E'*. The old equilibrium price was established at point *E*, or at a price of P_e. The new price of P_e' obviously lies below the old price.

What if the demand curve is relatively less elastic, such as *D'D'* (at *E*)? The new equilibrium price will then be established at *E''*, and the new equilibrium price will be P_e'', which is even lower than P_e'. We see, therefore, that when there is a shift rightward in the supply curve, the more inelastic the demand for agricultural products, the greater the decline in the market price. Conversely, for any shift leftward in the supply curve of agricultural products, the greater the inelasticity of demand, the greater the rise in the market price of agricultural products. For example, if there is a drought, we expect prices to rise rather substantially due to the relative inelasticity of demand for food. Thus, we see that the relative inelasticity of demand for agricultural products has also been one of the reasons that prices, and therefore farm incomes, have fluctuated more in agriculture than they have in other industries from year to year.

THE EFFECT ON FARMERS' INCOMES

So far we have only demonstrated that for any given shift in the supply curve, the more inelastic the demand for food products, the greater will be the resultant change in the market clearing price. Thus, when there is a bumper crop, the relatively inelastic demand for food results in a relatively substantial drop in the market clearing price for food products.

What, though, happens to farmers' incomes? Well, you have to go back to our discussion of the relationship between changes in price and changes in total revenues and consumer expenditures. This was discussed in Chapter 6. There we showed that any firm facing an inelastic demand would suffer a *decrease* in total revenues if it lowered price. This analysis holds for the total income in farming. Because farmers are facing an inelastic demand for food (that is, as a group they are undoubtedly operating in the inelastic portion of the *market* demand for food), a reduction in price—for example, from P_e to P_e'' in Exhibit 21-4—will result in a reduction in total farm income.

Concepts in Brief 21-1

- Over 50 percent of total farm sales is accounted for by about 8 percent of the farms. Small farmers constitute a large share of total farmers but do not produce a significant portion of farm output.
- The income elasticity of demand is the percentage change in amount of good purchased divided by the percentage change in income. Food products consistently have an income elasticity of demand that is very much below 1. Therefore, as income goes up, the percentage of total consumer expenditures going to food falls.
- For any shift in the supply schedule, a firm facing a relatively inelastic demand curve will experience a larger fluctuation in the price of the product. It is argued that since the demand for food is relatively price inelastic, the prices farmers receive for their products fluctuate more than in other sectors of the economy when there are shifts in supply.

History of the Farmers' Dilemma

Before World War I, there were at least 20 years of continuous agricultural prosperity in the United States. During the war, increased demand for agricultural products added to the "golden age of American farming." Many foreign countries demanded our agricultural products because they were using all their productive facilities to fight the war. The sharp depression in 1920 brought the "golden age" to an abrupt halt. Even though the economy picked up in 1921 and we went into the "roaring twenties," agriculture never did share in the remaining years of prosperity. Europeans reduced their demand for our agricultural exports as they increased their own productive capacities in farming. Also, the United States put high tariffs on all imported goods, thereby restricting the flow of imports. Since other countries were not able to export as many goods to us as before, they were in no position to import as much from us as before. Since exports are what any country uses to pay for its imports, the less it is able to export, the less it is able to import.

Then the Great Depression hit, and American farming was really hurt. Farm prices and farm incomes fell sharply. It was at this time that our massive farm programs were put into operation. In 1929, the Federal Farm Board was created and given a budget of $1.5 billion to begin price stabilization operations for poor farmers. The Farm Board was supposed to use the money to support the price of farm products so that farmers' incomes would not fall so much. Essentially it bought crops to keep their prices from falling. Then, when the Great Depression got into full swing, a system of **price supports** came into being. At one time or another, there have been some forms of price supports for wheat, feed grains, cotton, tobacco, rice, peanuts, soybeans, dairy products, and sugar. Let us now see if we can graphically analyze the effect of a price support system.

Price Supports

A price support system is precisely what the name implies. Somehow the government stabilizes or fixes the price of an agricultural product so that it can't *fall* below a certain level. Look at the supply and demand curves in Exhibit 21-5, showing the market demand and market supply of wheat. Competitive

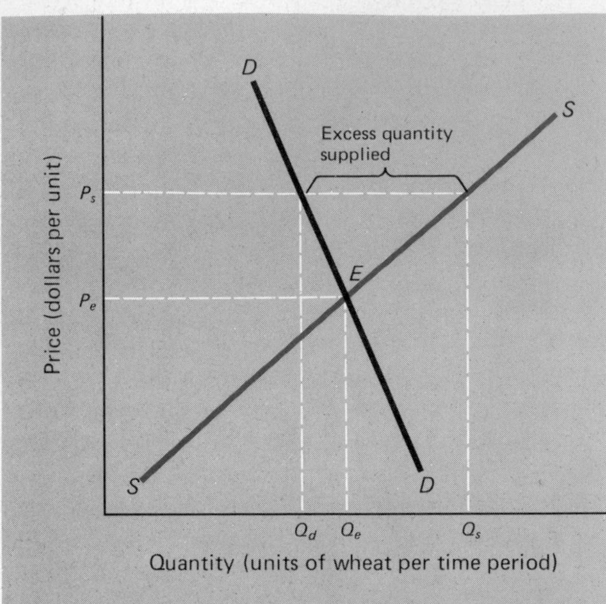

EXHIBIT 21–5
Price Supports. The quantity of wheat is measured on the horizontal axis and the price on the vertical axis. The domestic market demand and supply curves are given by *DD* and *SS*. Equilibrium is established at *E* with an equilibrium price of P_e and an equilibrium quantity of Q_e. However, the government steps in and sets a support price at P_s. At P_s the quantity demanded is Q_d and the quantity supplied is Q_s. The difference is the excess quantity supplied, or surplus, which the government must somehow take care of. It usually does this by storing the surplus or giving it away to foreign countries under one of our "food for peace" programs.

forces would yield an equilibrium price of P_e and an equilibrium quantity of Q_e. If the government sets the support price at P_e or below, obviously there will be no change, because the farmers can sell all they want at the market clearing price, P_e.

In many instances, however, the government will set the support price above P_e—say, at P_s. At P_s the quantity demanded is only Q_d, but the quantity supplied is Q_s. That is, at the higher price, there is a smaller quantity demanded but a larger quantity supplied. The difference is the excess quantity supplied. Producers respond to higher market prices by producing more. That's why we show the supply schedule as upward sloping. At the higher prices, farmers are able to incur higher production costs and still make a profit. They will keep producing up to the point where the support price cuts the supply curve. Since the government guarantees to purchase everything the wheat farmers want to sell at the price P_s, this price represents the marginal revenue to each farmer. Thus, each farmer will continue producing until marginal revenue equals marginal cost, or until the price support line intersects the summation of all the marginal cost curves above their respective average variable costs (that is, the industry supply curve).

HOW CAN SUPPORTS LAST?

How can such a situation last? If producers are producing more than consumers want to buy at the support price, what happens to all the surplus production? The government must buy the supplies if the price support is to work. The government acquires the surplus wheat, or the amount represented by the distance between Q_s and Q_d in Exhibit 21–5.

At one point back in the 1950s, things really got out of hand. The government was spending $1.1 million a day in storage costs for surplus wheat! The government acquired the wheat through the **Commodity Credit Corporation (CCC).** The Commodity Credit Corporation was given a **parity** price that it was allowed to offer for different products. Parity was called a "fair" price by farmers and politicians.[1]

Let's say that Congress set a fair, or parity, price of $5 a bushel, but the market price, where supply and demand would be in equilibrium, was $4.50 a bushel. But farmers would not sell at $4.50 a bushel; they would charge $5 a bushel and sell as much as they could at that price. Whatever they could not sell—the surplus—would be "sold" to the Commodity Credit Corporation.

In principle, the Commodity Credit Corporation merely "lent" each farmer the fair price times the number of bushels the farmer gave the CCC. The **loan,** however, was a **nonrecourse** one. That is, the CCC could never ask the farmer for the money back. The CCC kept the "surplus" wheat in its grain silos.

In economics, we find that the only way for a chronic "surplus" to exist is for there to be some

[1]The basic idea of parity is that if a bushel of wheat was exchanged for a pair of overalls 65 years ago, a bushel of wheat ought to be exchanged for a pair of overalls today. The base period used in these calculations is 1910–1914. Production goods, wages, and household items are included in the index of prices of articles *bought* by farmers. Thus, parity is a comparison of a price index for agricultural goods with a price index for goods that farmers buy. When farmers demand 100 percent parity, they are basically asking for an increase in the support price of agricultural commodities relative to the price of things that they buy. Note that the 1910–1914 base years were ones in which farmers received relatively high prices for their products. Thus, the concept of parity is, in fact, arbitrary. Another base set of years could have been chosen and parity prices would then be lower (or even higher).

EXHIBIT 21–6

Distribution of Income and Subsidies by Farm Size, 1976. Here we show the distribution of subsidies among farmers. We see that those farmers grossing less than $2,500 a year own 39 percent of all farms but receive only 4.9 percent of all direct subsidies. On the other hand, those farms with sales of over $100,000 constitute only 5.6 percent of all farms, but receive over 36 percent of all direct subsidies.

Annual Food Product Sales	*Percent of All Farms*	*Average Family Income*	*Percent of Income From Nonfarm Sources*	*Percent of All Farm Income*	*Percent of All Direct Subsidies*
$100,000 and over	5.6	$69,026	19.3	39.4	36.5
40,000–99,999	11.0	23,464	29.4	23.2	25.1
20,000–39,999	11.5	15,384	37.5	14.1	14.0
10,000–19,999	10.9	12,308	57.4	7.2	8.6
5,000–9,999	10.7	12,154	75.1	4.1	5.2
2,500–4,999	11.3	12,067	85.5	2.5	4.9
Less than $2,500	39.0	17,551	89.0	9.5	4.9
All Farms	100.0	19,059	58.6	100.0	100.0

Source: Economic Research Service, U.S. Department of Agriculture.

sort of price fixing. In an unrestricted market, a surplus can exist only temporarily. The forces of supply and demand will eventually eliminate the surplus by causing a decrease in the price.

WHO BENEFITS FROM PRICE SUPPORTS?

The argument of those favoring price supports has always been that it is a method to guarantee a decent income for low-income farmers. However, the evidence does not show that the price support system has helped small farmers very much, even during its heyday. Historically, the benefits of past price supports have been greatly skewed toward the owners of very large farms. Owners of farms with sales of less than $5,000, for example, received less than 10 percent of the benefits from price supports, as can be seen in Exhibit 21–6. Such statistics should not surprise you. The price support program is roughly equivalent to trying to help low-income people by giving everyone a cash subsidy equal to a percentage of his or her income. Poor people wouldn't get very much, would they?

Even more importantly, however, any benefit that conceivably could have been derived from the price support system would have ultimately accrued to landlords or landowners on which price-supported crops could be grown. The value of land went up when price supports were announced and put into effect (maybe even before, if the owners and potential buyers of land had anticipated that supports were going to be legislated). A recent study of past farm programs reached this conclusion. According to Professor D. Gale Johnson, "Most of the benefit of the farm program has been capitalized into the value of farmland."[2] This just means that the price of land went up in anticipation of higher revenues in the future.

A clear example of this capitalization phenomenon is the tobacco program, which has been around for some time.

TOBACCO

Support prices that are higher than equilibrium prices entice more people into farming because of the lure of higher incomes. However, the threat of new competition was squashed by tobacco growers about three decades ago. They got Congress to pass legislation that allotted the *then-current* half-million growers the right to grow tobacco on lands that were *then* in use. Since then, there has been no new land put into tobacco production, and for a very good reason. Any tobacco grown on unlicensed land is taxed at 75 percent of its value. This tax is prohibitive: Potential tobacco farmers cannot hope to make any income if they have to pay this tax—they're in competition with tobacco growers who do not have to pay it.

Perhaps, since tobacco farming is a monopoly today, you can make monopoly profits by buying some licensed tobacco-growing acreage? If you think so, you're wrong. The price of that licensed land was bid up long ago to levels that yield *new* owners only a competitive rate of return. Who benefits from the monopoly position granted by Congress? The owners of the land at the time the legislation was passed, of course. When they went

[2] *Farm Commodity Programs: An Opportunity for Change* (Washington, D.C.: American Enterprise Institute for Public Policy Research, May 1973), p. 3.

to sell their land, they found that its value, or market price, had increased by $1,500 to $3,000 per acre. Why? Because everyone knew that there was now a restriction on the amount of land that could be used for the production of tobacco. Higher tobacco prices were assured in the future because of this restriction on supply. The higher future profits in tobacco growing caused people to bid up the price of land that was licensed for tobacco production.

In addition to the restriction on acreage in tobacco growing, there are also tobacco price supports (that is, Commodity Credit Corporation nonrecourse loans). And just to make sure that not too much reaches the marketplace—that is, that there isn't a surplus—there are marketing quotas to keep output at a level consistent with price support objectives. The net results of the tobacco program have been:

1. A smaller supply of tobacco leaves than otherwise would have been grown.
2. A higher price for tobacco than would have prevailed under an unrestricted market situation.
3. A higher price for tobacco products than would have otherwise prevailed.
4. A higher price for tobacco acreage than would have otherwise prevailed.

Concepts in Brief 21-2

■ With the price support system, the government sets a minimum price at which certain agricultural products will be sold. Any farmer who cannot sell all that he or she produces at that price can "sell" the "surplus" to the government. Indeed, the only way that a price support system can last is for someone (such as the government) to buy up the excess quantity supplied at the supported price, which exceeds the market clearing price.

■ Since price supports benefit farmers directly in proportion to the amount of agricultural goods they produce, owners of large farms receive the bulk of payments.

■ The ultimate beneficiaries of price supports have been the owners of farmland, for the price of farmland has risen whenever price supports were announced.

■ The tobacco program involves price supports, production quotas, and a restriction on the total amount of land that can be used to grow tobacco.

■ The original owners of tobacco land reaped windfall capital gains, to the tune of $1,500 to $3,000 per acre.

Coping with the "Surpluses"

When the farm price support program was first instituted during the Great Depression, Exhibit 21-5 was appropriate. Later on, however, surpluses disappeared. At the end of World War II, there was an increased demand for U.S. farm products from abroad. For several years after the war, Europe continued to demand American agricultural products while using its productive capacity for reconstruction. The Korean War also helped to eliminate any problem of "surpluses" resulting from price supports. The rest of the world bought heavily from our farming production sector just in case there might be a need for large food inventories if the war spread. Finally, after the Korean War ended, the problem of excess capacity—surpluses—began to rear its ugly head.

By the mid-1950s, the Commodity Credit Corporation began to stockpile larger and larger inventories of the "surplus" farm products it had purchased. By 1954, there was a slight reduction in price support levels but not enough to eliminate the rising excess quantity from the farming sector. In 1952, the CCC purchased $1.3 billion worth of agricultural commodities. By 1955, it purchased $6.7 billion, and by 1959, almost $8 billion.

When John F. Kennedy came into office, one of his first major steps in changing farm policy was to raise support levels. We saw a substantial increase in farm income but also in potential surpluses due to the increases in the price supports. This increase in potential surpluses forced the Kennedy administration to institute some fairly drastic measures to reduce the amount of production that each farmer was allowed. Even before Kennedy, a **soil bank** had been created by the Eisenhower administration. Through this institution the government paid farmers *not to use* land for production. There were some experiments with mandatory controls on output, but increasingly the government came to rely on direct payments to farmers not to produce. This was called *purchasing acreage restrictions.* Let's now analyze the soil bank or land conservation program in agriculture.

GOVERNMENT REQUIRED ACREAGE RESTRICTIONS

In many cases, when farmers want to take advantage of the price support program offered to them by the government, they have to agree to participate in the acreage allotment program. Participating farmers agree to limit the number of acres they

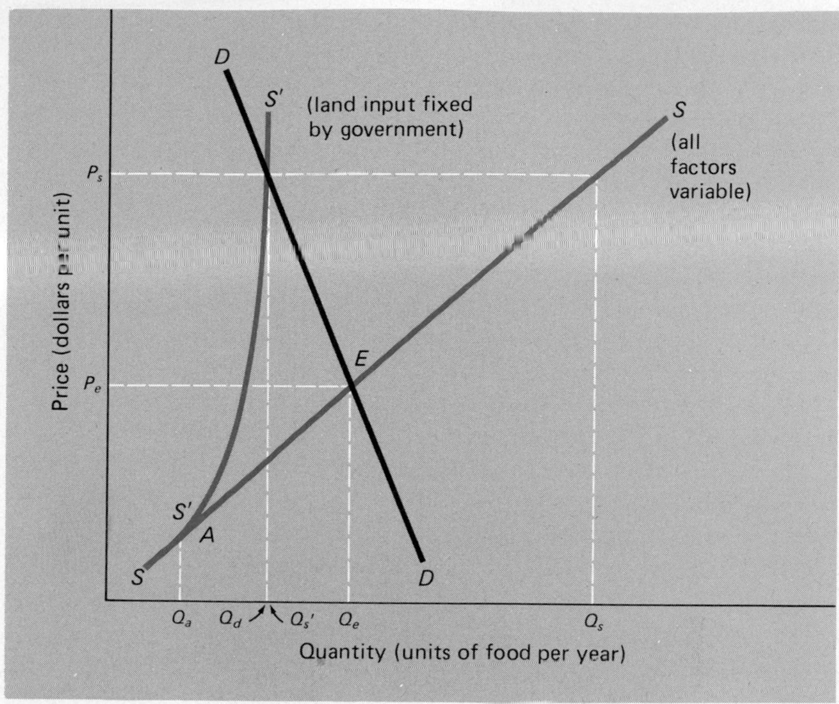

EXHIBIT 21–7
Acreage Restrictions. In an unrestricted situation, we have the demand curve *DD* and the supply curve *SS*, where *SS* is equal to the horizontal summation of all the marginal cost curves of the individual farmers when all factors can be varied. The equilibrium was established at *E*—at the intersection of *SS* and *DD*—and the equilibrium price would be P_e. The government decides to set a support price above the equilibrium price. The support price is P_s. At P_s the quantity demanded is Q_d and the quantity supplied would be Q_s. There would be a surplus equal to Q_s minus Q_d. In order to avoid the surplus, the government restricts the amount of land that can be cultivated. When land is restricted, we get a new supply curve. It is the old one up to point *A*, and then a new one, *S'S'*. We have drawn it in such a way that it intersects the demand curve at the support price. The government could conceivably keep restricting land until this happened. The reason the new supply curve is steeper than the old supply curve is that land is fixed and resources that would not otherwise be used in such large quantities, such as more fertilizer and more machines, will now be put to work on the restricted amount of land. We can see that the supply curve actually pivots at point *A*. Before point *A*, nothing happens to the supply curve because less land would be used than the government maximum, so the restriction has no effect. In the new equilibrium situation, the quantity demanded will be Q_d and the quantity supplied will be Q_s', which is equal to Q_d.

plant, so as to reduce surpluses caused by price supports. This acreage allotment program is slightly different from the soil bank program, where the Department of Agriculture actually rents the land from farmers. The rented land could be planted in timber or cover crops like grass, but with nothing that could be sold on the food market. In the acreage allotment program, there are no direct payments to farmers; the program is merely the entry fee that farmers must pay to be allowed to take advantage of price supports. In the soil bank program, the government actually gives direct payment to the farmer for *not* using part of his land, regardless of the farmer's participation in any other government program.

Let's graphically analyze the situation that occurs when the government restricts the use of land (one of the production factors in making food). Look at Exhibit 21–7. Here we have drawn the market demand curve and the market supply curve (above each firm's respective minimum average variable cost). Additionally, we have assumed one very important condition—that all factors of production can be varied. That is, farmers can use whatever amounts of labor, capital, and land they want to; they can vary the proportions. If it is more profitable to use less land, the farmers will do so; they will sell part of their land. If it is profitable to use more land, they will buy more land. The same holds with all other factors. The *SS* curve is drawn under the assumption that it represents the minimum cost combination of land, labor, and capital for producing any given quantity of the product in question. That is, it is assumed that farmers vary the proportions of their factors of production in such a way as to minimize the cost of production for any given quantity.

In the unrestricted market, the equilibrium price would be P_e and the equilibrium quantity would be Q_e. Now the government comes along and puts on a price support at P_s. If the government does nothing else, this will lead to an excess quantity supplied—that is, a surplus equal to the difference between Q_s and Q_d. In order to eliminate the surplus, the government requires more land to go into the acreage allotment program, where it can't be cultivated, and the government "rents" more land to put into the soil bank. The government wants to keep taking more land out of production until finally a new supply curve will intersect the stable demand curve at price P_s—or the support price. Look at Exhibit 21-7. Here we have shown a new supply curve, SS', and we have labeled it to show that land is fixed. Why does the supply curve *pivot* upward at point A? The reason is easy to see.

If farmers wanted to produce quantity Q_a, they would be at A on the supply curve. That is, an acreage restriction would have no effect if *only* Q_a were to be produced. The same small amount of land, labor, fertilizer, and machines would be used. But after Q_a, things are different. Land cannot be added in unrestricted quantities; there is acreage restriction. Any expansion beyond this point must come from *non*fixed inputs. Farmers will increase the use of all other *non*fixed inputs so long as the marginal revenue from doing so is greater than the marginal cost. Since the marginal revenue from doing so is always equal to P_s because that's the government support price, farmers will increase their use of other inputs until the marginal cost just equals P_s. That's why the supply curve pivots upward. It shows, for example, that at a price of P_s, it now "costs" P_s to produce the quantity Q_d. Before the soil bank program was instituted, it cost less in resources.

The soil bank and acreage allotment programs led to an inefficient use of resources—not from the point of view of the individual farmers, for it is assumed that they use their resources efficiently—but from the point of view of society. This is because the resources are being held out of economically productive uses.

HAVE ACREAGE RESTRICTION PROGRAMS BEEN SUCCESSFUL?

As you might expect, the government did not anticipate that production of agricultural crops would fall so little in comparison to the reduction in acreage. Farmers got rid of their worst land first and kept the best land in production. The remaining cultivated acres were worked more intensely; more and better seed was used. More and better fertilizers and insecticides and machines and workers were used. In 1953, 80 million acres of wheat were cultivated; 1.2 billion bushels grew. In 1960, only 55 million acres of wheat were cultivated; the output, however, was 1.4 billion bushels. A 30 percent reduction in the number of acres cultivated by 1960 was accompanied by an increase of 17 percent in output. Of course, the increase in output would have been even greater had there not been soil banks and acreage restriction allotments. The government should not have been too surprised about the increase in production on less land because, at the same time that it was restricting acreage, it was spending millions helping farmers improve productivity!

The soil bank program was phased out pursuant to the Agricultural and Consumer Protection Act of 1973. In 1978, however, a modified version of the soil bank program was started again. President Carter, under pressure from farmers complaining of disastrously low agricultural prices, started a "set aside" program to take out of production about 20 percent of wheat acreage.

Concepts in Brief 21-3

- One way to cope with an excess quantity supplied at higher than market clearing prices is to restrict the amount of land on which price supported crops can be grown.
- A soil bank requires that in order for farmers to receive price supports, or subsidies, they must not use a certain percentage of their available land for the production of crops to be sold in the food market.
- Analytically, the restriction on one factor of production—land—caused farmers to increase the intensity of use of other factors of production, such as seed, fertilizer, and machinery. Therefore, the supply curve rotated upward.
- The soil bank and the acreage allotment programs therefore led to inefficient use of resources from society's point of view—too little land and too much of other resources going to producing each unit of agricultural output.
- The soil bank program was phased out after 1973. In 1978, however, a modified version was reinstituted.

Moving into an Era of No Surpluses

The 1970s saw a shift in the farming situation. Instead of "surpluses," there were domestic and worldwide "shortages" of farm products. Because of this changing situation, Congress passed a new farm bill in 1973. This farm bill provided for something new in the agricultural sector.

TARGET PRICES

The Agricultural and Consumer Protection Act of 1973 provided a **target price** plan for grains and cotton for four years. Then-Secretary of Agriculture Earl L. Butz called the bill a historic turning

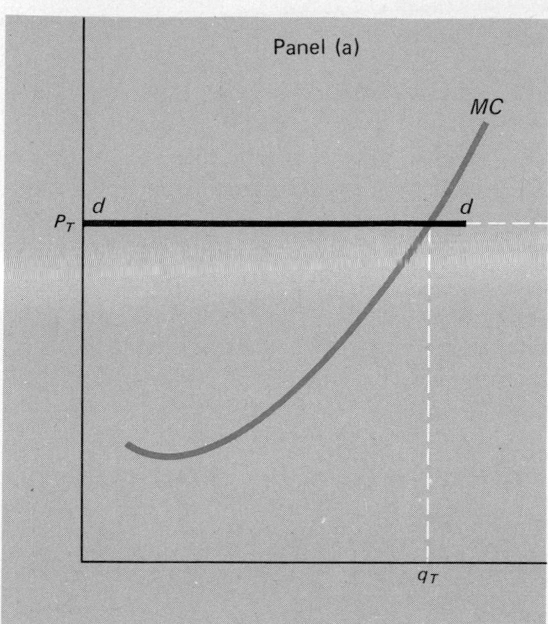

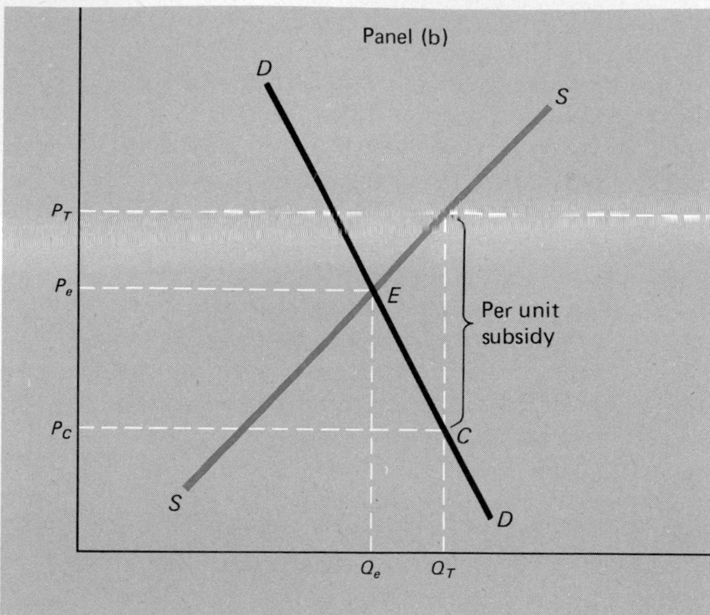

EXHIBIT 21–8

Target Prices. In panel (a) we show a representative marginal cost curve for a representative farm. In panel (b) we show the market demand curve, *DD*, and the market supply curve as *SS*. *SS*, as you will remember, is the horizontal summation of all of the marginal cost curves above their respective average variable cost. The intersection of *DD* and *SS* is at point *E* yielding a market equilibrium price of P_e and an equilibrium quantity of Q_e. The government, however, sets the target price, P_T, above the market equilibrium price. Farmers view this as, therefore, the firm demand curve, *dd*, in panel (a) at price P_T. Each representative farmer will therefore produce q_T. This results in a movement up the supply curve *SS* in panel (b) so that the total market quantity produced will be Q_T. But that quantity, Q_T, can only be sold if the price, P_C, is charged. Hence, the market clearing price is labeled P_C. That means that the government must pay a subsidy on each unit produced and sold of the vertical difference between P_C and P_T. This is labeled "per unit subsidy" in panel (b). Each farmer therefore receives a total subsidy of the per unit subsidy times the number of units sold.

point in farm program philosophy, which, he said, is now "geared to expanding output."

The concept of target prices for major crops was first proposed by Charles F. Brannan back in 1949, when he was Secretary of Agriculture under Truman. The 1973 bill allows for target prices that are relatively low compared to market prices. If at any time the market price falls below the target price, farmers will receive a direct payment from the government to make up for the difference. Thus, if the market price of wheat is $4 a bushel and the target price is $5 a bushel, farmers will receive $1 for every bushel they sell on the open market. That dollar will be paid as a subsidy to the farmer out of general tax revenues by the federal government.

GRAPHICALLY REPRESENTING THE TARGET PRICE

We have made reference to the market, or equilibrium, price for agricultural commodities. We have also talked about the support price that the government sets. And finally, we have discussed target prices. Now we will present target prices in a graphical format. We have already analyzed market price and the support price in Exhibit 36–5, where we showed that when the support price was greater than the market price, there would be an excess quantity supplied ("surplus") at the support price.

The concept of a target price is slightly different because it involves no direct purchase by government and, thus, no storage of the crop by government. Look at panels (a) and (b) in Exhibit 21–8. In panel (a) we show the individual firm demand curve and marginal cost curve. Assume that the target price is in effect. It is set at P_T. Every farmer is guaranteed that price for every bushel of wheat, for example. Thus, at P_T the demand curve is *dd*. The profit-maximizing perfect competitor looks at the intersection of marginal cost with marginal revenue (which in this case is average revenue, which is equal to P_T). Thus, the individual farmer produces q_T. In panel (b) we show the market demand and market supply, where the market supply curve SS is equal to the horizontal summation of all individual farmers' marginal cost curves. At price P_T, the quantity supplied will be equal to Q_T. At that quantity, however, consumers will only purchase it at P_C. Therefore, the subsidy to each farmer is equal to the vertical difference between P_T and P_C times the number of units that the farmer sells. We have labeled it "per unit subsidy" in panel (b). Target prices, therefore, lead to a greater use of resources, greater output, and greater consumption than in an unrestricted market. (Note, however, that these programs raise the long-run expected price to farmers and, thus, increase long-run production.)

A Further Analysis of Target Prices

We just pointed out that target prices lead to greater use of resources, greater output, and greater consumption than in an unrestricted market. Note, however, that comparing target prices to acreage restrictions would lead us to conclude that the consumer receives lower prices under a target price system.

Do not be fooled, however, into concluding therefore that target prices are "better." First of all, we are talking about policy; the ultimate decision about which program is "better" therefore rests on value judgments. The point we wish to make is that consumers of agricultural products nonetheless pay for the subsidy to farmers via target prices—in the form of taxes paid to the federal government.

Let us assume, for the moment, that the target price system is the "preferred" program to help farmers. The critical issue is where to set the target price. Corn and soybeans are substitutes in production. If the corn target price is too high, a "shortage" of soybeans may result. In other words, setting target prices while avoiding such problems is not an easy policy task. Ideally, the target price might be set at the point where the efficient firm is at least able to cover its average variable costs so as to prevent farmers from going out of business.

In any event, you should realize that for many years there was no direct cost of this target price program because market prices were above target prices.

> ***Concepts in Brief 21-4***
>
> ■ In the early 1970s, a reduction in the world production of agricultural products led to the end of the era of agricultural surpluses, at least temporarily.
>
> ■ World prices exceeded support prices so that there was no excess quantity supplied at the support price.
>
> ■ In 1973, target prices were instituted for various agricultural commodities. Farmers are paid the difference between the target price and the market clearing price whenever the latter is below the target price.

ISSUES AND APPLICATIONS

Is There an Impending Food Crisis?

> ***Concepts Applied***
>
> ■ Supply and demand, relative price changes

The Presidential Commission on World Hunger concluded in 1980 that a major world crisis worse than the energy crisis appears likely by 1990, unless food production is dramatically increased. The commission recommended that the United States "make the elimination of hunger the primary focus of its relationships with the developing countries."

First Surpluses, Then Shortages

In the 1950s, 1960s, and early 1970s, the American agricultural industry produced not shortages but surpluses—year in and year out. In fact, the surpluses became so embarrassing that the U.S. government at one time was dumping wheat into the Gulf of Mexico. Naturally, our less-developed neighbor nations, with untold numbers of undernourished individuals, found such activity appalling.

We obviously have solved the surplus problem—perhaps even for good. Thanks to unantici-

In many areas urban growth is spreading to envelop arable land that could be used for farming, but the total amount of farm land hasn't changed much nonetheless.

pated problems with agriculture throughout the world, shortages, not surpluses, were the order of the day. For a while, the specter of bread lines, similar to those for gasoline that occurred only a few years ago, seemed to be a real one. In fact, the Community Nutrition Institute of Washington stated that "sooner, but probably reluctantly later" the U.S. government would be forced to ration food. It's hard to believe, but the Los Angeles police force was some time ago even trained to handle riots that might occur over a food shortage.

If we look at what has happened to world grain reserves, we can get an idea of how serious the problem really is. In recent years the world has had to draw down its grain reserves with increasing frequency. This happened noticeably in 1966 and 1967 and became much more pronounced in the 1970s. The number of days of grain reserves has been falling, on the average, since the early 1960s. Where we will go from here is indeed a serious question.

A study by the Ford Foundation came up with a proposal for a world food reserve, with the United States contributing a large amount, but not 100 percent. This would be keeping in line with what the United States government has done in the past; since 1954 this country has given away, under Public Law 480, more than $25 billion worth of grain to numerous developing countries.

At a world food conference sponsored by the United Nations and the Food and Agricultural Organization a few years ago, 135 nations met to consider long-term measures to improve world food production. At the time this conference was meeting, an estimated 10,000 people a day were dying from starvation or diseases related to hunger. One of the attempts at the conference was to form a new system of international grain reserves similar to that proposed by the Ford Foundation. The international system would establish an emergency food aid bank and an agency to administer $5 billion worth of annual farm assistance. The concern of the United States—far and away the largest producer of food—was that the burden of holding surpluses for the whole world would fall to it.

The Organization for Economic Cooperation and Development seems to agree. Experts at the 24-nation Organization for Economic Cooperation and Development (OECD) believe that there is sufficient food for the world in the 1980s, but there won't be in the 1990s. Those experts believe that the big gains in productivity have started to decline. Agreeing with the OECD is Lester Brown, president of the Worldwatch Institute. While Brown agrees that world population growth peaked in 1970, he still maintains that the absolute number of people needing food is going up by 70 million a year. He points out that soil erosion is a major worry in the Soviet Union and nearly all of the Third World countries. He believes that one-fifth of the world's cropland is losing topsoil at a rate that is undermining its long-run productivity. Brown sees no major breakthroughs that would dramatically increase food supplies in the future.

Proposed Solutions

For the agricultural crisis that may occur, proposed solutions again draw heavily on improved production techniques to allow America, and indeed even underdeveloped countries, to dramatically increase their food production. However, there have been many suggestions to reduce the demand for food in years to come by drastically curtailing population growth. In some of those countries if growth rates were to continue at current rates (that cause the population to double every 20 years), there would hardly be enough room for every person to stand (let alone sit) by the year 2500.

But Is Everything Really Getting Worse?

If we look at what has actually happened to the world as a whole, we find some startling bits of information that tend to counter much of the concern over world food crises.

Are the deserts spreading? There has been concern that the deserts are spreading and that the world's arable land is steadily decreasing. Julian L. Simon[3] has found that the world's arable land increased by nearly 1 percent per year from 1950 to 1960 and by nearly .7 percent annually through 1970.

Are food supplies actually decreasing in Third World countries? Individuals concerned with famine seem to believe that food supplies are decreasing in less-developed countries. Per capita food production worldwide has increased by 25 percent in the last 25 years. Some countries have done worse than the average and, indeed, many of these countries are less developed. But other less-developed countries have done quite well. India can be used as an example; during the 1950s and 1960s, India required large imports of food to stave off mass starvation. Because of improved agricultural productivity, the situation is now reversed. India has substantial food reserve supplies.

[3] *Science*, June 27, 1980.

Is famine an increasing problem? Agricultural economist D. Gale Johnson of the University of Chicago contends that there is not increasing famine throughout the world. Indeed, he believes that there has been a "dramatic" decline in famine since World War II. From 1950 to 1974, 90 percent fewer people in the world died per year from famine than did in the period 1900–1950, in spite of the fact that we have a larger world population.

Is urban sprawl endangering prime agricultural land in the United States? One of the most common criticisms of urbanization is that prime agricultural land has been destroyed. In a recent government study in which 11 U.S. government agencies participated, the conclusion was "Every day in the United States, four square miles of our nation's prime farmlands are shifted to uses other than agriculture. The thief is urban spawl. . . . Ten years from now, Americans could be as concerned over the loss of the nation's prime and important farmlands as they are today over shortages of oil and gasoline."[4]

In total, almost 1 million acres of rural land are converted to urban use every year.

This is only one side of the picture, however. Every year there are less noticeable but dramatic increases in acres of cropland and in production per acre. In 1969, for example, the number of acres from which crops were harvested was 286 million. In 1979, it had risen to 337 million. From 1969 to 1979, yields per acre of cropland also rose at 1.7 percent per year.

Using a simple supply-demand analysis, the increase in cropland in use, as well as the increase in yields per acre, should result in a de-

[4] *Where Have All the Farmlands Gone?* Washington, D.C.: National Agricultural Land Studies, September 1979, pp. 1–2.

cline in the relative price of farm products. Except for the first half of the 1970s, when export demand rose sharply, this is exactly what happened.

Forget the Facts and Use Some Theory

We could probably recite many other facts in favor of and against the concept of an impending world food crisis. But perhaps that is the wrong tack to take. Just consider the problem as a simple economic one. There is a world demand for food and a world supply of food. At any point in time, there is an equilibrium price for food. That does not mean that everyone will be fed in a manner that concerned citizens throughout the world believe to be appropriate. What it means is that the market for food will be working. The problem in the past, today, and in the future will remain one of *distribution of income* throughout the world. Specifically, relatively well-off countries will have citizens who eat better than individuals in less-well-off countries. One way to solve that problem (and it is not a food crisis) is to improve per capita income in less-developed countries. This is a solution concerning economic development and economic growth of Third World countries. It has, basically, little to do with world food crises.

The worldwide demand for food is intimately tied to the growth in population, among other things. Population growth has slowed in the world. In fact, several European countries have experienced population declines recently.

In sum, one should suspect any analysis concluding that there will be a *permanent shortage* of some commodity. The model of supply and demand can be applied to any situation. In a world of relatively increasing food scarcity, we will see a rise in the relative price of food. This will elicit two responses: (1) there will be an increase in world production and (2) there will be a decreased quantity demanded. Typically, the analysis of world food crises assumes a fixed amount of food "needed" and a fixed amount of land on which food can be grown. To refute both precepts, we need simply look at (1) the varying caloric intake among the peoples of the world and (2) the varying intensity of land use throughout the world.

Questions

1. Why is land more intensively cultivated in countries like Switzerland than it is in the United States? In other words, why do we see small gardens in between railroad tracks in Switzerland?
2. What does a change in the relative price of farm products have to do with the notion of permanent food crises?

Definition of Terms

Price supports Minimum prices set by the government. To be effective, price supports must be coupled with a mechanism to rid the market of "surplus" goods that arise whenever the supported price is greater than the market clearing price.

Commodity Credit Corporation (CCC) A government agency that "lends" farmers an amount of money equal to the support price of crops times the amount offered as collateral for the loan.

Parity A concept applied to the relative price of agricultural goods. The federal government has established parity by using a formula in which the price of agricultural goods is compared with the price of manufactured goods during the period 1910–1914. A parity price today would give farmers the same relative price for their products (compared to what they buy) that they received during the period 1910–1914.

Nonrecourse loans Loans that never have to be repaid. The Commodity Credit Corporation gives nonrecourse loans to farmers. In other words, farmers never have to pay off the loan to the CCC. Thus, the CCC is "stuck" with the agricultural crops given it as collateral.

Soil bank A percentage of arable land that farmers must take out of production in order to receive price supports. In other words, it is a "bank" of unused soil.

Target price A price set by the government for specific agricultural products. If market clearing prices fall below target prices, a "deficiency" payment equal to the difference of the market price and the target price is given to each farmer who qualifies.

Chapter Summary

1. Even though average incomes are rising, the demand for farm products is not rising as rapidly. The income elasticity of demand for foodstuffs is less than 1, meaning that a 1 percent increase in income leads to a less than 1 percent increase in the quantity of farm products purchased, other things being equal.
2. Since farmers face a relatively inelastic demand for their products, any shift in the supply curve will cause a relatively large change in the market clearing price.
3. Price supports were started during the Great Depression. Under a price support system, the government sets a minimum price for food products. If the supported price exceeds the market clearing price, a surplus develops. In an unrestricted market, a surplus cannot last.
4. In order for the price support to be effective, the government must agree in some way to take the surplus off the market.
5. Our government has used nonrecourse loans offered by the Commodity Credit Corporation in order to boost prices of farm products.
6. Since price supports are tied to the volume of production, richer farmers receive the bulk of direct subsidy payments. For example, in 1976, farms with sales of over $100,000 received over 36.5 percent of all direct federal subsidies.
7. Another way to cope with surpluses is to restrict one of the inputs. Thus, we have seen a soil bank program in which farmers receiving "loans" from the Commodity Credit Corporation must agree not to cultivate a certain percentage of their arable land.
8. Briefly during the early and mid-1970s, we entered an era of no surpluses for food products. The world price of food products exceeded the support price.
9. In 1973, a target price system was instituted. Whenever the market clearing price falls below the target price, farmers are paid a deficiency payment, or subsidy, to make up the difference.

Selected References

Heady, Earl O. *A Primer on Food, Agriculture, and Public Policy.* New York: Random House, 1967.

Hopkins, R. F., ed. *Global Political Economy of Food.* Madison: University of Wisconsin Press, 1978.

Johnson, D. Gale. *World Food Problems and Prospects.* Washington, D.C.: American Enterprise Institute, 1975.

Answers to Preview and Study Questions

1. What is the farm problem?

It is misleading to talk in terms of the farm "problem." To a large extent, farming in the United States is a major success story. In 1776 some 80–90 percent of the people in this country worked on farms; this percentage has fallen steadily, and today fewer than 5 percent of the U.S. population work on farms. One farmer feeds the equivalent of 20 families in the United States—and is able to export food to other countries as well. Over the past decades technological advances have increased productivity more rapidly in the farm sector than in any other sector. Yet, there *are* some problems. There are about 800,000 small farms which produce and sell small quantities of goods. The largest 19 percent of the approximately 2.44 million farms account for about 78 percent of the value of total farm output. In short, a relatively small number of larger, more efficient farms produce the bulk of farm output, while many smaller, less efficient farms produce relatively small quantities. The farm "problem" largely revolves around attempts to aid the numerous low-income farmers.

2. How does the concept of elasticity help explain part of the farm problem?

The income elasticity of most farm goods is relatively low; as a consequence rising real incomes in the United States are spent proportionally more on nonfood goods. Combined with rapid technological advances that increase supply, this ultimately means fewer farmers will be necessary through time. Moreover, the price elasticity of demand for farm goods is relatively low over broad price ranges. Since farm outputs are subject to the vagaries of weather, the supply of farm goods is volatile. Thus, changing supply curves, given an inelastic demand for farm goods, lead to wide fluctuations in farm prices—and, therefore, in farmers' incomes. Part of the farm problem, then, consists of variable incomes; farmers go through periods of boom and bust.

3. How can price supports be maintained above market clearing levels?

A price support, in effect, guarantees a given price to farmers for their outputs. If the price support is *above* the market clearing price, a surplus will exist; at any price above the market clearing level, the quantity supplied will exceed the quantity demanded. What normally happens, then, is that sellers competing for sales will lower prices to induce increases in quantity demanded and reduce production in order to eliminate inventory increases. In free markets, then, surpluses will disappear as price reductions reduce quantity supplied and increase quantity demanded. How can a price support above the market clearing level be maintained? One way that the U.S. government maintained agricultural price support prices above market equilibrium was to purchase and store the surplus. Each year the U.S. government purchased the excess quantity supplied in order to maintain price supports—and surplus farm goods accumulated year by year.

4. How do the soil bank and acreage restriction plans help eliminate surpluses?

As the above question implies, growing surpluses could eventually be extremely costly—and politically embarrassing as surplus goods eventually rot. As a consequence various schemes were attempted that had as a goal the maintenance of price supports *without* the messy problem of the embarrassing surpluses. One obvious way to maintain price supports *and* not have surpluses is to reduce the supply of agricultural commodities; if supply were to shift leftward the proper distance, it would intersect demand at the support price and no surplus would exist. To this end the soil conservation program was enacted, whereby the government, in effect, paid farmers to *not* produce; the government "rented" a portion of a farmer's land and the farmer could not use it to produce crops that were supported. This program was abused by some farmers, who chose to rent their least fertile land to the government. Next followed the present acreage allotment programs, wherein farmers who wish to receive price supports must agree to set aside some land for that privilege. No *direct* rents are paid to farmers for setting aside land.

5. What is a target price, and how does it differ from other price support programs?

A target price is a politically determined "fair" price for farm goods. Unlike the other support programs mentioned, enactment of a target price program does *not* entail government purchases of surpluses if the market price falls below the target price. In essence, if market price falls below the target price, producers will receive the difference in this price times the number of units they produce. For example, if the market price of wheat is $6 per bushel, and the support price is $6.50 per bushel, farmers can sell their output on the private market for $6, and the government will pay them 50¢ for every bushel they sell. This program does not require direct government purchase of surpluses, which might then require storage. Nevertheless, it ultimately leads to inefficiencies because it raises the long-run average price of agricultural goods, and it entices more resource allocation to the farm sector than would otherwise have been forthcoming. Also, the subsidies to farmers must come from *somewhere;* they are paid by taxpayers. However, *given* a desire to subsidize all farmers, target prices may be the most efficient means of doing so.

Problem

(Answer at the back of the book)

1. Some people maintain that unless farmers are subsidized many will leave the farms and a small number of farms will take over the industry (an oligopolistic market structure) and prices will rise correspondingly. In 1981, it was estimated that 2.44 million farms were in existence in the United States, and that 19 percent of these farms accounted for 78 percent of the value of total farm output.

a. What is the number of farms accounting for this 78 percent of output?

b. In light of this fact, is it likely that an oligopoly will arise in the agricultural industry in the United States?

PART

V

INTERNATIONAL TRADE AND OTHER SYSTEMS

22

Comparative Advantage and International Trade

TOPICS FOR REVIEW

The topics listed below, which we have already analyzed, are applied in this chapter. You may find it worthwhile to review them. For your convenience, each topic is followed by the number identifying the specific "Concepts in Brief."

a. Specialization, comparative advantage (1–4, 2–3)

b. Disadvantages of specialization (2–4)

c. Equilibrium, surpluses, shortages (3–7)

FOR PREVIEW AND STUDY

1. Is international trade important to the United States?

2. How is an import demand curve derived?

3. How is an export supply curve derived?

4. How is international equilibrium for a commodity established?

5. What are some arguments against free trade?

Most people regard international trade as a gain to the United States economy when they are able to buy cheaper foreign products but as a loss to the economy when they see American workers put out of jobs because of foreign competition. In this chapter, we hope to ferret out the real issues involved in international trade. It is certainly true that you, as a consumer, gain from cheaper foreign products. It is also true that employees and stockholders of some industries are hurt by foreign competition. The question is: Are the gains from international trade worth the costs?

Putting Trade in Its Place

Trade among nations must somehow benefit the people of each nation by more than it costs them. The volume of world trade measured in terms of exports has been increasing at a compound growth rate of between 5 and 10 percent per year for quite a while. In 1800, world trade was a mere $1.4 billion in terms of 1981 purchasing power; just before the Great Depression, it reached almost $75 billion. That figure was again reached in 1950. Today, as seen in Exhibit 22–1, world trade exceeds $1 trillion a year. Most of the transactions involved take place voluntarily among individual citizens in different countries.

Exhibit 22–2 shows that the size of international trade in different countries varies greatly when measured as a percentage of each nation's GNP. Some countries export and import more than one-third of their GNPs. The United States ranks near the bottom of the list. In fact, the United States is the Western country that would suffer the least if

EXHIBIT 22–1
International Trade per Year in Nominal Dollars. International trade, measured in terms of exports, has grown rapidly over the last decade or so. By 1977, it had reached the one trillion dollar per year mark.

Source: U.S. Department of Commerce.

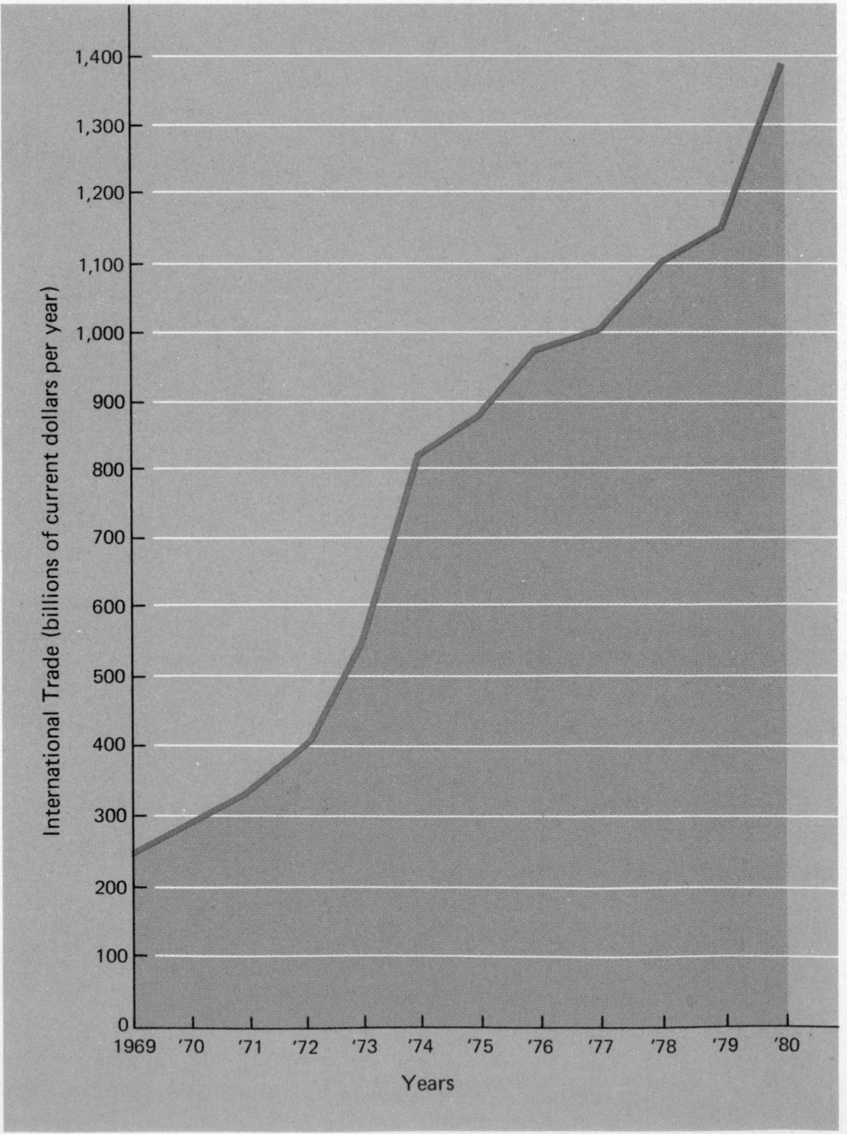

EXHIBIT 22–2
International Trade in Different Countries. Here we show the amount of international trade in different countries expressed in exports as a percentage of GNP. The U.S.S.R., where international trade represents only 5 percent of GNP, is the lowest on the list. Hong Kong, on the other hand, where world trade is a whopping 52 percent of GNP, is at the top of the list.

Country	*Percent of GNP*
Hong Kong	52
Netherlands	43
Canada	25
West Germany	22
United Kingdom	22
Italy	22
France	17
Japan	10
United States	8
U.S.S.R.	5

Source: U.S. Department of Commerce.

foreign trade were completely stopped. The change, however, would not go unnoticed.

IF FOREIGN TRADE STOPPED

If imports stopped, tea and coffee drinkers would have to switch to Postum or Pero. Chocolate would be out of the question: you'd have to switch to carob. You would have no bananas, no pepper, and no Scotch whiskey.

Many of our raw materials come from other countries. Over 90 percent of the bauxite from which we make aluminum is of foreign origin. All our chrome, cobalt, and the greater part of our nickel, platinum, tin, and asbestos are imported. If the world's trade stopped, we wouldn't be able to drink French wines; we wouldn't see Italian movies; and we wouldn't drive Datsuns.

EXPORTS

Imports, of course, are only half the story. We pay for imports either by exports or through an extension of credit from other countries. Some of our employment comes from export industries. Twenty percent of our cotton, 25 percent of our grains, and 25 percent of our tobacco are shipped abroad. A third of our sulfur and a fifth of our coal are sold in foreign countries. Over 16 percent of our auto production, 25 percent of our textile and metal work machinery, and 30 percent of our construction and mining machinery are exported. And there are perhaps 35 other industries in which at least 20 percent of the output is regularly sold abroad. All told, there are 3 to 4 million jobs involved in the production of exports.

Of course, if world trade ceased to exist, all those jobs wouldn't be lost and all the goods now imported wouldn't vanish from our shelves—we would simply alter our own production to take account of the situation. New industries would spring up to provide substitutes for the goods no longer imported. Workers who lost their jobs in export industries would probably get jobs later as we readjusted.

VOLUNTARY TRADE

We engage in foreign trade for only one reason: we benefit from it. All trade is voluntary, and a voluntary exchange between two parties has to benefit both of them. Otherwise the exchange would not take place. The reasoning behind this argument is so simple that it often goes unnoticed by politicians who complain about foreigners "underselling" us by offering relatively cheap goods.

Demand and Supply of Imports and Exports

Let's explore the mechanism that establishes the level of trade between two nations. We will assume that the world consists of only the two nations under study. Therefore, we are considering total world trade in our analysis. First we will need to develop a demand schedule for imports and a supply schedule for exports.

IMPORTS

We will try to calculate graphically how many liters of wine Americans will desire to import every year. We do this by deriving the **excess demand schedule** for wine. The left side of Exhibit 22–3 shows the usual supply and demand curves for wine in the United States. We draw parallel price lines starting at the equilibrium price and going down. At the equilibrium price of $2 per liter, there is no excess demand or excess supply for United States wine. In the right-hand portion of the figure, we again show that at the price of $2, *excess* quantity demanded is zero. If $2 were the world price of wine, there would be no net imports of wine. (In our two-country model, we're assuming that the world is comprised of France and the United States.) In other words, at $2 per liter, no wine trade would take place between these two countries.

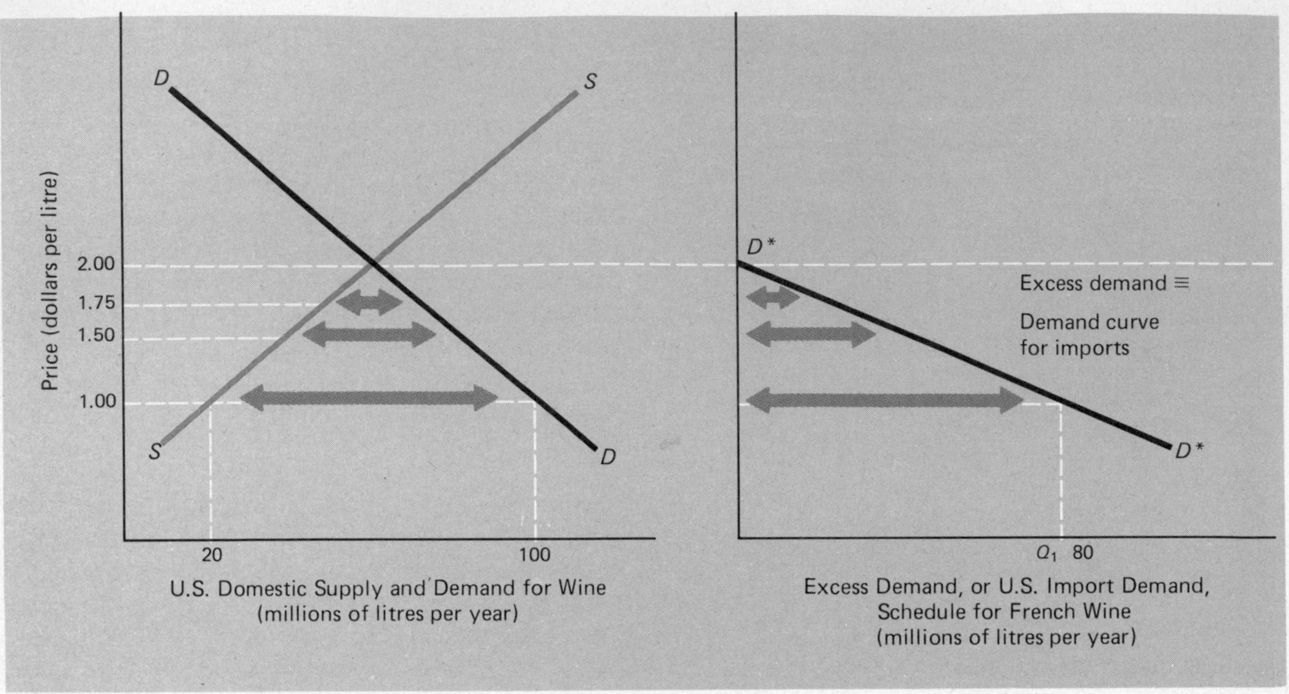

EXHIBIT 22–3
Derivation of Import Demand Schedule for the United States. On the left-hand side of the diagram, we show the U.S. domestic supply and demand schedules for wine. The demand schedule is *DD;* the supply schedule is *SS.* The equilibrium price is $2 per liter. At $2 per liter there will be no excess quantity of wine demanded. Therefore, the quantity of imports demanded will be zero. However, at a price of $1 per liter, there will be an excess quantity of wine demanded. The excess quantity demanded is represented by the longest arrow. We transfer that arrow to the right-hand graph to show the excess quantity of wine demanded at a price of $1. The curve, *D*D**, is the excess demand curve for wine. In other words, it is the U.S. demand for imports of French wine. If the world price were $1 per liter, we would demand the quantity Q_1 of imported wine. The excess demand curve for wine slopes down, starting at the domestic equilibrium price of wine—in this case $2 per liter.

But what about prices lower than $2? At a price of $1, there is an excess quantity demanded for wine in the United States. This is represented by the quantity (horizontal distance) between the domestic supply curve and the domestic demand curve at that price. We take that distance (indicated by the long arrow) and transfer it, at that price level, to the right-hand side of the figure. Here we draw the excess quantity demanded for wine at a price of $1 (the amount of wine represented by the length of the arrow). The length of the arrow is the same in both graphs. If we could continue doing this for all the prices below $2, we would come up with an *excess demand schedule for wine,* which is the same thing as the demand schedule for imports. We import wine because at prices below $2, American producers of wine are unwilling to supply the total quantity demanded by American consumers at those lower prices. Whatever the world price is, we can find out how much the United States will import. If the world price is established at $1, for example, we will bring in imports equal to Q_1. As we would expect, the excess demand schedule for imports is downward sloping, like the regular demand schedule. The lower the world price of wine, the more imports we will buy.

EXPORTS

What about the possibility of the United States exporting wine? Europeans, in fact, are starting to drink more California wines. The situation is depicted graphically in Exhibit 22–4, where we derive the **excess supply schedule.** Let's look at prices above $2. At a price of $3, the *excess quantity of wine supplied* is equal to the amount represented by the distance between the demand curve and the supply curve (again represented by the long arrow). The excess supply curve is shown on the right side of the figure. The supply curve of exports slopes up, like most supply curves. At a price of $2, there are no net exports from the United States. At any price

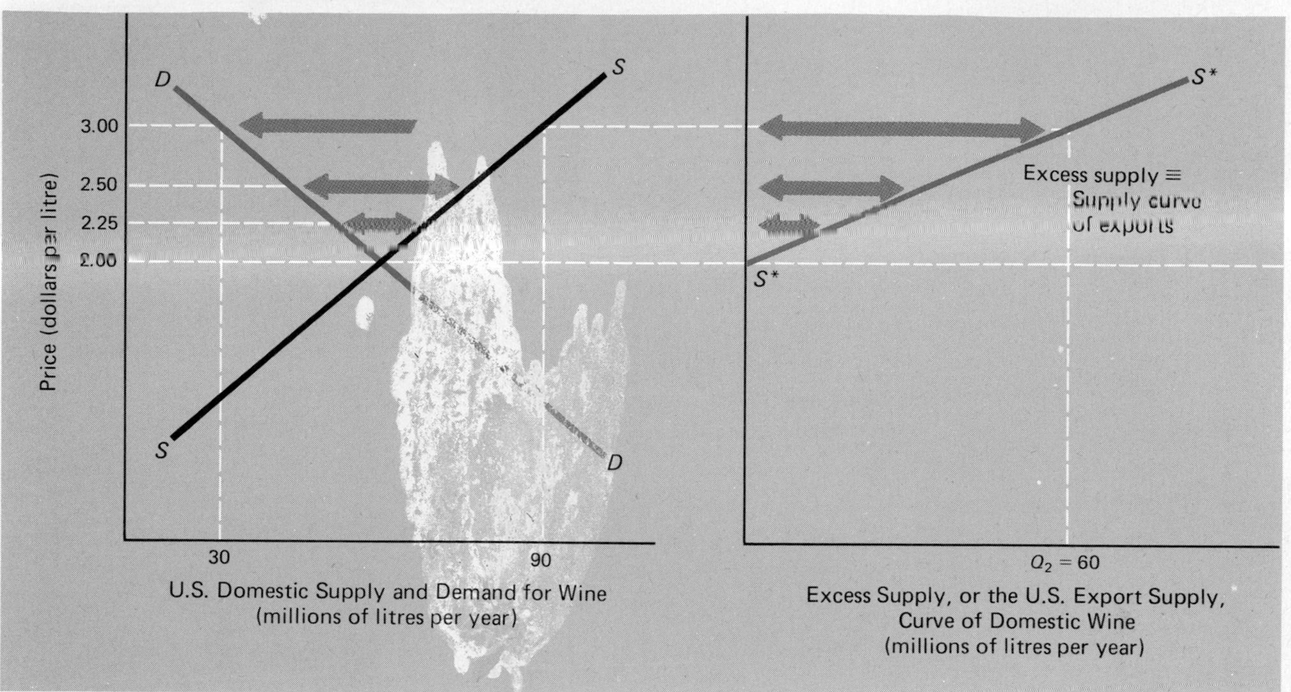

EXHIBIT 22–4
Derivation of Export Supply Schedule for the United States. The domestic demand and supply of wine is shown in the left-hand side of the figure. At an equilibrium price of $2, there is no excess quantity demanded or excess quantity supplied of domestic wine. In the right-hand graph, we show the excess supply of wine curve. At prices higher than $2, there is an excess quantity supplied of wine. The excess quantity supplied is represented by the three arrows. We transfer these arrows over to the right-hand graph to derive the amount of excess quantity supplied that can be used for export purposes. In this manner we derive the supply schedule of exports, *S*S**. It slopes upward, like most supply curves. If the world price of wine were $3, we would export the quantity, Q_2, to other countries.

above $3, however, there will be exports. The amount of these exports is represented by the length of the three arrows. Thus, if the world price rises above $2, the United States would become a net exporter of wine. The higher the world price, the more wine we would export. The lower the world price, the less wine we would export. Below a price of $2, we would start importing. The **zero trade price,** then, is $2. At a world price of $2, we will not engage in world trade. (Note that the world price is established by the interaction of total world demand and world supply.)

The Quantity of Trade in a Foreign Country

We can draw the graph in Exhibit 22–5 for France, our trading partner, in a similar manner. However, we have to establish a common set of measurements for the price of wine. Let's do this in terms of dollars and liters, and let's say that the exchange rate is 20¢ for 1 franc. We place the excess demand schedule for imports and excess supply schedule for exports on the same graph. Exhibit 22–5 shows a standard supply and demand schedule for French wine in terms of dollars per liter. The equilibrium price of French wine is established at $1 per liter. At a world price of $1 per liter, the French will neither import nor export wine. At prices below $1, the French will import wine; at prices above $1, they will export wine. We see in the right-hand portion of Exhibit 22–5 that the excess supply schedule of French wine slopes up, starting at $1 per liter. The French excess demand schedule for imports of wine slopes down, starting at $1 per liter.

International Equilibrium (in a Two-Country World)

We can see the quantity of international trade that will be transacted by putting the French and the American export and import schedules on one

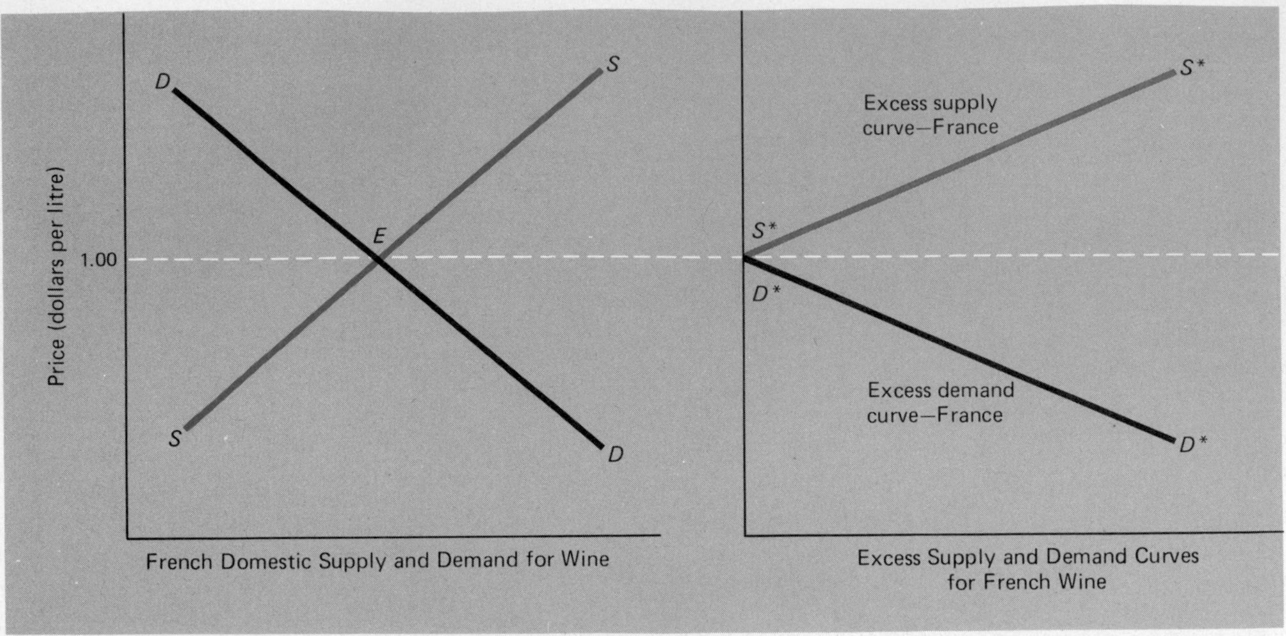

EXHIBIT 22–5
Derivation of Excess Demand and Supply of Wine for France. The left-hand side of the graph shows France's domestic demand and supply curves for wine. The domestic equilibrium price of wine in France, at an exchange rate of 20¢ per franc, translates into $1 per liter. At $1 per liter, France will have neither an excess quantity demanded nor an excess quantity supplied of wine. At higher prices it will have an excess quantity supplied—that is, it will *export* wine. At lower prices, it will have an excess quantity demanded—that is, it will *import* wine. On the right-hand side of the graph, we have drawn France's excess supply curve and excess demand curve. The export curve is S^*S^* and the import curve is D^*D^*.

graph. The zero trade price for wine in America was established at $2 per liter, whereas in France it was established at $1 per liter. We see in Exhibit 22–6 that the excess supply schedule of exports in France intersects the excess demand schedule for imports in the United States at point *E*, with an equilibrium world price of wine of $1.50 per liter and an equilibrium quantity of trade of 10 million liters per year. Here we see how much and the terms under which trade takes place. The amount is determined by the excess demand and supply schedules in each country and the point at which they intersect each other. If the tables were turned and America's no-trade price were below France's no-trade price, then Americans would be exporting wine and the French would be importing it.

In this example, the free-trade international equilibrium price will not fall below $1 per liter, nor will it rise above $2 per liter. Moreover, you should realize that the equilibrium price in this example turns out to be $1.50 because of the particular way the curves are drawn. If we were to do the example differently, we might come out with a somewhat different equilibrium price—although it would still lie between $1 and $2 per liter, given the no-trade price for each country in our example.

Concepts in Brief 22-1

- International trade represents a small part of U.S. GNP, but a large part of the GNPs of small countries, such as Belgium and the Netherlands.
- In order to derive the demand curve for imports, we construct an excess demand schedule showing the difference between domestic demand and domestic supply at prices below the domestic equilibrium price.
- The excess demand curve for imports is downward sloping.
- We derive the excess supply schedule by looking at the difference between domestic demand and domestic supply at prices above the equilibrium price. The excess supply schedule of exports is upward sloping.
- In a two-country world, international trade equilibrium occurs where one country's excess demand schedule intersects the other country's excess supply schedule; the quantity of imports demanded equals the quantity of exports supplied.

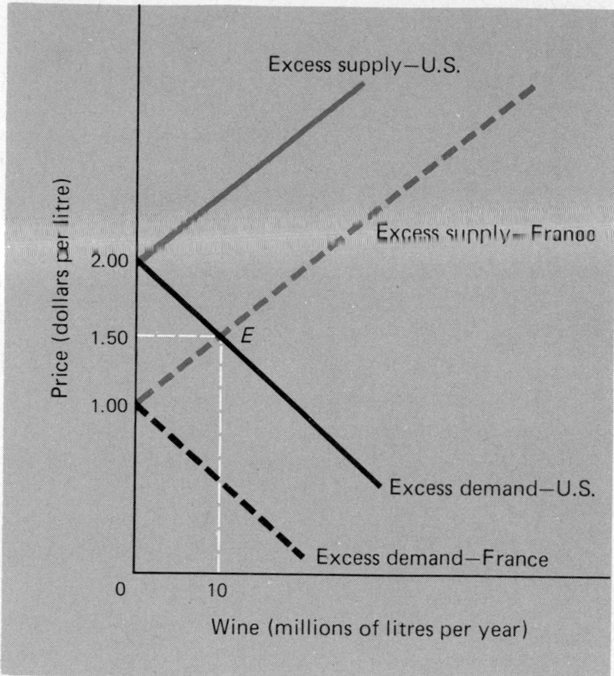

EXHIBIT 22–6
International Equilibrium. We plot France's excess demand and supply curves along with the United States' excess demand and supply curves. France's excess supply curve intersects our excess demand curve at point *E*, which establishes an equilibrium world price of wine. That world price is $1.50, which will be the price of wine everywhere. America will import 10 million liters of wine at that price, and France will export 10 million liters of wine.

Comparative and Absolute Advantage

The reason there are gains from trade lies in one of the most fundamental principles of economics: A nation gains by doing what it can do best *relative* to other nations. The United States benefits by *specializing* in only those endeavors in which it has a **comparative advantage.** (You were first introduced to this concept in Chapter 1.) Let's take an example to demonstrate this concept.

Let's look at France and the United States. We show in Exhibit 22–7 the comparative costs of production of wine and beer in terms of person-days. This is a simple two-country–two-commodity world where we assume that labor is the only factor of production. As you can see from Exhibit 22–7, in the United States it takes 1 person-day to produce 1 liter of wine and the same is true for 1 liter of beer. In France it takes 1 person-day for 1 liter of wine, but 2 person-days for 1 liter of beer. In this sense, Americans are more efficient in terms of labor productivity than the French: they have an **absolute advantage** in producing beer.

EXHIBIT 22–7
Comparative Costs of Production in Person-Days.

	United States	*France*
Wine (1 liter)	1	1
Beer (1 liter)	1	2

However, trade will still take place, which may seem paradoxical. That is to say, how can trade still take place if we can produce both goods at least as cheaply as the French can? Why don't we just produce both ourselves? To understand why, let's assume first that there is no trade and specialization and that the work force in each country consists of 200 workers. These 200 workers are divided equally in the production of wine and beer. We see in Exhibit 22–8 that 100 liters of wine and 100 liters of beer are produced per day in the United States. In France, 100 liters of wine and 50 liters of beer are produced per day. The total daily world production is 200 liters of wine and 150 liters of beer.

Now the countries begin to specialize. What can France produce most cheaply? Look at the comparative costs of production expressed in person-days in Exhibit 22–7. What is the cost of producing 1 liter more of wine? 1 person-day. What is the cost of producing 1 liter more of beer? 2 person-days. We can say, then, that in France the opportunity cost of producing wine is less than that of producing beer. We allow France to specialize in the activity that has the lowest opportunity cost. In other words, France specializes in her comparative advantage, which is the production of wine.

EXHIBIT 22–8
Daily World Output *Before* Specialization.

United States		
100 workers on wine	=	100 liters of wine
100 workers on beer	=	100 liters of beer
France		
100 workers on wine	=	100 liters of wine
100 workers on beer	=	50 liters of beer
World total output	=	200 liters of wine, 150 liters of beer

EXHIBIT 22–9
Daily World Output *After* Specialization.

United States		
200 workers on beer	=	200 liters of beer
France		
200 workers on wine	=	200 liters of wine
World total output	=	200 liters of beer, 200 liters of wine

According to Exhibit 22–9, after specialization, the United States produces 200 liters of beer, and France produces 200 liters of wine. Notice that the total world production per day has gone up from 200 liters of wine and 150 liters of beer to 200 liters of wine and 200 liters of beer per day. This was done without any increased use of resources. The world is better off when countries specialize in their comparative advantage and then trade, because world output is larger. Another way of looking at this is to consider the choice between two ways of producing a good. Obviously, each country would choose the least-costly production process. One way of "producing" a good is to import it, so that if in fact the imported good is cheaper than the domestically produced good, we will "produce" it by importing it.

ON FINDING ONE'S COMPARATIVE ADVANTAGE

It is important to understand the difference between the concept of comparative advantage, which we covered before in Chapter 1, and the notion of absolute advantage. Any time a country can produce a product with fewer person-hours of labor than another country, we say that it has an absolute advantage over the other in the production of that product. You, for example, may have an absolute advantage in doing a large variety of jobs. This does not mean, of course, that you divide your time equally among all these jobs. What you do is discover your area of comparative advantage and specialize in that area.

In general, people discover their own areas of comparative advantage by contrasting the return from doing one job with the return from doing another job. Let's assume you are an executive in a large corporation and you may have an absolute advantage in doing 15 different tasks for that company. For example, you may be able to type better than all the secretaries, wash windows better than any of the window washers, file better than any of the file clerks, and carry messages better than any of the messengers. Your comparative advantage, however, lies in being an executive. You know this because you are paid more for being an executive than you would be for any other job. The company willingly pays your salary as an executive because the value of your output in that job is at least as large as the salary paid to you. It would not pay you the same amount if you wanted to be a typist, for the going salary of typists may be one-fourth an executive's salary.

The key to understanding comparative advantage lies in realizing that total resources are fixed at any moment in time. You have only so much time in a day. A nation has only so many workers and machines. An individual, a company, or a nation must decide how it will allocate its available resources at a given moment. No one can use the same resource in two different jobs at the same time. Even if companies or nations are *absolutely* better at doing everything, they will still specialize in only those tasks in which they have a comparative advantage, because in that specialization they maximize the returns for the use of their time and resources. The United States may have an absolute advantage in producing computers and roller skates in the sense that we can produce both goods with fewer person-hours of labor than any other nation in the world. However, we let other countries produce roller skates because our comparative advantage lies in producing computers. We might be 25 percent more efficient in the production of roller skates but 60 percent more efficient in the production of computers—so we specialize in computers. We gain by exchanging the computers we produce for the roller skates that other countries produce.

Comparative Advantage and Opportunity Cost

We can also relate the concept of comparative advantage to the concept of opportunity cost. In fact, understanding comparative advantage will give you an important insight into all relationships involving exchange among individuals or among nations. Comparative advantage emphasizes the fact that cost means opportunities that must be foregone. If the United States decides to produce roller skates, it foregoes part of its opportunity to produce computers, because the resources used in producing roller skates cannot be used simultaneously in producing computers. The basic reason for the existence of comparative advantage among individuals, companies, cities, counties, states, countries, and continents lies in the fact that opportunity costs vary. It costs less for different parties to engage in different types of economic activities. Opportunity costs for different countries vary just as they vary for different individuals. Let's examine some of the reasons why opportunity costs and, hence, comparative advantages differ among nations.

DIFFERING RESOURCE MIXES

We know that different nations have different resource bases. Australia has much land relative to its population, whereas Japan has little land relative to its population. All other things being equal, one expects countries with relatively more land to specialize in products that use more land. One expects Australia, for example, to engage in extensive sheep raising but not Japan, because the opportunity cost of raising sheep in Japan is much higher. Since land in Japan is relatively scarce, its use carries a higher opportunity cost.

There are also differences in climates. We do not expect countries with cold, dry climates to grow bananas. The limitations of a resource base, however, do not always prohibit a country's actions. Watermelons require tremendous amounts of water; they are nonetheless grown in Arizona. (The federal government subsidizes water to watermelon growers in that state.)

ADVANTAGEOUS TRADE WILL ALWAYS EXIST

Since before the beginning of recorded history, there have been examples of trade among individuals. Since these acts of exchange have usually been voluntary, we must assume that individuals generally benefit from the trade. Individual tastes and resources vary tremendously. As a consequence, there are sufficient numbers of different opportunity costs in the world for exchange to take place constantly.

As individual entities, nations have different collective tastes and different collective resource endowments. We would expect, therefore, that there will always be potential gains to be made from trading among nations. Furthermore, the more trade there is, the more specialization there can be. Specialization in turn leads to increased output and—if we measure well-being by output levels—to increased happiness. (Admittedly, we are using the term *well-being* very loosely here.) Self-sufficiency on the part of individuals undeniably means that they forego opportunities to consume more than they could by not being self-sufficient. Likewise, self-sufficiency on the part of a nation will lower its consumption possibilities and therefore will lower the real-income levels of its inhabitants. Imagine life in Delaware if that state were forced to become self-sufficient!

COSTS OF TRADE

Trade does not come without cost. If one state has a comparative advantage in producing agricultural crops, other states may not be able to succeed as centers of agricultural production. Farm workers in states that are less efficient at agricultural production will suffer decreases in their incomes until they find other occupations or move to where the higher-paying jobs are.

As tastes, supplies of natural resources, prices, and so on change throughout the world, different countries may find their areas of comparative advantage changing. One example of this is the United States' production of steel. Japan has become increasingly competitive in steel products, and U.S. steelmakers are being hurt. The stockholders and employees in U.S. steel companies are feeling the pinch from Japan's ability to produce steel products at lower costs. In other words, foreign trade raises average and total income in each country, but some people may suffer ups and downs in their individual incomes.

Concepts in Brief 22-2

- Countries can be better off materially if they specialize in their comparative advantage.
- It is important to distinguish between absolute and comparative advantage: the former refers to the ability to produce a unit of output with fewer physical units of input; the latter refers to producing that output that has the lowest opportunity cost for a nation.
- On an individual basis, one can find his or her comparative advantage by seeking out the job for which the monetary rewards are highest.
- Different nations will always have different comparative advantages because of differing opportunity costs due to different resource mixes. Foreign trade may raise average and total incomes in each country, but it also can hurt certain groups in each country because of increased competition from abroad.

Arguments Against Free Trade

There are numerous arguments against free trade. Much of the time, however, these arguments are incomplete. They mainly point out the costs of trade; they do not consider the benefits or the possible alternatives for reducing costs while still reaping benefits.

INFANT INDUSTRY ARGUMENT

A nation may feel that if a particular industry were allowed to develop domestically, it could eventually become efficient enough to compete effectively in the world market. Therefore, if some restrictions were placed on imports, native producers would be given the time needed to develop their efficiency to the point where they would be able to compete in the domestic market without any restrictions on imports. In graphic terminology, we would expect that if the protected industry truly does experience technological breakthroughs toward greater efficiency in the future, then the supply curve will shift outward to the right so that the domestic industry can produce larger quantities at each and every price. This **infant industry argument** has some merit in the short run and has been used to protect a number of American industries in their infancy. Such policy can be abused, however. Often the protective import-restricting arrangements remain even after the infant has "matured." If other countries can still produce more cheaply, the people who benefit from this type of situation are obviously the stockholders (and specialized factors of production) in the industry that is still being protected from world competition. The people who lose out are the consumers, who must pay a price higher than the world price for the product in question. In any event, it is very difficult to know *beforehand* which industries will eventually survive. In other words, we cannot predict very well the specific "infant" industries that should be protected. Note that when we talk about which industry *should be* protected, we are in the realm of normative economics. We are stating a value judgment that comes from our heart.

Finally, critics of the "infant" industry argument in favor of tariffs point out that there really aren't any so-called infant industries threatened by foreign competition in the United States today.

NATIONAL SECURITY

It is often argued that we should not rely on foreign sources for many of our products because in time of war these sources might well be cut off and we would have developed few, if any, substitute sources. To make this point with an extreme and unlikely example, suppose that the Soviet Union can produce nuclear weapons more cheaply than we can; should imports of such Soviet-made commodities be restricted? A classic and more realistic example of using a national security argument to justify a trade restriction involves oil exploration. For national defense reasons (supposedly), President Eisenhower instituted at first a voluntary, and then a mandatory oil-import **quota** system, thereby restricting the amount of foreign oil that could be imported into the United States. The idea was to keep domestic prices up and thereby create an incentive for more exploration of American oil. Thus, in time of war, we would have a ready and available supply of oil for our tanks, ships, and bombers.

However, restricting the amount of foreign oil imported merely served to raise the price of oil in the United States. The people who benefited were obviously the stockholders in oil corporations; the people who lost out were the consumers of oil products. It has been estimated by various government officials that the oil-import quota program cost the consumer a staggering $7 billion a year in the form of higher oil product prices. Also, it was the poor who paid more, relatively, than the rich, since the poor spend a larger proportion of their incomes directly or indirectly on petroleum products than do the rich. And finally, it was absurd to think that restricting the amount of imported foreign oil would allow us to have more oil for a national emergency. Obviously, using more of our own finite sources would only lead to *less* for a national emergency.

STABILITY

Many people argue that foreign trade should be restricted because it introduces an element of instability into our economic system. They point out that the vagaries of foreign trade add to the ups and downs in our own employment level. However, if we follow this argument to its logical conclusion, we would restrict trade among our various states as well. After all, the vagaries of trade among particular states sometimes cause unemployment in other states. Things are sorted out over time, but workers suffer during the adjustment period. Nonetheless, we don't restrict trade among the states. In fact, there is a constitutional stricture against taxing exports and imports (*inter*state commerce) among the states.

As regards the international sphere, however, people somehow change their position. They feel that adjusting to the vagaries of *international* trade costs more than adjusting to the vagaries of domestic *interstate* trade. Perhaps people believe foreign trade really doesn't benefit us that much, and thus they argue against it, claiming that the stability of aggregate economic activity is at stake. (It may also be that individually we derive satisfaction from citizens in other states benefiting from trade among the states; but we do not derive any satisfaction from knowing that unrestricted trade has benefited those in other countries.)

We should note one difference between the domestic and international situations, however, that lends some truth to this argument. Labor is mobile among our states, but it is not as mobile among nations. Immigration laws prevent workers from moving to countries where they can earn the most income. There are also many differences in language and customs that prevent workers from freely moving from country to country. Therefore, the adjustment costs to a changing international situation may in fact be higher than the adjustment costs to a changing domestic situation. However, this may be an argument in favor of eliminating (or at least easing) immigration laws, rather than for restricting international trade.

PROTECTING AMERICAN JOBS

Perhaps the most often used argument against free trade is that unrestrained competition from other countries will eliminate American jobs because other countries have lower-cost laborers than we do. This is indeed a compelling argument, particularly for congresspersons from areas that might be threatened by foreign competition. For example, a congressperson from an area with shoe factories would certainly be upset about the possibility of constituents losing their jobs because of competition from lower-priced shoe manufacturers in Brazil and Italy. This argument against free trade is equally applicable, however, to trade among the several states. After all, if labor in the South is less expensive than labor in the North, southern industry may put northern workers out of jobs; but, again, we do not, and constitutionally cannot, restrict trade (at least not overtly) among states.

We can briefly point out that total American jobs depend on aggregate demand. Even though foreign competition may alter the *structure* of the demand for labor, it does not automatically change the *total* demand for labor.

Finally, we wish to point out here that virtually every attempt at protecting American jobs by imposing tariffs, quotas, and other restrictions on international trade leads to retaliation by our trading partners. In other words, they start imposing similar restrictions on trade with the United States. The result is that we save less productive employment at the expense of more productive employment.

We expand on this important topic in the following Issues and Applications section. There are numerous ways to hinder free trade, and there are numerous arguments in favor of restrictions on trade. Which of the arguments is most meaningful will now be discussed.

Concepts in Brief 22-3

- The infant industry argument against free trade contends that new industries should be allowed protection against world competition so that they can become technically efficient in the long run.
- The national security argument against free trade contends that we should not rely on foreign sources for crucial materials (such as oil) needed during time of war.
- Using the national security argument, President Eisenhower instituted an oil-import quota system.
- Some people argue that free trade increases instability in U.S. national income and business activity.

ISSUES
AND APPLICATIONS

Does International Competition Pose a Threat?

Concepts Applied
■ Quotas, excess demand, law of demand, and law of supply

This bill would discourage American business investment abroad and limit the flow of imports into this country. We can no longer afford to export American jobs and technology at the expense of our own industry all in the name of "free trade."

Imports of foreign-made, energy-efficient vehicles contributed to the huge financial losses in the U.S. automobile industry.

Such were the words contained in the preamble to one of the most debated bills introduced into Congress in the 1970s: the Burke-Hartke Foreign Trade and Investment Proposal. The preamble went on to state that the statute under consideration was to be interpreted as attempting to "ensure that the production of goods which have historically been produced in the United States is continued and maintained." Moreover, "to the extent that production of such goods has been transferred abroad, it is the intent of Congress that this production be encouraged to return to the United States."

Such words seem to be at odds with the underlying principles of economics. Specialization by people and countries in their areas of comparative advantage, coupled with trade, presumably allows for increased standards of material well-being. Why, then, would Senators Burke and Hartke want to stifle free trade? How could other senators introduce numerous other bills along the same lines—that is, seek to restrict the flow of goods and services between our nation and other countries? We already briefly touched on this phenomenon. It concerns protection—mainly what is called "job protection"—for those in industries hurt by foreign competition.

Getting Hurt by Free Trade

We have never said that free trade benefits everyone. What we did say on several occasions was that free trade allows for a higher *overall* material standard of living. This says nothing about how individuals may fare. Let's take a specific example. Suppose you are a worker in a shoe factory in Massachusetts. Suppose, also, that the industrialization in Brazil allows that country to produce shoes at a lower cost per pair than is possible in Massachusetts. In other words, given the relatively lower wage rate in Brazil, shoes can be produced there at a lower per unit cost. The importation of these low-cost Brazilian shoes into the United States might seriously threaten the profitability of the shoe manufacturing company for which you work. Suppose, in fact, there is no way for your Massachusetts company to compete effectively with the Brazilian shoe imports. In this case, your company will go out of business. As a worker in that company, you will lose your job. You will be upset and annoyed that "unfair" competition from "cheap" labor in Brazil has taken away what was "rightfully yours."

This is the crux of the argument against free trade, and it is the backbone of such bills as the Burke-Hartke one mentioned. Free trade does put some Americans out of work. Profits may fall and some firms may go out of business. Also, some workers, although not becoming unemployed, may see their wages rise at a lower rate than they would have without free trade. In a dynamic world where tastes change, resource bases change, technologies change, and everything else changes, the comparative advantages of individuals as well as of states and nations will change.

The fact, for example, that the United States has historically been a provider of high-technology goods for the rest of the world does not mean that the United States' comparative advantage won't change in the future toward some other good or service. This, in fact, is essentially what *has* happened with the United States, Japan, and Germany. Historically, the United States has had a comparative advantage in high-technology goods, but in recent years that comparative advantage has been eroded by the increasingly sophisticated products of such countries as Japan and Germany. Naturally, jobs have suffered in the United States. But this is what we call a *sectoral effect.* It affects a specific sector and not the entire American economy.

How We Pay for Imports

Strange as it may seem, if we reduce imports into the United States, we will also reduce exports from the United States, for we must ultimately pay for imports with exports. After all, the rest of the world is not interested in providing us with charity in the form of their exports (our imports). They want something in return. What they want in return, ultimately, is American goods and services. During certain periods of time, the rest of the world may be content to take, in exchange for the goods and services they provide the United States, such things as United States Treasury bonds and other dollar-denominated financial assets. But ultimately, the rest of the world will want to exchange whatever liquid or illiquid U.S. assets they hold for U.S. goods and services. In the very long run, the balance of trade must balance. Hence, if we stifle imports, we will in effect stifle exports.

How Trade Can Be Hindered

There are many ways that international trade can be stopped, or at least partially stifled. These include, among other things, quotas and taxes—the latter are usually called tariffs when applied to internationally traded items. Let's talk first about quotas.

Quotas. In the quota system, countries are restricted to a certain amount of trade. Consider an import quota system that has been in effect off and on in the United States. It concerns import quotas applied to sugar. We have, at different times, set a quota on the importation of sugar into the United States. Look at Exhibit 22–10. In panel (a) we present a supply and demand graph for sugar. The horizontal line, P_w, represents the world price line; this line also represents the world's supply of sugar to the United States. We draw this line horizontally because we assume that the United States buys only an extremely small fraction of the total world supply of sugar. Therefore, the United States can buy literally all the sugar it wants at the world price.

In the absence of world trade, the domestic (U.S.) price will be at the intersection of the domestic supply and demand schedules. The domestic quantity demanded will be determined at that intersection also. With world trade opened up, Americans will buy, in our example, 4 billion pounds of sugar in total; the domestic sugar producers (principally in Hawaii) will provide 3.5 billion pounds of this total. The difference between 4 billion and 3.5 billion represents the amount of sugar imported. This is an equilib-

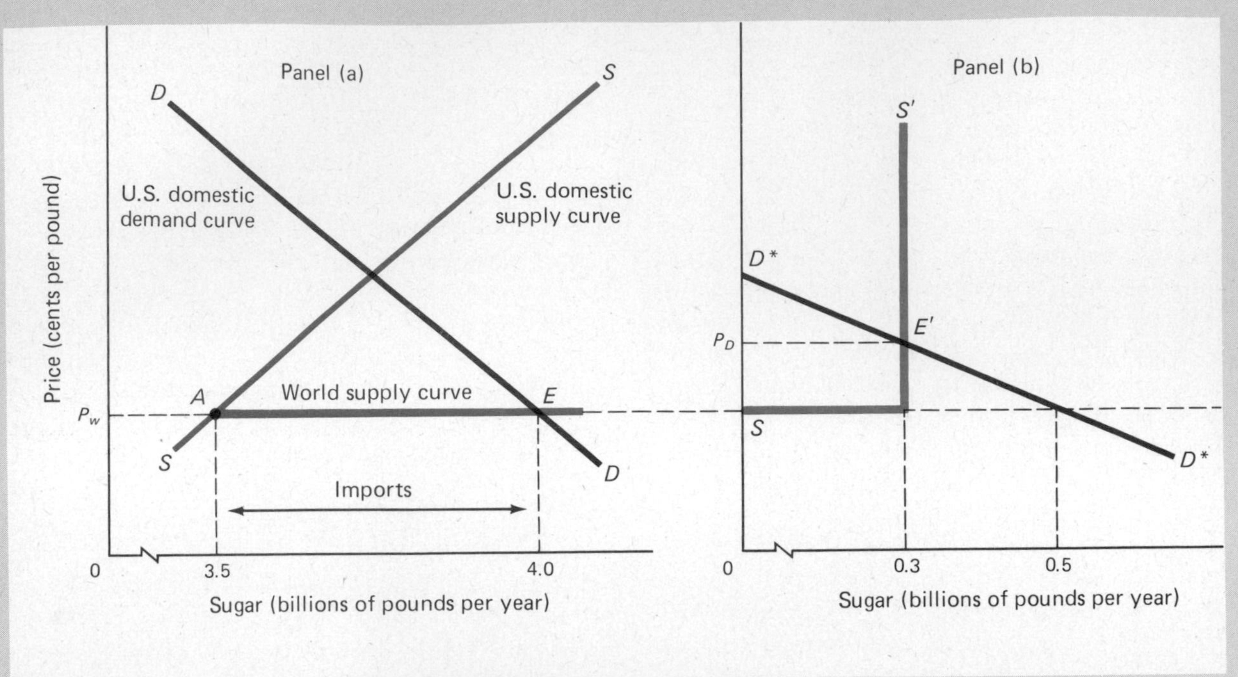

EXHIBIT 22–10
The Effect of a Sugar Import Quota System. The world price of sugar is established at P_w. We assume that the United States buys a very small part of the total world supply of sugar. The United States can buy all the sugar that it wants at the world price. The supply of imports curve faced by the United States, in effect, is the horizontal line at P_w, labeled "World Supply Curve." Our domestic supply curve is *SS* in panel (a) (left-hand portion of the graph) and our domestic demand curve is *DD*. At the world price of P_w, we will reach an equilibrium at *E*. This means that we will consume 4 billion pounds of sugar per year, of which 3.5 billion will be produced domestically. The difference is represented by imports. In the right-hand portion of the figure, panel (b), we show the excess demand for sugar as *D*D**; that is, *D*D** represents the demand curve for sugar imports. At the world price of P_w, the quantity demanded will be .5 billion pounds of sugar per year. The government, however, steps in and imposes an import quota of .3 billion pounds per year. The supply curve remains P_w until it hits the quota line of .3 billion pounds of sugar per year. Then it becomes vertical. The new supply curve is *SS'*. The new supply curve, *SS'*, intersects the demand curve for imports, *D*D**, at a new equilibrium of *E'*. With import quotas, P_D becomes the price on every pound of sugar—domestic or imported. Thus, the quota effectively raises the revenues to domestic sugar producers. It forces consumers to pay a higher price.

rium situation. The new, effective supply curve facing U.S. consumers is the domestic one below the price P_w, but becomes the horizontal P_w line at the price P_w. Thus, the effective supply curve facing U.S. consumers is a combination of the U.S. domestic supply curve and the world supply curve. It starts at *S*, goes to point *A*, then becomes horizontal at the world supply curve out through point *E* and beyond. The intersection of this effective supply curve facing U.S. consumers and the domestic demand curve is at *E*. Thus, we see that the quantity of imports demanded and supplied from the world market will be .5 billion pounds of sugar. The intersection of the combined supply curve and the domestic demand curve is at *E*, where it will stay if there are no restrictions.

Let's now look at the right-hand portion of the graph in panel (b). We draw the excess demand for imports; we put in the world price line, P_w, and we come up with the .5 billion pounds of sugar imported at the world price. Now we want to see what happens when a quota is instituted. Instead of allowing .5 billion pounds of sugar to be imported each year, the government says that only .3 billion pounds may be brought into the United States. We draw a vertical line at .3 billion pounds per year. The supply curve effectively becomes the world price line until it hits the import quota restriction at the vertical line.

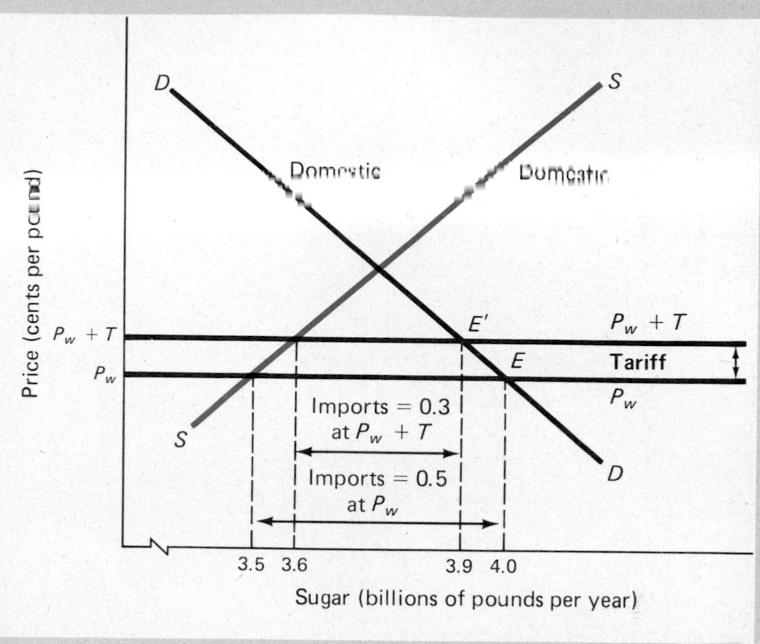

EXHIBIT 22–11

An Import Tariff. The domestic supply curve for sugar is *SS*. The domestic demand curve is *DD*. At a world price of P_w, the United States can buy all of the sugar it wants. Equilibrium is established at *E*, where the quantity demanded is 4 billion pounds per year. The quantity supplied domestically is 3.5 billion pounds. The difference is imports, or .5 billion pounds per year. Now the government puts a tariff, *T*, on every pound of sugar that enters the United States from abroad. No Americans can buy sugar at the world price, P_w. They must now pay $P_w + T$. This shifts the effective horizontal world supply curve up to the heavy solid line, $P_w + T$. At this price, the domestic quantity demanded is at the intersection of *E'*, or 3.9 billion pounds per year. The domestic quantity supplied increases to 3.6 billion pounds per year. Imports fall from .5 billion pounds per year to .3 billion pounds per year (the smaller shaded arrow). The government collects taxes equal to *T* times the new quantity of imports, .3 billion pounds. Domestic producers of sugar do not, however, pay any tariff on what they sell. Thus domestic producers get to keep all of the increase in the price of domestic sugar, but the government gets to keep all of the increase in the price of imported sugar—the tariff. This was not the case with the quota system discussed in Exhibit 37–10. There the domestic price went up because of the quota, but no government revenues were obtained.

The supply curve then follows the vertical line up; it is now *SS'*. The new equilibrium point is at *E'*, the intersection of the new supply schedule and the excess demand for imports. We see that at point *P'*, however, there is a higher price for all sugar consumed in the United States. And that price is P_D. You, the consumer, lose. The importers (who get the quota rights) and the domestic sugar industry gain.

Tariffs. We can use our graphic analysis to analyze the effect of a **tariff,** defined as a tax imposed by one country only on goods imported from other countries. The nature of a tariff is such that no similar tax is applied to identical goods produced domestically. A U.S. imposed tariff on an import raises the price of a product (in this case, sugar), both foreign and domestic, to United States residents. Let's assume that the tariff is 10 percent of the price of sugar entering this country. In Exhibit 22–11 we show the domestic supply and demand schedules for sugar, with the world price of P_w. Now we add a tariff.

The tariff, *T*, is equal to the difference between the world price, P_w, and the horizontal line above it ($P_w + T$). Domestic demanders of sugar must now pay the world price plus the tariff. They cannot get sugar any cheaper because everyone must pay the tariff. On domestically produced and sold sugar there is no import tariff. That means that the U.S. Treasury does not collect taxes on domestically produced sugar; the producers get to keep all of the revenues. Now that the price goes up to $P_w + T$, we move up the domestic supply curve and find that domestic producers are willing to increase the output of sugar from 3.5 billion to 3.6 billion pounds per year. On the other hand, consumers will demand a lower quantity at the higher price that now faces them. They will reduce the quantity demanded from 4 billion to 3.9 billion pounds per year. We see, then, that the level of imports will decrease from .5 billion to .3 billion pounds per year. This decrease in imports is similar to the one we discussed with a quota system; however, there are differences.

In both cases, the price is higher. In panel (b) of Exhibit 22–10, we saw that the price went up to P_D. In Exhibit 22–11, the price went up to $P_w + T$. In both cases, the quantity of imports fell from .5 billion pounds per year to .3 billion pounds. The big difference is that with the quota system, no government revenues (taxes) were collected. With the tariff system just described, the government keeps the tariff, T, times the quantity of imports (.3 billion pounds per year). These revenues can be used to reduce taxes or to increase government expenditures.

The U.S. experience. We see in Exhibit 22–12 that the United States has had a history of widely varying average tariff rates on *all* imported goods. The highest tariff rate came about during the Great Depression with the passage of the Smoot-Hawley Tariff in 1930. In recent years, our average tariff rates have been historically very low.

What the Future Holds

To be sure, the future will see a continuation of special-interest groups lobbying for protection

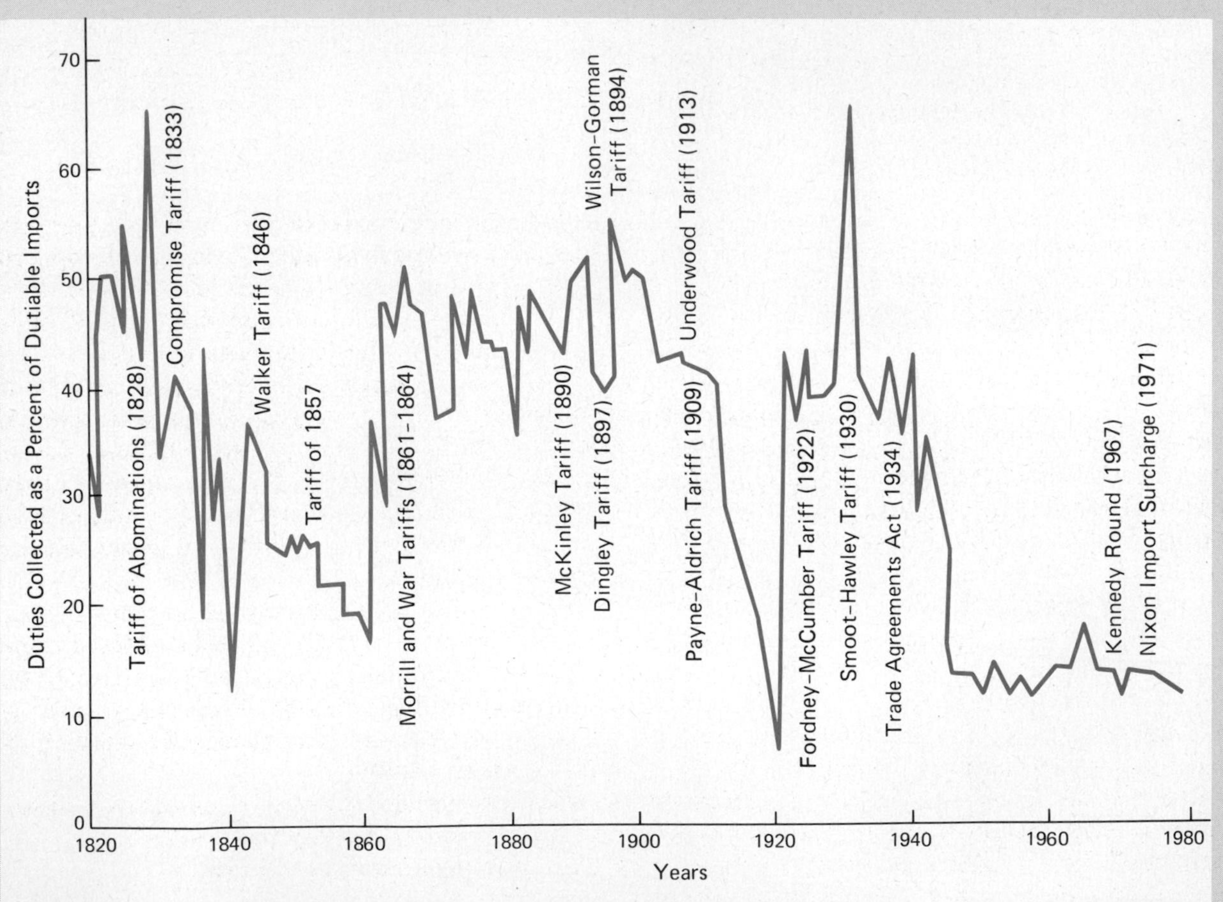

EXHIBIT 22–12
Tariff Rates in the United States Since 1820. Tariff rates in the United States have bounced about like a football, and, indeed, in Congress, tariffs do represent a political football. Import-competing industries prefer high tariffs. In the twentieth century, the highest tariff we have had was the Smoot-Hawley Tariff of 1930, which was almost as high as the Tariff of Abominations in 1828.

Source: U.S. Department of Commerce.

from international competition. It is difficult, though, for these groups to use the same arguments that they have used in the past—economic reality changes much too fast. For many years, the cry of "cheap Japanese labor" was heard, particularly from the U.S. labor movement. Lower-paid Japanese workers were undercutting American workers, and, in essence, we were exporting jobs to Japan. Japanese wages today, however, are far from being "slave" wages. Indeed, Japanese industry wage rates are on a par with U.S. industry wage rates.

What we must realize is that every economic action has a cost. It is indeed rare when everybody can be made better off by some policy. Any time that trade is stifled, there are gainers and losers. Economic analysis tells us that general material well-being will be reduced any time there are restrictions on trade. That is to say, import quotas and tariffs cause an inefficient allocation of resources. However, by the same token, specific groups will benefit from restrictions on foreign competition. It is impossible to argue, from a purely economic point of view, whether certain types of foreign trade should be restrained, because to do so would require a value judgment as to who should benefit or gain from a particular policy.

Questions

1. Mark Twain once said: "The free traders win all the arguments, but the protectionists win all the votes." Why?
2. Who loses from tariffs?

Definition of Terms

Excess demand schedule When applied to imports, a demand schedule derived from the difference between the quantities of a product supplied domestically and the quantities demanded at prices *below* the domestic "no-trade" equilibrium price.

Excess supply schedule When applied to exports, a supply schedule derived from the difference between the quantities of a product supplied domestically and the quantities demanded at prices *above* domestic "no-trade" equilibrium prices.

Zero trade price The price on an excess demand and supply diagram at which there is no foreign trade. At this price, the domestic demand and supply schedules intersect.

Comparative advantage An advantage arising out of relative efficiency, which follows from scarcity of resources. Comparative advantage is the advantage measured in terms of other goods that could be produced, not in terms of factor inputs. If a country has a comparative advantage in one good, it must have a comparative *disadvantage* in another. As long as the opportunity cost of doing the same job differs for different people or different countries, each will have a comparative advantage in something.

Absolute advantage The ability to produce more output from given inputs of resources than others can do. For example, America may have an absolute advantage in the production of agricultural goods in the sense that, per unit of labor, we can produce more bushels of wheat than any other country.

Infant industry argument An argument in support of tariffs: Tariffs should be imposed to protect (from import competition) an industry that is trying to get started. Presumably, after the industry becomes technologically efficient, the tariff can be lifted.

Quota A specified number of, or value of, imports allowed into a country per year.

Tariff A tax on imported goods.

Chapter Summary

1. In terms of current purchasing power, world trade has expanded from a mere $1.3 billion in the year 1800 to over $1 trillion in 1981. Trade rates differ among nations. The United States has one of the smallest amounts of world trade (which is expressed as exports as a percentage of GNP).
2. Although trade represents only 8 percent of

U.S. GNP, we would nevertheless notice a substantial change in our life-style if we were to cease trading with other countries.

3. Trade is usually voluntary among nations and among people. Therefore, it must be perceived to benefit everyone concerned if it is to continue.
4. We can draw an excess demand schedule for foreign goods by looking at the difference between the quantities demanded and the quantities supplied domestically at prices below our domestic equilibrium price.
5. The excess supply schedule of domestic goods is found by looking at the difference between quantities supplied and demanded at prices above our domestic equilibrium price. The excess supply schedule is our supply schedule of exports.
6. The world equilibrium price and quantity traded are established at the point where one country's excess demand schedule intersects another country's excess supply schedule. As long as the zero trade prices of two countries are different, there will be trade (in the absence of restrictions).
7. It is important to distinguish between absolute and comparative advantage. A person or country that can do everything "better" (with higher labor productivity) than every other person or country has an absolute advantage. Nevertheless, trade will still be advantageous because people will specialize in the things that they do relatively best. They will exploit their respective comparative advantage.
8. An individual's comparative advantage lies in that activity for which he or she is best paid. Comparative advantage follows from different relative efficiencies and from the fixed nature of our resources at any point in time.
9. Along with the gains, there are costs from trade. Certain industries and their employees may be hurt if trade is opened up. There are numerous arguments, therefore, against free trade.
10. There is also a national security argument for tariffs and import quotas. For example, the oil-import quota was imposed in the name of national security; presumably, by keeping out cheap foreign oil, we increase the incentive for domestic exploration of oil resources. Therefore, in time of war, we would have a sufficient amount to support our military effort.
11. An import quota restricts the quantity of imports coming into the country. It therefore raises the price. Depending on how the rights to importing are distributed, certain importers may gain; consumers always lose.
12. An import tariff raises the price of internationally produced goods. It therefore allows domestic producers to raise their own prices. The result is a higher price to consumers, a lower quantity of imports, and a lower volume of international trade.

Selected References

Caves, Richard E., and Ronald W. Jones. *World Trade and Payments: An Introduction.* 2nd ed. Boston: Little, Brown, 1977, chaps. 1–4.

Michaely, Michael. *Trade and Protection.* Chicago: University of Chicago Press, 1978.

Pen, Jan A. *Primer on International Trade.* New York: Random House, 1967.

Ricardo, David. *Principles of Political Economy and Taxation.* New York: Dutton, 1972.

Snider, Delbert A. *Introduction to International Economics.* 7th ed. Homewood, Ill.: Irwin, 1979, chaps. 1–6.

Answers to Preview and Study Questions

1. Is international trade important to the United States?

The direct impact of international trade on the United States, as measured by the ratio of exports to GNP, is relatively small (only about 8 percent)—compared to many other nations. Yet it is hard to imagine what life would be like without international trade. Initially many prices would rise rapidly, but eventually domestic production would begin on many goods we presently import. However, consider life without coffee, tea, bananas, and all foreign wines, motorcycles, automobiles, televisions, videotape recorders, and hundreds of other goods from food and clothing to electronics—not to mention vital imports such as bauxite, chromium, cobalt, nickel, platinum, tin, and asbestos.

2. How is an import demand curve derived?

An import demand curve can be derived from the domestic demand for the commodity in question. In effect, the import demand curve for some commodity is the domestic demand for the commodity in question minus the domestic supply—at all prices below equilibrium. Thus, at relatively low prices (below equilibrium), domestic suppliers will produce less than domestic buyers want to purchase (quantity demanded will exceed quantity supplied at all prices below domestic equilibrium). This excess demand for the commodity in question can be met by importing from abroad; the locus of all points, which shows the excess quantity demanded at all prices below equilibrium, defines the domestic import demand curve for the commodity in question.

3. How is an export supply curve derived?

An export supply curve can be derived from the domestic supply curve of the commodity in question. In effect, the export supply curve for some commodity is the domestic supply of the commodity minus the domestic demand—at all prices above the domestic equilibrium price. At relatively high prices (above domestic equilibrium), the domestic quantity supplied of this commodity will exceed the domestic quantity demanded. That is, a surplus will exist at all prices above equilibrium. If foreigners *are* willing to buy this domestically produced commodity at prices above equilibrium, then the excess supply can be exported to them. Thus, the domestic export supply curve is defined as the difference between domestic quantity supplied and quantity demanded—at all prices above equilibrium.

4. How is international equilibrium for a commodity established?

Consider a two-country world, each country with the capability of producing, say, videotape recorders. Country A has an import demand curve and an export supply curve (as derived in questions 2 and 3 above), and so does country B. Assuming that each country has different supply and demand conditions (and that each, therefore, has a different domestic equilibrium price level for videotape recorders), we can define the international equilibrium position. International equilibrium will occur where one country's excess supply curve intersects the other country's excess demand curve—at a price somewhere between country A's and country B's domestic equilibrium prices. At that intersection point, one country's exports will be equated with the other country's imports of videotape recorders; hence, international equilibrium will be established.

5. What are some arguments against free trade?

Many economists agree that free trade generates an efficient allocation of world resources; each country would produce those commodities in which it has a comparative advantage and import those commodities in which it does not. This, in general, leads to higher average and total incomes for all countries. Yet, despite this truth, there are many people who offer many arguments *against* free trade. First, there is the infant industry argument, which maintains that new industries developing domestically need protection from mature foreign competitors until they are mature enough themselves to compete with foreigners—at which time protection will be removed. One problem with this argument is that it is difficult to tell when maturity sets in, and domestic industries will fight against such weaning. Moreover, this argument is hardly one that U.S. industries can presently use. Another popular argument against free trade is the national security argument, which maintains that certain inputs or outputs are strategically important and should be developed domestically even if the cost of doing so is greater than importation. This will limit the domestic country's reliance on foreign sources that could be hazardous in times of crises. This argument is easily abused and is particularly attractive to domestic producers who stand to profit from protection. Moreover, other alternatives exist, such as finding substitutes and/or stockpiling of "strategic" resources. Finally, it is alleged (and is true to a large extent) that free trade leads to instability for specific domestic industries as comparative advantage changes in a dynamic world. Nations that traditionally have held a comparative advantage in the production of some goods occasionally lose that advantage (while necessarily gaining others). Regional hardships are a result, and protection of domestic jobs is demanded. Yet, if carried to its logical conclusion, this argument leads to restriction of trade between states, then between cities and towns *within* states, then between families! Some insecurity is a price that nations must pay for higher average and total incomes; nothing is free in this world.

Problems

(Answers at the back of the book)

1. The following is a hypothetical table of person-hours required to produce vodka and wheat in the United States and in Russia:

Product	*United States*	*Russia*
Vodka (qt)	6 person-hours	9 person-hours
Wheat (bu)	3 person-hours	6 person-hours

a. What is the opportunity cost to the United States of producing one quart of vodka? What is the opportunity cost to the United States of producing one bushel of wheat?

b. What is the opportunity cost to Russia of producing one quart of vodka? What is the opportunity cost to Russia of producing one bushel of wheat?

c. The United States has a comparative advantage in what? Russia has a comparative advantage in what?

2. The following is a hypothetical table of person-hours required to produce hemp and poppy seeds in Colombia and Turkey:

Product	*Colombia*	*Turkey*
Hemp (lb)	2 person-hours	1 person-hour
Poppy seeds (oz)	6 person-hours	2 person-hours

a. What is the opportunity cost to Colombia of producing one pound of hemp? One ounce of poppy seeds?

b. What is the opportunity cost to Turkey of producing one pound of hemp? One ounce of poppy seeds?

c. Colombia has a comparative advantage in what? Turkey has a comparative advantage in what?

3. Consider the international equilibrium situation for wine at right.
   a. What is the equilibrium price per liter of wine in the United States?
   b. What is the equilibrium price per liter of wine in France?
   c. What is the international equilibrium price per liter?
   d. Why won't $3 be the international equilibrium price?
   e. Why won't $4 be the international equilibrium price?
   f. Which country will export wine?

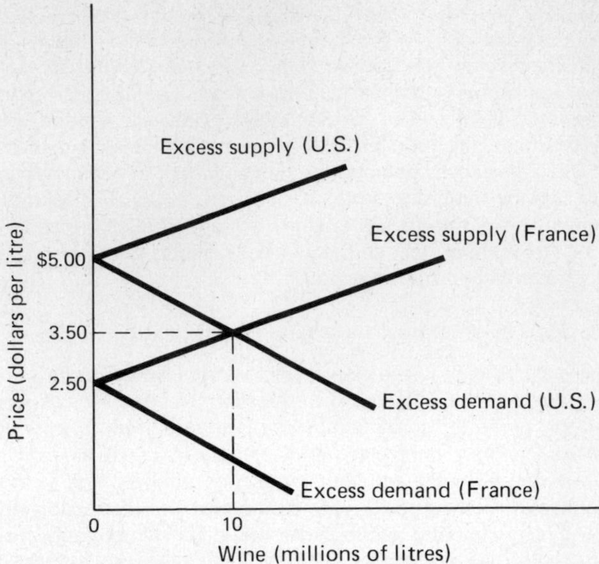

23 Other Economic Systems

TOPICS FOR REVIEW

The topics listed below, which we have already analyzed, are applied in this chapter. You may find it worthwhile to review them. For your convenience each topic is followed by the number identifying the specific "Concepts in Brief."

a. Mixed economy, capitalism (2–2)

b. What, How, For Whom (4–1)

c. Exploitation (14–3)

FOR PREVIEW AND STUDY

1. How can economies be classified?
2. What are the characteristics of a socialist command economy?
3. What is Marxian economics?
4. What are some problems facing command socialist economies?

This is the last chapter in this book. Throughout all of the other chapters, we have been looking at how things work in a mixed capitalist economic system—an economy in which both the decisions of the government and the free market together determine the behavior of consumers, producers, businesses, individuals, monopolies, and so on. Inherent in our mixed economic system is the principle that most of the means of production are owned by individuals. However, our capitalist system is not the only way that an economy can be run. Indeed, most of the world's population lives and works within economies that are not capitalistic.

Looking at the Spectrum of Systems

One possible way of comparing other economic systems in the world is to look at them according to how decentralized their decision-making processes are. In other words, to what degree do individuals make the decisions about what to produce, how to produce it, how much to produce, and for how much to sell it? In Exhibit 23–1, we have put on the extreme right-hand side of the scale pure free-enterprise capitalism, where all economic decisions are made by individuals without government intervention. On the extreme left-hand side of the scale, we have put pure command socialism, where economic decisions are made by some central authority such as a group of government planners or even a dictator. Somewhere in between would be the mixed economic systems such as those existing in the United States, Canada, Mexico, and the United Kingdom. The closer we go to a pure capitalist system, the less political centralization there is, and vice versa. Some economists like to distinguish economies according to whether or not they are a command economy or a decentralized economy. The word *command* refers to individuals within the economy being told what to do by some government authority or central planning agency.

SOCIALISM IN THEORY

Remember from Chapter 2 that the term *economic system* refers to the whole pattern of economic institutions that determine the allocation of resources. We made specific reference to a market, or price, system and talked about the capitalist system in more detail. Now we are trying to examine socialism, which is simply a different response to scarcity.

In Chapter 2, we attempted to define capitalism. The task was not easy. At that time, we didn't even enter into the subtleties among different capitalist systems. The task of defining socialism is even more difficult. Moreover, there are probably even more subtle ways of differentiating socialist systems. Clearly, any definition that we give for socialism will be inadequate. But we will nonetheless attempt to give some theoretical definitional aspects of **socialism.**

A socialist economy is sometimes called a command economy because there is an authority such as a central planning agency that commands what must be done with available resources such as land and machines and even labor. A central planning agency might, for example, decide that 20 percent of the workers should work in the coal mines, 10 percent should work in steel factories, and so on.

One of the most prevalent features in any theoretical socialist system is the attempt to redistrib-

EXHIBIT 23–1
Scale of Decentralization. On the extreme right-hand side of the diagram we find pure capitalism, which no country follows. On the extreme left-hand side is pure socialism, which again no country follows. In the middle are all of the mixed economies in the world. The United Kingdom, Mexico, and the United States are shown, with the United States being closer to pure capitalism, of course.

ute income more equally among the population. The socialist government has often used its taxing powers to reduce inherited wealth and relatively large incomes. Socialist systems usually have relatively larger welfare systems provided by the collective purse of the government than do mixed capitalist systems.

SOCIALISM AS A MOVEMENT

Socialism usually refers to a movement that aims to vest in society, rather than in the individual, the ownership and management of all capital goods used in any large-scale production. When we call socialism a movement, we imply that there exist organizations and programs at work to transform socialistic ideals into some actual economy in which certain property rights—specifically property rights in producer goods—are vested in "society as a whole." However, to speak of "society as a whole" is to assume the continued existence of some form of *organized* society—that is, a society organized on "democratic" principles. (Most socialist economies are not, however, *politically democratic* as we would define these terms.)

If the ownership of the means of production were vested in a group of people whose actions did not reflect the wishes of the masses, that would not be ownership by "society as a whole." Essentially, if the ownership and management of producer goods are to be vested in society as a whole, then the decisions concerning the use of those goods must be made "directly" by society rather than by individuals. Socialism as a movement, then, is really concerned with transferring decision-making powers from individuals to the state. Most theories of socialism assume that this transference of power takes place only for large-scale, not for small-scale, production. Land and tools used personally by their owners, for example, may not be subject to decision making by "society as a whole." In other words, in some socialist systems, a certain amount of land and tools can be owned by individuals privately.

ECONOMICS—THE CORE OF SOCIALISM

Obviously, the heart of socialism is economic. The central issues include who should have the property rights in producer goods, who should make decisions about the use of these goods, and how income should be distributed once it is created.

KEY ATTRIBUTES

Perhaps we can best isolate the key attributes of a socialistic system by seeing how it answers some basic questions. In a socialist system:

1. Although individuals are allowed to own many items of wealth, the government owns the major productive resources, such as land and capital goods. Individuals can own consumer goods and consumer durables, but they are not allowed to own factories, machines, and other things that are used to produce what society wants.
2. People are induced to produce by wage differentials. However, taxation of large incomes to redistribute income may reduce some of the incentives to produce as much.
3. The forces that determine the relative rewards people get from producing are usually set by the state, not by the market. That is, the government, rather than supply and demand, determines people's wage rates and who should be paid what in government-owned and operated factories.
4. Individuals are allowed to enter only certain endeavors. They cannot, for example, set up their own factories. They cannot become entrepreneurs or capitalists, for the state controls such enterprises.

This summary explanation of socialism is purely on the theoretical level. The real-world varieties of socialist systems seem to have only one thing in common: their governments control more factors of production than do capitalist governments.

Traditional socialism emphasized government ownership of the factors of production. Modern socialist thought appears to be heading in the direction of not necessarily government *ownership* of the factors of production, but rather government *control* over industry. Individuals in the private sector may personally own small businesses or be shareholders in corporations that form much of a country's industry. But the government, through its agencies and lawmaking abilities, can control many aspects of these businesses, such as the wages paid, the quantity and quality attributes of the goods produced, the working environment of the labor force, and the price that is charged for the product.

In this entire discussion, it is important to distinguish between economic control and political control. A socialist system could be as democratic as the political system in the United States. That would mean that government officials would be elected, and they would make decisions about the use of resources and particular producer goods. A socialist system could also come under the political control of a dictator. The same is true for a capitalist system. It can be democratic, as it is in the United States, or there could be a dictator ruling the land, but we could still have a free-enterprise system.

In a moment, we will turn to an analysis of Marxian economics.

> ***Concepts in Brief 23-1***
>
> - We can simplify the different types of economic systems by looking at them in terms of decentralization. Pure capitalism would be on one end of the scale; pure socialism on the other.
> - The key attributes of socialism are: (1) The government owns the major productive resources. (2) People are induced to produce by wage differentials, but taxation is often used to redistribute income, thereby reducing some incentive to produce. (3) The rewards for producing are usually set by the state rather than the market. (4) Individuals can enter only certain endeavors and cannot, for example, set up their own factories.
> - Traditional socialist thought emphasized government *ownership* of the factors of production, whereas modern socialist thought emphasizes government *control* over the factors of production.

Marxian Economics

Now, of course, socialist ideas have been around for a long time, but Karl Marx (1818–1883), perhaps more than anyone else in the history of economic thought, is responsible for the proliferation and importance of socialism as we know it today. One of the key analyses offered by Marx in his economic works was his theory of the exploitation of laborers by capitalists. Marx came up with the notion of surplus value. In his theory, he pointed out that workers spend part of every working day covering the costs of maintaining themselves and their families. These are, in fact, their wages. The rest of the day, it appears that they work without payment, creating surplus value, a source of wealth and profit for the capitalist class—the owners of the means of production. In other words, in Marx's world the value of any good or service is directly proportional to the amount of labor used to make it. That means that the worker will work all day to make, say, $50 worth of shoes, but he will be paid only, say, $30. The difference is surplus value and accrues to the capitalist. The workers will not get more because they supposedly only "require" wages that allow them to subsist. And the reason *this* is possible is that there is a **reserve army of unemployed.**

ECONOMIC CRISES

In Marx's world, capitalists strive continually to accumulate capital, and this creates one of the many contradictions within capitalism. As more and more things are produced and economic development continues, however, the reserve army of the unemployed will become depleted. Wage rates will have to rise. But capitalists will seek to increase their profits by introducing more sophisticated production equipment and techniques. Eventually, however, capitalists will no longer be able to sell their increased output. Layoffs and unemployment will result, thus reducing purchasing power. This will lead to a recession and depression. Marx saw continuous cycles of recessions and depressions in the capitalist economy, but these were different from the ones we've talked about in this book.

BUSINESS CYCLES

Marx's theory of the business cycle is one of explosion and collapse of capitalism where there is an eventual revolution of the working class. He predicted that the long-run tendency would be for the rate of profit to fall. Capital would become increasingly concentrated in fewer and fewer monopolistic firms. Wealth also would become concentrated in the hands of fewer and fewer capitalists. Laborers would become more and more exploited as production became more and more capital intensive—that is, as workers have more and more machines with which to work. Eventually, the workers of the world would unite and revolt. The whole system would be overthrown, and a more rational socialist economy would prevail:

> The revolt of a working class, a class always increasing in numbers and discipline, united, organized by the very mechanism of the process of capitalist production itself. Centralization of the means of production and socialization of labor at last reach a point where they become incompatible with their capitalist integument.

Karl Marx

GERMAN ECONOMIST (1818–1883)

GHOST OF WESTERN ECONOMICS

Karl Marx is the ghost that haunts establishment economics in the West. Because of his pointed critique of, and prophecies about, the economic system of capitalism, his adversaries among mainstream economists for the past century have continually felt obliged to refute his theories.

Marx was more than an economist. He was a revolutionary who was instrumental in developing the communist movement, a sociologist, and a historian. He marshalled all these talents for his analysis of capitalism and the ways in which this economic system affected social life. According to Marx (and his frequent collaborator Friedrich Engels), history is the struggle for power of competing classes based on their material interests in the production process. Unlike most economists since the time of Adam Smith, Marx saw capitalism as a specific and historically limited form of social organization. The internal dynamics of capitalism, he argued, would eventually create conditions ripe for its overthrow by the working class and the institution of a new form of social organization based on collective ownership.

Marx was a prolific writer, but the culminating work of his career is undoubtedly *Das Kapital,* the first volume of which appeared in 1867; the other two volumes were

published posthumously. In this gigantic text, Marx set out to do nothing less, he said, than "to lay bare the economic law of motion of modern society." Like Adam Smith and David Ricardo, Marx adhered to the labor theory of value—the theory that the value of commodities ultimately depends on the human labor time expended in their production. But to explain how profits could be generated in a society built on equivalent exchanges of commodities and money, Marx added a new concept—*surplus value.* Under capitalism, labor power is treated as a commodity like any other; workers are paid according to the cost of their reproduction and maintenance. But workers in fact can produce an equivalent to their subsistence in only part of a working day. The difference between the labor time workers spend producing for a capitalist and the labor time equivalent to the wages they actually receive Marx called *surplus value.* Here, he argued, was a scientific index of exploitation.

But it was, Marx argued, the workers who would get the last laugh. Capitalists, faced with competition, were continually driven to expand and mechanize production, thus eliminating some labor costs. But since labor is the ultimate source of value, capitalists, in effect, are cutting their own throats. Over the long term, Marx argued, the rate of profit would fall, while at the same time more and more people would be left without jobs. Through a combination of economic crises of increasing severity and the development of class consciousness among workers, capitalism would finally collapse.

The capitalist economic system appeared to partially break down in the 1930s depression, but Marx hadn't considered the possibility of Keynesian intervention by the state. Furthermore, the rate of profit hasn't fallen in the way he expected. But if the Marxian vision of capitalist breakdown hasn't taken place, Marx's analysis of the workings of capitalism contains many insights, some of which have only begun to be appreciated in the West.

> This integument is burst asunder. The knell of capitalist private property sounds. The expropriators are expropriated.[1]

Marx envisioned the fall of capitalism leading to the rise of socialism and eventually to the world of ideal communism where the state would wither away. In the world of communism, Marx foresaw a final state where the relations of production and distribution would be: "From each according to his ability, to each according to his needs."[2] In fact, in

[1] Karl Marx, *Das Kapital* (Moscow: Foreign Language Publishing House, 1961), Vol. 1, p. 763.

[2] A notion not too different from that in the New Testament.

the ideal communist world that Marx predicted would eventually emerge, there would be little or no need for government. Everything would take care of itself, for man's basic human nature would have been changed because the relations of production and distribution would no longer create class conflict and alienation would not occur. (We note here that Marx was basically a critic of capitalism rather than an architect of socialism. Marx did not spend time describing the perfect socialist or communist state.)

Lenin Takes Hold of the Torch

The most influential disciple of Marx's thought has been Vladimir Ilyich Lenin, who was able to lead the Russian Revolution in the name of Marxism. Lenin spent much of his time analyzing imperialism, which he called the highest stage of capitalism. In this stage, capitalist economies were completely dominated by monopolies. This, after all, was what Marx had predicted. Lenin considered monopolies to be any industries that were dominated by cartels, trusts, or a very few firms. Lenin used the experience of Germany as his example of what could happen with monopoly capitalism.

According to Lenin, as all the different capitalist countries in the world became more and more monopolized, their various governments would fight to gain access to protected markets within each other's boundaries. They would try to partition the world markets through international cartels, but competition would always rear its ugly head. National conflicts and wars would be the inevitable result. Lenin stated that:

> The epic of the newest capitalism shows us that certain relations are being established between capitalist combines, based on the economic division of the world: while parallel with this and in connection with it, certain relations are being established between political alliances, between states, on the basis of the territorial division of the world, of the struggle for colonies, of the "struggle for economic territory."[3]

Lenin was apparently as good a politician as he was a writer, for with the help of Leon Trotsky, Lenin's Bolsheviks obtained power in 1917 from the moderate regime that had recently overthrown the monarchy. What followed has been called "ten days that shook the world." Trotsky trained and organized an army, and the revolutionary forces took over town after town. A civil war ensued between the Bolshevik Communist Party (the Red Army) and their White Russian opponents (the White Army). In the end, the Bolsheviks, or Red Army, won. The world expected a necessary collapse of the new revolutionary government, but communism was here to stay and is still with us. Lenin didn't immediately get rid of all capitalist institutions in Russia. When the war was over, he instituted his New Economic Policy (NEP). He considered NEP a step backward in order to prepare for several steps forward. During the civil war, Lenin had supported antimarket policies. In order to get production back on its feet, he put antimarket policies aside, for his NEP allowed small industry and trade to go back into private hands. In the agricultural sector, forced requisitions were eliminated—the peasants no longer had to give away any products to the government or the army. The market was once again used. Peasant farmers found it profitable to sow fallow land in order to sell the crops. The NEP also involved a currency reform. The monetary economy that disappeared during the war reappeared. Only heavy industry, transportation, foreign trade, and banking remained in government hands. In retrospect, the NEP was a success. By 1928, industry and agricultural production surpassed prerevolutionary war levels. In 1924, however, Lenin died; Stalin took over and decided to take the "several steps forward" that Lenin had promised.

Stalin did not like the inability of central authorities to control the direction of the economy, which was the result of Lenin's having allowed so much of the economy to revert to private hands. Stalin felt that there were certain industries that should be treated favorably in order to get the economy growing rapidly. Thus, a course of economic development *in advance* was plotted in **five-year plans.** These plans were called five-year plans because they plotted a course of economic activity for the following five years. Special industries were picked for growth, which was to be "financed" by obtaining more agricultural produce to feed urban industrial workers. In order to obtain more agricultural products, collectivization was to be the key. Between 1928 and 1932, over 15 million peasant households were formed into over 200,000 collective farms. On the collectives, land and livestock were owned in common—that is, they were not private

[3] V. I. Lenin, *Imperialism: The Highest Stage of Capitalism* (London: Lawrence and Wishart, 1939), p. 69.

property. Land was also worked in common, since no one person owned it, and a system of wage payments to collective farmers was introduced. Communist Party control over the peasant was strengthened.

Agricultural collectivization was not an overwhelming success. Peasants slaughtered and then ate, sold, or traded much of their livestock rather than turn it over to the collectives. At the end of the first five-year plan, the number of livestock had fallen to half. Grain output also fell, perhaps because of the reduced incentive to produce, perhaps because of the problems of instituting collectives at the onset. Nonetheless, at the point of a gun more agricultural products flowed from the country to the city, and that was in fact the major objective of the first five-year plan. Clearly, since agricultural output had fallen, with more going to the city, much less was left for the peasants.

The Soviet System Today

The Soviet economy of today can be called socialistic, with its foundation in Marx's doctrines. But, remember, Marx spent much of his time writing about the faults of capitalism rather than laying out a blueprint for what a socialist economy should look like. Thus, we cannot really say that the current Russian system is exactly as Marx would have wanted it to be.

Concepts in Brief 23–2

- The Marxist theory of exploitation is that workers create a surplus value that is appropriated by capitalists. Surplus value is the difference between the value of the product in the marketplace and the wages paid the worker.
- Because of the existence of a reserve army of unemployed workers, Marx contended that at the initial stages of capitalism there would be little competition for workers, resulting in relatively low wages.
- In the Marxian world of capitalism, business cycles of boom or bust would occur and the long-run rate of profit would fall. Capital concentration would become more and more evident.
- Marx envisioned the fall of capitalism leading to the rise of socialism and eventually to a world of ideal communism in which the ruling principle would be: "From each according to his ability, to each according to his needs."
- Lenin believed that the world would become more and more monopolized and that nations would try to partition world markets through international cartels.
- He also believed that competition for increased markets (and raw materials) among nations would lead to wars.
- The New Economic Policy (NEP) formulated by Lenin was geared toward allowing a market economy to operate in all areas except heavy industry, foreign trade, transportation, and banking.
- Stalin instituted five-year plans that gave specific goals for industry and agriculture.

The Soviet Union Today

In the Soviet Union, the state owns almost all the factors of production. Workers receive wages, and they can choose, within limits, the jobs they prefer. However, Soviet citizens do not have as much geographic mobility as American citizens do, and they have to ask permission to take a job in another region or in another industry. They usually receive permission to move to a place where they think they can make higher wages; in fact, the current system now tries to attract workers to different locations by a system of wage differentials.

In the past, physical quotas were set for factories, but they caused too many problems: factories would put out numerous items, all of poor quality, just to meet the physical quota. The typical Soviet factory is now generally evaluated according to some overall concept of profitability. The government does not measure profitability in the same way a factory in the United States measures it, but it is moving in that direction. Within the factory itself, the managers—in addition to getting a higher-than-average paycheck—may obtain special benefits, such as travel expenses, a car, and other privileges. This is a centralized system, and although there seems to be a change toward more and more decentralization, there is an ever-present hierarchy within an individual firm and within economic life itself. Right now, there are regional economic councils, above them a council of ministers, and beyond that, planners who decide which industries should do what.

Resource Allocation

The decision as to how many of the available economic resources should be used in producing what consumers want as opposed to producing capital equipment—machines and the like—is a decision generally made by the planners. After the Russian Revolution, there was a distinct drop in the percentage of production going to satisfy consumer wants. That is one of the reasons Russia grew so rapidly: it spent a large amount of its resources in capital formation so that it would have a higher level of living in the future. Remember that in the United States, resources flow to where their relative rates of return are highest. If the highest rate of return is in making consumer durables, then resources will flow into making consumer durables. The decision as to how much should be saved and invested is made more or less by individuals. That is, the amount of saving that the economy actually engages in is determined basically by how much each individual decides he or she wants to put away and not consume today. Such is not the case in the Soviet Union.

Until recently, furthermore, very little market information was used to determine which consumer goods should be produced in the Soviet Union. The obvious resulted: lots of things were in short supply, and lots of other things were never bought at all. Today, however, central planners realize that when consumer goods are not bought, production should be slowed down; and when goods are bought rapidly, production should be increased. Russian planners are even starting to engage in marketing surveys to see what consumers really want.

THE PROBLEM OF COORDINATION

Since the Soviet Union is a command economy, it faces a fundamental problem of coordination. Even if a central plan mandates, for example, a 20 percent increase in steel production, planners must take additional steps to ensure that there are sufficient supplies, raw materials, and capital and labor for such an increase in steel output. For instance, if the iron-mining industry does not achieve its quota, the desired goal for steel production will not be met. Certainly there are problems in coordinating such economic endeavors nationwide.

Central planners somehow have to make sure that each of over 200,000 industrial enterprises in Russia today receives resources in correct amounts and at the right time to keep production moving smoothly. Millions, if not billions, of planning decisions must be made, and they are all interrelated. Mathematicians and computer experts have come up with advanced techniques to help the planners cope with such massive problems of coordination. For example, they analyze the relationship between inputs and outputs in different sectors of the economy and put their estimates into what are called input-output tables, a topic we covered in Chapter 17. The information in these tables tells planners how much input they require to change a specific output in a specific industry. This is one way they can avoid bottlenecks.

The planning techniques used in the Soviet Union are certainly too complicated to go into in this brief discussion. We know that priorities are established, with heavy industry given special status as a "leading link" and consumer goods assigned a lower priority. We also know that Soviet planners depend on large reserves or inventories of, for example, ball bearings, so that bottlenecks will be avoided. In any event, to get a command economy working, there is an enormous administrative problem. Once a command economy is working well, there are benefits to be derived. For example, externalities can be taken account of by planners in a way that is difficult in a decentralized system.

Other Variations of Socialism

While Russia may represent one of the largest testing grounds for the socialist-communist type of economics, there are variations that seem to have worked just as well. Without going into them in any detail, we can mention the Yugoslavian experiment in decentralized socialism. It is sometimes called Titoism, after the late party leader Josip Brozovitch Tito. For a while, Czechoslovakia tried its own experiment in decentralization, but Soviet intervention prevented the completion of that experiment. Hungary has its own form of socialism that is not too different from that of the Soviet Union. While one does not get a full panoply of economic systems within Communist Eastern Bloc countries, there are still variations to be studied.

There are certainly much milder forms of socialism than that of the Soviet Union. Britain has its own type of socialism, which seems, however, to vacillate between trends toward increased government ownership of the means of production and increased private ownership. For example, the steel mills have been nationalized and denationalized several times. Whenever the Labour Party gets into power, it tries to extend the welfare services of the state and redistribute income and wealth by progressive taxation. When the Labour Party came into power after World War II, it did an effective job of nationalizing the railroad, coal, and power industries. Today, however, there is considerable debate within the Labour Party itself as to the advisability of increasing socialist economic institutions within England. The same kinds of debates are raging in other countries that have experimented widely with socialism. These include Australia, Norway, Sweden, Denmark, and New Zealand. One might say that as the more socialist countries tend toward capitalism, the more capitalist countries tend toward socialism. The result is what we will call a mixed economy: neither socialism nor capitalism but a mixture of both.

Concepts in Brief 23-3

- The Soviet system of socialism involves profitability evaluations of factories. Managers in profitable factories get special benefits and higher-than-average paychecks.
- There are regional economic councils controlled by a council of ministers who, in turn, are controlled by central planners.
- After the Russian Revolution, there was less production of goods to satisfy consumer wants. More production went into capital formation.
- In any command economy, there are problems of coordination among different sectors. Millions of planning decisions must be made, and they are all interrelated.

ISSUES AND APPLICATIONS

Socialism: Pro and Con

Concepts Applied

- Economic efficiency, price system, and opportunity cost

In this chapter, we have attempted to define socialism both in theory and in practice. Now we wish to present the arguments for and against a socialist economic system. Proponents of socialism have long proclaimed its superiority over the other major competing economic system—capitalism. Socialism presumably "rationalizes" the market, taking away the problems of extreme decentralization (and presumed worker alienation) in a capitalist system. Moreover, socialism also presumably eliminates production for "mere profit" and replaces it with production for "society as a whole." Finally, socialism is supposed to eliminate the capitalist exploitation of workers. In a socialist system, its proponents argue, the real producers of products receive the full reward for their output.

The Efficiency of Socialism

Remember that when we use the term *efficiency*, we are referring to economic efficiency, where resources are being used in their highest-valued uses. When a system is perfectly efficient economically, it is impossible to rearrange the use of resources in such a way that a higher economic valuation of those resources results. We have shown that in a system of perfect competition, a capitalist economy is completely economically efficient. We want first to compare efficiency under perfect competition in capitalism with efficiency under some sort of perfect socialism. (Then we would want to compare efficiency under *actual* capitalism and *actual* socialism.) One economist who attempted to demonstrate the superiority of socialism was Oskar Lange. He set forth his ideas in a series of articles entitled "On the Economic Theory of Socialism." He proposed a system in which socialist managers of each firm would essentially imitate the behavior of managers under *perfectly* competitive capitalism. Central planners would be around, but their

Pictures of Marx and Lenin remind a science student about the fathers of socialism.

major function would not be to issue commands. Rather they would be there to set prices for goods, services, and factors of production. Socialist firm managers would then take these prices into account. The actual operation of their firms would be made in accordance with two rules:

1. The rate of output will be set where the marginal cost of production is equal to the assigned price of a product.
2. Factors will be chosen in such combinations that the value of the marginal physical product of each factor will be equal to the value of the marginal physical product of any other factor.

In other words, Lange's market socialist system does not involve planners setting physical goals or quotas for individual firms. Individual socialist firm managers would do their own planning of physical output and input.

Thus, under Oskar Lange's market socialist system—which he considered the ideal socialist system—economic efficiency could be assured. Central planners would adjust prices to market clearing equilibrium levels, and managers would make proper adjustments in marginal product and marginal cost. Lange further went on to attempt to demonstrate that his perfected socialist system would do better in the real world than a capitalist system, which does not operate, to be sure, under perfectly competitive conditions in the real world. Lange pointed out that numerous monopolies exist. Thus, in numerous industries in capitalist countries, price is not set equal to marginal cost. Price exceeds marginal cost, because monopoly managers equate marginal cost with marginal revenue rather than with price. In the Lange system, managers will always follow the same rule of marginal cost equaling price, no matter whether there is one firm in the market or 100. Finally, Lange pointed out that externalities could be taken account of by central planners in the setting of prices. This is not possible under most circumstances in capitalist countries today. Thus, the appropriate penalties or incentives can be built into the prices in a market socialist system.

Market socialism is not perfect, however. There have been many critics of Lange's attempt to demonstrate the theoretical superiority of market socialism over real-world capitalism. For example, critics contend that Lange's central planners would have to engage in a trial-and-error pricing system that might be unstable and that would certainly be time consuming. Also, how does a central planner use trial-and-error methods for unique goods, such as highly complex industrial equipment made specifically for a single firm? Also, even if Lange's system can be shown to be more economically efficient than real-world capitalism, critics contend that efficiency is not the most important criterion for evaluating different economic systems. Critics of socialism further contend that under such a system, economic growth would be less than under real-world capitalist systems.

Freedom of choice. In contrasting socialism, whether it be market or otherwise, with a market economy, we cannot forget the freedom-of-choice question. If someone in a market economy wants, for example, a complex stereo system more than anything else, the chances are fairly good that such a system will be produced. In a centrally planned (normally socialistic) economy the planners may decide that a complex stereo system is not necessary; it will not be produced. Centralized planning under socialism involves many all-or-nothing choices, whereas in a market economy we end up with a little of some and a little of another. In the market system we observe proportional-dollar voting so that even dollar votes that add up to one ten-thousandths of 1 percent of a total market may generate, if it is profitable, a particular product to satisfy those dollar votes. Such is definitely not the case in a centrally planned socialist system.

Growth

What if the standard for comparison or evaluation of two different systems involved the ability of each to generate economic growth? Remember that economic growth involves an increase in the production potential of the economy. Growth depends in part on the amount of saving, the increases in knowledge and technological progress, and the ability of entrepreneurs to desire and to take advantage of business opportunities.

Proponents of socialism believe that the absence of patent rights would speed the spread of innovations in the economy. In other words, if no one could maintain a monopoly because of a patent, then any advance in knowledge could be used freely by anyone in the economy.

Socialist proponents also contend that economic growth under socialism is greater than under capitalism because of the socialist system's ability to mobilize better the factors of production. Further, socialist planners can divert a larger share of national income into saving and investment than might be forthcoming under a capitalist system. It has been argued that that has been exactly what has happened in Russia and China. In a sense, there has been forced saving that has led to a higher rate of growth than might have occurred otherwise, other things being equal. Socialist planners can also increase the intensity of the use of factors of production. They can require or at least encourage longer hours of work and a greater degree of labor force participation by women, teenagers, and otherwise retired individuals.

What the critics have to say. Socialist critics contend that the area of economic growth is where socialism falls down the most. Economic growth requires that entrepreneurs take advantage of opportunities when they arise. Effective entrepreneurship therefore requires the use of knowledge about the appropriate time and place to take a risk. When should investment funds be risked in a new business venture? The price system makes such information generally available. The opportunity cost of alternative actions is readily available to all individuals immediately. Even with Lange's artificial price system, it might take some time to get this information; and certainly in the real-world examples of socialism where planners decide physical input and output quotas, the information about where and when to innovate is very difficult to come by. Moreover, entrepreneurs need independence of action, which by definition they do not have in a socialist system (to the extent that entrepreneurship is allowed at all). Additionally, entrepreneurs require an incentive to take risks. In the capitalist system, the incentive is the ability to earn economic profits if correct decisions are undertaken. Under socialism, all workers are essentially civil servants; they have little incentive to take risks because the reward may be trivial if they succeed. The incentive under a socialist system is for the worker to "not rock the boat."

Other Factors Important

We have just referred to several economic concepts for which we could generate standards of comparison between socialism and capitalism. But much of the argument for or against socialism does not directly have to do with economic performance under each system. Economic *justice,* however it is defined, may be more important to the proponents of socialism (or capitalism) than any avowed superior economic *performance.*

Socialists, for the most part, equate economic justice with equality: From each according to his or her ability, to each according to his or her need. In a strictly capitalist system, workers are paid the value of their marginal product. That is not equivalent to "to each according to his or her need." Additionally, socialist economic justice presumably eliminates economic exploitation. According to many socialists, only wages are *bona fide* factor payments. Profits, rents, and interest presumably are "unearned" and should be eliminated. Thus, some socialists oppose the nonsalary earnings of even small-scale landlords, bankers, and shopkeepers, even if these individuals earn very low nonwage incomes. Thus, no matter how strong opponents' arguments against socialism are in terms of economic inefficiency, proponents of socialism can always retort that such inefficiency is a small price to pay for their notion of economic justice.

Questions

1. What incentives induce people to take risks in a capitalist system? In a socialist system?
2. What does it mean to say that a socialist system can engage in "forced saving"? Can the same thing occur in a capitalist system?

Definition of Terms

Socialism Any of a number of economic doctrines, or philosophies, that include at least the following major precepts: a major share of the factors of production (except labor) are owned by the state or in common, and incomes are distributed more equally than under a purely capitalist system.

Reserve army of unemployed In Marxian terminology, the mass of unemployed workers, the size of which will grow as workers become more and more exploited by the capitalists.

Five-year plans Economic plans set up by the central government in a country that plots the future course of its economic development. The first five-year plan was devised in Russia by Stalin after Lenin's death.

Chapter Summary

1. We can look at the spectrum of economic systems in terms of how politically centralized economic decision making is. At one extreme is pure command socialism; at the other extreme is purely decentralized capitalism. In between lie all economic systems.
2. Socialism is difficult to define, but we can state that its key attributes are: (a) Individuals may own tools and land, but government owns the major productive resources; (b) people are induced to produce by wage differentials, but taxation of large incomes in order to redistribute income can reduce incentives to produce; (c) wage rates are not determined by the market, but rather by central decision makers; and (d) individuals are not free to enter all trades.
3. Marx felt that capitalists received surplus value, which was the difference between wage rates and the market value of products produced by workers.
4. Marx argued that low wage rates could be paid because of a large reserve army of unemployed. This army, however, would eventually disappear as capitalists competed among each other.
5. Marx's theory of the business cycle was an explosive one in which there were continuing recessions and depressions that finally led to a total collapse of the capitalist system.
6. Lenin instituted his New Economic Policy, eliminating most antimarket provisions in Russia's economy. The NEP also included a currency reform.
7. Stalin instituted five-year plans that "looked forward." Agriculture was collectivized with a larger percentage of total output going to the cities.
8. In Russia today there are wage incentives for workers, but not to the extent that they exist in capitalist systems. The country has a centralized system with regional economic councils, a council of ministers, and central planners.
9. A command economy can in principle take care of externalities that would not be taken care of in a decentralized capitalist system.
10. Market socialism requires that signals be given to managers that are consistent with the price signals that would exist in a perfectly competitive system.

Selected References

Balinky, Alexander. *Marx's Economics: Origin and Development.* Lexington, Mass.: Heath, 1970.
Bornstein, Morris, and Daniel R. Fusfeld, eds. *The Soviet Economy.* 4th ed. Homewood, Ill.: Irwin, 1974.
Heilbroner, Robert L. *Marxism: For and Against.* New York: Norton, 1980.
Lange, Oskar, and Fred M. Taylor. *On the Economic Theory of Socialism.* New York: McGraw-Hill, 1964.
McAuley, Alastair. *Economic Welfare in the Soviet Union.* Madison: University of Wisconsin Press, 1979.
Spulber, Nicholas. *Organizational Alternatives in Soviet-Type Economies.* Cambridge, England: Cambridge University Press, 1979.

Answers to Preview and Study Questions

1. How can economies be classified?

As we stated in Chapter 4, all societies must answer the three fundamental economic problems: what, how, and for whom. One way to classify economies is to categorize them according to the manner in which they answer these questions. In particular, we can classify them according to the degree to which *individuals* are allowed to make these decisions. At the polar extremes exist pure command socialism and pure market capitalism. Under pure command socialism, practically all economic decisions are made by a central authority; under pure capitalism, practically all economic decisions are made by private individuals pursuing their own economic self-interests. Of course, in the real world no economies can be classified as either one of these polar extremes; all real-world economies are mixed. Yet, most economies lie close enough to one or the other of these extremes to be classified as "capitalistic" or "socialistic."

2. What are the characteristics of a socialist command economy?

A main characteristic of a socialist command economy is government control over the (large-scale) means of production; as a practical matter, private ownership of *small-scale* enterprises is usually permitted. Another major characteristic of command socialist economies is central planning; most resources are allocated according to a centrally directed economic plan. Finally, command socialist economies are usually characterized (at least in theory) by wide-scale redistribution of income programs. Workers are usually permitted some freedom of choice on jobs and, as expected, usually choose the higher-paying jobs; yet redistribution is carried on by a system of taxing high-income earners and transferring to low-income earners.

3. What is Marxian economics?

Marxian economics is a method of analyzing economics and is derived from the approach taken by a nineteenth century economist, Karl Marx. Marx's scheme consisted mostly of criticizing capitalism and predicting that it would eventually collapse and be replaced by socialism, which would itself evolve into communism. Marx felt that this "progression" was "inevitable." Marxists feel that laborers, under capitalism, are exploited by capitalists. Marx defined exploitation as a situation in which laborers are paid subsistence wages—the difference between these wages and the value of what they produce (surplus value) going to capitalist exploiters. A reserve army of the unemployed makes it possible for capitalists to get away with paying such low wages. Certain "inherent contradictions" in capitalism, and a long-run tendency for profits to fall, inevitably lead (say Marxists) to the collapse of capitalism. Socialism, under which laborers are still paid according to their productivity, replaces capitalism. Socialism eventually evolves into communism, under which the distribution system is "From each according to his ability, to each according to his needs." Marx really did not elaborate on what the communist economy would be like.

4. What are some problems facing command socialist economies?

Economic planning was hailed as the wave of the future; rational planning was supposed to be economically superior to the anarchy of the marketplace; under planning, goods are produced for "use," not for profit. However, planning, to date, has not been conspicuously successful; living standards within the planned economies are lower than (and economic growth rates are generally slower than) within the welfare-state–mixed-capitalist economies. A major problem of planning is that enormous administrative problems exist; in Russia hundreds of millions of planning decisions must be made in order to keep over 200,000 industrial enterprises running on schedule. Planned economies have simplified this process by devising a system of priorities—but such a scheme is admittedly crude. Moreover, there is a tendency for laborers and enterprise directors to follow the *letter* rather than the *spirit* of official planning rules or "commands." Laborers and enterprise directors are not particularly cooperative, especially since incomes are low due to low productivity—and redistribution of income programs. In the 1980s the world is still awaiting the promise of economic planning.

Problem

(Answer at the back of the book)

1. Suppose you are an economic planner and you have been told by your country's political leaders that they want to increase automobile production by 10 percent over the previous year. What other industries will be affected by this decision?

Answers to Problems

CHAPTER 1

1. There are, of course, a very large number of possible factors that might affect the probability of death. Perhaps the most common would be age, occupation, diet, and current health. Thus, your model would show that the older someone is, the greater the probability is of dying within the next five years; the more risky the occupation, other things being equal, the greater the probability of dying within five years; and so forth.
2. The law of increasing costs does seem to hold because of the principle that some resources may be more suited to one productive use than to another. In moving from butter to guns, the economy will first transfer those resources most easily sacrificed by the butter sector, holding on to the very specialized (to butter) factors until the last. Thus, different factor intensities will lead to increasing relative costs.

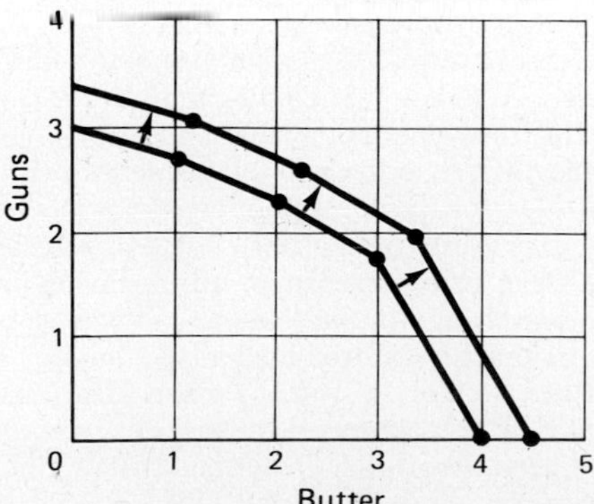

Production Possibilities Curve for Guns and Butter (and after 10 percent growth)

3. Neither has an absolute advantage, therefore neither has a comparative advantage. As a consequence, total output would not change if specialization occurred.
4. Ms. Jones has an absolute advantage in jacket production; she can produce twice as many as can Mr. Jones. Mr. Jones does not have an absolute advantage in anything; he is less productive than Ms. Jones at jacket production and equally productive at tie production. Ms. Jones has a comparative advantage in the production of jackets; she is twice as productive as Mr. Jones in jacket production and equally productive in the production of ties. Mr. Jones has a comparative advantage in the production of ties; he is just as productive in tie production and only half as productive in jacket production. If Ms. Jones specializes in jackets and Mr. Jones specializes in ties, total production equals 16 jackets and 24 ties; tie output remains the same but jacket production increases from 12 to 16.

CHAPTER 2

1. Consumer sovereignty might not exist because: (a) there is insufficient information about characteristics and qualities of consumer products in the marketplace; (b) there is an overwhelming amount of fraud and misrepresentation so that consumers cannot find out about the qualities of consumer products; or (c) there is insufficient competition among firms in the economy to provide the desired assortment of goods and services. Consumer sovereignty relates to the output mix in the economy being determined by consumer dollar votes. Consumer choice, on the other hand, relates to the freedom to choose among the goods and services that can be produced in the economy. It is possible to

have a situation where consumer sovereignty exists but little consumer choice does because of, for example, government restrictions on the manufacture and sale of certain products. The drug industry might be a case in point. Consumers conceivably could be sovereign in that their dollar votes for various drugs would determine what was produced. They do not, however, have complete choice because government restricts which drugs can be purchased without prescription. Furthermore, government controls which drugs can be sold even with a prescription.

2. Customs, habits, ethics, and laws in a nation constitute the institutions that mold production and exchange. Virtually all institutions change somewhat over time. For example, there has been a change in religious customs in the United States since the beginning of colonial settlement. Gradually, religious sentiment grew weaker concerning work performed on the Sabbath. This has had the effect on our economic system of allowing stores to remain open on Sunday.
3. Private property, free enterprise and choice, self-interest, competition, a price system, limited role for government.
4. Large capital stock, specialization, use of money.

CHAPTER 3

1. The equilibrium price is $30. The quantity supplied and demanded is about 10.5 million skateboards per year.

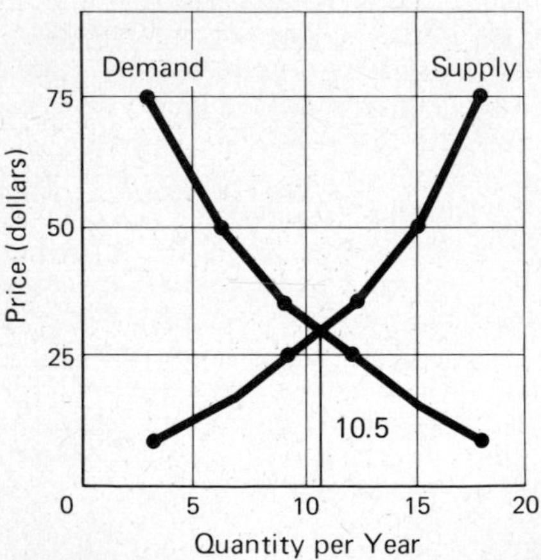

Graph of Supply and Demand for Skateboards

2. No. In many countries, particularly where virtually all drugs are sold without a prescription, drugs are a substitute for physicians' services. Instead of going to a doctor, the patient will go to the drugstore and try one or more drugs to cure an illness.
3. (a) The demand curve for vitamin C will shift outward to the right because the product has taken on a desirable new quality. (b) The demand curve for stenographic services will shift inward to the left because the substitute good, the tape recorder, is now a lower-cost alternative (change in the price of a substitute). (c) The demand curve for beer will shift outward to the right because the price of a complementary good, pretzels, has decreased. Is it any wonder that tavern owners often give pretzels away? (Change in the price of a complement.)
4. The *absolute* price of heating oil has doubled, while the price of natural gas has quadrupled. The *relative* price of heating oil has decreased; that of natural gas has increased. Consumers will start buying more heating oil and less natural gas.
5. As the diagram below indicates, demand doesn't change, supply decreases, the equilibrium price of oranges rises and the equilibrium quantity falls.

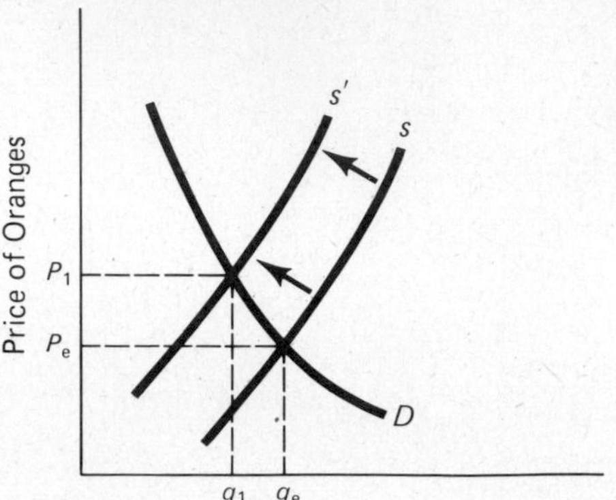

CHAPTER 4

1. The relative price of tequila in relation to beer has fallen from 10 beers per tequila quart to 9 beers per quart. Although the absolute prices of beer and tequila rose, the relative prices of both commodities fell in relation to all other goods and services, because neither rose by as much as 70 percent. The relative price of beer in 1984 is equal to $\frac{100}{170} \times \$.70 = \$.41$. The relative (or constant) price of tequila is equal to $\frac{100}{170} \times \$6.30 = \$3.71$.
2. Transactions costs are the costs of engaging in a transfer of goods, over and above the sale price of the goods. In the purchase of a home, some of these costs are the costs of gasoline and travel during the search; the opportunity cost of the time of the buyers who are searching; the fees that must be paid for checking the validity of the title; the fees paid to the realtor, if one is used; the fees paid to a lawyer to draw up the contract; the costs of securing a loan, if the house is to be mortgaged, including the costs of searching for the most attractive credit terms; the costs of moving family and furniture into a new home and community; the costs of adapting or remodeling the house to your tastes; and the costs of disposing of the residence being given up for the new location. Each of these costs, and others that you may think of, may present possibilities of economizing. Organizing the search effort, hiring an agent to do the searching, finding lawyers and realtors who handle legal matters at reduced rates, buying a new house that can be built to your own specifications, contributing more or less of your own capital to defray credit costs—all are potential transactions costs reducers.
3. (a) The firm will choose technique *C* because it incurs the lowest cost of the three methods at the prices given, $107, as opposed to $120 for *A* and $168 for *B*.

(b) The firm's maximum profit will be \$65. (c) If labor increases to \$4 per unit, technique A becomes the most profitable, because its cost increases to only \$132, less than the \$143 that C now costs. Therefore A would be chosen. Profits would drop to \$40.

4.

Advantages	Disadvantages
a. economic freedom	a. externalities
b. efficiency	b. insufficient output of social goods
	c. highly unequal distribution of income
	d. lack of competition

Although the list of disadvantages is larger than the list of advantages, one cannot say that a price system is not worthwhile or preferable to an alternative system. Value judgments as to how much *weight* to attach to each item in each list are necessary.

CHAPTER 5

1.

Plant	Firm	Industry
McDonald's	General Motors	Steel, Aluminum, Metals,
Factory	All Ford Plants	Autos, Trucks, Buses, etc.
Drugstore	Prudential Insurance Co.	

2. Advantages of incorporation: easier to raise money capital, limited liability, unlimited life, specialized and professional management. Disadvantages: double taxation, increased governmental control.
3. Advantages of financing by issuing stock: low risk since stockholders only receive *residual* profits, no legal obligation to repay stockholders in the future or to make dividend payments. Disadvantages: dilution of ownership, double taxation, expensive selling costs.

CHAPTER 6

1. a.

Quantity Demanded/ Week	Price/ Oz.	(Elasticity)
1000 oz.	\$ 5	
		$\frac{1}{3}$ or .33
800	10	
		$\frac{5}{7}$ or .714
600	15	
		$\frac{7}{5}$ or 1.4
400	20	
		$\frac{9}{3}$ or 3
200	25	

b. There are several different ways to explain why elasticity is greater at higher prices on a linear curve. At higher prices, a given price change will result in a smaller percentage price change. The smaller resulting denominator of the elasticity ratio leads to a larger overall ratio. Similarly, as prices rise, quantities fall, thereby implying greater percentage quantity changes for a given absolute quantity change, and a larger numerator. Alternatively, the sizes of total revenue changes first increase, then decrease, as price is lowered throughout a linear demand curve, thus implying declining elasticity.

2. The average value of the price elasticity over this price change is $(\frac{1}{5}) \div (\frac{2}{5}) = \frac{1}{2} = .5$. The demand schedule is price inelastic. Total revenue is greater at the higher price.
3. Using the midpoint elasticity equation, the income elasticity of demand for videotape recorders is .6666 divided by .2857, or 2.33. Hence, we refer to it as being income elastic, and it is presumably a luxury good.

CHAPTER 7

1. For you, the marginal utility of the fifth orange is equal to the marginal utility of the third ear of corn. Apparently, your sister's tastes differ from yours; for her, the marginal utilities are not equal. For her, corn's marginal utility is too low, while that of oranges is too high; that's why she wants you to get rid of some of the corn (raising its marginal utility). She would have you do this until marginal utilities, for her, were equal. If you follow her suggestions, you will end up with a market basket which maximizes *her* utility subject to the constraint of *your* income. Is it any wonder that shopping from someone else's list is a frustrating task?
2. The statement is correct because of the law of diminishing marginal utility. As more is consumed, the additional unit leads to a smaller increase in total utility than the previous unit did. Therefore, in order to increase marginal utility, consumption must be decreased.
3. 100; 200; 50; divide marginal utility by price per unit.
4. a. Group Demand Schedule

Price per Hamburger	Quantity Demanded per Unit of Time
\$2.00	2
1.50	4
1.00	6
.50	8

b. See graph.

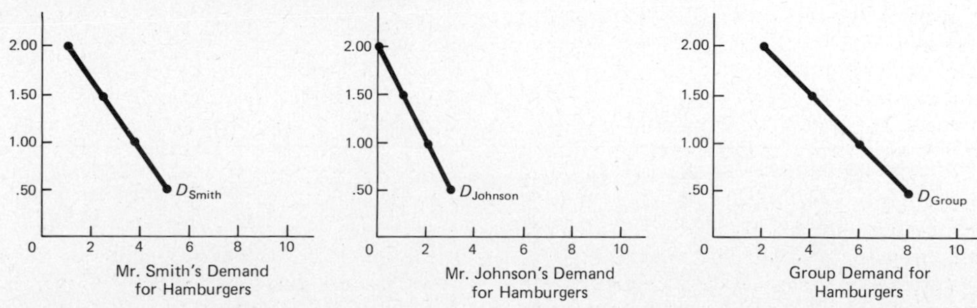

c. They might have different incomes, tastes for hamburgers (marginal utility schedules), wealth, expectations, and so on.

CHAPTER 8

1. What is being ignored is the opportunity cost of continuing to possess the van. For example, if the van could be sold without much problem for $10,000 and you could earn 10 percent per year by investing that $10,000 in something else, then the opportunity cost of keeping the van is $1,000 per year.
2. a. 8 hours; approximately 4 hours each (since the second laborer can produce 2 batches of 2 in 8 hours); they will have fewer labor hours embodied within them.
   b. 8 hours (the twelfth person hired produces 20 units in 8 hours); the next batch of 20 costs 32 man-hours (4 people working 8 hours); additional batches of 20 cost more in labor hours.
   c. When the marginal product of labor is rising, equal increases in output require fewer labor hours; when the marginal product of labor is falling, equal increases in output require more labor hours.
3. (a) $1; (b) 5¢; (c) $1; (d) 10¢; (e) MC is rising; (f) when the marginal product of labor is rising, marginal cost of output falls; when the marginal product of labor is falling, the marginal cost of output rises.
4. (a) .500; (b) it fell from .800 to $\frac{85}{110}$ = .773; (c) rising from .500 to .600; (d) even though their marginal performance is rising it is still below average; hence, average falls from .800 to .773 to $\frac{91}{120}$ = .758.
5. a. The AFC curve remains unaffected by the unit tax, because the tax is imposed only if there is some output. The AVC curve shifts upward by a constant $5 throughout its domain, because a unit tax imposes a constant charge per unit. The ATC curve shifts a constant vertical distance for the same reason, as does the MC curve. The tax imposes an extra $5 cost for each additional unit produced. (See graph.)

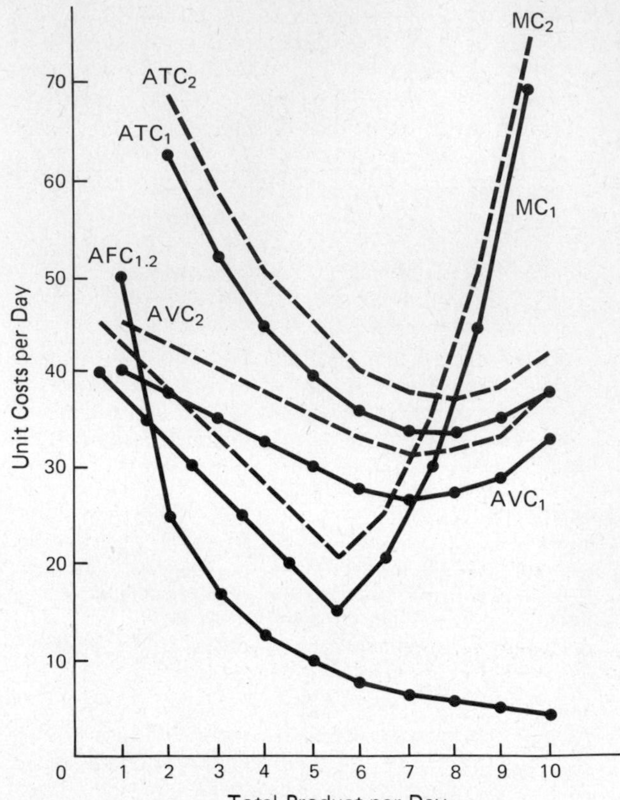

Effect of a Unit Tax on the Cost Curves of Sunshinsea Surfboards. (Subscript$_1$ refers to pre-tax levels, subscript$_2$ refers to post-tax levels.)

b.

Total Costs per Day					Unit Costs per Day			
(a) TP	(b) TFC	(c) Tax Bill	(d) TVC	(e) TC	(f) AFC	(g) AVC	(h) ATC	(i) MC
0	$50	$ 0	$ 0	$ 50				
1	50	5	45	95	$50.00	$45.00	$95.00	$45
2	50	10	85	135	25.00	42.50	67.50	40
3	50	15	120	170	16.67	40.00	56.70	35
4	50	20	150	200	12.50	37.50	50.00	30
5	50	25	175	225	10.00	35.00	45.00	25
6	50	30	195	245	8.33	32.50	40.83	20
7	50	35	220	270	7.14	31.43	38.57	25
8	50	40	255	305	6.25	31.88	38.13	35
9	50	45	305	355	5.56	33.89	39.44	50
10	50	50	380	430	5.00	38.00	43.00	75

CHAPTER 9

1.

Output	Fixed Cost	AFC	Variable Cost	AVC	Total Cost	ATC	MC
1	$100	$100	$ 40	$40	$140	$140	$40
2	100	50	70	35	170	85	30
3	100	33.33	120	40	220	73.33	50
4	100	25	180	45	280	70	60
5	100	20	250	50	350	70	70
6	100	16.67	330	55	430	71.67	80

a. The price would have to drop below \$35 before the firm would shut down in the short run.
b. \$70 is the short-run break-even point for the firm. The output at this price would be 5 units per period.
c. At a price of \$76, the firm would produce 5 units and earn a profit of \$30 (\$6 per unit over 5 units).

2. (a) D; (b) D''; (c) D'; (d) MC above point B; (e) P_3.

CHAPTER 10

1. a. The rectangle that shows total costs under ATC_1 is $0WCQ$. Total revenue is shown by $0XBQ$. This monopolist is in an economic profit situation. MC = MR is the output at which profit—the difference between total cost and revenue—is maximized.
   b. With ATC_2, the rectangle showing total costs is $0XBQ$. The same rectangle, $0XBQ$, gives total revenue. This monopolist is breaking even. MC = MR shows the only quantity that does not cause losses.
   c. Under ATC_3, total costs are represented by rectangle $0YAQ$, total revenue by $0XBQ$. Here the monopolist is operating at an economic loss, which is minimized by producing where MC = MR.

2.

Price	Quantity Demanded	Marginal Revenue
	0	
		\$1,000
\$1,000	1	
		840
920	2	
		780
840	3	
		520
760	4	
		400
680	5	
		160
600	6	
		40
520	7	
		−20
440	8	
		−470
350	9	
		−550
260	10	

3. Probably low-income patients have higher elasticities of demand for the services of a physician than do high-income patients; low-income patients are probably more willing to substitute inferior medical care or none, than are high-income patients. Thus two distinct groups with differing elasticities exist. Moreover, the services of a physician to a patient are usually nontransferable, so markets can be separated. After all, can you sell your appendectomy to someone else?
4. Given the output rate at which MR = MC, a monopolist's price will be determined. A higher price would create a shortage, a lower price a surplus.

CHAPTER 11

1. The marginal revenue of this ad campaign was \$1,000. There was an addition of 40 cars per week at \$25 per car. To determine whether profits have risen, we would have to know how much additional cost was incurred in the tuning of these cars, as well as the cost of the advertisement itself.
2. (a) q; (b) P_1; (c) B; (d) F; (e) higher than ($B > F$); (f) greater than ($B > A$).
3. (a) Approximately 64 percent (\$525,000,000 ÷ \$825,000,000); (b) the ratio would rise as the industry is more narrowly defined and fall as it is more broadly defined. Since an "industry" is arbitrarily defined, concentration ratios may be misleading.

CHAPTER 12

1. (a) Quantity produced would be q_b, and price would be P_c; (b) $P_b\,BC\,P_c$.
2. a. Small quantity users would pay higher prices per unit.
   b. Large businesses are likely to purchase more kilowatts of electricity.
   c. Large businesses are likely to have a higher elasticity of demand, since it could potentially be profitable for them to substitute their own power generators for the public utility's power.
   d. Yes. Households and businesses have different price elasticities of demand; and businesses, who are charged lower per unit rates, are legally restricted from reselling to households.

CHAPTER 13

1.

Quantity of Labor	Total Product per Week	MPP	VMP
1	250	250	\$500
2	450	200	400
3	600	150	300
4	700	100	200
5	750	50	100
6	750	0	0

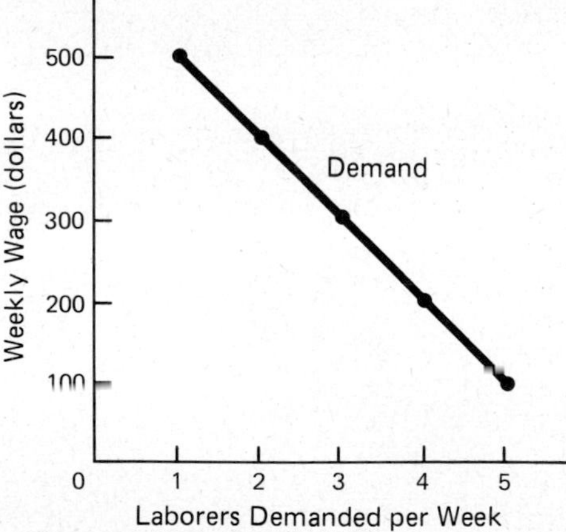

a. Demand schedule for labor:

Weekly Wage	Laborers Demanded per Week
\$500	1
400	2
300	3
200	4
100	5

b. If five workers were hired, the firm would be willing to pay no more than \$100 for each one.
c. At \$200 per week, four laborers would be hired.

2.

Quantity of Capital (machine weeks)	Total Product (units/week)	Marginal Product of Capital (units/week)	Product Price ($/week)	VMP ($/week)
0	0		$10	
1	25	25	10	$250
2	45	20	10	200
3	60	15	10	150
4	70	10	10	100
5	75	5	10	50

If the price of capital is $90 per machine-week, the firm will use four units of capital. If the price rises to $300 per week, the firm will not use any capital; it will not produce. At $300, capital costs would not be covered by any amount of production, for the greatest value of its marginal product is $250.

3. (a) 15 million man-hours per unit of time; (b) 11 million per unit of time; (c) buyers can get all the labor they want at W_1; laborers can't sell all they want to sell at W_1; (d) since a surplus of labor exists, the unemployed will offer to work for less and industry wage rates will fall toward W_e.

4. (a) 10 million man-hours per unit of time; (b) 17 million man-hours per unit of time; (c) sellers of labor are working as much as they care to at W_2, but buyers of labor cannot get all they want at that rate; (d) since a shortage of laborers exists, buyers of labor will compete for labor and drive wage rates up toward W_e; (e) W_e, since neither a surplus nor a shortage exists at that wage rate.

CHAPTER 14

1. (a) VMP; (b) S; (c) Q_A; (d) W_A; (e) $W_E - W_A$; that is, the VMP of the Q_A unit of labor minus the equilibrium wage rate.

CHAPTER 15

1. The statement is false. Although there may be a substantial portion of rent in the revenues from these museums, we would have to assume that the museums are absolutely costless to keep in their current use in order to make the statement that *all* revenues are economic rent. The most obvious expenses of keeping the museums operating are the costs of maintenance: cleaning, lighting, and other overhead costs. But these may be minor compared to the opportunity cost involved in keeping the museum *as a museum*. The buildings might make ideal government office buildings. They may be on land that would be extremely valuable if sold on the real estate market. If there are any such alternative uses, the value of these uses must be subtracted from the current revenues in order to arrive at the true level of pure economic rent. Foregoing these alternative opportunities is as much a cost of operating the museum as is the monthly utility bill.

2. We already know that any payment above that which is required to keep a resource in its current use is an economic rent. It must follow, then, that there is some economic rent going to the superstars if they are receiving more than their next best opportunity would provide. To make the argument in this question, it is necessary to draw on the distinction between short-run and long-run supply and demand. Human beings are not eternally durable. They grow old and step aside for more popular and more productive younger talent. It is possible that younger talent in the entertainment field is not attracted by "scale" wages that are paid to the majority who never reach stardom. Rather it is the *chance* of making the astronomical salary that draws great talent. Without this possibility, potential actors and athletes would seek other employment. Even as they continue to work at mediocre scale wages, young performers may be deriving nonmoney income because they are building and investing in their own talent and they are buying the opportunity to be available when stardom calls. Thus, although the high salaries may be more than is necessary to keep current talent performing (their short-run supply curve is inelastic), such prizes may be needed to attract future talent (their long-run supply curve is elastic).

CHAPTER 16

1. Whites might invest more in human capital; blacks might receive less, and lower-quality education and/or training; blacks in the work force may, on average, be younger; discrimination may exist; and so on.

2. (a) A; (b) C; (c) inward toward A; the Lorenz curve tends to overstate income inequality unless these, and other, adjustments are made.

CHAPTER 17

1. (a) P_e; (b) shortage; (c) surplus; (d) unstable, because a price above equilibrium creates a shortage, and a price below equilibrium creates a surplus; in each case price will move further away from P_e.

2. Partial equilibrium analysis: c, d.
General equilibrium analysis: a, b, e, f.

CHAPTER 18

1. When the external costs are added to the supply curve (which itself is the sum of marginal costs of the industry), the total (private plus public) marginal costs of production are above the private supply schedule. At quantity Q_1, marginal costs to society are greater than the value attached to the marginal unit. The demand curve is below the social supply curve. To bring marginal cost and marginal benefit back into line, thus promoting an economically efficient allocation of resources, quantity would have to be reduced to Q_2 and price raised to P_2.

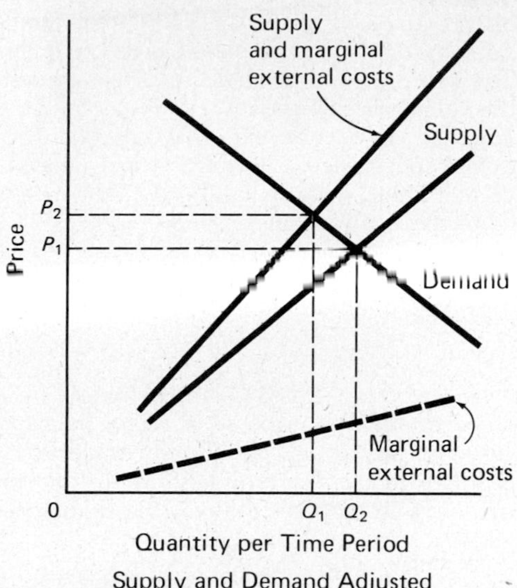

Supply and Demand Adjusted
for External Costs

2. The analysis is similar for the case of external benefits. Instead of adding to the private costs of production, now we are adding other consumers' demand curves (marginal external benefits) to the demand curve of the individuals actually engaged in the transaction. (Note that we add vertically, instead of horizontally, because we are talking of one good satisfying more than one consumer.) Before taking external benefits into consideration, we reach equilibrium at Q_1, where consumers place a higher value on an additional unit of the good than that additional unit costs. Allocative efficiency would be enhanced by expanding production to the point Q_2. At this point, the product is more costly, but ideally this cost could be divided between the private and external demanders. The private consumers could pay P_{2P}, while the third parties could pay P_{2E}.

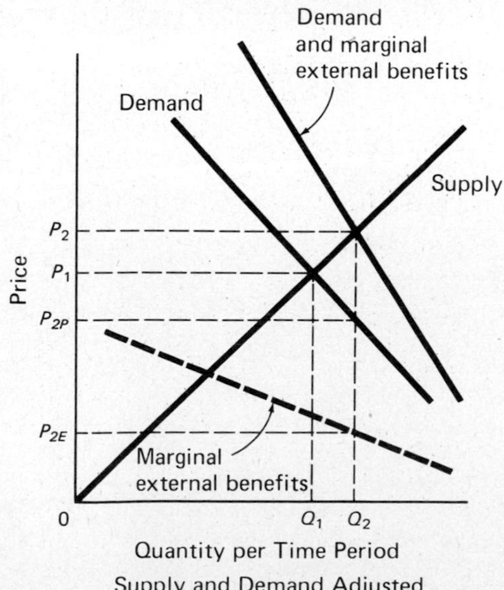

Supply and Demand Adjusted
for External Benefits

3. a. the price of polluting should be set according to the marginal economic damage imposed by polluters; this means that similar quantities of pollution will cost polluters different prices in different parts of the country; pollution will be more costly in New York City than in Little Town, Mid-America.
   b. Those firms which find it cheaper to treat will do so; those firms which find it cheaper to pay to pollute will pollute; this is a sensible solution to the problem: who should treat, who should pollute?
   c. Yes, some firms will be forced to shut down due to increased costs; this is efficient, in that the true costs to society of their operations were not paid by them and their customers; they were only able to remain in business by imposing costs on third parties.
   d. This might be good because now those who are using the resources will be forced to pay for them—instead of imposing costs on others. Those who are *not* using these products were, in effect, subsidizing lower prices to those who were. This new solution seems "fair"—it certainly is efficient.
4. The problems involved are too complex for free markets (and for governments too!); contracting costs would be prohibitive and enforcement impossible. Firms would go into the business of being paid *not* to pollute, individuals would claim all sorts of damages from pollution, and so on. Moreover, determining *marginal* costs and benefits for specific firms and individuals would be difficult indeed.

CHAPTER 19

1. (a) $P = \dfrac{\$1}{(1+i)}$; (b) $P = \dfrac{\$1}{(1+i)^2}$

   (c) $P = \dfrac{\$1}{(1+i)^t}$

   (d) it falls; (e) falls; (f) yes, just plug in a zero where appropriate.
2. Walking, car pooling, bike riding, motorcycling, buying smaller or more fuel-efficient cars, combining gasoline with other fuels, using autos run on steam or electricity, and many other means.

CHAPTER 20

1. (a) 50 women plus 500 men equal 550 people; (b) one; (c) 550 people; (d) remaining constant, since the net reproduction rate equals 1.

CHAPTER 21

1. (a) 19 percent of 2.44 million is 463,600 farms; (b) no.

CHAPTER 22

1. a. The opportunity cost to the United States of producing one quart of vodka is two bushels of wheat. The six hours that were needed to make the vodka could have been used to grow two bushels. The opportunity cost of producing one bushel of wheat is half a quart of vodka.
   b. The opportunity cost to Russia of producing one

quart of vodka is $1\frac{1}{2}$ bushels of wheat. The opportunity cost of producing a bushel of wheat in Russia is two-thirds of a quart of vodka.

c. The United States has a comparative advantage in wheat, because it has a lower opportunity cost in terms of vodka. Russia has a comparative advantage in vodka. Less wheat is foregone to produce a quart of vodka in Russia.

2. a. The opportunity cost to Colombia of producing one pound of hemp is one-third ounce of poppy seeds. The opportunity cost of one ounce of poppy seeds is three pounds of hemp.

b. The opportunity cost to Turkey of producing one pound of hemp is one-half ounce of poppy seeds. The opportunity cost of one ounce of poppy seeds is two pounds of hemp.

c. Colombia has a comparative advantage in hemp, because the poppy seed sacrifice is less. Turkey has a comparative advantage in poppy seeds.

3. (a) \$5; (b) \$2.50; (c) \$3.50; (d) at \$3 per liter the quantity demanded by the United States exceeds the quantity supplied of French wine; hence, a shortage will exist and the dollar price will rise; (e) at \$4 per liter the quantity supplied of French wine exceeds the U.S. quantity demanded; hence, a surplus exists and the dollar price of French wine will fall; (f) France will export wine to the United States.

CHAPTER 23

1. Steel (and coal and coke), glass, tire (and rubber), plastic, railroad (and steel!), and possibly radio, hubcaps, air conditioner, to mention a few. Moreover, decisions on resource allocations concerning labor and other inputs for each of *these* (and the many other) industries must be made.

Indexes

Index of Names

Index of Glossary Terms

Index of Subjects

MICROECONOMIC PRINCIPLES

LAW OF DEMAND

At higher prices, a lower quantity will be demanded than at lower prices, other things being equal.

LAW OF SUPPLY

At higher prices, a larger quantity will generally be supplied than at lower prices, other things held constant.

MOVEMENT ALONG VERSUS SHIFTS IN A CURVE

If the relative price changes, we *move along* a curve—there is a change in quantity demanded and/or supplied. If something else changes, we *shift* a curve—there is a change in demand and/or supply.

THE DETERMINANTS OF THE PRICE ELASTICITY DEMAND

1. The existence and closeness of substitutes.

2. The "importance" of the commodity in the total budget.

3. The length of time allowed for adjustment to changes in price.

INCOME ELASTICITY OF DEMAND

$$\text{income elasticity of demand} = \frac{\text{percentage change in the amount of good purchased}}{\text{percentage change in income}}$$

PRICE ELASTICITY OF DEMAND

$$e_d = \frac{\text{percentage change in quantity demanded}}{\text{percentage change in price}}$$

AVERAGE AND MARGINAL COST

$$\text{Average Total Cost (ATC)} = \frac{\text{total cost}}{\text{output}}$$

$$\text{Average Variable Cost (AVC)} = \frac{\text{total variable cost}}{\text{output}}$$

$$\text{Average Fixed Cost (AFC)} = \frac{\text{total fixed cost}}{\text{output}}$$

$$\text{Marginal Cost (MC)} = \frac{\text{change in total cost}}{\text{change in output}}$$

ELASTICITY OF SUPPLY

$$e_s = \frac{\text{percentage change in quantity supplied}}{\text{percentage change in price}}$$

RELATIONSHIP BETWEEN PRICE ELASTICITY OF DEMAND AND TOTAL REVENUES

When price elasticity is	*Demand is called*	*Thus, if price changes*	*Quantity demanded changes (in opposite direction of price)*	*So that total revenues on the good (P × Q)*
Greater than 1	Price elastic	$P\uparrow$	More than in proportion	Fall
		$P\downarrow$	More than in proportion	Rise
Equal to 1	Unitary elastic	$P\uparrow$	In exact proportion	Remain constant
		$P\downarrow$	In exact proportion	Remain constant
Less than 1	Price inelastic	$P\uparrow$	Less than in proportion	Rise
		$P\downarrow$	Less than in proportion	Fall

MICROECONOMIC PRINCIPLES

THE PROFIT-MAXIMIZING COMBINATION OF RESOURCES

VMP of labor = price of labor (wage rate)

VMP of land = price of land (rental rate per unit)

VMP of machines = price of machines (cost per unit of service)

MONOPOLY AND MONOPSONY EXPLOITATION

$VMP_L - MRP_L$ = monopolistic exploitation

$MRP_L - w_m$ = monopsonistic exploitation

$VMP_L - w_m$ = total exploitation

PROFIT

accounting profits = total revenues − total costs

economic profits = total revenues − total opportunity cost of all inputs used

LAW OF DIMINISHING RETURNS

As successive equal increases of the variable factor of production, such as labor, are added to a fixed factor of production, such as capital, there will be a point beyond which the extra or marginal product that can be attributed to each additional unit of the variable factor of production will decline.

THE LEAST-COST, OR COST MINIMIZATION, RULE

$$\frac{\text{marginal physical product of labor}}{\text{price of labor}} = \frac{\text{marginal physical product of machines}}{\text{price (rental value) of machines}}$$

$$= \frac{\text{marginal physical product of land}}{\text{price (rental value) of land}}$$

= and so on

RULE FOR HIRING

The firm hires workers up to the point where the additional cost associated with hiring the last worker is equal to the additional revenue generated by that worker.

SHERMAN ANTITRUST ACT

Section 1: Every contract, combination in the form of trust or otherwise, or conspiracy, in restraint of trade or commerce among the several states or with foreign nations, is hereby declared to be illegal.

Section 2: Every person who shall monopolize, or attempt to monopolize, or combine or conspire with any other person or persons to monopolize any part of the trade or commerce . . . shall be guilty of a misdemeanor.

COMPARING MARKET STRUCTURES

Market Structure	*Number of Sellers*	*Unrestricted Entry and Exit*	*Ability to Set Price*	*Long-run Economic Profits Possible*	*Product Differentiation*	*Examples*
Perfect competition	Numerous	Yes	None	No	None	Agriculture
Monopolistic competition	Many	Yes	Some	No	Considerable	Toothpaste, toilet paper, soap, retail trade
Oligopoly	Few	Partial	Some	Yes	Frequently	Automobiles, steel
Pure monopoly	One	No	Considerable	Yes	The product is unique	Electric company, telephone company

82 83 84 85 9 8 7 6 5 4 3 2